Deluxe Education Edition

MULTIMEDIA FOR THE WEB: REVEALED

Creating Digital Excitement

By Calleen Coorough and Jim Shuman

Multimedia for the Web: Creating Digital Excitement – Revealed, Deluxe Education Edition

By Calleen Coorough and Jim Shuman

Managing Editor:
Marjorie Hunt

Senior Product Managers:
Christina Kling Garrett, Karen Stevens

Associate Product Manager:
Emilie Perreault

Editorial Assistant:
Shana Rosenthal

Production Editor:
Pamela Elizian

Developmental Editor:
Pam Conrad

Composition House:
GEX Publishing Services

QA Manuscript Reviewers:
Jeff Schwartz, Danielle Shaw, Ashlee Welz, Susan Whalen

Marketing Manager:
Joy Stark

Text Designer:
Ann Small

Illustrator:
Philip Brooker

Cover Design:
Steve Deschene

Printed in the United States of America.

1 2 3 4 5 6 7 8 9 BU 09 08 07 06 05

For more information, contact Thomson Course Technology, 25 Thomson Place, Boston, Massachusetts, 02210.

Or find us on the World Wide Web at: www.course.com

ISBN 1-4188-3953-1

Revealed Series Vision

The Revealed Series is your guide to today's hottest multimedia applications. These comprehensive books teach the concepts and skills behind the application, showing you how to apply smart design principles to multimedia elements, such as dynamic graphics, animation, Web sites, and video.

A team of design professionals including multimedia instructors, students, authors, and editors worked together to create this series. We recognized the unique learning environment of the digital media or multimedia classroom and have created a series that:

- Gives you comprehensive explanations
- Offers in-depth explanation of the "why" behind a skill
- Includes creative projects for additional practice
- Explains concepts clearly using full-color visuals

It was our goal to create a book that speaks directly to the multimedia and design community—one of the most rapidly growing computer fields today.

This series was designed to appeal to the creative spirit. We would like to thank Philip Brooker for developing the inspirational artwork found on each chapter opener and book cover. We would also like to give special thanks to Ann Small of A Small Design Studio for developing a sophisticated and instructive book design.

—The Revealed Series

Author's Vision

Writing a textbook on multimedia for the Web is extremely challenging. How do you adequately cover all of the concepts and provide the necessary hands-on experiences that bring the concepts to life?

Our goal is to provide a comprehensive, yet manageable, introduction to multimedia for the Web while having you use some of the most popular applications as you work though the various projects. Our desire is that you'll become fascinated with the conceptual material and get so caught up in the activities and projects that you'll be pleasantly surprised with the level of skills and knowledge you've acquired at the end of each chapter. As you will see the Revealed Series is a great format for teaching and learning.

We would like to thank the reviewers who provided invaluable feedback and guidance as we were developing this title: Thomas Ahlswede, Central Michigan University; Kathleen Harmeyer, The Community College of Baltimore County; Constance Humphries, AB-Technical Community College; and Mete Kok, Borough of Manhattan Community College.

What a pleasure it has been to be part of such a creative and energetic team. We would like to thank Nicole Pinard for providing the vision for the project; Christina Kling Garrett and Karen Stevens for their management expertise; and Marjorie Hunt and all those at Thomson Course Technology for their professional guidance. A special thanks goes to Pam Conrad, Developmental Editor, for her meticulous eye, attention to detail, editorial expertise, and most important, her kind manner.

— Calleen Coorough and Jim Shuman

The Authors

I would like to thank my co-author, Calleen, who has an incredible knowledge of multimedia and the Web and a talent for conveying this knowledge through her writing. I also want to give a heartfelt thanks to my wife, Barbara, for her patience and support.

—Jim Shuman

Special thanks go to Jim Shuman, co-author, for his exceptional insight, creativity, and hard work. This book is dedicated to my son, Declan. Thank you for always bringing me back to the moment and for always making me smile. As always, my husband, Barclay Berry, deserves recognition for his patience and his pervasive support and endurance. I would also like to thank my students as well as my friends and colleagues for feeding my soul and spirit.

— Calleen Coorough

Introduction

Welcome to *Multimedia for the Web: Creating Digital Excitement—Revealed, Deluxe Education Edition*. This book builds a foundation in multimedia design and concepts to foster student creativity. This text is organized into two sections—one dedicated to a conceptual understanding of multimedia for the Web and the other to hands-on, step-by-step lessons that allow you to put into practice the concepts you just studied. The chapters cover all aspects of multimedia on the Web: in-depth discussions of planning and designing multimedia for the Web; software for implementing your multimedia design; and important design principles for working with text, graphics, animation, sound, and video. Design tips and sidebars address topics related to chapter content. The discussion is followed by several hands-on projects, including an ongoing case, The Inn at Birch Bay Web site, and Project Builders that are independent of the ongoing case.

CONCEPT 2

UNDERSTAND
Fonts

What You'll Learn

In this lesson, you will learn about different font classifications and styles. You will also understand the importance of adjusting the font size, spacing, color, line length, and alignment of text on a Web page.

Good typography is anything but boring. There are literally thousands of fonts on the market today. Slight differences between two fonts can create vast differences in the look and feel of a Web site. There are times when it is difficult to describe what distinguishes one font from another in technical terms, yet fonts often have a certain look or feel associated with them—in much the same way that colors often have emotions associated with them. See Figure 5-5 for examples of feelings associated with fonts. Regardless of how you describe them, each one would lend an entirely different mood to a Web site.

Emphasis can be added by varying the font, including the style, size, or color used. Special effects and drop shadows can be used to give the feeling of three dimensions. The subtleties of type foster a variety of impressions and can change the entire feeling of a Web site. Look at the typography in the three examples shown in Figure 5-6. It is obvious that the fonts used in these three examples were selected in part because of the mood they create. The fonts used lend meaning to the Web sites. They communicate a feeling to the user. It is important to remember that different fonts evoke different emotional responses.

FIGURE 5-5
Each of these fonts creates a different mood

162 Multimedia Element—Text Chapter 5

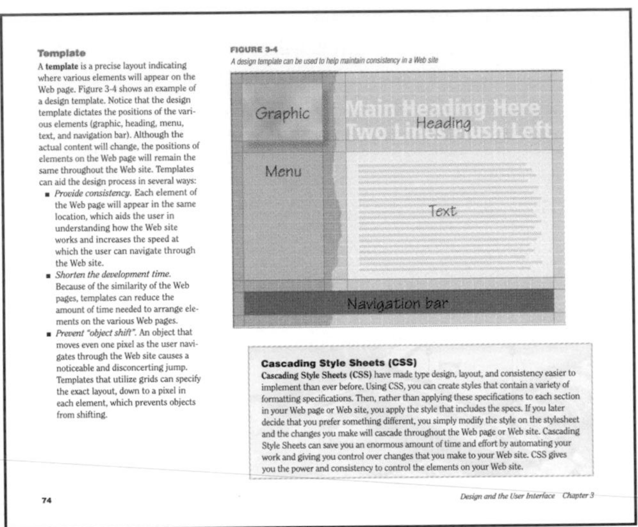

Template

A **template** is a precise layout indicating where various elements will appear on the Web page. Figure 3-4 shows an example of a design template. Notice that the design template dictates the positions of the various elements (graphic, heading, menu, text, and navigation bar). Although the actual content will change, the positions of elements on the Web page will remain the same throughout the Web site. Templates can aid the design process in several ways:

- *Provide consistency.* Each element of the Web page will appear in the same location, which aids the user in understanding how the Web site works and increases the speed at which the user can navigate through the Web site.
- *Shorten the development time.* Because of the similarity of the Web pages, templates can reduce the amount of time needed to arrange elements on the various Web pages.
- *Prevent "object shift".* An object that moves even one pixel as the user navigates through the Web site causes a noticeable and disconcerting jump. Templates that utilize grids can specify the exact layout, down to a pixel in each element, which prevents objects from shifting.

FIGURE 3-4
A design template can be used to help maintain consistency in a Web site

Cascading Style Sheets (CSS)

Cascading Style Sheets (CSS) have made type design, layout, and consistency easier to implement than ever before. Using CSS, you can create styles that contain a variety of formatting specifications. Then, rather than applying these specifications to each section in your Web page or Web site, you apply the style that includes the specs. If you later decide that you prefer something different, you simply modify the style on the stylesheet and the changes you make will cascade throughout the Web page or Web site. Cascading Style Sheets can save you an enormous amount of time and effort by automating your work and giving you control over changes that you make to your Web site. CSS gives you the power and consistency to control the elements on your Web site.

74 Design and the User Interface Chapter 3

What You'll Learn

The beginning of every concept features a What You'll Learn bullet and graphic. The bullet gives you an at-a-glance look at the concept covered in the chapter so that before you start each concept, you will know what "territory" it will cover. Above the bullet is a "sneak preview" of part of a screen or a piece of artwork from the concept.

Chapter Introduction

A chapter introduction lays the groundwork for the concepts that follow. These introductory pages give a brief historical perspective on the chapter topic, leading up to the present time, and/or explain relevant terminology and processes that help you understand the context of the concepts that follow.

Software Overview

The majority of the chapters describe the leading software packages in a given area; in these chapters, the first concepts always discuss the multimedia element and related design principles when appropriate. These concepts are followed by a discussion of the major industry software players as they relate to this multimedia element discussed at the beginning of the chapter. Major features of the software and, often, screens showing the software are presented. This way you learn what the major industry players are in each software category and why you might select one over another to meet your particular needs.

Software Discussion and Instructions

The discussion of the software packages provides a broad overview of the software. Sometimes, steps describing how to perform certain tasks are included in the discussion; these steps are generic and are not tied to any particular Data File. Combined with explanations of selected tools and other interface elements, these discussions give you a view of the software package's basic capabilities, help you appreciate a program's strengths, and prepare you for a more comprehensive course in the application.

Summing It Up

At the end of the last concept in each chapter, a one- or two-page **Summary** provides a concise overview of the major points covered in the chapter.

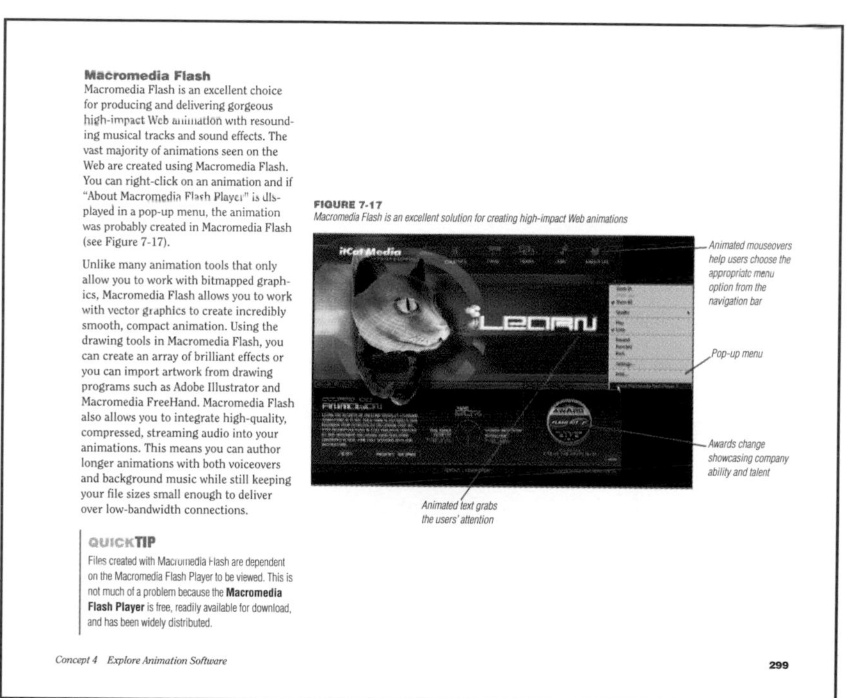

Macromedia Flash

Macromedia Flash is an excellent choice for producing and delivering gorgeous high-impact Web animation with resounding musical tracks and sound effects. The vast majority of animations seen on the Web are created using Macromedia Flash. You can right-click on an animation and if "About Macromedia Flash Player" is displayed in a pop-up menu, the animation was probably created in Macromedia Flash (see Figure 7-17).

Unlike many animation tools that only allow you to work with bitmapped graphics, Macromedia Flash allows you to work with vector graphics to create incredibly smooth, compact animation. Using the drawing tools in Macromedia Flash, you can create an array of brilliant effects or you can import artwork from drawing programs such as Adobe Illustrator and Macromedia FreeHand. Macromedia Flash also allows you to integrate high-quality, compressed, streaming audio into your animations. This means you can author longer animations with both voiceovers and background music while still keeping your file sizes small enough to deliver over low-bandwidth connections.

QUICKTIP

Files created with Macromedia Flash are dependent on the Macromedia Flash Player to be viewed. This is not much of a problem because the **Macromedia Flash Player** is free, readily available for download, and has been widely distributed.

FIGURE 7-17
Macromedia Flash is an excellent solution for creating high-impact Web animations

iCat Media
Animated mouseovers help users choose the appropriate menu option from the navigation bar
Pop-up menu
Awards change showcasing company ability and talent
Animated text grabs the users' attention

Concept 4 Explore Animation Software 299

PREFACE

Projects

This book contains a variety of end-of-chapter material for additional practice and reinforcement. The **Key Terms** list includes all boldfaced terms and concepts covered in the chapter, letting you review the terms to check your mastery of the chapter material. The **Matching Questions** and **Discussion Questions** provide material for self-assessment and in-class discussions.

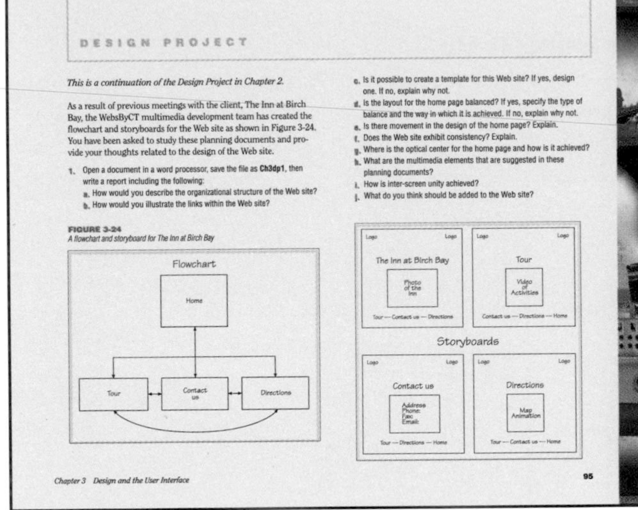

DESIGN PROJECT

This is a continuation of the Design Project in Chapter 2.

As a result of previous meetings with the client, The Inn at Birch Bay, the WebsByCT multimedia development team has created the flowchart and storyboards for the Web site as shown in Figure 3-24. You have been asked to study these planning documents and provide your thoughts related to the design of the Web site.

1. Open a document in a word processor, save the file as **Ch3dp1**, then write a report including the following:
   a. How would you describe the organizational structure of the Web site?
   b. How would you illustrate the links within the Web site?
   c. Is it possible to create a template for this Web site? If yes, design one. If no, explain why not.
   d. Is the layout for the home page balanced? If yes, specify the type of balance and the way in which it is achieved. If no, explain why not.
   e. Is there movement in the design of the home page? Explain.
   f. Does the Web site exhibit consistency? Explain.
   g. Where is the optical center for the home page and how is it achieved?
   h. What are the multimedia elements that are suggested in these planning documents?
   i. How is inter-screen unity achieved?
   j. What do you think should be added to the Web site?

FIGURE 3-24
A flowchart and storyboard for The Inn at Birch Bay

Chapter 3 Design and the User Interface 95

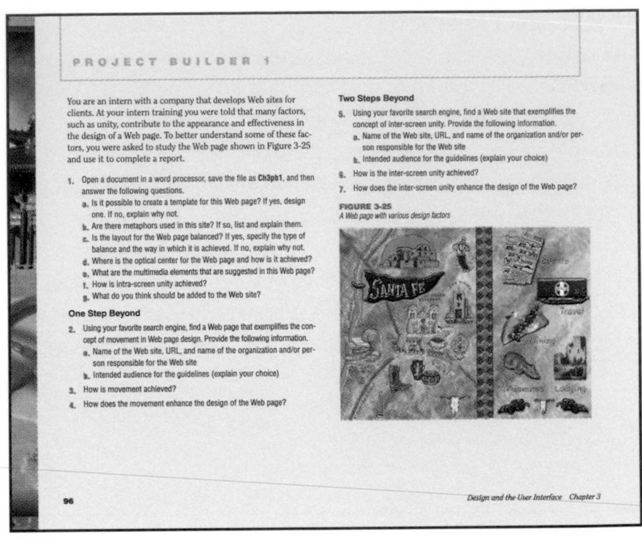

PROJECT BUILDER 1

You are an intern with a company that develops Web sites for clients. At your intern training you were told that many factors, such as unity, contribute to the appearance and effectiveness in the design of a Web page. To better understand some of these factors, you were asked to study the Web page shown in Figure 3-25 and use it to complete a report.

1. Open a document in a word processor, save the file as **Ch3pb1**, and then answer the following questions.
   a. Is it possible to create a template for this Web page? If yes, design one. If no, explain why not.
   b. Are there metaphors used in this site? If so, list and explain them.
   c. Is the layout for the Web page balanced? If yes, specify the type of balance and the way in which it is achieved. If no, explain why not.
   d. Where is the optical center for the Web page and how is it achieved?
   e. What are the multimedia elements that are suggested in this Web page?
   f. How is intra-screen unity achieved?
   g. What do you think should be added to the Web site?

One Step Beyond

2. Using your favorite search engine, find a Web page that exemplifies the concept of movement in Web page design. Provide the following information.
   a. Name of the Web site, URL, and name of the organization and/or person responsible for the Web site
   b. Intended audience for the guidelines (explain your choice)
3. How is movement achieved?
4. How does the movement enhance the design of the Web page?

Two Steps Beyond

5. Using your favorite search engine, find a Web site that exemplifies the concept of inter-screen unity. Provide the following information.
   a. Name of the Web site, URL, and name of the organization and/or person responsible for the Web site
   b. Intended audience for the guidelines (explain your choice)
6. How is the inter-screen unity achieved?
7. How does the inter-screen unity enhance the design of the Web page?

FIGURE 3-25
A Web page with various design factors

96 Design and the User Interface Chapter 3

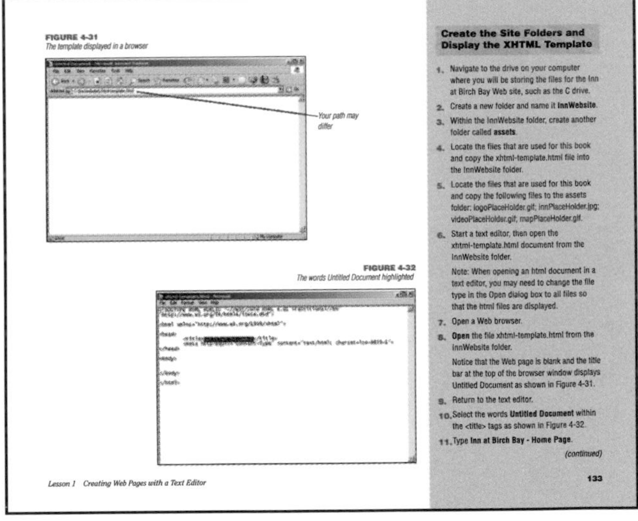

FIGURE 4-31
The template displayed in a browser

FIGURE 4-32
The words Untitled Document highlighted

Create the Site Folders and Display the XHTML Template

1. Navigate to the drive on your computer where you will be storing the files for the Inn at Birch Bay Web site, such as the C drive.
2. Create a new folder and name it **InnWebsite**.
3. Within the InnWebsite folder, create another folder called **assets**.
4. Locate the files that are used for this book and copy the xhtml-template.html file into the InnWebsite folder.
5. Locate the files that are used for this book and copy the following files to the assets folder: logoPlaceHolder.gif; innPlaceHolder.jpg; videoPlaceHolder.gif; mapPlaceHolder.gif.
6. Start a text editor, then open the xhtml-template.html document from the InnWebsite folder.
   Note: When opening an html document in a text editor, you may need to change the file type in the Open dialog box to all files so that the html files are displayed.
7. Open a Web browser.
8. **Open** the file xhtml-template.html from the InnWebsite folder.
   Notice that the Web page is blank and the title bar at the top of the browser window displays Untitled Document as shown in Figure 4-31.
9. Return to the text editor.
10. Select the words **Untitled Document** within the <title> tags as shown in Figure 4-32.
11. Type **Inn at Birch Bay - Home Page**.

(continued)

Lesson 1 Creating Web Pages with a Text Editor 133

The chapter concludes with three projects: one Design Project and two Project Builders. The **Design Project** offers step-by-step instruction in building a Web site, The Inn at Birch Bay, from scratch. Each chapter provides the opportunity to integrate additional multimedia components. The **Project Builders** prompt you to consider the concepts and software skills you have learned in the chapter. The One Step Beyond and Two Steps Beyond features let you extend your knowledge further into the concepts and skills.

What Instructor Resources Are Available with This Book?

The Instructor Resources CD-ROM is Thomson Course Technology's way of putting the resources and information needed to teach and learn effectively into your hands. All the resources are available for both Macintosh and Windows operating systems, and many of the resources can be downloaded from *www.course.com*.

Instructor's Manual

Available as an electronic file, the Instructor's Manual is quality-assurance tested and includes chapter overviews and detailed lecture topics for each chapter, with teaching tips. The Instructor's Manual is available on the Instructor Resources CD-ROM, or you can download it from *www.course.com*.

Syllabus

Prepare and customize your course easily using this sample course outline (available on the Instructor Resources CD-ROM).

PowerPoint Presentations

Each chapter has a corresponding PowerPoint presentation that you can use in lectures, distribute to your students, or customize to suit your course.

Figure Files

Figure Files contain all the figures from the book in bitmap format. Use the figure files to create transparency masters or include them in a PowerPoint presentation.

Data Files for Students

To complete the design project and some of the project builders in this book, your students will need Data Files. Put them on a file server for students to copy. The Data Files are available on the Instructor Resources CD-ROM and the Review Pack, and can also be downloaded from *www.course.com*. See the inside back cover for directions on downloading Data files.

Solutions to Exercises

Solution Files are provided for each phase of the design project and for the project builders. Use these files to evaluate your students' work. Or, distribute them electronically or in hard copy so students can verify their work.

Test Bank and Test Engine

ExamView is a powerful testing software package that allows instructors to create and administer printed, computer (LAN-based), and Internet exams. ExamView includes hundreds of questions that correspond to the topics covered in this text, enabling students to generate detailed study guides that include page references for further review. The computer-based and Internet testing components allow students to take exams at their computers, and also save the instructor time by grading each exam automatically.

BRIEF CONTENTS

CONTENTS

CHAPTER 1 INTRODUCING MULTIMEDIA FOR THE WEB

CHAPTER 2 PLANNING THE MULTIMEDIA WEB SITE

CONTENTS

CHAPTER 4 HTML, XHTML, AND WEB AUTHORING

CHAPTER 5 MULTIMEDIA ELEMENT—TEXT

CONTENTS

CHAPTER 6 MULTIMEDIA ELEMENT—GRAPHICS

CHAPTER 7 MULTIMEDIA ELEMENT—ANIMATION

CHAPTER 9 MULTIMEDIA ELEMENT—VIDEO

Intended Audience

This text is designed for beginning Web design and development students who want an overview of multimedia concepts, as well as an introduction to the most widely used software packages in multimedia.

Approach

This text is unique in its approach. It is a conceptual presentation of design principles and multimedia applications. Where possible, the available packages are compared and contrasted so that students will feel comfortable discussing the benefits and features of each one in a work environment. The conceptual presentation is enriched by the Design Project, which is a step-by-step, hands-on experience with some of the software discussed in the chapters. The Design Project is intended to give students an opportunity to work with major software packages in each area of multimedia, and in the process, create a fully functional, multimedia-enhanced Wed site. This title provides an introductory presentation to multimedia concepts; after completing this book, students will be able to continue on to more specific texts and courses for each. The end-of-chapter material contains:

- **Key Terms/Chapter matching questions and discussion questions** to help students check their understanding of major chapter concepts.
- **Design Projects** that use industry-standard software and develop one case through the book. As students complete the Design Project at the end of each chapter, they build a professional Web site that integrates various multimedia components, from text and images to animation, sound, and video.
- **Project Builders** that use the skills taught in the chapters, sometimes modifying supplied Data Files. These exercises assume that students will have access to a more detailed application text, if they want to take their projects further. Project Builders also feature One Step Beyond and Two Steps Beyond, which allow students to extend their knowledge and experience.

Figures

The screen shots in this text were taken on a computer running Windows XP; for applications that are also on the Macintosh platform, screens will vary slightly. Conceptual art is included to help deepen students' understanding of specific concepts.

Software

This book uses a variety of software programs to create the multimedia components:

HTML: a text editor and Macromedia Dreamweaver MX 2004

Browser: Internet Explorer 6

Images: Adobe Illustrator and Adobe Photoshop

Animation: Macromedia Flash

Sound: Macromedia Flash

Video: Windows Movie Maker 2 (PC); iMovie 3/4 (Mac)

If you are using versions of the software other than those listed here, steps and figures may vary.

The .htm file extension and the .html file extensions are interchangeable. Your Dreamweaver files might be saved using either file extension.

Data Files

The Design Project exercises and selected Project Builders ask students to open files supplied in the Data Files for this text. See the inside back cover of this book for information on how to obtain Data Files. Students download the files to a location they select, such as a hard drive, a network server, or a Zip drive.

Student Online Companion

The Student Online Companion is a Web page containing links to Web sites discussed in the chapters. Because the Web is such a dynamic environment and URLs change frequently, the text tells student to "Connect to the Internet, go to www.course.com, navigate to the page for this book, click the Student Online Companion link, then click the link for this chapter." Directing students to the Student Online Companion link allows the URLs to be as current as possible. The site also contains references to supplementary resources the authors feel will assist students who want to learn more on a particular area, and selected additional materials.

Other Notes

If you have installed Windows XP Service Pack 2, you might need to allow blocked content to view the Web site you develop. To allow blocked content, click the Internet Security bar, and then select Allow Blocked Content. Specific directions regarding screen size are included in the Design Project Introductions, when appropriate.

NR'328

chapter 1

INTRODUCING MULTIMEDIA
For the Web

1. Define Multimedia
2. Understand the Benefits of Multimedia
3. Discuss Web-based Multimedia Categories
4. Discover Careers in Web-based Multimedia

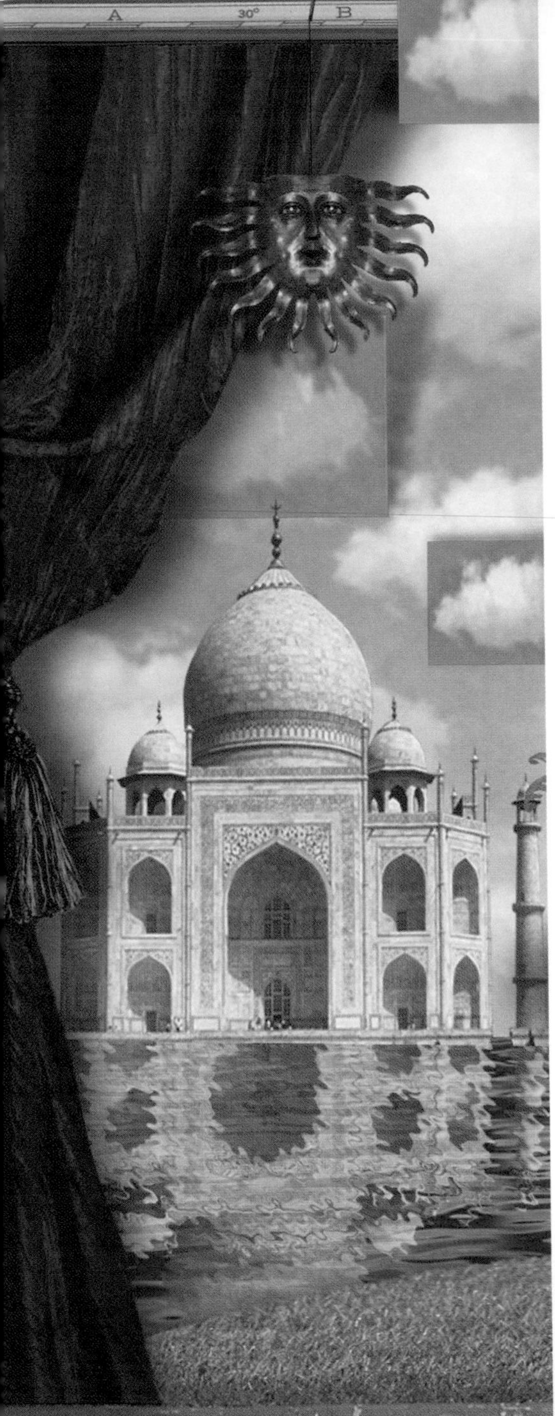

chapter 1 INTRODUCING MULTIMEDIA For the Web

Introduction

Welcome to the wonderful world of interactive **Web-based multimedia**!

Multimedia Web sites are all around you. Chances are you see or interact with one or more Web sites almost daily. Society depends on information, and the **Web** is an effective way to present it. By providing a consistent, user-friendly interface, the **Web browser** makes information easily accessible to the multitudes. Adding multimedia to Web sites makes the content accessible, as well as interactive and fun. See Figure 1-1.

In this chapter, you will be introduced to the concept of Web-based multimedia. You will also learn about the media elements that comprise today's multimedia Web sites and how interactivity is an integral part of a successful online multimedia Web site. You will learn why Web-based multimedia has become so pervasive. You will learn about the four basic categories of multimedia Web sites. In addition, you will see examples of multimedia Web sites and learn about careers in the field.

FIGURE 1-1
Multimedia-based Web sites are more interactive and more fun than static sites

In a generic sense, multimedia is simply the use of more than one media element. You have encountered multimedia if you have listened to a music clip from an online music store, played interactive games on the Web, or purchased a product or service using an interactive form at an e-commerce Web site. But what exactly is Web-based multimedia? For the purpose of discussion in this book, Web-based multimedia is defined as an online, interactive experience that incorporates two or more media elements including text, graphics, sound, animation, and video. As illustrated in Figure 1-2, a fundamental feature of most Web-based multimedia is **interactivity**, which gives the user some control over the content.

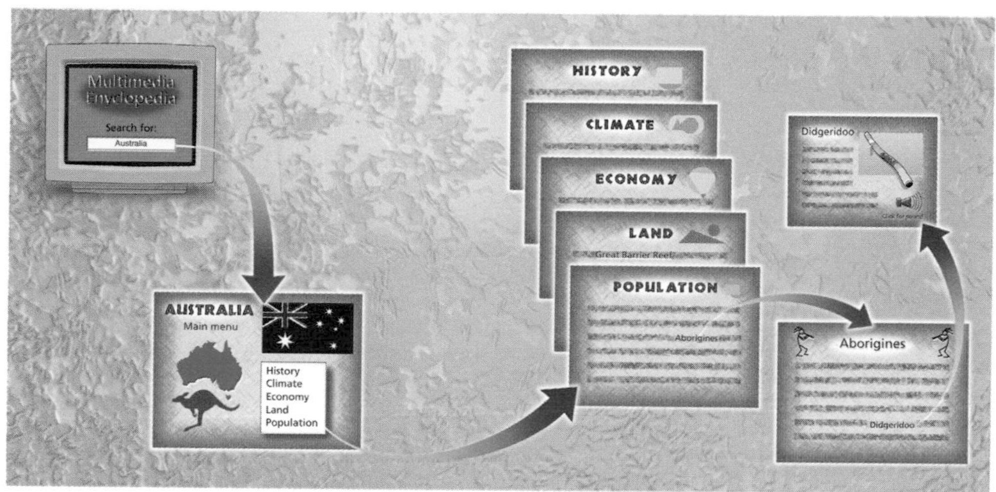

FIGURE 1-2
Multimedia interactivity

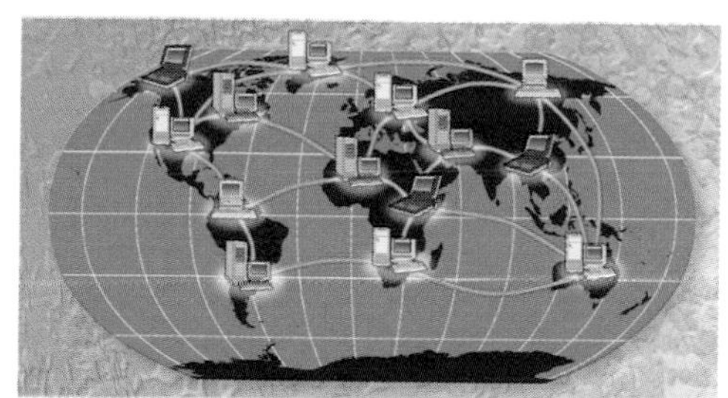

FIGURE 1-3
Browsers enable the distribution and sharing of information around the world

Explain the evolution of multimedia for the Web

The Internet grew out of a project called **ARPANET**, which was started by the military in the 1960s. Today, the **Internet** is a network of networks that connects millions of computers and people around the globe. The **World Wide Web** (also called the Web), a system that permits the distribution and sharing of information around the world, began in May 1991. Via the Internet, the World Wide Web offers the fastest-growing method for multimedia delivery.

In 1993, **Mosaic**, the first cross-platform, graphical-user interface Web browser (also called a browser) that fully exploited the Web's **hypermedia** capability, was released. Browsers provide a visual interface that interprets and displays the text and other multimedia elements, such as graphics, animation, sound, and video, included and referenced within Web pages. The development of browsers played a key role in influencing the explosive growth of the Web by providing a means to deliver hyperlinked content and multimedia via the Internet. See Figure 1-3.

CONCEPT 1

DEFINE
Multimedia

What You'll Learn

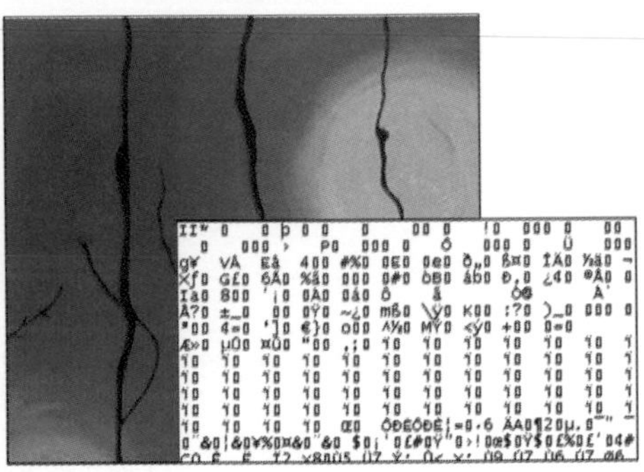

In this lesson, you will learn about multimedia and interactive multimedia, and how each of these terms is defined. You will understand the meaning of digitized media and will be introduced to the various multimedia elements. You will also get an overview of the different types of search engines.

Multimedia is not new. As a society, people are very accustomed to viewing text combined with graphics and photographs. Movies with sound replaced silent movies more than fifty years ago, but even in their day, silent movies incorporated multiple media by using video and text captions together. Today, we have full-length animated movies for children and adults, and people can view trailers, shorts, and full-length features on Web sites from companies such as Pixar (see Figure 1-4) and Disney.

The growth of Web-based multimedia has exploded over the past few years. There are many reasons for this growth. Computer processing power and technology have improved making it easier and more fun to work with media elements on the computer. People in many industries have found new and beneficial ways of using multimedia applications, thereby creating a demand for multimedia technology. The growth of the Web has spurred the growth of multimedia as more multimedia applications are designed for the Internet and the World Wide Web. Undoubtedly, this growth in Web-based multimedia will continue at a rapid rate as the technology continues to improve and people find more reasons to use it.

At the most basic level, multimedia means using more than one media. It refers to the integration of text, graphics, animation, sound, and video. Today, this integration is accomplished by digitizing different media elements and then manipulating them with computer software.

FIGURE 1-4

Web sites from companies, such as Pixar and Disney, provide opportunities to view trailers and shorts of full-length feature films

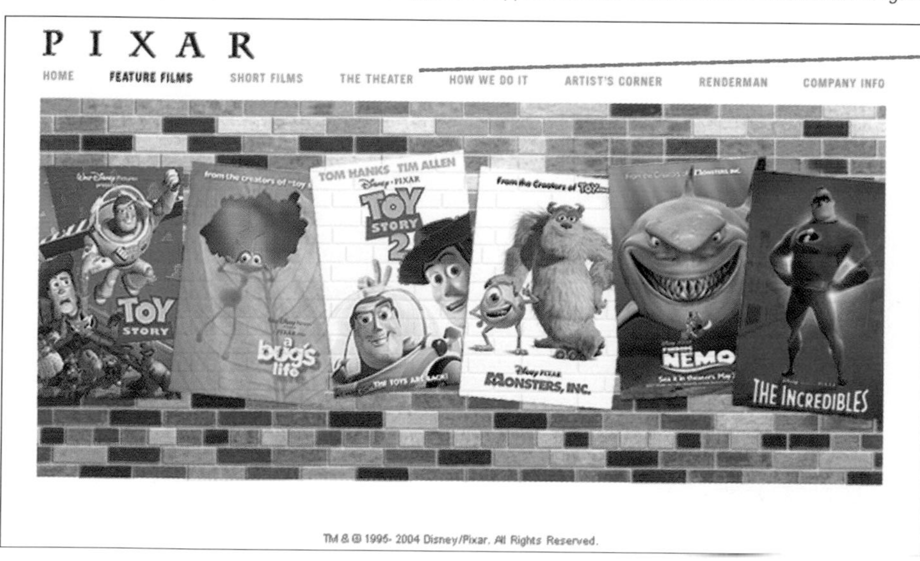

Click to access multimedia shorts and trailers

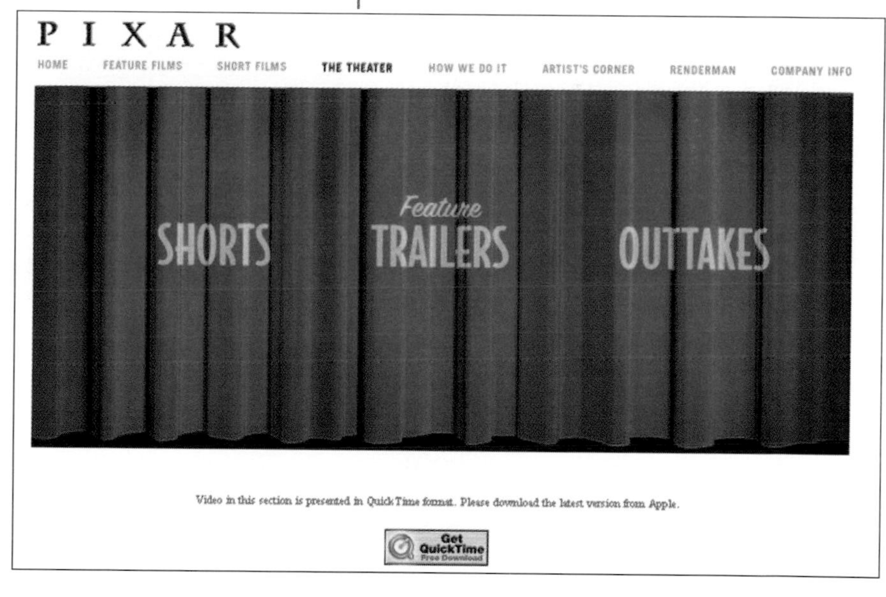

Working with media elements that have been **digitized** means the media elements have been captured in a code the computer can understand (see Figure 1-5). People can send and receive media elements across networks, developers can create and modify elements in ways they never dreamed possible, and users can interact and control these media elements for greater personalization. As a result of digitized media elements, a variety of uses for multimedia has been created within a multitude of industries. Consequently, people are surrounded by multimedia Web sites.

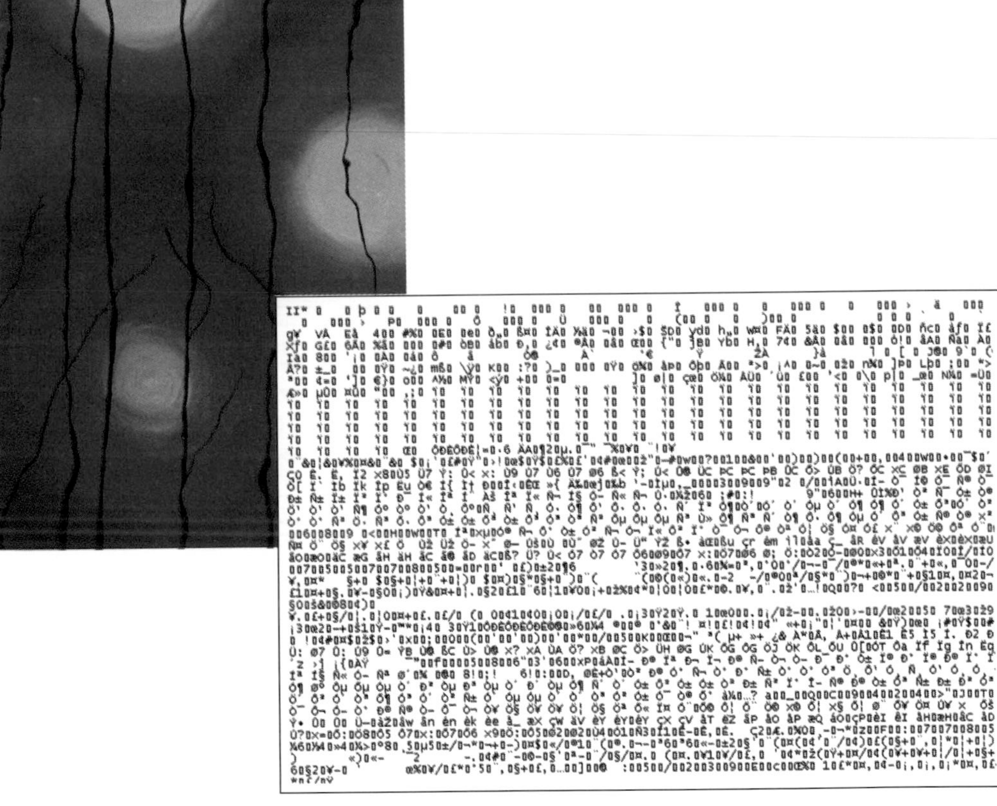

FIGURE 1-5
Digitized media elements have been converted to code that can be interpreted by the computer

Some multimedia Web sites are **linear**. In other words, users start at the beginning and progress through a set sequence of events until they reach the end. Most digital slide shows and plays are examples of linear media. The idea behind the Web, of course, is that the order of events should be left to the discretion of the user. To facilitate this idea, most Web sites use a **nonlinear** approach to navigation. Because there is generally no established or predefined order, users have more control over what they are interested in pursuing, as well as at what point they enter and exit a Web site.

Interactive multimedia enables the user to directly respond to and control any or all of the media elements at the Web site. Users of interactive multimedia applications become active participants instead of passive recipients of information. The user determines what content is delivered, when it is delivered, and how it is delivered. Interactivity provides multimedia range and depth because it requires creativity on the part of both the designer and the user. It also frees users by giving them choices.

The Web and multimedia on the Web have grown far beyond anyone's wildest expectations. Today there are billions of Web sites through which people share information around the world. Web pages are documents that can contain text, graphics, photographs, animation, sound, video, software, applications, and forms for data handling and **e-commerce**. Web-based multimedia has evolved into a billion-dollar industry, and it is still growing at an incredible rate. Because of increased bandwidth, improved compression, more powerful processors, and better software, it is becoming easier and easier to include multimedia on Web pages.

DESIGNTIP Using forms to add interactivity

Up to this point, we have been focusing primarily on delivering media to users. Yet in order to be truly interactive, Web pages should also allow us to get information from users. Forms invite users to interact with a Web site. Online forms allow you to receive immediate feedback from your users. You can use forms for surveys, orders, and guest books. If you are using a database for a transaction or any kind of search that will be initiated from a Web page, you will also need to set up an online form.

Interactivity is created within the form when users are given choices. In creating interactivity, intuitive, user-friendly stimuli are important. Methods of interactivity should be obvious to the user. There are many ways to design interactivity into your forms, including hyperlinks, buttons and icons, menus, keyboard commands, text boxes, check boxes, radio or option buttons, drop-down list boxes, and drag-and-drop functionality.

Using search engines

As the number of Web pages has increased into the billions, users often find they need help locating the information they want. Search engines make finding information possible. There are thousands of search engines available today. Although each search engine has its own little quirks and methods for dealing with keywords and performing advanced searches, there are really just three major categories of search engines. A **spider-based search engine** automatically roams the World Wide Web adding the contents of the Web sites it visits to its database. A **directory-based search engine** is selective, meaning that humans choose which sites to add to the database. A **pay-per-click** search engine gives priority placement to sites offering top bidding for keywords.

In order for users to find a Web site, it must usually be registered with search engines. The process of registering a Web site is discussed later in the book.

CONCEPT 2

UNDERSTAND THE BENEFITS of Multimedia

What You'll Learn

Aeolian Wind Harp
Originating in ancient Greec
and flourishing throughout th
era, Aeolian Harps are rare,
instruments designed to be
wind; free of the touch of hu
Wind Harps transpose the s
into spontaneous, multi-laye
time to nature's rhythms. Th
voices sing pure harmonic t
from deep, pulsing bases to
sopranos. A variety of winds
string tunings combine on th
recordings to produce an ec
of definitive music.
Greg Joly has been building
of various sizes for over 20 y
range from smaller harps tha
and window openings, to the
pictured at left. Visit Greg's
www.harmonicwindharps.
Click here to listen to a
Grand Harp.
ctured above) stands 7.5'

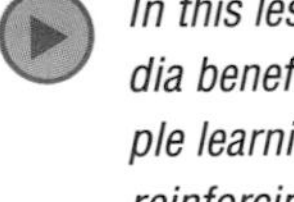

In this lesson, you will learn how multimedia benefits the user by addressing multiple learning styles, conveying content, reinforcing ideas, creating rich experiences, giving life to flat information, enhancing user enjoyment, improving retention, and enabling user control.

The importance of interactive multimedia can be summarized by the Chinese proverb, "Tell me and I will forget; show me and I may remember; involve me and I will understand." Why? Because each person learns differently and each person is inspired by something different. The use of multimedia allows Web developers to tap into these differences. For example, some people are visual learners. They learn or are inspired by reading, seeing, or visualizing. Other people are auditory and learn best by listening. And, there are kinesthetic learners who learn by doing. Many people learn through a combination of these learning styles.

Although each person has a preferred learning style, learning experiences for everyone are enhanced when each learning style is accommodated. In fact, research shows that people remember only 20 percent of what they see and 30 percent of what they hear. When they see it and hear it, they remember 50 percent. When they see it, hear it, and interact with it, they remember 80 percent. That is a big difference, which certainly supports the increased use of Web-based multimedia. Figure 1-6 summarizes some benefits of using Web-based multimedia.

Web sites that include multimedia enable Web designers to create rich, multisensory experiences that accommodate multiple learning styles and enhance the user's enjoyment at a site. In addition, retention improves when people are able to see, hear, and interact with the content.

FIGURE 1-6
Benefits of using Web-based multimedia

- Addresses multiple learning styles (visual, auditory, and kinesthetic)
- Provides an excellent way to convey content
- Uses a variety of media elements to reinforce one idea
- Activates multiple senses creating rich experiences
- Gives life to flat information
- Enhances user enjoyment
- Improves retention
- Enables users to control Web experience

An excellent way to convey content is to use a variety of media elements to reinforce *one* idea. In other words, use multiple media to direct the user's attention to one concept or idea. Figure 1-7 illustrates this concept as it uses a balance of text, graphics, photographs, and sound to convey information about a particular musical instrument. When designing for the Web, we have to be careful not to overwhelm the user by trying to use multiple media to convey *multiple* ideas simultaneously. Finding the right balance and relationship between the media elements is critical.

When multiple media are incorporated into an application, more senses are activated. Consequently, one reason to use multimedia is to give life to flat information. Multimedia encourages users to embrace, internalize, and glean more from information because users can undertake the information from multiple directions. In other words, users of multimedia applications have an opportunity to read about information, as well as to see it, hear it, and watch it move. Today, most multimedia Web sites consist primarily of elements that involve the eyes and ears, but this too is changing as research on touch and smell continues to be explored.

In the future, multimedia will provide greater opportunities and options to control the Web environment whether it is for entertainment, research, education, or conducting business. In an effort to accommodate an increasingly mobile society, multimedia will continue to evolve into an extremely rich and powerful information environment that will be easily shared across networks and experienced on hand-held devices that are getting smaller and more portable each day.

FIGURE 1-7

All of the different elements on this screen convey information about one idea, the Aeolian wind harp

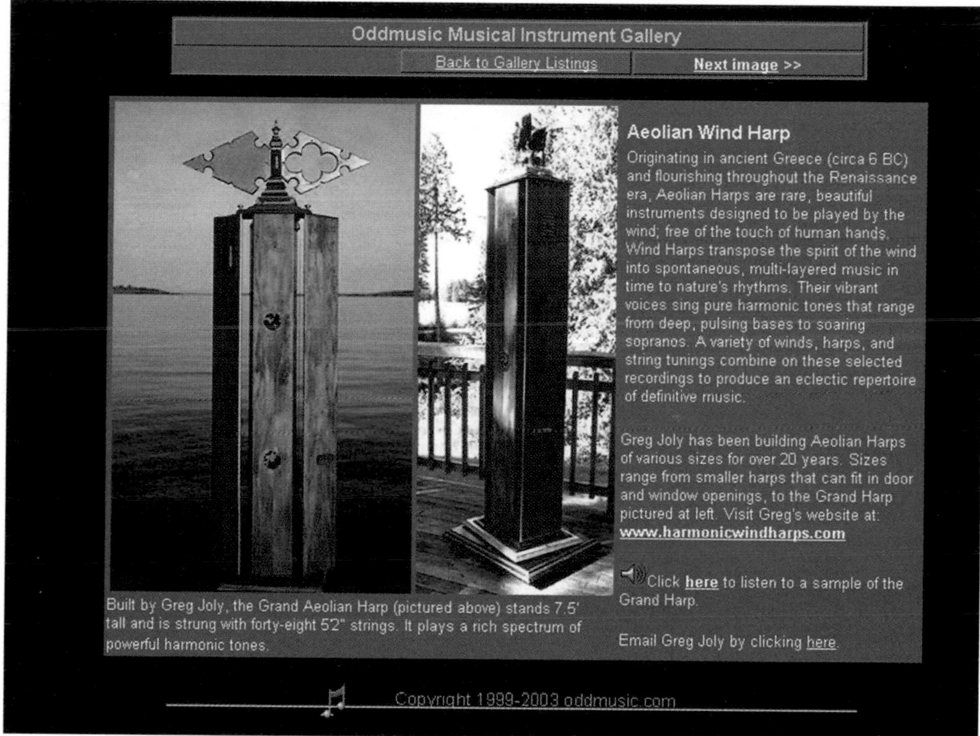

Oddmusic Musical Instrument Gallery
Back to Gallery Listings
Next image >>
Aeolian Wind Harp
Originating in ancient Greece (circa 6 BC) and flourishing throughout the Renaissance era, Aeolian Harps are rare, beautiful instruments designed to be played by the wind; free of the touch of human hands. Wind Harps transpose the spirit of the wind into spontaneous, multi-layered music in time to nature's rhythms. Their vibrant voices sing pure harmonic tones that range from deep, pulsing bases to soaring sopranos. A variety of winds, harps, and string tunings combine on these selected recordings to produce an eclectic repertoire of definitive music.
Greg Joly has been building Aeolian Harps of various sizes for over 20 years. Sizes range from smaller harps that can fit in door and window openings, to the Grand Harp pictured at left. Visit Greg's website at: www.harmonicwindharps.com
Click here to listen to a sample of the Grand Harp.
Email Greg Joly by clicking here.
Built by Greg Joly, the Grand Aeolian Harp (pictured above) stands 7.5' tall and is strung with forty-eight 52" strings. It plays a rich spectrum of powerful harmonic tones.
Copyright 1999-2003 oddmusic.com

CONCEPT 3

DISCUSS WEB-BASED Multimedia Categories

What You'll Learn

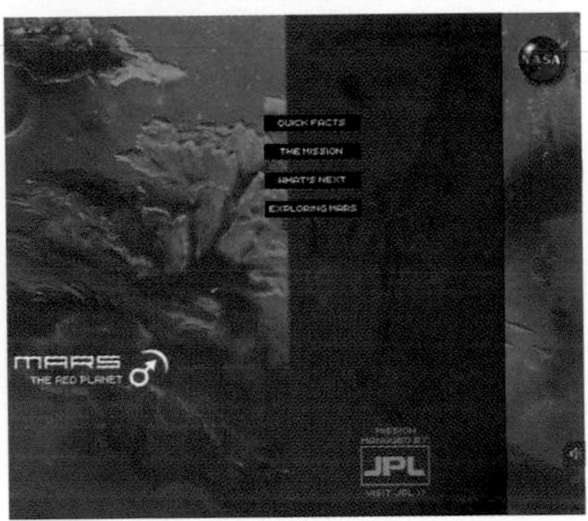

In this lesson, you will learn about the role of multimedia Web sites in e-commerce, Web-based training and distance learning, research and reference, and entertainment and games.

From e-commerce to distance learning to research to games, multimedia Web sites offer a variety of applications to a range of industries. In the past, the entertainment industry was the primary creator and disseminator of multimedia. However, the surge of activity on the World Wide Web has caused multimedia to become more prevalent via the Internet. The Web has opened the doors of multimedia production to a variety of users and has expanded the application of multimedia outside the world of entertainment.

Once it was considered exemplary simply to have a presence on the Web. Today, in order to get a visitor to return to your Web site, you need more than good content. For this reason and because it is easier to include multimedia on a Web page, multimedia Web sites are becoming increasingly important. Hyperlinks allow users access to resources from around the globe. Graphics and animation convey information, reinforce content, and guide the user. Audio and video clips involve additional senses thus improving understanding and giving depth to a flat page.

Software packages empower users to create multimedia Web sites. These software programs help users create Web pages with multimedia elements for online games, interactive forms, electronic magazines, reference materials, entertainment, and more. As bandwidth issues pose less of a concern, the use of multimedia on the Web will continue to grow.

E-commerce

The Web has caused a revolution in the way most companies do business (see Figure 1-8). E-commerce is one category in which Web-based multimedia plays a critical role. E-commerce involves using the Web to serve clients and customers and is one way to provide solutions for companies, small or large, that wish to sell products or services online. E-commerce is about setting up your business on the Web, giving potential customers access to your Web site, and allowing them to peruse a virtual catalog of your products or services online. When customers decide to buy something, they simply add it to their virtual shopping cart. Items can be added to or deleted from the virtual shopping cart until the customer is ready to check out. At the point of checkout, the customer's total is calculated and the information is securely transmitted.

Companies have moved to e-commerce for a number of reasons. By using the Web to sell and market their products, they can significantly expand their customer base, reaching a larger number of customers from all over the world. Businesses are also able to stay open 24 hours a day, 7 days a week without the burden of maintaining a traditional business operation. By expanding their market and making use of technology to sell products and services, many companies have been able to increase sales significantly. In addition, if they are able to reduce overhead or operate without a traditional storefront they can cut costs, thereby increasing profits. If e-commerce is used effectively, companies can improve the efficiency of order processing, reduce inventory and warehousing expenses, and lower the actual dollar cost of sales transactions, all of which result in higher profit margins.

The use of multimedia elements is helping companies sell their products and services online because multimedia elements are much more likely to grab attention than text alone. Multimedia elements are used extensively in advertising and marketing. Web designers employ multimedia-authoring software to create unique, attention-getting advertisements with animated text and graphics. Animated logos and banners advertising products, services, and links to other sites are everywhere on the Web. E-commerce Web sites rely heavily on multimedia elements, such as a site search feature that visitors use to find products they want and online forms that visitors use to submit their orders.

QUICKTIP

Data handling and security are also important aspects of e-commerce.

Two types of companies do business on the Internet: those companies that augment a traditional business with an online storefront, and those companies that use the Internet exclusively to reach potential customers. This second type of company is one that exists solely on the Internet and does not have a traditional storefront from which to conduct business in a more traditional fashion.

FIGURE 1-8

The ability to buy products and services online has changed the way consumers shop

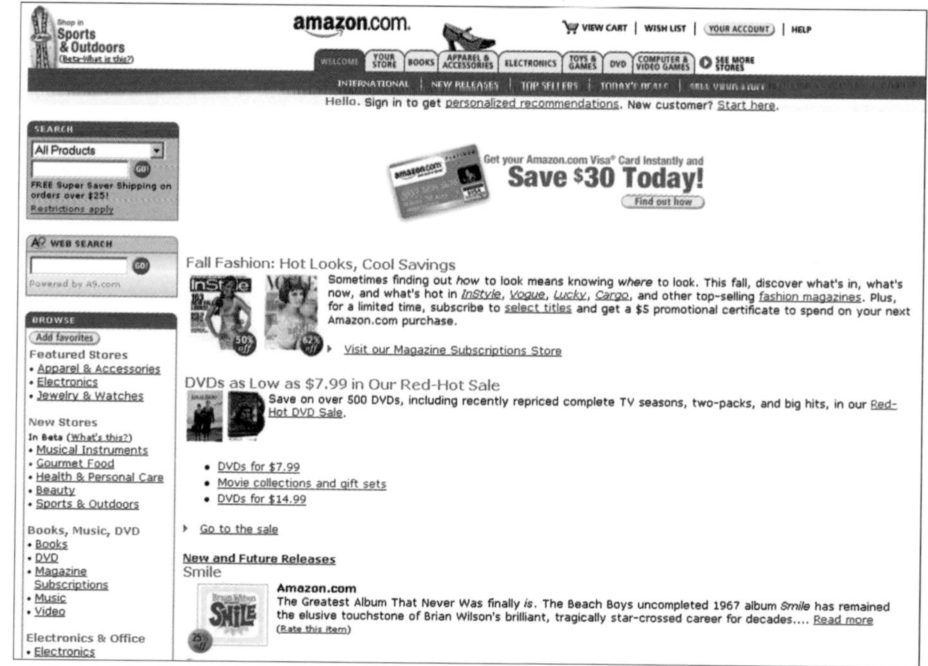

Because the way companies do business has changed, so too has the way consumers shop and buy. Record numbers of businesses are using the Web to market their goods and services online. Electronic catalogs and malls offer users variations to traditional shopping experiences. From name brands to obscure specialty shops and legal services, there really is something for everyone to buy or sell online. As seen previously in Figure 1-8, Amazon.com's Web site makes it easy to buy books and other products via the Web.

E-commerce is all about using technology to streamline business, increase efficiency, and improve sales. It is about lowering costs and establishing closer, more responsive relationships with customers, suppliers, and partners.

Web-based Training and Distance Learning

A second category Web-based multimedia is affecting is education, especially in the areas of **Web-based training** and **distance learning**. The Web offers many options for delivering and receiving education over a distance. Faced with training and retraining millions of workers, businesses around the globe are using Web-based training programs to prepare workers effectively and efficiently. Web-based training is training or instruction delivered over the Internet using a Web browser. The advantages of online distance learning include freedom of location, open entry/open exit, self-paced instruction, immediate feedback, assessment, simulated experiences, and varied learning environments.

The rise of digital media has also transformed higher education. Academic institutions are using Web-based distance learning courseware created by curriculum designers and technicians, and computer-based evaluation and self-assessment to educate and test students. Distance learning has enabled students to take courses, as well as complete certificates and degrees, online. Educational institutions also find Web-based exams useful in ensuring that students have achieved a certain level of mastery before they advance to the next level (see Figure 1-9). Research on distance learning strongly suggests that it is an effective means for delivering instruction. Through online distance learning, professors become facilitators and coaches. Learners interact globally through the Web, which provides an extensive multimedia communications network.

FIGURE 1-9

Online exams provide students with the opportunity to test their knowledge

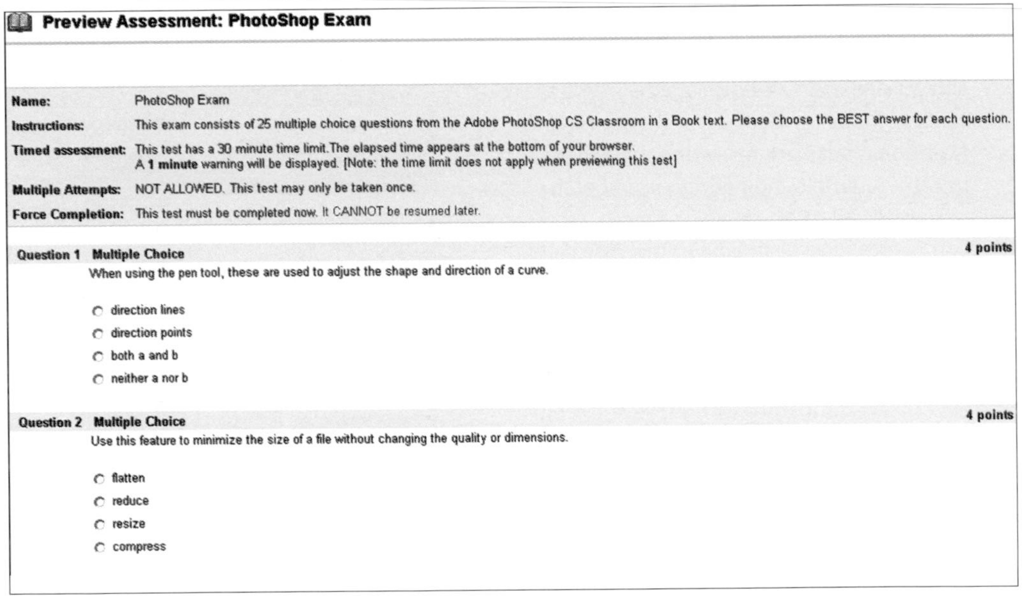

Preview Assessment: PhotoShop Exam

Name:	PhotoShop Exam
Instructions:	This exam consists of 25 multiple choice questions from the Adobe PhotoShop CS Classroom in a Book text. Please choose the BEST answer for each question.
Timed assessment:	This test has a 30 minute time limit.The elapsed time appears at the bottom of your browser. A **1 minute** warning will be displayed. [Note: the time limit does not apply when previewing this test]
Multiple Attempts:	NOT ALLOWED. This test may only be taken once.
Force Completion:	This test must be completed now. It CANNOT be resumed later.

Question 1 Multiple Choice **4 points**

When using the pen tool, these are used to adjust the shape and direction of a curve.

- direction lines
- direction points
- both a and b
- neither a nor b

Question 2 Multiple Choice **4 points**

Use this feature to minimize the size of a file without changing the quality or dimensions.

- flatten
- reduce
- resize
- compress

Research and Reference

A third category in which Web-based multimedia is expanding is in the area of research and reference. Today, newsletters, newspapers, magazines, books, encyclopedias, and other reference materials are being offered online via the Web. In many cases, they represent "electronic" versions of existing research and reference materials. The challenge to the developer is to make it easy for the user to find the desired information, as well as to use other multimedia elements such as sound, video, and animation to enhance the user experience effectively. Research Web sites and reference Web sites, such as Discovery.com and Nasa.gov (see Figure 1-10), offer full multimedia features including full-text search engines, graphics, audio, and video.

QUICKTIP

Web designers and developers rely on content specialists to ensure that the information on a Web site is accurate. However, there is no guarantee that all of the information on the Web is accurate or reliable. Be sure to verify information you read.

FIGURE 1-10

The NASA Web site offers children and adults a wealth of information

An increasing number of self-help and how-to guides are also being offered as interactive multimedia applications on the Web. Access to online counselors (see Figure 1-11) and psychologists, both real and simulated, are quite popular, as are guides to help you build a deck, repair a car, and plant a perennial garden.

Some advantages to offering reference materials in a Web-based multimedia format follow:

- *Cross-referencing*. Multimedia research and reference materials provide links that give the user immediate access to related information.
- *Expanded search capabilities*. Access to search engines enables users to locate specific topics of interest.

> **QUICKTIP**
>
> To hone in on a specific topic or reference requires wisdom, effort, creativity, and diligence. The ability to restrict and expand a search using appropriate keywords as well as advanced search techniques and Boolean operators is of paramount importance to today's information seeker.

- *Multisensory experiences*. By providing information through the use of graphics, sound, animation, and video, the research or reference material comes to life and is often more enjoyable and more memorable than text alone.

FIGURE 1-11
Virtual counselors are often less intimidating and more accessible than a real person is

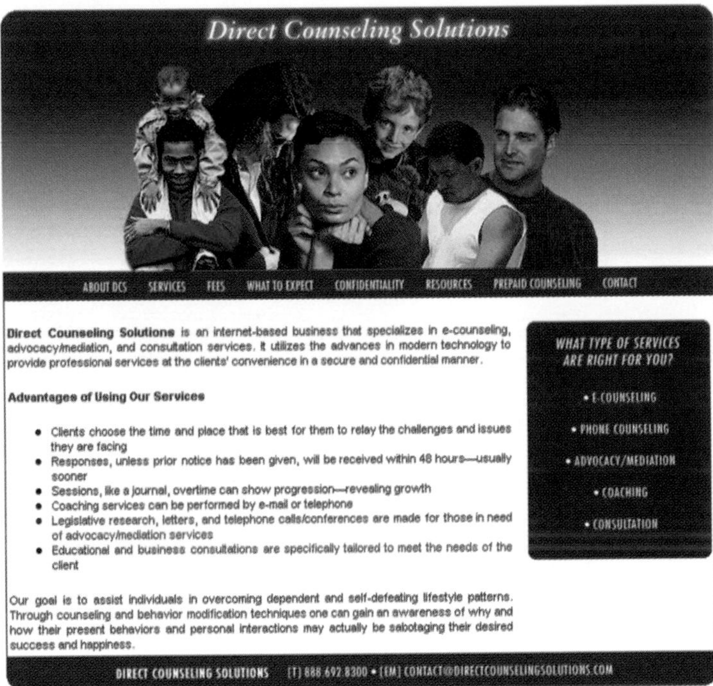

Entertainment and Games

A fourth category in which Web-based multimedia is making a significant impact is in Web game and entertainment sites. In fact, when people think of Web-based multimedia, these sites are the first to come to mind because they are examples of some of the most popular and most varied interactive multimedia sites available. Game sites often offer multilevel, multiplayer entertainment that simulates real or imaginary worlds in which characters are controlled, obstacles are encountered, and goals are achieved. From solitaire and dartboards to sites that involve more interactivity, entertainment and game Web sites are bursting with multimedia (see Figure 1-12).

Although the primary purpose of most games is entertainment, many Web sites are designed to educate as well as entertain. Again, examples abound and there is something for everyone. At Crayola.com (see Figure 1-13) kids can, among other things, mix colors and test their color IQ.

FIGURE 1-12

Puzzles, cards, trivia, action — you can find many different types of games on the Web

FIGURE 1-13

Web sites are often educational as well as entertaining

CONCEPT 4

DISCOVER CAREERS IN
Web-Based Multimedia

What You'll Learn

In this lesson, you will learn about the varied careers in Web-based multimedia and how to prepare for these careers through the development of a professional portfolio.

As more industries are discovering the value of and creative uses for the Web, consumers are demanding a wider variety of interactive Web-based multimedia products and services. To respond to this demand, industries must employ people who can help them deliver the Web presence consumers want. Opportunities for individuals with Web-based multimedia skills are varied.

Preparing for a career in Web-based multimedia is a bit like trying to hit a moving bull's-eye. Because the technology changes so rapidly, Web professionals must thrive on change and chaos, love learning, take initiative, and engage actively in self-education. Because Web design and development can be time-consuming, successful Web designers and developers not only must be good at what they do but must also love what they do, or they will quickly tire of it.

QUICKTIP

If you are interested in a career in Web-based multimedia, be prepared to be a lifelong learner. Keeping up with the latest technologies by reading, experimenting, and teaching yourself is of paramount importance. Consider doing this through conferences or seminars, which can be expensive, or through free resources such as the Web.

In the past, Web professionals were self-taught and entered the wonderful world of the Web from various backgrounds. Today, many colleges and universities offer classes, certificates, and degrees in Web design and development (see Figure 1-14).

When looking for a job, your most important asset may be your **electronic portfolio** (also called an **ePortfolio**). A compelling **portfolio** of sample work and projects to share with potential clients and employers will provide depth to your interviews (see Figure 1-15). A Web search using the keyword "portfolio" should provide links to sample portfolios to analyze and review.

As you plan and prepare your portfolio, think about the type of work that you would like to do. If your goal is to write code for a living, then develop a portfolio with an emphasis on Web page development. If your goal is to design original artwork, then ensure that your portfolio emphasizes your abilities as a graphic artist.

> **QUICKTIP**
>
> It is helpful to include a list of clients in your portfolio. Testimonials or references lend credibility to your work and prove that you can work with clients to complete a project. Even if the jobs that you have completed thus far are the result of an unpaid internship, they should still be listed.

In addition to developing a compelling portfolio of your work, be prepared to prove yourself on the spot. Many employers are asking prospective employees to prove that they have the requisite skills to complete a job. During the interview process, do not be surprised if you are asked to take a test. Depending on the type of position you are seeking, you may be asked to optimize images, create an intriguing animation, or design a Web site.

FIGURE 1-14

Most colleges and universities now offer classes, certificates, and degrees in Web design and development

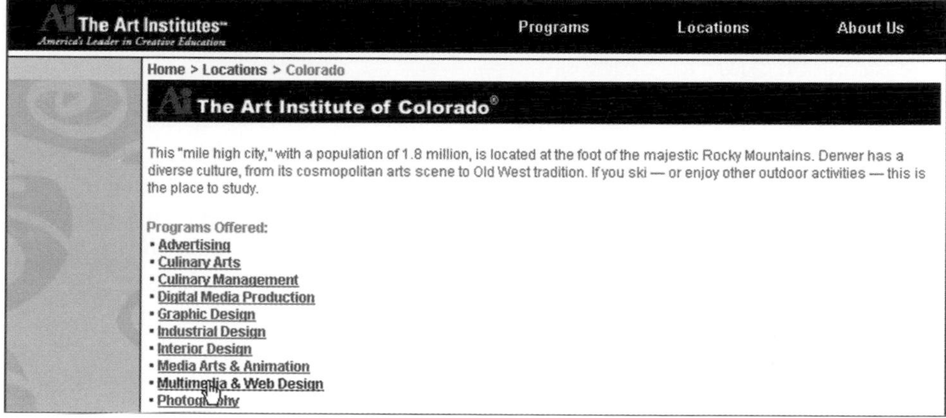

FIGURE 1-15

A compelling portfolio that showcases your talents will be paramount in launching your career in Web design

QUICKTIP

Plagiarism is the act of using someone else's ideas as your own without crediting the proper source. Résumé padding is the act of stretching the truth on your résumé, such as padding your accomplishments or education. When developing your portfolio or résumé, always be truthful.

A few years after the inception of the Web, there were Web masters who did everything. They designed, developed, and maintained the entire site. Today, very few people are able to do it all alone. Some people work independently and contract with small companies to develop simple Web sites. However, beyond simple Web sites, even people who are independent contractors generally end up developing specialty areas and contracting or subcontracting portions of a job. Regardless of the industry, creating a multimedia Web site is usually a team effort (see Figure 1-16).

QUICKTIP

Keep in mind that a project team will rarely include someone for every potential position. At times, the same person will fill several positions within a project. For example, the audio specialist may also be responsible for the video on a project.

Determining if you are the right candidate for a job

Most potential employers include a laundry list of skills in their job announcements. Even if you do not have every skill in the list, consider applying. Obviously, you will need to have most of the skills listed if you want to be considered, but if you are missing one or two, don't hesitate to give it a go. Of course, you should always be honest about your existing skill level, but if you are willing to learn and have most of what a company is seeking, you may be hired. In addition to technical skills, do not underestimate the value of soft skills including excellent communication and interpersonal skills, a strong work ethic, and the ability to work with clients and as part of a team. These skills are always highly sought after and valued.

FIGURE 1-16

Today's Web sites are generally created by teams of specialists

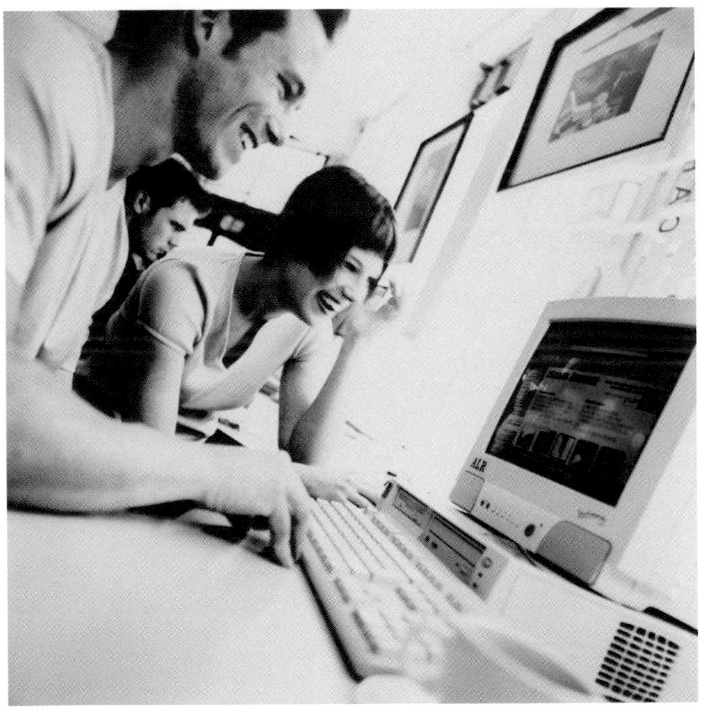

As is true in most new industries, the job titles encountered in the Web world are varied and constantly changing. There are position announcements for Web master, Web designer, and Web developer. Within specialty areas there are listings for graphic artists, graphic specialists, graphic designers, animation specialists, animation designers, and directors of animation.

Position titles and job duties vary depending on the industry and even within the same industry. Some of the more common team member categories and their corresponding duties are listed in Figure 1-17 (Note: Careers have been grouped into broad categories and general skills associated with those categories listed). Not all jobs in a category will require all the skills listed and not all skills required are listed, but the information presented in Figure 1-17 provides a broad overview of Web-based multimedia careers.

- *Management-related positions.*
  Executive Producer: The primary role of the executive producer (also called **producer**) is to move a project into and through production. This person will work with clients and is particularly active in the development and delivery stages of the application. This person is the team leader.
  Project Manager: The project manager (also called **production manager**) is responsible for forming a project, moving it into production, and overseeing its creation. This involves working with clients, developing original concepts, preparing budgets and schedules, hiring personnel and assembling project teams, assembling resources and equipment, managing conceptual design, and managing production. This person will have a closer day-to-day working relationship with the project team than the executive producer/producer will have.

FIGURE 1-17
Categories for careers in Web-based multimedia and their associated skills

Category	Sample of skills these jobs require
Management-related positions	Management skills, high-level communication skills, the ability to see the big picture, understanding of Web-based multimedia tools, knowledge of copyright and other laws, negotiation skills, and human resource skills
Production-related positions	Skills in markup, scripting and programming languages, as well as Web-based multimedia authoring programs; excellent graphic and typography skills; artistic talent and a good understanding of design; good communication skills; and expertise with Web-based multimedia programs and creation tools
Art-related positions	Good graphic editing skills; a talent for layout and design; expertise in working with various drawing and paint programs; and a basic knowledge of Web authoring tools
Content-related positions	Excellent writing, editing, and planning skills; research skills; and attention to detail
Support-related positions	Communication skills; attention to detail; and excellent human relations skills

- *Production-related positions.*
  Audio specialist: The audio specialist works with musical scores, sound effects, voice-overs, vocals, and transitional sounds, and is responsible for recording, editing, and selecting voices, sounds, and music. The audio specialist should have an in-depth knowledge of digital sound, skills in sound editing, and knowledge of streaming technologies and multimedia authoring tools.
  Computer programmer: The programmer creates the underlying code that makes the Web site interactive and responsive to the user's actions. Programmers help craft and implement the project by writing lines of code that define the structure, interactions, and technical implications of certain decisions. Computer programmers are the foundation of the project because they help the Web team realize its collective vision.
  Video specialist: The video specialist manages the process of capturing and editing original video. Today's Web-based video specialists need in-depth skills in digital video and video production as well as an extensive knowledge of streaming technologies.
  Web designer: The Web designer develops or refines a design process and efficiently creates a cohesive and well-planned Web site from the front-end. The Web designer is both an artist and a technician and needs a talent and eye for creating an effective color scheme and layout. The Web designer must ensure that all of the multimedia elements on the Web site are high quality and consistent with the purpose and goals of the overall theme of the site.
  Web developer: The Web developer ensures that the communication between the front-end of the Web site and the back-end of the Web site is working. It is the responsibility of the Web developer to make sure that data input from users is properly verified and transmitted.
  Web master: The Web master is responsible for making sure the Web page is technically correct and functional on the Web server and that the Web server remains accessible to the user.

- *Art-related positions.*
  Animation specialist: The animation specialist creates two-dimensional and three-dimensional animation by taking a sequence of static images and displaying them in rapid succession on the computer screen. This creates the illusion of motion. The animation specialist must have graphic design skills and skills in the newest animation programs.
  Art director: The art director's responsibility is to coordinate the creation of the artwork for the project. Traditionally, art directors have primarily worked with visual and graphic artwork. However, with interactive media, the art director may also be responsible for sound, animation, and video.
  Graphic artist/designer: The graphic artist is responsible for creating and designing all of the graphic images for a project. This includes buttons, bars, backgrounds, type, illustrations, 3-D objects, logos, and photographs. The graphic designer works closely with the interface designer and the Web designer to create a unified and cohesive look for the Web site.
  Interface designer: The interface designer is responsible for the look of the Web site's interface and navigation method. Interface designers create and design icons, buttons, and the other onscreen elements that are used to navigate the site. In addition, this person is responsible for what users hear, touch, and feel. Interface designers need to understand both the human cognitive process and how to develop intuitive human interfaces. Consequently, these people will generally have a background in psychology with an emphasis on human factors.
  Photographer: The photographer shoots and captures appropriate, compelling, and high-quality photos to be used on the Web site.
  Videographer: The videographer shoots and captures appropriate, compelling, and high-quality video footage to be used on the Web site.

- *Content-related positions.*
  Content specialist: The content specialist is responsible for providing authenticity and accuracy to the information on a Web site. Clients often serve as content specialists, particularly when a Web site is being created for an e-commerce business.
  Instructional specialist: The instructional specialist is an expert in designing instructional projects. This person's responsibilities include defining learning objectives and outcomes, as well as establishing the delivery and flow of a project around the best educational strategies. Instructional specialists should have a background in educational theory and curriculum development as well as knowledge of the basic principles of multimedia authoring. Most Web-based distance learning packages were designed with the aid of one or more instructional specialists (see Figure 1-18).
  Writers/editors: Depending on the purpose of the Web site there may be technical writers, scriptwriters, creative writers, or journalists involved in the project. Because most Web sites are interactive and nonlinear, Web writers must learn to bridge the gap between journalistic reporting and traditional writing. Editors work closely with the Web writers to ensure that the text is grammatically correct and that the content flows in a logical fashion.
- *Support-related positions.*
  Production positions: An entry-level production position may involve tasks such as scanning and cleaning up photographs or optimizing images for the Web. Entry-level production positions provide an excellent learning environment and an opportunity to learn the real-world aspects of the job. In addition, these positions give the company an opportunity to evaluate the work habits and skills of potential employees.
  Quality-assurance: A **tester** is responsible for testing the Web site on multiple platforms using different versions of different browsers. Testers also evaluate the design of the site and the intuitiveness of the user interface.
  Sales/marketing: Sales and marketing people are involved in providing input and feedback on the site. Once the Web site is completed, **customer support personnel** respond to users who have questions and problems.

FIGURE 1-18
Instructional specialists assist in the development of distance learning Web sites

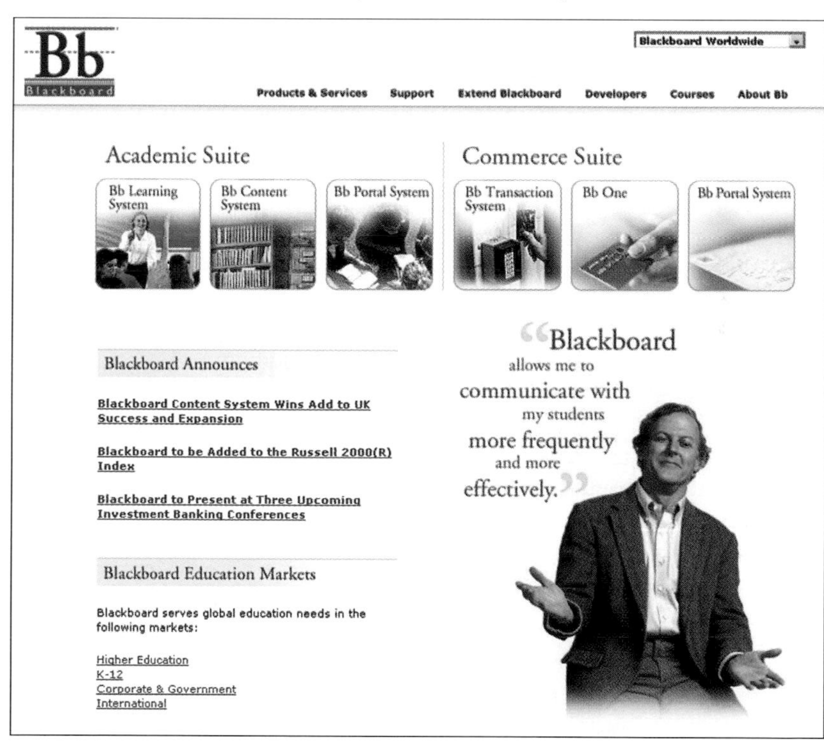

SUMMARY

Our society depends on information, and the **Web** has become the most efficient and effective way for users to get it. Adding multimedia to the Web has enabled users to become active participants who can shop, conduct business, research, or simply play a game. **Web-based multimedia** is all around you. A fundamental feature of Web-based multimedia is **interactivity**.

The Web has grown far beyond anyone's wildest expectations and today there are billions of Web sites. Because of increased bandwidth, improved compression, more powerful processors, and better software, it is also becoming easier to include multimedia on Web pages. **Multimedia** means using more than one media. Today, it implies using the computer to digitize and integrate text, graphics, animation, sound, and video. Multimedia can be **linear**, but it is more often **nonlinear**. **Interactive multimedia** enables users to directly respond to and control these **digitized** media elements making them active participants in the Web site.

Web sites that include multimedia enable Web designers to create rich, multisensory experiences that accommodate multiple learning styles and enhance the user's enjoyment at a site. In addition, retention improves when people are able to see, hear, and interact with the content.

Multimedia Web sites are as varied as the users they target and are developed for **e-commerce**, **Web-based training** and **distance learning**, research and reference, as well as entertainment and games. As improvements in technology and bandwidth continue, the use of multimedia on the Web will also grow.

Opportunities for individuals with Web-based multimedia skills are diverse. Position titles and job duties vary depending on the industry and even within the same industry. Regardless of the industry, creating a multimedia Web site is usually a team effort. Careers in multimedia include the following: **executive producer**, **project manager**, **audio specialist**, **computer programmer**, **video specialist**, **Web designer**, **Web developer**, **Web master**, **animation specialist**, **art director**, **graphic artist/designer**, **interface designer**, **photographer**, **videographer**, **content specialist**, **instructional specialist**, **writer/editor**, **production**, **quality-assurance**, and **sales/marketing**.

Preparing for a career in Web-based multimedia is a bit like trying to hit a moving bull's-eye. The successful candidate must be a lifelong learner because Web technologies and tools are constantly changing. In the past, most Web professionals were self-taught and entered the world of the Web from various backgrounds. Today, many colleges and universities offer classes, certificates, and degrees in Web design and development. When looking for a job, your most important asset will likely be your **electronic portfolio**.

In addition to developing a compelling portfolio of your work, you may be asked to complete a hands-on test during the interview process. Be prepared to prove that you have the requisite skills to complete a job. Do not underestimate the value of soft skills including excellent communication and interpersonal skills, a strong work ethic, and the ability to work with clients and as part of a team. These skills are highly valued by all employers.

KEY TERMS

animation specialist
ARPANET
art director
audio specialist
computer programmer
content specialist
customer support personnel
digitized
directory-based search engine
distance learning
e-commerce
editor
electronic portfolio
ePortfolio
executive producer
graphic artist
graphic designer
hypermedia
instructional specialist
interactive multimedia
interactivity
interface designer
Internet
linear
Mosaic
multimedia
nonlinear
pay-per-click
photographer
portfolio
producer
production manager
production position
project manager
quality-assurance
sales/marketing
spider-based search engine
tester
video specialist
videographer
Web
Web-based multimedia
Web-based training
Web browser
Web designer
Web developer
Web master
World Wide Web
writer

MATCHING QUESTIONS/DISCUSSION QUESTIONS

Match each term with the sentence that best describes it.

a. ARPANET	**b.** directory-based	**c.** distance learning
d. e-commerce	**e.** interactivity	**f.** interface designer
g. Mosaic	**h.** multimedia	**i.** nonlinear
j. pay-per-click	**k.** portfolio	**l.** project manager
m. spider-based	**n.** tester	**o.** Web developer

_____ **1.** Search engines that give priority placement to those offering top bidding for keywords.

_____ **2.** This browser was the first cross-platform, graphical-user interface Web browser that fully exploited the Web's hypermedia capability.

_____ **3.** Search engines that automatically roam the World Wide Web adding the contents of the Web sites they visit to their database.

_____ **4.** Most Web sites use this navigation approach, in which there is no established or predefined order for viewing the contents of a Web site.

_____ **5.** Search engines that are selective, meaning that humans choose which sites to add to the database.

_____ **6.** This person evaluates the design of the site and the intuitiveness of the user interface.

_____ **7.** This term describes working with more than one type of digitized media element.

_____ **8.** This person generally has a psychology background and is responsible for designing the onscreen elements with which the user will interact.

_____ **9.** This feature gives the user control over the content.

_____ **10.** Term used to describe solutions for companies, small or large, that wish to sell products or services through the Internet.

_____ **11.** This person is responsible for forming a project, moving it into production, and overseeing its creation.

_____ **12.** This is a collection of sample work and projects that can be shared with potential customers and employers.

_____ **13.** This person ensures that data input from users is properly verified and transmitted.

_____ **14.** The Internet was a result of this project.

_____ **15.** This multimedia application allows students to take courses online.

Answer each question either in writing or in a class discussion as directed by your instructor.

1. How does multimedia aid learning?
2. What are four Web-based multimedia categories? How do these categories aid users?
3. In what ways do spider-based search engines, directory-based search engines, and pay-per-click search engines differ?
4. How do Web developers, Web designers, and Web masters differ?
5. What are some practical applications of a portfolio? What should be included in a portfolio?

DESIGN PROJECT

You have been hired recently by WebsByCT. Your first project will be to design a Web site for The Inn at Birch Bay. Your first task is to review resort Web sites to understand how they are designed. You begin your research for this project by studying the Web site shown in Figure 1-19 and completing the following questions. For each question indicate how you determined your answer.

1. Connect to the Internet, go to *www.course.com*, navigate to the page for this book, click the Student Online Companion link, then click the link for this chapter.
2. Open a document in a word processor, save the file as **Ch1dp1**, then answer the following questions:
   a. Whose Web site is this?
   b. What is the purpose of the site?
   c. Who is the target audience?
   d. What multimedia elements are used in this site?
   e. How are the multimedia elements used to enhance this site?
   f. Do you think that the use of multimedia is effective? Why or why not?
   g. What suggestions would you make to further enhance the site using multimedia and why?

FIGURE 1-19
Sample Web site with multimedia elements

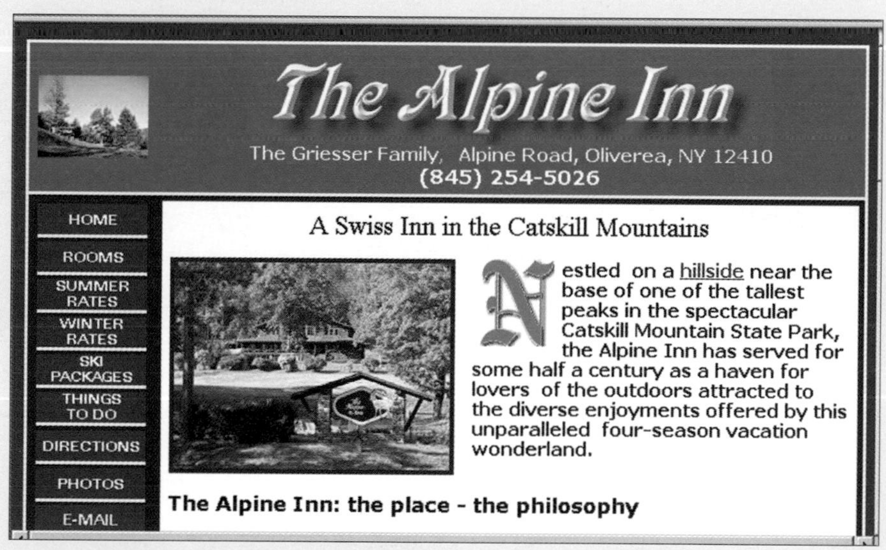

PROJECT BUILDER 1

You are an intern with a company that develops multimedia-rich Web sites for clients. At your intern training you were told that there are numerous companies in the business of developing Web sites for others, and that many of these companies use multimedia in their own Web site to promote themselves, as shown in Figure 1-20. You have been asked to conduct the following research and to write a report of your findings.

1. Use your favorite search engine to locate three of these companies.
2. Open a document in a word processor, save the file as **Ch1pb1**, then fill in the following information for each company:
   a. Company name
   b. Contact information (address, phone, and so on)
   c. Web site URL
   d. Company mission
   e. Services provided
   f. Sample list of clients
   g. Describe three multimedia elements the company has used in its site. Were these elements effective? Why, or why not?
   h. Describe three applications of multimedia the company included in its portfolios (or showcases or samples). Were these effective? Why, or why not?
   i. Would you work for this company? Why, or why not?
3. Compare your three analyses. Of the three companies you reviewed, name the company you would recommend to develop a multimedia-rich Web site and explain why.

One Step Beyond

4. Create a table using a word processing program. Use the column heads: Multimedia element, Description, Advantages, Disadvantages.
5. List the multimedia elements you identified on the three sites you reviewed. Provide a brief description of each element. Then list the advantages and disadvantages of using each element in a Web site.

Two Steps Beyond

6. Continue to review Web sites and their use of multimedia elements. Add new elements you find to the table you created in step 4. Include the URL for a site containing a new multimedia element so you can easily revisit the site.

FIGURE 1-20
Sample Web site of a company that develops multimedia

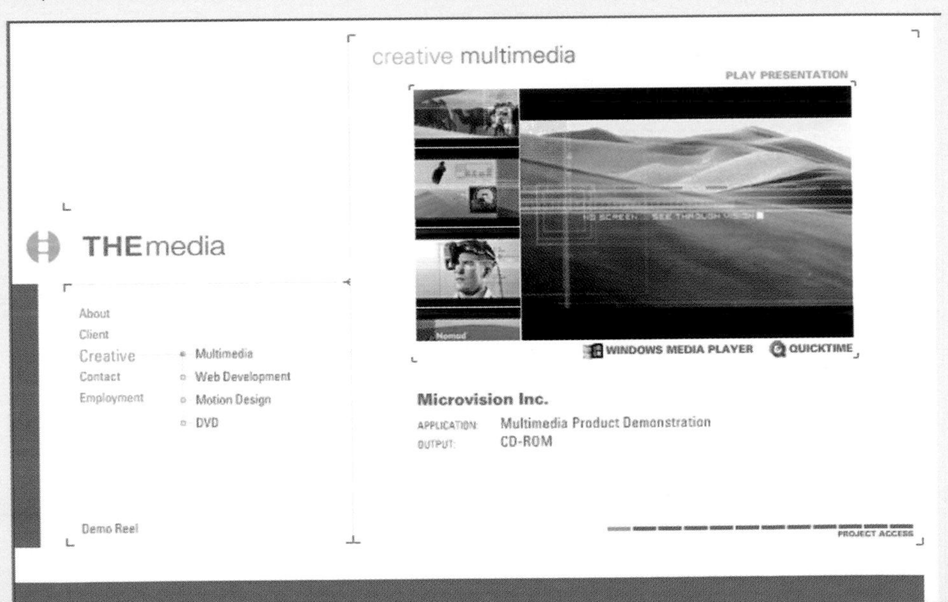

PROJECT BUILDER 2

You have strengths in many areas, and so at this time, you are still undecided about which multimedia career path to follow. You decide to use an online job-search Web site to help you research career opportunities in multimedia, including job requirements. You know that a portfolio will be a critical part of your job application, so you also decide to investigate portfolios.

1. Review the job titles listed in this chapter. Select one that you would like to find out more about as a career possibility.
2. Complete an online job search for jobs with the title you selected using a Web placement service such Monster.com, as shown in Figure 1-21. This particular site allows you to specify an area of interest such as graphic artist; a company, if desired; a location, and an industry category.
3. Open a document in a word processor, save the file as **Ch1pb2**, then answer the following questions:
   a. What information did you provide in order to conduct your search?
   b. List three jobs listed in your search results and specify why each one interests you.
   c. Describe each job including the job description, title, company, salary, and other useful information.
   d. What are the requirements? (technical skills, soft skills, education, and so on)
4. Conduct an online search for sample portfolios. Choose one that you could use as a template when creating your portfolio, which you might want to include with job applications.
   a. Describe why the portfolio you selected would be a good template.
   b. Take two or more screen shots of the portfolio site and include them as part of this report, or include the Web address of the site in this report.

One Step Beyond

5. Identify one job in multimedia from the three you identified in step 3 that interests you. Write a description of that career. List skills and education required to secure that job. Conduct additional research to provide a comprehensive list of skills.
6. Write a concluding paragraph explaining how your talents are suited for that job. Provide concrete examples.

Two Steps Beyond

7. Begin designing your own portfolio. Based on your research in step 4, identify what you would include in your personal portfolio.
8. Identify items in the list that you have already completed and items that you will be working on as you pursue your career in multimedia.

FIGURE 1-21
Sample job-search Web site

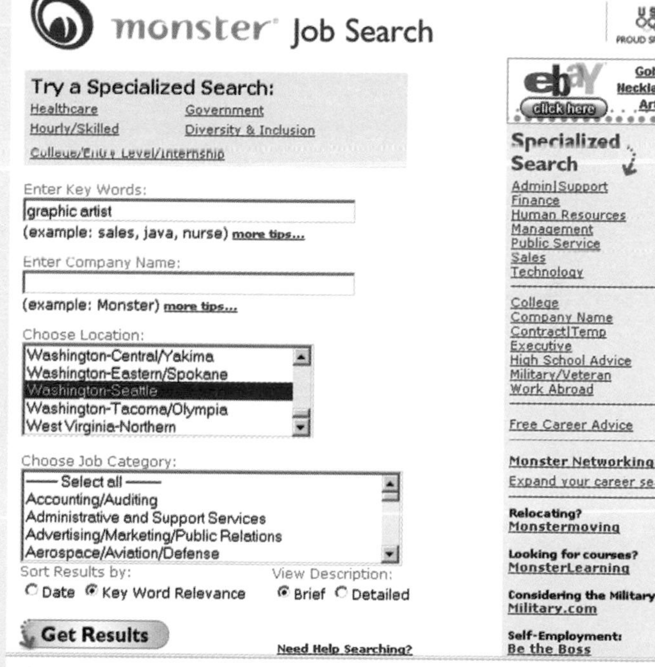

PEPPER
SALT
C 10 D 0 E 10 F 20 G 30

chapter 2

PLANNING THE MULTIMEDIA Web Site

1. Understand the Design Strategy
2. Identify Web Site Categories
3. Define the Planning Documents
4. Explore Organizational Structure
5. Investigate Navigational Structure
6. Discuss Additional Web Site Tasks

chapter 2 PLANNING THE MULTIMEDIA Web Site

Introduction

Web site development is a project-based process. There are three parts to the project: planning, development, and implementation (see Figure 2-1). Chapter 2 focuses on the planning phase. The planning phase is the most important phase in developing a multimedia Web site. The more complex and interactive your Web site becomes, the more important the planning phase becomes. Resist the urge to delve into a project without developing the plan first.

Successful multimedia Web sites are built from a plan, and they are successful because of the plan. Time spent planning and preparing will pay off in the long run. A well-developed plan will save you time, money, and lots of potential agony. The rule of thumb for multimedia development is 80% planning and 20% production.

Following a well-defined development process that places the actual production in perspective helps ensure a successful project.

A plan provides the structure for the other phases of the project. Within the Web development industry, this plan is often called **Web architecture** (site architecture or information architecture). In essence, the plan is the blueprint around which a consistent and functional Web site is developed. This blueprint includes the purpose, the target audience, the organizational and navigational structures, the multimedia elements, the user interface, the layout, and the design. It ensures that the user knows where to go and what to do, and it helps guarantee that the user's experience is positive so that he or she will want to return to the Web site.

FIGURE 2-1

The phases of Web-based multimedia development

Figure 2-1: Development Phases of a Multimedia Web Site

Phase 1: Planning the Web site

- Develop the design strategy
- State the purpose
- Identify the target audience
- Develop the specifications
- Create the wireframes and storyboards
- Determine the organizational structure
- Design the navigational structure and user interface
- Register the domain name
- Obtain a Web host
- Prepare to register with search engines

Phase 2: Develop the Web site

- Develop the structure behind the site
- Create multimedia elements: text, graphics, animation, sound, video
- Add the content
- Write additional scripts

Phase 3: Implement the Web site

- Post the Web site
- Test the Web site
- Make adjustments
- Retest
- Register the Web site with search engines

CONCEPT 1

UNDERSTAND THE DESIGN Strategy

What You'll Learn

In this lesson, you will learn about the importance of developing a design strategy that will be presented in a written creative brief and includes a definitive purpose and an identified target audience.

To ensure the success of your Web site, all of the people involved in its creation should collectively develop a **design strategy**. The design strategy will help ensure that your Web site evolves into a product that effectively achieves its purpose for the intended audience. At the onset of a project, the multimedia team should meet with the client to develop a sense of shared **vision** surrounding the project. Together, the multimedia team and the client should clarify the **purpose** of the Web site and identify the **target audience**.

Purpose

Before building your Web site, the Web site's purpose must be clearly stated and pervade the planning documents. The multimedia team and the client must have a clear understanding of the multimedia Web site's purpose. Without a clear statement of purpose the project may wander off course. A succinct purpose is crucial to the success of the Web site.

The purpose is defined further by **goals** and **objectives**. The goals support the purpose. The objectives, which must be clear, measurable, and obtainable, are developed from the goals. Writing the goals and objectives of a multimedia Web site is perhaps the most critical step in Web-based multimedia planning because they guide the development process. The goals and objectives provide a way to evaluate the Web site both during and after its development. Because multimedia development is a team process, goals and objectives are necessary to keep the team focused, on track, on budget, and on time.

To determine the purpose of a multimedia Web site, the development team should ask questions such as the following:

- How will users be using this Web site?
- Why will users want to visit this Web site?
- What will users gain from this Web site?
- Which browser and platform will users likely use to access this Web site?
- What types of features will be most useful to the users of this Web site?

If the Web site is being designed for a client, the development team must work with the client to understand the Web site's purpose. Although there are no guarantees that what you perceive to be the purpose of the Web site will be identical to what your client perceives, your chance of being successful is greater if you ask your client lots of questions and listen carefully to your client's answers. There is nothing worse than spending many hours working on a Web site only to discover that it is not what your client wanted. It is imperative that you find out what your client wants in advance. Agreeing with the client on the design strategy helps to keep the client from continually requesting changes and additions to the site as it is being developed. This is called **feature creep** and it can add time and cost to the development process.

To ensure the development team understands the client's purpose, goals, and objectives for the Web site, ask the client to answer questions such as the following:

- What do you want your Web site to do?
- Is there anything special that you want to be included in your Web site?
- Do you want to sell something on this Web site, and if so, what?
- How do you plan to handle secured transactions?
- How do you plan to advertise, market, and support this Web site?
- What is the primary action you wish your target audience to take after viewing your site?
- Do you have a domain name in mind? Is it already registered?
- Do you have a budget for this Web site? What are the limitations of the budget?

Part of your job in planning the Web site is to educate your clients about what is practical, possible, and eye-catching. There will also be times when your best efforts to educate your clients fail, and you will perceive their decisions as illogical. If this happens, you will need to continue to work with the client to reach a shared understanding of the point in question. If you do not do this, your implementation may fall short of the client's expectations. In essence, the client is the visionary of the Web site. If the client is struggling with the vision, the multimedia team can help by providing concrete examples the client can use to help articulate the vision. In the end, everyone should have a definitive picture of the vision, and this vision should be articulated into a well-stated purpose similar to those shown in Figure 2-2.

FIGURE 2-2

A well-articulated purpose statement will help to ensure that the client and the multimedia team understand the direction that the Web site is to take

Sample Purpose Statement #1

"The Web site will help position us as a leader in our industry in the use of state-of-the-art technology by providing a dynamic, multimedia-rich experience for our customers. They will be able to quickly access product information, view video demonstrations, listen to testimonials, and conduct online transactions."

Sample Purpose Statement #2

"The Web site will give students access to all course requirements including a syllabus, a list of assignments, due dates, and staff information. In addition, students will be able to communicate with one another via chat and e-mail as well as post messages to a shared discussion board."

Target Audience

A Web site must always be designed with the target audience in mind. When designing Web sites, you absolutely must make it your goal to create a product that represents what the audience wants and needs. If you have prepared any type of public presentation, you know how important it is to consider your audience in planning the presentation. If you do not consider your audience, your presentation will be a flop. The same holds true when preparing a Web site. It is more important to focus on the user and what the user wants than it is to focus on what you, as a designer, think is cool.

Always take a user-centered approach when you are establishing the purpose and objectives of the multimedia Web site. As a Web designer, you should attempt to visualize and understand the target audience. The more you know about the target audience, the better you can design a multimedia Web site that appeals to its unique interests, beliefs, and goals. Your users are the key to your project's success. Therefore, the more you can define the target audience, the more you can tailor your Web site to meet its needs and wants. The publishers of *Muscle & Fitness* magazine online are targeting a different audience than the publishers of the Web site for *Better Homes and Gardens* (see Figure 2-3), although there may be users who are interested in both Web sites.

FIGURE 2-3

Online magazines create very different looks for their Web sites in order to appeal to their target audiences

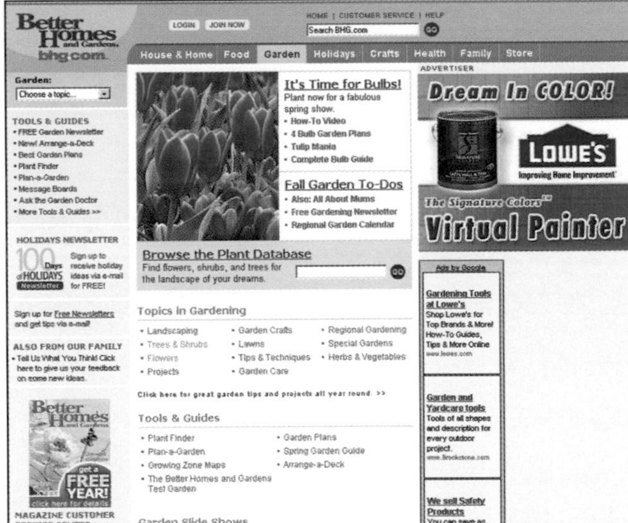

In the Web world, there are different ways to create a **user profile**. A user profile creates a picture about the people who will be using the Web site—their online and offline habits. The best way to design and develop a multimedia Web site is to survey potential users to determine how they will use your Web site. Find out where (e.g., home or office) they access the Web, how often they go online, and why they go online. Discover what they do in their spare time when they are not online. There are different ways to survey potential users. You can use online surveys, in-person interviews, focus groups, or even observations from office or home visits.

In order to define the target audience, that is, find out who the target audience is, you need to find answers to questions such as the following to create your user profile:

- What are the demographics of the target audience?
- How computer savvy is the target audience?
- What interests, beliefs, and values does the target audience have in common?
- For what purpose does the target audience use the Web?
- What type of Web sites does the target audience frequent?
- How does the target audience spend its time, both online and when not online?

The more clearly you can see your Web site through the eyes of your users, the more successful your Web site will be. This becomes even more crucial when designing interactive multimedia Web sites. Because your users will be interacting with your Web site as well as viewing it, use information from the user profile to understand how your target audience expects to use your Web site, and then design the Web site to exceed those expectations. If you do this, your multimedia Web site will be a success! For example, the designers of quakeroatmeal.com (see Figure 2-4) have created a successful Web site that engages a health-conscious target audience by providing information on its products and good nutrition.

When visiting a Web site, users like to feel they are in control. Give your users the opportunity to choose or create their own experience by designing your multimedia Web site to give them the control they want. One option is to design multiple Web sites so that your users can then choose how they want to experience the Web site. For example, if your Web site includes streaming media, you might provide users links to indicate how they want to view the media—via a dial-up connection, a broadband connection, or a wireless mobile connection. Once the user makes the selection, the Web page will adapt to accommodate that choice.

FIGURE 2-4

Quaker Oatmeal has created an effective Web site that markets its products to a health-conscious target audience

One area of target audience analysis that is often difficult to determine is the technology that the target audience will have available for viewing your Web site. If your Web site is designed to reach a very broad target market, then make sure that the technology needed to experience the Web site is minimal or provide options so the user can match the Web site experience to his or her available technology. Similarly, if your target audience is technologically astute, then you can include more cutting-edge multimedia elements and technologies on your Web site based on the assumption that your users will have the most up-to-date hardware, browsers, and plug-ins. For example, Web sites that target developers, such as the Sun Microsystems Developers' Web site shown in Figure 2-5, can safely assume that the target audience is technologically savvy.

Many of your potential users may rely on adaptive technologies. Blind and vision-impaired people have made extensive use of the Web because it gives them the freedom and ability to access information that was not previously available to them or that would be available only after being converted to Braille. A screen reader is an adaptive technology that synthesizes text and sounds included on Web sites. Unfortunately, most

FIGURE 2-5
It is appropriate for Web sites that target the technologically savvy user to incorporate cutting-edge technologies based on the assumption that the user will have an up-to-date system

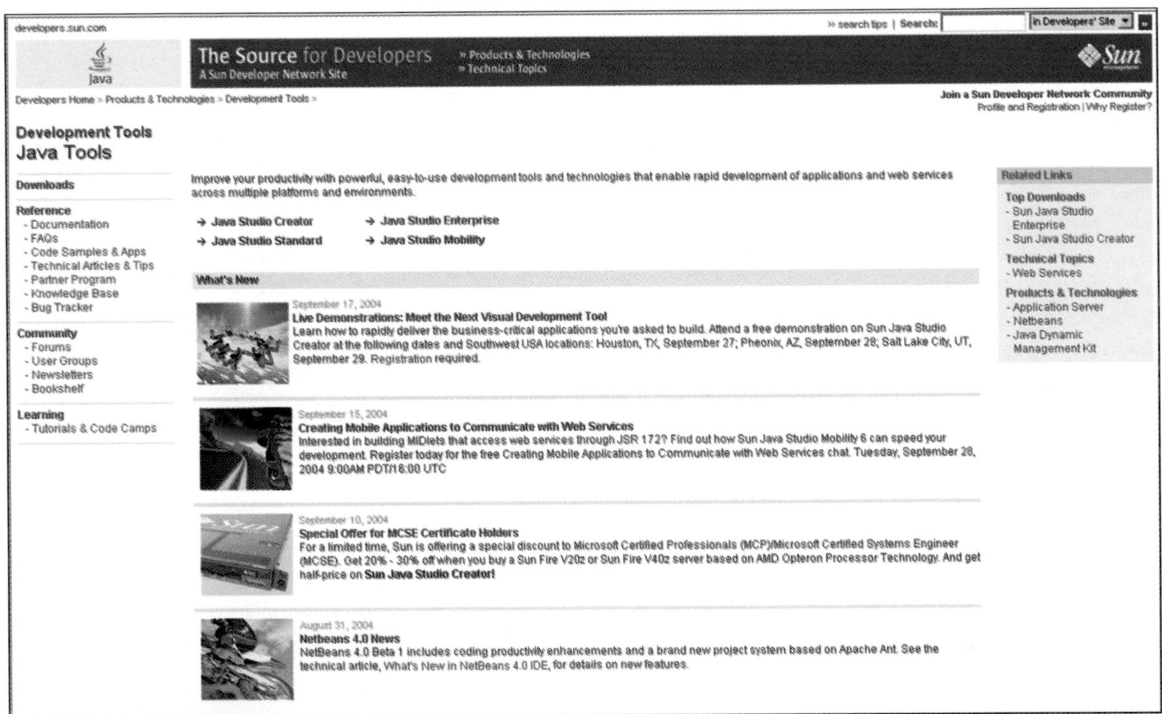

multimedia elements including any graphics, animation, and movies are useless as far as this particular audience is concerned unless **alternate text** is associated with each of these elements. The Leader Dogs for the Blind Web site (see Figure 2-6) uses alternate text. Alternate text is text assigned to a graphical element so that if the Web site is being viewed with a screen reader, the screen reader can read the text when the user's cursor passes over the graphical element. If your target audience includes people with special needs, be sure to design your Web site with features that make it accessible to them.

The purpose and target audience largely determine the look and feel of the Web site. More specifically, they determine the tone, approach, metaphor, and emphasis of the site.

- *Tone*. The **tone** of a Web site might be humorous, serious, light, heavy, formal, or informal. It can often be used to "make a statement"—for example, projecting a progressive, high-tech, well-funded corporate image.
- *Approach*. What **approach** will be taken? How much direction will be provided to the user? Some multimedia Web sites, especially children's games, focus on exploration. Other multimedia Web sites provide a great deal of direction in the form of menu choices or a "guide" that is available to assist the user. Other Web sites simply have a Help button that can be used to display a Help screen.
- *Metaphor*. Will a **metaphor** or a theme be used to provide interest or aid in understanding the Web site? For example, providing a shopping cart in which users place items they want to purchase.
- *Emphasis*. How much **emphasis** will be placed on the multimedia elements? For example, a company may want to develop an informational Web site that shows the features of its new product line, including video clip demonstrations of how each product works. The budget might not allow for creating the video segments, so the emphasis would shift to still images with text descriptions that might already be available for use via the company's printed catalogs.

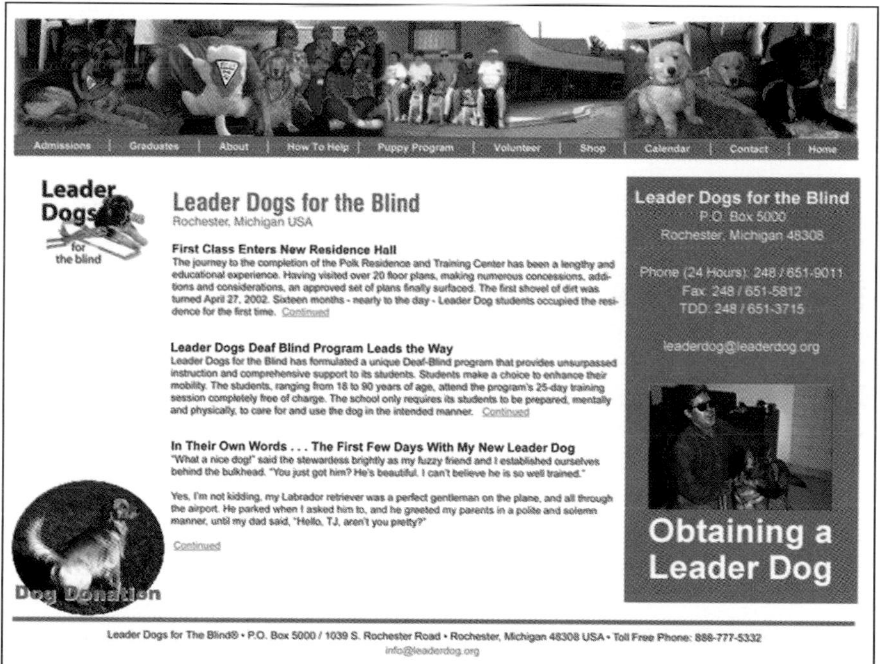

FIGURE 2-6

Make sure the Web site will be accessible to all users, even those who are accessing the site through the use of adaptive technologies, such as screen readers

Because it is important to analyze your audience not only from a demographic perspective, but also from the perspective of the technology it will use to access the Web, **specifications** are written as part of the technology analysis. The specifications of a multimedia Web site state what will appear on each Web page, including the arrangement of each element and the functionality of each object (for example, what happens when you click the button labeled Next). The specifications include several parts:

- *Playback system*. The specifications for the **playback system** should always include the operating systems, bandwidth speeds, and the browsers for which the Web site is to be developed.
- *Multimedia elements to be included*. The specifications should include details about the elements to be included in the Web site. What fonts, font sizes, and type styles will be used? What are the colors for the various elements on the site? At what speed should sound be recorded (44 MHz, 16-bit, stereo)? At what resolution should the graphics be designed? What should the playback speed be for video? Questions such as these need to be addressed so that all members of the development team are creating elements of comparable quality.
- *Functionality*. The specifications should describe the **functionality**—how the program reacts to an action, such as a mouse click, by the user. For example, clicking a door (object) might cause the door to open (an animation) or a doorbell to ring (sound). In addition, the specifications should indicate how the object itself changes based on a user action, such as how a button changes when a user clicks it.
- *User interface*. The **user interface** involves designing the appearance—how each object is arranged on the screen—and the interactivity—how the user navigates through the multimedia Web site.

In determining whether your Web site will be technologically appropriate for your target audience and the specifications you have outlined can be met, you should ask questions such as the following:

- Which operating system is the target audience most likely to use?
- Which browser is the target audience most likely to use?
- What type of hardware is the target audience likely to own?
- What bandwidth is the target audience most likely to use?
- Are there any specific adaptive technologies that might be utilized?

Web Sites on an Intranet

Designing a Web site for an **intranet** is generally much easier than designing a Web site for the Internet. Because an intranet is a network set up to be used by employees within the same organization, the client will be able to tell you which browser the company supports as well as the minimum and maximum hardware, software, and bandwidth issues that your Web site will need to endorse. In addition, the client can answer many questions regarding the target audience. When designing a Web site for the Internet, however, you will need to rely heavily on the user profile to better define the target audience.

Creative Brief

After the purpose, goals, objectives, and specifications of the Web site have been thoroughly analyzed and a target audience based on a user profile has been established, a document similar to the one in Figure 2-7 should be prepared. Different corporations call this document by different names including **creative brief** (also called document summary, design brief, or design summary). In essence, this document is a summary of the design strategy, and it should be available at all times as a reference for the multimedia team as well as the client. At any point and at any stage, it may be necessary to revisit the creative brief if the multimedia team or client is uncertain about some aspect of the Web site, or if the general direction of the Web site appears to be off track or off target.

FIGURE 2-7

The creative brief provides a summary of the design process including objectives, purpose, and target audience of the Web site

Creative Brief

Note: Include all relevant information. You need not complete every item on this form.

Client: Lone Star Software Date: 7/12/2007

Contact: Mark Leonard Phone: 310-555-1701

Project: New Product Launch (code name "Enterprise")

Media (check all that apply): ☒ Mail ☒ Space (Size: Various) ☐ Collateral
☒ Web ☐ CD-ROM ☐ Catalog ☐ Other
Type: ☒ Business to business ☐ Consumer ☒ Load Generation
☐ Traffic Building ☒ Awareness
☐ Solo ☒ Campaign ☐ New component in existing campaign

Objectives:

1. Quickly generate high awareness for new product in target market
2. Achieve first- and second-quarter sales goals as outlined in marketing plan (attached)

Purpose/Business Problem to Be Solved:

Break in to competitive market currently dominated by Paragon Corp's flagship products "Advantage 5.0" and "Cloaker 2.2." Although Enterprise is a more robust, feature-rich product, Paragon products have a wide acceptance, considerable brand loyalty, and proven effectiveness, Lone Star Software enters this battle for market share as the underdog.

Offer:

30-day free trial: sweepstakes, additional prizes on Web (prize structure TBD)
Offer deadline 60 days after launch

Target Audience:

IS managers, network managers, application developers

CONCEPT 2

IDENTIFY WEB SITE Categories

What You'll Learn

In this lesson, you will learn about the differences between static Web sites and dynamic Web sites.

From the creative brief, the multimedia team should be able to identify the most appropriate type of Web site to fulfill the client's vision. Today's Web sites can be divided into two broad categories, each with increasing scope and sophistication. Determining the category of the Web site will give you a better understanding of the project's depth.

Static

Static Web sites serve the purpose of self-branding. They are most often designed to promote or provide information about a department, a business, a corporation, an organization, an idea, or a belief. These Web sites convert existing information to Web pages and are an electronic copy of a company brochure. There is generally little or no interactivity. Because they are quite passive, they require few design or technology changes, although the content will need to be updated as new information becomes available.

Static Web sites are often a point of departure for a future project that will incorporate interactivity. The Movement Arts Web site in Figure 2-8 is an information-only Web site. Its only interactivity is the use of hyperlinks, which allows the page to remain uncluttered and the user to view each page randomly rather than sequentially.

FIGURE 2-8

This Web site is a brochure in an electronic format—user interaction with the Web site is limited to the use of hyperlinks

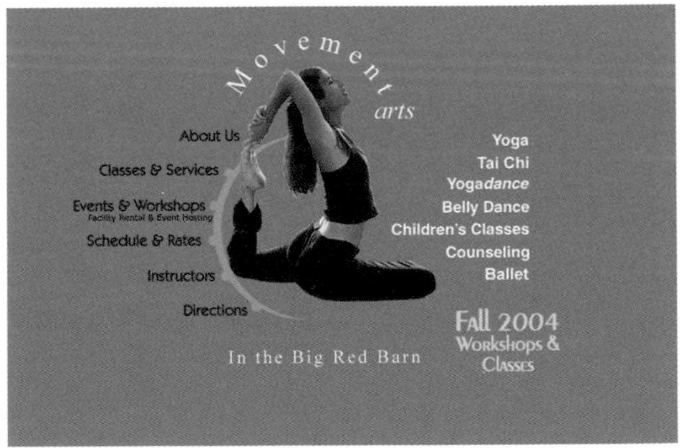

Dynamic

Dynamic Web sites provide information and offer some form of interactivity such as e-mail, searches (see Figure 2-9), questionnaires, and order processing. In addition, users are often able to customize the Web site to meet their own personal needs. Dynamic Web sites can be complex. Dynamic Web sites should answer questions such as the following: Are search features available to locate information on a particular topic? How do I purchase products/services through the Web site? Are forms available for data exchange?

More advanced dynamic Web sites are developed so that the interaction between the user and the Web site is fully automated. For example, when an order is placed from a menu of products via an e-commerce Web site, an invoice is generated, the inventory is adjusted, and the item is pulled and shipped—the entire process is automated. The user accesses features that make the Web site dynamic (such as selecting the item to be purchased and paying for it online), while other features are implemented behind the scenes based on user input (such as generating and updating the invoice). E-commerce Web sites can be used to distribute goods to fill supplier and customer orders and will answer questions such as the following: What is the status of my order? How much is the invoice? When will I receive the shipment?

FIGURE 2-9

Any Web site that enables users to perform a search is considered an interactive Web site (top); more advanced interactive Web sites actively engage the user, for example, allowing the user to select a model to try on clothing (bottom)

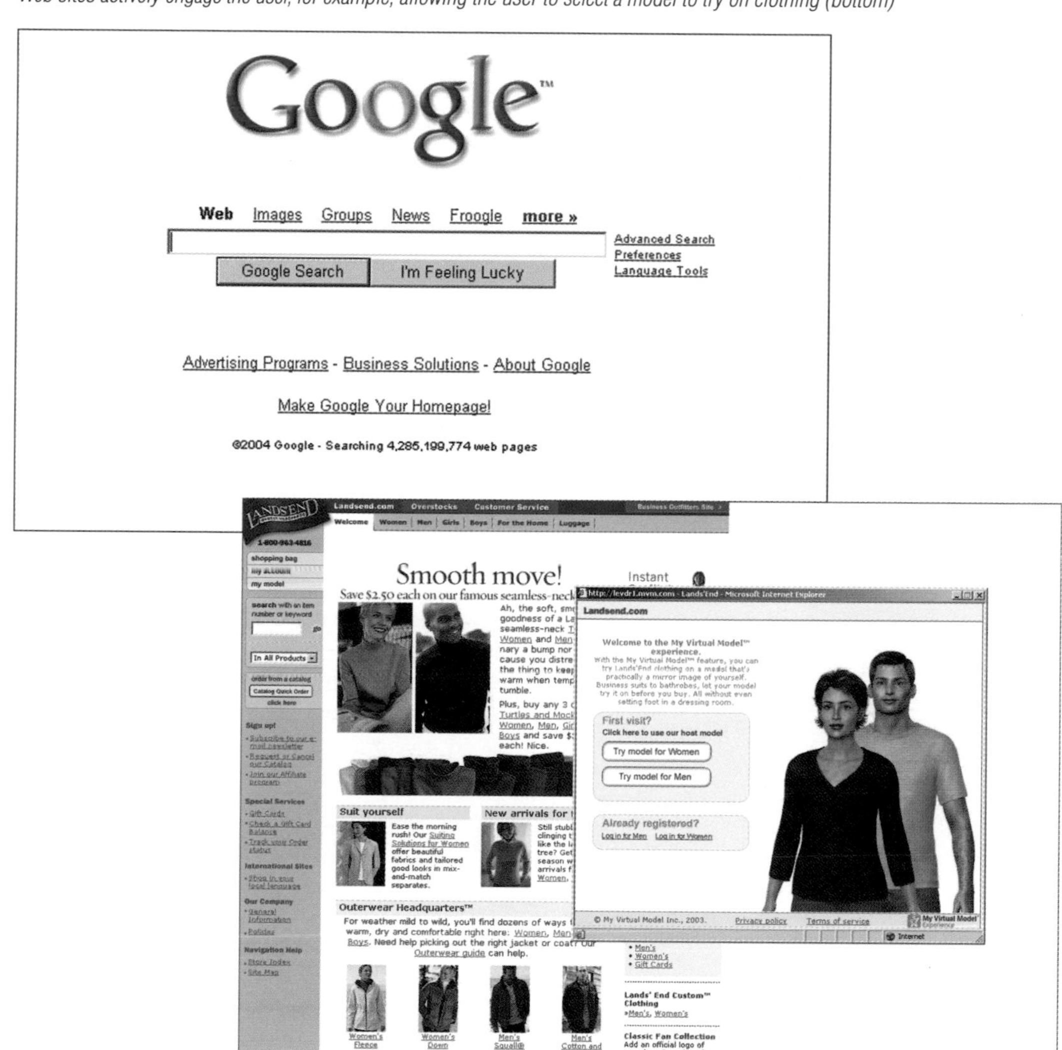

CONCEPT 3

DEFINE THE PLANNING Documents

What You'll Learn

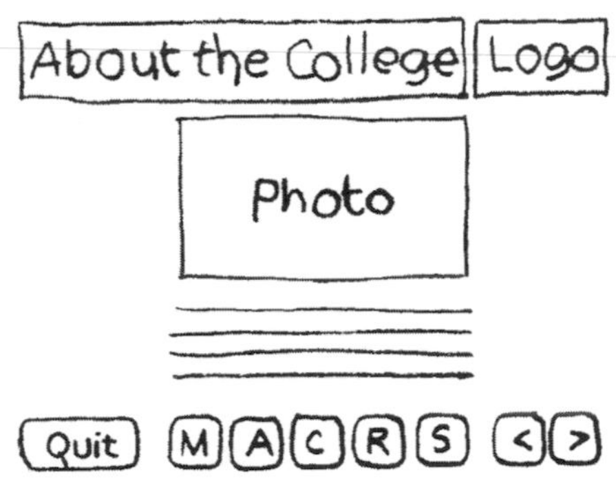

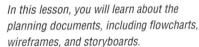

In this lesson, you will learn about the planning documents, including flowcharts, wireframes, and storyboards.

Determining how your Web site will look and function is an important step in the design process. **Planning documents**—including flowcharts, site maps, link maps, wireframes, and storyboards—are key to the creation and maintenance of a successful multimedia Web site. Although these documents may need to be altered as work on the project progresses, they serve as a point of departure for the multimedia team. These planning documents also provide the multimedia team with a concrete reference that will help them maintain a focus so that the goal of the project does not get lost in the creative process. As a Web site grows larger and more complex, the planning documents used to establish the scope and feel of the site become increasingly important.

Flowcharts

Flowcharts provide a visual guide of your entire Web site. They provide a graphical representation of how the information within your Web site is organized as well as how it flows. Although you should prepare a flowchart very early in the planning process of your multimedia Web site, keep in mind that the flowchart is a flexible document that will change as your Web site evolves. Be willing to incorporate changes and modify the flowchart as you go.

In addition to giving you a visual representation of your Web site, flowcharts are also an excellent way to illustrate interactivity. Interactive Web sites are more difficult to plan because there are multiple possibilities that may result from user decisions. Flowcharts make it is easier to track the possibilities of the decision-making process (see Figure 2-10).

Flowcharts can be created by hand, however, there are also software programs available that help you to create flowcharts using the computer.

Wireframes and Storyboards

Wireframes are created to answer the "what" questions related to a Web site and **storyboards** are created to answer the "how" questions related to the Web site. A wireframe is a text-only skeletal structure of every click-through possibility of your Web site. Storyboards are diagrams of the layout of each page of the Web site. They describe the content and sequence of each page and specify how the text, graphics, animation, and other multimedia elements will be positioned on each screen (see Figure 2-11). In addition, the navigational structure and links are designated on the storyboards. Although information contained in a storyboard will vary for each page, each screen usually includes these key elements: a sketch and description of the multimedia (text, graphics, animation, audio, video, navigation, links), time allotted for each element, and a page number. In addition, the storyboard may include information about transitions, tools to be used to create the multimedia elements for each page, budget information, and general comments.

Wireframes and storyboards are extremely important when planning a complex multimedia Web site. Multimedia team members refer to these planning tools as they design the Web site. These documents help the members of the team to visualize the Web site and to work out problems before the Web site is developed. Using these documents, design changes can be made before money is spent on development. In addition, these documents keep the project moving because most of the potential problems were anticipated and resolved through the planning process. Like the other planning documents, wireframes and storyboards can be designed using drawing programs and other application software.

FIGURE 2-10

Flowcharts provide a visual representation of a multimedia Web site and are an excellent way to illustrate interactivity

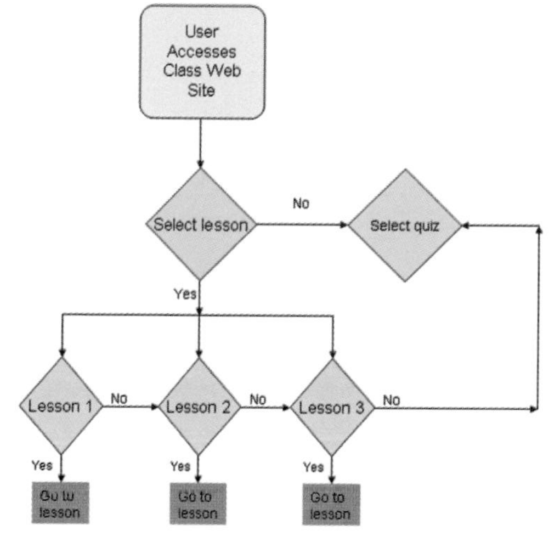

QUICKTIP

When designing storyboards for Web sites, create a layout that matches the shape and size of the browser window so that the final product does not have to be repositioned in order to make everything fit.

FIGURE 2-11

Storyboards provide a detailed overview of the layout of each page of the Web site

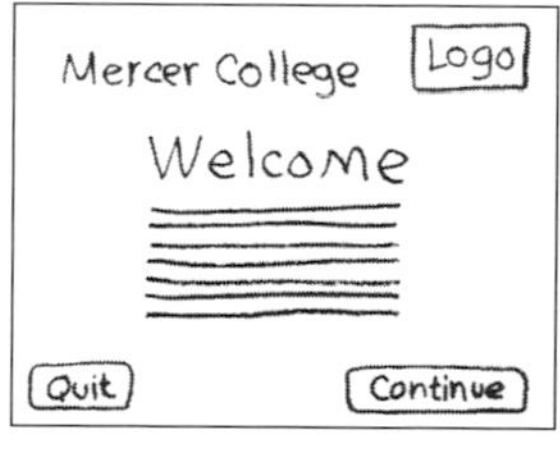

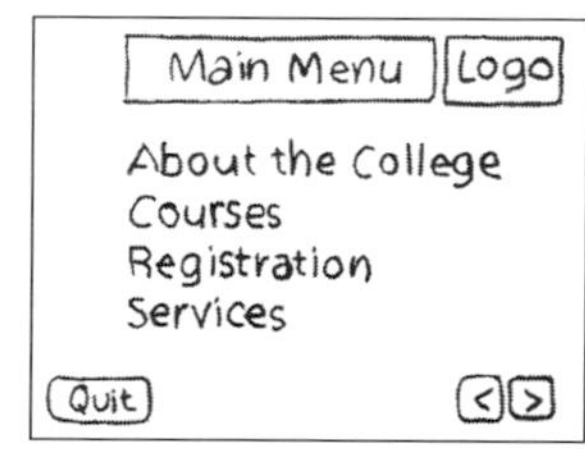

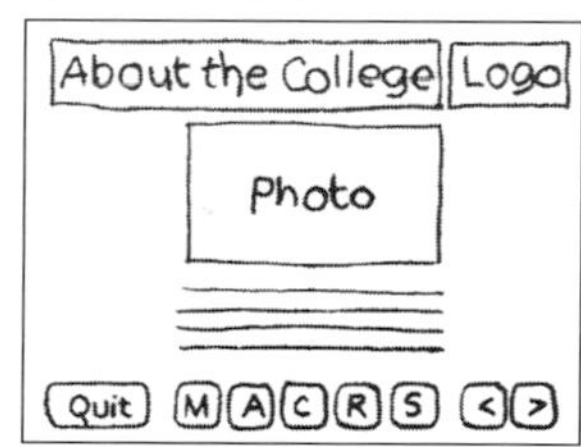

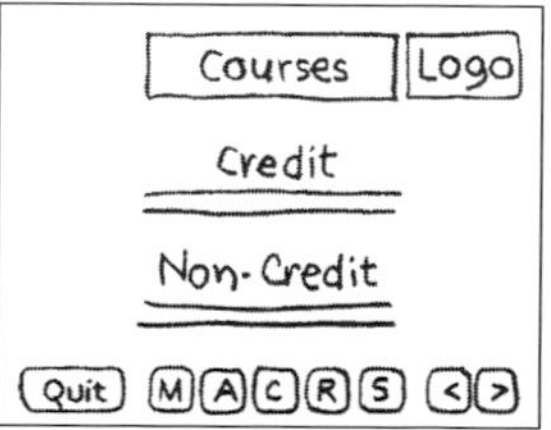

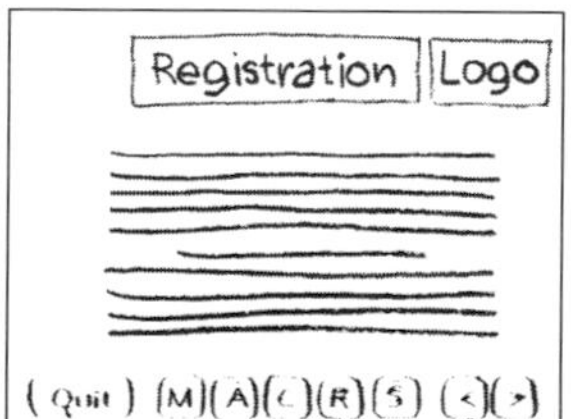

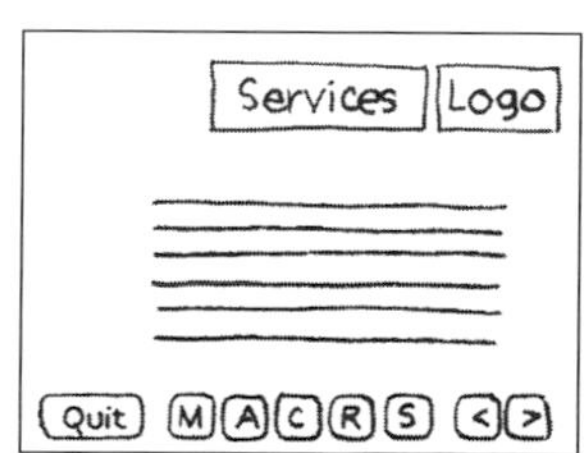

CONCEPT 4

EXPLORE ORGANIZATIONAL Structure

What You'll Learn

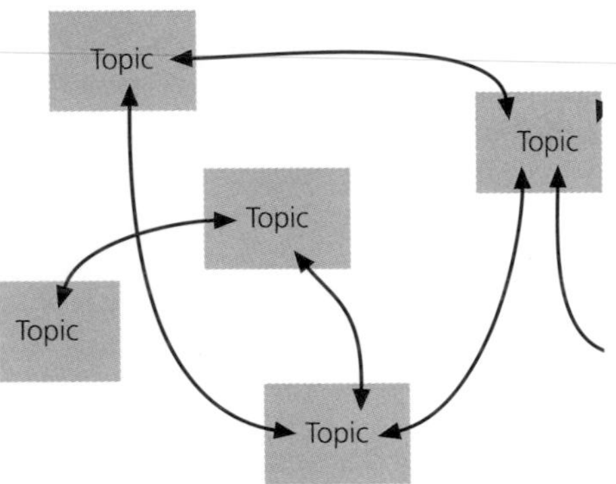

In this lesson, you will learn about the ways in which information can be organized. The different Web site organizational structures include hierarchical, nonlinear, linear, and database-driven.

Part of planning the Web site and developing the Web site structure involves developing an effective organizational structure. **Organizational structure**, the way in which information is organized, is important from the perspective of the human cognitive process—our human brains like order. A discussion of different ways to organize information follows.

Hierarchical

The **hierarchical organizational structure** organizes data using a top-down approach. This is a common organizational structure because most data can be easily and naturally broken down into sets and subsets that form a hierarchy. Chunks of information are ranked and then categorized based on interrelationships. Once the information is chunked, a hierarchy from most important or general to least important or more specific can be created. This method of organization is very common on the Web because most Web sites start with a home page that provides general information and has links to information that becomes increasingly more specific.

The hierarchical method is sometimes referred to as the tree-method or a gopher-style approach because users start at the top and burrow down until they locate the information they need. Hierarchical systems can be broad and shallow as illustrated in Figure 2-12 or deep and narrow as illustrated in Figure 2-13.

Nonlinear

A **nonlinear organizational structure** uses no prescribed or sequential path. Most information on the World Wide Web consists of information that is read nonsequentially. In a nonlinear organizational structure, the information is organized so that there are links from one discrete piece of information to another as shown in Figure 2-14.

FIGURE 2-12
A broad and shallow hierarchical organizational structure provides a little information on many topics

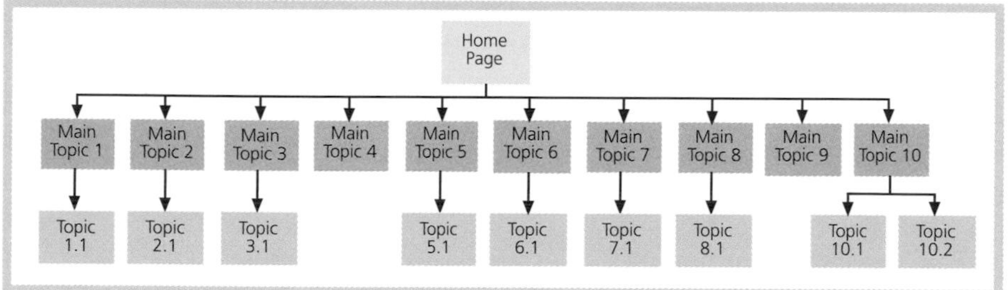

Broad and shallow sample

FIGURE 2-13
A narrow and deep hierarchical organizational structure provides deep knowledge on a few topics

Narrow and deep sample

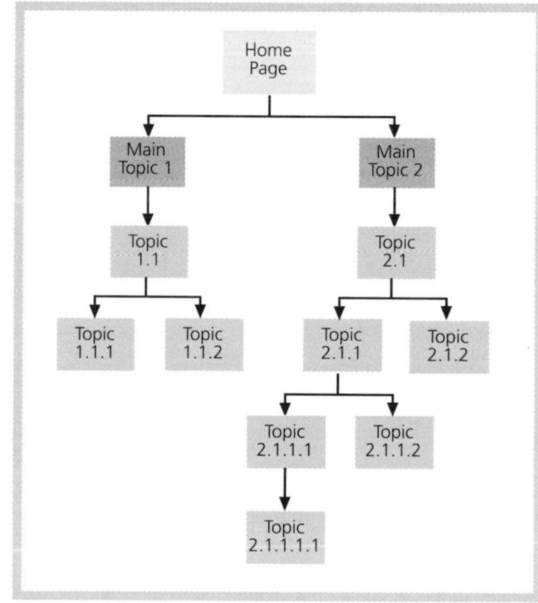

FIGURE 2-14
Most information on the Web is read nonsequentially, so most Web sites use a nonlinear organizational structure similiar to the one shown here

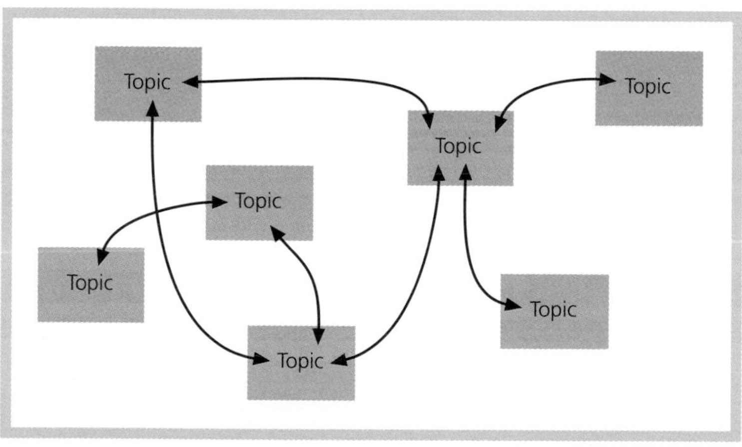

Users of a nonlinear organizational structure generally expect to find a discrete unit of related information that has been filtered, but not erratically subdivided. As a general rule, fewer than three paragraphs of text probably should not be divided. If the information is more than three printed pages, it may need to be further divided. Obviously, there are times when it makes sense to keep long documents as single Web pages or one integrated unit of information, particularly when users may want to print a page.

Linear

The **linear organizational structure** organizes information sequentially as illustrated in Figure 2-15. This is the traditional method of navigation used in Web pages that have a set sequence that must be followed in order for the information to make sense. For example, a Web site with an online slide show falls into this category, as do plays and other stories that may be retold via the Web. Another example would be a Web site used for training, where one lesson builds on another and completing a lesson is a prerequisite for moving to the next one. Although this is the most common organizational structure used in most analog media (such as videos and printed books), it is a very uncommon organizational structure on the Web.

Database-Driven

The **database-driven organizational structure** has become increasingly popular because of the large volume of short bits of information that must be organized on some multimedia Web sites. Any Web site that uses an internal search engine uses the database-driven organizational structure. This organizational structure is very common on library and research-type Web sites as well as e-commerce Web sites. As illustrated in Figure 2-16, this organizational structure organizes data into containers or tables that can then be accessed upon request from the user.

In the real world, most Web sites use a combination of these organizational structures. For example, some information may be organized using a database-driven organizational structure so it is accessible upon user request via a Web site search, while primary information is also organized using the nonlinear organizational structure.

FIGURE 2-15
The linear organizational structure is an uncommon method for organizing information on the Web because most Web sites have no set path or sequence that must be followed

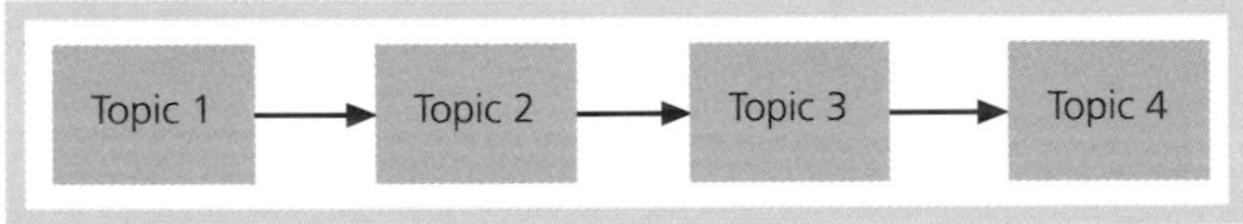

FIGURE 2-16
Any Web site that includes an internal search engine uses a database-driven organizational structure

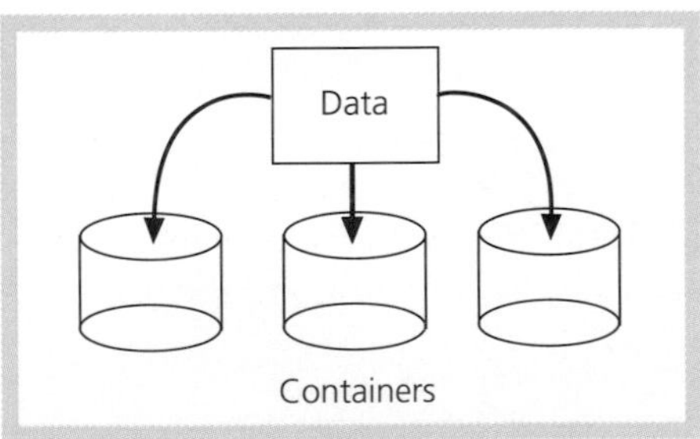

Site and Link Maps

Regardless of which organizational structure or combination of organizational structures you use, a uniform format for organizing and presenting information helps users predict how an unfamiliar section of a Web site will be organized. When organizing information, remain flexible and subdivide bits of information using common sense, logic, and a user-centered approach at all times. Discrete and short bits of information are appropriate for online viewing. Because very few Web users will spend time reading long passages of text onscreen, users appreciate short bits of information that can be scanned quickly.

Site maps provide an overview of the organizational structure of a Web site. They can be used at the planning stage to help the designer see the big picture, and they are often included on Web sites so users can view the overall structure of the Web site. Site maps on Web pages may be graphical in nature, or as the site map in Figure 2-17 shows, they may be in a text-based menu format. In addition, many Web-authoring programs will generate site maps.

A **link map** (refer again to Figure 2-17) is another planning document that serves as a schematic illustrating the interconnectivity of Web pages within the Web site as well as the links to external sites and all of the multimedia elements (graphics, animation, sounds, and video) included within the Web site.

FIGURE 2-17

A site map (top) provides an overview of the Web site's structure; a link map (bottom) provides an overview of the Web site's links

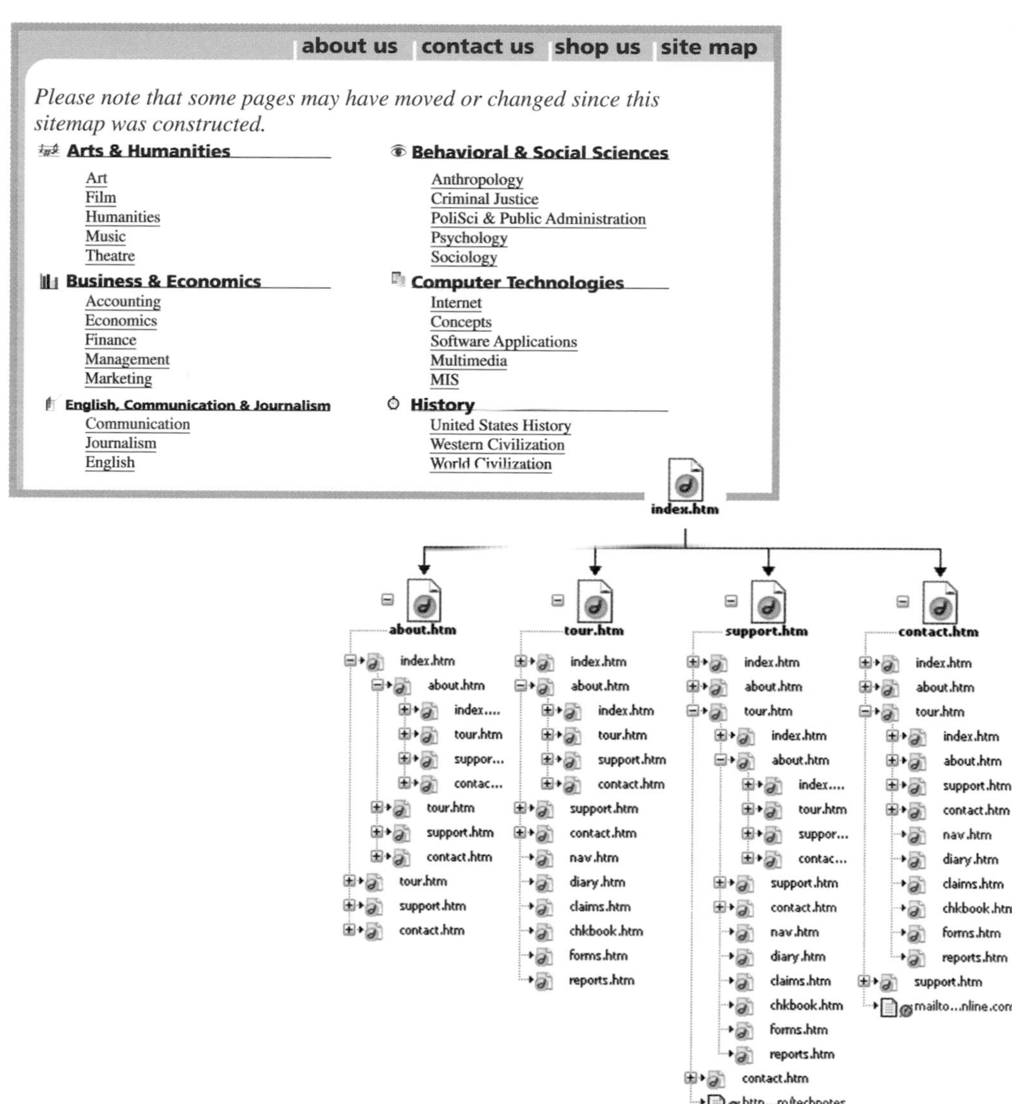

CONCEPT 5

INVESTIGATE NAVIGATIONAL Structure

What You'll Learn

In this lesson, you will learn about the different Web site navigational structures—frames, navigation bar, hub and spokes, search, and directed.

The organizational structure and the navigational structure are different, yet related. To create a Web site that is easy to navigate you must have a clear picture of the organizational structure—hierarchical, nonlinear, linear, database-driven, or combination of these structures. After you have determined how the information in your Web site is organized, you can create the **navigational structure** or means through which the users will know where they are, where they have been, and where they want to go.

The way you arrange the content of your multimedia Web site is often the most important part of the design. For example, psychologists have determined that most people can store only about four to seven discrete pieces of information in short-term memory. This is an important piece of information from a Web site design perspective. As a designer, you should attempt to limit the amount of data that the user must keep in short-term memory. Research has also shown that users prefer small, discrete units of information to long, undifferentiated units. Web surfers rarely read long contiguous passages of text and will be annoyed if they are forced to scan long blocks of text to find what they want. It does not matter if you have really cool-looking graphics and animation if nobody can find them. A clearly structured multimedia Web site should offer simple, consistent navigation that is available from every page within the Web site. You should not make your users learn how to navigate your Web site at each new page. By keeping your navigation consistent, users will grow accustomed to it and will quickly become skilled at maneuvering within your Web site. If you change the navigational structure from screen to screen, they will be forced to learn anew from one page to the next. Obviously, this leads to frustration and is ineffective in both function and form.

Frames

One way to establish a navigational structure is to use frames. **Frames** divide a screen into multiple pages, enabling one region of a screen to remain constant, while other regions of the screen change. A Web site can be designed so that one frame (Web page) contains the navigational elements or links that will appear on every screen of the Web site, while the other frames change as the links are clicked. The Web site in Figure 2-18 uses a frame-based navigational structure. On this screen, the frame on the left is a Web page that contains all of the buttons that the users can click to link to a different page. When the user clicks a button, the left frame remains on the screen and the right frame displays the newly clicked Web page.

In the Web world, frames are a somewhat controversial subject. There are definitely both pros and cons associated with frames. For example, true frame-based code can cause problems if users want to print a frame and do not realize that they must first click inside the frame in order for this to happen. In addition, you cannot bookmark a specific page. Bookmarks will always refer to the entire frameset. Despite these concerns, frames can be used effectively for navigation.

There are now ways to represent a frame-based navigational structure without coding frames. These methods provide all of the advantages of consistent navigation through the use of a frame-based navigational structure without the disadvantages presented by frame-based code.

FIGURE 2-18

This frame-based Web site uses the left frame to establish a consistent navigational structure that remains constant from screen to screen

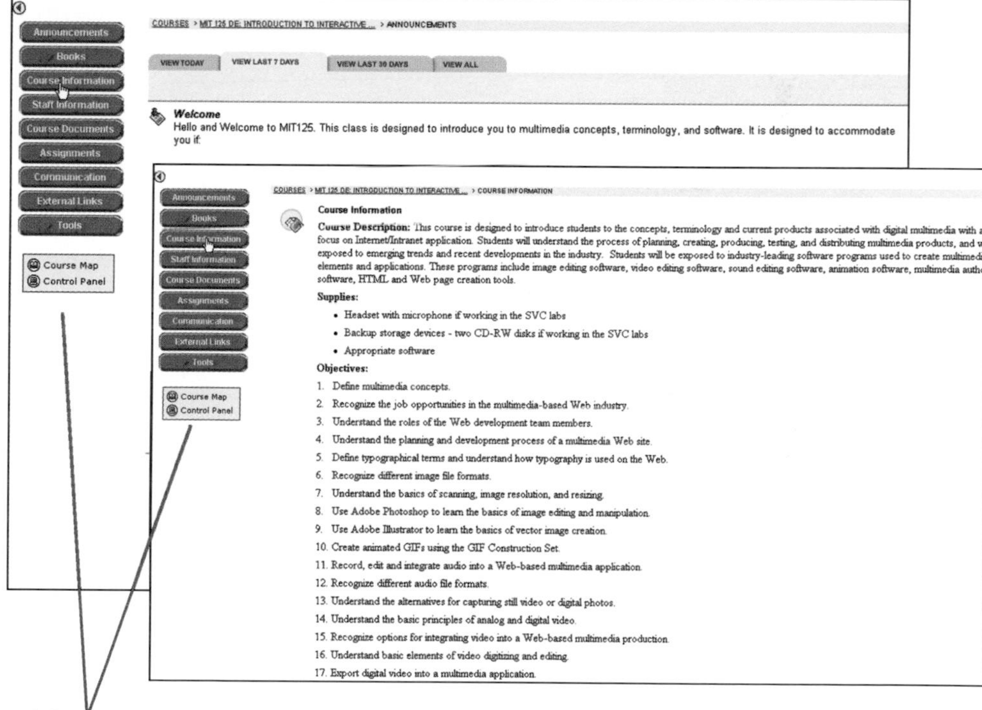

Navigation Bar

Like frames, a user-friendly **navigation bar** strategically placed and accessible from every page of the Web site is an excellent navigational choice. In fact, navigation bars are found in one form or another on almost every Web site. As illustrated in Figure 2-19, there are many different ways to design a navigation bar. Some Web sites use a text-only navigation bar because most users easily understand this type of navigation bar and it is also practical for vision-impaired users who rely on screen readers. Although useful, text-only navigation bars can be dull. Thus, they are often used in addition to or in conjunction with icons and images. Navigation bars designed with images or combinations of text and images are generally more appealing than text alone. Other Web sites are designed with navigation bars that take the form of tabs or buttons. However, there are potential drawbacks to image-based navigation bars. These drawbacks include a larger file size that may make the page slower to download, and image-only navigation bars are not as accessible to screen readers unless alternate text has been assigned to each image.

Regardless of how the navigation bar is created, it should be consistently positioned on every page of the Web site in order to serve as a friendly helper to the user. It will not take users long to familiarize themselves with a good navigation bar. Remember to keep the navigation bar intuitive, simple, functional, and, most importantly, consistent. In addition, you will want to keep the number of navigation links to a minimum so that users can quickly navigate to any location on the Web site.

FIGURE 2-19

There are many different types of navigation bars, including text only, buttons, and tabs

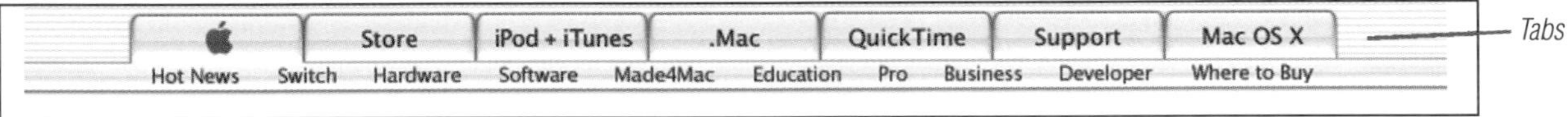

Tabs

WebAuthor * Web Graphics *Web Multimedia * Web Developer * Web Manager
Java Programming * Perl Programming * Visual Basic Programming

Text only

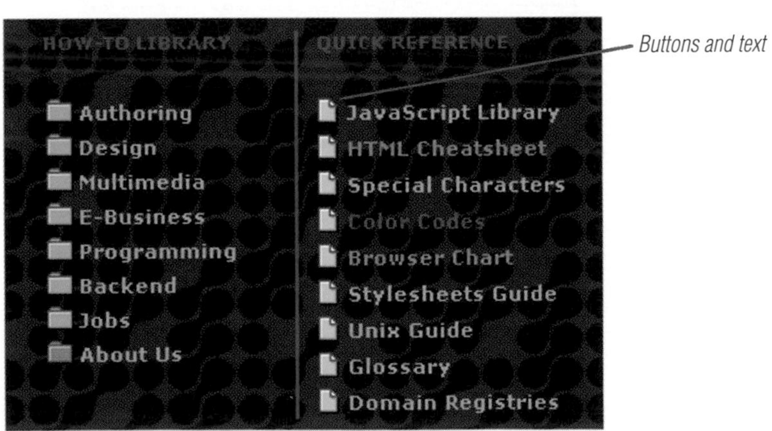

Buttons and text

Hub and Spokes

All multimedia Web sites are organized around a **home page** that serves as a point of entry into the Web site. All pages of the Web site should contain a direct link back to the home page. However, most navigational structures permit users to go to other pages of the Web site without first returning to the home page. In a **hub and spokes navigational structure**, as illustrated in Figure 2-20, users must return to the home page to go to the other pages of the Web site.

The hub and spokes navigational method is a bit cumbersome because it relies too heavily on the browser's Back button. It can be somewhat effective if it fits with the metaphor of the Web site or if the site is small. Under most circumstances, however, the hub and spokes navigational method should be avoided.

FIGURE 2-20

The hub and spokes navigational structure should be avoided because it forces the user to rely too heavily on the browser's Back button

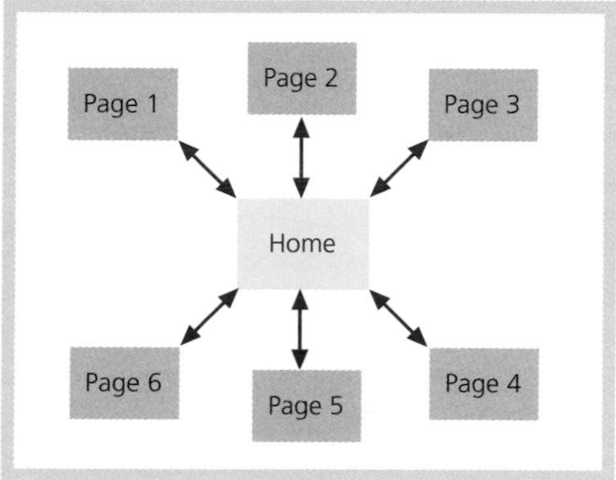

Hub and spokes navigation

DESIGNTIP Intuitive Navigational Structures

You cannot assume that users will grasp the structure of your Web site. You must make it easy for them to find their way around and go where they want to go. At all times, users should know exactly where they are and how to get back to where they were. At the same time, you should not have to provide them with a complex set of instructions to help them navigate. If the multimedia Web site is well designed, the navigational structure should be transparent to the user.

Search

As your Web site grows larger and more complex, making it easy for users to find what they need becomes increasingly challenging. One way to enable users to navigate directly to the content that is most appealing to them is to use a **search navigational structure**, which essentially means incorporating a search feature into your Web site. Web sites using a **search feature** generally use a text box or form in which users enter specific **search terms**—words or combinations of words. The search engine uses the search term entered by the user to search the Web site, then displays a list of matches and links to those specific sections or pages of the Web site.

Well-designed search features follow standard search guidelines and provide a simple and intuitive user interface for more complicated searches. Adobe's search form is shown in Figure 2-21. This simple form helps eliminate potential frustration by enabling users to restrict their searches using the four different options shown. When you include a search feature in your Web site, be sure to make it simple, and if necessary provide a brief explanation of how to use the tool along with a list of query examples.

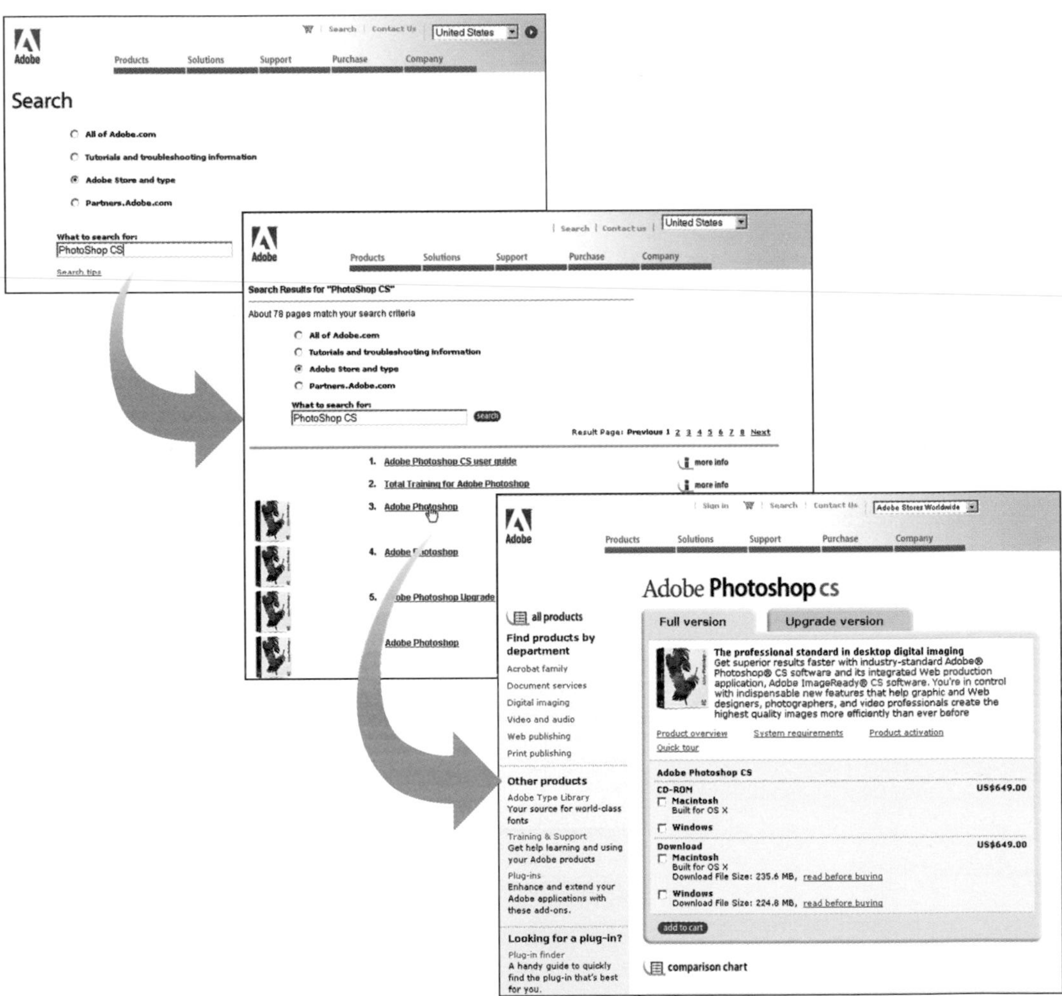

FIGURE 2-21

In addition to enabling users to enter keywords, this form allows them to narrow their search by choosing specific categories within the Adobe Web site

Directed

A **directed navigational structure** is a simple, yet efficient example of tailoring the Web site to the user. Upon entering the Web site, the user is asked to provide information. Based on the information entered, the user is directed to a specific area of the site. For example, at hollywood.com shown in Figure 2-22, the user enters his or her city or zip code and, based on the information entered, the user is directed to a Web page of movies playing in the local area or region. This type of navigational structure is perfect for those Web sites that provide different information or different features based on the user's location, gender, age, or other characteristics. Directed navigational structures are common on airline, hotel, and other Web sites designed around making reservations.

FIGURE 2-22

Directed navigation makes choices for the user based on the user's input

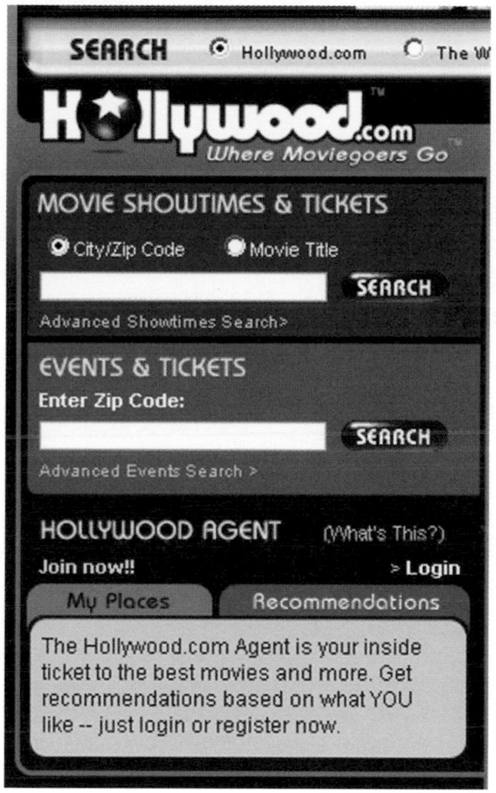

CONCEPT 6

DISCUSS ADDITIONAL Multimedia Web Site Tasks

What You'll Learn

In this lesson, you will learn about domain names, Web hosting, and marketing your Web site through the use of search engines.

In addition to preparing the creative brief and planning documents as well as determining how the Web site information will be organized and navigated, it is also wise to determine early in the planning process where the Web site will reside and how it will be located and accessed by the users.

Domain Name Selection

Every Web site on the Internet has a numeric address called an **IP (Internet Protocol) address**. Similar to a standard mailing address, an **IP address** points to a specific location or Web page on the Internet. A standard IP address might look similar to 134.39.42.57. Although it is easy for computers to locate and remember these long, complicated sequences of numbers, most humans find it a bit more challenging to remember the IP address of every Web site they wish to visit.

In an attempt to make surfing the Web easier, the **domain name system** was invented. This system allows people to use easy-to-remember names instead of long, complicated sequences of numbers to get to specific Web sites. In short, a **domain name** is a pointer to a numeric Web address (see Figure 2-23).

FIGURE 2-23

A domain name is really just a pointer to an IP address, a numeric address of a Web site on the Internet

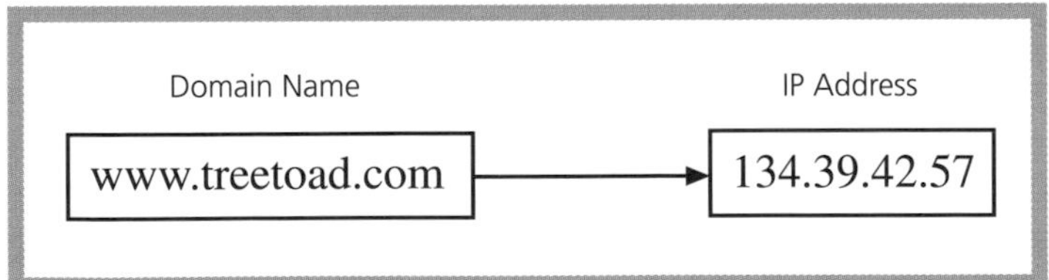

Domain names are organized according to a specific hierarchy, called the **DNS naming hierarchy**. The DNS naming hierarchy is a structured arrangement of ascending authority. Each domain represents a unique piece of the hierarchy. The root of this hierarchy is referred to as "." (dot) and directly beneath it are the top-level domains. Examples of top-level domains are shown in Figure 2-24. For domains outside the United States, two-letter ISO (International Organization for Standardization) country codes are used.

A domain name is a powerful marketing tool. Many companies and organizations now register multiple domains in an effort to secure their Web identity. You want to select a name that will be easy for your customers and clients to remember. The obvious choice would be to use your business name. However, if your company name is quite lengthy, you might want to try abbreviating the domain name for simplicity. In addition, the domain name you want may already be registered and therefore unavailable for you to use. To find out if the domain name you are considering has already been registered, you can search the domain name registration database at various sites, such as the one shown in Figure 2-25.

FIGURE 2-24
Examples of top-level domains within the DNS naming hierarchy

Top- Level Domain	Original Purpose	Who Can Register It
.com	Commercial Companies	Anyone–Unrestricted
.edu	Educational Institutions	Restricted–4-yr. Institutions
.gov	Government Agencies	Restricted–Government
.mil	Military Agencies	Restricted–US Military
.net	Network Providers	Anyone–Unrestricted
.org	Not-for-Profit Organizations	Anyone–Unrestricted

FIGURE 2-25
To find out if the domain name you are considering has already been registered, you can search the domain name registration database

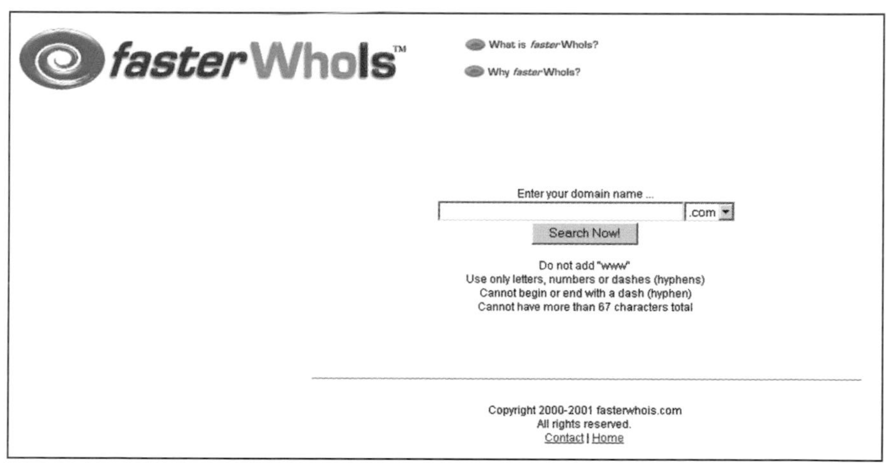

In order to own a domain name, you must register it with a registry authorized to issue and license domain names. The **Internet Consortium for Assigned Names and Numbers (ICANN)** is the organization that is charged by the U.S. Department of Commerce to control authorized domain registries. Many domain name registration companies such as register.com (shown in Figure 2-26), provide a fully automated service that handles the entire registration process for a small fee. In addition to the small fee that a domain name registration company may charge, you may also pay a small annual fee to maintain the domain name license.

Web Site Hosting

Once the Web site has been designed, it must be uploaded to a Web server that is accessible by the Internet community. In other words, the site must reside somewhere on the Internet so users from around the world can access it. This is called **Web site hosting**. You can buy a Web server and host your Web site in-house, or you can outsource the entire operation to a Web-hosting company such as hosting.com.

For most businesses, particularly small businesses, the choice to outsource Web hosting is the best decision for several reasons. Most Web-hosting services can have your site up and operational almost immediately while it could take several months to set up an in-house operation. A Web-hosting company will maintain the server, network connections, and security of your site on a 24-hour basis, which relieves you of the need for additional equipment, connectivity, and technical personnel. Because many Web-hosting companies have fast servers and connections, customers and clients will be able to access your Web site quickly.

If you choose to outsource your Web site hosting, you must decide on a company. Fortunately, the Web-hosting business is extremely competitive. There are hundreds of companies available to choose from. You will find, however, that there are differences in quality, service, and price. To effectively compare Web-hosting companies based on price, you have to determine which services you need.

Web-hosting companies generally offer tiered-service packages that include the most popular features. These packages are a good place to start, although you might want to determine whether they offer a la carte pricing if you have specific needs that are not accommodated in a package. Many Internet Service Providers offer basic or limited Web-hosting services as part of the monthly fee that you pay for Internet access and offer full services for an additional fee. There are also free sites at which you can post your Web pages. Most of these sites have limitations on what is allowable as well as how much space you can use on the server. In addition, you may be required to accommodate advertising

FIGURE 2-26

Register.com provides a fully automated service that handles the entire domain name registration process

banners if you choose to post your Web site through a free service. To determine the service that is best for you, it might be easier to use a checklist similar to the one shown in Figure 2-27 to compare services.

QUICKTIP

Free Web-hosting services are generally best reserved for nonprofessional Web sites.

Before you choose a Web-hosting company, consider the following points. It is important to understand the overall capabilities of the Web server, as well as the connections to the server, so that you know what you can and cannot do.

- *Storage space*. Different Web-hosting companies and packages allot varying amounts of disk **storage space** for your Web site. Although each individual Web page should actually be quite small, if the Web site is at all extensive, these small individual pages and their multimedia elements can quickly add up.
- *Bandwidth*. **Bandwidth** plays an important role in delivering a multimedia or e-commerce Web site. It is imperative that you choose a Web-hosting company that offers sufficient bandwidth and connection speed to deliver your site effectively. In addition, some Web-hosting companies meter bandwidth and charge you additional fees if you exceed the limit. Find out what your Web-hosting company's policies are if your site becomes too popular and how many other Web sites share your server. This could be a concern if your customers cannot get through to your site because the other Web sites on your server are flooded with visitors.
- *Peering*. If pages included on a Web site take too long to download, users simply will not wait. Your Web-hosting company should offer fast connections. **Peering** is when your host has multiple Internet connections and can automatically route traffic to the fastest line out.
- *Performance*. These factors must be considered when assessing **performance**. Minimum and optimal hardware requirements should be considered before you choose a Web-hosting company. The processor, bus structures, memory, and other hardware on the server storing and delivering the multimedia Web site must be powerful enough and fast enough to effectively process and return user data, access and deliver multimedia elements, and run programs or connect with other computers that will. If the server is too slow or is not powerful enough to deliver, animation and video may appear choppy.
- *Technical support*. If you are not a technical guru, **technical support** should be one of your primary considerations when choosing a Web-hosting company. You need to know that tech support is available 24 hours a day, 7 days a week. In addition, you should find out how many support staff are available compared to how many customers they have to support.

FIGURE 2-27

Web-hosting companies generally offer similar services. You may find it easier to rate them by using a checklist

Sample Web Hosting Service Checklist

	Service 1	Service 2	Service 3
Storage Space	✓	✓	
Bandwith	✓	✓	✓
Peering		✓	✓
Performance		✓	✓
E-commerce	✓	✓	✓
Technical support	✓	✓	
Service/scripts/software		✓	✓
Site administration	✓	✓	✓
Security		✓	✓
Customer service		✓	✓
Price		✓	
Total	5	11	8

- *E-commerce*. If you are going to sell products or services online, make sure your hosting service offers the services you will need. Many Web-hosting services (see Figure 2-28) offer everything you need to build an online storefront including data base management services, shopping-cart scripts, credit card merchant accounts, and a secure site for transmitting electronic transactions.
- *Scripts and software*. A top-notch Web-hosting company should have a broad library of **scripts** and **software** that you can use to add guestbooks, forms, statistics, counters, and other features to your site. The host should also be able to support current programming and server extensions, secure transactions, and other utilities.
- *Co-location*. **Co-location** facilities offer customers a secure place to physically house their hardware in a location other than in their offices or warehouse where the potential for fire, theft, or vandalism is much greater. Co-location facilities offer high security, including cameras, fire detection and extinguishing devices, multiple connection feeds, filtered power, backup power generators, and other items to ensure high availability, which is mandatory for all Web-based, virtual businesses. Although the company maintains ownership of the hardware and equipment, storage and maintenance are the responsibility of the Web hosting company.
- *Site administration*. Web sites are dynamic environments. **Site administration** is important so that you can update your pages, manage files, collect orders, retrieve data from forms, get statistics, and perform other maintenance chores on your Web site. You will want to choose a Web-hosting company that offers simple and secure site management capabilities so that it is easy for you to modify the contents of your site whenever and wherever necessary.
- *Security*. **Security** is always an important consideration. You will want to know that your data is secure from hackers. For some businesses, this is even more important than it is for others. Find out what security features your host offers or supports. Find out if your data is safe and how often backups are performed.
- *Customer services*. The Internet market is suited for the old saying "you get what you pay for." A quality hosting service should offer **customer services**, such as an online area with FAQs (frequently asked questions), guides, tips, and other resources.
- *Price*. Remember, cheaper is not always better, but the most expensive company is not necessarily the best choice either. You will have to carefully compare features in order to effectively compare price.

FIGURE 2-28
Many Web-hosting services offer everything you need to build an online storefront

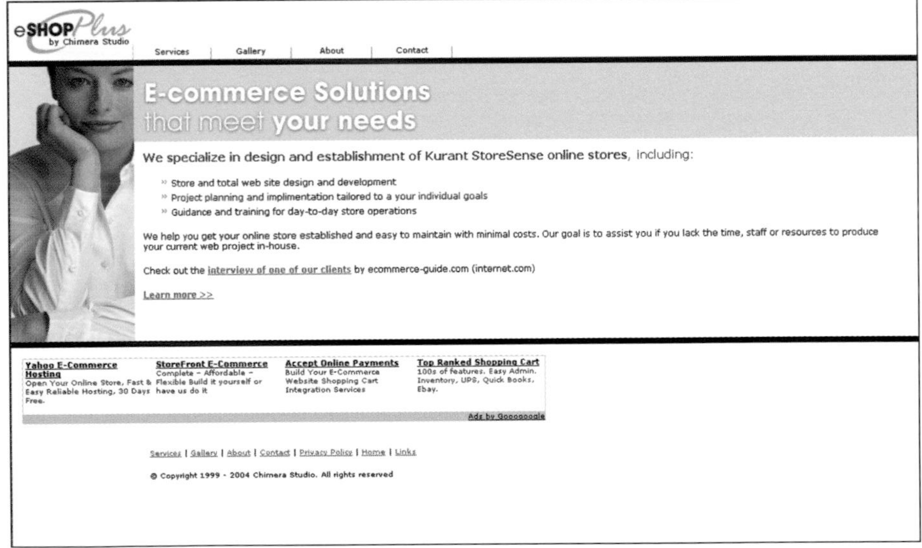

As you attempt to choose a quality Web-hosting company that offers what you feel is important to the success of your site, be prepared to do some research. It is wise to check your Web-hosting company's track record, and remember good service, support, and connections are worth a lot to your company's image.

Search Engine Registration

One of the most important aspects of Internet marketing is the search engine. From a Web designer/developer perspective, you will want and need to register your Web site with search engines in order for users to find your multimedia Web site. If your site is not coming up in at least the top 30 for your chosen keywords, then people may never find you. The process of registering a Web site can be time-consuming, but it is fairly simple. Again, there are businesses and individuals who specialize in registering Web sites, and they will register your Web site for you if you are willing to agree to their terms. There are also automated software programs and online services like addme.com (see Figure 2-29) that will register your Web site with search engines.

If you choose to register your Web site manually, you may want to prepare a text document that includes basic information about your Web site. You can copy and paste from this document to the registration form. Each search engine operates differently. The registration forms at some sites are easier to complete and submit than they are at other sites. Some search engines are quick at listing your pages while others take weeks or months before your Web site will be registered.

FIGURE 2-29

Automated online services like addme.com will register your Web site with different search engines

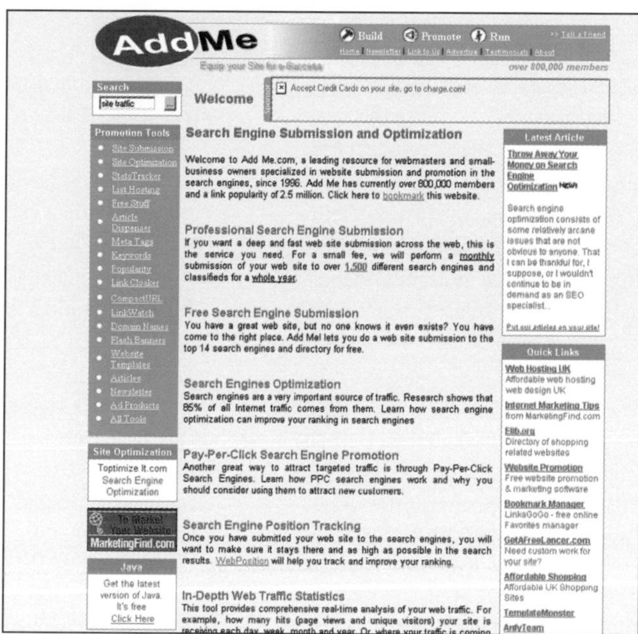

> ### Marketing Your Web Site
>
> In addition to marketing your Web site through search engines, you can also market your Web site through other Web sites or portals. **Web portals** are high-traffic Web sites that serve as gateways to a multitude of other sites. Marketing your Web site in this manner is most often accomplished by renting a piece of another Web site's screen to post an advertising banner, graphic, or link to your Web site.
>
> Before you market your Web site, make sure you have developed and designed a good one. Do not submit your site until you feel it is ready. Focus on a single topic or purpose. Make your site the best you can. Avoid long downloads, especially on the home page. Make it easy to get around and find your way back. Repair all broken links. Update often.

SUMMARY

Planning is the first and most critical phase in the multimedia development process. A plan provides the structure for the other phases of the project. The plan is often called **Web architecture**, site architecture, or information architecture. A **design strategy** helps ensure the success of your Web site. The multimedia team and the client should develop a sense of shared **vision** surrounding the project. They should discuss the **target audience** and clarify the **purpose**, as well as the **goals** and **objectives** of the project in order to avoid **feature creep.**

A **creative brief**, or summary of the design strategy, should be prepared. In addition, a **user profile** should be generated so that the Web site can be tailored to meet the needs and desires of the target audience, which will help set the **tone**, **approach**, **metaphor**, and **emphasis**. Designing a Web site for an **intranet** is generally much easier than designing a Web site for the Internet. If your target audience relies on adaptive technologies such as screen readers, remember to include **alternate text**. The technology analysis will determine the **specifications** of the Web site.

Today's Web sites can be divided into two broad categories. **Static Web sites** serve the purpose of self-branding. **Dynamic Web sites** provide information and offer some form of interactivity such as e-mail, searches, questionnaires, and order processing.

Planning documents, including **flowcharts**, **site maps**, **link maps**, **wireframes,** and **storyboards,** are key to the creation and maintenance of a successful multimedia Web site. Information can be organized in different ways. The **hierarchical organizational structure** organizes data using a top-down approach. In a **nonlinear organizational structure** there is no prescribed or sequential path. In a **linear organizational structure** information is organized sequentially. The **database-driven organizational structure** is becoming more and more popular because of the volume of short bits of information found on the Web.

One way to establish a **navigational structure** is to use frames. **Frames** divide a screen into multiple pages. Like frames, a user-friendly **navigation bar** that is strategically placed and accessible from every page of the site is an excellent navigational choice. In a **hub and spokes navigational structure** users must return to the **home page** to go to the other pages of the Web site. As Web sites grow larger and more complex, the **search navigational structure** enables users to enter specific words or combinations of words, and the search engine will then display a list of matches and links to specific sections of the Web site. **Directed navigation** asks users to provide information. Based on the data entered, they are directed to specific areas of the site.

Every Web site on the Internet has a numeric address called an **IP address**. Because most humans find it difficult to remember IP addresses, the **domain name system** was invented. A **domain name** is a pointer to a numeric Web address and domain names are organized according to the **DNS naming hierarchy**. In order to own a domain name, you must register it with a registry authorized to issue and license domain names by the **Internet Consortium for Assigned Names and Numbers (ICANN).**

Once the Web site has been designed, it must be uploaded to a Web server accessible by the Internet community. This is called **Web hosting**. Before choosing a Web-hosting company, do some research. It is wise to check your Web-hosting company's track record and remember good service, support, and connections are worth a lot to your company's image. One of the most important aspects of Internet marketing is the **search engine**. You will need to register your Web sites with search engines.

KEY TERMS

alternate text
approach
bandwidth
co-location
creative brief
customer service
database-driven organizational structure
design strategy
directed navigational structure
DNS naming hierarchy
domain name
domain name system
dynamic Web site
emphasis
feature creep
flowchart
frame
functionality
goal
hierarchical organizational structure
home page
hub and spokes navigational structure
IP address
Internet Consortium for Assigned Names and Numbers (ICANN)
intranet
linear organizational structure
link map
metaphor
navigation bar
navigational structure
nonlinear organizational structure
objective
organizational structure
peering
performance
planning document
playback system
purpose
scripts
search engine
search feature
search navigational structure
search term
security
site administration
site map
software
specifications
static Web sites
storage space
storyboard
target audience
technical support
tone
user interface
user profile
vision
Web architecture
Web portal
Web site hosting
wireframe

MATCHING QUESTIONS/DISCUSSION QUESTIONS

Match each term with the sentence that best describes it.

a. creative brief	**b.** database-driven	**c.** directed
d. domain name	**e.** dynamic	**f.** frames
g. hierarchical	**h.** hub and spokes	**i.** ICANN
j. intranet	**k.** static	**l.** storyboards
m. user profile	**n.** Web architecture	**o.** wireframe

1. Using this navigational structure, users must return to the home page to go to the other pages of the Web site.
2. The blueprint around which a consistent and functional Web site is developed.
3. This will help you define your target audience.
4. This provides a summary of the design strategy.
5. The name of the Web site category that includes little or no interactivity.
6. Pointer to a numeric Web address.
7. A text-only skeletal structure of every click-through possibility of your Web site.
8. Web sites that use an internal search engine have this type of organizational structure.
9. Organization charged by the U.S. Department of Commerce to control authorized domain registries.
10. These are diagrams of the layout of each page of the Web site.
11. This is the navigational structure that divides a screen into multiple Web pages.
12. This is the navigational structure that prompts users for data upon entry to the Web site.
13. A network set up to be used by employees within the same organization.
14. This category of Web site provides information and offers some form of interactivity such as e-mail, searches, questionnaires, and order processing.
15. This type of organizational structure organizes data using a top-down approach.

Answer each question either in writing or in a class discussion as directed by your instructor.

1. What are some questions you should ask your client in an effort to develop a design strategy?
2. What is a user profile, and why is it important to develop one?
3. What is the difference between static and dynamic Web sites?
4. What are the different types of navigational structures?
5. What are some of the key traits you should look for when choosing a Web-hosting company?

DESIGN PROJECT

This is a continuation of the Design Project in Chapter 1.

As a result of previous meetings with the client, The Inn at Birch Bay, the WebsByCT multimedia development team has created the Creative Brief shown in Figure 2-30. You have been asked to study this brief, then research and recommend a Web-hosting service and domain name for the inn.

1. Open a document in a word processor, save the file as **Ch2dp1**. Using your favorite search engine, find three companies that offer Web hosting. For each company use their least expensive plan and write a report that includes the following:
   a. Company name
   b. URL
   c. Cost per month
   d. Storage space
   e. E-mail accounts
   f. Bandwidth
   g. Technical support
   h. Customer service
   i. Other (you feel is important)
   j. Name the company you would recommend and specify why.
2. Based on your knowledge of The Inn at Birch Bay, add the following to your report:
   a. Suggest a domain name for the inn
   b. Provide a rationale for choosing that name
   c. Use a domain name registration service to verify that the name is available

FIGURE 2-30
A creative brief for The Inn at Birch Bay

WebsByCT

Creative Brief

Client: The Inn at Birch Bay
Contact: Pat Kruse
Phone: (206) 555-1212
E-mail:pkruse@ctwired.com
Project: Web site
Type: Business to consumer

Vision Statement:
"This Web site will help to promote the Inn while fostering an image of a family facility that provides a relaxing, yet recreational outdoor setting. Also, the Web site will help position the Inn as a quality resort at a reasonable price and as an alternative to hotels and motels. Incorporating multimedia into the Web site will provide the viewer with a pleasant Web experience and reinforce the concept of a new, progressive resort."

Objectives:
1) Provide information on the Inn to prospective visitors
2) Foster an image of a family Inn providing a relaxing, yet recreational outdoor setting
3) Become the primary medium for generating follow-up e-mails, phone calls, and postal inquiries

Purpose/Business Problem to Be Solved:
The Inn at Birch Bay is a new facility set in a remote area of Washington state, along the shores of the bay. There is a need to promote the Inn and yet the budget is modest. The client requests a Web site that can be found, using popular search engines, by those interested in staying at a resort in the Birch Bay area. The Web site would provide, at a minimum, images of the Inn and surrounding area, as well as facilities, contact information, and directions. Awareness is of utmost importance, as well as speed in getting the Web site up and running. The focus for the first version of the Web site will be on providing information rather than on providing a full-service Web site with reservation capabilities.

Target Audience:
Middle to higher income families, couples, and singles who enjoy the outdoors.

PROJECT BUILDER 1

You are an intern with a company that develops Web sites for clients. At your intern training you were told that there are various ways to organize a Web site. You were also told that one way to study a Web site's structure is to create a flowchart as you navigate through it. The purpose of the flowchart is to illustrate the various pages on the Web site and how they are linked. Figure 2-31 shows a straightforward Web site that can be used to study a Web site's structure.

1. Connect to the Internet, go to *www.course.com*, navigate to the page for this book, click the Student Online Companion link, and then click the link for this chapter.
2. Using a pencil and paper, sketch a flowchart to represent this Web site. Be sure to indicate the links between the pages and any external links.

One Step Beyond

3. Using a pencil and paper, sketch a storyboard for each page.

Two Steps Beyond

4. Search for a Web site that includes a site map.
5. Open a document in a word processor, save the file as **Ch2pb1**, and then answer the following questions.
   a. How does the site map help you to understand how this Web site is organized?
   b. Do you think every Web site needs a site map? Why, or why not?

FIGURE 2-31
A Sample Web site with a straightforward organizational structure

1898
CONNOR
HOTEL
OF JEROME
164 Main Street, P.O. Box 1177, Jerome, AZ 86331
1-800-523-3554
From overseas: 928-634-5006
Welcome to the Connor Hotel of Jerome, located in the West's most delightful former ghost town. Our 10 historic rooms have been renovated to the highest standards of comfort and convenience, while maintaining their authenticity with antique furnishings and decor. Each room features a private bathroom, coffemaker.
Step out the front door, and Jerome awaits you with its great choice of eateries, saloons and unique shops. Venture a bit further, and the world is at your feet. Breathe the cool mountain air, and make Jerome your home base for exploring Northern Arizona. Perched high in the hills overlooking the spectacular Verde Valley. The Connor

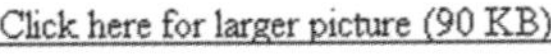

PROJECT BUILDER 2

You have been studying Web development. You have decided to create your own personal Web site that will function as your online portfolio. Visualize a multimedia Web site that you would like to create.

1. Open a document in a word processor, save the file as **Ch2pb2**, and then create a report with the following:
   a. A one-page creative brief
   b. A description of the organizational structure that you plan to use to organize the content of your Web site
   c. A flowchart of your Web site that includes a minimum of three Web pages and shows any links to external Web sites
   d. A storyboard of each page
   e. A description of the different types of multimedia elements that will be included in your Web site; specify why these will be included

One Step Beyond

2. Brainstorm domain names for your Web site, select one, make sure that it has not already been taken, and then provide a rationale for why you chose it.
3. Research two Web-hosting companies including one that offers free hosting such as the Web site shown in Figure 2-32. Compare the two based on the following, then choose one and provide a rationale for your choice.
   a. Company name
   b. URL
   c. Cost per month
   d. Storage space
   e. E-mail accounts
   f. Bandwidth
   g. Technical support
   h. Customer service
   i. Other (you feel is important)

Two Steps Beyond

4. Interview a representative at your school's placement office and obtain information on the process for using the office's resources. Ask for their opinion on the value of online portfolios when job hunting and their advice on developing an online portfolio.
5. Interview a representative of a placement service who specializes in the type of career you are targeting. Obtain information on the process for using their resources. Ask for their opinion of the value of online portfolios when job hunting and their advice on developing a portfolio.
6. Summarize your findings in a short report to be submitted to your instructor.

FIGURE 2-32

A company that offers free Web hosting

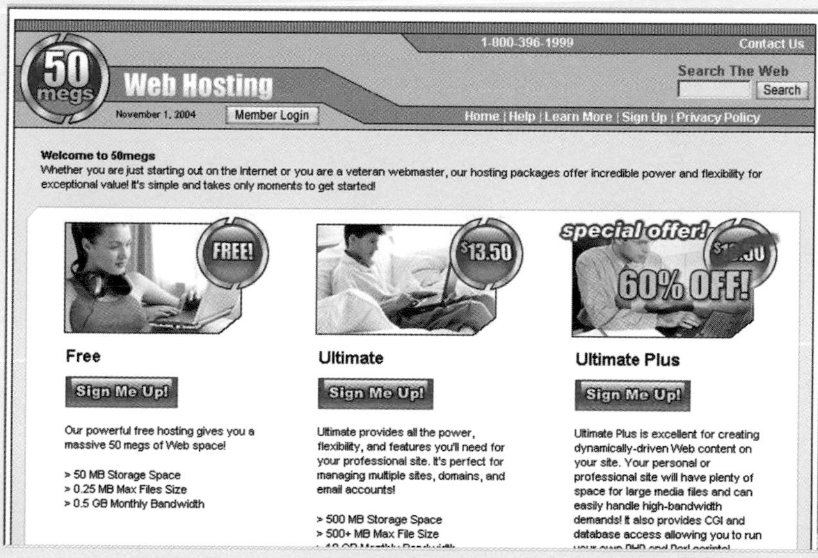

lu lu

chapter 3

DESIGN AND THE USER Interface

1. Understand Design Guidelines: Appearance
2. Understand Design Guidelines: Interactivity

chapter 3 DESIGN AND THE USER Interface

Introduction

Web design is a tricky topic. The novelty of Web design should never cause you to toss aside basic standards of design. In fact, sometimes the best Web designs are the ones that go unnoticed because they are so cohesive and functional. As discussed in Chapter 2, the key to designing any Web site begins at the planning phase. A plan provides the structure for all phases, including the design phase. Once a design strategy and planning documents have been developed and while the multimedia elements are being prepared, the overall look and feel of the Web site should begin to take shape. Figure 3-1 shows one planning document for a Web site on the San Juan Islands. This document helps the development team see the big picture for the Web site.

During the planning phase, a design strategy should have been established with input from the client and all members of the team. As you develop the look and feel of the Web site, always refer to the design strategy and always focus on the user. Your design must be user-centered, not designer-centered. It must be focused on what the user wants and needs, not what you think is cool. The planning documents developed during the planning phase serve as the foundation for the design of the project. Although the planning documents should always be considered works in progress, the design strategy should be solid. The planning documents serve as a perpetual reference guide that will help the multimedia team stay focused on the design.

The development team should make the design simple, easy to understand, and easy to use. The entire design process is undertaken for the benefit of the user. The user should not have to be taught how the navigation scheme and media controls work—these components of the multimedia Web site should be intuitive. From the moment the first Web page appears and throughout the interactive process, users should know where they are and where they can go (unless the Web site is designed to be exploratory, such as a mystery- or adventure-type game). The home page, which is the entry page to the Web site, should indicate what is contained in the Web site and how to navigate through it.

In addition to the design strategy, the design team should follow the principles of multimedia design that have been established over time. Developers use these principles as design guidelines, which are based on the target audience, content, and type of Web site, rather than as absolute design rules. Multimedia design guidelines help the developer achieve the overriding design consideration from which the entire Web site flows. The design guidelines fall into two broad categories: appearance and interactivity. This chapter discusses selected multimedia design guidelines in more detail.

FIGURE 3-1

This planning document serves as the foundation for the design of the project

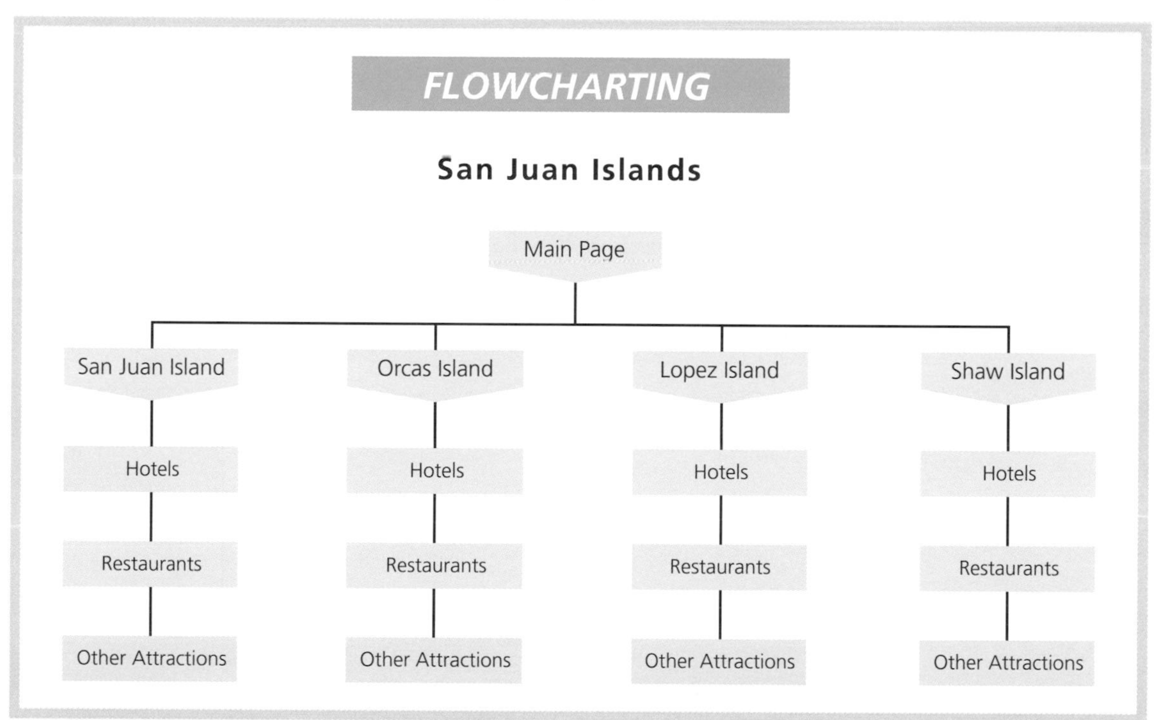

CONCEPT 1

UNDERSTAND DESIGN
Guidelines: Appearance

What You'll Learn

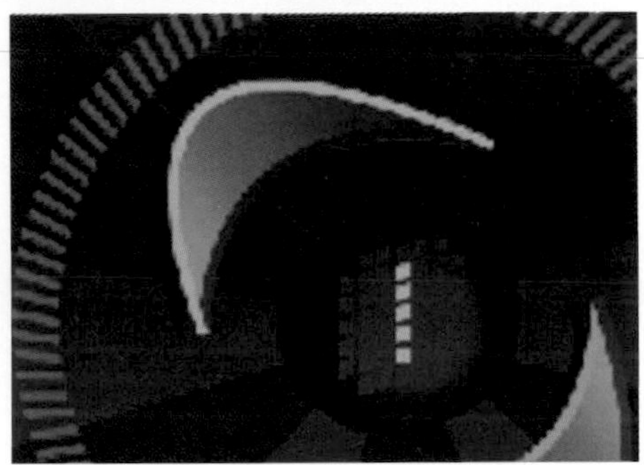

In this lesson, you will learn about the design guidelines related to the overall appearance of a Web site. These guidelines include metaphor, template, content, balanced layout, movement, color scheme, independence, functionality, and unity.

If you want your Web site to be credible, you have to design each page of the Web site just as carefully as you would create any piece of company or organizational correspondence. An accurate Web site with superb visual design and high editorial standards will inspire confidence in your users. One of the most powerful aspects of any Web site design is its appearance, including the important "extras" that are designed for users. The discussion that follows focuses on aspects of Web site design related to appearance. This discussion is not inclusive, but hopefully will provide a springboard to implementing your creativity and ingenuity as you design Web sites.

Metaphor

A **metaphor** is a figurative representation that links the content of your Web site to an established mental model. For example, one of the established metaphors for e-commerce is the electronic shopping cart. See Figure 3-2.

FIGURE 3-2

One of the established metaphors for an e-commerce Web site is the electronic shopping cart

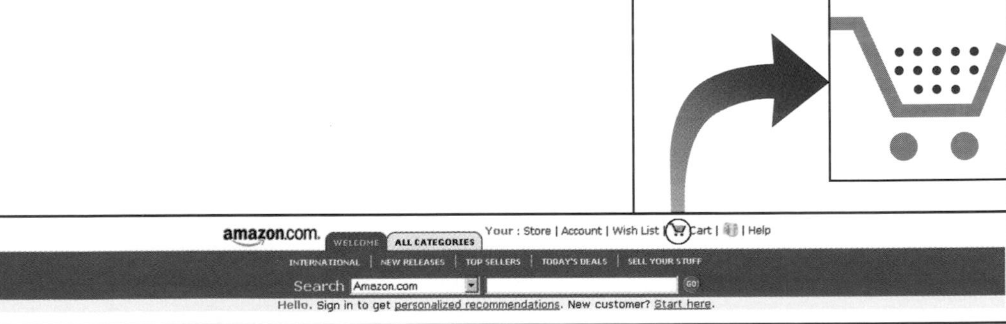

Well-designed and targeted metaphors can be powerful communication tools, but deciding whether to use a metaphor is not a simple task. The best approach for developing a metaphor is to collaborate with the client and prospective users. To be effective, metaphors must be concrete and obvious. All of the Web page images, including icons and pointer symbols, as well as the navigation process, should complement one another and be consistent with the Web site's content. In addition, they must be appropriate; otherwise, they may mislead and confuse the user. Poorly designed and inappropriate metaphors are distasteful and unnecessary. If the metaphor reinforces the message and appeals to the target audience without detracting from the content and navigability of the Web site, you should consider using it.

Consistency

Consistency is an especially important component of a Web site. It applies to both the appearance of each Web page and how the navigation scheme works. Figure 3-3 shows how a consistent look is achieved as the user navigates from one Web page to another. In this example, the user clicks one of the tabbed links in the navigation bar at the top of the page to move to the next page of the site. Notice how the navigation bar remains consistent from one page to the next.

FIGURE 3-3

Maintaining a consistent look from Web page to Web page is an important design consideration

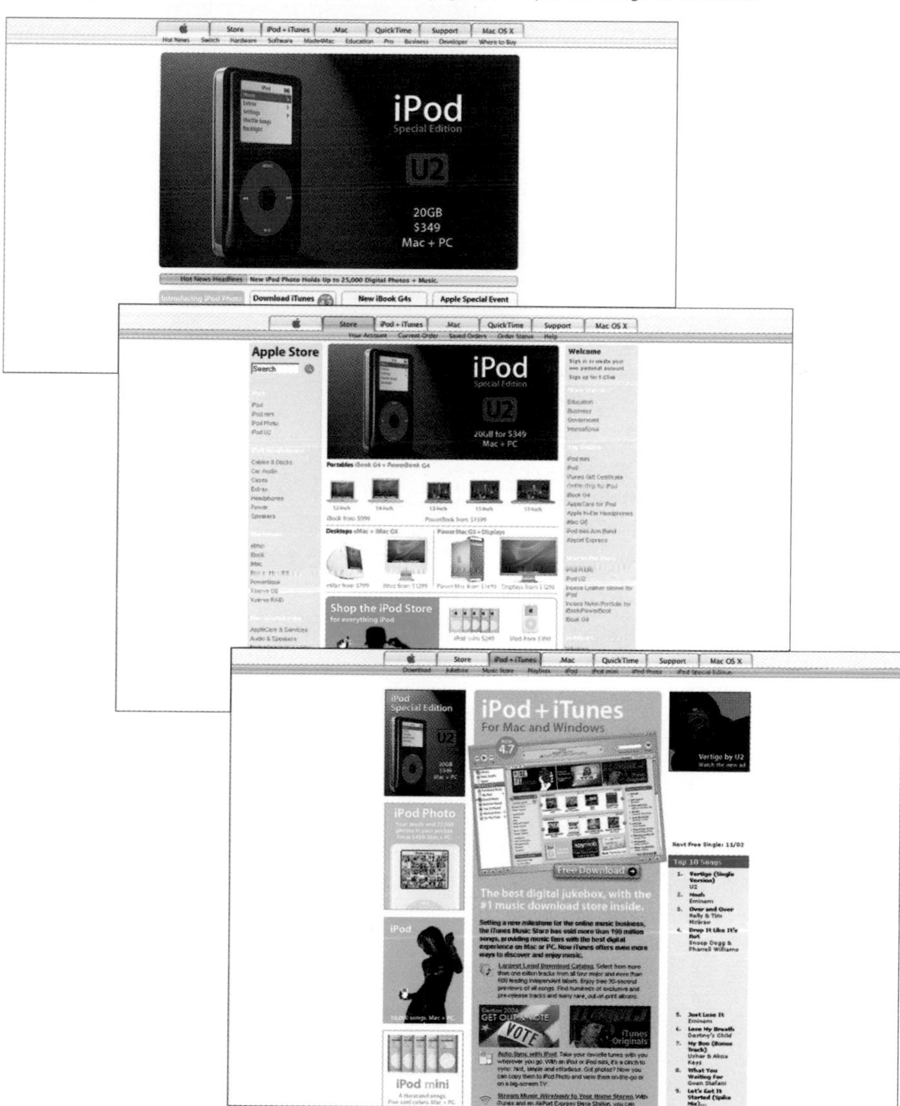

Template

A **template** is a precise layout indicating where various elements will appear on the Web page. Figure 3-4 shows an example of a design template. Notice that the design template dictates the positions of the various elements (graphic, heading, menu, text, and navigation bar). Although the actual content will change, the positions of elements on the Web page will remain the same throughout the Web site. Templates can aid the design process in several ways:

- *Provide consistency.* Each element of the Web page will appear in the same location, which aids the user in understanding how the Web site works and increases the speed at which the user can navigate through the Web site.
- *Shorten the development time.* Because of the similarity of the Web pages, templates can reduce the amount of time needed to arrange elements on the various Web pages.
- *Prevent "object shift".* An object that moves even one pixel as the user navigates through the Web site causes a noticeable and disconcerting jump. Templates that utilize grids can specify the exact layout, down to a pixel in each element, which prevents objects from shifting.

FIGURE 3-4

A design template can be used to help maintain consistency in a Web site

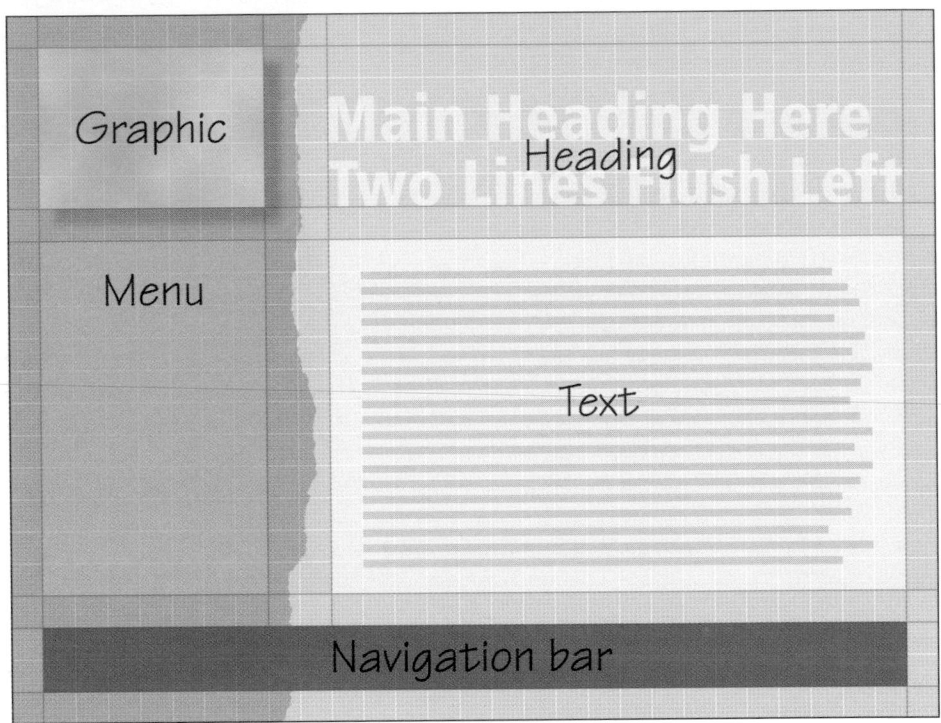

Cascading Style Sheets (CSS)

Cascading Style Sheets (CSS) have made type design, layout, and consistency easier to implement than ever before. Using CSS, you can create styles that contain a variety of formatting specifications. Then, rather than applying these specifications to each section in your Web page or Web site, you apply the style that includes the specs. If you later decide that you prefer something different, you simply modify the style on the stylesheet and the changes you make will cascade throughout the Web page or Web site. Cascading Style Sheets can save you an enormous amount of time and effort by automating your work and giving you control over changes that you make to your Web site. CSS gives you the power and consistency to control the elements on your Web site.

Content

In general, people visit your Web site because they are interested in the information or content you have to offer. Keep this in mind when designing your Web site—all multimedia elements: text, graphics, animation, sound, and video—should complement the content of a Web page. The media elements should enhance the content and not be the focus, unless the goal of the Web site is to entertain or showcase artwork.

A major consideration in designing a Web site is determining what content and how many levels users must navigate. On Web pages, less text is usually better. So, just as you should always strive to include content that users may want or need, you should also strive to remove content that they do not want or need. When there is a lot of content, the tendency is to add more levels. The more levels, however, the greater the chance for confusion and frustration by users as they try to determine where they are, how they got there, and how they can return to the starting point.

You can reduce the number of levels in many ways, for example, by providing **hyperlinks** (also called **links**) that skip several levels, by replacing parts of the original Web page with new content but leaving the shell of the Web page intact so that users have a frame of reference, by using pop-up windows that display additional information, by using scroll bars (for text-intensive Web sites), or by providing tabs or bookmarks that indicate where the user has been and that allow the user to return quickly to a previously viewed Web page. Hyperlinks extend the capabilities of Web pages by allowing users to link to related topics. Links allow designers to keep text on each page to a minimum. By setting up links, users can click to get to another page if they want to read more about the particular topics that interest them.

Regardless of the amount of content, make sure the content is always accessible. Users generally do not read a Web page, instead, they simply scan it. They look for keywords and links. Consequently, providing too much information on a page or cluttering it with too many graphics or animations may hinder the user.

First-time visitors to a Web site generally spend less than 60 seconds on the Web page. During that time, the Web site must capture the visitor's interest, and the visitor must understand what the Web site is about, how to navigate through it, and how to obtain the desired information, especially considering that users come to a Web site in many ways. Users might access your Web site through a search engine list, through a link from another Web site, or by surfing. The Web site must be designed in a way that makes it easy for the users to learn the purpose of the Web site quickly.

Text is still the primary element used to convey information on Web pages. Fonts, color, style, and special effects can enhance text, but the bottom line is that your text must be readable. Be careful of tiled backgrounds and light text on a dark background. See Figure 3-5. Always test your color and background combinations.

FIGURE 3-5
Make sure your background enhances your text and does not make your text difficult to read, as shown here

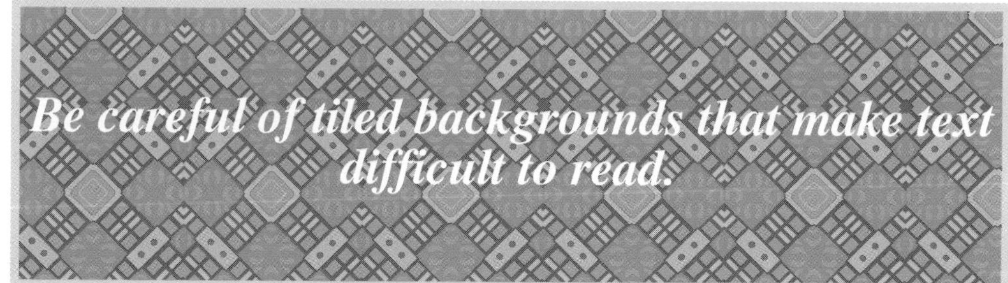

Balanced Layout

Web pages may include text, photographs, buttons, icons, and animation all on the same Web page. The goal to laying out an effective Web page is to design it so that it is balanced, but not boring. **Balance** in Web page design refers to the distribution of optical weight in the layout. **Optical weight** is the ability of an element (such as a graphic, text, headline, or subhead) to attract the user's eye. Each element has optical weight as determined by its nature and size. The nature of an element refers to its shape, color, brightness, and type. For example, a stunning color photograph of Mount Everest has more weight than a block of text of equal size.

Balance is determined by the weight of the elements and their position on the Web page. That is, if you divide the Web page into two parts, a balanced layout has about the same weight for each part. A Web page can have symmetrical balance, asymmetrical balance, or no balance. **Symmetrical balance** is achieved by arranging elements as horizontal or vertical mirrored images on both sides of a center line. See Figure 3-6. **Asymmetrical balance** is achieved by arranging nonidentical elements on both sides of a center line, as shown in Figure 3-7. A **no balance** design has elements arranged on the Web page without regard to the weight on both sides of the center line.

FIGURE 3-6
A balanced layout using symmetrical design

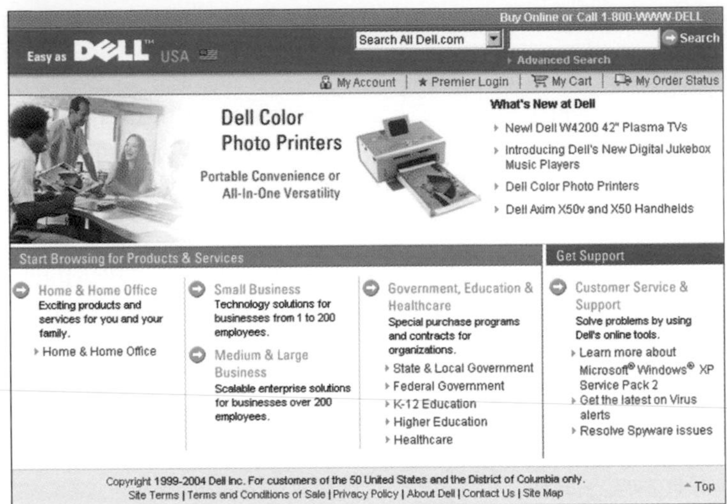

FIGURE 3-7
A balanced layout using asymmetrical design

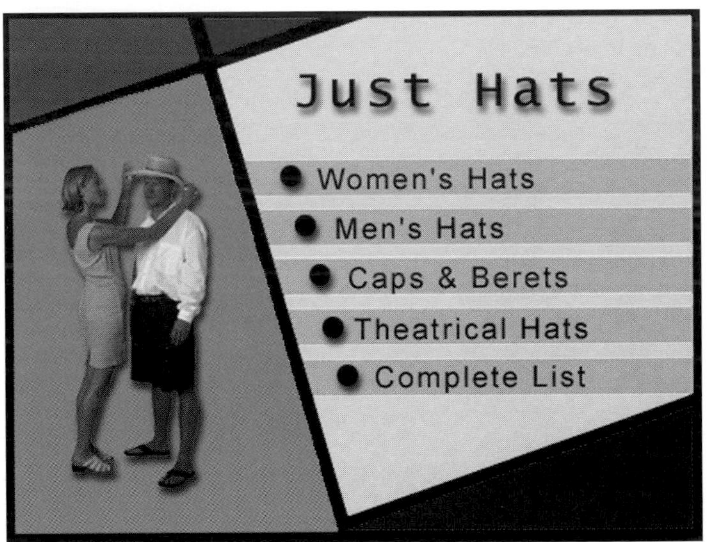

In general, symmetrical design is static and suggests order and formality. It might be appropriate for multimedia Web sites that highlight the corporate image of conservative organizations such as banks and insurance companies. On the other hand, asymmetrical design is dynamic and suggests diversity and informality. It might be appropriate for entertainment Web sites for which a feeling of movement and discovery are important.

Though you do want a consistent method of navigation, you do not want to develop a monotonous rhythm of graphic, text, animation, and sound. The goal is to grab the user's attention but still maintain a balanced look. One way to achieve balance without monotony is to consider how the elements work together. Position text carefully to achieve a good balance with the other multimedia elements. For example, you can wrap text around a related graphic to create an attractive, well-balanced paragraph with visual appeal. Make sure text flows around the appropriate graphic and that readability is considered. Text is easier to read when it flows around the top, bottom, or to one side of a graphic. In addition, do not forget **white space**, the blank areas on a page where text and other media elements are not found. Remember that white space does not have to be white. See Figure 3-8. In general, users like space between elements. Too much on the Web page at one time can be unsettling. White space is an important element in Web page design.

Movement

In addition to balance, the Web designer must consider movement. In general, **movement** relates to how the user's eye moves through the elements on the Web page. When a Web page appears on the monitor, the viewer's eye is drawn to a particular location. In a balanced design, this point might be the **optical center**—a point somewhat above the physical center of the Web page. In Western culture, the tendency is to move through the contents of the Web page by going from the upper left to the lower right. As we design for the global community, however, it is critical to include visual clues such as arrows that help direct the viewers' movement on the page.

FIGURE 3-8

The designers of the Colgate Web site use white space between media elements—the white space in this example includes the blue area around the products

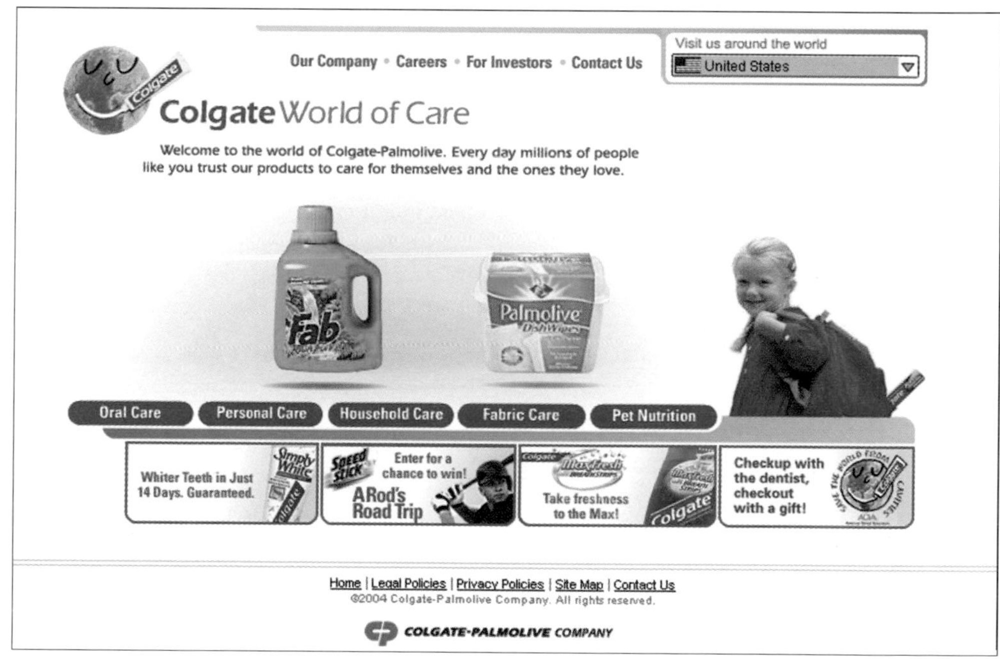

Movement is especially important in training and educational Web sites, especially if the designer wants the user to work through the content in a more structured way. In these cases, the designer tries to affect the movement and emphasize various elements by doing one or more of the following:

- Controlling where the user starts on the Web page—for example, by placing emphasis on a graphic or headline
- Using lines or objects that point the user in a certain direction
- Using color gradients that go from a light shade to a dark shade
- Having people or animals looking in the direction the user should look
- Emphasizing an element—for example, making it a different shape or color, surrounding it with white space, using a different font or type style, creating borders, or using different backgrounds for selected objects

Color Scheme

Most people take color for granted, but as a Web designer you cannot. Color is a powerful communication tool. Color schemes immediately convey information and set the mood or tone of the Web site. Colors and words are similar in that both have great power and are used to communicate. If you choose the wrong colors you may communicate the wrong message, just as if you had selected the wrong words.

Receptors in our eyes translate different wavelengths of light to our brains, which then interpret the light and identify it as a distinct color. **Hue** is color in its purest form. **Shades** of color occur when light is added to it or subtracted from it. In addition to just identifying colors, our brains pass judgment on colors based on both instincts and knowledge. This is important information for a Web designer.

Color evokes emotion and associations. See Figure 3-9. These associations are common in Western culture. There are, however, individual and regional variations. Before you choose a color scheme, it is imperative that you conduct some research on the colors you intend to use and that you test your color scheme on a group of users who are representative of your target audience.

QUICKTIP

Some designers prefer to select colors from a color wheel, while others arrive at color combinations by looking at nature.

In the beginning, Web designers used color sparingly and relied almost entirely on black and gray tones. Because adding color changes the look of Web pages without adding graphics and increasing file size, it was not long before designers began to use color to complement the

FIGURE 3-9
Color evokes emotion and associations

White is associated with the words *innocent*, *clean*, and *good*.
Black is associated with the words *evil*, *fear*, and *death*.
Brown is associated with the words *dirty* and *earthy*.
Yellow is associated with the words *warm*, *coward*, and *caution*.
Red is associated with the words *hot*, *passion*, and *stop*.
Green is associated with the words *envy*, *nature*, and *go*.
Blue is associated with the words *cold*, *sad*, and *sky*.

other media elements on the Web site, increase visual appeal, improve readability, and signal changes in context.

As a beginner, one technique that may help you design an effective color scheme is to avoid trying to work with too many colors at one time. Restricting a palette is a very good way to make colors work together and to keep your Web site from disappearing among the clutter. Working with fewer colors will help you create a cleaner, more tasteful look. You can begin by designing in black and white. Because black holds the highest contrast to white, it is easy to see black text or elements on a white background. Once you feel you have achieved a nice design concept in black and white, then you can begin adding one or two colors. Another technique is to design with different shades of one color as shown in Figure 3-10. Web sites created with a **monochromatic** color scheme can be incredibly appealing. The idea is to use a color scheme that is pleasing to your audience and conveys the desired message and mood.

FIGURE 3-10
A monochromatic color scheme is designed with various shades of a single color

Generally, it is easier to work with dark objects on a light background than it is to work with light objects on a dark background. In the hands of experienced and knowledgeable Web designers, the use of dark backgrounds can be quite stunning, but it takes time and experience to create an effective contrast. As a beginning designer, if you want your messages to stand out, consider using dark on light instead of light on dark. Using these color combinations will make it easier for you to effectively create contrast. And, consider beginning with a main color and adding a few lighter and darker variations together with a few contrasting colors.

Many Web authoring programs include preset color schemes that can be applied to Web pages and entire Web sites. These color schemes have settings for the background and text, as well as for active and visited links. Other authoring programs include themes. A **theme** contains a color scheme and more. It generally consists of unified design elements for bullets, fonts, images, navigation bars, and other media elements. Many third-party vendors sell and distribute themes that can be used in Web-authoring environments. See Figure 3-11.

FIGURE 3-11
A theme contains a color scheme that has unified design elements for bullets, fonts, images, navigation bars, and other media elements

Color schemes and themes can be used to give your Web pages an attractive and consistent appearance. However, unless color schemes and themes have been customized, they sometimes appear amateurish. They offer a great place to start and an excellent source for ideas and inspiration, but the color schemes and themes prepared for most professional Web sites are custom built from the ground up.

Independent and Functional

Users want consistency in design and navigation so they do not get lost on a Web site; and yet, they do not want the Web site to be stale. So in addition to designing the Web site right the first time, you must also build in design elements that will allow you to keep the Web site fresh and functional.

Web sites are by nature interactive. They include internal and external links that must be maintained. And because the Web is dynamic, the layout of each Web page will need to be closely analyzed and programmed to ensure that the links work and that the transition to the next page is effective. You will need to check links periodically to be sure that they are still working properly, and that the content at the linked Web page is still relevant to your users' needs. Developers realize they cannot redesign their Web sites too often, so they rely on updating the content and changing the multimedia elements, especially the graphics and animations, to keep the Web site fresh. This can be done by linking the Web site to a database of images and other content that is updated periodically. Figure 3-12 provides additional Web development tips for keeping the Web site functional.

Web pages are different from traditional print documents because hypertext allows users to access a single Web page in a nonlinear manner. As a result, Web pages need to be more freestanding than pages in traditional print. This means that certain information may need to appear on every page of a Web site simply because a single Web page may be the only page of the Web site viewed by some users. This is really no different than using headers and footers, or repeating dates, volumes, and issue numbers in magazines and newspapers. See Figure 3-13.

FIGURE 3-12

A sampling of Web site development tips for keeping a Web site fresh and functional

- √ Users should be able to display any page within three to five clicks of the mouse button and return to the home page in one click.
- √ Navigation options (often presented in button or table formats) should be labeled clearly.
- √ Text links should be color-coded.
- √ A site map that lists and provides links to the major topical areas is a quick reference for the viewer.
- √ A search feature is a useful tool for finding desired information.

FIGURE 3-13

You should consider including contact information, last modified date, and a link to the home page on every page of your Web site

Title of Web Page | Company Name | Name of Contact Person

Link to Home Page

This Page Was Last Modified On: Date

The best design strategy is to include basic information such as the following consistently on every Web page of your Web site.

- *Contact information*. All well-designed Web sites provide information on how users can contact the company or organization. This is usually done through a "Contact Us" button and page that includes simple information such as company or organization name, address, phone/fax numbers, and e-mail address. In addition, you should always provide a direct link to the Web master's e-mail address.
- *Last modified date*. On any Web page, the last modified date reference is indicative of how dynamic the page is. Users need to know when a page was last updated so that they have confidence that the information they are viewing is current. The Web is home to billions of pages, many of which are outdated. The last modified date provides assurance that the content being accessed is relevant and timely. You can manually change the last modified date on your Web pages, but a better option is to set the date to change automatically using a scripting language. Although it never hurts to include this date on every page of the Web site, at minimum you should include it on all main pages that serve as gateways or portals to other pages of the Web site.
- *Copyright notice*. All original creative works are **copyright** protected and fall under the guidelines and regulations of the **Copyright Act of 1976**. In 1998, this act was reformed to become the **Digital Millennium Copyright Act (DMCA)**. This act updates U.S. copyright law for the digital age. As a user, even if a Web site does not expressly indicate that it is copyright protected, you should consider the content copyright protected. As a designer, it is always wise to include a copyright notice on your Web site. To further substantiate a potential copyright infringement you may also want to apply for a copyright.
- *Link to home page*. Using search engines, users may enter a Web site from a page other than the home page. Consequently, it is important that the designer set up a link to the home page from all other pages of the Web site so that users can be quickly directed to the page that was intended to be the introductory page of the multimedia Web site.

In addition to the basic information on every page, a **Frequently Asked Questions (FAQs)** page can be helpful. This page is a great place for users to go before they contact the company or organization through e-mail or with a phone call. See Figure 3-14.

FIGURE 3-14

A well-thought-out FAQs list can save both the users and the company time and money

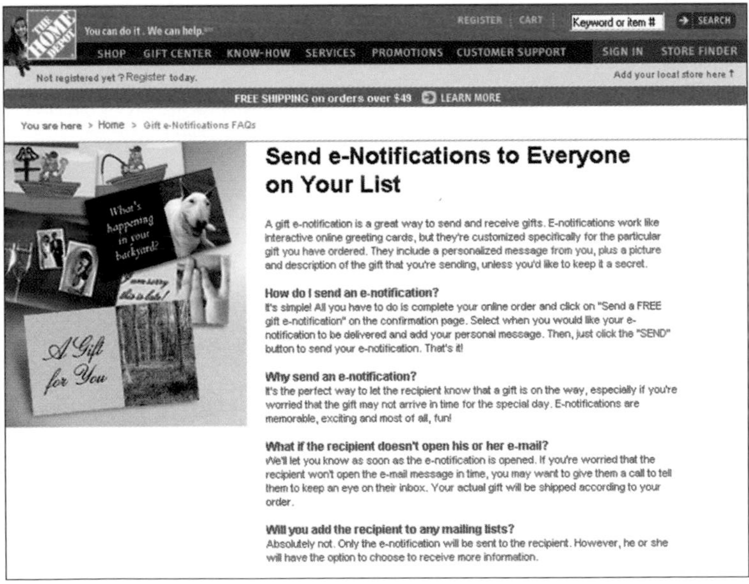

Unified Piece

Finally, the Web site must be presented as a unified piece. A Web designer must be concerned about two types of **unity**: intra-page unity and inter-page unity.

Intra-page unity has to do with how the various page elements relate. That is, do all the elements "fit in"? An element that seems out of place can be disconcerting to the user, and it can prevent the design from achieving the desired effect for a particular Web page. **Inter-page unity** is the interactive design that users encounter as they navigate from one Web page to another. It provides consistency throughout the entire multimedia Web site.

Unity is a desirable design goal in multimedia Web sites and can be achieved by maintaining consistency in shapes, colors, text styles, and themes. All of the multimedia elements created for the Web site must come together and complement one another in the final application. The goals of the Web site must be considered and the underlying theme and mood of the piece must be obvious and well established. All of the multimedia elements should be designed to work with one another and the Web site in its entirety. Consequently, none of the individual media elements can be designed without considering the Web site as a whole. In games and other entertainment Web sites, however, where exploration and surprise are important considerations, a unified design may be perceived as rather dull.

QUICKTIP

Sequence and synchronize your multimedia elements so that the Web site becomes a unified piece — a flowing work of information art.

Unless you are trying to achieve some special effect, all of the multimedia elements used within the Web site should work together. They should all play a role in achieving the purpose and goals of the piece. They should also appeal to the target audience and match the overall mood of the project. Your users will appreciate the help of a common metaphor, color scheme, and navigation method as they transition from page to page. See Figure 3-15.

FIGURE 3-15

All of the multimedia elements at the Starbucks Web site work together to create a unified piece

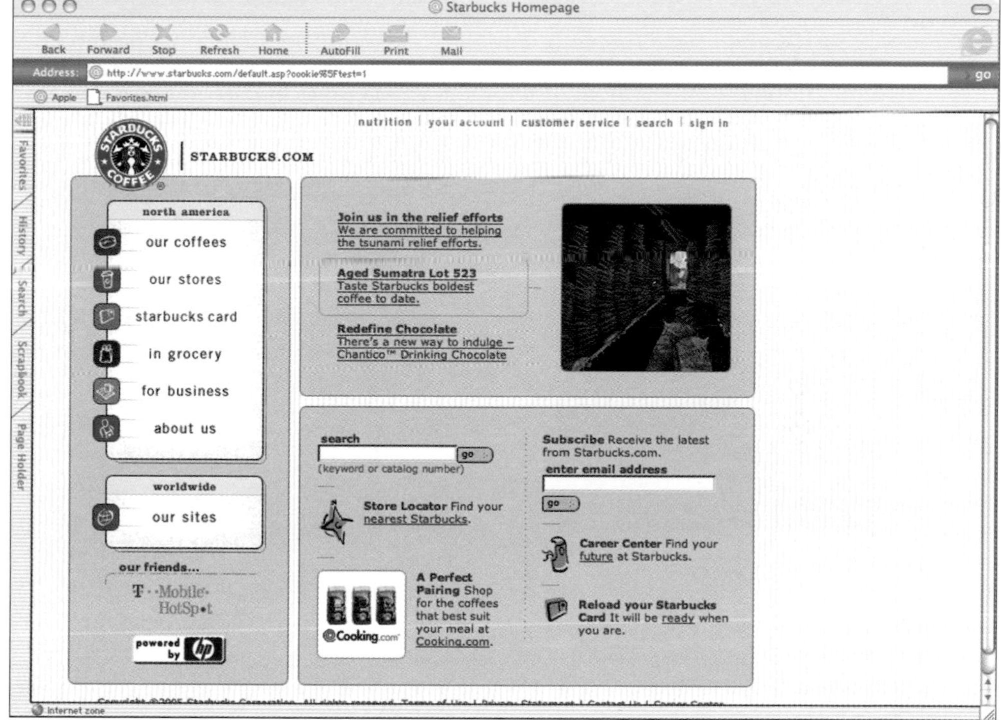

UNDERSTAND DESIGN
Guidelines: Interactivity

What You'll Learn

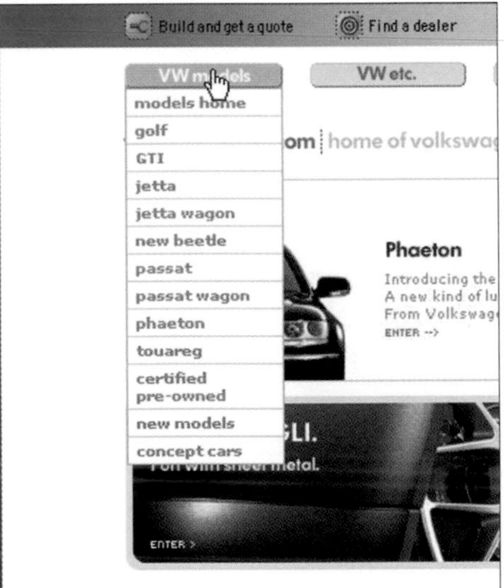

In this lesson, you will learn about the design guidelines related to the interactivity of a Web site including the user interface, optimizing user access and control, download speed, effective linking, sense of context, providing choices and escapes, opportunities for feedback/dialog, and equal access.

In addition to designing the appearance of a Web site, developers must design the Web site's interactivity. The interactive design needs to be user-centered. The interface must support user control that works with the content while addressing the needs of the user (for example, if a sound is played, the user should be able to adjust the volume). So, in addition to guidelines for multimedia design that affect the visual appearance of a Web site, guidelines that affect the navigation of the Web site must also be established.

These guidelines are not absolute interactive design rules, but rather help the developer achieve the overriding interactive design consideration from which the entire Web site flows. That is, they help the developer design the interactivity of the multimedia Web site so that it is user-friendly while enhancing the overall design. This lesson presents selected interactive design guidelines in more detail.

The User Interface

Putting together and designing the **user interface** for the Web site is crucial. Web users do not just look at information on a Web site, they interact with it. Research on the needs and demographics of the target audience are very important to designing the interface. It is impossible to create a functional user experience if you do not understand your users' wants and needs. When you design the user interface, you are literally establishing the foundation of the Web site. You are creating the means through which the user will navigate and interact with your Web site.

User interfaces are designed to give users direct control over the Web site. The user interface includes the interaction metaphors, images, and concepts that are used to convey function and meaning. It is the detailed visual characteristics of every interface component, together with the functional method of interaction, that produce the "look and feel" of a Web site.

Design and visual appeal are not just used to embellish Web pages. They are an integral part of the user's experience with your Web site. In interactive documents it is impossible to fully separate design from function. In other words, there is no such thing as function over form or form over function. Function is part of form. It is part of good design. A well-designed Web site like the Disney Web site shown in Figure 3-16, must not only look good—it must also be functional to the user. Even if all of the other multimedia elements have been exquisitely created and designed, if the final Web site is not user-friendly and functional, the work done by the other media specialists will be wasted.

Users expect a certain degree of function and sophistication from all interfaces, including Web interfaces. The goal is to fulfill the needs of all potential users without requiring them to simply conform or work around an interface full of needless obstacles. As you will recall from Chapter 2, there are many different navigational structures to choose from, including frames, navigation bars, and search features. Regardless of the method chosen, it should be transparent to the user. If the user interface is well designed, the user will be able to interact with the Web site without even thinking about it.

FIGURE 3-16
The Disney Web site is visually appealing, functional, and user-centered

Optimize User Access and Control

Most user interactions on Web sites involve linking between Web pages. As users navigate from page to page, the main interface challenge for multimedia designers is to ensure that users know where they are within the overall structure of the Web site. If this is not accomplished, users become frustrated because they do not know how to get where they want to go, they do not know where they are, and they do not know how to get back to where they were before. Many Web sites use tabs or button bars as their navigation tool, which provide a consistent look and feel from Web page to Web page. See Figure 3-17.

Users want quick and easy access to the content at your Web site. At all times, they should be able to easily return to your home page or to other major pages. Every page should contain at least one link. Pages that dead-end and offer no links to other pages on your Web site are frustrating to users. If users have reached these pages without first visiting other pages of the Web site, they may not realize that there is more to your Web site than a dead-end page. If pages do not contain links back to a home page or to the other major pages of the Web site, the user will be unable to access the remainder of your Web site. Consequently, they may be forced to leave your Web site entirely, particularly if these pages are buried within the hierarchy of the Web site.

If you can give users a sense of control, you will maximize the number of pleasurable experiences that they have at your Web site and they will return again and again. We have already discussed the importance of a user-centered design and a transparent user interface. You can also optimize user access and control by making your pages quick to load, linking effectively to content, establishing a sense of context, providing choices and escapes, providing an opportunity for feedback, and giving access to everyone.

Quick to Load

Users will not tolerate delay. They become impatient when it comes to waiting for Web pages to appear. They become frustrated and may even abort the process after a short time. Research has shown that the threshold of frustration for any computer-related task is about 10 seconds. Even the

FIGURE 3-17
Many Web sites use tabs or a button bar as part of the user interface

Tabs

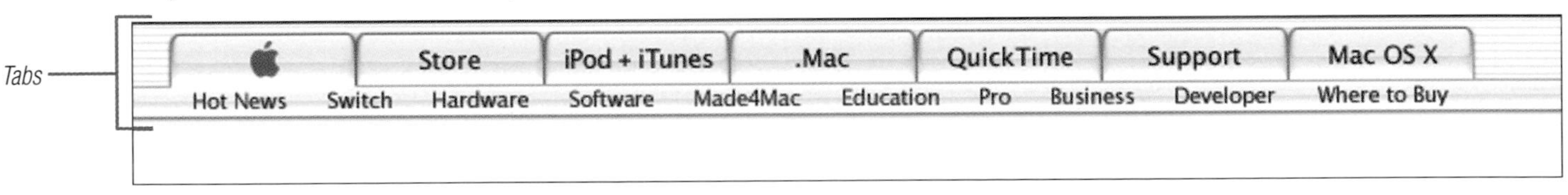

Button bar

most stunning Web sites will go unvisited if they are not quick to load. Users simply will not wait.

Techniques to improve download times include the use of **optimized graphics** and **thumbnail images.** Optimized graphics have been fine-tuned to download more rapidly. A thumbnail image is a miniature display of an image that is linked to a larger version of the same image. Optimize your multimedia elements and files as much as possible without sacrificing too much quality. Keep your graphics, animation, and video files as small as possible, as smaller files will take less time to transmit from the Web server.

QUICKTIP

To keep your Web pages quick to download at all connection speeds, try to keep graphics below 30K each and Web pages below 100K each.

Although **broadband** connections and improved **compression** and **streaming** have made it possible to deliver multimedia via the Web, download speed is still a major issue in Web page design. In addition to **bandwidth** and file size, speed is also dependent upon the user's computer as well as the server hosting the Web site. Therefore, it is important to learn as much as possible about a Web-hosting service before you agree to do business with it.

There are many different speeds at which users are connected to the Internet. If you are fortunate enough to be building an intranet Web site where most users will be accessing your Web pages at faster connections, you do not need to be as concerned about using multimedia elements sparingly and making your Web pages as small as possible. However, if you are designing a Web site for the Internet community at large, the pressure is on you as a designer to keep files small so that they will download quickly over any kind of connection with standard equipment and hardware. If users must wait for your page to load, warn them of the wait and give them a status update as the page loads. See Figure 3-18.

FIGURE 3-18

Provide a status message, similar to the examples shown here, if a multimedia element will take time to load

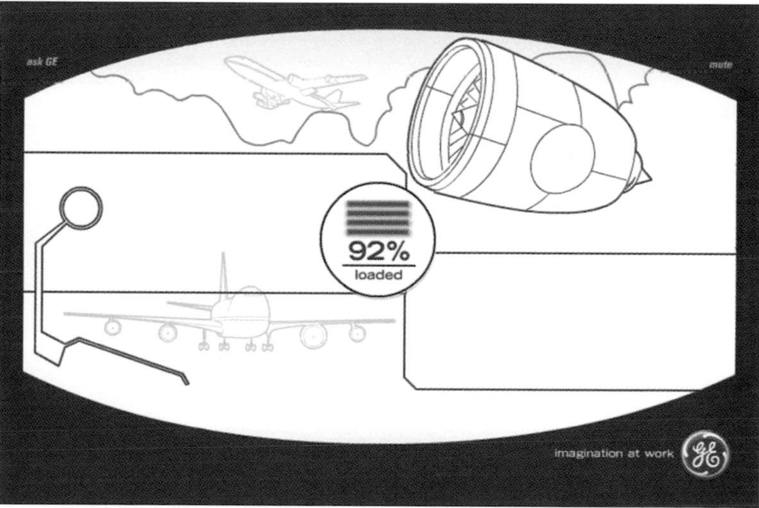

Link Effectively

Keep the number of links on a Web page manageable. Studies on interface design have shown that users favor menus with a minimum of five to nine links. See for example the Beringer Web site (see Figure 3-19), which has eight primary links available through the button bar. In addition, users favor a few Web pages with lots of choices over many Web pages with few choices. One way to create those additional links is through the use of a **mouseover**—a technique that results in a change of the **hot spot** the mouse is moving over. It might be that the text changes color, that a pop-up window opens, or that an image is swapped for text. The goal is to provide users with the information they want in the fewest number of steps possible, in the shortest amount of time, while using the least amount of screen real estate.

To minimize the number of steps through the available choices to the information, you must design efficient organizational and navigational structures as discussed in Chapter 2. The bottom line is that users should be able to quickly locate and access information at your Web site, as well as be able to return to the starting point without hassle.

The entire premise of the Web is based on **cross-linking** or cross-referencing. Using the Web, users have the ability to click text or a graphic and be transported to another Web page within the same Web site or to an entirely different Web site stored on a computer in an entirely different part of the world. The ability to link to related Web sites is a great benefit of using the Web.

At the same time, if your goal is to get users to your Web site and then keep them at your Web site, the last thing you want them to do is click a link that transports them off of your Web site the moment they arrive. If you wish to provide your users with links to other Web sites, create an entirely separate page of external links clearly identified as links to other Web sites. By establishing a clearly identified page of external links, users will not unknowingly leave your Web site. You can also have external links open in a separate browser window so your Web site always remains open in its own browser window.

FIGURE 3-19

At the Beringer Web site, there are eight primary menu links

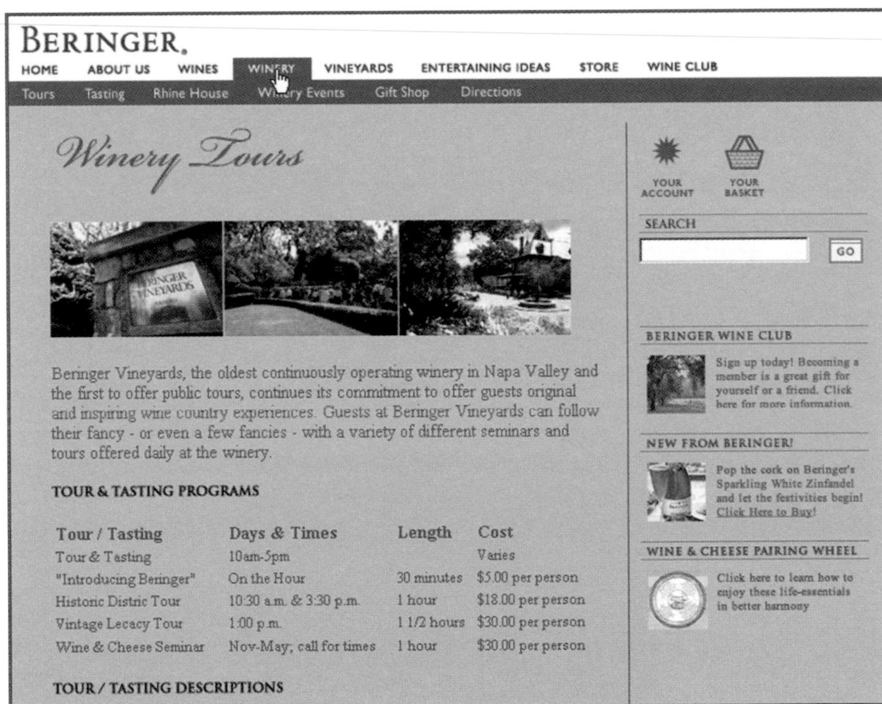

Sense of Context

Just as readers use context to help them assess their place in a printed document, Web users rely on context to help them determine where they are within the hierarchy of information at a Web site. The **contextual clues** on a Web page, however, are different than those found in printed copy. When you read paper copy, you get a sense of context from the layout, the graphic design, the organization of text, and the physical dimensions of the object you are reading. These cues are not always available on Web pages. Because users do not see the entire Web site at one time, but instead see it one page at a time, there are fewer cues to indicate where they are going and what they will find once they get there. In addition, if the Web site is poorly designed, the individual Web pages may not fit on a standard computer screen. Consequently, many users are restricted from viewing an entire Web page at one time.

As the Web-page designer, you need to provide functional and **contextual cues** for the user. To let users know that they are still within the same Web site you should establish and create familiar and intuitive icons, a common color scheme, a consistent method of navigation, and graphic similarity. For example, a bar of navigation buttons that appears at the top of every page of the Web site helps assure readers that they are still in the right place. At the Volkswagen Web site, shown in Figure 3-20, every page of the Web site includes the same drop-down list boxes so that users know at all times where they are and how to get where they want to be.

A consistent approach to the layout of titles, subtitles, footers, and links also reinforces the user's sense of context. In addition, text-based overviews and summary screens help users find exactly what they are looking for without wasting time. By providing a consistent and predictable set of navigation buttons and contextual cues, you give your users the confidence to explore your Web site and all it has to offer.

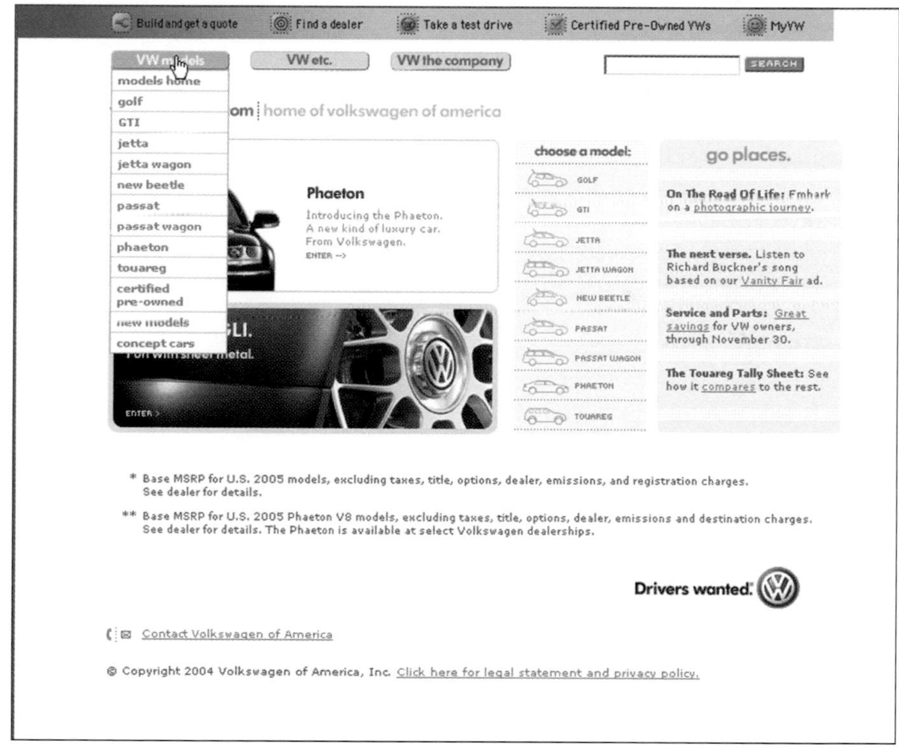

FIGURE 3-20

A drop-down list box is associated with each button; list boxes provide contextual clues to the Web site content

Provide Choices and Escapes

One of the guiding principles of interactivity is that the user should have control. With that principle in mind, consider the following: avoid long introductions of automatically scrolling text, narration, music, or credits. Do not make the user view a video or animation, or listen all the way through sound clips that he or she might already have heard; provide a way for the user to skip or escape viewing these elements. Always provide ways for the user to control the playing of animations, sound, and video. See Figure 3-21. If video (or animation or sound) is used, then decisions that affect interactive design must be considered. For example: Who controls the video? Does the video play automatically or can the user stop and start it? Can the user adjust the sound volume? If the user has viewed the video previously, what controls are needed to allow the user to bypass the video?

Opportunity for Feedback

A well-designed Web site gives users the opportunity to establish an ongoing relationship with the company or organization. As part of this relationship, users need to be able to communicate with the company or organization online. See Figure 3-22.

The establishment of an opportunity for dialog, together with an expedient and professional response, helps guarantee the success of the Web site.

FIGURE 3-21
Video controls allow the user control when viewing a video element

FIGURE 3-22
At the Nordstrom Web site, users have many vehicles for communicating with the company

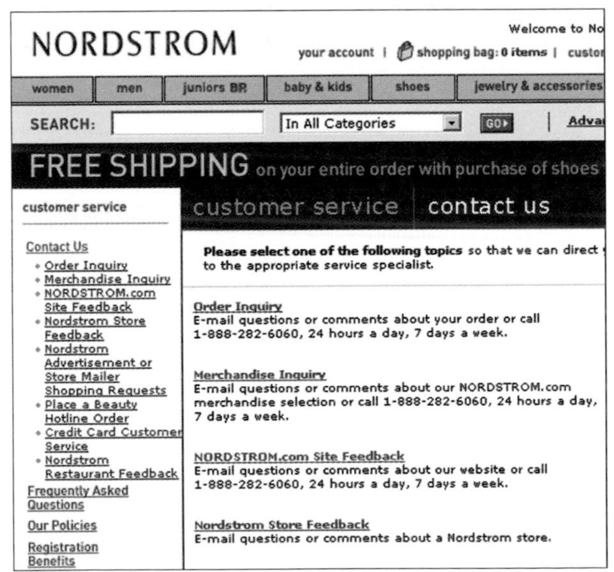

Equal Access

Millions of people throughout the world have disabilities that prevent them from taking advantage of all of the media elements that you have designed for your Web site. Many visually impaired individuals use a text-based Web browser to get information from the Internet. Using special software and a screen reader, the visually impaired can hear the text on your Web pages being read. For visually impaired users to take full advantage of your content, it must be in a text-based format. Screen reading devices can only recognize text, not graphics, unless alternative text has been assigned to a graphic (such as the phrase "List of phone numbers" associated with a picture of a phone). If alternative text has been assigned, the screen reader reads the alternative text when the cursor is moved over the graphic of the phone, or, in some cases the text is read automatically after the Web page is loaded in the browser.

At this time, there are laws in place that require Web sites that receive federal funding to be accessible by people with disabilities. The laws are always changing so you will want to check government Web sites or the World Wide Web Consortium (w3.org) Web site to stay current on these changing laws and ensure that the Web sites you design are compliant. See Figure 3-23.

FIGURE 3-23

Stay current on accessibility laws to ensure that the Web sites you design are compliant

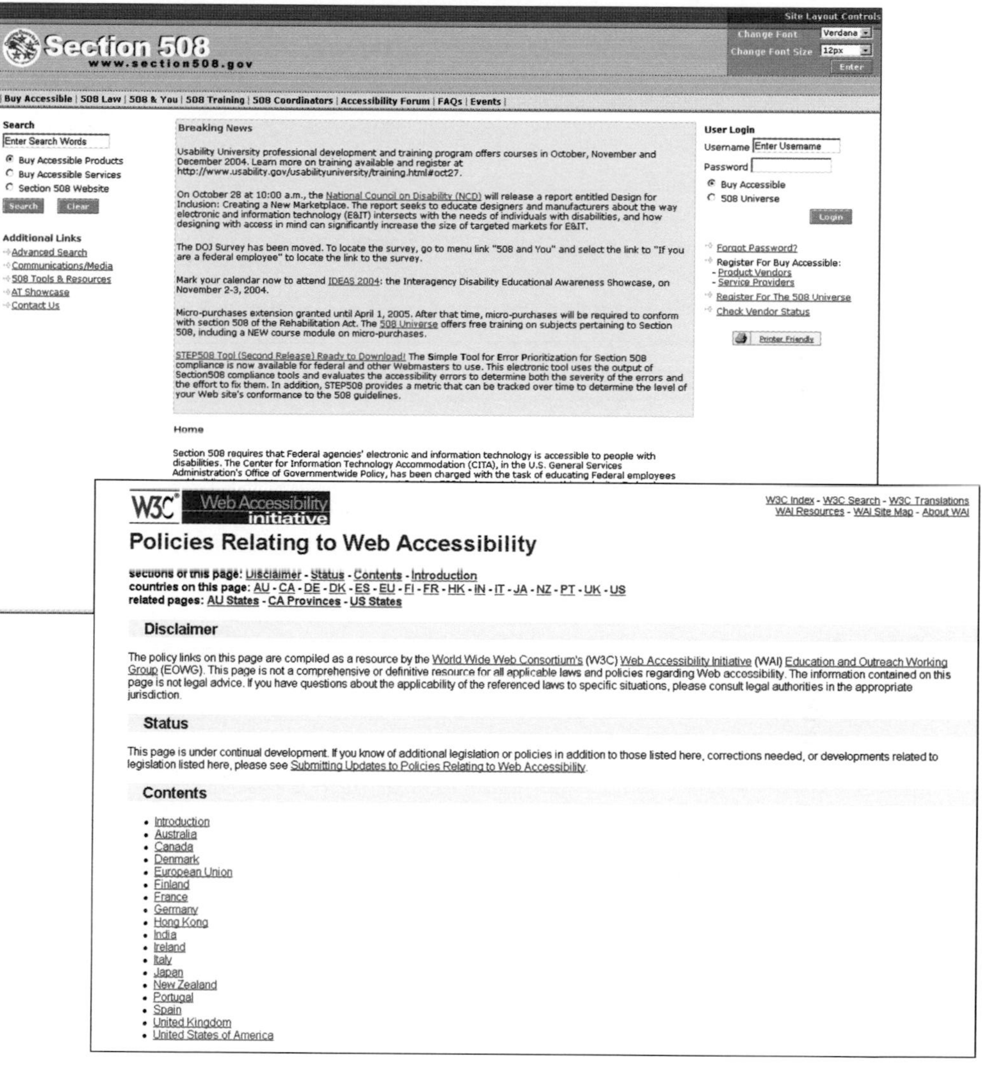

SUMMARY

One of the most powerful aspects of any Web site design is its appearance. A **metaphor** is a figurative representation that relates the content of your Web site to an established mental model. Another important aspect of good Web page design is consistency. **Cascading Style Sheets (CSS)** have made type design, layout, and consistency more possible. A **template** is another layout tool used to ensure consistency. A major consideration in designing a Web site is determining what content and how many levels users must navigate. **Hyperlinks** (also called **links**) extend the capabilities of Web pages by allowing users to link to related topics. Links allow designers to keep text on each page to a minimum.

The goal to laying out an effective Web page is to design it so it is balanced, but not boring. **Balance** in screen design refers to the distribution of **optical weight** in the layout. Each element has optical weight as determined by its nature and size. A Web page can have **symmetrical balance**, **asymmetrical balance**, or no balance. In addition, consider the use of **white space** and **movement**. When a Web page appears on the monitor, the viewer's eye is drawn to a particular location. In a balanced design, this point might be the **optical center**.

As a Web designer, you cannot take color for granted. All of the **hues** and **shades** of color convey information and set the mood or tone of the Web site. **Monochromatic** color schemes are appealing. Many Web-authoring programs include preset color schemes and **themes**. The final Web site must be presented as a unified piece. A Web designer must be concerned about two types of **unity: intra-page unity** and **inter-page unity**.

The **user interface** for the Web site needs to be user-centered. Web users do not just look at information on a Web site, they interact with it. You can optimize user access and control by making your pages quick to load, by linking effectively to content by establishing a sense of context, by providing choices and escapes, by providing an opportunity for feedback/dialog, and by giving equal access to everyone.

Users will not tolerate delay. Techniques to improve download times include the use of **optimized graphics** and **thumbnail images**. Although **broadband** connections and improved **compression** and **streaming** have made it possible to deliver multimedia via the Web, download speed is still a major issue in Web page design. In addition to **bandwidth** and file size, speed is also dependent upon the user's computer as well as the server hosting the Web site.

The Web is based on **cross-linking** or cross-referencing. A button bar with additional links or **hot spots** with **mouseovers** helps users access information in the fewest number of steps possible, in the shortest amount of time, while using the least amount of screen real estate. Just as readers use context to help them assess their place in a printed document, Web users rely on **contextual clues** to help them determine where they are within the hierarchy of information on a Web site. Always provide ways that the user can control the playing of animations, sound, and video, or escape viewing these elements.

Millions of people throughout the world have disabilities that prevent them from taking advantage of all of the media elements that you have designed for your Web site. At this time, there are laws in place that require Web sites that receive federal funding to be accessible by people with disabilities. The laws are always changing so you will want to check government Web sites or the World Wide Web Consortium (w3.org) Web site to stay current on these changing laws and ensure that the Web sites you design are compliant.

KEY TERMS

asymmetrical balance
balance
bandwidth
broadband
Cascading Style Sheet (CSS)
compression contextual clue
contextual clue
copyright
Copyright Act of 1976
cross-linking
Digital Millennium Copyright Act (DMCA)
Frequently Asked Questions (FAQ)
hot spot
hue
hyperlink
inter-page unity
intra-page unity
link
metaphor
monochromatic
mouseover
movement
no balance
optical center
optical weight
optimized graphic
shade
streaming
symmetrical balance
template
theme
thumbnail image
unity
user interface
white space

MATCHING QUESTIONS/DISCUSSION QUESTIONS

Match each term with the sentence that best describes it.

a. Cascading Style Sheet	**b.** contextual cue	**c.** cross-linking
d. FAQs	**e.** hue	**f.** last modified date
g. metaphor	**h.** monochromatic	**i.** mouseover
j. optimized graphic	**k.** symmetrical balance	**l.** template
m. theme	**n.** thumbnail image	**o.** user interface

_____ **1.** A miniature display of an image that is linked to a larger version of the same image.

_____ **2.** The means through which the user will navigate and interact with the Web site.

_____ **3.** Information that helps users determine where they are within the hierarchy of information on a Web site.

_____ **4.** Process of arranging elements as horizontal or vertical mirrored images on both sides of a center line.

_____ **5.** A precise layout indicating where various elements will appear on the Web page.

_____ **6.** Color in its purest form.

_____ **7.** Color scheme designed with all different shades of one color.

_____ **8.** A color scheme and unified design elements for bullets, fonts, images, navigation bars, and other media elements.

_____ **9.** A figurative representation that relates the content of a Web site to an established mental model.

_____ **10.** Formatting specification that has made type design, layout, and consistency easier to implement.

_____ **11.** Premise on which the Web is based.

_____ **12.** Lists of questions and answers that can save both the users and the company or organization time and money.

_____ **13.** A technique in which a hyperlink appears as the cursor moves over a hot spot, such as an image or text.

_____ **14.** Item that should be included on each Web page as assurance that the content being accessed is relevant and timely.

_____ **15.** Images that have been fine-tuned to download more rapidly.

Answer each question either in writing or in a class discussion as directed by your instructor.

1. What is a metaphor? What are some examples of metaphors that are used on the Web?
2. What are five fundamental design guidelines that apply to Web page design?
3. Why is the color scheme important to Web page design? What are some basic guidelines beginners should follow when they are trying to select a color scheme for a Web site?
4. What factors should be considered when designing the user interface?
5. What are five ways to optimize user access and control?

DESIGN PROJECT

This is a continuation of the Design Project in Chapter 2.

As a result of previous meetings with the client, The Inn at Birch Bay, the WebsByCT multimedia development team has created the flowchart and storyboards for the Web site as shown in Figure 3-24. You have been asked to study these planning documents and provide your thoughts related to the design of the Web site.

1. Open a document in a word processor, save the file as **Ch3dp1**, then write a report including the following:
   - **a.** How would you describe the organizational structure of the Web site?
   - **b.** How would you illustrate the links within the Web site?
   - **c.** Is it possible to create a template for this Web site? If yes, design one. If no, explain why not.
   - **d.** Is the layout for the home page balanced? If yes, specify the type of balance and the way in which it is achieved. If no, explain why not.
   - **e.** Is there movement in the design of the home page? Explain.
   - **f.** Does the Web site exhibit consistency? Explain.
   - **g.** Where is the optical center for the home page and how is it achieved?
   - **h.** What are the multimedia elements that are suggested in these planning documents?
   - **i.** How is inter-screen unity achieved?
   - **j.** What do you think should be added to the Web site?

FIGURE 3-24
A flowchart and storyboard for The Inn at Birch Bay

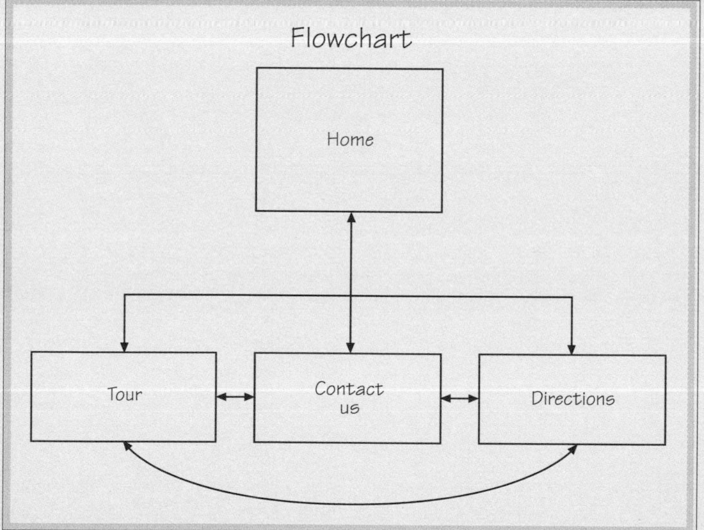

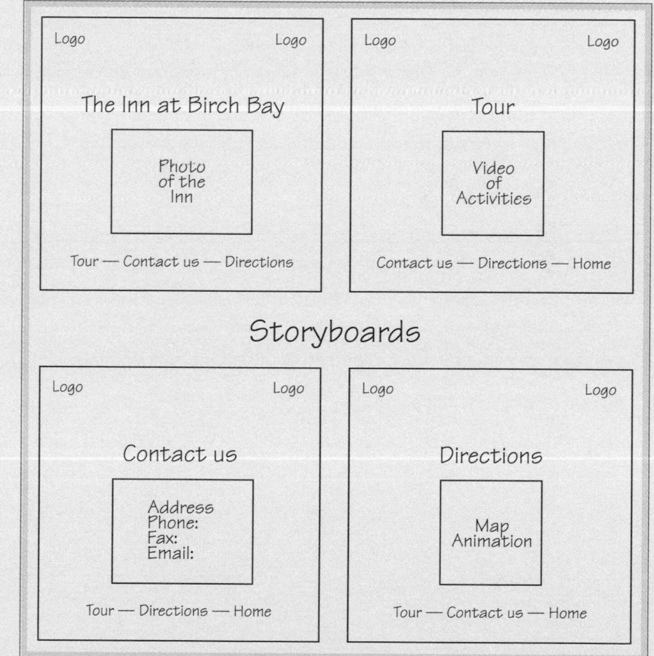

PROJECT BUILDER 1

You are an intern with a company that develops Web sites for clients. At your intern training you were told that many factors, such as unity, contribute to the appearance and effectiveness in the design of a Web page. To better understand some of these factors, you were asked to study the Web page shown in Figure 3-25 and use it to complete a report.

1. Open a document in a word processor, save the file as **Ch3pb1**, and then answer the following questions.
   a. Is it possible to create a template for this Web page? If yes, design one. If no, explain why not.
   b. Are there metaphors used in this site? If so, list and explain them.
   c. Is the layout for the Web page balanced? If yes, specify the type of balance and the way in which it is achieved. If no, explain why not.
   d. Where is the optical center for the Web page and how is it achieved?
   e. What are the multimedia elements that are suggested in this Web page?
   f. How is intra-screen unity achieved?
   g. What do you think should be added to the Web site?

One Step Beyond

2. Using your favorite search engine, find a Web page that exemplifies the concept of movement in Web page design. Provide the following information.
   a. Name of the Web site, URL, and name of the organization and/or person responsible for the Web site
   b. Intended audience for the guidelines (explain your choice)
3. How is movement achieved?
4. How does the movement enhance the design of the Web page?

Two Steps Beyond

5. Using your favorite search engine, find a Web site that exemplifies the concept of inter-screen unity. Provide the following information.
   a. Name of the Web site, URL, and name of the organization and/or person responsible for the Web site
   b. Intended audience for the guidelines (explain your choice)
6. How is the inter-screen unity achieved?
7. How does the inter-screen unity enhance the design of the Web page?

FIGURE 3-25
A Web page with various design factors

PROJECT BUILDER 2

You have been studying Web development. You decide it would be useful to apply design guidelines to the development of your Web site portfolio.

1. Open a document in a word processor, save the file as **Ch3pb2**, and then create a report with the following:
   a. A user interface template for your portfolio Web site or the user interface for each page of the Web site.
   b. Using Figure 3-26 as a guide, explain how you plan to apply each design guideline. If you do not plan to apply a guideline, explain why not.

One Step Beyond

2. Using your favorite search engine, find three Web sites that provide information on guidelines for Web site design and user interfaces. Provide the following for each Web site:
   a. Name of the Web site, URL, and name of the organization and/or person responsible for the Web site.
   b. Intended audience for the guidelines (explain your choice).
3. Choose one Web site as the most useful and explain your choice.

Two Steps Beyond

4. Compare the guidelines for the Web site you have chosen to those in this book.
   a. Are all the guidelines covered in this book also mentioned on the Web site? If not, list guidelines covered in this book that are not covered on the Web site?
   b. Does the Web site provide additional guidelines that are not mentioned in the book? If so, list these additional guidelines.

FIGURE 3-26
Design and user interface guideline categories

Guideline	Application
Metaphor	
Consistency	
Content (Explain how multimedia elements will complement the content)	
Balanced layout (explain how the type of balance will be achieved)	
Movement (explain how movement will be achieved)	
Color Scheme	
Independent and functional (include plan for keeping content fresh and external links current)	
Unity	
User Control	
Link effectively	
Sense of Context	
Choices and escapes	
Feedback/Dialog	
Equal Access	

Hanoi

chapter 4

HTML, XHTML, AND Web Authoring

1. Describe HTML and XHTML
2. Identify Conversion Tools
3. Explain How Web Page Editors Are Used
4. Explain How Web Authoring Programs Are Used
5. Discuss How to Upload Files to a Web Server

chapter 4 HTML, XHTML, AND Web Authoring

Introduction

After you have established the purpose and target audience of your Web site and you have developed a thorough plan including a creative brief, flowcharts, wireframes, and storyboards, you are ready to begin development of the multimedia Web site. A Web site is made up of Web pages that are linked together. Each Web page is displayed in the browser based on its underlying source code. See Figure 4-1. The **source code** provides the information the browser needs in order to display the Web page correctly.

As Web pages have become more complex and as more browsers have become available, standards have been developed that help Web designers create source code that can be interpreted by many browsers. There is an official standards committee for the Web called the **World Wide Web Consortium (W3C)** that maintains Web standards and specifications. However, many browser developers have ignored the sanctions established by the W3C and developed their own proprietary HTML specifications, which is why Web pages that work or display properly on one browser may not work on another.

In developing your Web sites, it is important to understand basic Web development standards so that you can develop your site to display properly on the broadest range of browsers, if that is your objective. You can develop your Web site by writing all of the source code from scratch or you can use tools to help you write the source code. Tools are readily available that enable you to design and develop multimedia Web sites.

This chapter focuses on the different methods and tools that can be used to create Web sites.

FIGURE 4-1
A Web page and its underlying source code

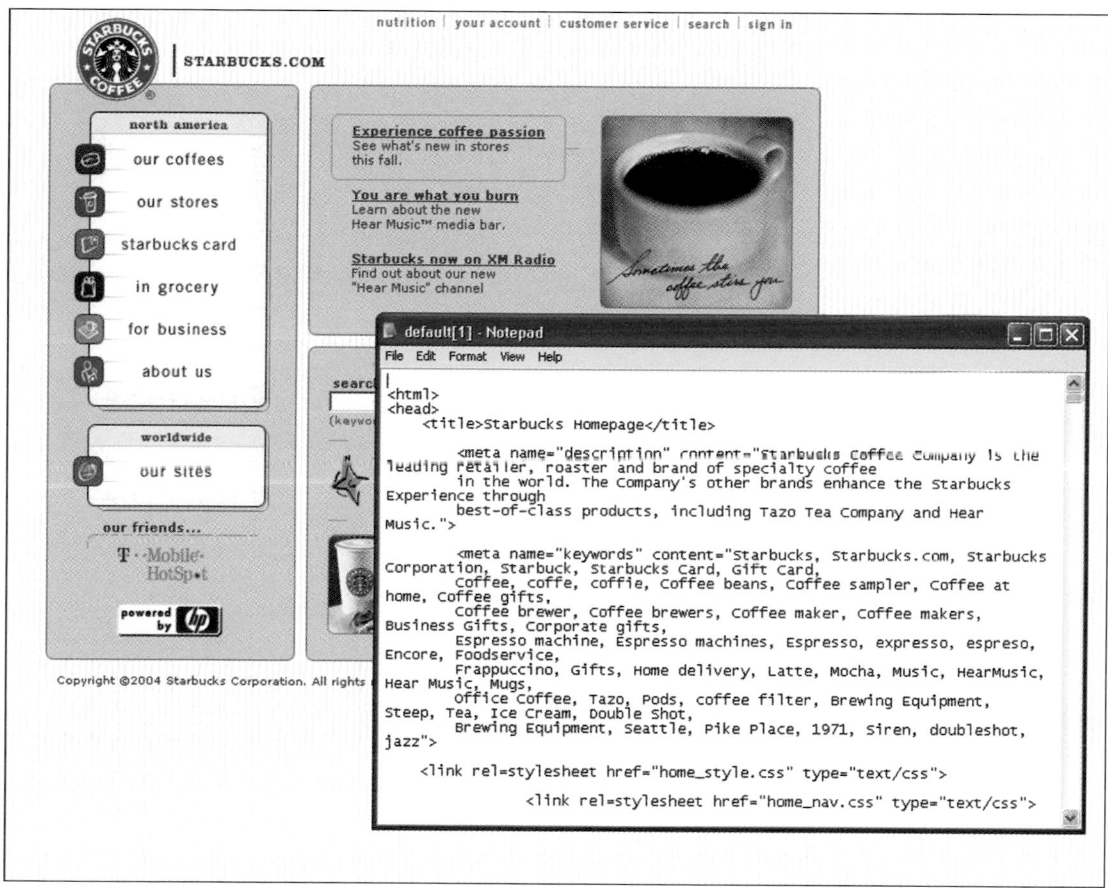

CONCEPT 1

DESCRIBE HTML and XHTML

What You'll Learn

```
page="http://www.macromedia.com/
" width="400" height="200">
```

In this lesson, you will learn about the advantages and disadvantages of creating Web pages by writing HTML and XHTML code from scratch using a text editor.

HTML stands for **Hypertext Markup Language.** This is the standard language used to create Web pages. It is a **markup language**. Markup languages are used to specify or describe the structure, content, or formatting of a document. HTML is designed to be a platform-independent markup language that enables different computers running different operating systems and using different browsers to display the same page. Today, the Web has grown to be an incredibly intricate and sophisticated environment. As a result, there is more to Web page design and development than HTML. However, every Web page has its roots as an HTML document regardless of what it includes and how it is created. Therefore, if you plan to design or develop Web pages, you should understand at least the fundamentals of HTML. Fortunately, HTML is really quite simple to learn.

HTML continues to develop and evolve. There are different versions of HTML. Each new version has supported increased Web page functionality as seen in Figure 4-2. The most recent version, **Extensible Hypertext Markup Language (XHTML)** conforms to **Extensible Markup Language (XML)** rules. XML is a markup language that describes the structure and content of a document and conforms to much stricter coding standards than HTML. In addition, XML allows you to define your own markup tags.

XHTML includes the benefits of the formatting features of HTML and the stricter coding standards of XML. These stricter coding standards help ensure that Web pages created in XHTML will be consistently interpreted by many different browsers and devices (Web browsers, cell phones, and so on). Because XHTML is a more structured markup language than HTML, the same document will be viewable using different browsers and multiple devices simply by referencing style sheets (you will learn more about style sheets later in the book). Even though you can still use HTML to create Web pages, throughout the remainder of this book, we will use the term *XHTML* because it is the most current markup language standard for creating Web pages.

> **QUICKTIP**
>
> XHTML is a markup language not a programming language or a scripting language. **Programming languages** are used to create executable programs. **Scripting languages** are used to write code that is interpreted by a Web browser. You will learn more about programming languages and scripting languages in Chapter 10.

Specifying the look of a Web page is accomplished through the use of markup tags. **Markup tags** specify how the browser will display text and other multimedia elements. Tags are paired and consist of a beginning tag that specifies the application of the effect and an ending tag that marks the end of the effect. Ending tags are basically the same as beginning tags except they include a forward slash (/) in front of the tag name. Each pair of tags contains information between the tags, and so a pair of tags is often called a **container**.

The information between two tags is the content that will be affected by the tags. For example, in the following container, `<b>This text will be bold</b>`, the beginning tag is `<b>`, the ending tag is `</b>`, and the information between the tags "This text will be bold" is what will be affected. The tags `<b>`...`</b>` instruct the browser to display the information between the tags in bold on a Web page.

Attributes, such as align, color, and width, can also be included within a container to add a modification to information within a container. In general, a **value** follows an attribute. The value determines the result of the attribute. For example within the container

<p align="center"> This text will appear center aligned</p>

<p is the beginning tag and it stands for paragraph, *align* is the attribute that determines how the paragraph will be modified and *center* is the value. It is the value that determines which type of alignment (left, center, or right) will be used. An **element** is the combination of a beginning tag along with its attributes and values. See Figure 4-3.

FIGURE 4-2
A basic overview of HTML versions

Version	Description
HTML 1.0	Ability to create hyperlinks
HTML 2.0	Added support to display inline images and interactive forms
HTML 3.0	Included support for tables and extended formatting capabilities
HTML 4.0	Included support for cascading style sheets (CSS)
XHTML	Conforms to Extensible Markup Language (XML) rules

FIGURE 4-3
In this element, the tag body, the attribute bgcolor, and the value "yellow" set the background color of the body of the Web page to yellow

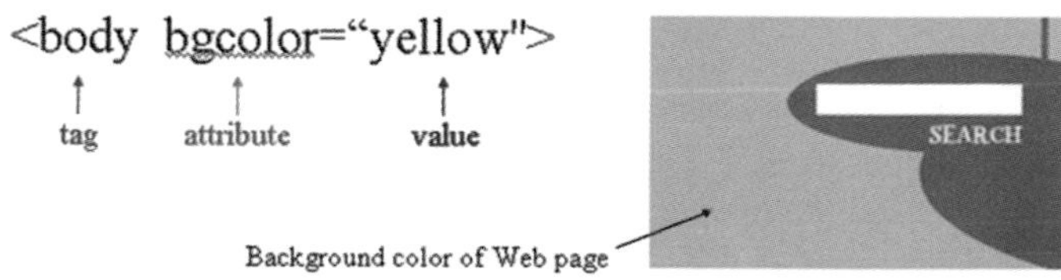

All XHTML documents are formatted using markup tags. Figure 4-4 provides examples of some basic XHTML tags. There are tags to format most anything you can imagine on your Web pages. Unfortunately, however, even if you use these tags properly, your pages still may not display as expected because the configuration of the browser and the user's equipment are also factors that determine the final appearance of the Web page. This makes testing your Web pages under different conditions (e.g., different operating systems, browsers, and monitor settings) imperative.

FIGURE 4-4
Examples of XHTML tags

XHTML tags	
Basic tags	
<html>	Creates an XHTML document
<head>	Defines the title and other information that is not part of the Web page itself
<body>	Defines the Web page itself
Header tags	
<title>	Defines the page title, usually displayed in the browser's title bar
<base href="URI" />	Defines the base URL for this page
Body attributes	
<body background="URI">	Sets the page background image.
<body bgcolor="rgb">	Sets the page background color, either by name ("black"), or hex value ("#RRGGBB").
<body text="rgb">	Sets the page text color.
<body link="rgb">	Sets the color for hyperlinks.
<body vlink="rgb">	Sets the color for visited (previously followed) links.
<body alink="rgb">	Sets the color for activated (clicked) links.
Block tags	
<p>...</p>	Defines a text paragraph.
 	Defines a forced linebreak.
<blockquote>	Defines a quoted, indented text block.
<h1>...<h6>	Defines a level 1-6 heading.
<div>	Defines a page section.
<table>	Defines a tabular section.
<form>	Defines a Web form.
<ol>	Defines an ordered list (1, 2, 3, ...).
<ul>	Defines an unordered, bulleted list.
<li>...</li>	Defines a list item in an ordered or unordered list.
<dl>	Defines a definition list, with terms and their definitions.
<dt>	Marks the term to be defined.
<dd>	Marks the definition of the term.

Advantages of Writing XHTML

- *Power/Control.* If you know XHTML you will have greater power and control over your Web pages. In addition, it will be easier for you to find and fix problems.
- *Clean Code.* To write XHTML, all you need is a simple text editor such as Notepad on the Windows platform and TextEdit on the Macintosh. In general, if you write your own XHTML code, your pages will be cleaner and more fine-tuned.
- *Not Dependent on a Tool with Limitations.* It is to your advantage to learn the basics of XHTML in order to comprehend the placement and use of tags in existing documents, as well as for editing documents that you or someone else has created using other

applications. If you do not know any XHTML, you will be dependent on a tool that may contain bugs or limitations, and you won't know what is and what is not possible at the code level. This can be frustrating. It is important to realize that a great deal of Web development work involves site maintenance. Often there is only one minor adjustment that needs to be made in a Web page and editing the code is easier and quicker than using an application.

Eventually, if you are a serious Web developer, you may want to master a Web site development tool such as Dreamweaver. Learning the basics of XHTML is crucial to understanding how these tools work.

QUICKTIP

When naming HTML and XHTML files, follow standard naming conventions to ensure that the files will function properly when uploaded to a Web server.

- Do not use spaces
- Avoid capital letters
- Avoid illegal characters, such as \ / : * ? < > |

Disadvantages of Writing XHTML Code

- *Learning Curve.* One disadvantage to writing XHTML is that you have to learn it. Although learning XHTML may seem daunting at first, most people find it very easy to learn once they understand the basics.
- *Time-consuming to Write.* Typing all of the symbols and characters into a text document is much more time-consuming than using a program that writes the code for you.
- *Easy to Make Mistakes.* It is easy to make careless mistakes as you write XHTML code, but mistakes are also fairly easy to troubleshoot and fix.

QUICKTIP

As is true with anything, the more you do it, the easier it will be and the more proficient you will become. In addition, developing an XHTML template that provides the basic structure for all your Web pages can help overcome the disadvantages.

Examples

There are too many tags, attributes, and values to include all of them in this textbook. In addition to the ones shown in Figure 4-4, a few examples follow that will help you understand tags.

A common tag used to include multimedia elements on a Web page is the `<embed>` tag. For example, if you want to include sound on a Web page you might insert XHTML code similar to the following:

```
<embed src="sound.mp3"
autoplay="true"> </embed>
```

This code instructs a browser to retrieve a sound file named "`sound.mp3`". The attribute *autoplay* and the value *true* cause the sound file to begin playing without the use of a controller. The ending tag `</embed>` completes the container.

To include images, graphics, and animated gif files on your Web pages you use the <img> tag (See Figure 4-5). The XHTML code

```
<img src="at_the_beach.gif"
border="0" width="353"
height="238" >
```

instructs a browser to display a graphic file named "`at_the_beach.gif`" on the Web page. The attribute *border* and value *0* mean that the image will have a border or frame of 0 pixels (no border). The rest of the code `width="353"` and `height="238"` represents the measurement of the image in pixels.

In XHTML, all tags, must have a termination or ending tag. In older versions of HTML, some tags were commonly used on their own without an ending tag. Empty tags are special single tags such as *img*. Because these tags do not come as a set, in XHTML, a termination must be specified within the tag itself. This is done by entering a space and forward slash into the tag. Example: <img src="imagename.gif" />.

Helper Applications

In the early days of the Web, any file that was not in an HTML format had to be downloaded, saved, and opened at a later time with a separate application. As time went on, browsers began to launch **helper applications** to play non-native HTML content. Today, many multimedia elements require the use of **plug-ins** or **players** in order for the user to see or hear the media element included on the Web page.

FIGURE 4-5

The <img> tag instructs a browser to display a graphic on your Web pages

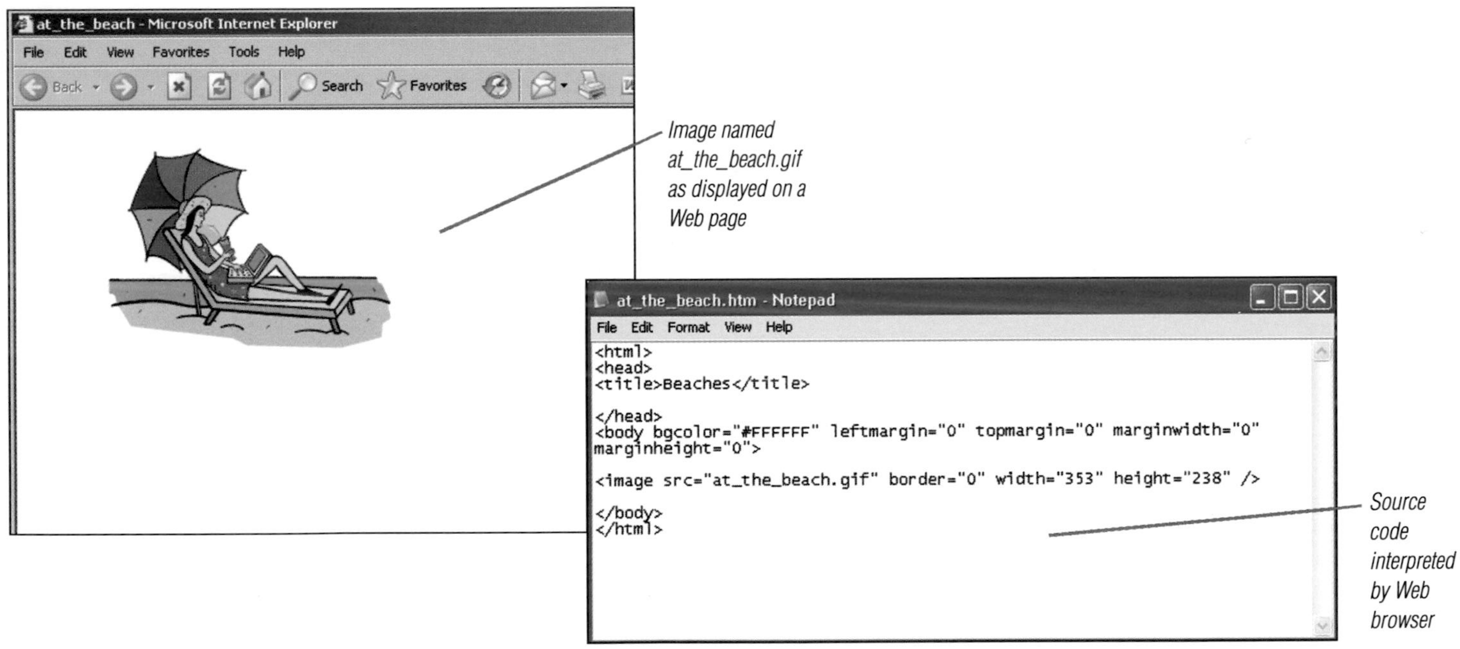

Plug-ins or players allow users to play media content within the browser window. The **pluginspage** attribute shown in Figure 4-6 makes it possible for the Web page designer to better accommodate users by making it easy for them to download and install the appropriate plug-in or player if they do not already have it on their computer system. In this example, the embed element has several attributes with associated values as follows:

embed: an XHTML element allowing a media object to be played in the Web page

src: an attribute (specifies the file to play)

"ridetolive.swf": a value (the file name)

pluginspage: an attribute (specifies the location of the Web page providing the plug-in or player)

"http://www.macromedia.com/shockwave/download/": a value (the URL for the download Web site)

type: an attribute (specifies the type of plug-in or player needed to play the file)

"application/x-shockwave-flash": a value (the plug-in or player type)

width: an attribute (specifies the width of the object to be displayed on the screen)

"400": a value (width)

height: an attribute (specifies the height of the object to be displayed on the screen)

"200": a value (height)

As Web page formatting becomes more complex and graphics, animation, audio, and video are included in interactive multimedia Web pages, the XHTML coding also becomes more complex. Converters, editors, and authoring programs can be used to simplify this process. These tools allow you to design your multimedia Web pages visually using graphical user interface or **What You See Is What You Get (WYSIWYG)** applications that generate the XHTML code for you.

FIGURE 4-6

In this element, the attribute pluginspage *opens a download page for the Macromedia Flash player so the user can decide if he or she wants to download it*

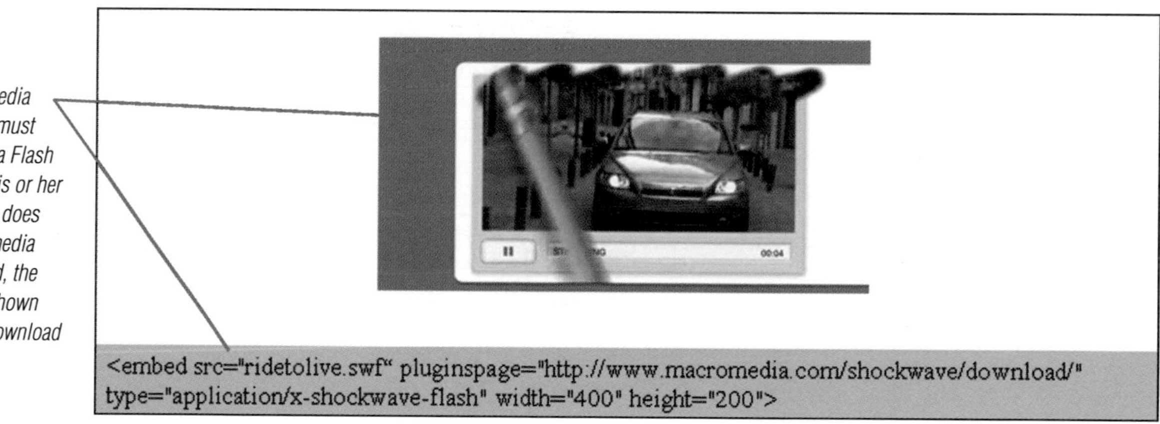

<embed src="ridetolive.swf" pluginspage="http://www.macromedia.com/shockwave/download/"
type="application/x-shockwave-flash" width="400" height="200">

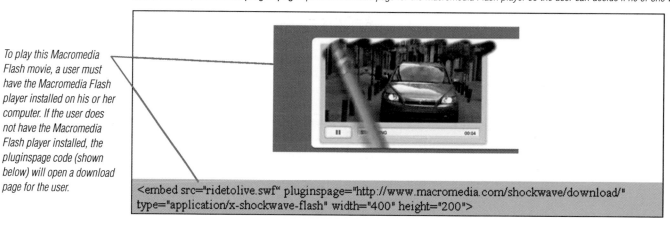

To play this Macromedia Flash movie, a user must have the Macromedia Flash player installed on his or her computer. If the user does not have the Macromedia Flash player installed, the pluginspage code (shown below) will open a download page for the user.

CONCEPT 2

IDENTIFY CONVERSION Tools

What You'll Learn

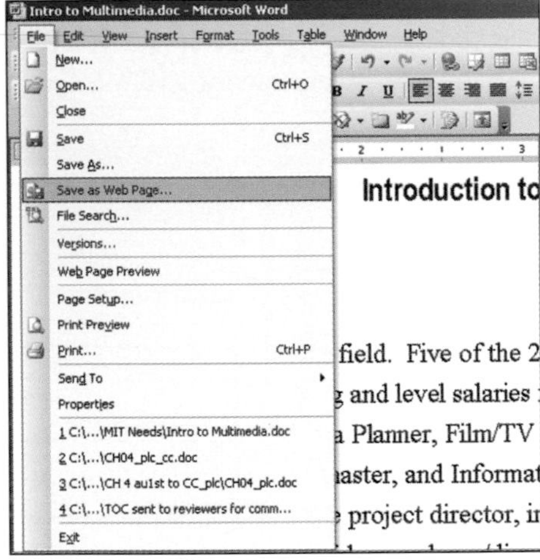

In this lesson, you will learn about conversion tool software as well as the advantages and disadvantages associated with using these tools for Web design and development.

Though it is possible to create an incredibly complex XHTML document using nothing more than a text editor, it can also be extremely laborious and time consuming. For this reason, many software programs are Internet-aware or Web-ready. This means that most programs now include converters that enable Web page creation and publishing capabilities within an existing software program.

Conversion tools translate existing document formats into XHTML. In other words, these programs make it possible for you to generate a Web page from an existing document without knowing a single XHTML tag. In fact, to convert your document the process is very simple and straightforward. Generally, it is as simple as changing the file type in the Save As dialog box to an XHTML format or choosing Save as XHTML or Save as Web Page from the menu. See Figure 4-7. Conversion tools can be convenient and can be real time-savers.

Advantages of Using Conversion Tools

- *No Learning Curve.* If you already know a program or have files in a format recognized by that program, there is no need to learn a new program in order to prepare your documents for the Web nor do you have to buy a separate program to author your Web pages.
- *Additional Features/Themes.* In addition to a straight conversion, many of these programs also include features such as templates that allow you to enhance your documents for the Web while still using the common features of a program that you already know.
- *Convenient/Time-Saving.* Using conversion tools, many of the documents that you have already created for the print world can be quickly published to the Web by merely saving the file in an HTML format and then uploading it to a Web server.

Disadvantages of Using Conversion Tools

- *Limited.* Though conversion tools make it easy for you to convert documents to a format that can be published to the Web as well as use familiar features to create new Web pages, they do have limitations. Generally, conversion tools will not enable you to do everything that you could do if you were writing the XHTML code. In addition, because XHTML is dynamic and regularly updated, conversion tools may not include the most recent tags, which could limit functionality.
- *Alter Document Format.* Much of the formatting you have included in your document will be altered. Fonts, margins, and indentations may be changed. This occurs because all XHTML markup tags are added automatically when your document is converted to XHTML. If there is no XHTML markup tag and attribute to exactly match the formatting you have specified with another application, your Web page format will be altered.
- *Extraneous Code.* In addition, many conversion tools write extraneous XHTML code into your Web pages, making them less efficient than pages written directly in XHTML. Extraneous code increases page size, reduces performance, adds to page complexity, and hinders editing. This unnecessary code can also make troubleshooting problematic if you decide to tweak your XHTML source code after it has been converted from another application.

FIGURE 4-7

To convert a Microsoft Word document to XHTML, simply choose Save as Web Page

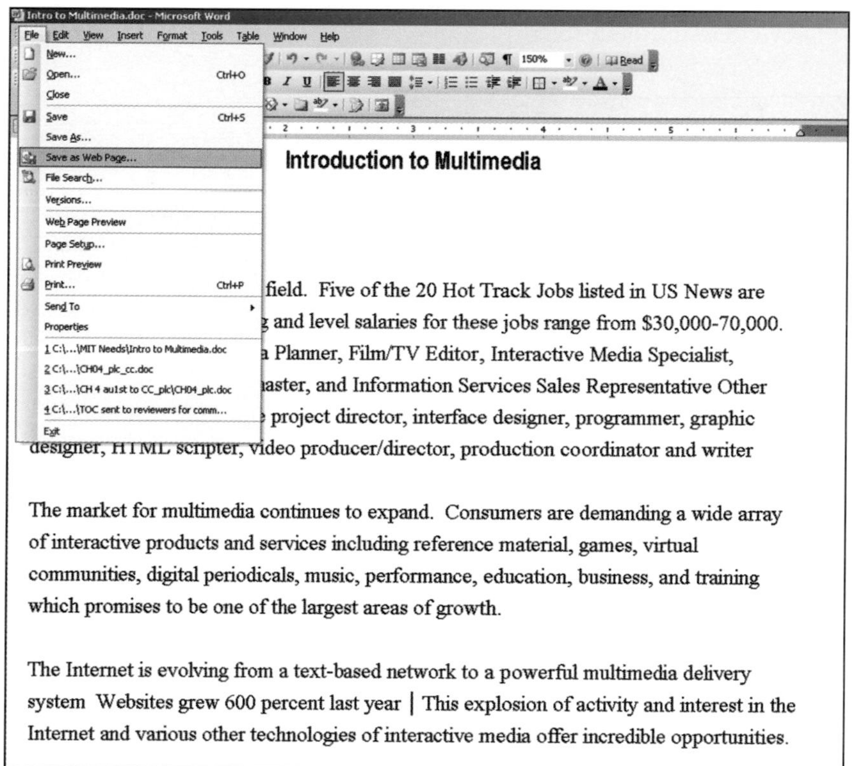

Software

Because the Web has fast become the communication environment used by most businesses and organizations as well as many individuals, nearly all software developers have included features that allow users to convert proprietary file types to XHTML and other Web-ready formats. For example, all of the applications within recent versions of **Microsoft Office** have been specifically designed to make creating Web-ready documents easier than ever. In addition to converting existing Microsoft Office documents to XHTML, you can also save any document to an XHTML format with the click of a button.

Microsoft Word offers themes for creating a Web site that has a consistent background, color scheme, and images for every page of the site (see Figure 4-8). In addition, once you have saved a document as a Web page, you can format the page using features specifically created for the Web such as bullets and horizontal rules. Frames are even available for organizing different pages and graphics on a single screen.

FIGURE 4-8

Microsoft Word's Theme feature makes it easy to create a visually appealing Web site

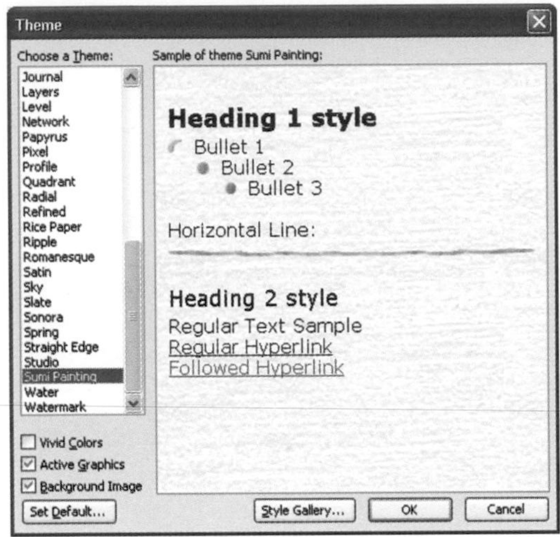

Microsoft Word Themes

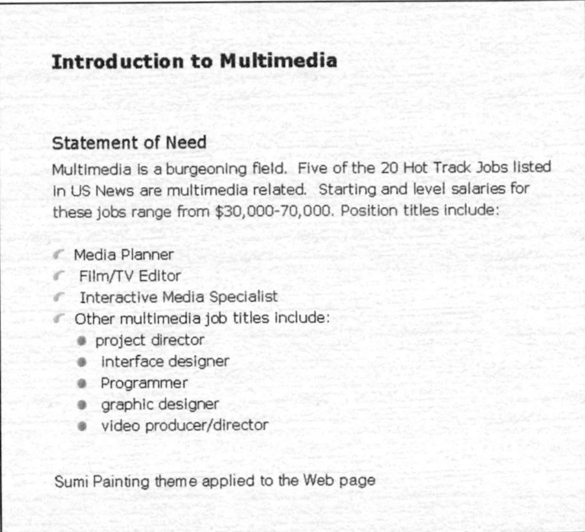

Sumi Painting theme applied to the Web page

Microsoft PowerPoint can be used to create Web pages and animated Web presentations. Like Word, PowerPoint includes various templates and themes for creating visually appealing and effective online presentations. PowerPoint makes it easy to create professional-looking slide presentations that include text, graphics, animations, sound, and even full-motion video. PowerPoint also makes it easy to include these multimedia elements within an online presentation (see Figure 4-9).

Microsoft Excel can be used for publishing numeric data and charts to the Web. See Figure 4-10. In addition to publishing static Web pages, Excel makes it possible for you to create interactive Web pages. For example, you can choose to include functionality that allows users to insert and format numeric data within an online spreadsheet or even change the appearance of a chart. Formulas will automatically compute user data in specific cells even on the Web.

FIGURE 4-9

An example of a PowerPoint presentation embedded in a Web page

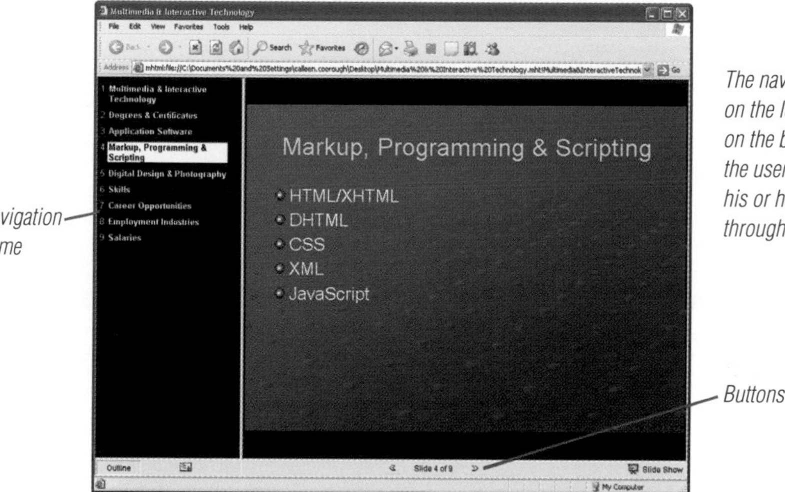

FIGURE 4-10

Microsoft Excel can be used to publish numeric data and charts to the Web

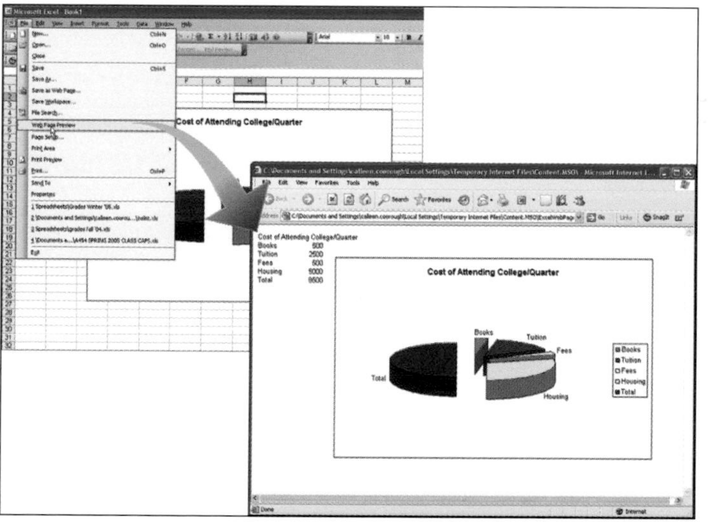

CONCEPT 3

EXPLAIN HOW WEB PAGE Editors Are Used

What You'll Learn

In this lesson, you will learn about several common Web page editors as well as the advantages and disadvantages of using this software to design and develop multimedia Web sites.

Like conversion tools, **Web page editors** make designing Web pages simple and practical. Web page editors allow you to create and design Web pages using toolbars containing menus and buttons that represent XHTML tags. Web page editors make it extremely easy for you to format Web pages. For example, if you want text to be bold, you don't have to use the `<b>` and `</b>` tags around the text, you simply highlight it and select the Bold command. In addition to tags and basic formatting, most of these tools provide extensive and sophisticated functionality beyond XHTML.

Advantages of Using Web Page Editors

- *Extensive Functionality.* Web page editors provide precise layout control and total design flexibility, while delivering the latest Web technologies. In addition, most of these tools provide checking and validation features that ensure the functionality of your Web pages before you upload them to a Web server.
- *Clean Code.* XHTML Web page editors let you build great Web sites in less time while maintaining pure XHTML code. Unlike converters and authoring programs, editors do not add any code to the XHTML page other than what is necessary for display through a browser. These programs are created for serious Web developers who want clean code fast.
- *Time Saving.* Web page editors save you time because they enable you to choose tags and attributes from lists, menus, and dialog boxes, rather than having to type the tags and attributes yourself. As a result, you are also less likely to make mistakes. Web page editors are an obvious choice for building a clean, efficient, well-designed Web site.

Disadvantages of Using Web Page Editors

- *Learning Curve.* Unless you know XHTML, Web page editors will not help you much. They are designed to make Web page development and editing with XHTML a faster, easier process than typing it from scratch using a text editor. However, without a basic understanding of XHTML, you will be lost when using a Web page editor.
- *Imperfect Tool.* Because you are using a software program to write the code rather than typing it in yourself, there is always the possibility that the program will contain bugs or unintuitive features.

Software

There are many different professional, shareware, and freeware editors on the market. Some of the more well-known Web page editors include BBEdit for the Macintosh and HomeSite for the Windows platform.

BBEdit

BBEdit is a high-performance text and XHTML editor for the Macintosh. See Figure 4-11. It is designed for editing, searching, transforming, creating, and manipulating files for the Web. It offers a wide array of useful features specifically developed to meet the needs of Web designers and developers. In addition to XHTML features, BBEdit supports a number of programming and scripting languages.

BBEdit offers a variety of XHTML-specific features including extensive tag lists (see Figure 4-12) available from menus and drop-down list boxes. In addition, you have the ability to store custom text, tags, and scriptable XHTML authoring preferences.

FIGURE 4-11
BBEdit is a high-performance XHTML editor for the Macintosh

FIGURE 4-12
BBEdit includes extensive tag lists available from menus and drop-down list boxes

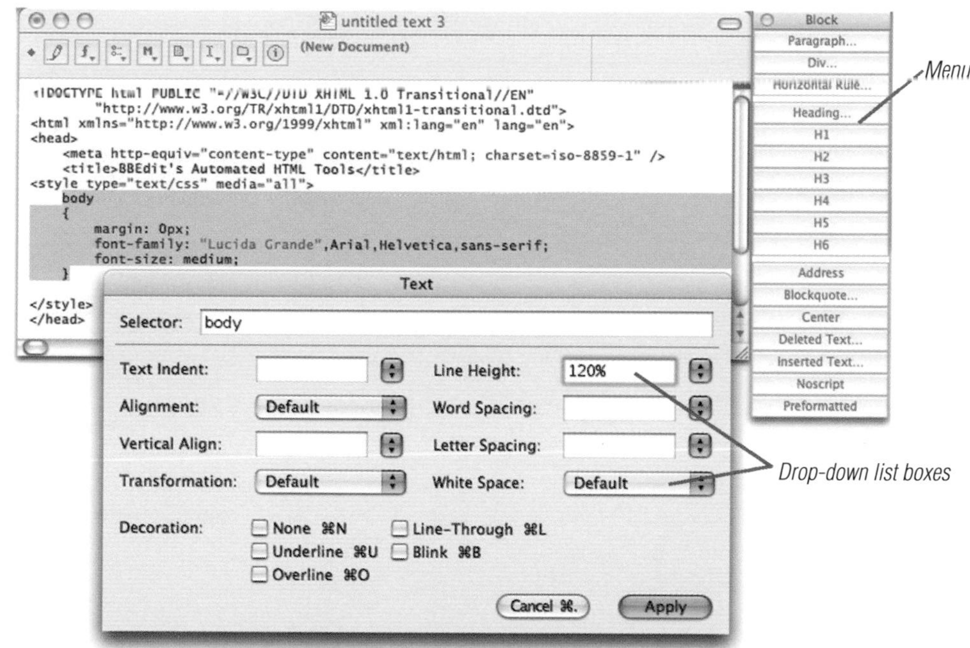

With a single click, you can view your Web pages within BBEdit's preview window or in any browser. BBEdit also includes multiple undo and multi-file Find & Replace features as seen in Figure 4-13.

Before you publish your Web pages you can use the XHTML-aware spell checker as well as the standards-based XHTML document and site syntax checker (see Figure 4-14) to ensure that your Web pages are professional and functional. From the File menu, you can directly open from and save to Web servers for quick Web publishing.

FIGURE 4-13

BBEdit improves productivity through the use of its multi-file Find & Replace features

FIGURE 4-14

The Check Syntax feature in BBEdit helps ensure your Web pages are functional before you upload them to a Web server

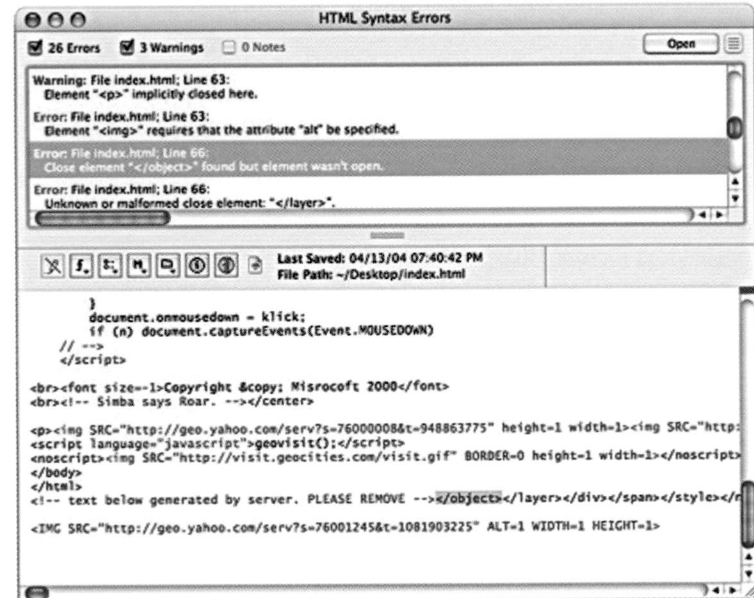

HomeSite

HomeSite by Macromedia is the industry-leading professional XHTML editor for Windows. It offers an intuitive interface complete with all of the necessary site-building tags and tools (see Figure 4-15). HomeSite is flexible and powerful and offers all of the functionality Web builders need.

HomeSite conforms to XHTML specifications. When you select a template provided by HomeSite (see Figure 4-16), a new document is created by HomeSite, which generates the code necessary for the Web page. Using HomeSite you can quickly lay out pages and make changes in design view, a visual development environment within HomeSite. Features are available for incorporating tables, scripting, CSS, and streaming media into your pages.

FIGURE 4-15

Tag editor dialog box in HomeSite

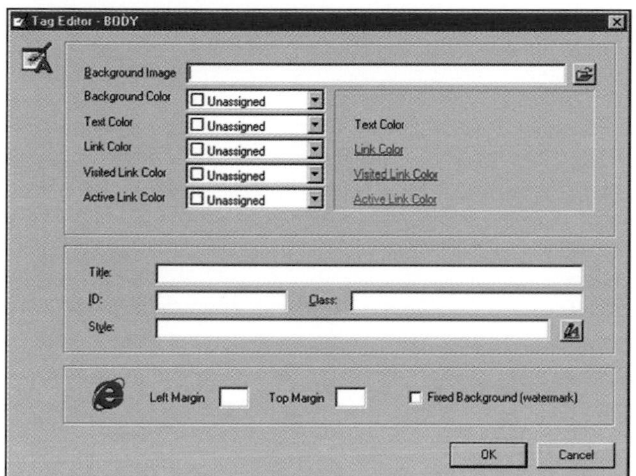

FIGURE 4-16

By selecting a HomeSite template, all of the code necessary to start developing your Web page is automatically generated

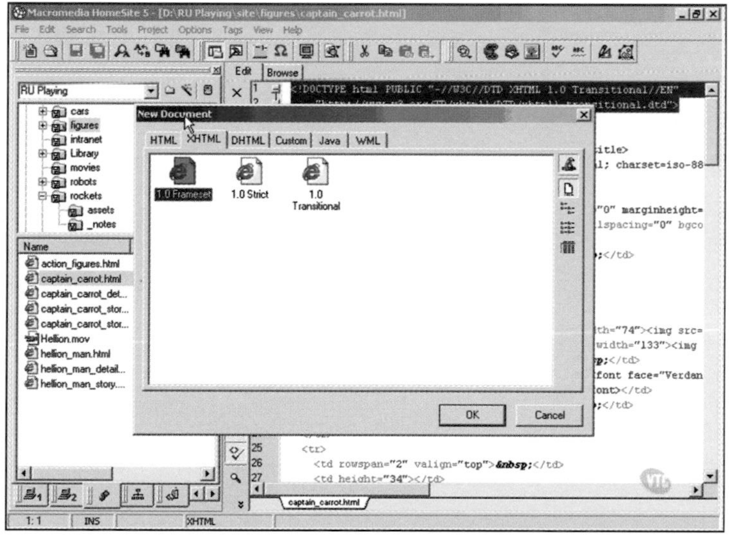

CONCEPT 4

EXPLAIN HOW WEB Authoring Programs Are Used

What You'll Learn

In this lesson, you will learn about Web authoring programs. The most commonly used Web authoring programs will be introduced and the advantages and disadvantages of using Web authoring programs will be discussed.

The goals and functions of all Web authoring programs are basically the same—to provide Web designers and developers with a user-friendly WYSIWYG interface in which to create Web pages. **Web authoring programs** use a graphical interface instead of forcing you to type or even choose XHTML markup tags and attributes from menus. Web authoring programs are very similar to working with word processing applications such as Microsoft Word. They write XHTML code for you. However, rather than converting a non-native XHTML file, they are designed with the specific purpose of developing Web pages.

Advantages of Using Web Authoring Programs

- *Immediate Results.* Because these programs offer WYSIWYG features, designers and developers can see the results of formatting changes immediately. They can spend a greater amount of time creatively manipulating and tweaking design features rather than writing and revising XHTML code.
- *Convenient/Time-saving.* Web authoring programs can be huge time-savers. When you use these tools, you do not have to learn or write XHTML. The program writes the code for you.
- *No XHTML Knowledge Required.* Although most Web authoring programs allow you to switch between a code view and a design view so that you can tweak and write code manually, you don't have to know the markup language to use these programs.

Disadvantages of Using Web Authoring Programs

- *Limited.* Although these programs have certainly improved over time and the functionality available today is extremely extensive, there are times when these programs are still somewhat limiting. They do not always allow you to do exactly what you want to do and what you could do with XHTML.

- *Extraneous Code.* Like converters, some Web authoring programs generate extraneous and proprietary code, which has no value to the Web browser. In addition, this unnecessary code increases file size, reduces performance, adds to page complexity, and hinders editing.
- *Not up-to-date.* Web and multimedia technologies change and evolve at a remarkably rapid rate. For this reason, Web authoring programs may not be as up-to-date as the most current markup and programming languages. Therefore, if you need to implement new techniques and take advantage of the latest technologies, you will want to know basic XHTML.

Web page authoring programs are user-friendly and sophisticated. They save Web designers and developers countless hours. They continue to become more and more extensive and feature-rich every day. These tools can be used for designing a quality Web site. If you also know basic XHTML, you can troubleshoot some of the problems that these programs generate or are incapable of solving, which means you will be even happier with the results generated from these tools.

Software

Although the goals of all Web authoring programs are basically the same, the features and the ways in which elements are manipulated vary dramatically. Some programs are easier to learn, yet limited, while other programs have a higher learning curve, yet provide much greater functionality. While some of these programs are targeted to the consumer market, there are also much more sophisticated applications developed for professionals.

Analyzing the features of several different Web authoring programs should help you determine which one will best meet your needs. Depending on your computer experience and expertise, you may find it helpful to learn a simple Web authoring program at the onset and progress to a more sophisticated application later. In addition, keep in mind that you may want to learn several of these programs so that you can use the best tool at the time depending on your needs, purpose, and target audience.

Once again, there are a number of professional, shareware, and freeware Web authoring programs available. Free demo and trial versions of many of these programs can be downloaded. Some of the more well-known programs include Adobe GoLive, Macromedia Dreamweaver, and Microsoft FrontPage.

Adobe GoLive

Adobe GoLive is Adobe's professional Web authoring and site management tool offering both content-creation and site-management tools (see Figure 4-17). This program is beneficial for both designers and developers, who need to design, develop, and maintain high-profile Web sites.

GoLive is tightly integrated with other Adobe applications including Photoshop and Illustrator. Layout grids, boxes, and rulers are available for precise layout and placement of objects. You can visually create and modify tables and forms. You can even create and control animation using this application.

FIGURE 4-17
Adobe GoLive is a professional Web authoring and site management tool

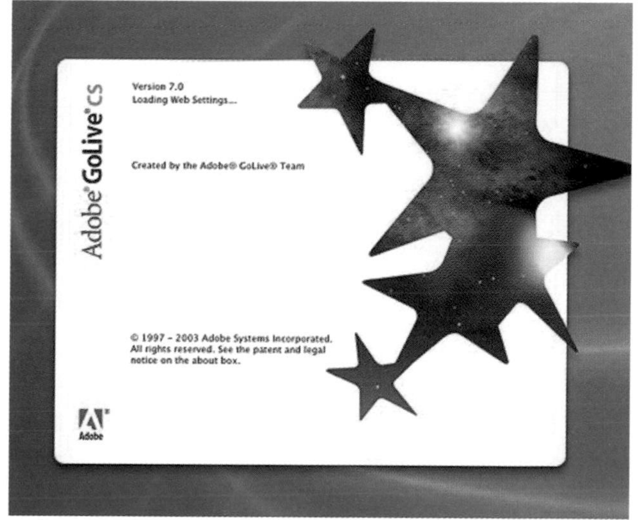

When starting a Web site from scratch, there are many professional design templates available from which to begin (see Figure 4-18). Although this is a WYSIWYG Web authoring program, you can also view, write, and edit pure XHTML source code. There are features available to automatically check XHTML syntax, including compatibility with different browsers. You can even use GoLive to write scripts and cascading style sheets.

In addition to creating and editing individual Web pages, Adobe GoLive also features advanced site management capabilities including site map generation. You can design, create, edit, and view an entire site or import an existing site. You can also check for and repair broken links before uploading or downloading individual Web pages or an entire Web site. There are even features that support the deployment of content for mobile devices (see Figure 4-19).

FIGURE 4-18
Adobe GoLive offers a variety of design templates

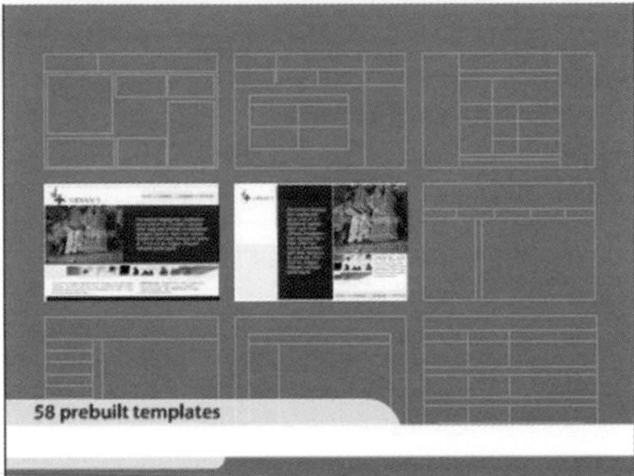

FIGURE 4-19
New features in Adobe GoLive support deployment of content for mobile devices

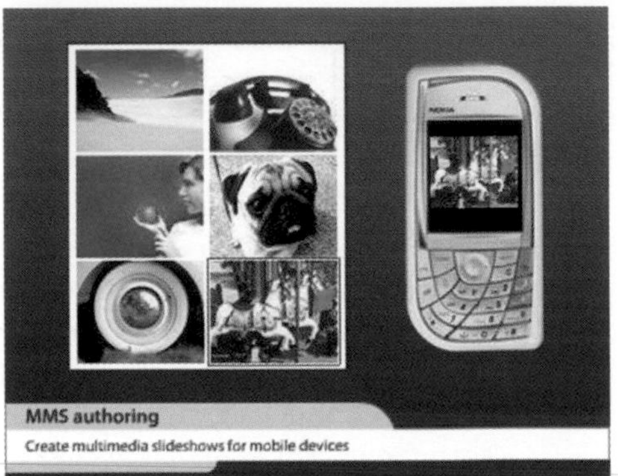

Macromedia Dreamweaver MX 2004

Macromedia Dreamweaver MX 2004 is the Macromedia solution for professional Web site design and production. See Figure 4-20. Similar to GoLive, you can use Dreamweaver to develop, edit, automate, and maintain Web sites. Dreamweaver is the tool of choice among professional Web designers and developers because it delivers powerful standards-based control and offers a world-class design and code editor in one tool.

FIGURE 4-20
Dreamweaver is the Macromedia solution for professional Web site design and production

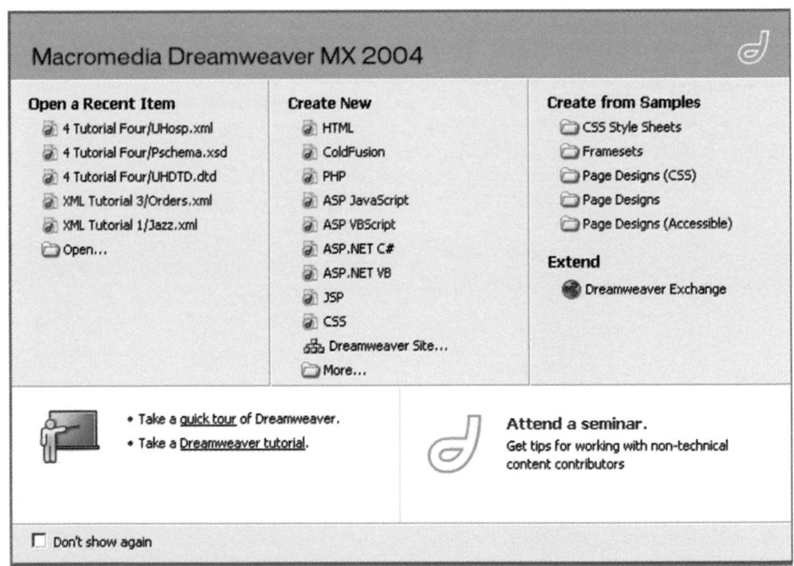

Macromedia Dreamweaver enables designers and developers to enhance productivity by providing tight integration with all Macromedia products. The Macromedia suite of integrated Web development products includes Dreamweaver, **Macromedia Flash** (for animations and user interactivity), and **Macromedia Fireworks** (for image editing). Used together these tools allow creation of Web sites that include compelling graphics, animations, and interactivity. Recognizing that development of a Web site often involves team members with varying expertise (graphic designers, animators, programmers, and so on), Macromedia designed these products so that they integrate easily. This integration allows movement from one tool to another as the elements of a Web site are brought together. For example, an animation can be created using Macromedia Flash, imported into Dreamweaver, and then edited from the Dreamweaver environment. Although the products can stand alone, they have a similar look and feel, with common features and interface elements that allow skills to transfer from one program to the other. Dreamweaver also supports database functionality and integration with **Macromedia ColdFusion**, Macromedia's database management system.

Dreamweaver supports cross-browser validation. Using **roundtrip** XHTML and XHTML editing, Dreamweaver lets you visually design your Web site without completely sacrificing control over the source code. Roundtrip code is pure; it contains no unnecessary or proprietary code. Dreamweaver championed roundtrip XHTML and includes a cross-browser validation feature that has built-in intelligence to determine which tags, attributes, and CSS constructs work within the browser combination you need to support (see Figure 4-21). Even if you import hand-coded XHTML into Dreamweaver it will remain pure. In addition, you can edit the XHTML source code directly in the code view environment.

You can use Dreamweaver to quickly build and format tables using predefined colors and layouts to create appealing table designs (see Figure 4-22). In addition, Dreamweaver provides professional-quality, prebuilt layouts and code, including site structures, forms, accessible templates, and script functions for client-side interactivity. There also is a Site Setup Wizard for designers and developers who need to jumpstart the production process.

FIGURE 4-21

Results of cross-browser validation

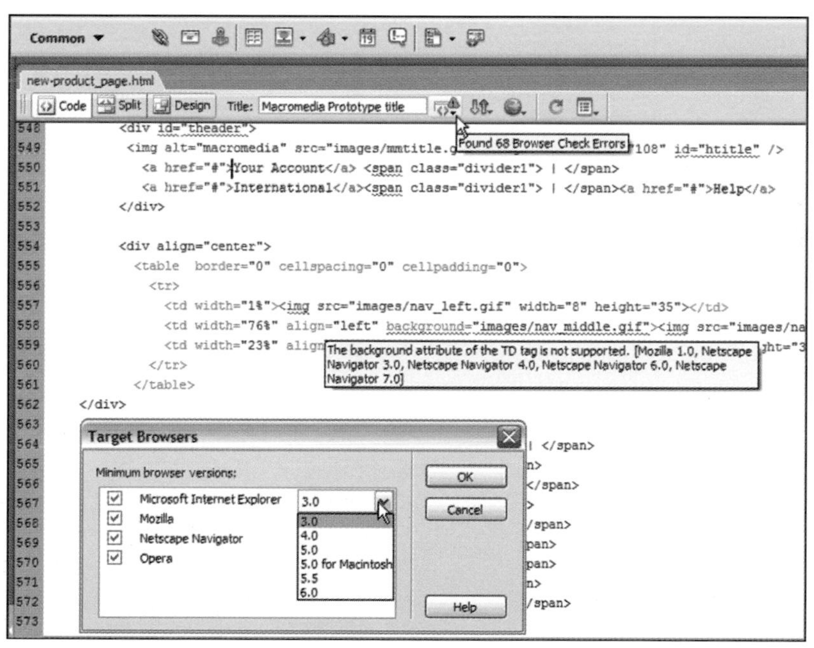

You can start an external HTML or text editor from Dreamweaver to edit the code for the current document and then switch back to Dreamweaver to continue editing graphically. Dreamweaver detects any changes that have been saved to the document externally and prompts you to reload the document upon returning. You can use the following integrated HTML editors: **Macromedia HomeSite** (Windows only) or BBEdit (Macintosh only). You can also use any text editor such as Notepad and TextEdit.

Of course, Dreamweaver also supports CSS, which enables you to easily configure character and paragraph level styles for greater flexibility and control over the formatting of your entire Web site (see Figure 4-23). Dreamweaver Web pages can be further customized using the most recent scripting languages. Dreamweaver also makes it easy for Web designers and developers to create accessible Web sites because it provides compliance-checking features for pages and sites so that they will comply with U.S. law and international standards.

Macromedia Dreamweaver also supports site management. You can create and use site maps for quick site design and reorganization. In addition, you can change the location or name of any file in your site, Dreamweaver will track these changes and automatically update applicable links.

FIGURE 4-22

Example of visual feedback using the table-editing feature in Macromedia Dreamweaver

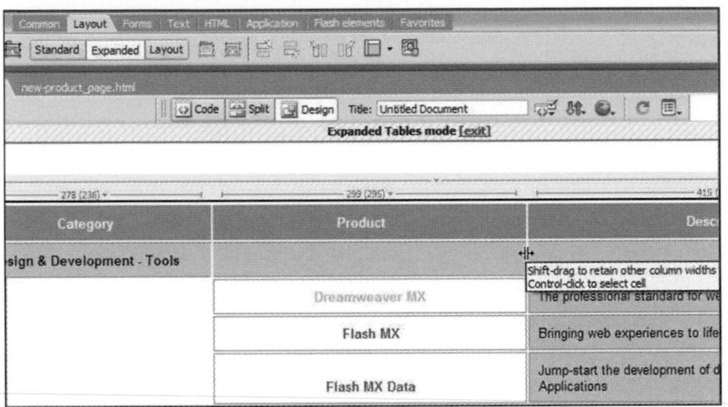

FIGURE 4-23

Macromedia Dreamweaver CSS rule inspector tool

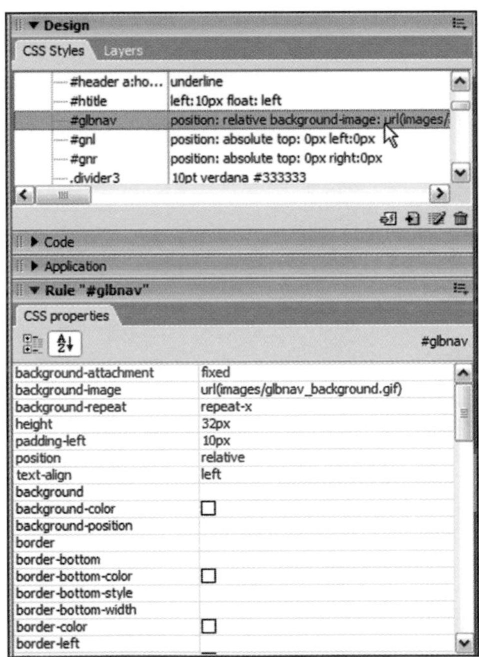

As shown in Figure 4-24, secure FTP is available to fully encrypt all file transfers and prevent unauthorized access to data, files, usernames, and passwords.

Microsoft FrontPage

Microsoft FrontPage is yet another well-known Web site creation and management tool (see Figure 4-25). FrontPage is integrated with the rest of Microsoft Office. If you are familiar with any of the Microsoft Office applications, it will be easy for you to learn and use Microsoft FrontPage.

Microsoft FrontPage allows you to create, edit, manage, and update your site using multiple views. As expected, you can use Microsoft FrontPage to create tables, and add hyperlinks, graphics, thumbnail images, frames, search forms, hit counters, and numbered or bulleted lists. Ready-made templates or design themes are available that enable you to get started immediately.

FIGURE 4-24
Dreamweaver offers secure FTP for full file encryption

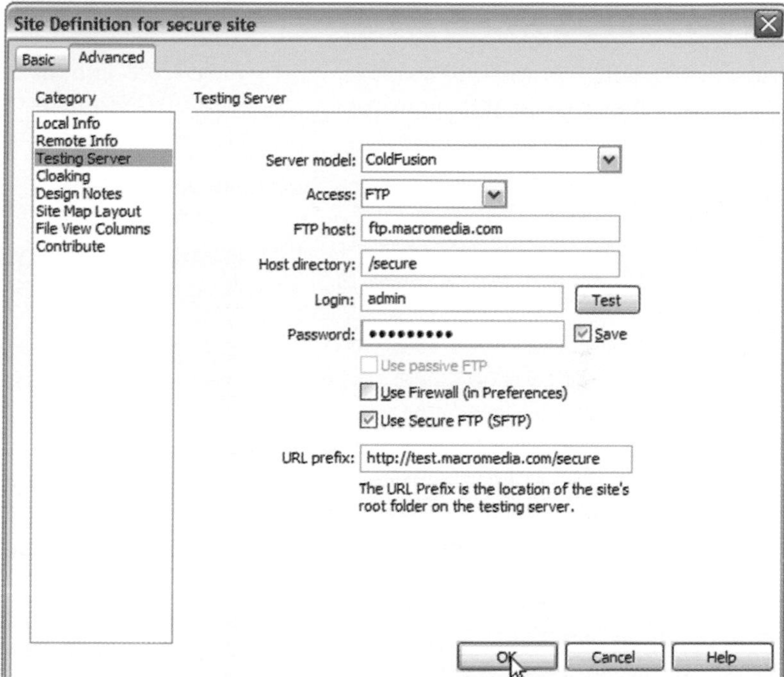

FIGURE 4-25
Microsoft FrontPage is a Web site creation and management tool

You can choose from a variety of themes that apply a distinctive and consistent look to your pages. You can also customize any theme with your own banner, colors, graphics, backgrounds, and buttons or you can download additional themes from the Web for free or for a small fee (see Figure 4-26).

QUICKTIP

When you create a Web page or Web site using FrontPage, specific extensions must be installed on the Web server in order for your FrontPage Web pages to work properly. Check with your Web hosting service before you develop in FrontPage to make sure that the FrontPage extensions will be available.

You can use Microsoft FrontPage to add cross-browser scripting as well as Cascading Style Sheets to control formatting, place graphics exactly where you want them, and create consistent formatting on a single page, multiple pages, or across an entire site. FrontPage also supports pixel-precise positioning.

As shown in Figure 4-27, Microsoft FrontPage allows you to view and edit your XHTML source code in code view. You can use the split view to divide the screen so that you can see both the design of the site in a WYSIWYG format as well as the source code behind it. Microsoft FrontPage will not modify imported or edited source code. You can also choose which browser, which version of the browser, and which server platforms in which you want your site to be both viewable and functional. After making these specifications, FrontPage restricts features that will not function properly under the specified conditions.

FIGURE 4-26

Ready-made FrontPage templates and themes can be downloaded from the Web for free or for a small fee

FIGURE 4-27

Microsoft FrontPage allows you to view and edit your XHTML source code in code view or split view

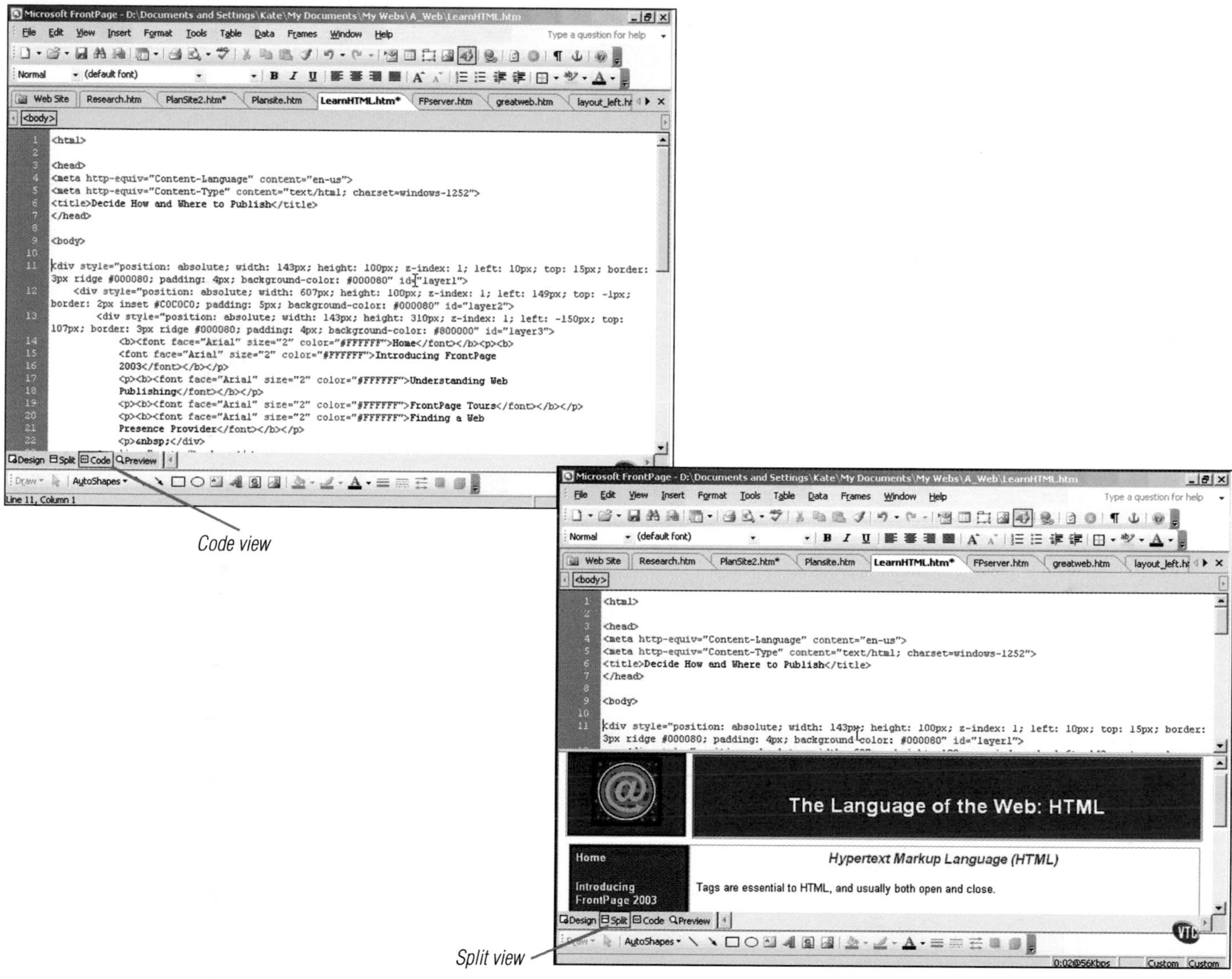

CONCEPT 5

DISCUSS HOW TO UPLOAD Files to a Web Server

What You'll Learn

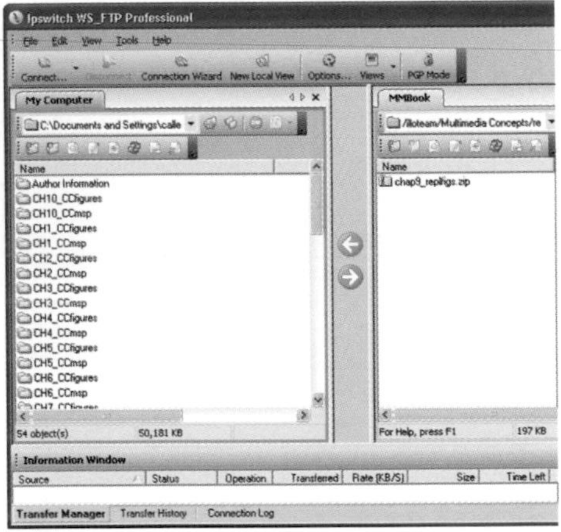

In this lesson, you will learn about the process of uploading Web site files to a Web server using File Transfer Protocol (FTP) software.

In order for the Internet community to access your Web site you must upload all of your HTML and other media element files to a Web server. In other words, you will need to transfer all of the files associated with the Web site from your computer's hard drive to a remote Web server.

Because there are different Web server platforms and software, you should contact your Web-hosting company for details regarding naming conventions and other specifics before you upload your files to the Web server. In general, if you adhere to the following guidelines your Web site will be more likely to function properly after you upload your files.

- *Index.htm.* Name the home page of your Web site or the first file you want your users to see "index.htm". Most Web server software automatically recognizes index.htm as the first page of the Web site to be loaded.
- *Case Sensitive.* Many operating systems on Web servers are case sensitive when handling file names. Therefore, you should pay attention to case when you name your files and when you reference them or link them from one Web page to another. The general recommendation is that file names be saved in all lowercase. If your files do not have the proper case, you may have problems viewing them from your Web browser after they are uploaded. Remember, index.htm, Index.htm, index.HTM, INDEX.htm, INDEX.HTM are all considered unique files. As such, they may be referenced differently once they are uploaded to the server.
- *Naming Conventions.* In addition to case, some operating systems and browsers conform to particular naming conventions. To further

ensure that your Web pages will work properly after they are uploaded, it is best to conform to these conventions by naming your files following the appropriate guidelines for that OS and avoiding illegal characters. For example, it is best to avoid the use of spaces (use an underscore if you wish to show a separation between parts of a file name) as well as other unacceptable characters, such as \ / : * ? < > | in your file names.

Before you can upload your properly named files to a Web server, your Web-hosting company will need to supply you with a host address, username, and password. These security controls will allow you access to the Web server so that you can upload your files there. You will have to specify the following:

- **Host Address:** www.domainname.com
- **Username:** your login username
- **Password:** your login password

The process by which files are transferred to the Web server is called **File Transfer Protocol (FTP)**. You can transfer your files using an FTP program or utility such as the one shown in Figure 4-28.

In addition to using a separate FTP program to upload your files to a server, most Web page editors and Web authoring programs also include FTP capabilities. For example, as shown earlier in Figure 4-24, you can use the Secure FTP feature in Macromedia Dreamweaver to upload files. Once again, you will have to supply a URL and provide a username and password.

Commitment to a maintenance program is important to the success of a Web site. You want visitors to come back often, but if they see no change or if it has not been updated, they may not return. Failure to update your site and remove broken links implies neglect and disinterest. FTP allows you to easily upload changes to your site, which allows you to keep the site fresh and interesting to your visitors.

FIGURE 4-28

You can transfer your files from your hard drive to a Web server using an FTP program or utility, such as WS_FTP

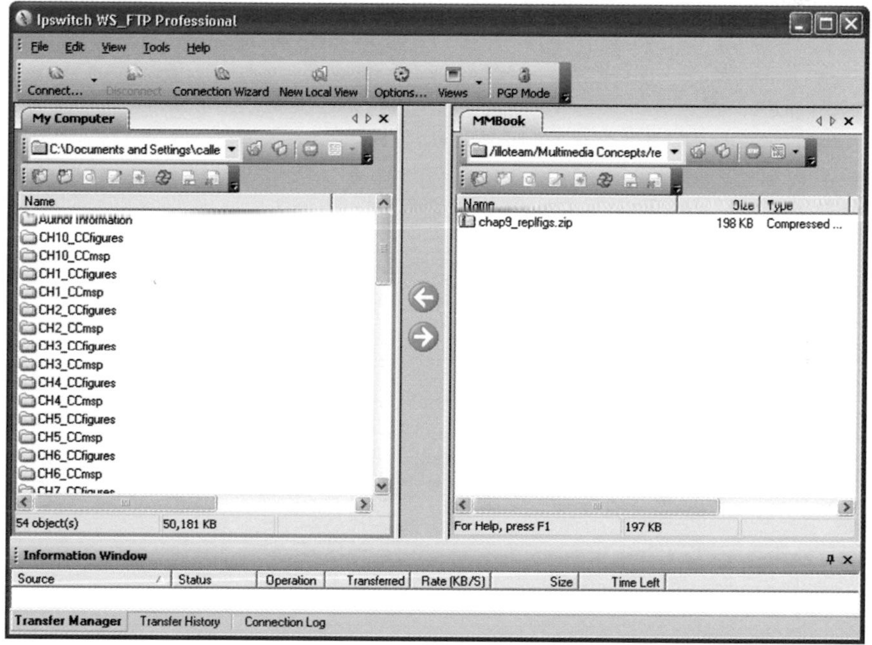

SUMMARY

Hypertext Markup Language (HTML) is the standard language used to create Web pages. HTML was designed to be a platform-independent language that enables different computers running different operating systems and using different browsers to display the same page. All Web pages are based on **source code**.

HTML is a **markup language**, not a **scripting** or **programming** language. The most recent version, **Extensible Hypertext Markup Language (XHTML)**, is a reformulation and replacement of HTML that conforms to **Extensible Markup Language (XML)** rules. The **World Wide Web Consortium (W3C)** controls changes and additions to HTML.

Markup tags, **attributes**, and **values** are used to create the formatting behind Web pages. **Tags** specify how the browser will display text and other media. The opening and closing tags together are often called **containers**. **Attributes** modify tags and **values** determine the results of the modification. Combined, these three items (tags, attributes, and values) are considered an **element**.

To view or hear multimedia elements on your Web pages, users may need a **helper application**, a **plug-in**, or a **player**. The **pluginspage** attribute makes it possible for the Web page designer to accommodate users by making it easy for them to download and install the appropriate plug-in or player.

Conversion tools translate existing document formats into Web pages. Conversion tools offer convenience and savings in time. The biggest disadvantages to using these programs are that the formatting of the document may be altered and extraneous code may be included in your Web pages. Most applications now include conversion tools. All of the Microsoft Office applications, such as **Word**, **Excel**, and **PowerPoint**, are Web-ready and allow you to convert existing formats to XHTML.

Web page editors allow you to create and design Web pages using menus and buttons that represent XHTML tags. XHTML editors let you build great Web sites in less time while maintaining pure XHTML code. You must understand XHTML to make use of Web page editors. Although there are many different editors on the market, **HomeSite** and **BBEdit** are two of the most popular.

Web page authoring programs use a graphical interface instead of forcing you to type or even choose XHTML markup tags and attributes from menus. Most now include the ability to edit the source code from within the program, which provides the flexibility of a **WYSIWYG** (What You See Is What You Get) environment with the control of writing pure XHTML code.

There are a number of programs available for Web page and Web site creation, editing, and management. Some of the more wellknown programs include **Adobe GoLive**, **Macromedia Dreamweaver**, and **Microsoft FrontPage**. The Macromedia suite of integrated Web development products includes **Dreamweaver**, **Flash**, and **Fireworks**. Used together these tools allow creation of Web sites that include compelling graphics, animations, and interactivity. Using **roundtrip** XHTML and XHTML editing, Dreamweaver lets you visually design your Web site without completely sacrificing control over the source code. Dreamweaver also supports database functionality and integration with **ColdFusion**, Macromedia's database management system.

In order for the Internet community to access your Web site you must upload all of your files to a Web server. Your Web-hosting company will need to supply you with a host address, username, and password. The process by which files are transferred to the Web server is called **File Transfer Protocol (FTP)**. FTP can be accomplished using FTP software. In addition, some authoring programs and browsers include built-in FTP capabilities.

KEY TERMS

Adobe GoLive
attribute
BBEdit
container
conversion tool
element
Extensible Hypertext Markup Language (XHTML)
Extensible Markup Language (XML)
File Transfer Protocol (FTP)
helper application
Hypertext Markup Language (HTML)
Macromedia ColdFusion
Macromedia Dreamweaver
Macromedia Fireworks
Macromedia Flash
Macromedia HomeSite
markup language
markup tag
Microsoft Excel
Microsoft FrontPage
Microsoft Office
Microsoft PowerPoint
Microsoft Word
player
plug-in
pluginspage
programming language
roundtrip
scripting language
source code
value
Web authoring programs
Web page editor
What You See Is What You Get (WYSIWYG)
World Wide Web Consortium (W3C)

MATCHING QUESTIONS/DISCUSSION QUESTIONS

Match each term with the sentence that best describes it.

a attributes	b. container	c. conversion tool
d element	e. FTP	f. helper application
g. img	h. index.htm	i. markup
j. player	k. pluginspage	l. source code
m. W3C	n. Web page editors	o. XHTML

_____ **1.** Process by which files are transferred to the Web server.

_____ **2.** The most recent version of HTML.

_____ **3.** Official standards committee for the Web.

_____ **4.** A beginning and ending tag with something in the middle.

_____ **5.** The combination of a tag, an attribute, and a value.

_____ **6.** Tag used to insert an inline image.

_____ **7.** This attribute makes it possible for the Web page designer to accommodate users by making it easy for them to download and install the appropriate plug-in or player.

_____ **8.** Program that allows users to play media content within the browser window.

_____ **9.** Program that translates existing documents into XHTML.

_____ **10.** This provides the information the browser needs to display the Web page correctly.

_____ **11.** Programs that let you build great Web sites while maintaining pure XHTML code.

_____ **12.** Prior to plug-ins and players, these programs were launched to play non-native HTML content.

_____ **13.** Name most often recognized by Web server software as the home page or first page of a Web site.

_____ **14.** These are used to modify tags.

_____ **15.** These languages specify the structure, content, or formatting of a Web page document.

Answer each question either in writing or in a class discussion as directed by your instructor.

1. What are four different methods used to create Web pages?
2. What is XHTML? Why is it important to learn XHTML?
3. What are conversion tools? What are some advantages and disadvantages of using these tools?
4. What are Web page editors? What are some advantages and disadvantages of using Web page editors? What are some key features found in the well-known Web page editors?
5. What are Web authoring programs? What are the advantages and disadvantages associated with these programs? What are some key features found in most Web authoring programs?

Creating a Web Site

1. Create Web Pages with a text editor
2. Create a Web Site with Macromedia Dreamweaver

Introduction

This is a continuation of the Design Project in Chapter 3.

The client The Inn at Birch Bay has reviewed the planning document, including the flowchart and storyboards, and has given approval for the development of the site. You have been asked to create the Web pages for the site. The WebsByCT multimedia development team has decided that this project would be just right for you to master XHTML coding as well as learn an authoring program. To complete the lessons in this design project, you will be using a text editor, such as Notepad, and the authoring program, Macromedia Dreamweaver MX 2004, to develop the Web pages and the Web site. You will use the text editor when you complete the steps to create the Web pages. The multimedia elements for the Web site, such as the logo, photo of the inn, video, et cetera, will be created in a later design project. So, you will use placeholders that have been provided.

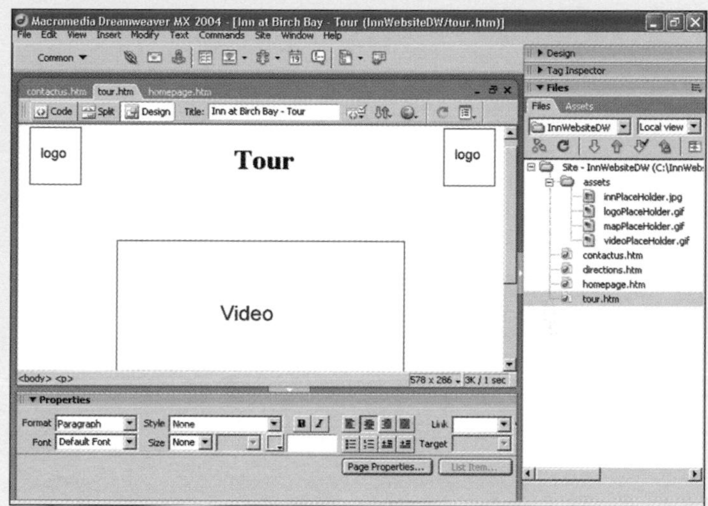

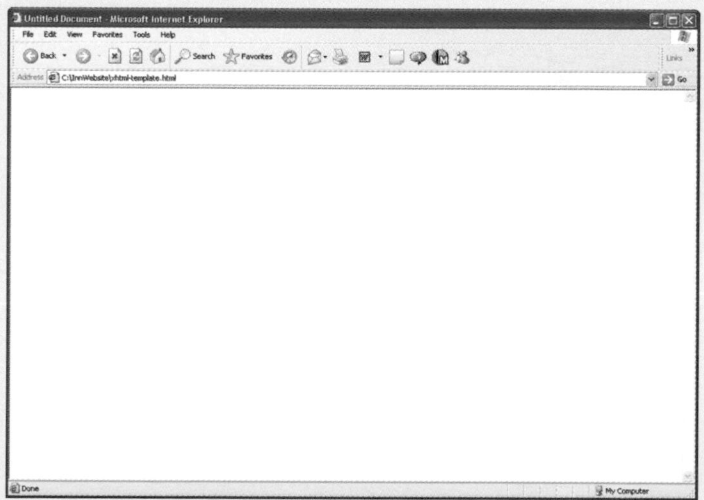

LESSON 1

CREATING WEB PAGES with a Text Editor

What You'll Do

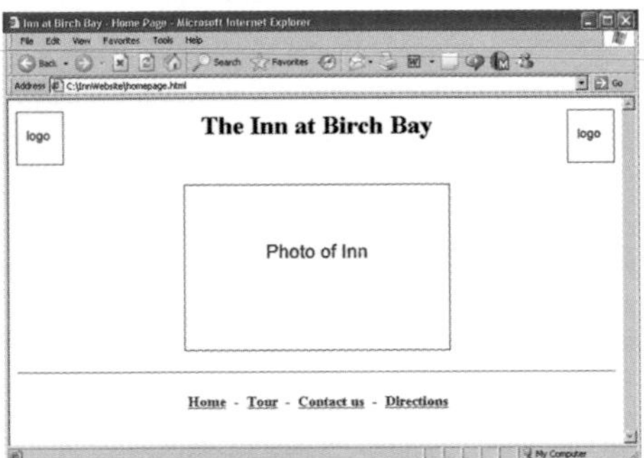

In this lesson, you will learn how to create XHTML pages using a text editor. You will begin by preparing folders for a Web site, then you will create an XHTML document, save the document, and display it in a browser.

The Structure of an XHTML Document

Figure 4-29 shows a template that can be used when creating an XHTML document. The structure of a Web page is commonly divided into three sections: the Declaration, the Head, and the Body.

Declaration. Several types of HTML (including XHTML) and numerous W3C standards, have been developed over the years. Web browsers need to know which type and which standards to apply so that when they translate the XHTML code the Web page displays correctly. There are two statements, <!DOCTYPE...> and <html xmlns...>, that are used to declare the type and the standards. WebsByCT has asked you to use the statements shown in Figure 4-29. Notice that xhtml is specified in the <html xmlns...> statement.

FIGURE 4-29
An HTML template

```
<!DOCTYPE HTML PUBLIC "-//W3C//DTD HTML 4.01 Transitional//EN"
"http://www.w3.org/TR/html4/loose.dtd">

<html xmlns="http://www.w3.org/1999/xhtml">

<head>
        <title>Inn at Birch Bay - Home Page</title>
        <meta http-equiv="Content-Type" content="text/html; charset=iso-8859-1">
</head>

<body>








</body>

</html>
```

Head. The Head section is where, among other things, you can include information used by search engines, write scripts, add style sheets, and specify a title for your Web page. The Head section typically has two nested tags, the <title> tag and the <meta...> tag. The <title> tag is used to specify a title that appears in the title bar of the browser and in the list of Favorites when a user bookmarks the Web page. Some search engines use the title to index the Web page. The title is the only part of the Head section visible to the user. The <meta...> tag is used for specifying the character set (the characters recognized by the browser). Although we are accustomed to working with the letters in the English language, other languages use various other characters, such as accented characters. The iso-8859-1 character set provides all of the characters that are normally used in the English language. CSS code, such as the code to specify an external style sheet, would be included in the Head section of your XHTML document.

Body. The Body section contains the code (that is, in addition to any style sheets referenced in the Head section) needed to format the document and display content including all multimedia elements.

Follow these guidelines as you develop your Web page documents.

- Proper XHTML code requires closing tags with a forward slash (/). In most cases the closing tag is separate from the opening tag, such as <title>...</title>. In some cases the opening and closing are within one tag, such as <img src="bay.gif" />. In a few cases a closing tag is not required, such as <hr> which displays a horizontal rule line in the Web page.
- All tag names should be in lowercase.
- Be sure to properly nest any elements that are within other elements. To format the text heading "The Inn at Birch Bay" so it is displayed with a heading size 3 and centered the proper nesting would be:

  <h3><center>"The Inn at Birch Bay"</center></h3>

  Improper nesting would be:

  <h3><center>"The Inn at Birch Bay"</h3></center>
- Use indentation to aid readability.
- Extra spaces and tabs that are typed into an XHTML document are compressed into a single space when displayed in the browser.

The Folder Structure for a Web Site

The more complex (large number of Web pages, multimedia elements, etc.) a Web site is, the more important the folder structure used to store the various files becomes. With a less complex Web site only two folders may be required—one folder is the site folder (that contains the files and folders for the site) and the other folder is an assets folder that contains the multimedia elements, such as graphics files, video files, sound files, etc., as shown in Figure 4-30.

FIGURE 4-30
The folder structure for a Web site

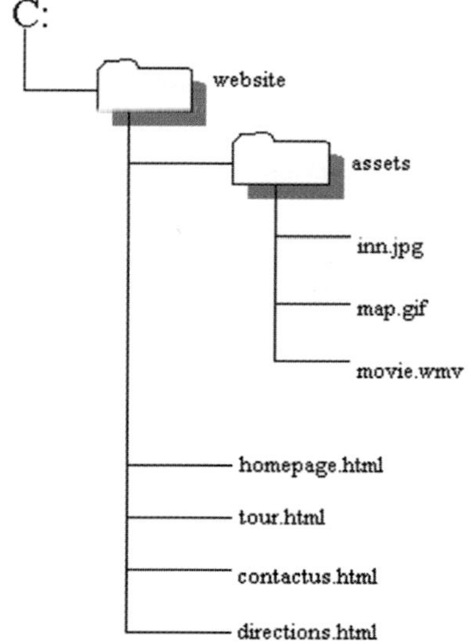

XHTML Tags and Attributes That Will Be Used in This Lesson

<!DOCTYPE...> and <html ...>: Declaration statements as explained earlier.

<head>...</head>: Section used to provide information, scripts, and titles as explained earlier.

<title>...</title>: Specifies text that appears in the title bar of the browser window.

<meta.../>: Specifies the character set and keywords for the document.

<img .../>: Inserts an object, such as a graphic, into a document and specifies properties such as the dimensions and alignment of the object. Attributes are used to define these properties.

Attributes:

src – Specifies the name of the object.

align – Specifies the object alignment (left or right) within the Web page.

Example: the following XHTML code causes the image named bay.jpg to appear at the right side of the Web page. Note: In this case the file bay.jpg is located in a folder named assets.

```
<img src="assets/bay.jpg" align="right" />
```

<center>...</center>: Centers the content that is between the tags.

<h1>...</h1>: Applies a predefined style (font and size) to the text between the tags.

<a href...>...</a>: Creates a link. For example the following code creates a link from the active Web page to the tour.html Web page. When the user clicks the word *Tour*, the tour.html page is displayed. Because no folder is specified, the assumption is that both Web pages are in the same folder.

```
<a href="tour.html">Tour</a>
```

<p>...</p>: Starts and ends a new paragraph

: Creates a line break

 : Inserts a space (equivalent to pressing the spacebar)

QUICKTIP

When saving an XHTML document from a text editor, be sure to specify the .html file extension (e.g., homepage.html). Otherwise, the text editor will append its own file extension, such as homepage.txt, and these types of documents cannot be displayed in a Web browser. Note: You can also specify .htm as the file extension because .htm and .html extensions are interchangeable.

QUICKTIP

The exercises in this chapter were created with the screen resolution set at 800 × 600. If your computer's screen resolution has a different setting, the figures in the book may appear different. You may want to verify the screen resolution on your computer and set it to 800 × 600, if necessary.

FIGURE 4-31
The template displayed in a browser

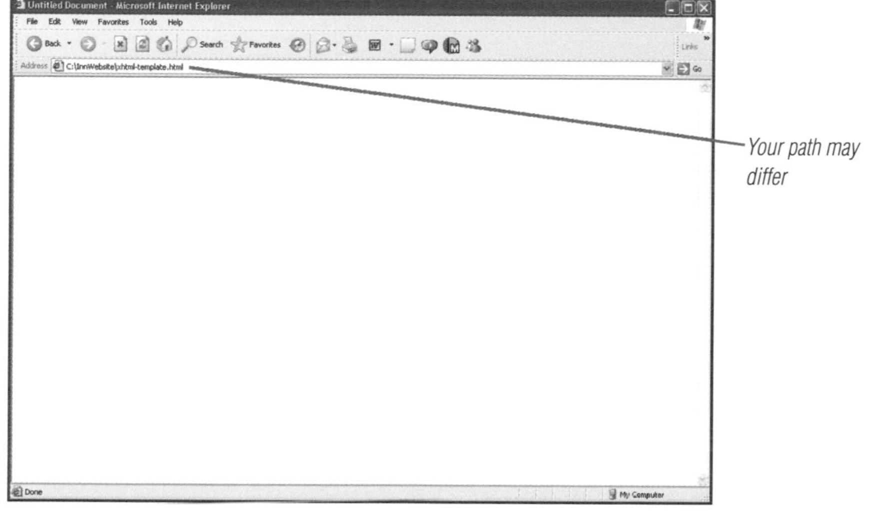

FIGURE 4-32
The words Untitled Document highlighted

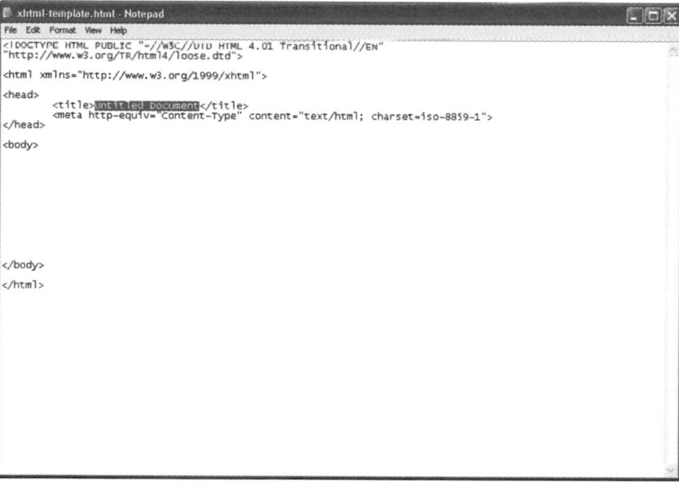

Create the Site Folders and Display the XHTML Template

1. Navigate to the drive on your computer where you will be storing the files for the Inn at Birch Bay Web site, such as the C drive.
2. Create a new folder and name it **InnWebsite**.
3. Within the InnWebsite folder, create another folder called **assets**.
4. Locate the files that are used for this book and copy the xhtml-template.html file into the InnWebsite folder.
5. Locate the files that are used for this book and copy the following files to the assets folder: logoPlaceHolder.gif; innPlaceHolder.jpg; videoPlaceHolder.gif; mapPlaceHolder.gif.
6. Start a text editor, then open the xhtml-template.html document from the InnWebsite folder.

   Note: When opening an html document in a text editor, you may need to change the file type in the Open dialog box to all files so that the html files are displayed.
7. Open a Web browser.
8. **Open** the file xhtml-template.html from the InnWebsite folder.

   Notice that the Web page is blank and the title bar at the top of the browser window displays Untitled Document as shown in Figure 4-31.
9. Return to the text editor.
10. Select the words **Untitled Document** within the <title> tags as shown in Figure 4-32.
11. Type **Inn at Birch Bay - Home Page**.

(continued)

12. Save the document to the InnWebsite folder with the file name **homepage.html**.
13. Open the homepage.html document in a browser and notice Inn at Birch Bay - Home Page is displayed in the title bar of the browser window.
14. Return to the text editor.

You have created folders for the Web site, opened a template, created, saved, and viewed a Web page.

Edit the Home Page Using a Text Editor

Figure 4-33 shows the completed XHTML document for the Inn at Birch Bay home page.

1. With the homepage.html document displayed in the text editor, click the insertion point beneath <body>.
2. Type **<img src="assets/logoPlaceHolder.gif" align="right" />.**
3. Save the document, then display it in a browser.

   Notice how the logo placeholder is aligned to the right of the Web page.
4. Return to the text editor.
5. Click the insertion point below the img src line, then type **<img src="assets/logoPlaceHolder.gif" align="left" />**.
6. Save the document, display it in a browser, verify the logo placeholder is left aligned, then return to the text editor.
7. Click the insertion point below the second img src line, then type **<center><h1>The Inn at Birch Bay</h1></center>**.

(continued)

FIGURE 4-33
The completed XHTML document for the home page

homepage.html - Notepad

File Edit Format View Help

```
<!DOCTYPE HTML PUBLIC "-//W3C//DTD HTML 4.01 Transitional//EN"
"http://www.w3.org/TR/html4/loose.dtd">

<html xmlns="http://www.w3.org/1999/xhtml">

<head>
        <title>Inn at Birch Bay - Home Page</title>
        <meta http-equiv="Content-Type" content="text/html; charset=iso-8859-1">
</head>

<body>
<img src="assets/logoPlaceHolder.gif" align="right" />
<img src="assets/logoPlaceHolder.gif" align="left" />
<center><h1>The Inn at Birch Bay</h1></center>
<br /><br />
<p>
<center><img src="assets/innPlaceHolder.jpg"/></center>
</p>
<p>
<hr>
<h3><center>Home - Tour - Contact us - Directions</center></h3>
</p>

</body>

</html>
```

FIGURE 4-34

The lines to be typed

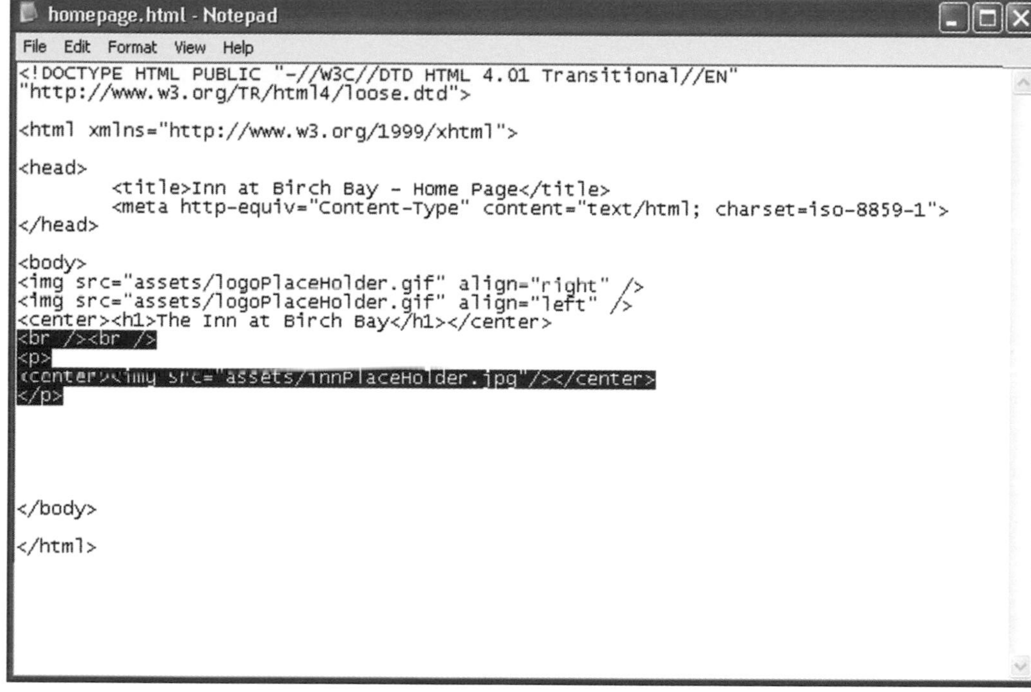

8. Save the document, display it in a browser, verify the inn text is center aligned, then return to the text editor.
9. Click the insertion point below the <center> line, then type the lines highlighted in Figure 4-34.
10. Save the document, display it in a browser, verify the inn placeholder is center aligned, then return to the text editor.
11. Click the insertion point below the </p> line, type **<p>**, press **[Enter]** (PC) or **[return]** (Mac), then type **<hr>**.
12. Save the document, display it in a browser, verify a horizontal line appears, then return to the text editor.
13. Click the insertion point below the <hr> line.
14. Type **<h3><center>Home - Tour - Contact us - Directions</center></h3>**, press **[Enter]** (PC) or **[return]** (Mac), then type **</p>**.
15. Save the document, display it in a browser, verify the four labels are centered under the horizontal line, then return to the text editor.

You have created a home page using a text editor.

Create Additional Web Pages Using a Text Editor

1. With the home page document displayed in the text editor, save the document to the InnWebsite folder with the file name **tour.html**.

   Because all four pages of the Web site are similar, you can use the home page document as a template to create the other three pages by simply replacing selected sections.

(continued)

2. Select the words **Home Page** within the <title> tags as shown in Figure 4-35, then type **Tour**.
3. Select the words **The Inn at Birch Bay** within the <h1> tags, then type **Tour**.
4. Select the file name **innPlaceHolder.jpg**, then type **videoPlaceHolder.gif**.
5. Save the document, display it in a browser, verify the Tour title and video placeholder appear in the browser, then return to the text editor.
6. With the tour document displayed in the text editor, save the document to the InnWebsite with the file name **directions.html**.
7. Select the word **Tour** within the <title> tags, then type **Directions**.
8. Select the word **Tour** within the <h1> tags, then type **Directions**.
9. Select the file name **videoPlaceHolder.gif**, then type **mapPlaceHolder.gif**.
10. Save the document and display it in a browser, verify the Directions title and map placeholder appear in the browser, then return to the text editor.
11. With the directions document displayed in the text editor, save the document to the InnWebsite with the file name **contactus.html**.
12. Select the word **Directions** within the <title> tags, then type **Contact us**.
13. Select the word **Directions** within the <h1> tags, then type **Contact us**.

(continued)

FIGURE 4-35

The highlighted words

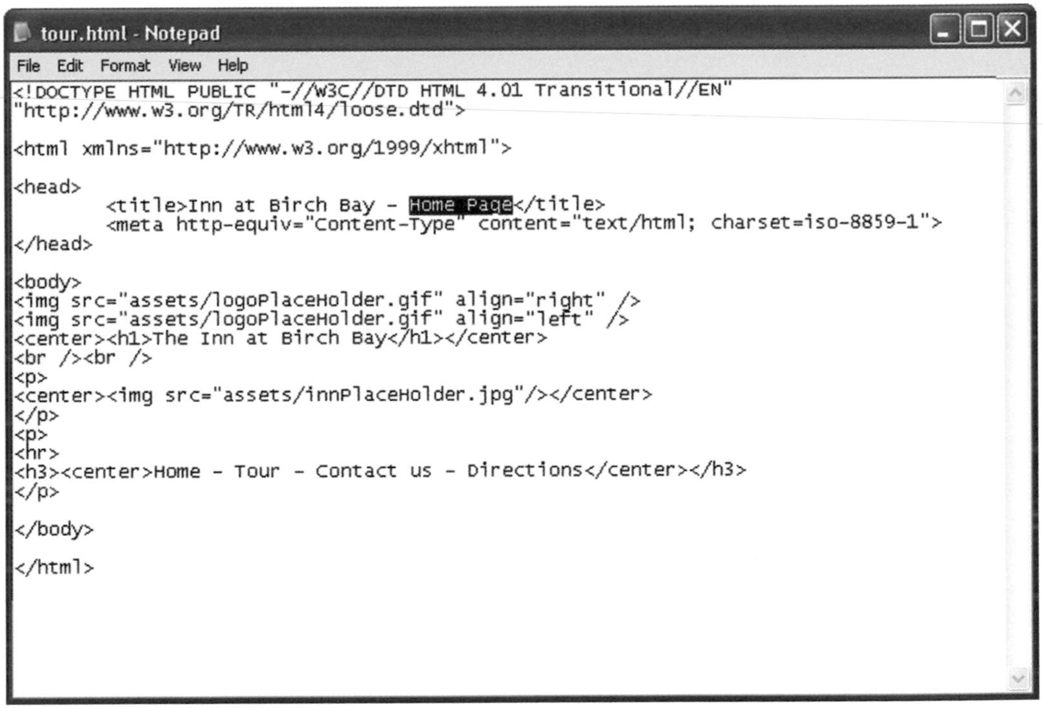

tour.html - Notepad

File Edit Format View Help

```
<!DOCTYPE HTML PUBLIC "-//W3C//DTD HTML 4.01 Transitional//EN"
"http://www.w3.org/TR/html4/loose.dtd">

<html xmlns="http://www.w3.org/1999/xhtml">

<head>
	<title>Inn at Birch Bay - Home Page</title>
	<meta http-equiv="Content-Type" content="text/html; charset=iso-8859-1">
</head>

<body>
<img src="assets/logoPlaceHolder.gif" align="right" />
<img src="assets/logoPlaceHolder.gif" align="left" />
<center><h1>The Inn at Birch Bay</h1></center>
<br /><br />
<p>
<center><img src="assets/innPlaceHolder.jpg"/></center>
</p>
<p>
<hr>
<h3><center>Home - Tour - Contact us - Directions</center></h3>
</p>

</body>

</html>
```

FIGURE 4-36
The completed contactus.html document

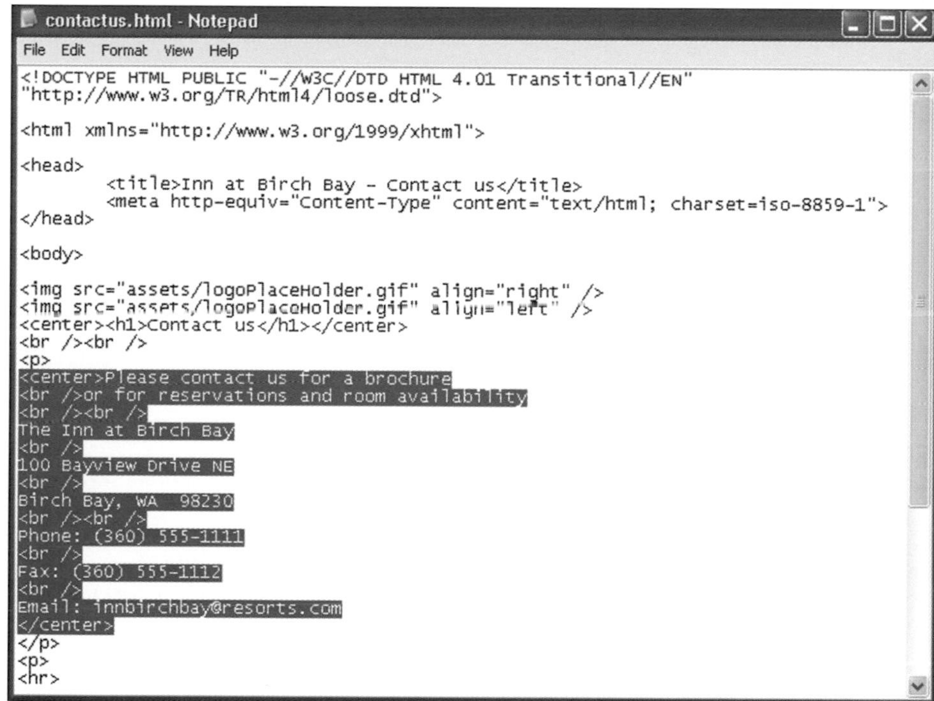


```
<!DOCTYPE HTML PUBLIC "-//W3C//DTD HTML 4.01 Transitional//EN"
"http://www.w3.org/TR/html4/loose.dtd">

<html xmlns="http://www.w3.org/1999/xhtml">

<head>
        <title>Inn at Birch Bay - Contact us</title>
        <meta http-equiv="Content-Type" content="text/html; charset=iso-8859-1">
</head>

<body>

<img src="assets/logoPlaceHolder.gif" align="right" />
<img src="assets/logoPlaceHolder.gif" align="left" />
<center><h1>Contact us</h1></center>
<br /><br />
<p>
<center>Please contact us for a brochure
<br />or for reservations and room availability
<br /><br />
The Inn at Birch Bay
<br />
100 Bayview Drive NE
<br />
Birch Bay, WA  98230
<br /><br />
Phone: (360) 555-1111
<br />
Fax: (360) 555-1112
<br />
Email: innbirchbay@resorts.com
</center>
</p>
<p>
<hr>
```

14. Select the line **<center><img src="assets/mapPlaceHolder.gif" /></center>**, then press **[Delete]**.

15. Type the highlighted lines shown in Figure 4-36.

16. Save the document, display the document in a browser, verify the contact information appears in the browser, then return to the text editor.

You have created additional Web pages for the Inn at Birch Bay Web site.

Create Linked Web Pages Using a Text Editor

1. Open the homepage.html document in a text editor.
2. Select **Home - Tour - Contact us - Directions </center></h3>**, then press **[Delete]**.
3. Press **[Enter]** (PC) or **[return]** (Mac), then type **<a href="homepage.html">Home</a>**.
4. Press **[Enter]** (PC) or **[return]** (Mac), then type ** - **.

   The   causes a space to be displayed. So, this code displays a space after the word *Home*, then a - (hyphen), then another space.
5. Press **[Enter]** (PC) or **[return]** (Mac), then type **<a href="tour.html">Tour</a>**.
6. Press **[Enter]** (PC) or **[return]** (Mac), then type ** - **.
7. Save the document, then display it in a browser.

   Notice that Home is followed by a -, then Tour, then another -. Also, notice that the words are in blue and underlined indicating that they are links.

(continued)

8. Click **Tour** to display the tour.html Web page.
9. Return to the text editor and the homepage.html document, then complete the other two links using the code shown in Figure 4-37.

   After clicking a word to go to the linked page and then returning to the original page, the word will have changed color indicating that the linked page has been visited.
10. Press **[Enter]** (PC) or **[return]** (Mac), then type **</center></h3>**.
11. Save the document, display it in a browser, verify that the Contact us and Directions links appear in the browser, then return to the text editor.
12. Select the code shown in Figure 4-38, then copy it.
13. Start your text editor again so that a new page opens in a new window, then open tour.html.
14. Delete **Home - Tour - Contact us - Directions</center></h3>**.
15. Click the insertion point after <h3><center> if necessary, then press **[Enter]** (PC) or **[return]** (Mac).
16. Paste the copied code into the document, save the document, display it in a browser, then verify the four links appear in the browser.
17. Click the **Home** link, then return to the text editor.
18. Repeat steps 13 through 16 for the contactus.html and directions.html pages.
19. Check all links for all Web pages, then close the text editor and browser windows.

You have linked the Web pages for the Inn at Birch Bay Web site.

FIGURE 4-37

Code used to complete the links

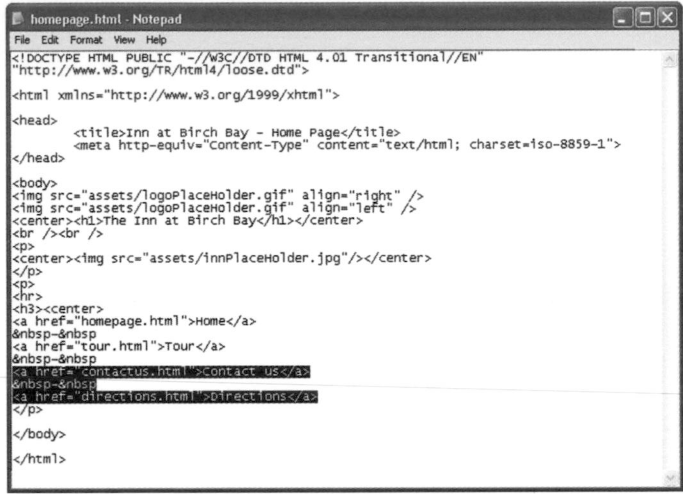

```
<!DOCTYPE HTML PUBLIC "-//W3C//DTD HTML 4.01 Transitional//EN"
"http://www.w3.org/TR/html4/loose.dtd">

<html xmlns="http://www.w3.org/1999/xhtml">

<head>
	<title>Inn at Birch Bay - Home Page</title>
	<meta http-equiv="Content-Type" content="text/html; charset=iso-8859-1">
</head>

<body>
<img src="assets/logoPlaceHolder.gif" align="right" />
<img src="assets/logoPlaceHolder.gif" align="left" />
<center><h1>The Inn at Birch Bay</h1></center>
<br /><br />
<p>
<center><img src="assets/innPlaceHolder.jpg"/></center>
</p>
<p>
<hr>
<h3><center>
<a href="homepage.html">Home</a>
 - 
<a href="tour.html">Tour</a>
 - 
<a href="contactus.html">Contact us</a>
 - 
<a href="directions.html">Directions</a>
</p>

</body>

</html>
```

FIGURE 4-38

The highlighted code

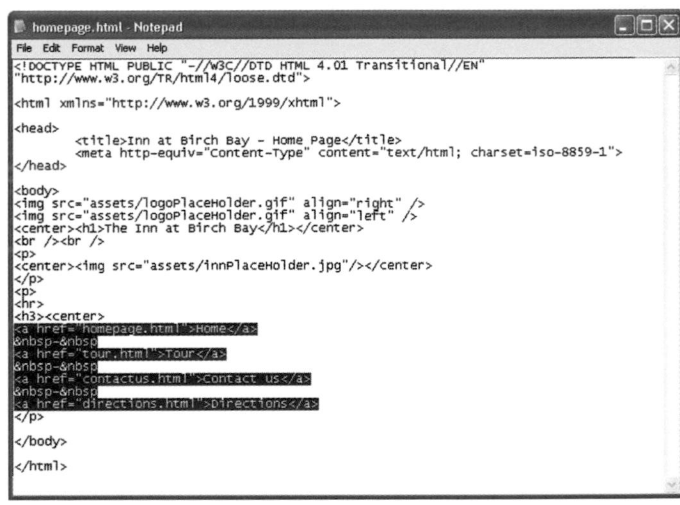

```
<!DOCTYPE HTML PUBLIC "-//W3C//DTD HTML 4.01 Transitional//EN"
"http://www.w3.org/TR/html4/loose.dtd">

<html xmlns="http://www.w3.org/1999/xhtml">

<head>
	<title>Inn at Birch Bay - Home Page</title>
	<meta http-equiv="Content-Type" content="text/html; charset=iso-8859-1">
</head>

<body>
<img src="assets/logoPlaceHolder.gif" align="right" />
<img src="assets/logoPlaceHolder.gif" align="left" />
<center><h1>The Inn at Birch Bay</h1></center>
<br /><br />
<p>
<center><img src="assets/innPlaceHolder.jpg"/></center>
</p>
<p>
<hr>
<h3><center>
<a href="homepage.html">Home</a>
 - 
<a href="tour.html">Tour</a>
 - 
<a href="contactus.html">Contact us</a>
 - 
<a href="directions.html">Directions</a>
</p>

</body>

</html>
```

LESSON 2

CREATING A WEB SITE with Macromedia Dreamweaver

What You'll Do

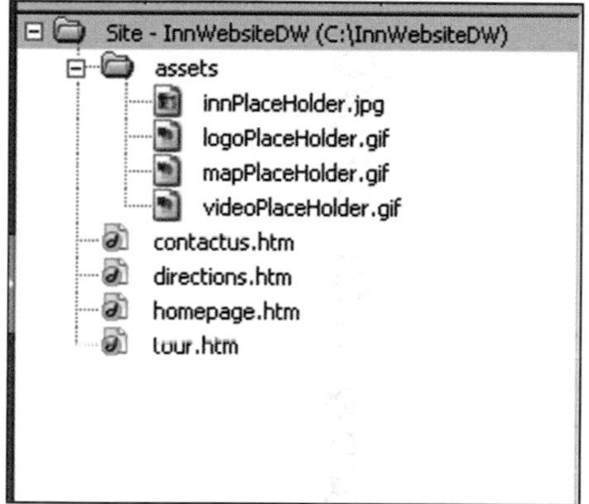

In this lesson, you will learn how to create a Web site using Macromedia Dreamweaver.

Using Macromedia Dreamweaver MX 2004

Macromedia Dreamweaver MX 2004 is a Web design and development tool that allows you to create Web pages as well as to create and maintain entire Web sites. Dreamweaver provides a WYSIWYG (What You See Is What You Get) development environment. That is, what appears in the Dreamweaver document window is the same as what is shown in a browser window. Figure 4-39 shows an XHTML document in both the Dreamweaver window and a browser window. You create a Web page by typing and formatting text, and inserting and aligning graphics in much the same way as you accomplish these tasks using a word processing program. As you are creating the Web page, Dreamweaver is generating the XHTML code.

Macromedia Dreamweaver MX 2004 is an extremely powerful program with many features. In this lesson you will learn the basics of Dreamweaver as you develop the Inn at Birch Bay Web site. The process involves creating the folder structure for the site, defining the site, then creating and linking the Web pages. Upon completion of this lesson you will have created a Web site with Web pages similar to those created using a text editor.

The Folder Structure for the Macromedia Dreamweaver Web Site

Earlier you created the folders that were used when developing the Web pages with a text editor. In this lesson you will create and use another set of folders in order to keep the files for the two sites separate. Then as you proceed through the book, you can use the folders created in this lesson to update the site using Macromedia Dreamweaver MX 2004.

Defining a Web Site

After creating the folders and adding files to them, you define the Web site in Dreamweaver. When you define a Web site you specify a name for the site and indicate the folder where the Web site will reside, that is, the folder you created for the site. Then, any files within the folder become available to be used in the Web pages you create.

FIGURE 4-39

An XHTML document in both the Dreamweaver MX 2004 window and a browser window

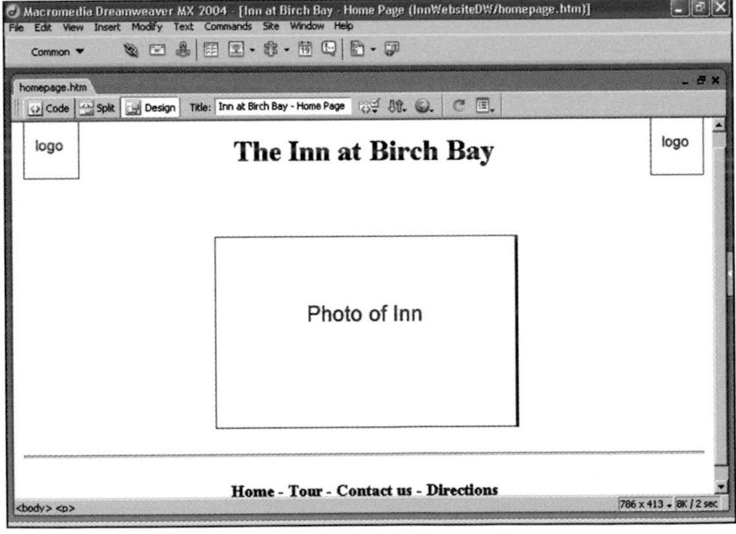

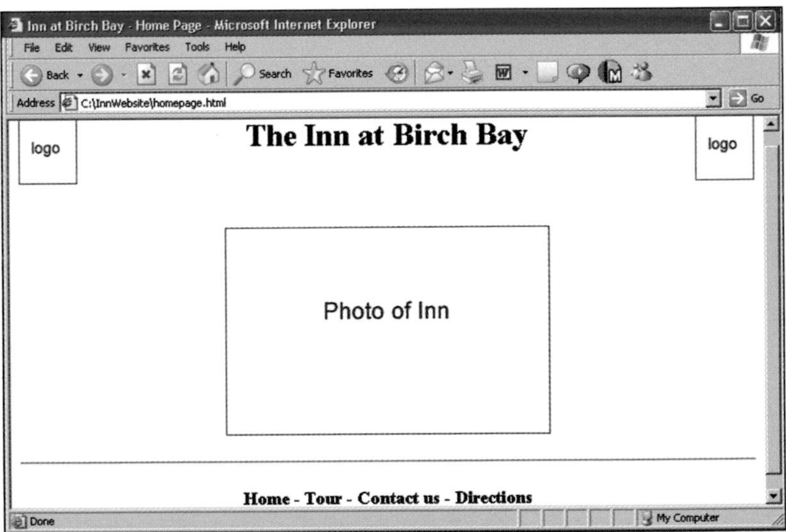

The Macromedia Dreamweaver Environment

Figure 4-40 shows the Dreamweaver MX 2004 workspace. The major components are:

- Title bar – Displays the program name and the file name for the current document.
- Menu bar – Provides the standard menu categories.
- Insert bar – Provides shortcuts to such features as inserting images and tables.
- Document toolbar – Contains buttons used to change the current work mode and a box to enter a title for the Web page.
- Document window – Each open document has a window with a tab specifying its name, and a toolbar that allows you to, among other things, switch views and specify a title. There are three ways to view a document in the document window. The Design view shows the Web page as it will appear in the browser. The Code view shows the underlying XHTML code for the Web page. The Code and Design view is a combination of the other views.
- Property inspector – A panel that allows you to change the properties of a selected item. For example, if text is selected, you could change its font, font size, font color, and so on.
- Files panel – A panel used to display the folders and files that have been previously defined. Image files that appear in this panel can be dragged into the Document window to be inserted into a Web page. Also, Web page files can be dragged to the Document window to be opened. As Web pages are created and saved, they appear in this panel. This allows you to easily switch between documents in the site.

FIGURE 4-40

Macromedia Dreamweaver MX 2004 workspace

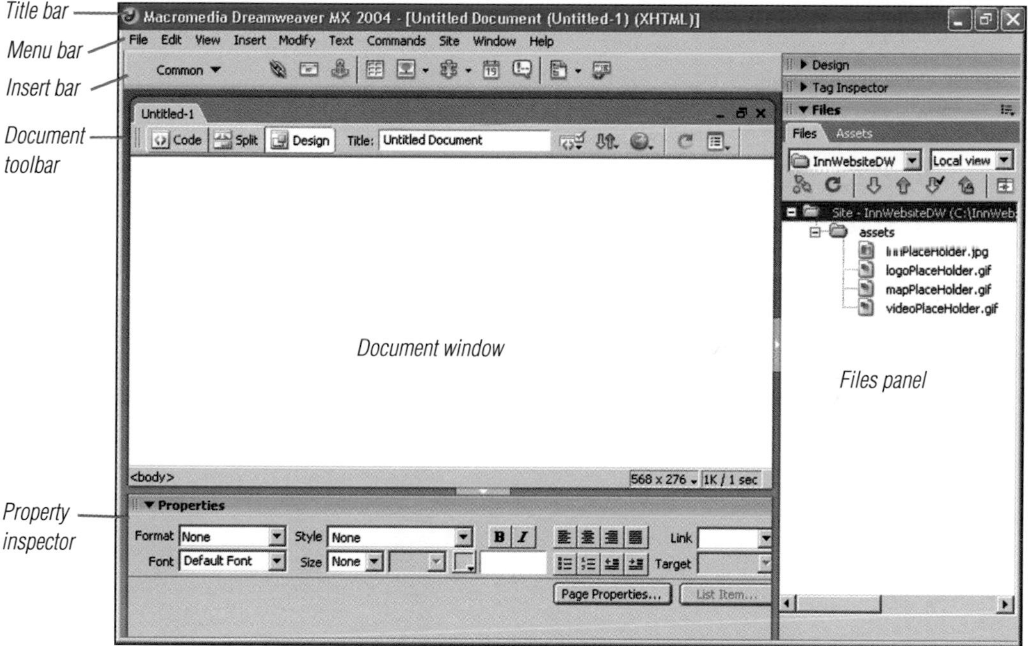

Create the Folders for the Web Site and Define the Web Site Using Dreamweaver MX 2004

1. Navigate to the drive on your computer where you will be storing the files for the InnWebsite.
2. Create a new folder and name it **InnWebsiteDW**.
3. Within the InnWebsiteDW folder, create another folder called **assets**.
4. Locate the files that are used for this book and copy the following files to the assets folder: logoPlaceHolder.gif; innPlaceHolder.jpg; videoPlaceHolder.gif; mapPlaceHolder.gif.
5. Start Macromedia Dreamweaver MX 2004.
6. The Dreamweaver opening screen appears allowing you to choose a recently saved or a new document to open.

   Note: If the opening screen does not appear, click File on the menu bar, click New, click Create, and then skip step 7.
7. Click **HTML** beneath Create New.

(continued)

FIGURE 4-41
The InnWebsiteDW folder

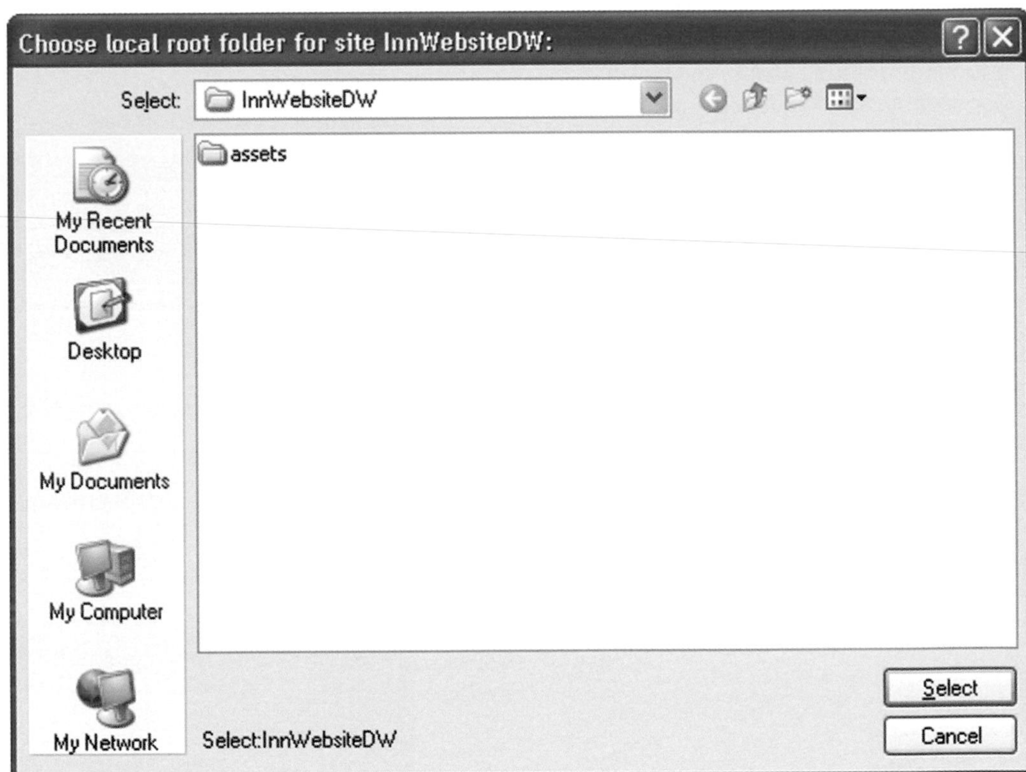

FIGURE 4-42
The Files panel displaying the InnWebsiteDW folder

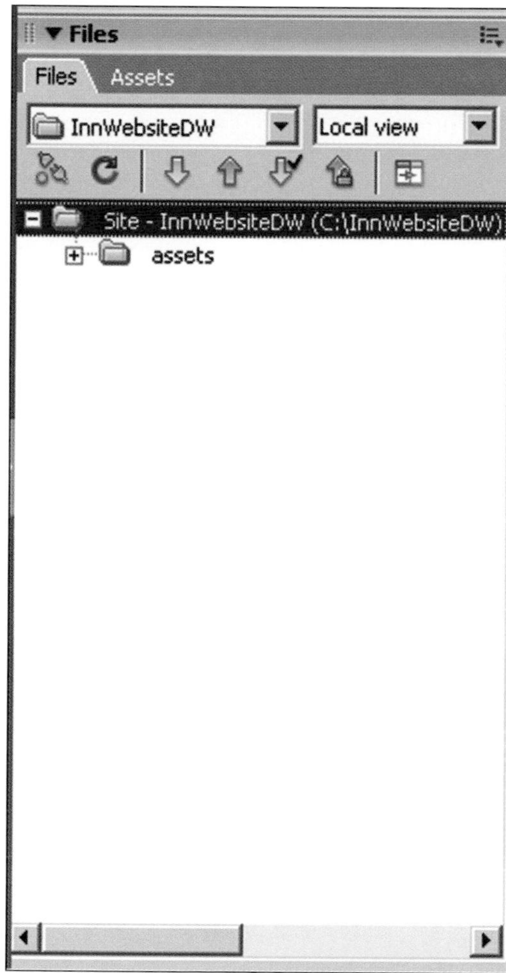

8. Click **Site** in the menu bar, then click **Manage Sites**.
9. Click **New** in the Manage Sites dialog box, then click **Site**.
10. Verify the Advanced tab is selected, then type **InnWebsiteDW** in the Site name box of the Site Definition dialog box.
11. Click the **Local root folder icon** .
12. Navigate to the InnWebsiteDW folder as shown in Figure 4-41.
13. Click **Select** (PC) or **Choose** (Mac), click **OK** in the Site Definition dialog box, then click **Done** in the Manage Sites dialog box.

    The Files panel appears as shown in Figure 4-42.
14. Click the + (PC) or ▶ (Mac) in the assets folder in the Files panel to reveal the files in this folder.

You created the folders for a Web site and defined a Web site in Dreamweaver.

15. Drag the pointer to select the text.

16. Click the **down list arrow** in the Format box in the Property inspector, then click Heading 1.

17. With the text still selected, click the **Align Center button** in the Property inspector.

18. Click the insertion point to the right of the word Bay, then press **[Enter]** (PC) or **[return]** (Mac).

19. Hold down **[Shift]**, then press **[Enter]** (PC) or **[return]** (Mac) twice.

    Holding down [Shift] and pressing **[Enter]** (PC) or **[return]** (Mac) inserts a line break using the <br /> tag. You can repeat the <br /> tag as many times as needed to get the desired spacing between lines. Pressing **[Enter]** (PC) or **[return]** (Mac) inserts a blank line using the paragraph tag <p>. Repeating the <p> tag has no effect on spacing between lines. So, you use only one <p> tag at a time.

20. Drag the innPlaceHolder.jpg icon from the Files panel to the document just below the insertion point as shown in Figure 4-45.

21. Press **[Enter]** (PC) or **[return]** (Mac).

(continued)

FIGURE 4-45

Positioning the icon

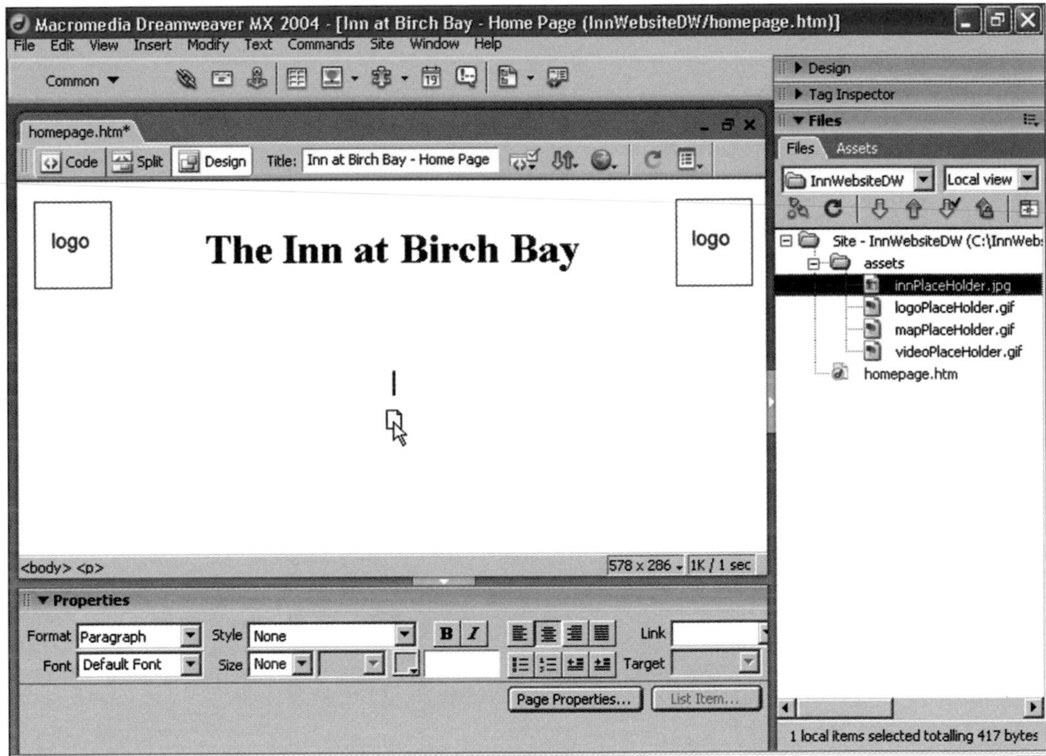

FIGURE 4-46

Specifying a heading style

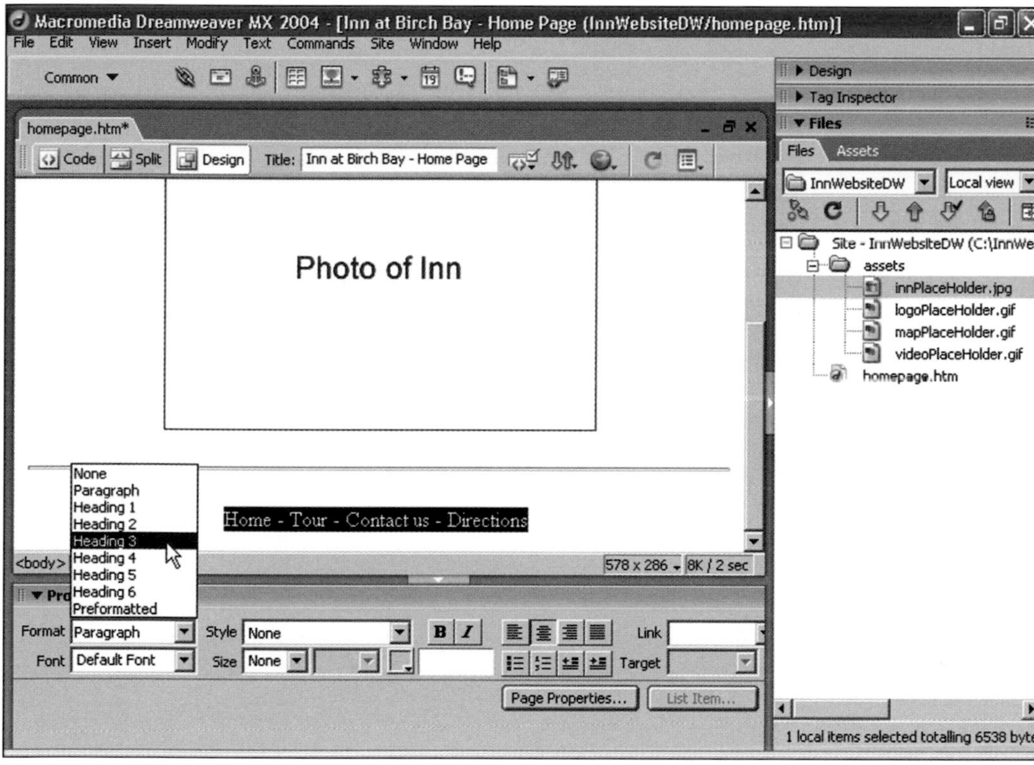

22. Click **Insert** on the menu bar, point to **HTML**, then click **Horizontal Rule**.

23. Click the insertion point at the end of the horizontal rule line, then press the **down arrow** on the keyboard once to position the insertion point below the horizontal rule line.

    Inserting a horizontal rule causes the rule line to be placed above the <p> tag. Therefore, you can use the down arrow key to position the insertion point below the rule line without using **[Enter]** (PC) or **[return]** (Mac).

24. Type **Home - Tour - Contact us - Directions**.

25. Select **Home - Tour - Contact us - Directions**, click the **down list arrow** in the Format box in the Property inspector, then click **Heading 3** as shown in Figure 4-46.

26. Save the document.

27. Click **File** in the menu bar, point to **Preview in Browser**, click **iexplore** (PC) or **Internet Explorer** (Mac) or another browser, then verify the document appears in the Web page the way it appears in Dreamweaver.

28. Close the browser, then return to Dreamweaver.

You created a home page in Dreamweaver.

Create Additional Web Pages Using Dreamweaver

1. With the homepage.html document displayed in Dreamweaver, click **File**, click **Save As** in the menu bar, then save the document to the InnWebsiteDW folder with the file name **tour**.
2. Select **Home Page** in the Title box on the Document toolbar, then type **Tour**.
3. Select **The Inn at Birch Bay** heading in the Document window, then type **Tour**.
4. Click the **Photo of Inn image**, then press **[Delete]**.
5. Drag the **videoPlaceHolder.gif** icon to the insertion point as shown in Figure 4-47.
6. Save the document.
7. With the tour.html document displayed in Dreamweaver, click **File**, click **Save As** in the menu bar, then save the document to the InnWebsiteDW folder with the file name **directions**.
8. Select **Tour** in the Title box on the Document toolbar, then type **Directions**.
9. Select the **Tour heading** in the Document window, then type **Directions**.
10. Click the **video image**, then press **[Delete]**.
11. Drag the **mapPlaceHolder.gif icon** to the insertion point.
12. Save the document.
13. With the directions.html document displayed in Dreamweaver, click **File**, click **Save As** in the menu bar, then save the document to the InnWebsiteDW folder with the file name **contactus**.

(continued)

FIGURE 4-47
Positioning the icon

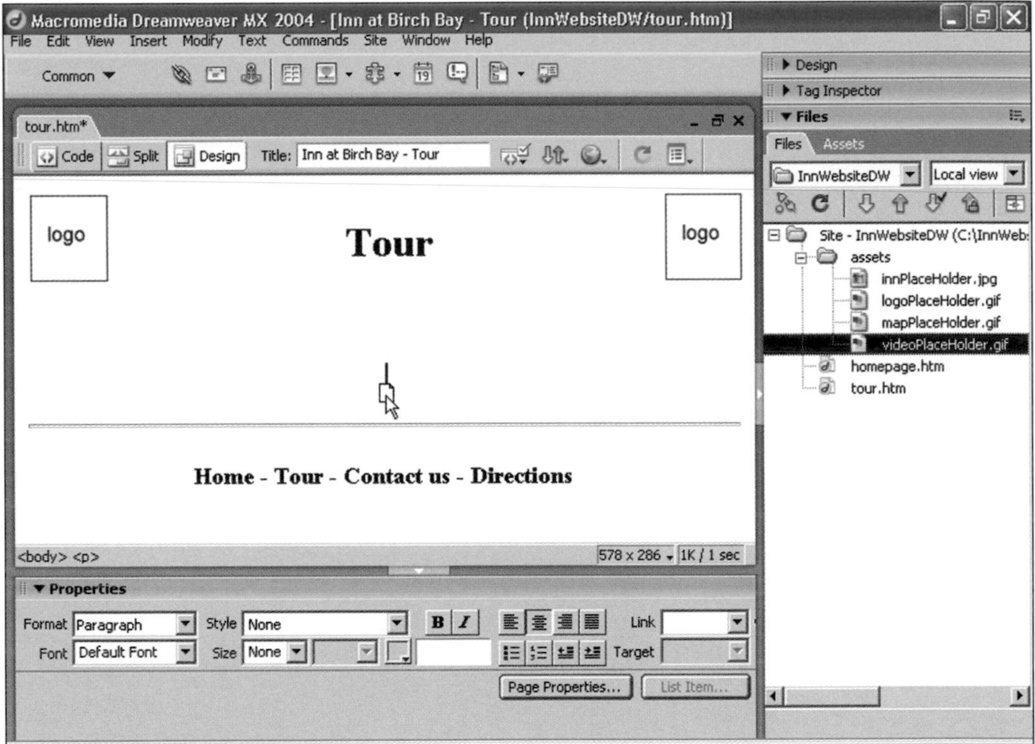

FIGURE 4-48
The contactus.htm document

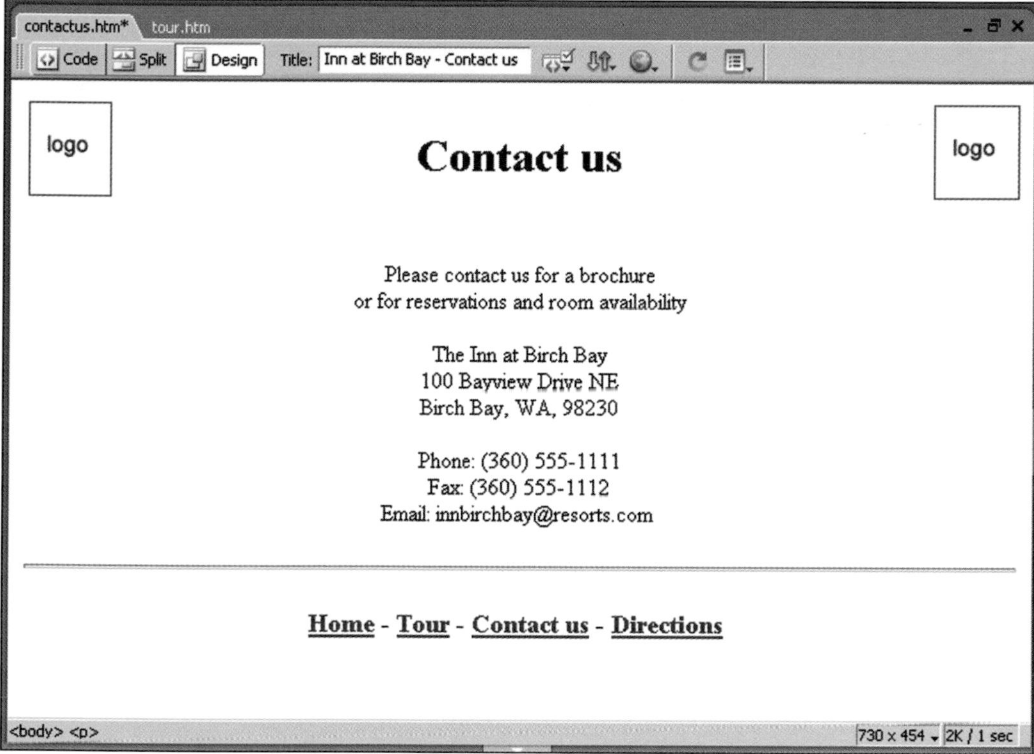

14. Select **Directions** in the Title box on the Document toolbar, then type **Contact us**.
15. Select the **Directions heading** in the Document window, then type **Contact us**.
16. Click the **map image**, then press **[Delete]**.

    Figure 4-48 shows the completed contactus.html document. Refer to the figure as you complete the following steps.
17. Type **Please contact us for a brochure**, then hold down **[Shift]** and press **[Enter]** (PC) or **[return]** (Mac).
18. Type **or for reservations and room availability**, then press **[Enter]** (PC) or **[return]** (Mac).
19. Type **The Inn at Birch Bay**, then hold down **[Shift]** and press **[Enter]** (PC) or **[return]** (Mac).
20. Type **100 Bayview Drive NE**, then hold down **[Shift]** and press **[Enter]** (PC) or **[return]** (Mac).
21. Type **Birch Bay, WA, 98230**, then press **[Enter]** (PC) or **[return]** (Mac).
22. Type **Phone: (360) 555-1111**, then hold down **[Shift]** and press **[Enter]** (PC) or **[return]** (Mac).
23. Type **Fax: (360) 555-1112**, then hold down **[Shift]** and press **[Enter]** (PC) or **[return]** (Mac).
24. Type **Email: innbirchbay@resorts.com**.
25. Save the document, display it in a browser, verify the document appears in the browser as it appears in Dreamweaver, then return to Dreamweaver.

You used Dreamweaver to create additional Web pages.

Link Web Pages Using Dreamweaver

1. With Dreamweaver open, double-click the **homepage.htm icon** in the Files panel to display the home page.
2. Drag the scroll bar down to display the bottom of the Web page if necessary, then double-click **Home** to select it.
3. Click in the **Link box** in the Property inspector as shown in Figure 4-49.

   To create a link so that when a user clicks on an object (text or image) another Web page is displayed, select the object and type the file name of the Web page in the Link box in the Property inspector panel.
4. Type **homepage.htm**, then press **[Enter]** (PC) or **[return]** (Mac).
5. Double-click **Tour**, click in the **Link box**, type **tour.htm**, then press **[Enter]** (PC) or **[return]** (Mac).
6. Select **Contact us**, click in the **Link box**, type **contactus.htm**, then press **[Enter]** (PC) or **[return]** (Mac).
7. Double-click **Directions**, click in the **Link box**, type **directions.htm**, then press **[Enter]** (PC) or **[return]** (Mac).
8. Save the document.

(continued)

FIGURE 4-49
The Link box

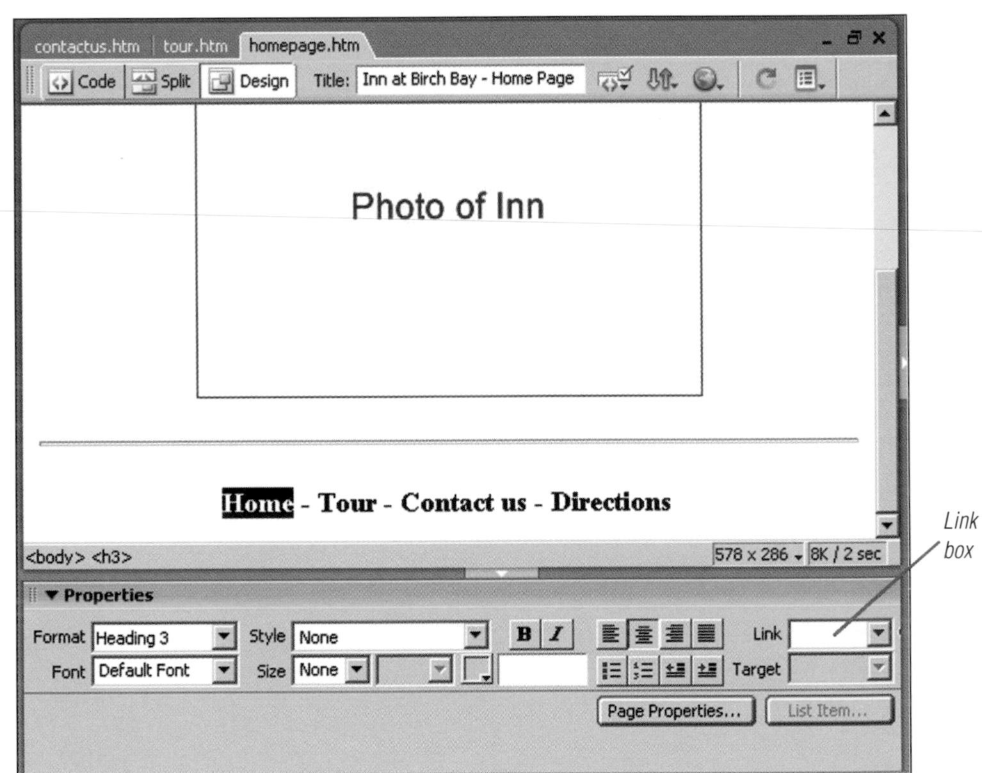

FIGURE 4-50

The tour.htm icon in the Files panel

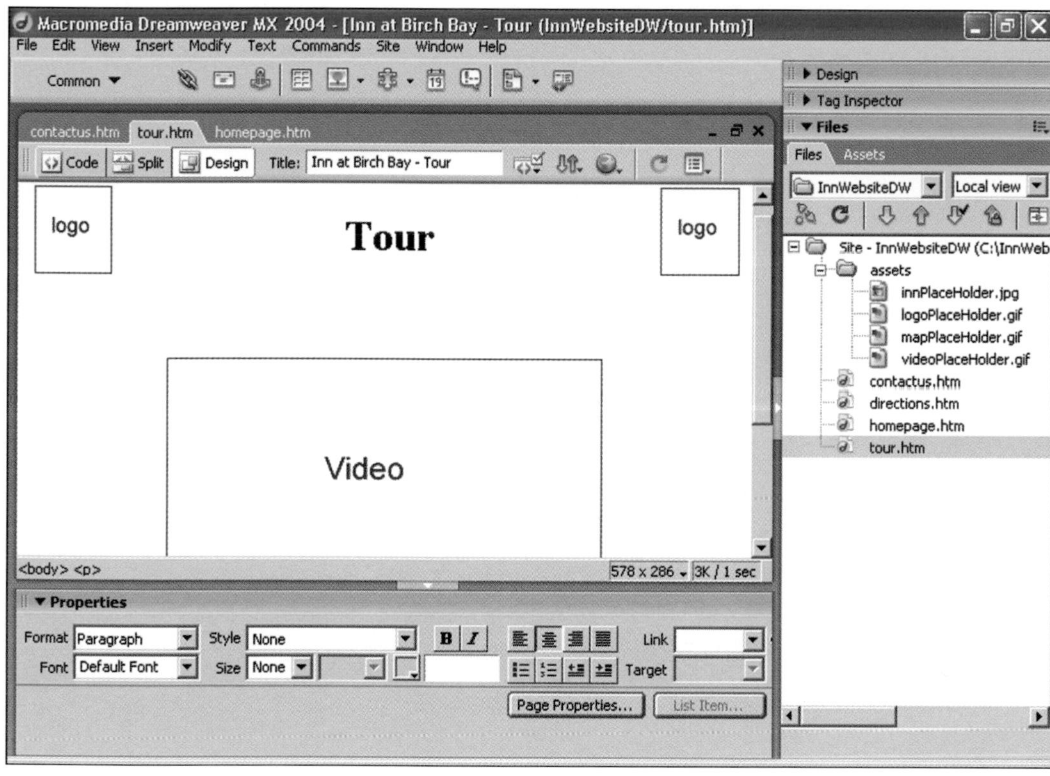

9. Double-click the **tour.htm icon** in the Files panel to display the Tour page as shown in Figure 4-50.
10. Repeat steps 2 through 7, then save the document.
11. Double-click the **contactus.htm icon** in the Files panel to display the Contact us page.
12. Repeat steps 2 through 7, then save the document.
13. Double-click the **directions.htm icon** in the Files panel to display the Directions page.
14. Repeat steps 2 through 7, then save the document.
15. Open the home page in a browser, test the links, then close the browser.

You used Dreamweaver to link Web pages.

PROJECT BUILDER 1

You are an intern with a company that develops Web sites for clients. During your internship training you learned the basics of XHTML and Macromedia Dreamweaver. You have been asked to prepare a report that compares the Web site development process using a text editor and a Web development authoring program.

1. Open a document in a word processor, save the file as **Ch4pb1**, then develop and complete a table similar to Figure 4-51.

One Step Beyond

2. Go to the Macromedia Web site and display the Dreamweaver Home page. List the topics that are linked to the page.
3. List and briefly describe three features of Dreamweaver presented in the site.

Two Steps Beyond

4. Navigate to the Web page that describes the Macromedia Studio MX 2004. List and briefly describe the products included in Macromedia Studio MX 2004.

FIGURE 4-51
Evaluating text editors and Web development authoring programs

Which process	Using a text editor	Using an authoring program
Is the quickest to develop Web pages? Explain.		
Allows you to define a Web site? How is this done?		
Is considered WYSIWYG? How is this useful?		
Helps you understand how XHTML works? Explain.		
Is best for troubleshooting problems with XHTML code? Explain.		
Is best for working with more than one Web page at a time? Explain.		
Is the least expensive tool to use? Explain.		

PROJECT BUILDER 2

You have been studying Web development. You decide it is time to create your Web site portfolio.

1. Create a Web site folder structure, similar to Figure 4-52, on your hard drive with a minimum of two folders—one folder containing the entire site and the other folder (called assets folder in the figure) containing the multimedia elements.
2. Open a document in a text editor, save the file as **Ch4pb2.html**, then create a Home Page for your portfolio Web site with at least the following:
   a. A text heading
   b. An image or placeholder
   c. Navigation buttons in the form of text

One Step Beyond

3. Create one or more additional Web pages for your portfolio site.
4. Link all of the Web pages.

Two Steps Beyond

5. Create another Web site folder structure on your hard drive with a minimum of two folders. One folder contains the entire site and the other folder contains the multimedia elements.
6. Using Macromedia Dreamweaver, duplicate the Web site you developed using a text editor.

FIGURE 4-52
A folder structure for a Web site

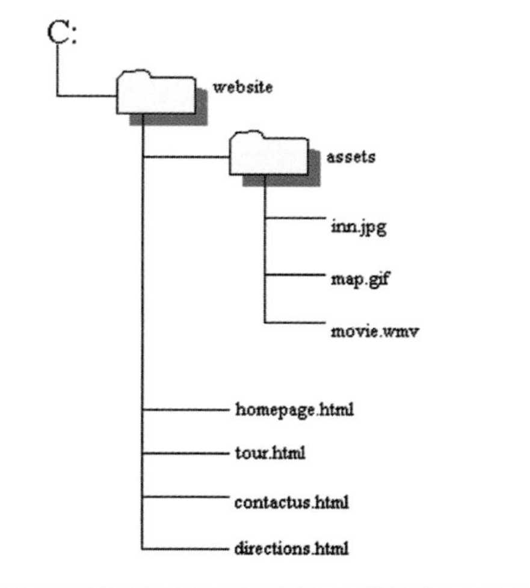

STOP
ONLY
ONLY

chapter

5 MULTIMEDIA ELEMENT—Text

1. Discuss Fonts
2. Understand Fonts
3. Define Cascading Style Sheets (CSS)
4. Explain Additional Options for Implementing Text on the Web

chapter 5 MULTIMEDIA ELEMENT—Text

Introduction

At one time, all Web content was disseminated with text. Although graphics and other media elements have since been added, text is still the primary vehicle for communicating content on Web pages because written words are an effective way to communicate. Similar to the way text is used in print, text on Web pages is used for headlines, subtitles, captions, and body copy. In addition to supplying content on Web pages, text can be used as a hyperlink, linking content and concepts within a Web page and between Web pages. Text-based menus and buttons provide navigational tools that help guide users through a Web site. Popular Web-based products, such as electronic books, magazines, and reference materials, use text to inform and educate.

The effective use of text on Web pages is dependent upon typography and the typefaces used. **Typography** is type design; it is the typeface used and the way the type is arranged to communicate an idea.

> **QUICKTIP**
>
> Technically, according to Wikipedia, *typography* is defined as "the art of arranging letterforms in space in any medium (including the printed page, Web pages, television, film, etc.), usually using a recognized typeface, in order to achieve a combination of both aesthetic and functional goals."

A **typeface** is a set of characters, usually made up of alphabet letters, numerals, and symbols, that all follow the same rules within the set. A **font** is a set of characters within a typeface that has specific characteristics associated with it, especially with

> **A Brief Look at Typography**
>
> Typography is more than 300 years old. During that period, many aspects to type design have evolved and grown into an expansive collection of knowledge. Entire books have been devoted to typography and type design. It would be wise to extend your research of typography beyond the scope of this book. Type design is an incredible art form and a wonderful communication tool.

respect to size (the height of the characters), weight (how dark the characters appear), and style (such as italic or condensed). Fonts belong to a **font family** such as Times New Roman. For example Times New Roman 12 point, bold, condensed is one font, and it is in the same font family as Times New Roman 16 point, light, expanded.

Good typography is as important on a Web page as it is on paper. Text should be easy to read and visually pleasing. One challenge of using text on a Web page is getting the message across in an exciting, creative, and visual way. Meeting this challenge means recognizing how text is used differently on the Web than in print. Although the results need to be the same, print typography and Web typography are very different. Why? Because Web designers need to design for computer screens of various sizes and resolutions, which carries with it a unique set of issues. In addition, the variety of browsers and platforms used by the Web community makes Web typography an even greater challenge. To top it all off, markup languages do not provide the control designers need and want to effectively implement Web typography. HTML was established for cross-platform distribution of functional text not visually appealing typography. This issue has been greatly resolved in XHTML and with the use of Cascading Style Sheets (CSSs).

People who work with print know that when the copy is printed, it does not always print the way it looked on screen in a desktop publishing program. This difference in print material can occur for a number of reasons: the printer may not be properly calibrated, which means the color may be off-register and print outside the intended image, making text blurry, or the text may bleed on the paper. The print designer can correct these problems and end up with a printed piece that remains consistent each time it is printed. A Web designer, however, does not have this luxury. The Web is an elastic medium that must work across different computer platforms, screen sizes, and available font sets. As a Web designer, it will be your job to understand these issues and to try to control them or at least minimize their negative impact.

This chapter focuses on the appropriate use of text in multimedia Web sites (see Figure 5-1) as well as some considerations and guidelines to keep in mind when working with text on the Web.

FIGURE 5-1

Effective use of text in a multimedia Web site: the use of type size, color, and font in the EURO RSCG Web site communicates a contemporary feel and quickly guides the user to key points about the company

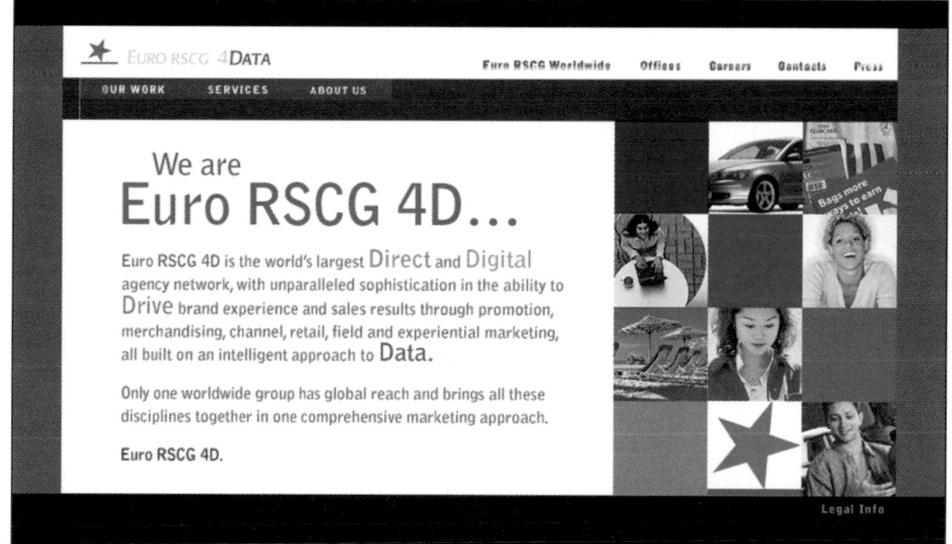

CONCEPT 1

DISCUSS
Fonts

What You'll Learn

In this lesson, you will learn about fonts, default fonts, and how fonts vary from one computer to another. You will also learn to choose fonts to ensure that the text on a Web page will display as intended.

When your content is mostly text, the way you use typography to create readable and visually interesting text is of paramount importance. Unfortunately, the wonderful world of typography is somewhat muddled and confusing. You must understand many issues to effectively control how text appears on the Web. For example, users may not have the fonts you specify in your XHTML document installed on their computers. This means that if you use fonts haphazardly, what you see on your screen may not be anything close to what your users see on their screens.

Although readability is a vital part of type design, most Web designers also want the ability to use different fonts to help create the desired look and feel of the site for the target audience. Different fonts, when used properly, can help focus attention on certain text on the screen, enhance readability, set a tone (serious, light-hearted), and project an image (progressive, conservative).

There are **default fonts** that come pre-installed with each operating system (such as with Windows or Mac OS). See Figure 5-2 for a list of common default fonts currently pre-installed on Windows and Macintosh computers. Unless a user has specifically deleted a default font, these default fonts will be available for displaying text on a Web page.

QUICKTIP

Use default fonts to maintain consistency and obtain a certain degree of insurance that the text will appear on the Web page as you intended.

As you work with fonts, you will probably begin to recognize which fonts are the more commonly used default fonts. You can also view the fonts installed on a specific computer from the Fonts folder on that computer. The Fonts folder is located in the Windows folder on a PC and in the System folder on a Macintosh.

QUICKTIP

Macintosh users can obtain the versions of the major Windows fonts by downloading and installing Microsoft Internet Explorer.

FIGURE 5-2

Refer to this list of common default fonts when choosing fonts to be used for text delivery on the Web

Common Default Fonts	
Arial	Helvetica
Arial Black	Monaco
Arial Narrow	MS Dialog
Arial Rounded MT Bold	MS Dialog Light
Book Antique	MS LincDraw
Bookman Old Style	MS Sans Serif
Century Gothic	MS Serif
Century Schoolbook	**MS SystemX**
Chicago	New York
Courier	Palatino
Courier New	Times
Garamond	Times New Roman
Geneva	Verdana
Georgia	

In addition, you can right-click on the font in Windows and choose Properties for additional details on the font (see Figure 5-3) or press CTRL and click on the Mac and choose Get Info.

An important consideration in selecting fonts for use on a Web page is whether the user has the same fonts available on his or her computer. From a Web designer perspective, you need to realize that all computer users will have a different set of fonts installed on their computers. Macintosh and Windows users will have a different set of installed fonts on their computers because a different set of default fonts comes with each operating system. Even users with the same platform may have different fonts installed on their computers. In addition to the operating system installing default fonts, most software programs come with default fonts that are installed when the programs are installed. Users rarely have the exact same software installed on their computers so that means available fonts vary from one computer to the next.

To further complicate matters, font sets can be downloaded from the Internet or purchased on CD. Many font designers sell or

FIGURE 5-3
The Fonts folder and Font Properties dialog box in Windows

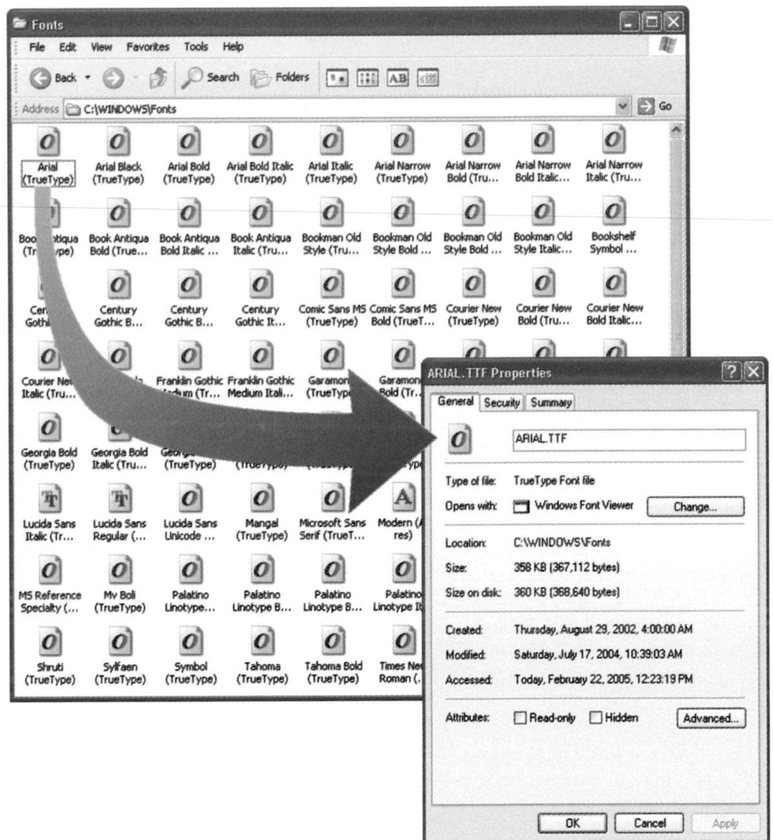

offer royalty free fonts via the Web. For example, you can purchase font sets from the Fonthead Web site shown in Figure 5-4. There are many more sites on the Web similar to Fonthead. Take time to visit some of these sites.

Although using exotic fonts can be amazingly fun and beneficial if you plan accordingly, if you use these fonts as standard Web-based text, you are asking for trouble. If you choose a font that is not on a user's computer, then, when he or she views the Web page, the system will substitute a default font. The system will try to match the developer's font with a substitute font that resembles it. Unfortunately, even a close match can have disastrous effects on the appearance of the text—for example, it might change word spacing, wrap the text inappropriately, or even alter the size of the text. Ways to minimize these potential problems are discussed later in the chapter.

> **QUICKTIP**
>
> The font tag used in HTML to control typography has been deprecated and is being replaced by Cascading Style Sheets (CSS).

Remember that fonts are original creations. If you purchase the rights to use the font, be sure to read the licensing agreements very carefully. If you do not purchase the rights to use the font, make certain it is royalty free.

FIGURE 5-4

Web sites, such as fonthead.com, sell fun and quirky font sets

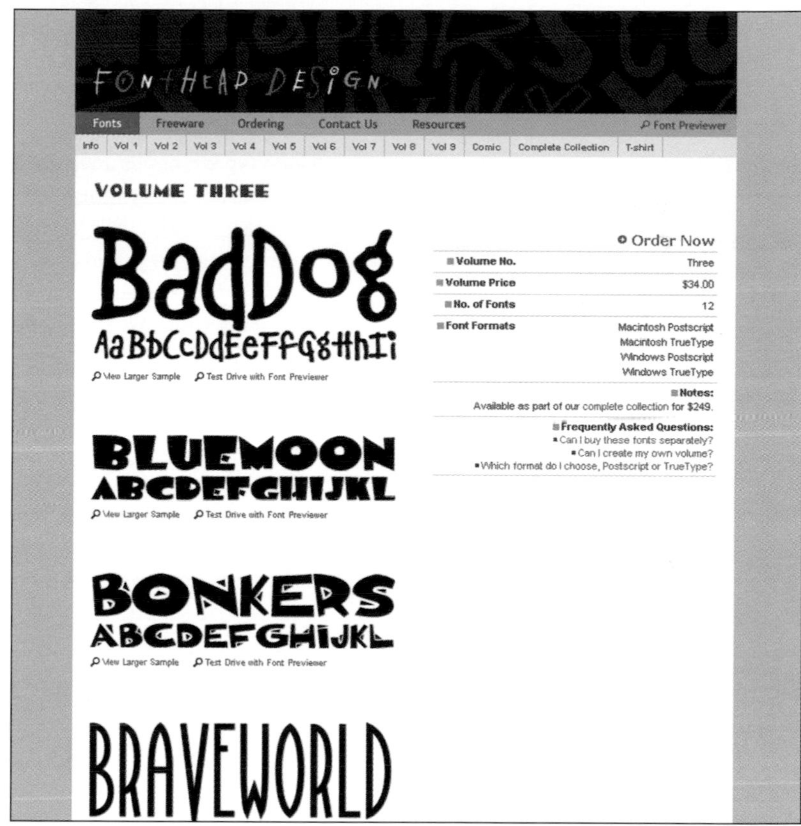

UNDERSTAND Fonts

What You'll Learn

In this lesson, you will learn about different font classifications and styles. You will also understand the importance of adjusting the font size, spacing, color, line length, and alignment of text on a Web page.

Good typography is anything but boring. There are literally thousands of fonts on the market today. Slight differences between two fonts can create vast differences in the look and feel of a Web site. There are times when it is difficult to describe what distinguishes one font from another in technical terms, yet fonts often have a certain look or feel associated with them—in much the same way that colors often have emotions associated with them. See Figure 5-5 for examples of feelings associated with fonts. Regardless of how you describe them, each one would lend an entirely different mood to a Web site.

Emphasis can be added by varying the font, including the style, size, or color used. Special effects and drop shadows can be used to give the feeling of three dimensions. The subtleties of type foster a variety of impressions and can change the entire feeling of a Web site. Look at the typography in the three examples shown in Figure 5-6. It is obvious that the fonts used in these three examples were selected in part because of the mood they create. The fonts used lend meaning to the Web sites. They communicate a feeling to the user. It is important to remember that different fonts evoke different emotional responses.

FIGURE 5-5
Each of these fonts creates a different mood

FIGURE 5-6

The typography in these examples illustrates how type helps set the mood of a Web site

Business/professional

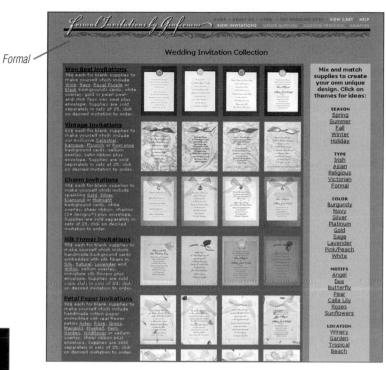

Wedding Invitation Collection

Mix and match supplies to create your own unique design. Click on themes for ideas:

SEASON: Spring, Summer, Fall, Winter, Holiday

TYPE: Irish, Asian, Religious, Victorian, Formal

COLOR: Burgundy, Navy, Silver, Platinum, Gold, Sage, Lavender, Pink/Peach, White

MOTIFS: Angel, Bee, Butterfly, Pear, Calla Lily, Roses, Sunflowers

LOCATION: Winery, Garden, Tropical, Beach

Formal

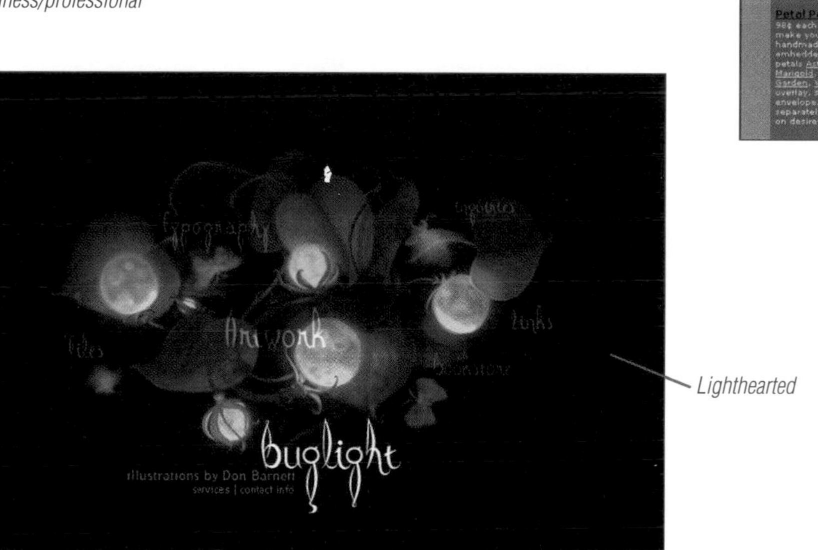

Lighthearted

Serif, Sans Serif, Decorative

Fonts are classified as either **serif**, **sans serif**, or **decorative**. As shown in Figure 5-7, serif fonts have feet or short lines at the ends of the strokes of the letter, whereas sans serif fonts do not. *Sans* means "without", so a sans serif font is one without serifs or without feet. A decorative font may have a combination of serif and sans serif fonts or it may be one that cannot be categorized either way.

Perhaps the overriding concern with text is readability. In print, serif fonts are used for long or dense bodies of texts, such as paragraphs, because, according to readability studies, serif fonts are more readable than sans serif fonts. The research indicates that the serifs create an imaginary line at the top and bottom of a text line, which helps guide the eye across the page. Generally, people in western culture are accustomed to reading text set with serif fonts because they use the little feet to track or lead their eyes along the horizontal line. Many people think serif fonts are easier to read on screen as well, however, other users believe that the serifs actually interfere with readability on the screen. Although more research needs to be done in the area of readability on the Web, there are still text guidelines, as discussed in this chapter, that you can follow to help ensure your Web pages will be readable.

Sans serif fonts do not create the imaginary line, so the eye has difficulty reading along the text line; it wants instead to leave the text line and wander through the body of text. Sans serif fonts are most often used for headings, titles, and callouts because they are more likely to draw attention. They are also considered more recognizable at a glance than serif fonts, which makes them perfect for short bits of text. This is true both in print and on the Web.

Both serif and sans serif fonts can be used on Web pages. Serif fonts tend to be more traditional fonts so they are great for Web sites designed to set a conservative tone, while sans serif fonts tend to convey a more contemporary and modern feel. Because much of our text in multimedia applications is often quite short, sans serif fonts are used extensively on multimedia Web sites.

FIGURE 5-7
Sans *means "without" so sans serif fonts are without serifs*

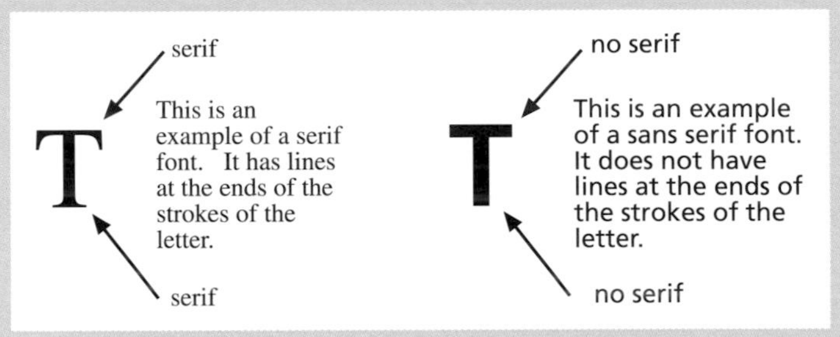

QUICKTIP

Because there are differences between serif and sans serif fonts in print versus on screen, entire font sets specifically for the Web are being created from the ground up. Generally these can be downloaded for free or for a fee.

It is acceptable, and even preferred, to use both font types on one Web page (see Figure 5-8), but it is not good practice to use too many different fonts on a single page or within a single Web site. As in print, it is best to choose one serif font and one sans serif font or two different sans serif fonts and use them consistently throughout the site. In addition, you should always test for readability and legibility. According to some Web designers, Georgia (a serif font) and Verdana (a sans serif font) tend to be more readable on screen than the commonly used Times (a serif font) and Arial (a sans serif font). See Figure 5-9 for a comparison of these fonts. Once again, however, you must remember that the font has to be installed on the user's computer in order to display on a Web page on a user's computer. If the font is not available on a user's computer, a default font will be used in its place.

FIGURE 5-8

This Web page follows the traditional recommendation from the print world—serif fonts for body copy and sans serif fonts for titles

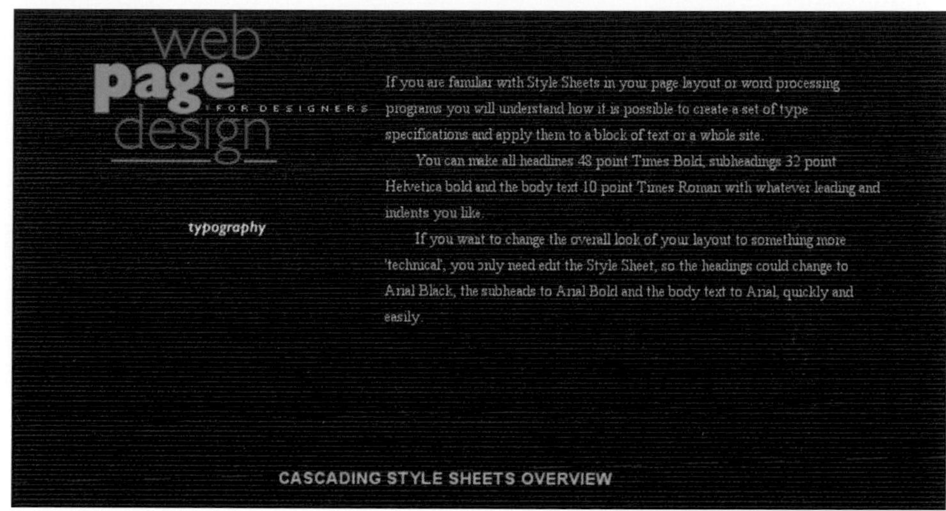

FIGURE 5-9

Comparing fonts

Serif	Sans Serif
This is an example of the Georgia font.	This is an example of the Verdana font.
This is an example of the Times font.	This is an example of the Arial font.

Monospaced vs. Proportional

Monospaced fonts are those in which each character takes up the exact same amount of horizontal space. For example, the letter "i" would take up the same amount of horizontal space as the letter "w" although it is obviously not as wide as a "w". Refer to Figure 5-10 for an example of a monospaced font. Monospaced fonts were commonly used on typewriters, and therefore they tend to appear "old-fashioned." They are rarely used on Web pages.

Most fonts used in Web pages today are **proportional fonts**. Each character takes up a varying amount of horizontal space. Because the letter "i" does not require as much space as the letter "w", it does not consume as much horizontal space. Figure 5-11 provides an example of a proportional font.

Style

There are many ways to emphasize a word or phrase, for example by using a different font, by changing the font size, or even by animating a word or phrase in a Web page. In essence, the goal of emphasizing a word or phrase is to set that specific text apart from the other text on the screen.

In the print world, designers generally draw attention to a word or phrase by applying a **style** to it. They use *italic*, **bold**, and underline to provide emphasis. On the Web, however, these three simple styles do not always achieve the same effect. For example, although the italic style works well on a printed page, italicized words pixelate (appear as a series of small dots) on a computer screen. Italicized fonts do not generally read well on screen.

QUICKTIP

You should avoid italic fonts because monitors display pixels based on a square grid, which works against slanted fonts.

Underlining has special meaning on Web pages. An underlined word or phrase usually indicates a hyperlink. Users automatically assume an underlined word or phrase can be clicked to access new information. Unless the text is a hyperlink, avoid the use of underline for emphasis or you will confuse and frustrate your users.

FIGURE 5-10
By using a monospaced font, the letters line up in columns

```
In this paragraph the letters
take up the exact same amount
of space. See how the letters
line up in columns, one below
the other?
```

FIGURE 5-11
By using a proportional font, the letters take up only the amount of horizontal space they need

In this paragraph the letters take up varying amounts of horizontal space. Consequently, the letters do not line up in columns, one below the other.

The case of the text also affects its readability. Sentence case (the first word begins with a capital letter), title case (each word begins with a capital letter), and lowercase (no word begins with a capital letter) are much easier to read than uppercase (all letters are capital letters) text. As shown in Figure 5-12, the use of all capital letters in body copy reduces the readability. This is because readers generally read by recognizing the shape of words; they do not read by examining individual letters and then assembling a recognizable word. Words created with capital letters are basically all the same size and shape, which means the shape of the words is not distinct enough to make the words easily recognizable.

FIGURE 5-12

The use of all caps in body copy reduces the readability

THE CASE OF THE TEXT ALSO AFFECTS ITS READABILITY. SENTENCE CASE, TITLE CASE, AND LOWERCASE ARE MUCH EASIER TO READ THAN UPPERCASE. WE READ BY RECOGNIZING THE SHAPE OF WORDS NOT BY EXAMINING INDIVIDUAL LETTERS AND THEN ASSEMBLING THE LETTERS INTO A RECOGNIZABLE WORD. WORDS CREATED WITH CAPITAL LETTERS ARE BASICALLY ALL THE SAME SIZE AND SHAPE. THE SHAPE OF THE WORDS ISN'T DISTINCT ENOUGH TO BE RECOGNIZABLE.

Size

Fonts are most often measured in point sizes. In print, there are 72 points per inch. Ten and 12 points are common point sizes for type displayed on a Web page. Choosing the proper point size depends on how the font is to be used—that is, as a title, as body text, and so on. Text that appears as a title at the top of a screen may be relatively large, whereas text that is used on a button might be quite small. Some guidelines regarding font size follow:

Use	Point Size
Headings	14–48
Subheadings	Half the heading size, with a minimum that is not smaller than the body text
Body text	10–12

Headings and subheadings are used to attract attention and provide the user with quick identification of the screen content, while body text provides the substance. Subheadings must never be smaller than the body text.

A font with a specific size assigned to it may look different from one computer monitor to the next because the resolution of the user's computer monitor, as well as the operating system installed on the computer, impacts how the font size is rendered on the final Web page. Text displayed on a monitor that is set to a higher resolution will appear smaller than text displayed on a monitor that is set to a lower resolution. In addition, type displayed in a Web browser on a Windows computer will look two to three points larger than it will on a Macintosh computer. This difference in font rendering can have a major impact on your Web pages, particularly the layout of Web pages. This difference is most notable when you are laying out your multimedia elements as the text may wrap unexpectedly forcing the layout to break down. It is important to test your Web pages on different monitors set to different resolutions, as well as on computers running different operating systems.

Although it may be tempting and certainly easy to use a variety of fonts, sizes, and styles, it is important to exercise restraint and to be consistent. Avoid too many font sizes and styles on one Web page. In addition, try to maintain consistency. For example, if several Web pages have a similar heading, use the same font, size, and style for all of the headings at this same level.

Spacing

Kerning is the term used to specify the amount of space between characters. Figure 5-13 shows some character pairs before and after kerning has been applied. **Leading** is the amount of space between lines of text. Kerning and leading are important in making text readable and are somewhat dependent on the font size and how the text will be used on the Web page.

Unlike familiar commands used in desktop publishing software to adjust character and line spacing for printed material, adjusting the spacing between characters and lines in an HTML document was a nightmare. In fact, there were no HTML tags available to adjust leading and spacing. As a result, many Web designers learned to use other tags to trick the HTML code into doing what they wanted it to do. These tricks included the use of tables and invisible graphics set to any number of pixels high or wide, which they would insert into a Web page to control spacing.

Fortunately, with newer Web technologies, such as Cascading Style Sheets (CSS) and features in Web authoring programs, kerning and leading of text used on Web pages is not only possible but extremely precise and easy to deploy. With CSS, Web designers can use the **letter-spacing property** to control kerning and the **line-height property** to control leading. These properties use a number of different **relative** or **absolute length units**, as shown in Figure 5-14, to create precise placement of text. A **length unit** is used to define the length of an object. Relative length units define the length of the object relative to another property, such as the size of the font. Absolute length units are dependent on the viewing medium (monitor resolution, for example) and are useful only if you know the properties of the viewing medium. In general, using relative units rather than absolute units provides a better design because there are no assumptions about screen resolution and window size.

FIGURE 5-13

Proper kerning makes text more readable

Unkerned pairs	AT	AY	Fo	Jo	Ke	To	Ve	Wo	r,	y,	115
Kerned pairs	AT	AY	Fo	Jo	Ke	To	Ve	Wo	r,	y,	115

FIGURE 5-14

Web designers use relative or absolute length in CSS to precisely control character and line spacing

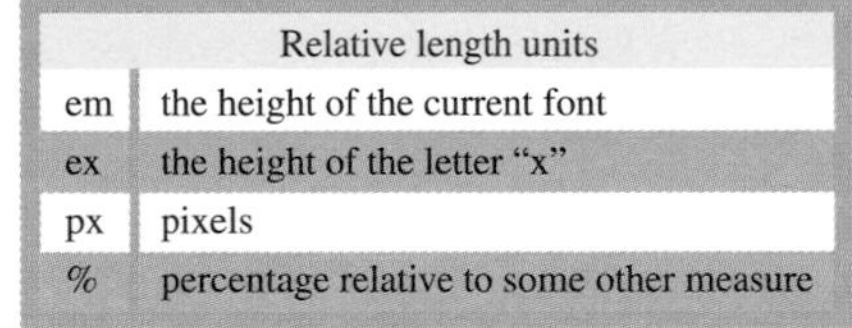

Relative length units	
em	the height of the current font
ex	the height of the letter "x"
px	pixels
%	percentage relative to some other measure

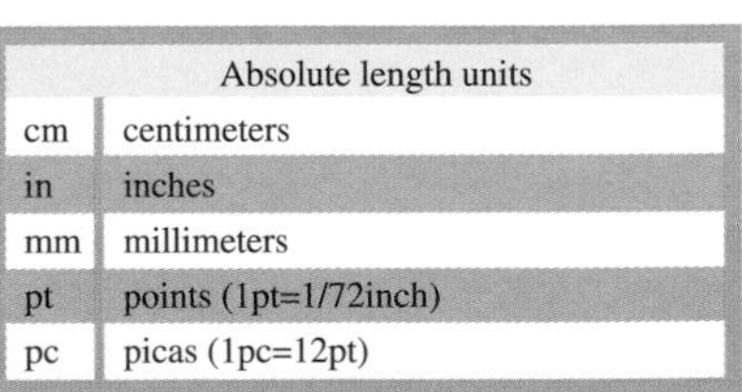

Absolute length units	
cm	centimeters
in	inches
mm	millimeters
pt	points (1pt=1/72inch)
pc	picas (1pc=12pt)

Color

Anything that deviates from the norm creates emphasis by causing a visual disturbance—the greater the visual disturbance, the greater the emphasis. Look at the Web site in Figure 5-15 and pay attention to what grabs your attention and where your eye travels as you look at this page. Does color impact your eye movement?

It is extremely important that you make your text readable. Good typography depends on the visual contrast between fonts, as well as the contrast between body text and white space. Strong contrast attracts the eye and engages the brain of the viewer. Creating strong contrast, however, requires careful design. It is very disturbing to encounter text on the Web set in a color that does not have enough contrast with the background color to make it readable. Text color can also be used to create a hierarchy of importance. Provided the other characteristics of the type are identical, text set in a color that has a greater contrast to the background than other text on the page will be noticed first. Which text color in Figure 5-16 do you notice first?

FIGURE 5-15

On a Web page, color can be applied to text for emphasis

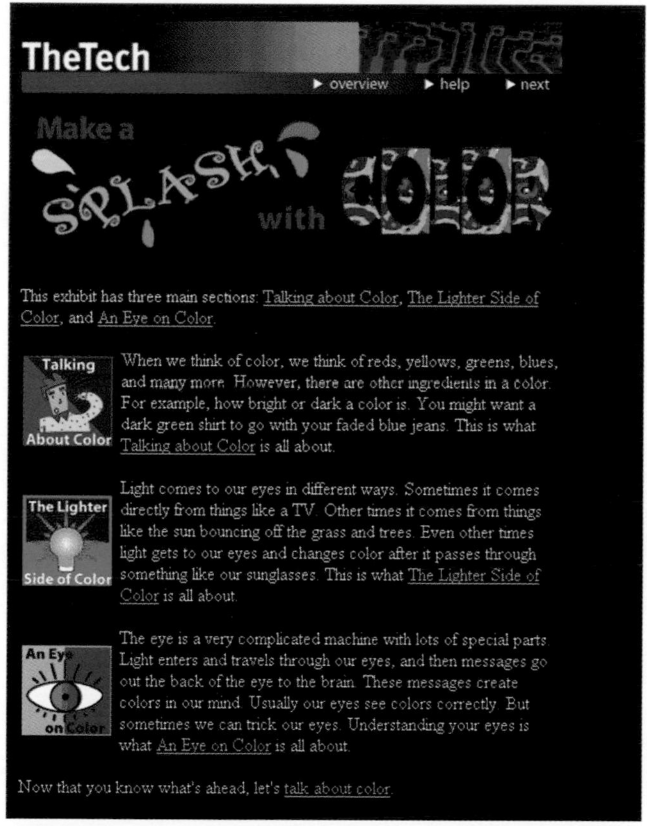

Along with the other colors used to design a Web site, color applied to text contributes to the overall mood and tone of the site. Color also conveys messages, impacts creativity, and influences responsiveness. A great deal of research has been compiled on color. Before you begin applying color to your type, it would definitely be worthwhile to review some of this research. Color scheme palettes, tools, and software are available to assist you in choosing just the right color for the fonts on your Web site.

FIGURE 5-16

The greater the contrast between the type color and the background, the more the type will be noticed

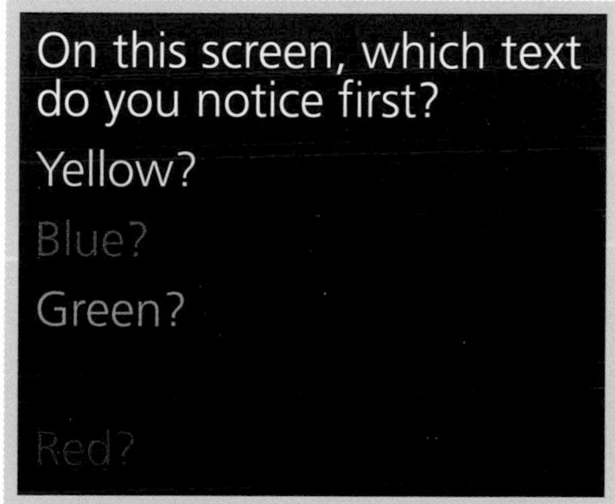

For example, some programs provide an eyedropper tool that lets you pick up the color in an object, such as a corporate logo, so the program can analyze the color and provide the **hexadecimal values** from the base-16 numbering system (see Figure 5-17) used to reference color on a Web page.

> **QUICKTIP**
>
> Adding color to text on your Web page does not cost a dime. Consider adding color to your text to create emphasis and to contribute to the mood of the piece.

If you are working with clients, you may find that they have established corporate colors that they would like to use for the text on their Web site. They might be surprised to learn that the colors they have selected may not display the same on a Web page as they do in print. There are many reasons for color variations that occur including the computer's video card, monitor, and platform. For example, the **gamma settings** influence how bright items on the screen appear and the gamma settings vary from platform to platform. The gamma settings on Macs are lower than they are on PCs, which makes color on Macintosh computers appear brighter. To further complicate the Web designer's life, even within the same platform no two monitors are calibrated the same. Remember that there are no absolutes and that testing the colors you choose on your Web sites is of utmost importance.

Alignment

Layout and alignment are important typographic considerations. In fact, when your content is primarily text, typography is used to create patterns of organization on the page. The first thing your reader will notice is the overall pattern and contrast of the Web page, not the title or the details. The user will scan your Web page in an effort to quickly organize the information and increase legibility.

Text can be left aligned, right aligned, center aligned, and justified. In general, body text is left aligned. Attempting to align text using markup tags was once an extremely painful process because HTML was not designed for layout. It was designed for cross-platform transmission of simple text. However, using Cascading Style Sheets, Web designers now have the control they need to follow basic design principles for aligning text.

> **QUICKTIP**
>
> In general, you should not center align body text because it is difficult to read. Center alignment should primarily be reserved for titles, headings, and callouts.

FIGURE 5-17

The six-digit hexadecimal value is used to reference color on a Web page

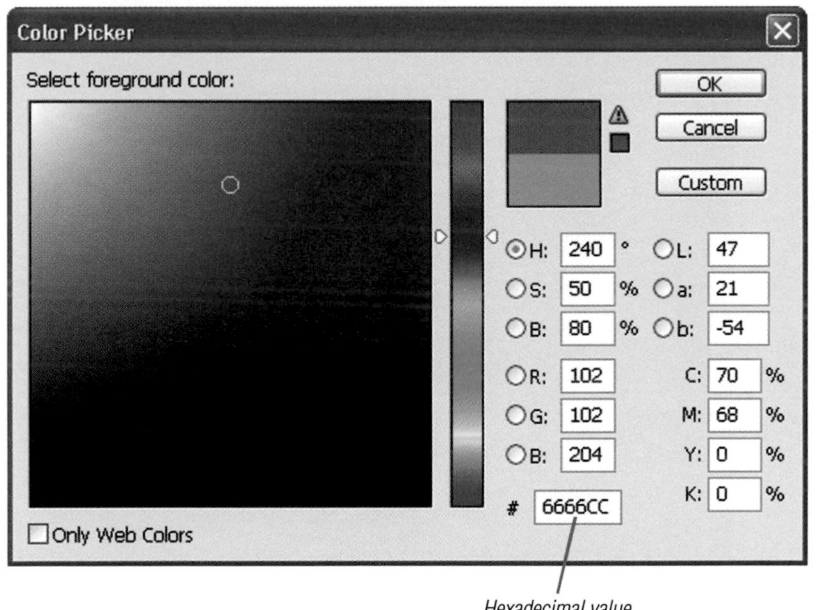

Line Length

Many Web pages include lines of text that are much too long. Long lines of text are difficult to read. This is because many Web pages are almost twice as wide as the viewer's eye can span naturally, which is about 3 inches. If you look at magazines and newspapers, you will notice that the text is almost always organized into narrow columns. This is because columns are more readable. Print designers try to keep long passages of text in columns no wider than the reader's comfortable eye span, and the guideline is the same for the layout of long passages of text on the Web. Compare the readability between the two passages of text in Figure 5-18. If you are like most people, you will find the text set in narrower columns to be more readable.

In traditional print layout, it is recommended that designers allow for 30 to 40 characters per line. On the Web, your lines can be slightly longer. Although it is sometimes difficult to predict the exact number of characters per line due to variations in display across different platforms and browsers, setting a goal of approximately 50 characters per line should help you create an acceptable line length for reading text on screen.

QUICKTIP

Creating shorter lines of text will encourage your Web site visitors to read an online document instead of printing it or avoiding it altogether.

FIGURE 5-18

Narrow columns of text are easier to read online just as they are easier to read in print

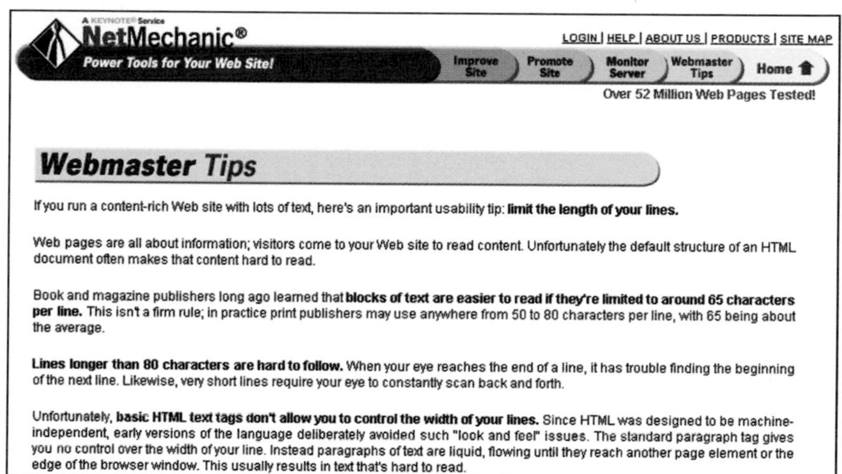

Wide column

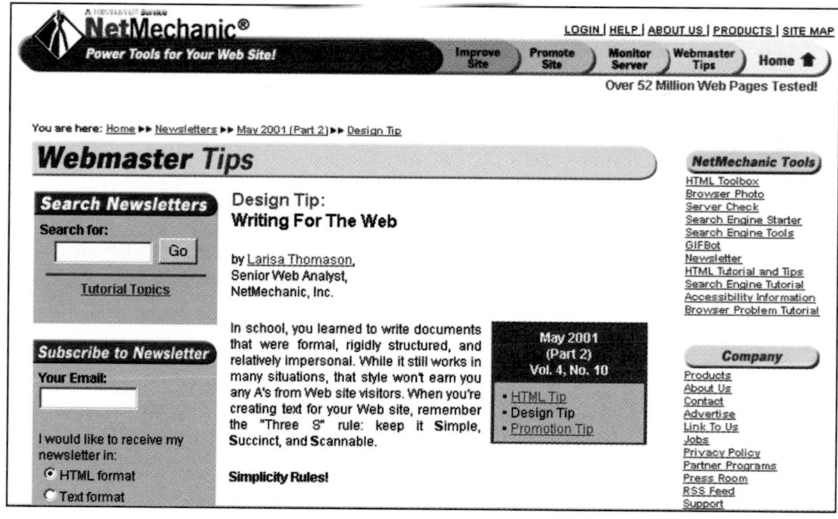

Narrow column

CONCEPT 3

DEFINE CASCADING Style Sheets (CSS)

What You'll Learn

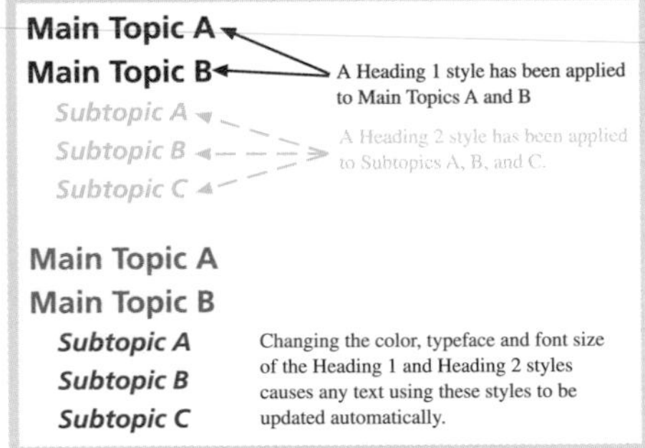
Main Topic A
Main Topic B
A Heading 1 style has been applied to Main Topics A and B
Subtopic A
Subtopic B
Subtopic C
A Heading 2 style has been applied to Subtopics A, B, and C.
Main Topic A
Main Topic B
Subtopic A
Subtopic B
Subtopic C
Changing the color, typeface and font size of the Heading 1 and Heading 2 styles causes any text using these styles to be updated automatically.

*In this lesson, you will learn about the four different types of **Cascading Style Sheets (CSS)**—inline, embedded, linked, and imported. You will also learn about some of the advantages of using CSS to design Web sites.*

If you have ever used styles in a word processing or desktop publishing program then you know how useful they can be, particularly when you are working with large volumes of text or many pages with similar formatting. A Cascading Style Sheet is similar to a style used in a word processing program in that it defines the appearance of the text on a Web page. When the Cascading Style Sheet is applied to a Web page, the Web page displays the text and other style formats based on the information in the style sheet. For example, as shown in Figure 5-19, using CSS you can create a style named Heading with a font of Georgia, a font size of 48 points, and a .5 inch indent from both sides. Rather than applying these specifications to eachheading in your Web page or Web site, you apply the Heading style that includes these specifications. If you later decide that you prefer Times, Bold, 36 point, no indent instead of Georgia, 48 point, indent, you need only to modify the Heading style and the changes you make will cascade through the Web page or the entire Web site depending on the type of style sheet used. After changing the style sheet, all headings will appear in Times, Bold, 36 point, no indent.

Fortunately for Web designers, improvements in Web authoring programs and the inclusion of CSS have made many typography features more palatable, more predictable, and much easier to develop and modify. CSS is a set of type specifications that can be applied to a block of text, a single Web page, or an entire Web site. With CSS, you can control basic typographic needs, such as font, leading, kerning, font size, color, and alignment, which gives you control over how your text is displayed.

As explained earlier, even using CSS, you will still be restricted by the availability of fonts on the user's system. However, CSS can save development time and effort by automatically modifying any text to which a style has been applied. Web designers can apply CSS to all pages on a Web site or to selected pages or even selected sections of pages within a Web site so that the formatting is applied consistently in the desired areas. Using CSS provides consistency of style throughout a Web site and enables the Web designer to update all pages of a Web site simultaneously simply by modifying the style sheet. In addition to making global changes, it is also possible to deliver the same content with different specifications according to the browser used. This makes it possible to optimize the user experience by calling for a different set of styles to be used based on the browser in which the Web page is displayed.

There are four different types of CSS (inline, embedded, linked, and imported), each with its own benefits depending on your goals as well as the type of Web site you are creating.

FIGURE 5-19

A style contains type specifications, such as font, color, and size; modifying the style causes any text using that style to change

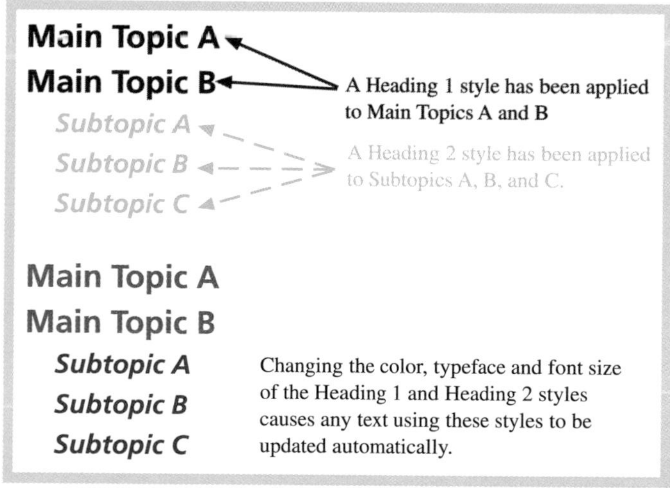
Main Topic A
Main Topic B
A Heading 1 style has been applied to Main Topics A and B
Subtopic A
Subtopic B
Subtopic C
A Heading 2 style has been applied to Subtopics A, B, and C.
Main Topic A
Main Topic B
Subtopic A
Subtopic B
Subtopic C
Changing the color, typeface and font size of the Heading 1 and Heading 2 styles causes any text using these styles to be updated automatically.

Inline

When you insert a style sheet in the middle of your markup code, the style is considered an **inline style**. An example of an inline style is shown in Figure 5-20.

The biggest disadvantage of inline styles is that they have to be added to each tag you want to modify. Inline styles are not as powerful as the other types of CSS. However, you can use more than one type of style within a Web site, so you might use an inline style to override another type of style. The power of using styles comes from combining them.

FIGURE 5-20

Inline styles must be applied each time they are used

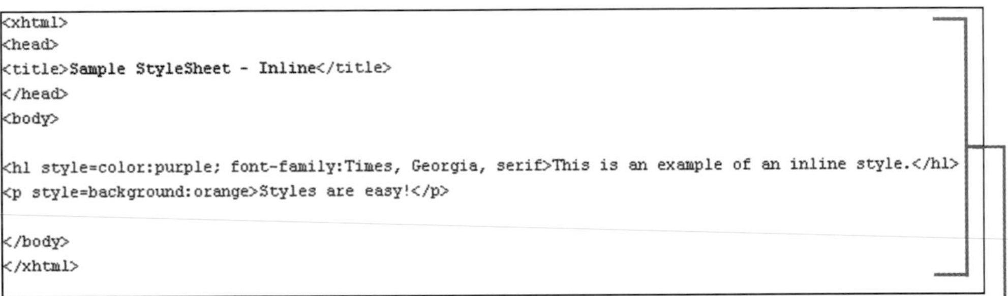

```
<xhtml>
<head>
<title>Sample StyleSheet - Inline</title>
</head>
<body>

<hl style=color:purple; font-family:Times, Georgia, serif>This is an example of an inline style.</hl>
<p style=background:orange>Styles are easy!</p>

</body>
</xhtml>
```

CSS code in XHTML file directly before text the style will be applied to

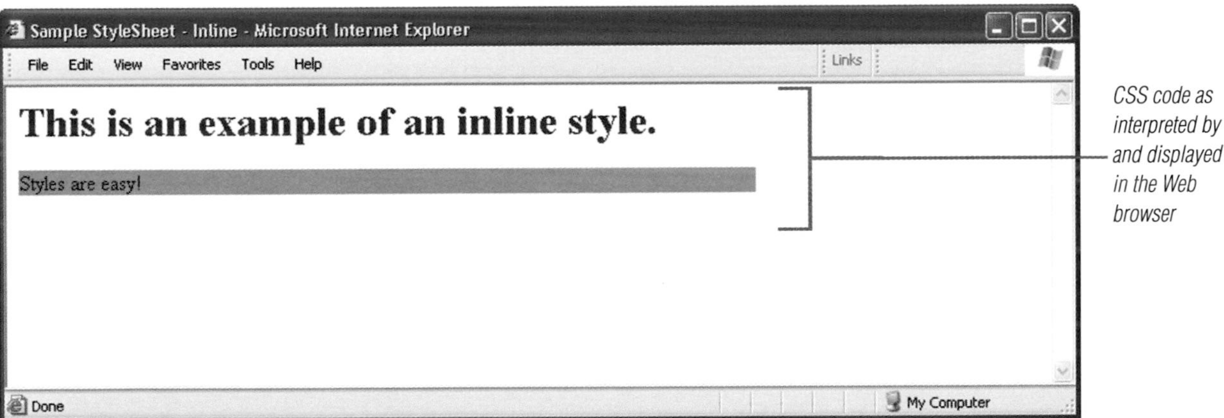

Embedded

When you use an **embedded** or **internal style** all of the style information appears at the top of the XHTML document in the <head> section of the XHTML file, and it is separate from the <body> of the XHTML code (see Figure 5-21). Code in the <head> section of an XHTML file is applied to the entire file. Browsers recognize and use the styles from an embedded style sheet throughout the entire Web page. The style type="text/css" attribute and the comment tags (<!-- and -->) allow older browsers that do not support CSS to ignore the style sheet code. Web page designers use embedded styles when they want to add style sheets one page at a time.

FIGURE 5-21

Embedded style sheet code appears at the top of the XHTML document in the <head> section

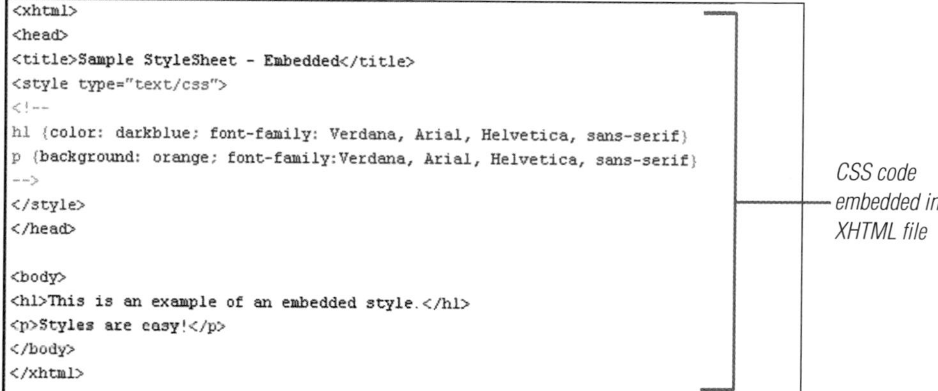

```
<xhtml>
<head>
<title>Sample StyleSheet - Embedded</title>
<style type="text/css">
<!--
h1 {color: darkblue; font-family: Verdana, Arial, Helvetica, sans-serif}
p {background: orange; font-family:Verdana, Arial, Helvetica, sans-serif}
-->
</style>
</head>

<body>
<h1>This is an example of an embedded style.</h1>
<p>Styles are easy!</p>
</body>
</xhtml>
```


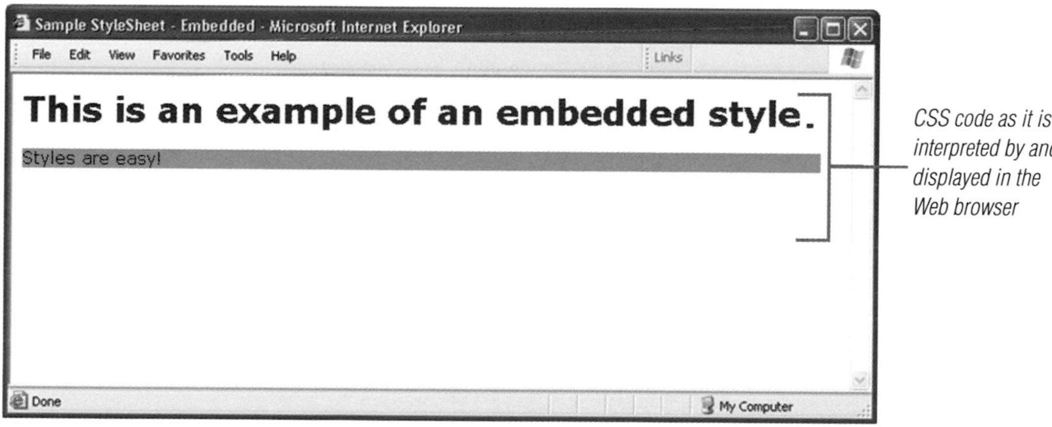

Linked

Linked styles are more powerful than inline or embedded styles. Linked styles are sometimes called **external styles**. Unlike embedded styles where the style code is inserted within the <head> section of each XHTML document one page at a time, linked styles direct multiple XHTML files to one common style sheet document. This external or linked file contains the specifications that will be used for all Web pages linked to the external style sheet. If you modify any detail of any style in the external style sheet file, all of the Web pages linked to that file will instantly reflect the change. Figure 5-22 provides an example of an external style sheet (named sitestyles.css), how the linked style sheet is referenced from within the XHTML file, and how the code is interpreted and displayed by the browser.

Any Web page can use the <link> tag to link the Web page to an external style sheet and the style specifications within it. There is no limit to the number of Web pages that can be linked to an external CSS file. This feature is priceless in maintaining a large site.

Imported

There is a fourth method of applying a style sheet to your pages. A style sheet may be **imported** with the @import statement, which may be used in a .css file or inside the <style> tag. In some ways a linked style sheet and an imported style sheet are very similar, but there is one major difference between them. By importing an external style sheet, you get the benefits of linking and you can use the other types of styles as well. This allows you to use one style sheet that you can override using inline, embedded, and linked styles.

FIGURE 5-22
Code in the <head> section of a Web page links the Web page to an external style sheet, which contains all the style specifications for the Web page and all other Web pages in the Web site that contain a link to the same external style sheet

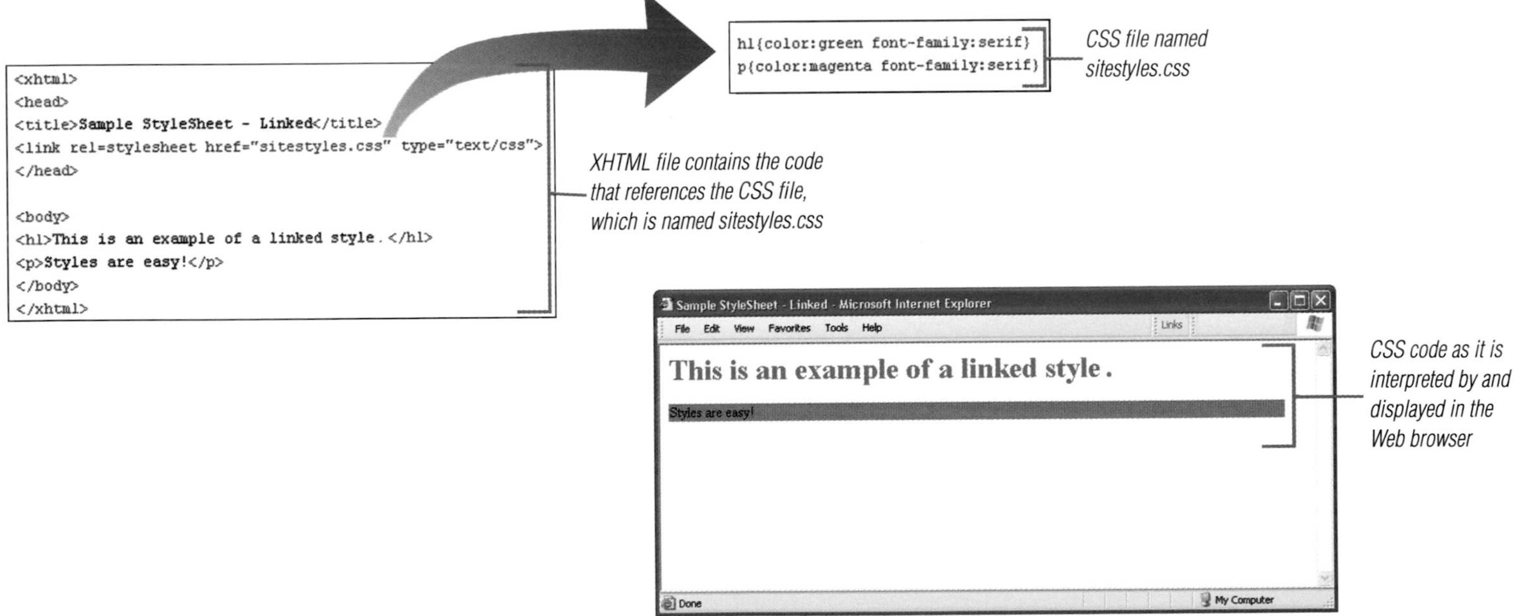

h1{color:green font-family:serif}
p{color:magenta font-family:serif}
CSS file named sitestyles.css
<xhtml>
<head>
<title>Sample StyleSheet - Linked</title>
<link rel=stylesheet href="sitestyles.css" type="text/css">
</head>
<body>
<h1>This is an example of a linked style.</h1>
<p>Styles are easy!</p>
</body>
</xhtml>
XHTML file contains the code that references the CSS file, which is named sitestyles.css
Sample StyleSheet - Linked - Microsoft Internet Explorer
File Edit View Favorites Tools Help
Links
This is an example of a linked style.
Styles are easy!
Done
My Computer
CSS code as it is interpreted by and displayed in the Web browser

To view the code used to import a CSS, see Figure 5-23.

When multiple styles are used, the browser determines the order of importance according to the official specification of CSS. The order of importance is as follows:

1. Inline styles
2. Embedded styles
3. Linked styles
4. Imported styles
5. Default browser styles

This means that inline styles override embedded styles, which override linked styles, and so on. It is important to know this order because if you use a linked style sheet and then use inline styles, the linked style sheet will be ignored and the inline styles applied.

Cascading Style Sheets are an incredible tool. They provide control over the layout of Web pages. They allow Web designers and developers to quickly, efficiently, and consistently modify and maintain large Web sites. They can be used to customize the user experience through a design that is browser-friendly as well as browser-specific. And because the style specifications can be in an external file, CSS files can be used to create smaller XHTML files that are quick to download.

The biggest disadvantage to using CSS is that older browsers do not support CSS and therefore, as with any other Web page design technology, you need to test your Web site on as many different computers and browsers as possible.

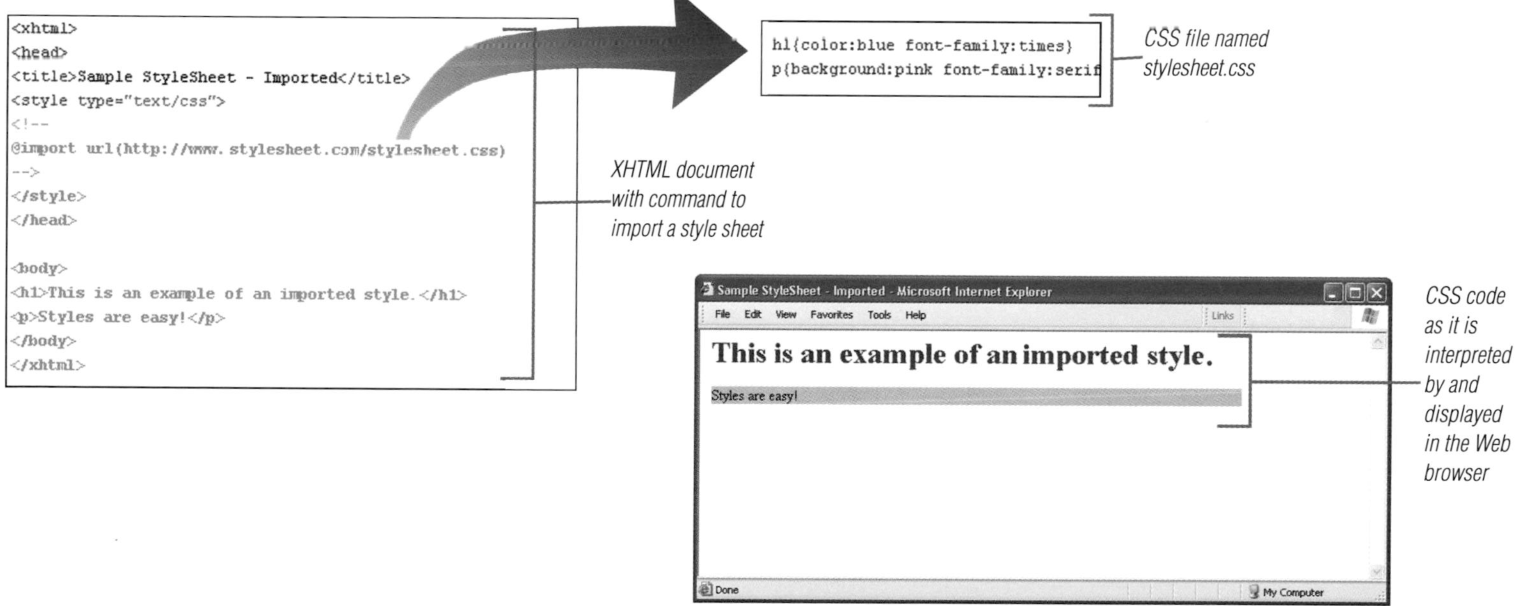

FIGURE 5-23
A CSS may be imported with the @import statement

CONCEPT 4

EXPLAIN ADDITIONAL OPTIONS for Implementing Text on the Web

What You'll Learn

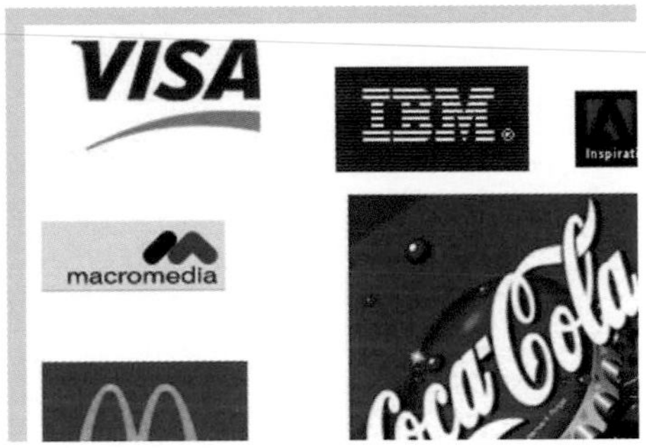

In this lesson, you will learn about the advantages and disadvantages of using graphic-based typography and Portable Document Format (PDF) files on your Web pages.

There are times when the multimedia Web site must include a great deal of text—for example, in reference Web sites such as encyclopedias. Combining other elements with text can often reduce the amount of text needed to convey a concept. There are ways to accommodate large amounts of text without overwhelming the user.

- First, consider if there are other ways to communicate the message. For instance, can you show an animation or use narration rather than text to present the idea?
- Second, consider including a small amount of text and then allowing the user to obtain more information as desired via a hyperlink (see Figure 5-24). A hyperlink, allows the user to select a button (or word, graphic, or other element) that "jumps" or connects to another Web page or an entirely different Web site where more text and other information about the concept is presented.
- Third, consider using drop-down boxes with scroll bars and list arrows, which will display more text when clicked by the user. See Figure 5-25.

In addition to those just named, there are other options and technologies that enable Web designers to work with larger amounts of text, have better control over the text, and have greater assurance that the text will display on the Web page as the Web designer intended. Those options are discussed next.

FIGURE 5-24

A hyperlink can be used to display additional text

The Web page on the left has a minimal amount of text, which is used to describe each link. The Web page on the right shows the text that appears when the link in the Web page on the left is clicked.

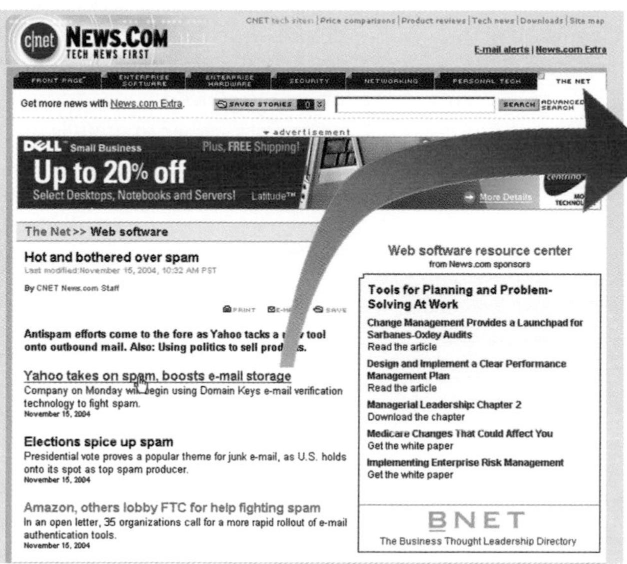

This Web page has the expanded story, that is, the full text associated with the link.

FIGURE 5-25

Text boxes can be used to save screen real estate and accommodate larger amounts of text

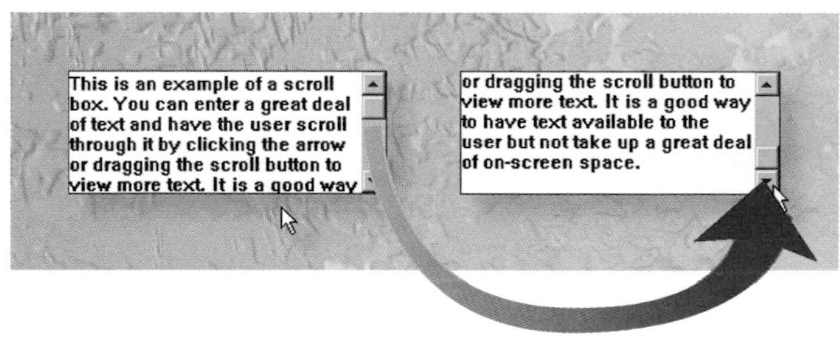

Drag the scroll box to read the text

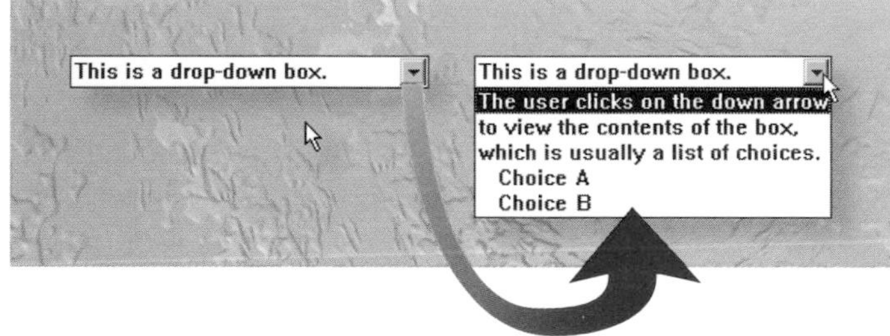

Click the down list arrow to show the drop-down menu

Graphic-based Typography

The Web may be the only text-based medium in which designers do not have complete control over the appearance of type. Although CSS helps control some of the uncertainties of text on the Web, it is still no help if a requested font is not on the user's computer. One way to ensure that text will be displayed in a specific format is to change the text into an image—that is, to create the text and save it as a graphic.

There are problems with this approach. For example, more development time is often needed, which increases development costs. In addition, graphic files are much larger than text files, which may increase download time. Obviously converting entire paragraphs of body copy to graphics would be an unreasonable proposition, however, converting text such as that used in logos, headings, and titles to graphics works great. In fact, this is one of the best options to use if you really must have a particular font. As seen in Figure 5-26, a particular font is often associated with a logo. Converting the logo to a graphic ensures the company branding will not be altered in any way.

QUICKTIP

Provided you can keep the file size down to a few kilobytes, consider turning stylized type into a graphic and saving it in one of the graphic file formats supported on the Web.

In addition to creating a larger file, there is one other disadvantage to using graphics instead of XHTML-based text. The vision-impaired and site visitors who may be using text-only browsers, or individuals who have their browsers set so that they do not display graphics, will not be able to see or read your graphic-based type. If you choose to convert your text to graphics, always remember to include alternate text that can be read by a screen reader.

Portable Document Format

The **Portable Document Format (PDF)** was developed so documents could be transported and viewed without the requirement that the users viewing the documents own or have access to the software with which the document was created. In order for this to work, users need a reader that allows them to view the document in its original layout with all of the proper fonts and

FIGURE 5-26

Because the font used in most company logos is important, company logos are usually converted to graphic-based type for use on the Web

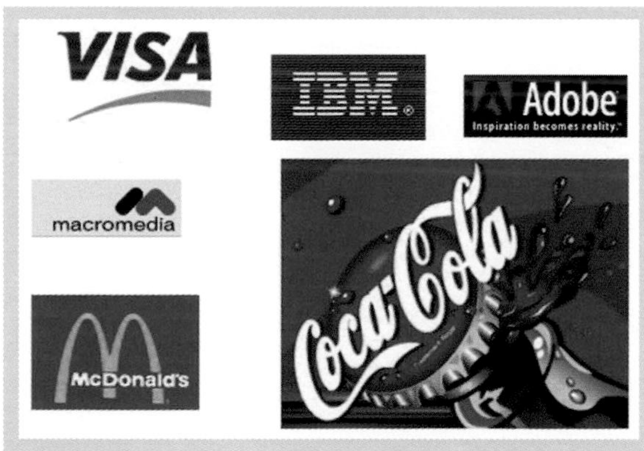

graphics. PDF readers can handle any font and any layout. PDF files can be viewed from any type of computer. This makes this file format extremely versatile.

Portable document software enables you to create, edit, and read PDF files. Many traditional document file formats, such as Microsoft Word or Adobe InDesign files, can be converted to a PDF format. Adobe Acrobat is the most common portable document application and reader used on the Web. The reader is available as a free download from Adobe, as shown in Figure 5-27. In addition, up-to-date versions of most browsers include the Adobe Reader plug-in, which enables users to save PDF files and view them offline or view them directly in the browser window provided the Acrobat Reader plug-in is available and has been properly configured in the Web browser. Thoughtful designers who have included PDF files on their Web sites should also include a direct link to the address from which the Adobe Reader can be downloaded.

Although the PDF file format was available long before the Web, it has become incredibly popular on the Web because of its versatility and the fact that it uses a reader, which helps guarantee that the original document will be seen by the user as it was intended. It is particularly popular for distributing forms and other documents that require specialized styles.

Although the PDF format is an incredible technology for delivering content via the Web, it is not a replacement for XHTML nor is it the best option for traditional online delivery. If the reader is not already available, it will have to be downloaded and installed. This can be time-consuming and confusing for beginners. In addition, unlike content within XHTML files, spider-based search engines do not automatically catalog the contents of PDF files. This means that the content within a PDF is not likely to be returned as a hit from a keyword search in a spider-based search engine. The PDF format is not a substitute for XHTML content, but it is a great option for distributing any file that needs to maintain its original formatting or that might need to be printed.

FIGURE 5-27
The Adobe Reader is available as a free download

Adobe Reader

Free software to view and print Adobe PDF files

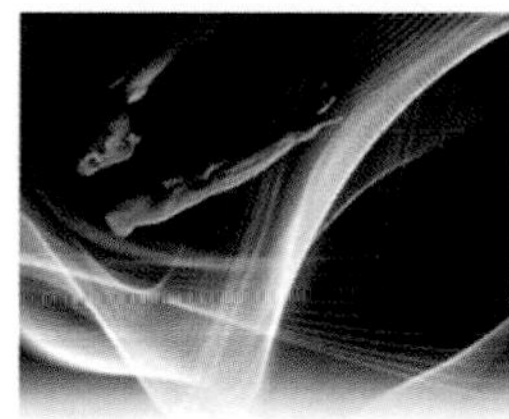

Adobe® Reader® 6.0 is free software that lets you view and print Adobe Portable Document Format (PDF) files on a variety of devices and operating systems. This new version of the familiar Adobe Acrobat® Reader provides a host of rich features that enable you to:

- Submit Adobe PDF forms that are created with fillable form fields in such applications as Adobe Acrobat 6.0 Professional and Adobe Designer
- Play back a variety of embedded multimedia content, such as QuickTime and MP3 files
- Read and organize high-fidelity eBooks
- Activate search and accessibility capabilities built into your PDF files
- Display Adobe Photoshop® Album slide shows and electronic cards and export images for online photo processing (online photo services vary regionally)

Other Reader products

Adobe Reader for Palm OS
View PDF files on your Palm OS device.

Acrobat Reader for Pocket PC
View PDF files on your Pocket PC device.

Acrobat Reader for Symbian OS
View Adobe PDF files on your Nokia Communicator 9210/9290 device.

Highlights

Find out why InfoWorld says "Adobe PDF has become the gold standard for electronic documents."

Adobe Reader inducted into CNET Download.com's Hall of Fame
New program recognizes "...the most popular, high-quality, and time-tested software products in its online software library."
- Read the CNET press release.

SUMMARY

Typography denotes the communication of a message using **typefaces**. Although good typography is as important on a Web page as it is on paper, print typography and Web typography are entirely different. Unlike the print medium, the Web is an elastic medium and the text must work across different computer platforms, screen sizes, and font sets. **Fonts** affect readability and visual interest. Fonts usually belong to a **font family**.

There are many issues that Web designers must understand in their ongoing effort to control type on the Web. Not all users will have the same fonts on their computers so you must specify fonts with caution. **Default fonts** come pre-installed with the operating system software and, unless the user has deleted one, these fonts should be available to display on a Web page.

There are thousands of fonts on the market today. Fonts are classified in a variety of different ways, such as **serif**, **sans serif**, or **decorative**. Serif fonts have short lines at the ends of the strokes of the letter. In the print world, serif fonts are generally used for larger bodies of text because they are considered more readable, however, some Web designers believe they are actually harder to read on screen. Sans serif fonts do not have short lines at the ends of the strokes and tend to be considered contemporary and quicker to recognize than serif fonts.

Fonts are also classified as **monospaced** or **proportional**. Monospaced fonts are those in which each character takes up the exact same amount of horizontal space. Most computer fonts are proportional, which means that each character takes up a varying amount of horizontal space.

Some of the typical **styles** applied to fonts used in print are unacceptable on the Web. For example, the italic style pixelates on the computer screen and the use of italics should be avoided. Because underlining on a Web page generally indicates a hyperlink, the use of underlines for emphasis or as a font style should be avoided and reserved for hyperlinks. If you use underlining on text that is not a hyperlink, you will frustrate and confuse your readers. Case is also important on Web pages. The use of all capital letters should be avoided because the shape of words typed in uppercase is not distinct enough to be recognized easily.

Type size is also important. Choosing the proper font size depends on how the font is to be used, that is, as a title, as body text, and so on. The same size font may look different from one computer monitor to the next. The resolution of the user's computer monitor as well as the operating system installed on the computer will impact how the font size is rendered on the final Web page. This difference in font rendering can have a major impact on the layout of your Web pages.

Kerning is the term used to specify the amount of space between characters. **Leading** is the amount of space between lines of text. Controlling the spacing on a Web page is challenging if you are using basic HTML. XHTML supports **Cascading Style Sheets (CSS)**, which makes it possible and much easier to control how text looks through the use of the **letter-spacing property** and the **line-height property**, both of which permit the use of either **absolute** or **relative length units**. A **length unit** is used to define the length of an object.

Contrasts between text colors can be used to create emphasis, as well as a hierarchy of importance. In addition, color contributes to the mood of a piece as well as its psychological impact. The use of color should be carefully researched and analyzed before its **hexadecimal value** is used on a Web page. If clients want corporate colors included on a Web site, you may need to help them understand that the colors may not display the same on a Web page as they do in print. **Gamma settings**, computer platform, and monitor calibration will impact how the color appears on screen.

Long lines of text are difficult to read. A viewer's natural eye span is about 3 inches. To make longer passages of text more readable on a Web page use columns with lines that are approximately 50 characters long. Layout and alignment are important typographic considerations. The first thing your reader will notice is the overall pattern and contrast of the Web page. HTML was not designed for layout, but Cascading Style Sheets make it possible for Web designers to control text alignment.

More recent technologies enable Web designers to work with larger amounts of text, have better control over text, and have greater assurance that the text will display on the Web page as intended. Cascading Style Sheets (CSS) have made many type design features more palatable, more predictable, and much easier to develop and modify. CSS are a set of type specifications that can be applied to a block of text, a single Web page, or an entire Web site. There are four different types of CSS including **inline**, **embedded** (also called **internal**), **linked** (also called **external**), and **imported**. Each type has its own benefits depending on your goals, as well as the type of Web site you are creating.

Another way to control typography on the Web is to convert text to graphics. Because graphic files are much larger than text files, converting entire paragraphs of body copy to a graphic is unreasonable. However, converting logos, headings, and titles to graphics works great. This is one of the best options to use if you really must have a particular font.

The **Portable Document Format (PDF)** enables users to view a document using a reader that maintains the document's original layout with all of the proper fonts and graphics included. Because these files are not dependent on a browser to interpret XHTML, documents displayed in a PDF reader look as they were designed to look. PDF files can handle any font and any layout. They can be viewed from any type of computer, which makes this file format extremely versatile. There are a few pitfalls to it, however. The reader may have to be downloaded and installed for the document to be read. In addition, content within PDF files may not be found by spider-based search engines using a keyword search. Like many Web technologies, PDF files are not designed as a replacement for XHTML but an enhancement to it. When you need a guarantee that your page will appear as you designed it or you have a long document that users might be inclined to print, PDF files are a perfect option. PFD files are created using **portable document software**. Adobe Acrobat and Adobe Reader are two popular PDF programs.

KEY TERMS

absolute length unit
Cascading Style Sheets (CSS)
decorative
default font
embedded style
external style
font
font family
gamma settings
hexadecimal value
imported style
inline style
internal style
kerning
leading
length unit
letter-spacing property
line-height property
linked style
monospaced font
Portable Document Format (PDF)
portable document software
proportional font
relative length unit
sans serif
serif
style
typeface
typography

MATCHING QUESTIONS/DISCUSSION QUESTIONS

Match each term with the sentence that best describes it.

a. CSS	**b.** default	**c.** font
d. internal	**e.** italics	**f.** kerning
g. leading	**h.** monospaced	**i.** PDF
j. relative	**k.** sans serif	**l.** serif
m. typeface	**n.** typography	**o.** underline

_____ **1.** Fonts that come pre-installed with the operating system on the user's computer.

_____ **2.** A set of characters that all follow the same rules within the set.

_____ **3.** Fonts that have feet or short lines at the ends of the strokes of each letter.

_____ **4.** Fonts in which each character takes up the exact same amount of horizontal space.

_____ **5.** Style that should be avoided because it pixelates on the computer screen.

_____ **6.** Fonts that are generally considered more contemporary and modern.

_____ **7.** Style that should be reserved for hyperlinks.

_____ **8.** The art of arranging letterforms in space in any medium.

_____ **9.** The amount of space between characters.

_____ **10.** The amount of space between lines of text.

_____ **11.** File format that requires a reader in order to be displayed.

_____ **12.** Set of type specifications that can be applied to a block of text, a single Web page, or an entire Web site.

_____ **13.** This CSS length unit makes no assumptions about screen resolution and window size.

_____ **14.** A set of characters within a typeface that has specific characteristics associated with it.

_____ **15.** This is another name for an embedded style.

Answer each question either in writing or in a class discussion as directed by your instructor.

1. What are some factors you should consider when selecting a font to be used on a Web page?
2. List and describe the different type design features. How can these different type design features be used to enhance a Web page?
3. What are the four types of Cascading Style Sheets and when would it be appropriate to use each type of style sheet?
4. How can graphic-based typography be useful on the Web?
5. What is a PDF file and what are some advantages and disadvantages of using PDF files on the Web?

DESIGN PROJECT

Working with Text

1. Working with Text in an XHTML Document Using Macromedia Dreamweaver

Introduction

This is a continuation of the Design Project in Chapter 4.

The client The Inn at Birch Bay has reviewed the Web pages and has asked that additional content be provided on the Tour page. They would like the following:

- A few paragraphs describing the area
- A list of recreation activities available
- A notice that the new conference center is open

You have been asked to modify the tour.htm Web pages. The WebsByCT multimedia development team has decided that this project would be ideal for you to master XHTML coding that relates to text, especially the use of style sheets. To complete the lesson in this design project, you will be using the authoring program, Macromedia Dreamweaver, to enhance the Tour Web page.

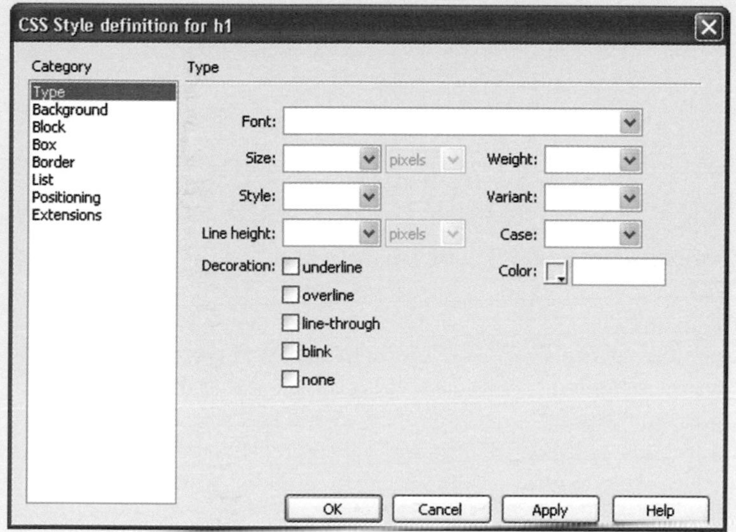
CSS Style definition for h1
Category
Type
Type
Background
Block
Box
Border
List
Positioning
Extensions
Font:
Size:
pixels
Weight:
Style:
Variant:
Line height:
pixels
Case:
Decoration:
underline
overline
line-through
blink
none
Color:
OK
Cancel
Apply
Help

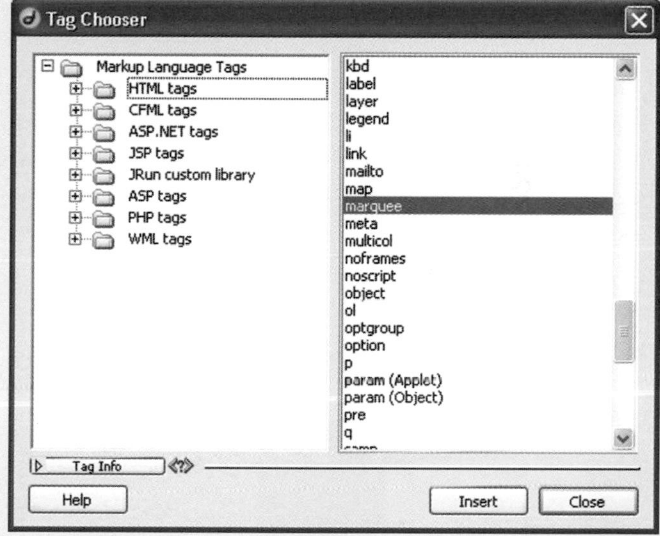
Tag Chooser
Markup Language Tags
HTML tags
CFML tags
ASP.NET tags
JSP tags
JRun custom library
ASP tags
PHP tags
WML tags
kbd
label
layer
legend
li
link
mailto
map
marquee
meta
multicol
noframes
noscript
object
ol
optgroup
option
p
param (Applet)
param (Object)
pre
q
Tag Info
Help
Insert
Close

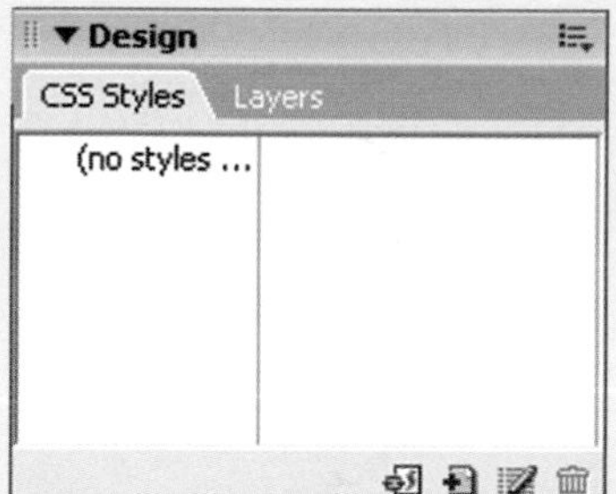
Design
CSS Styles
Layers
(no styles ...

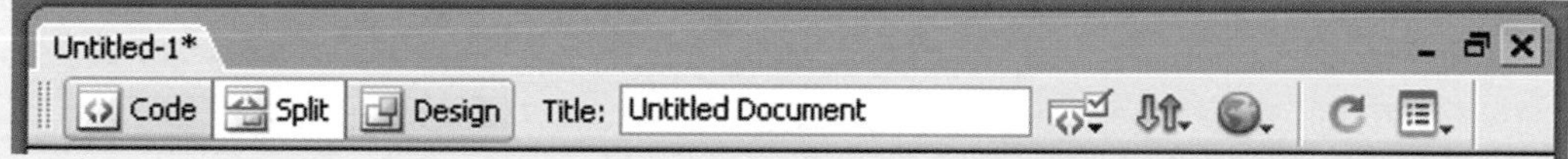
Untitled-1*
Code
Split
Design
Title:
Untitled Document

LESSON 1

WORKING WITH TEXT IN AN XHTML Document Using Macromedia Dreamweaver

What You'll Do

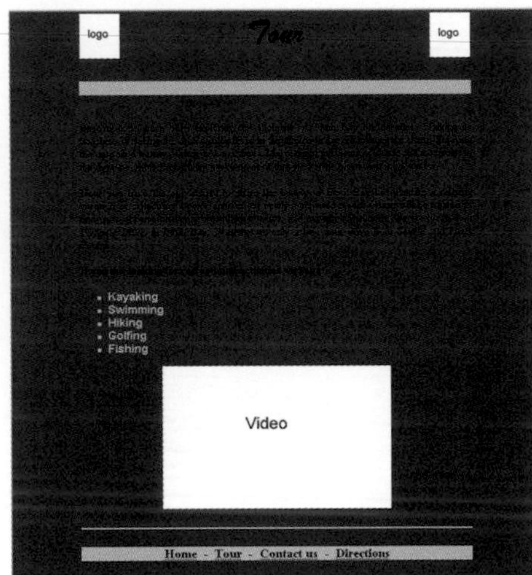

In this lesson, you will learn how to use Macromedia Dreamweaver to format and to change the appearance of text. You will also learn about the code view in Dreamweaver as a way to quickly make minor changes in the XHTML code within the document window.

Formatting and Enhancing the Appearance of Text

Because of the WYSIWYG nature of Macromedia Dreamweaver, it is relatively easy to work with text, whether aligning paragraphs, setting margins, applying colors to text or to text backgrounds, creating lists, specifying fonts and font sizes, or any number of other enhancements. In many cases, you can simply select the text and use the Property inspector to apply the desired effect. However, for more extensive changes that may affect several sections of a Web page or an entire Web site, it may be more efficient to create a style sheet, either internal or external.

Style Sheets

Earlier versions of HTML required you to write the code for defining the appearance of text individually. For example, the <h3> header tag caused text to display with a specific font and font size. Now, with style sheets, you can redefine existing tags, for example, by adding a specified color to the text.

Style sheets are made up of rules that have two main parts: the selector and the declaration. The selector identifies the tag to be formatted and the declaration provides the property and values. Figure 5-28 shows an example of a style rule that defines the <h3> tag as formatting text with a green color.

FIGURE 5-28
A style rule

Selector — Declaration

```
h3 {color:green;}
```

tag — Property — Value

Notice that there are specific symbols used in a rule. The tag is followed by a left-facing brace ({), then the property is followed by a colon (:), then the value is followed by a semi-colon (;), then a closing right-facing brace (}). Additional properties (such as a font type) can be added after the semi-colon.

You can create internal style sheets, which are included in the coding for each Web page, or external style sheets, which are created in a separate text document and linked to a Web page. The advantage of an external style sheet is that you can make a change in just one document (the style sheet) and have it affect any number of Web pages in a site. Figure 5-29 shows a style sheet named mystyles.css linked to a Web page. The css filename extension indicates that this is a Cascading Style Sheet, which is the standard for XHTML coding. The code used to create the link between the two documents is placed in the <head> tag of the Web page: **<link href="mystyles.css" rel="stylesheet" type="text/css" />**. This code instructs the browser to use the style sheet (which is a text css type) named mystyles.css. In this example, the mystyles.css file is placed in the same folder as the Web page.

FIGURE 5-29
An external style sheet

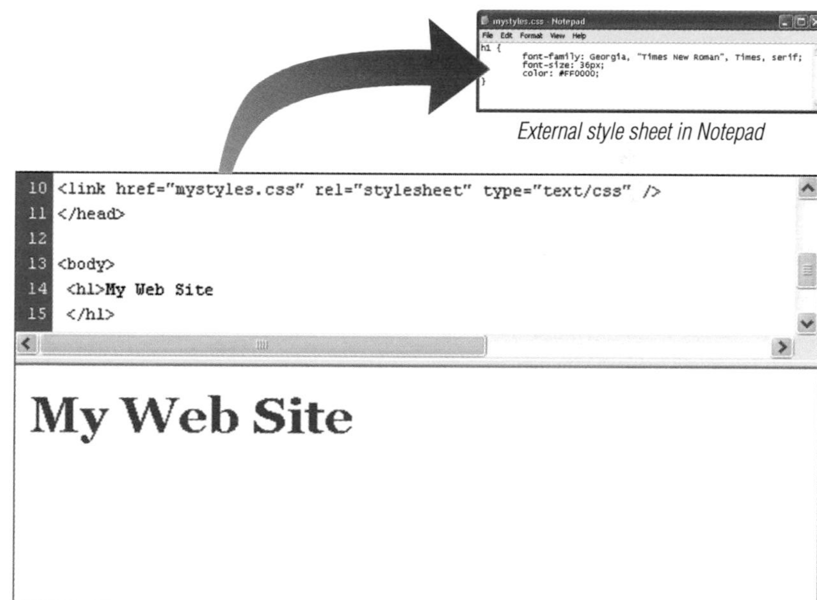

External style sheet referenced in XHTML code

Preview of style applied

Internal style sheet rules use the <style> tag as shown in Figure 5-30. The <style> tag is placed within the <head> tag of individual Web pages. Any number of rules can be placed within the <style> tag using the same format as for external style sheets. Style sheets save time in creating and updating Web sites as well as helping to ensure consistency in the appearance of the site.

In Macromedia Dreamweaver, creating style sheets is done using the Design palette and completing dialog boxes to indicate the tags, selectors, and declarations. External style sheets appear in the Files panel making it easy to display and edit them.

Working with Colors

Colors for text and backgrounds can be specified using six characters that represent the values of three colors (red, green, blue), referred to as RGB. When these colors are combined in various ways they can represent a spectrum of colors. The values are in a hexadecimal format (base 16), so they include letters and digits (A - F + 0 - 9 = 16 options), and they are preceded with a pound sign (#). The first two characters represent the value for red, the next two for green, and the last two for blue. For example, #000000 represents black (lack of color); #FFFFFF represents white; #FF0000 represents red, #00FF00 represents green, and #FFCC33 represents a shade of gold.

QUICKTIP

You don't have to memorize all the numbers for all the colors. There are reference manuals available for looking up colors, and most Web-authoring programs allow you to set the values visually by selecting a color from a palette.

FIGURE 5-30
An internal style sheet

```
<!DOCTYPE HTML PUBLIC "-//W3C//DTD HTML 4.01 Transitional//EN"
"http://www.w3.org/TR/html4/loose.dtd">

<html xmlns="http://www.w3.org/1999/xhtml">

<head>
        <title>Inn at Birch Bay - Tour</title>
        <meta http-equiv="Content-Type" content="text/html; charset=iso-8859-1">
        <style type="text/css">
                p {text-align:justify}
        </style>
</head>
```

Additional XHTML Tags and Attributes That Will Be Used in This Lesson

<ul>...</ul>: Used to create an unordered list.

<li>...</li>: Specifies the text for each bulleted item in a list.

<marquee>...</marquee>: Causes text to scroll across the screen.

<b>...</b>: Applies a bold emphasis to text.

Attributes:

font-family — Specifies the font to apply to the text.

font-weight — Specifies the emphasis to apply to the text, such as bold.

color — Specifies the color to apply to the text.

background color — Specifies the color to apply to the Web page or selected text.

margin-left(-right) — Specifies a left (or right) margin.

justify — Causes paragraphs to be formatted using the justify alignment.

square — Causes the bullets in a list to be displayed as squares.

Displaying the XHTML Code in the Dreamweaver Document Window

Macromedia Dreamweaver provides three views when working with the document window: Design, Code, and Split. You have been working in the Design view, which displays the document in a WYSIWYG format. The Code view shows the XHTML code that has been generated as you are developing the Web page. The Split view splits the view between Design and Code. Using the Split view you can select an area within the document design, and the corresponding code will be displayed as shown in Figure 5-31. This makes it easy for you to edit the code without having to use a text editor. You switch between the views using the buttons on the document toolbar.

QUICKTIP

The exercises in this chapter were created with the screen resolution set at 800 x 600. If your computer's screen resolution has a different setting, the figures in the book may appear different. You may want to verify the screen resolution on your computer and set it to 800 x 600, if necessary.

FIGURE 5-31
The Split view in the Dreamweaver document window

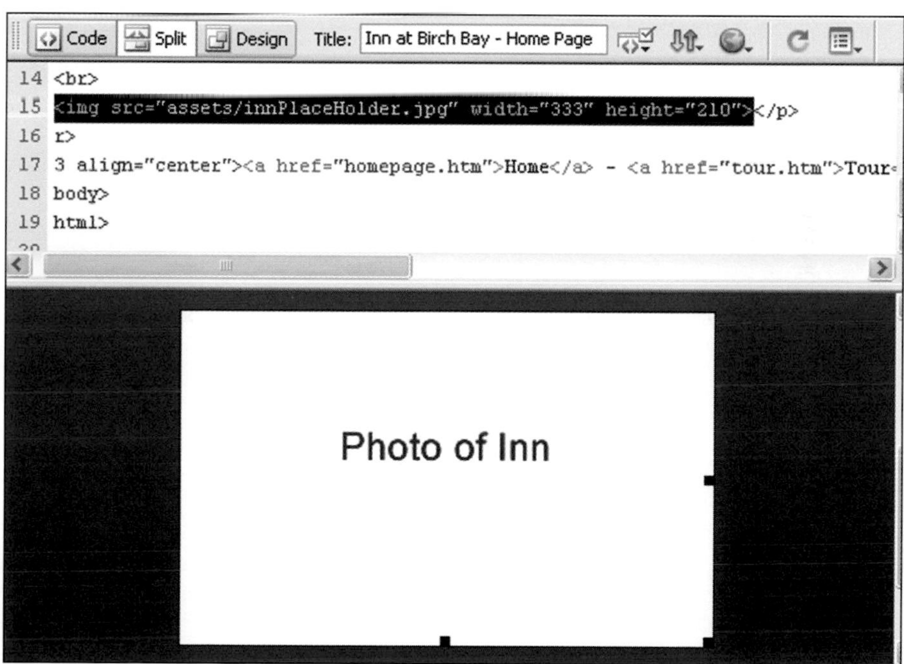

Copy text into an XHTML document

1. Start Dreamweaver MX 2004, then open the tour.htm document in the InnWebsiteDW folder created in Chapter 4.
2. Locate the files that are used for this book and copy the tourtext.txt file into the InnWebsiteDW folder you created in Chapter 4.
3. Start a text editor, then open the tourtext.txt document from the InnWebsiteDW folder.
4. Select all the text as shown in Figure 5-32, then copy the text.
5. Return to the Dreamweaver document window, position the insertion point above the Video placeholder, click, then click the **Align Left button** in the Property inspector as shown in Figure 5-33.

   Note: the Video placeholder will align to the left. This will be fixed later.
6. Paste the copied text.
7. Position the insertion point just in front of Now near the middle of the copied text, click, then press **[Enter]** (PC) or **[return]** (Mac).
8. Position the insertion point just after Sound., click, then press **[Enter]** (PC) or **[return]** (Mac).
9. Save the document, preview it in a browser, verify the text has been added, then return to the Dreamweaver document window.

You copied text from a text editor to a Web page document.

FIGURE 5-32
The selected text in the text editor

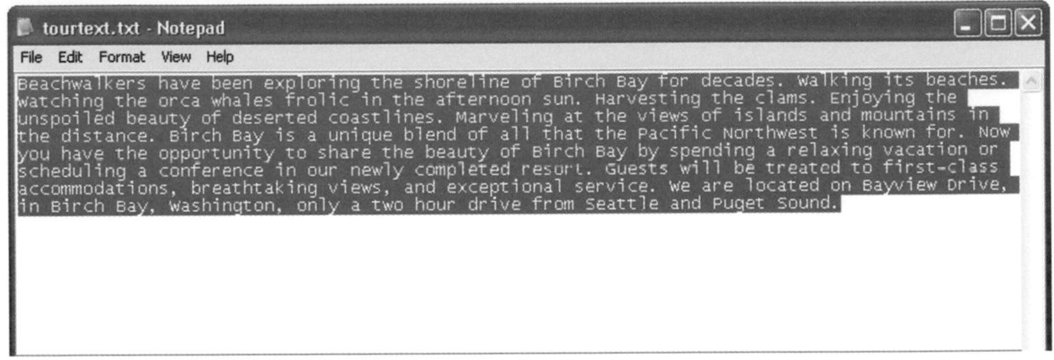

FIGURE 5-33
The Property inspector panel

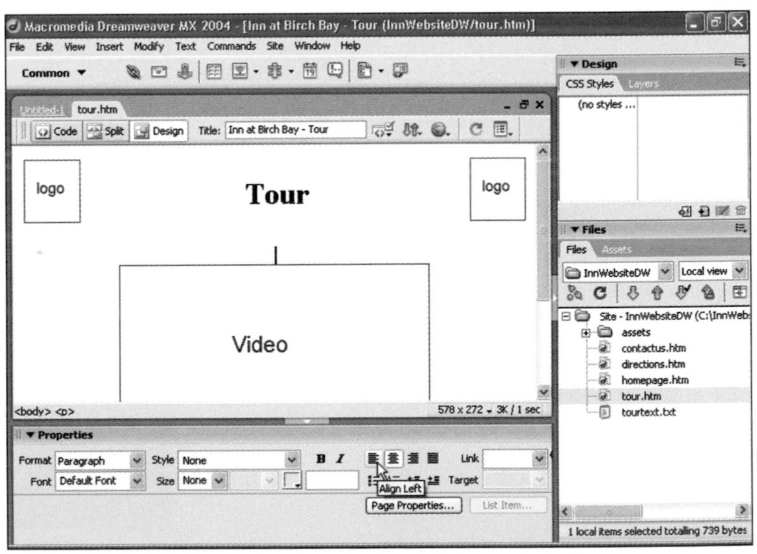

FIGURE 5-34

The down arrow in the Design panel

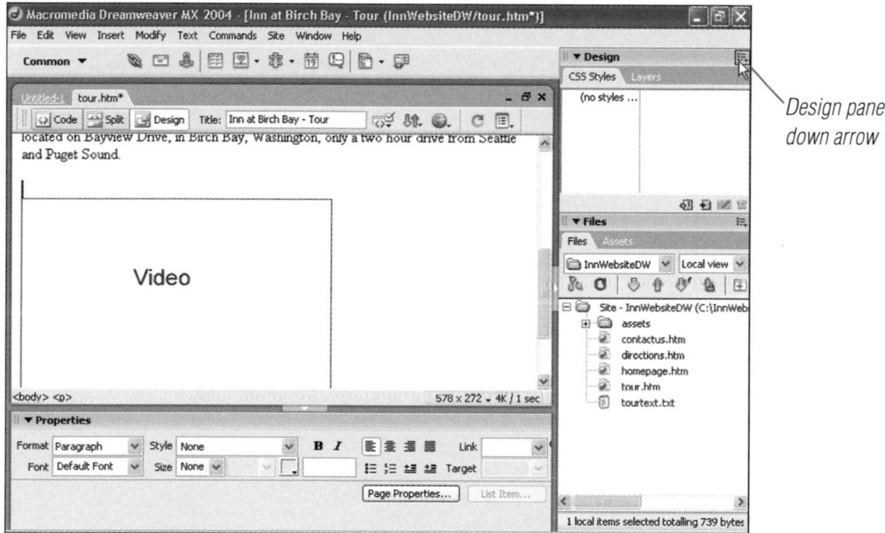

Create an internal style

1. Click **Window** in the menu bar, then click **CSS Styles** if it is not already selected.
2. Click the **down arrow** in the Design panel, as shown in Figure 5-34, then click **New**.

   The New CSS Style dialog box appears, allowing you to specify the tag to be defined and whether this is an external or internal (This document only) style.
3. Delete any text in the Name box, type **p** in the Name box, click **Tag**, click **This document only**, then click **OK**.
4. Click **Block** in the CSS Style definition for p dialog box.
5. Click the **down arrow** for the Text align option, click **justify**, then click **OK**.
6. Save the document, then display it in a browser.

   Notice how the paragraphs are formatted using the justify alignment. Also, notice that the Video placeholder has lost its center alignment. This is because the placeholder was within a <p> tag and the style was applied to it. You will fix this in the next objective.
7. Return to the Dreamweaver document window.

You created an internal style element to format text displayed on this page.

Use the split view to edit code

1. Click the **Video placeholder** to select it.
2. Click the **Split button** [Split] on the document toolbar.

   Notice that the <img...> tag is selected. Just above the tag is the <p align="left"> tag. This <p> tag needs to be deleted and the image centered.
3. Select **<p align="left">** as shown in Figure 5-35, then press **[Delete]**.
4. Click the **Design button** [Design] on the document toolbar.
5. Click the **Video placeholder** to select it, then click the **Align Center button** in the Property inspector panel.
6. Save the document, preview it in a browser, then verify the Video placeholder is center aligned.
7. Return to the Dreamweaver document window.

You used the Split view to edit code in a Dreamweaver document.

Create an unordered list

1. Position the insertion point after Puget Sound. in the body text, then click.
2. Hold down **[Shift]**, then press **[Enter]** (PC) or **[return]** (Mac) twice.
3. Type **If you are looking for recreational activities we have:**, then press **[Enter]** (PC) or **[return]** (Mac).
4. Type **Kayaking**, then press **[Enter]** (PC) or **[return]** (Mac).

(continued)

FIGURE 5-35
The selected code

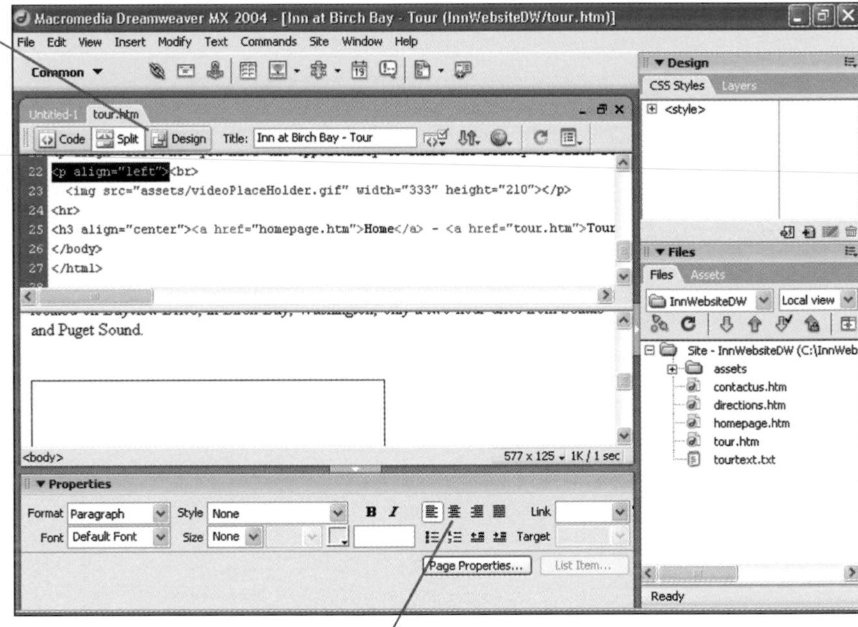

FIGURE 5-36

The Unordered List button in the Property inspector panel

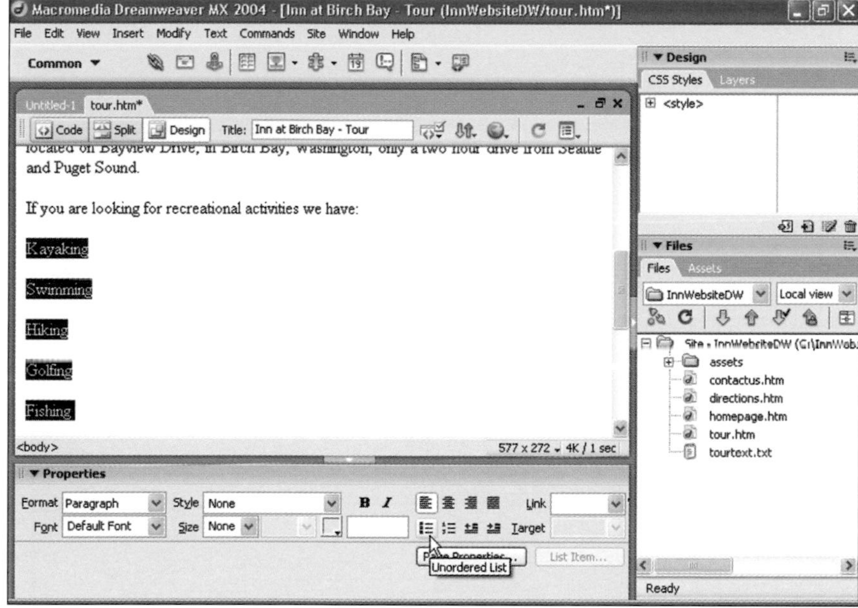

5. Type **Swimming**, then press **[Enter]** (PC) or **[return]** (Mac).
6. Type **Hiking**, then press **[Enter]** (PC) or **[return]** (Mac).
7. Type **Golfing**, then press **[Enter]** (PC) or **[return]** (Mac).
8. Type **Fishing**.
9. Select the five items, then click the **Unordered List button** in the Property inspector panel, as shown in Figure 5-36.
10. Select **If you are looking for recreational activities we have:**, then click the **Bold button** **B** in the Property inspector panel.
11. Save the document, preview it in a browser, then verify that bold and bullets have been added.
12. Return to the Dreamweaver document.

You created an unordered list and applied a bold style to text.

Apply a style to a list

1. Click a **blank area** in the document window to deselect the text.
2. Click the **down arrow** in the Design panel, then click **New**.
3. Type **ul** in the Tag box, click **Tag** and **This document only** if necessary, then click **OK**.
4. Click the **down arrow** for the Font option, then click **Arial**, **Helvetica**, **sans-serif**.
5. Click the **down arrow** for the Weight option, then click **bold**.

(continued)

6. Position the insertion point in the Color box, click, then type **#C0C0C0**.

   Your dialog box should resemble Figure 5-37.

7. Click the **List option** in the Category box.
8. Click the **down arrow** for the Type option, click **square**, then click **OK**.
9. Save the document, preview it in a browser, then verify the list uses square bullets.

   Note: The list is displayed in gray when viewed in the browser.

10. Return to the Dreamweaver document window.

You created a style for an unordered list.

Create and apply an external style sheet

1. Click the **down arrow** in the Design panel, then click **New**.
2. Type **h1** in the Tag box, verify that **New Style Sheet File** is selected, then click **OK**.
3. Verify the Save in folder is InnWebsiteDW, then type **sitestyles** in the File name box (PC) or Save As text box (Mac).

   The external style sheet file that you are creating will be named sitestyles.css and will be placed in the InnWebsiteDW folder.

4. Click **Save** to display the CSS Style Definition dialog box.
5. Position the insertion point in the Font box, click, then type **Brush Script MT, Arial, sans-serif**.

(continued)

FIGURE 5-37
The CSS Style definition dialog box

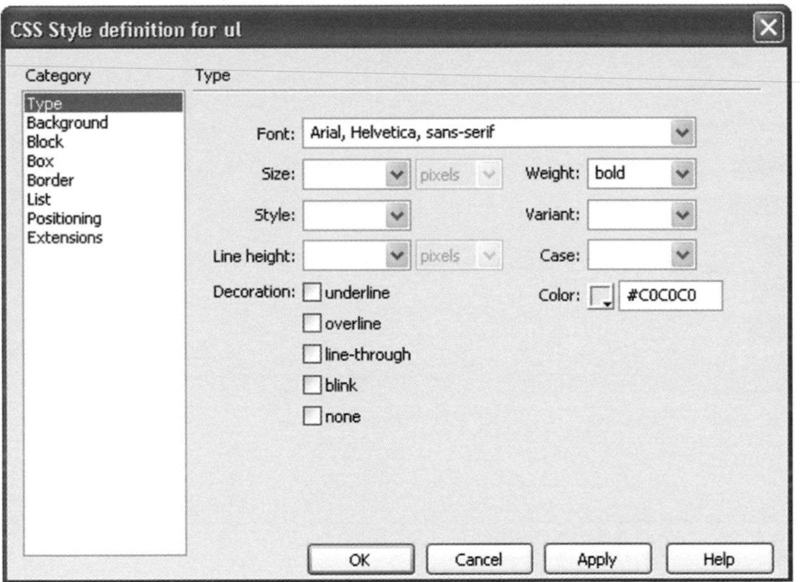

FIGURE 5-38
Completing the CSS Style Definition dialog box

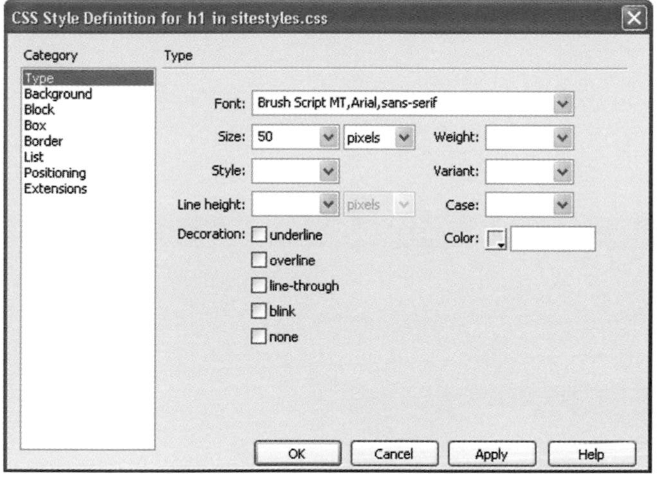

FIGURE 5-39
The completed code

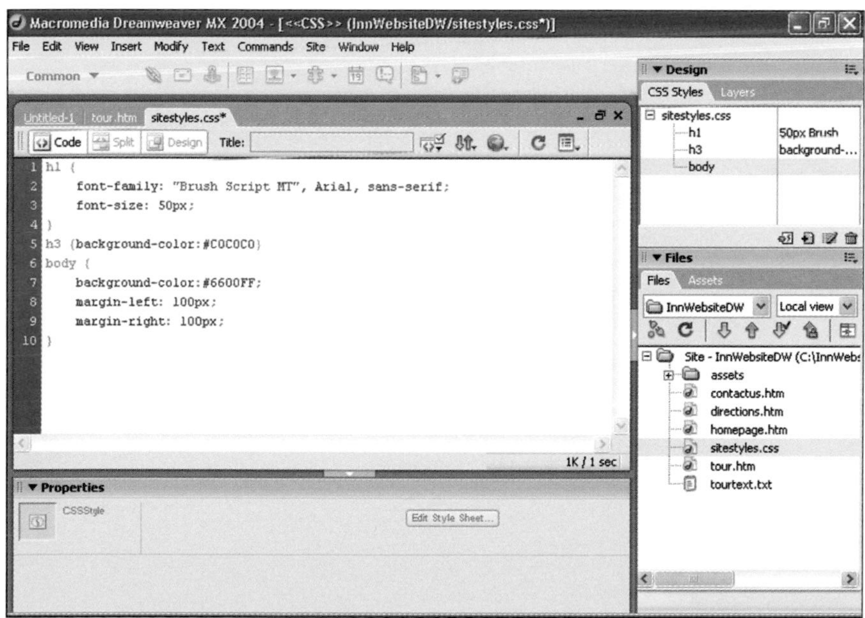

6. Position the insertion point in the Size box, click, then type **50** as shown in Figure 5-38.

   This code defines the <h1> heading, which will display text using the Brush Script MT font in a font size of 50 points. Per the code specifications, if the Brush Script MT font is not available on the user's computer, Arial is used, and if Arial is not available a generic sans-serif font is used.

7. Click **OK**, save the Dreamweaver document, preview it in a browser, then verify the heading appears per the code specifications.

8. Return to the Dreamweaver document window.

You created and applied an external style sheet.

Edit an external style sheet

1. Double click **sitestyles.css** in the Files panel to open the document in Dreamweaver.

2. Type the following text as shown in Figure 5-39.

```
h3 {background-color:#C0C0C0}
body {
        background-color: #6600FF;
        margin-left: 100px;
        margin-right: 100px;
}
```

   This code creates two styles, one for the <h3> tag and one for the body tag. All text formatted with an <h3> style will have a silver (#C0C0C0) background color. The background for the page will be blue (#6600FF), and there will be left and right margins of 100 pixels.

(continued)

3. Save the style sheet document, then click tour.htm at the top of the document window.
4. Preview tour.htm in a browser.

   Notice the page background color, the margins, and the background color for the navigation text at the bottom of the page (this background color may not show on a Mac). Applying a background to <h3> text displays a colored bar, in this example silver per the code (#C0C0C0), across the page.
5. Return to the Dreamweaver document window.

You edited an external style sheet.

Create a marquee

1. Position the insertion point before the word Beachwalkers in the body text, then click.
2. Press **[Enter]** (PC) or **[return]** (Mac), then press the **up arrow**.
3. Type **Our new Conference Center is now open!**.
4. Select the text, then click the **Tag Chooser icon** in the Insert bar (click **Window**, **Insert** if this bar is not open) as shown in Figure 5-40.
5. Click **HTML tags**, then scroll to display marquee.
6. Click **marquee**, click **Insert**, then click **Close**.
7. Using the Split view, position the insertion point between the e and > in the first marquee tag, click, press the Spacebar, then type **loop="2"**.
8. Click the **Design button** [Design] in the document toolbar to display the Design view.

(continued)

FIGURE 5-40

The Tag Chooser icon in the toolbar

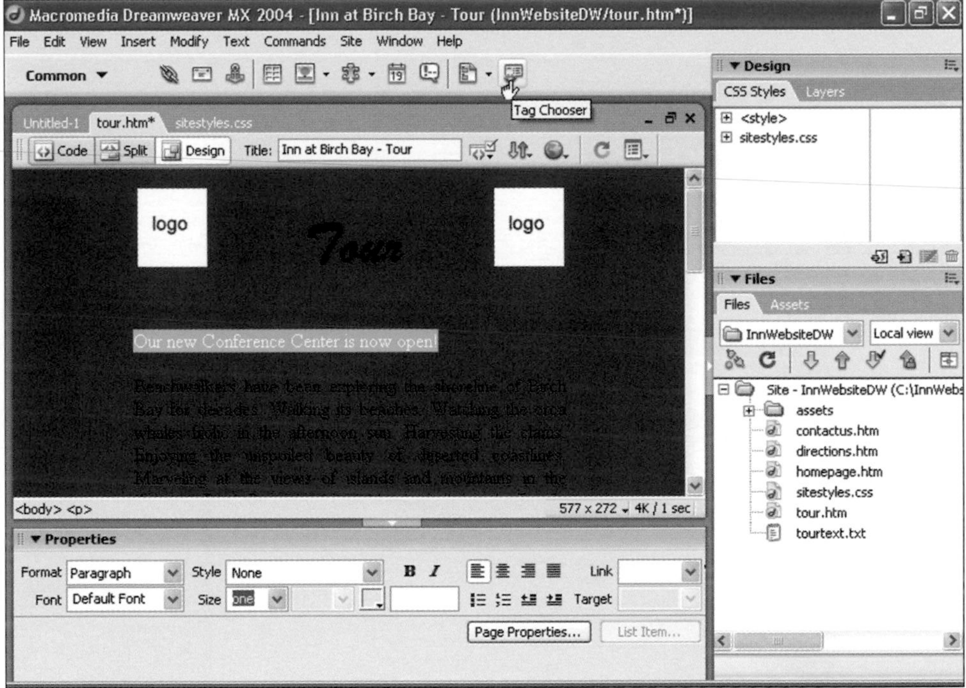

9. Select the text **Our new Conference Center is now open!**, click the **down arrow** for the Format option in the Property inspector, then click **Heading 3**.
10. Delete the entry in the Text Color box, click, type **#008000**, then press **[Enter]** (PC) or **[return]** (Mac).
11. Save the document, preview it in a browser, verify the marquee appears, then return to the Dreamweaver document window.

You created a marquee.

FIGURE 5-41
The completed dialog box

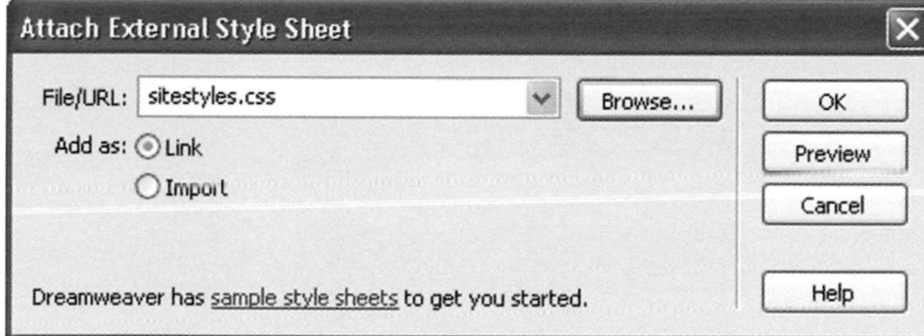

Attach the style sheet to other Web pages

1. Double-click **homepage.htm** in the Files panel to display the document.
2. Click the **down arrow** in the Design panel, then click **Attach Style Sheet**.
3. Click the **Browse button** , then navigate to the InnWebsiteDW folder.
4. Select the **sitestyles.css file**, then click **OK** (PC) or **Choose** (Mac).
5. Click **OK** in the Attach External Style Sheet dialog box as shown in Figure 5-41.
6. Save the document, preview it in a browser, verify the styles, such as background color, have been applied, then return to the Dreamweaver document window.
7. Repeat steps 1 and 2, then 5 and 6 for the contactus.htm and directions.htm documents.

You copied the style code to the other Web pages in the Web site.

PROJECT BUILDER 1

You are an intern with a company that develops Web sites for clients. During your internship training you learned how important text is in the development of Web pages. One of the most important considerations when evaluating how to utilize text is the target audience. The variance in text is evident in different Web sites that target adults and children, and even in Web sites that target both. You have been asked to write a report that compares how text is used within a Web site that has different target audiences.

1. Connect to the Internet, go to *www.course.com*, navigate to the page for this book, click the Student Online Companion link, then click the link for this chapter.
2. Navigate through the Web site (see Figure 5-42) and study the use of text for the Web pages targeting kids and for those targeting adults. (Note: In the kids section of the Web site there is a link in the upper-right corner for the parents. This directs adults to the home page for the site.)
3. Open a document in a word processor, save the file as **Ch5pb1**, create a table with these column heads: topic, adult viewer, child viewer; then create one row for each topic that follows:
   a. Amount of text used
   b. Fonts (serif, sans-serif, decorative)
   c. Font sizes
   d. Text colors
   e. Text emphasis (bold, italic, underline)
4. Complete the table by comparing the Web pages based on the topics listed in your table.

One Step Beyond

5. Do you think the use of text was appropriate for each target audience? Why, or why not?
6. What recommendations would you make to improve the use of text?

Two Steps Beyond

7. Conduct a Web search for two online encyclopedias. List the URL for each site.
8. Choose one subject and search for it in each Web site. Specify the subject.
9. Briefly describe the use of text (amount, font, font sizes, colors, and so on) for each site.
10. For the subject you choose:
    a. Do you think the use of text was appropriate for encyclopedia Web sites? Why, or why not?
    b. What recommendations would you make to improve the use of text?

FIGURE 5-42
A Web site targeting children

PROJECT BUILDER 2

You have been studying Web development. You decide it would be useful to apply various text features to a portfolio Web site. Complete the following steps to create a Web page similar to the one shown in Figure 5-43.

1. Start Dreamweaver, then open mysite.htm and edit as follows.
2. Type your name and type at least four lines of body text.
3. Separate the body text into two or more paragraphs.
4. Create an unordered list of at least four items using the heading: "My areas of interest:".
5. Create internal style sheet rules to format:
   a. list items to display with square bullets, Arial font, and bold emphasis
   b. paragraphs using the justify alignment
   c. <h2> tags as center aligned
6. Create an external style sheet as follows:
   a. <h3> tag to display
      i. fonts: Georgia, Arial, sans-serif
      ii. size: 20 pixels
      iii. alignment: center
      iv. color: #330099
   b. <h1> tag to display
      i. alignment center
      ii. color: #330099
   c. body
      i. background color: #CCCCCC
      ii. left and right margins: 75 pixels
7. Save the document with the file name **mysitexx.htm** (where *xx* are your initials).

One Step Beyond

8. Create a second Web page named Contact me with the same formatting as the main page.
9. Use your contact information where the body text appears.
10. Link the two pages.

Two Steps Beyond

11. Using a text editor, duplicate the Web site you developed using Macromedia Dreamweaver, and save it as **Chpb2_texx.html**.

FIGURE 5-43
The completed Web page

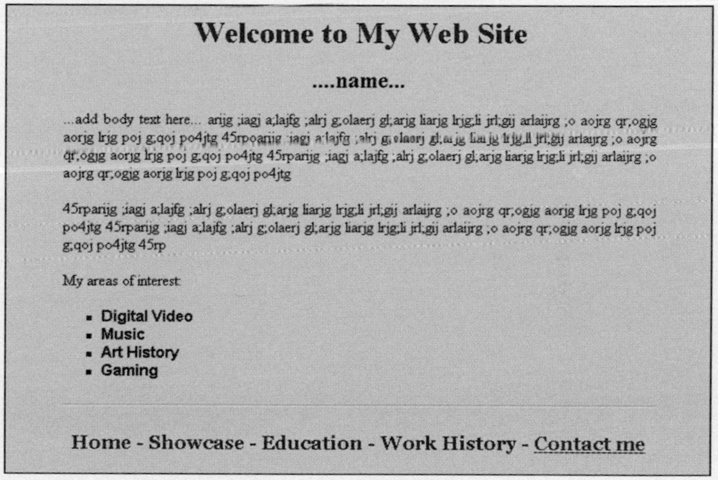

Welcome to My Web Site

....name...

...add body text here...

My areas of interest:

- **Digital Video**
- **Music**
- **Art History**
- **Gaming**

Home - Showcase - Education - Work History - Contact me

7530

chapter 6

MULTIMEDIA ELEMENT — Graphics

1. Examine the Sources of Digital Images
2. Identify Image Types
3. Understand Image Quality
4. Explore Graphics Software
5. Discuss Web Graphic File Formats

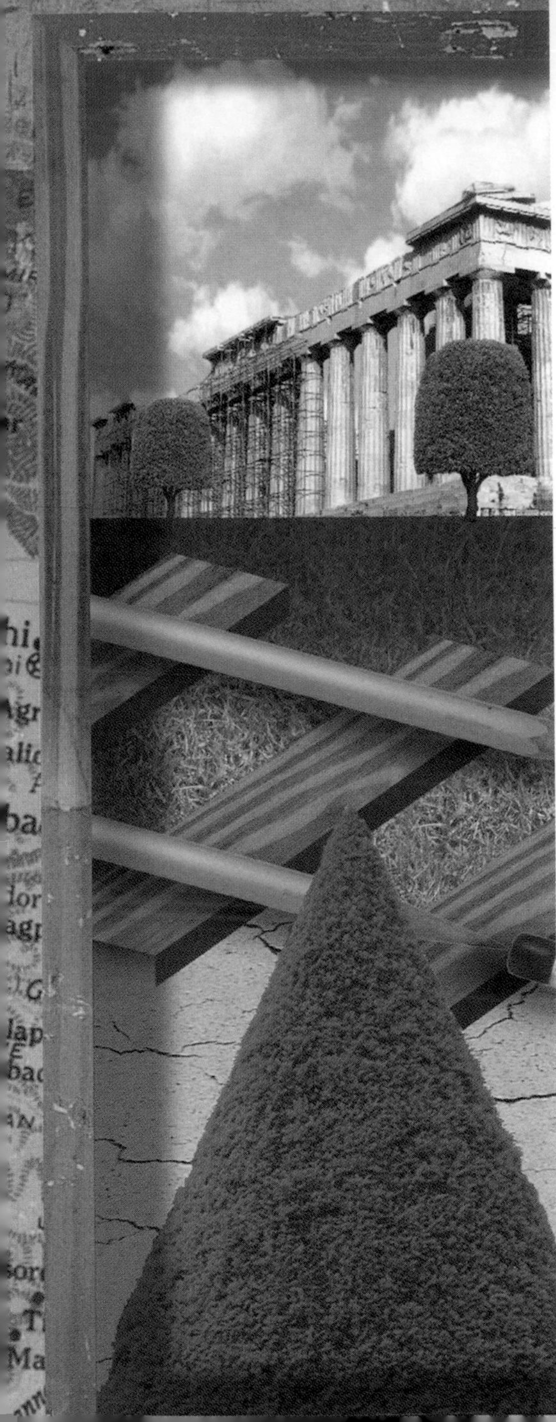

chapter 6 MULTIMEDIA ELEMENT — Graphics

Introduction

Graphics are vital to multimedia Web sites. Web pages are filled with them. An image can be very simple or very complex—in which case, a picture really can be worth a thousand words. A single table, chart, graphic (see Figure 6-1), or photograph can illustrate what might take many pages of narrative text to communicate. In the end, the image may still do a better job of creating a lasting impression or establishing a mood. On the Web, communicating information quickly is crucial, which means the importance of graphic elements in multimedia Web sites cannot be overstated.

A compelling image on a Web page is as important to the overall appeal of a Web site as the right image is in print. However, in print, the reader is not concerned with how quickly the image downloads or whether it pixelates when it is displayed. Just as preparing type for the Web is a very different process from preparing type for print, preparing images for the Web is quite different from preparing images for print due to differences in computer screens, browsers, platforms, and bandwidth.

Graphics can be used on Web pages as images, backgrounds, buttons, icons, navigational items, maps, and logos. In addition to being able to use graphics in many different ways within a multimedia Web site, developers also have a variety of sources from which they can obtain the graphics they use in their designs. Scanners, video capture cards, and digital cameras allow Web designers to create different types of digital images for multimedia Web sites.

FIGURE 6-1
Graphics are used on the Web to illustrate complex ideas

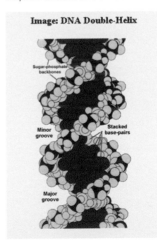

Image: DNA Double-Helix
Sugar-phosphate backbones
Minor groove
Stacked base-pairs
Major groove

Graphics are also available for download from the Web or on a CD.

Because still images are so vital to a Web site, care and time in searching for or creating just the right image is important. When searching for just the right image for your Web pages, you should first create a list and description of the images you need for your project. Once you know what you want, you can choose to create the images yourself, obtain the images from a commercial image provider, or hire a graphic designer to create them for you. Regardless of which source you use to obtain your images, you should keep track of the vital information and correspondence surrounding each image you have selected. It is good practice to create a multimedia image log, similar to the one shown in Figure 6-2, to record the information.

Today's software programs allow Web designers and developers to combine text and images to create almost any work of art imaginable. The first step is for the Web designer or developer to acquire the images. These images can be obtained in a number of ways, including being created using paint and drawing software. After the images are in a digital format, the images may need to be manipulated using image editing software, such as **Adobe Photoshop**. The final step in preparing images for the Web is to optimize the files.

Because the technology used to create and manipulate images changes almost daily, as a Web designer, it is not always practical or even wise to find or create your own image. If you are working as part of a multimedia production team, graphic artists will be part of the team. If you are not working as part of a team, you may want to hire a graphic artist if you feel you cannot find or create the image you need or if you do not have the time or skill level to do it yourself. Many professional graphic artists and photographers do freelance work, and they use the computer and technology as tools to express their creativity. You can usually hire them by the hour, by the day, or by the project.

QUICKTIP

When hiring professionals, ask them for recommendations and samples of their work. Also inquire about additional expenses, such as travel, and determine up front who will pay those expenses.

Remember, graphic artists are responsible for creating images for all different types of Web pages. They must have a clear understanding of the Web site and how the images will be used. Web designers must ensure that the project contains high-quality images that have been optimized for the Web. This chapter focuses on a discussion of graphics used for multimedia Web sites and the programs used with those graphics.

FIGURE 6-2

Use a Multimedia Image Log to track vital information about the images used in your multimedia Web site

MULTIMEDIA IMAGE LOG			
Description	Source	Rights Negotiated	Amount Paid

CONCEPT 1

EXAMINE THE SOURCES of Digital Images

What You'll Learn

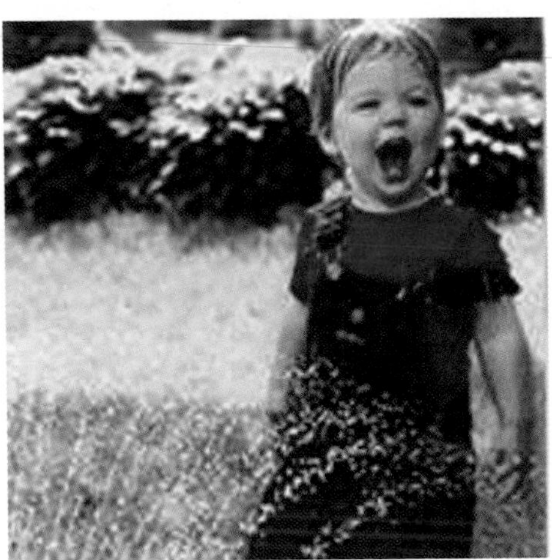

In this lesson, you will learn about the different sources of digital images including scanning, digital cameras, digital video cameras, Photo CD, stock photography, clip art, and original artwork. The chapter will also provide a general overview of copyright law.

To be used on a multimedia Web site, images must be in a digital format. **Digitizing** is the process of converting images into a format that the computer can recognize and manipulate. There are many different sources of pre-existing digitized images, or you can digitize images that are currently photographs, slides, or line art.

Many different companies, including Agfa, Epson, and Hewlett Packard, manufacture scanners. Depending on the quality and features, scanners range in price from as little as one hundred dollars to thousands of dollars. As shown in Figure 6-3, scanning software is used to digitize images, such as photos and illustrations.

Scanned Images

Scanning images provides a way to generate images for Web sites. **Scanners** digitize already developed images, including photographs and drawings. Once these images have been converted to a digital format, they can be interpreted and recognized by the computer. Scanners look like small photocopiers that record millions of colors. **Slide scanners** are also available for converting a slide or a negative to a digital image.

FIGURE 6-3

Scanning software is used to digitize images, such as photos and illustrations

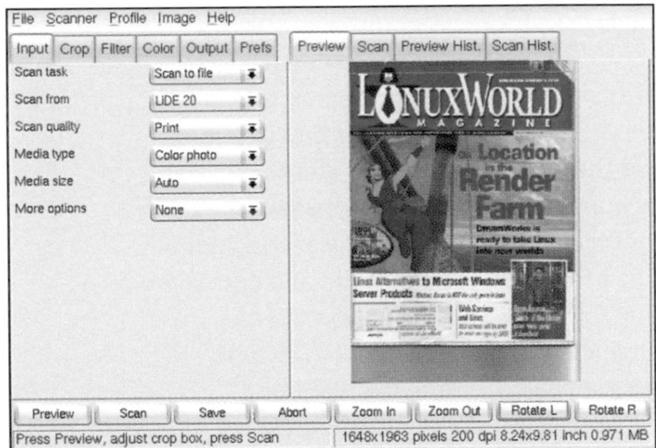

To scan an image, usually you place the material on the glass surface of the scanner and run the scanning software. Depending on the type of scanner and the sophistication of the program, you can zoom in and select specific parts of the image before capturing or digitizing it. You can edit the image by adjusting colors, contrast, and brightness.

When purchasing image-capture equipment such as scanners, make sure the resolution at which it captures the image is at least two times higher than the final output. Most monitors will only display a resolution of 72 dpi (dots per inch), so make sure the equipment will capture at least 150 dpi. Remember that you can always scale back. You will learn more about resolution later in this chapter. When scanning images:

- Always work from the original image.
- Capture the image at the highest resolution required to get the best reproduction of the image being scanned.
- Lower the resolution of the image to 72 ppi (pixels per inch) before you export the scanned image to a Web page.
- Do not increase image resolution after it has been lowered. Some of the original color will have been deleted so the image will not be as sharp.

QUICKTIP

Check the speed at which you will be able to scan images. If you will be scanning large volumes, a faster scanner will pay for itself in a very short time period.

Still Images

Digital cameras capture images in a digital format. Unlike regular still cameras, photographs are not stored on film but instead are stored in memory. Photographs can be imported directly from the camera to the computer where they can be manipulated and added to any Web page.

Digital cameras are generally small and lightweight and range from consumer to professional models, as shown in Figure 6-4. They are easy to use and include many of the same features found on a regular camera. Features such as auto focus and auto flash make using a digital camera a snap. Transferring the photos to the computer is also quite simple. By connecting the camera to a port on the computer and using the software that comes with the camera, you can easily transfer the images to any computer. After the image is transferred, you can immediately include it on your Web page or edit it using image editing software, such as Adobe Photoshop.

Nikon, Canon, Olympus, and many other companies manufacture digital cameras. Prices range from under one hundred dollars to thousands of dollars for high-end, studio-quality cameras. The cost of these cameras can be quickly recovered from savings in film development and processing. The quality produced from digital cameras varies between the portable and studio units, but even the quality of the photographs taken with inexpensive, portable digital cameras is generally adequate for use on Web pages. The number of photographs that can be stored in the camera depends on the resolution selected and the amount of storage available. Digital cameras are fast, quiet, convenient, inexpensive, and environmentally friendly—an excellent choice for taking photographs for Web pages.

FIGURE 6-4

Digital cameras range from consumer to high-end professional models

QUICKTIP

When snapping pictures:

- Photograph people from many different angles and in many different poses so you can choose from a number of different images or create sequences.
- Shoot people in indirect light.
- Shoot in the morning or evening when the light is filtered through the clouds, as midday light creates too many contrasts.
- Use a variety of angles and perspectives to record details and panoramas.
- Shoot objects both indoors and outdoors, from a variety of angles, and play with the light and color to get the effect you want to create.

If you choose not to take your own pictures, there are other alternatives. You can purchase photographs in a digital format from commercial image providers or stock photographers. You can also hire a photographer to take pictures for you. Additionally, many professional-quality photographs are available with commercial software packages, on CD, or from the Web.

Video Images

Digital video cameras can also be used to capture frames of video or still images. Although regular camcorders store video on film, digital video cameras store images as digital data. Similar to digital cameras, video footage from digital video cameras can be transferred to the computer where individual frames can be saved as a graphic image, which can then go directly onto the Web page.

Digital video cameras range in price from under one hundred dollars for small desktop cameras up to hundreds of thousands of dollars for high-end equipment. Digital video cameras are usually a more expensive means of adding images to your multimedia Web sites than digital cameras, however, if you want to purchase one device that will take both still and video images, this is a good option. If you need video only occasionally, consider the use of professional companies, who specialize in selling video footage.

Photo CD

As shown in Figure 6-5, another excellent method of storing and using photographic digital images is a **Photo CD**. All you need is a camera, a roll of film, and an authorized service provider to process your roll of film and supply you with digitized images on a CD.

FIGURE 6-5

Photo CDs, such as Kodak's Picture CD, store hundreds of digital photographs

There are many advantages to using a Photo CD. The quality of these images is usually very good and the authorized service provider or developer will usually include each image in several sizes on the Photo CD. Photo CDs are relatively inexpensive, and they provide a convenient and near-permanent storage medium. Photo CDs can hold hundreds of images and can be read by most computers equipped with a CD-ROM drive.

Stock Photography

Commercial image providers or **stock photography houses** create or secure and sell the rights to images. **Stock photography** refers to the photographs available on CD or on Web sites, such as iStockphoto.com shown in Figure 6-6. Some of these images are available for a price while others are royalty free. Diverse and innovative images from multiple collections are accessible using keyword and category searching. Thumbnails of photos are provided from a variety of categories including family, business, people, secluded beaches, lifestyle, sports, and kids.

CD and Web site catalogs allow you to search for an image using descriptive words. If you want photos of sunsets, you might search using "sun" or "sunsets." A list of photos appears based on the keyword search. Today it is easier than ever to access images from around the world simply by accessing the Web and taking a few minutes to download the image.

Keep in mind that in most situations commercial image providers are selling only the rights to use the image, they are not selling the image itself. In other words, they may sell you the right to use the image within one Web site, but the image does not become your property. If you want to use it again on a different Web site, you may have to pay another royalty. Other companies may allow you to use the photos on a Web site without paying a royalty. Sometimes the purchase agreement requires you to give notice that you obtained the image from the company that provided the image. The agreements vary depending on the image, the original artist, and the commercial image provider. Be cautious and be sure to read the licensing agreement carefully. Just because you purchased the CD or were given access to the image on the Web does not necessarily mean you own or can use the image whenever you want. Because the **copyright** and licensing agreements on images will vary from one stock photography house to another as well as from photograph to photograph, it is imperative that you read the licensing agreement carefully and record specific information about every image you intend to use on a Web site.

FIGURE 6-6

Millions of high-quality photographs are available from stock photography Web sites

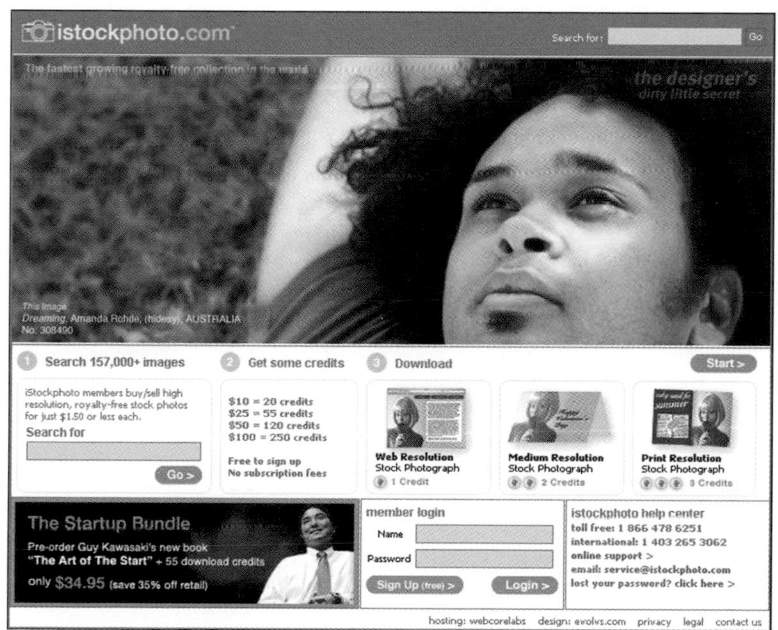

Always make sure that you understand the terms of the agreement before you incorporate any image in your Web site.

QUICKTIP

When obtaining digital images:

- Make sure the file is in a format that is Web ready.
- Make sure the size and resolution are appropriate for your Web page.

Clip Art

Clip art refers to a collection of drawings or illustrations, which are generally organized by category. Extensive clip art libraries are available with some software packages, on CD, or from Web sites such as clipart.com as shown in Figure 6-7. Due to the growth of the Web and the need for Web-ready graphics, most clip art images are now available in a file format that will allow you to immediately include them on your Web pages.

Clip art is an excellent alternative if you are not an artist, do not have time to create your own images, or do not have the money to hire a graphic artist. Although clip art images are great in a pinch, you will want to make sure that the images are appropriate for your Web site and that the quality of the images is high. If you do not take care in selecting clip art images, they may make your Web site appear amateurish.

Some graphic images available as part of a clip art library are **public domain**. When images are in the public domain, it means you can use these images at your discretion for no charge (other than what you may pay up front to purchase the clip art library). Others, however, have restrictions and charge royalties. Royalties are more commonly charged if you plan to use the graphic for commercial purposes. The royalty may be charged each time you use the image or it may be a one-time fee. Be sure to read the licensing agreement carefully before you include someone else's clip art on your multimedia Web site.

FIGURE 6-7
Clip art from clip art libraries is available for download from the Web

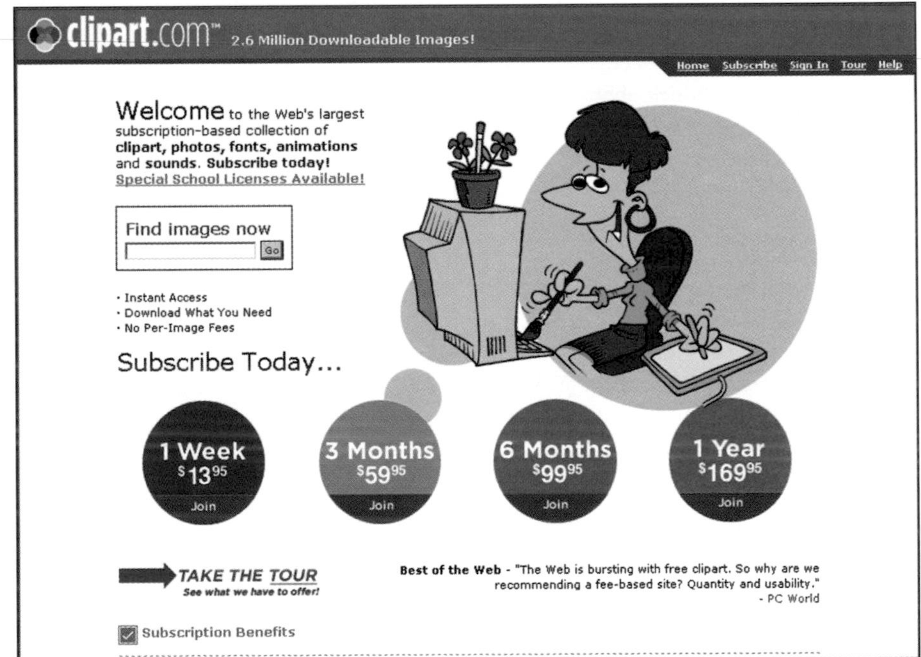

Original Artwork

With a little time and effort you can generate your own digital images. This chapter explores some software programs that enable you to create and edit original artwork. There are many drawing, paint, and image editing programs available for you to use. Some are intended for creating graphics, while others are designed for editing existing images. There are many advantages to creating original artwork. For example, you do not have to worry about copyright and licensing agreements, and you do not have to settle for a graphic that is not exactly what you want.

Although there is obviously a learning curve any time you set out to master a new software program, the ability to create original artwork or edit existing images will undoubtedly prove to be an invaluable skill. If you intend to master the art of designing Web graphics that are consistent with the purpose of your Web site, you will need to know how to use these tools at least at an introductory level.

If you do intend to use these tools on a regular basis, you should consider buying a digitizing or graphics tablet, such as the one shown in Figure 6-8. A **digitizing tablet** or **graphics tablet** is a touch-sensitive board that converts points, lines, and curves drawn with a stylus or digitizer device to digital data. Each location on the graphics tablet corresponds to a specific location on the screen.

Using a **stylus** is similar to using a pen and is much easier to draw with than a mouse, trackball, or touchpad. Designers, such as graphic artists, professional architects, engineers, and mapmakers, who need to create drawings or precisely trace sketches and photographs often use a stylus in conjunction with a digitizing or graphics tablet. Like most hardware devices, graphics tablets range in size and quality as well as price, from less than one hundred dollars to thousands of dollars.

In addition to creating original drawings, you may want to use charts or graphs to present numerical data. Charts provide a much more effective means of communicating data than text alone. People are much more likely to grasp trends over time or the relationship between the parts to the whole by looking at a line graph or pie chart than by reading only text.

FIGURE 6-8

Digitizing tablets are excellent for tracing or drawing objects to be recognized by the computer

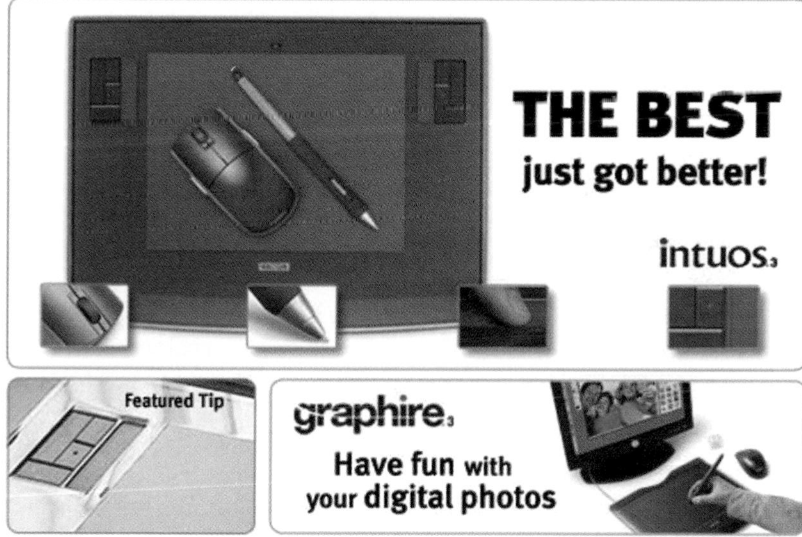

If chart-making tools are not available in the authoring software you are using to create your Web page, you can generally develop the chart with an electronic spreadsheet such as Microsoft Excel. As shown in Figure 6-9, electronic spreadsheets contain excellent tools for preparing two-dimensional and three-dimensional charts. Once the chart or graph is developed, you can either export it to your application or take a screen capture of it and save the screen capture in an appropriate Web graphics file format. Many programs now include integrated chart-making tools.

FIGURE 6-9

Data in spreadsheet programs can be visualized using content-appropriate chart types

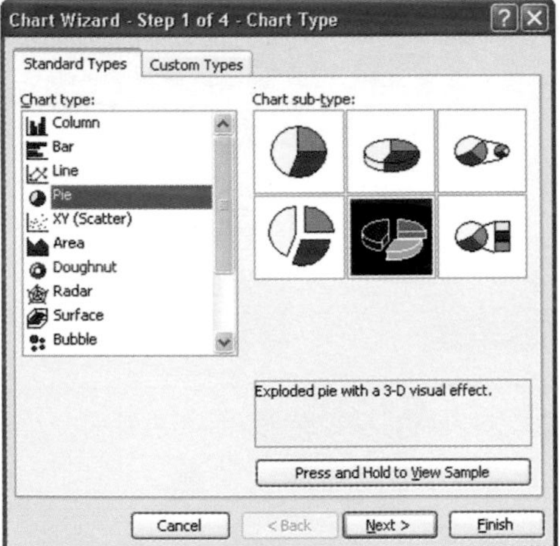

In fact, some of these programs even allow you to animate charts. For example, in an animated chart, different pieces of the chart may fly into the screen as you click the mouse.

Maps are used to illustrate locations and are becoming increasingly prevalent on the Web. More companies are including maps on their Web pages so that people are able to locate their offices or stores. If you just need a general map, there may be clip art to meet your needs. If you need a more detailed map and you have the map in an analog format, you can scan the map. Provided the original map, your scanner, and your scanning software are of high enough quality, this should work fine. A third and more exacting option is to use **mapping software**. By selecting the geographic area, scale, and proposed perspective, you can use mapping software to create a custom map illustrating precisely what you want viewers to see.

In addition, screen capture software programs are available that enable you to capture the entire contents of the computer screen or a selected area of the computer screen and save it as a graphic that can be used on a Web page. If you do not have access to screen capture software, you can use the [Print Scrn] key to capture the screen on a PC; and the Command + [Shift] + 3 keys to capture the screen on a Mac.

Copyright Law

The ease with which material can be copied, digitized, manipulated, and incorporated into a multimedia Web site has raised concerns about the adequacy of existing copyright laws. When you include graphic images and different multimedia elements on your Web pages, it is important to understand **copyright law**. Copyright laws are designed to protect intellectual property rights and provide potential monetary rewards for inventiveness and hard work. In this way, they foster creativity. Original material is copyright protected. Copyright law protects all art forms, including electronic art forms. Drawings, photographs, sound files, video clips, and even maps are protected by copyright law. The copyright holder can choose to freely distribute the material, license it, sell it, or withhold it from a particular use.

The 1976 Federal Copyright Act stipulates that copyrighted artwork is the property of the creator from the time it is created to 50 years beyond his or her life. If the creator is a corporation or business, the artwork is the property of the creator up to 75 years after publication or 100 years following creation, whichever is shorter. However, concerns have been expressed that copyright laws that apply to printed material cannot be applied to digitized material. A recent law, the **Digital Millennium Copyright Act of 1998**, was passed in an effort to better control copyright as it relates to digital media. In addition to or in place of the © symbol, some digital images may include an embedded signature or a digital watermark (see Figure 6-10). An embedded signature or digital watermark cannot be seen when the image is displayed or printed, but it does serve as proof of artistic ownership if needed.

If an image is copyright protected, you must obtain permission from the artist, publisher, or owner of the piece in order to copy or use it, even if you plan to use only part of it. If you fail to obtain permission to use someone else's work, you are violating copyright law, and you could be liable for damages including statutory damages, legal fees, and compensation to the artist. After obtaining a release to use a piece, be sure to read the agreement carefully. Though you can use some elements royalty free on any Web site, with others, you will need to pay the creator a royalty for each application in which you use it. As further insurance, you should always keep a log of your multimedia elements and the releases that accompany each piece.

QUICKTIP

Assume all creative endeavors that are not your original work are copyright protected. This is true even if the copyright symbol is not explicitly included. Do not try to get away with merely altering an image. There may be an embedded signature or a digital watermark within the image.

Materials that have no copyright are said to be in the public domain and can be manipulated and used without the artist's permission and without having to pay the artist any royalties for using it. When images or other copyright protected works are used strictly in news reporting, parody, research, and education, copyright permission may not be necessary. This exclusion is referred to as **fair use**. There are many factors that determine when this exception applies and when it does not.

In summary, the only time you can alter or manipulate artwork is if:

- you receive permission from the original artist, publisher, or owner of the piece
- you create the piece yourself
- the creative work is clearly public domain
- the creative work is being used strictly for instructional purposes or falls within the restrictions of fair use

FIGURE 6-10

Digital watermarks provide identity information about the creator or owner of an image that is invisible to the viewer

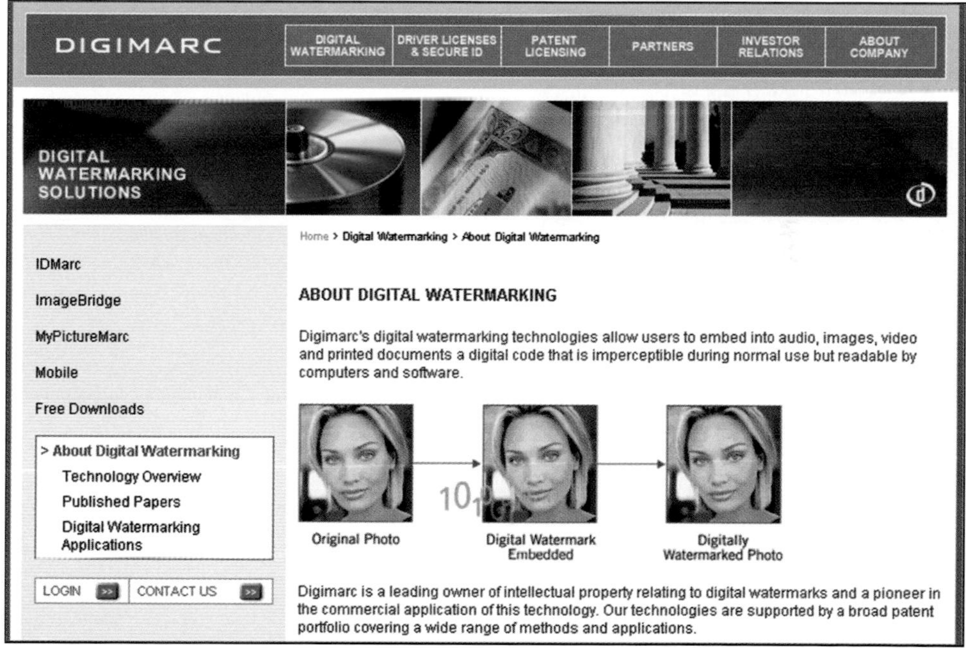

CONCEPT 2

IDENTIFY IMAGE Types

What You'll Learn

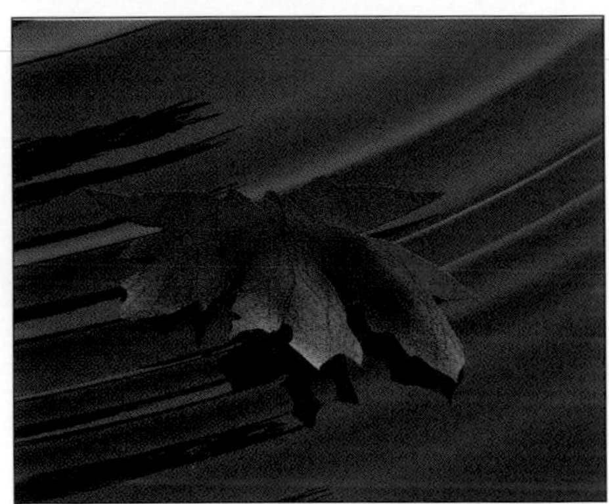

In this lesson, you will learn about the different types of digital images including line art, continuous-tone images, 2-D and 3-D images, hypergraphics, and image maps.

There are many different types of images used in Web-based multimedia production. A solid understanding of the terminology associated with these different types of images will help you work as part of a multimedia team.

Line art is the term used to describe drawings that contain flat colors without tonal variations. These images generally contain only black and white pixels; however, they could also be drawings that incorporate different colors. An example of line art is shown in Figure 6-11.

Continuous-tone images are graphics that have tonal variations, such as color photographs. A **grayscale image** is a continuous-tone image consisting of black, white, and gray data only. This is an image comprised of a range of grays, typically up to 256 levels of gray.

FIGURE 6-11

Drawings that contain flat colors, usually black and white, are considered line drawings

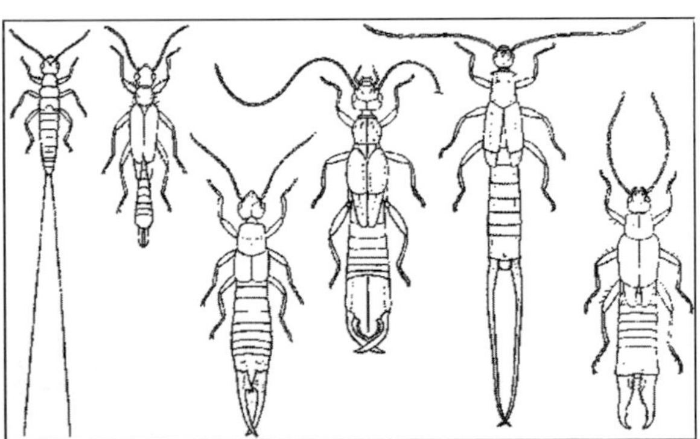

Images can also be classified as **two-dimensional (2-D)** or, by adding depth to them, they become **three-dimensional (3-D)**. As illustrated in Figure 6-12, three-dimensional images are much more lifelike than two-dimensional images. However, they are more difficult to create and they require greater computer resources to work with and display.

Actually, 3-D graphics on the computer merely represent a three-dimensional scene in two dimensions because a flat computer monitor allows images to be viewed in only two dimensions. Because the real world is three-dimensional, the 2-D interface is often stifling, particularly for Web sites designed for education, architecture, games, and training simulators. Some people predict that the 2-D desktop may eventually be replaced by a 3-D desktop. As evidence of this trend, 3-D environments are becoming increasingly common on the Web.

On Web pages, a graphic, no matter what type, can be used as a link just as text can be used as a link. Clickable graphics are called **hypergraphics**. When a graphic is a link, the pointer will usually change to a pointing finger when it is placed on a hotspot. Each graphic can contain one link or several links. Graphics that contain more than one link are called **image maps**. A single image usually takes less time to download than do multiple images, which is why image maps are commonly used on the opening menu screens of Web pages. However, image maps can be more difficult to create and maintain than single images. The image map shown in Figure 6-13 is a single graphic that has been set up with multiple hotspots. Each hotspot links the user to different information depending on the region clicked.

FIGURE 6-12

Three-dimensional images are more lifelike than two-dimensional images, but they also require greater computer resources

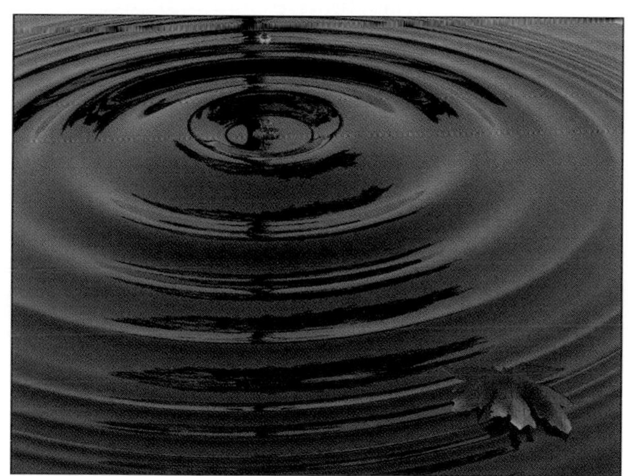

FIGURE 6-13

An image map is a single graphic that has been set up with multiple hotspots

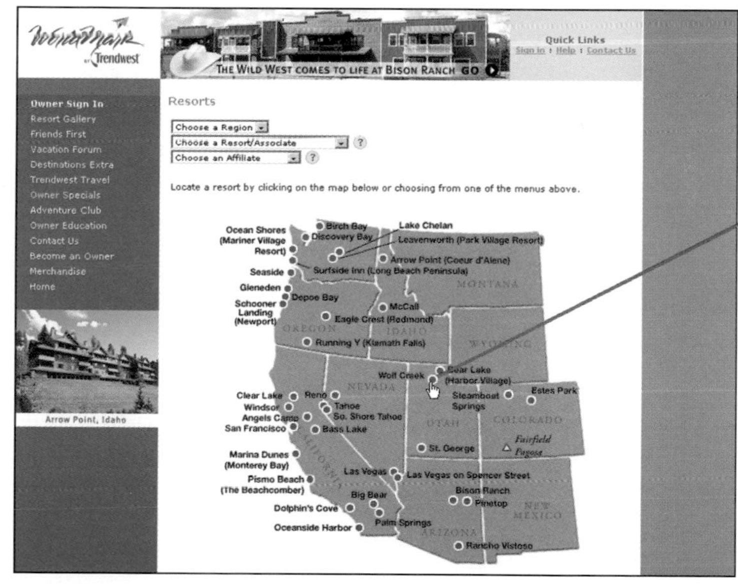

Clicking a hot spot (blue dot in this image) links the user to related information

CONCEPT 3

UNDERSTAND IMAGE Quality

What You'll Learn

In this lesson, you will learn how color resolution, image resolution, and compression impact the quality of an image.

Several factors affect image quality: color resolution, image resolution, and compression. In addition, images are dependent on the equipment used to display them. Although you cannot completely control the way an image displays on the user's monitor due to differences in gamma settings, dot pitch, and display settings such as monitor resolution and color, there are factors that you can control. Due to bandwidth considerations, Web designers must constantly weigh the cost of improving image quality with the cost of increasing file size and therefore time to download. It is an endless trade-off that you must learn to balance in order to create functional Web graphics.

When it comes to multimedia, resolution can be a confusing term. This is because it is used with several different multimedia elements, and it means something slightly different each time it is used. In other words, there are many different types of resolution. This chapter is concerned with resolution as it relates to the image itself. A discussion of color resolution and image resolution follows.

Color Resolution

All Web graphics, whether bitmap or vector, are displayed on a computer monitor. This monitor is an array of pixels. This array is referred to as a **bitmap**. Each pixel within the bitmap contains **bits** of information about the graphic. **Color resolution** measures the number of bits of stored information per pixel, which means it determines how many tones or colors every pixel in a bitmap can have. Color resolution is also called bit resolution, pixel resolution, color depth, bit depth, or pixel depth. If you want to understand Web graphics, you need to understand color resolution.

How is the range of colors available for each pixel determined? The number of colors is determined by information associated with the pixel. The information is coded in bits, which means binary digits. Color resolution ranges from 1-bit color (2 colors) to 32-bit color (16.7+ million colors) with the most common ranges being 8-, 16-, and 24-bit. Look at Figure 6-14. Notice that the total number of possible colors is calculated by raising 2 to the number associated with the color resolution (2, 4, 8, 16, and so on). So, for example, to determine how many colors can be displayed per pixel using 4-bit color resolution, take 2 (which is the number of colors for 1-bit color) and raise it the 4th. This number per bit is the number of colors each pixel can display, which ranges from one color to millions of colors. The higher the bit depth, the greater the number of colors stored in the image.

An image with a greater color resolution will be more colorful and of higher photographic quality. While 32-bit color depth will produce a higher quality image, it will also make the file size much larger because more information must be stored for every pixel. Therefore, as shown in Figure 6-15, there is a trade off between color depth and file size.

FIGURE 6-14
Color resolution, or bit depth, ranges from 1-bit to 32-bit color

Color Resolution		
32-bit	2^{32}	16.7+ million colors plus an 8-bit (256-level) grayscale mask
24-bit	2^{24}	16.7+ million colors
16-bit	2^{16}	65.5 thousand colors
8-bit	2^{8}	256 colors
4-bit	2^{4}	16 colors
2-bit	2^{2}	4 colors
1-bit	2^{1}	2 colors

FIGURE 6-15
As the bit depth increases, so does the size of the file

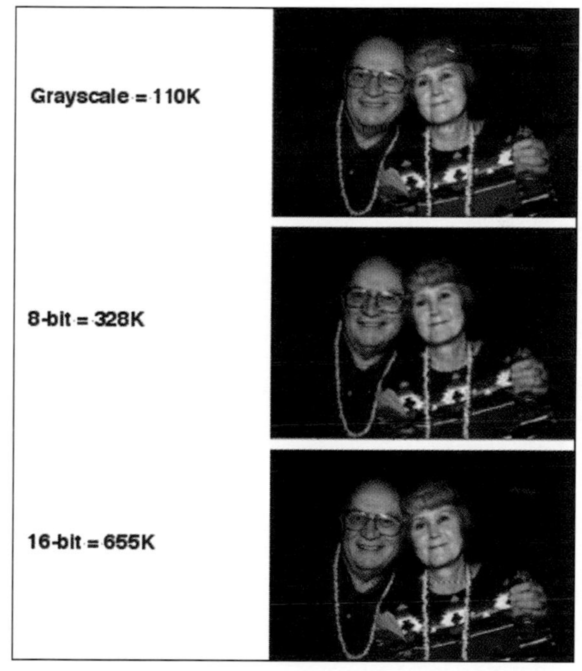

The colors that make up the image are referenced to a **palette**. Notice how the palette in Figure 6-16 changes as the bit depth of the image changes. The main point to remember is that the number of colors available in the palette is determined by the color resolution of the image.

Because the colors available to display the image are dependent on the bit depth of the image as well as the color resolution of the user's monitor, there is no guarantee that your image will display as you planned. If you save an image as 24-bit color but your user's monitor is set to display only 256 colors (or 8-bit color), the colors in your image will be converted to a fixed palette. This conversion can result in drastic changes in the way your image appears.

Although the 256-color limitation is due to the viewer's 8-bit video card, the browser sets the color palette for the image. The fixed palette shared by the most popular browsers contains 216 common colors and is called the **browser-safe** or **Web-safe color palette**. Instead of selecting colors from the image, if a 16-bit or 26-bit image is viewed on a monitor that will display only 8-bit color, the browser converts the image to this 216-color fixed palette. Again, this conversion process can have a drastic effect on your image.

FIGURE 6-16

As the bit depth changes, so does the color palette

1-bit color = 2 colors

4-bit color = 16 colors

8-bit color = 256 colors

Web-safe color = 216

When an image with millions of colors is converted to an image with only 256 colors, some colors have to be removed from the image. This is accomplished either by **dithering** or **banding** the image. Dithering is the process of positioning different colored pixels side-by-side to create the illusion that no colors are missing. For example, placing red and blue pixels next to each other would create the illusion of purple. Banding reduces the colors without dithering, which results in areas of solid colors. Although neither of these options is ideal, as you can see from Figure 6-17, dithering is generally a better option than banding.

One way to guard against the potential hazard of the browser converting your 24- or 32-bit image to 256 colors is to save your images using the 216 colors found in the Web-safe color palette. Because these colors are recognized across browsers, operating systems, and platforms, you will not have to worry about the colors within your image changing. Because most video cards today will display millions of colors, many Web designers find the Web-safe color palette archaic and limiting and therefore choose to ignore it. Always remember that color resolution is a factor in determining the quality of an image.

FIGURE 6-17
Dithering is generally better than banding

Image Resolution

Image resolution refers to the amount of information stored for each image, which means the number of pixels making up the image. Typically, image resolution is measured in pixels per inch (ppi). Images must be at a certain minimum resolution to avoid a pixelated or out-of-focus appearance. Although a high image resolution is extremely important if a graphic is to be printed, the same is not true for graphics used on a Web site. Web graphics can be set to 72 ppi because most computer monitors cannot display more than 72 ppi Setting Web graphics any higher than 72 ppi only makes them larger both in file size and on screen. See Figure 6-18.

When deciding on an appropriate resolution for your image, keep in mind that a higher image resolution will display a superior image but it will also result in a larger file size. This means the file will require more storage space and it will take longer to download and display. When creating images for Web pages, there are times when some quality must be sacrificed in order to ensure that the graphic file sizes are small enough to download quickly.

The present Web audience consists of people accessing the Web via dial-up as well as higher-speed broadband connections. At low connection speeds, a modest 36K graphic on your Web page could take 10 seconds or longer to download. Actual data transmission rates vary depending on the amount of traffic on the network, the speed of the Web server, the type of Internet connection used, and other factors. However, the overall point is clear: the more graphics you use, the longer your reader will have to wait to see your page. Therefore, something must be done to optimize your images and make them as small as possible. Most images can be optimized if you do the following:

- Reduce the color resolution (number of colors) to the minimum necessary for the image
- Reduce the image resolution to no more than 72 ppi (pixels per inch)
- Choose and apply the image size (in pixels) that you will need for your final Web page
- Crop to the smallest area possible

Each of these steps will reduce your image's file size by a discrete amount and the smaller the file size the faster the image will load. In addition, there are software programs designed specifically for image optimization that will greatly assist you in maintaining high-quality graphics while significantly

FIGURE 6-18

Image resolution is a factor in determining the size of the image on screen

Resolution: 72 ppi

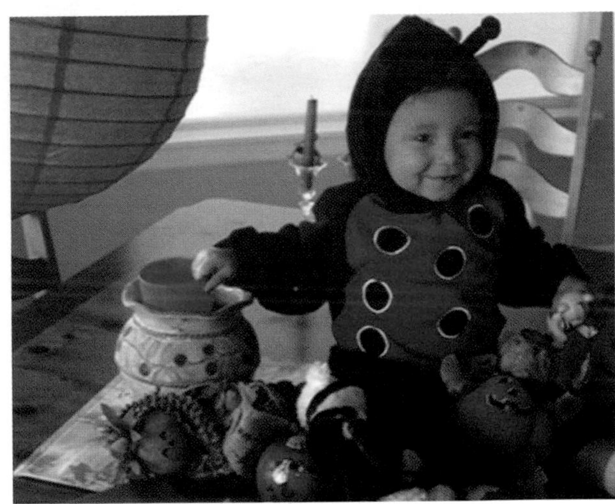

Resolution: 150 ppi

reducing the file size. Determining how much quality you are willing to sacrifice for a smaller file requires a judgment call that you will have to make regularly. As a general guideline, Web graphics should not exceed 30K. However, there are always exceptions to rules so be prepared to experiment, optimize, and make decisions about what is acceptable in terms of both image size and quality.

Image Compression

In general, graphics consume a lot of storage space. Because graphic files consume a lot more storage space than text, they also take longer to transfer or download from the Web server to the user's computer. One way to solve this problem is to compress the files. **Compression** is simply an algorithm that is used to create smaller file sizes. File compression reduces the file size of a graphic and therefore reduces the transfer time to the user's computer. Files are compressed before they are sent to the user's computer and decompressed before they are displayed. In fact, the standard graphic file formats for the Web are compressed automatically when they are created.

There are two types of compression: **lossless** and **lossy**. With lossless compression, none of the data is actually lost during compression. Instead, mathematical algorithms eliminate redundant data. If there is not a lot of redundant data, the file size may not be significantly reduced. In fact, in some instances file size will actually be increased. Many graphic formats and compression utilities, such as WinZip and StuffIt, use lossless compression. Lossless compression is important for text where you need to maintain the same appearance before and after compression.

In lossy compression some of the data is lost. The idea behind lossy compression is that some of the data is not important to an image and therefore that data is expendable. For example, in Figure 6-19, notice how the color palette changes when the file is saved using lossy compression. The colors that are not needed within the image are expendable and although this decreases the size of the file it does not significantly impact the quality of the image.

FIGURE 6-19

Lossy compression removes expendable data to create a smaller file size

Uncompressed 655K

Compressed 110K

CONCEPT 4

EXPLORE GRAPHICS Software

What You'll Learn

In this lesson, you will learn about the different types of graphics programs used to create and edit bitmapped, vector, and 3-D images.

There are many **graphics programs** available that allow a graphic artist or Web designer to create and modify two-dimensional images for multimedia Web sites. These graphics programs include drawing, paint, and image editing programs. You will probably need to use a combination of these programs when designing a multimedia Web site. In addition, there are programs, called 3-D-modeling programs, that allow you to create or modify three-dimensional images.

Because features available in graphics programs vary, you should ask yourself questions such as those listed in the table in Figure 6-20 when analyzing which graphics program to use. High-end

FIGURE 6-20

Ask yourself questions, such as those listed in this table, when analyzing which graphics program to use

FEATURE	QUESTIONS
Image manipulation	Does the graphics program allow you to stretch, skew and rotate an image?
Filters	Does the graphics program have filters for sharpening, softening, and styling the image?
Anti-aliasing	Does the graphics program support anti-aliasing? Anti-aliasing smoothes edges by blending the colors on the edge of the image with the adjacent colors. Because bitmaps are made up of rectangular pixels, the outside edge of the image can appear jagged. Anti-aliasing adjusts for this problem.
Text support	How extensive is the text support? Does the graphics program support manipulation of PostScript and TrueType fonts?
Graphics tablets	Does the graphics program support pressure-sensitive graphics tablets, which are periphial devices that can be used for freehand drawing?
Open architecture	Does the graphics program support open architecture? Is it compatible with third-party software such as programs that provide special effects?

graphics programs address all of the issues raised in these questions.

There are many advantages to creating your own images. When you create them, you own them, and you do not have to worry about copyright, permission, and royalties. You can edit and manipulate the images in any way you desire. If you have a clear vision of the images you want, you may find it easier to create them yourself rather than explain them to someone else who may find it difficult to understand your vision. With today's tools, you can either create the images using drawing, paint, image editing, and 3-D modeling software, or you can draw them, paint them, and edit them using traditional methods and then digitize them with a camera or scanner.

Typically, to create on-screen graphics in one of these programs, you use a **tool palette** similar to those shown in Figure 6-21. Each tool palette contains electronic drawing tools such as pencils, paintbrushes, and erasers. Once you have created or modified images using the available drawing tools, you can resize, move, rotate, or change the shape of images. Once completed, the images can be incorporated into a Web page.

A discussion of different types of graphics programs, including features of each, follows.

FIGURE 6-21

These tool palettes contain electronic drawing tools used to create and modify graphic images

Adobe Photoshop *Adobe Illustrator* *Adobe ImageReady*

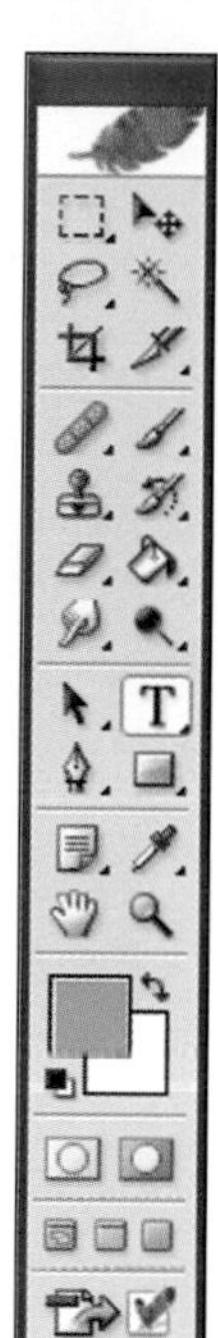

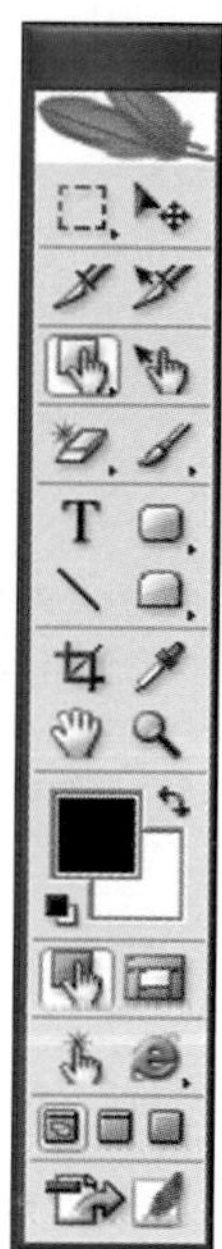

Paint Programs

When you use a **paint program**, the image you create is a **bitmapped image**. Paint programs allow you to edit images at the pixel level as shown in Figure 6-22. This means paint programs can be used to accomplish effects such as changing colors in photographs pixel by pixel.

Because bitmapped images are pixel-based, when you enlarge these images the squares simply get bigger. In other words, because bitmapped images have a specific resolution or number of pixels per inch, if the image is enlarged without adding extra pixels, the size of each pixel is increased. Consequently, the pixels are larger, but there are fewer pixels per inch. Obviously, this decreases the resolution. Enlarging an image too much may result in **staircasing**, or **jaggies**, such as those shown in Figure 6-23. Jaggies are the stair-stepped edges that result when you enlarge a bitmapped image too much.

When you reduce the width and height of a bitmapped image, the opposite occurs. Pixels become smaller, therefore, there are more of them per inch. Although this increased resolution is aesthetically pleasing, it may create an unnecessarily large file size.

FIGURE 6-22
Zoom in to edit a bitmapped image pixel by pixel

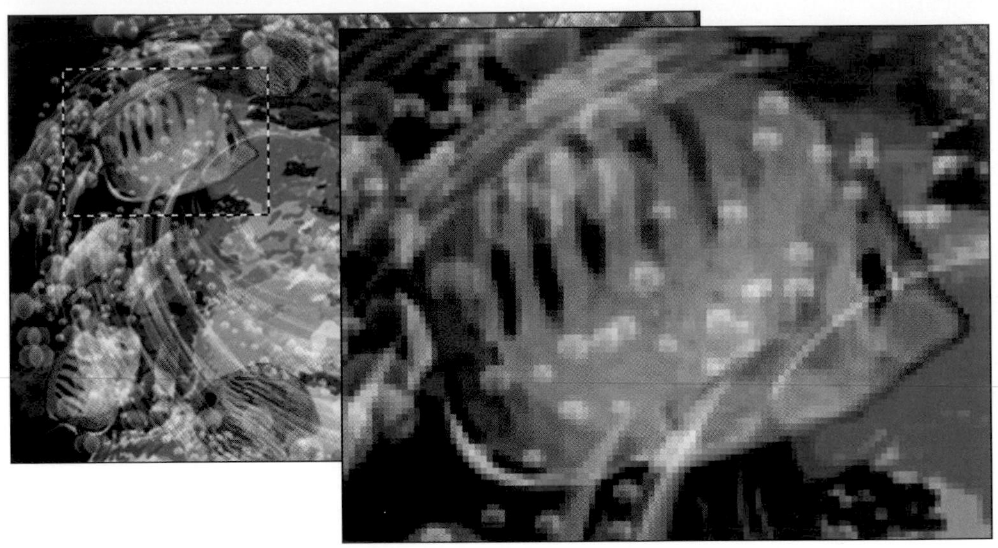

FIGURE 6-23
The original bitmapped image has been enlarged too much and so the smooth edges have been replaced by jaggies

Features of Paint Programs

Although all paint programs are slightly different, they do share many common features.

Geometric figures. With paint programs, there are many tools available that allow you to create and combine geometric figures and shapes to create forms. For example, you can choose the line tool, the rectangle tool, the oval tool, and the freeform tool to create images like the ice cream cone in Figure 6-24.

Edit. All paint programs offer some method of editing mistakes; the eraser tool is one of the more common tools for removing mistakes. If you place a line where you later decide you do not want one or if you draw the line too long, you can use the eraser tool to remove it. In addition, the undo feature enables you to undo what you have done.

Add color and patterns. After you have created the image, you can add color to it using Fill and Paintbrush tools. Fill tools enable you to cover entire areas with solid color or special patterns of color whereas Brush tools apply color or spray patterns of dots to an area based on the size and type of brush selected. Combined, these tools allow you to apply color to objects and backgrounds.

Selection. Using selection tools you can select any part of an image. This selected area can then be copied, moved, modified, or deleted without impacting the rest of the pixels in the image.

FIGURE 6-24

Lines and other geometric figures available on the tool palette can be used to create images like this ice cream cone

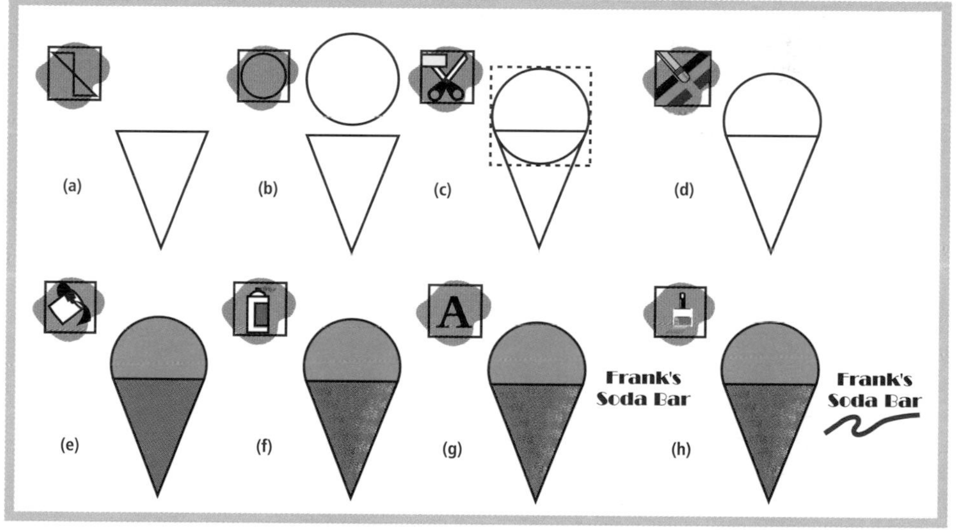

Rotate. The horizontal or vertical position of an image can easily be modified. In some programs, you can flip the image only horizontally or vertically. However, as shown in Figure 6-25, more sophisticated paint programs allow you to specify the direction and number of degrees to rotate an image.

FIGURE 6-25

Paint programs allow you to specify the direction (clockwise or counterclockwise) and the number of degrees to rotate an image

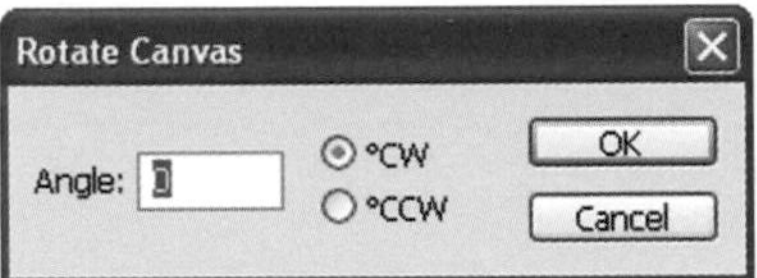

Drawing Programs

Drawing programs allow you to create **vector graphics**, which are created and re-created from mathematical models. These models actually create the image as a series of mathematical formulas that connect vectors or simple geometric shapes such as lines and arcs that ultimately become circles and boxes. Vector graphics can be resized or contorted without losing the quality of the image (see Figure 6-26). Vector graphics are smoother and more precise than bitmapped graphics. In general, they also require less memory. Because vector graphics are more versatile and more precise than bitmapped images, professionals in art and drafting often use them. In addition to drawing programs, most 3-D graphics programs and computer-aided design (CAD) programs also produce vector graphics.

Drawing programs excel as art production and illustration tools for creating original artwork. They are useful in creating designs where precise dimensions and relationships are important.

FIGURE 6-26

This image can be changed at any point without losing the quality of the image

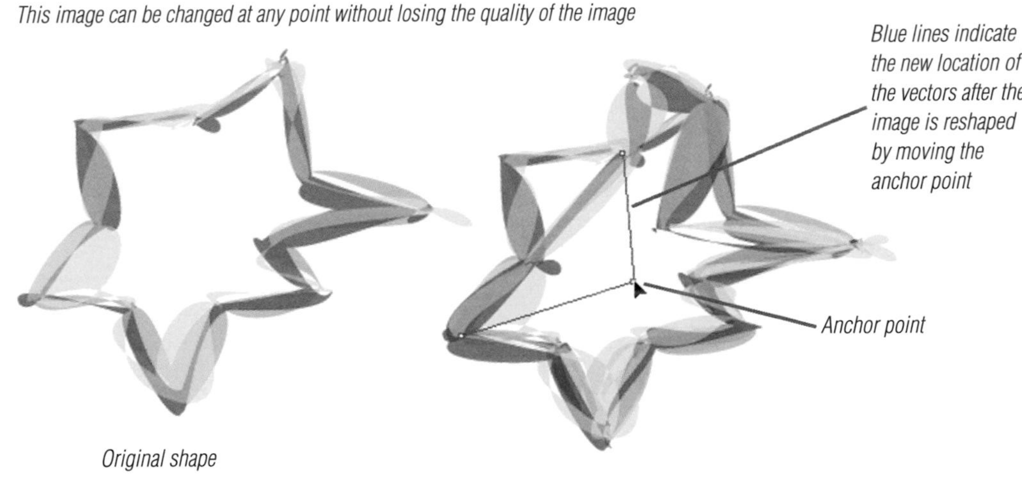

Features of Drawing Programs

Common drawing programs used today are **Adobe Illustrator** and **Macromedia FreeHand**. Common features found in Adobe Illustrator, an industry-standard drawing program, are discussed next.

Fully editable shapes. Adobe Illustrator contains different tools that can be used to create a variety of shapes, such as a 30-point star or a 15-sided polygon. Though you could also create these shapes in a paint program, it would require a lot more time and patience. In addition, when shapes are created with a drawing program, they are fully editable. Bitmapped graphics can only be edited pixel by pixel.

Bézier curves. Creating curved lines is much easier in a drawing programs than it is in a paint program. This is because all curves in Adobe Illustrator and most drawing programs are **Bézier curves**. These are curves, named after Pierre Bézier, that are defined mathematically by four control points. The control points are the two directional nodes at the end of each line, and the handles tangent to each curve (see Figure 6-27). These control points allow you to fine-tune a curve.

Freehand drawings created in a drawing program are converted into Bézier curves. In Illustrator, freehand drawings are created using the Pen tool (see Figure 6-28), which is the industry's most powerful tool for creating precise paths.

FIGURE 6-27
Change the shape of a Bézier curve by moving its handles

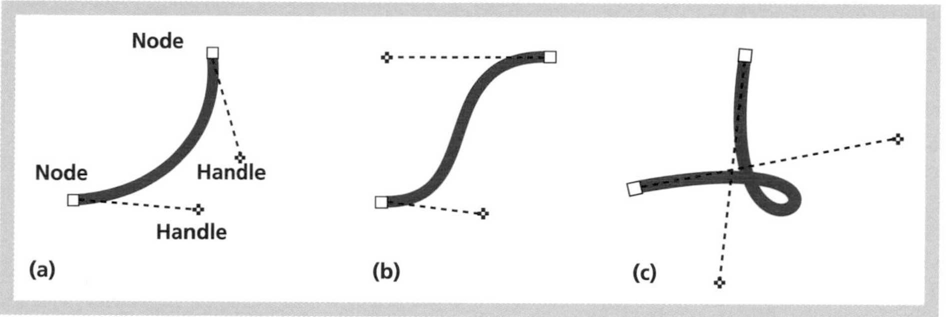

FIGURE 6-28
Bézier curves can be created and modified using the Pen tool in Adobe Illustrator

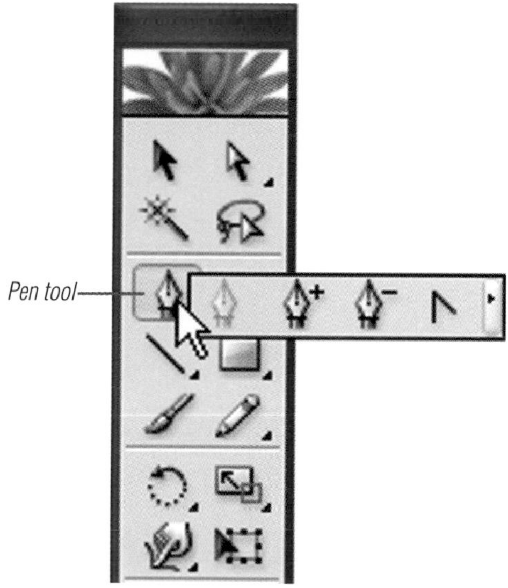

Gradient fill. Both draw and paint programs use **gradient fills**, which provide a graduated blend between colors. This blending can be either linear or it may radiate from a specific point. This blending may occur between a single starting and ending color, or it may consist of multiple intermediate blends between colors as shown in Figure 6-29. The gradient fill feature makes an object look more professional by giving it a 3-D effect.

Blending. **Blending** allows you to create a series of intermediate colors and shapes between two selected objects so that one seems to blend into the other. This process is often called **morphing**.

Grouping objects. When you use a drawing program to create a graphic image, each part of the image is considered a separate component (see Figure 6-30). If you want to resize, reshape, or rotate the entire image, you would have to modify each component of the image separately. Because this is an inefficient and time-consuming way of working with an object, drawing programs allow you to **group** the components together. After individual components are grouped together, the components become one object. The drawing program and other programs recognize all of the components of the object as one unit. You can also group and **ungroup** components within the image to have fewer components with which to work.

FIGURE 6-29
The gradient fill added to this polygon consists of blends between different colors

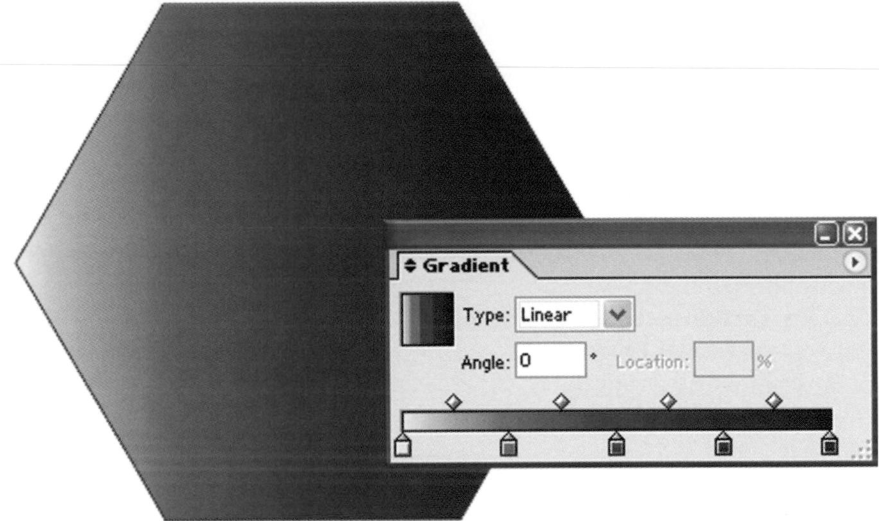

Rasterize. Each time items on a Web page change, the entire screen must be redrawn. This is called the **refresh rate**. Because performance is critical in multimedia Web sites, a fast refresh rate is also critical. On a Web page, bitmapped graphics are sometimes considered superior to vector images because the refresh rate of a screen containing bitmapped images tends to be faster than the refresh rate of a Web page containing vector images. With vector images, the computer must recalculate all of the vectors each time the screen is redrawn. As you might imagine, this can take time depending on the complexity of the image. For this reason, most of the graphic file formats supported by Web browsers are bitmapped file formats. Many drawing programs, including Adobe Illustrator, allow images to be exported to a bitmapped format so that they can be used on a Web page. This feature gives you the best of both worlds. You can edit your images with the flexibility of a drawing program yet export them as bitmapped graphics for the Web. The process of converting a vector image to pixels is called **rasterizing**, and the resulting bitmapped graphics are often called **raster graphics**.

Drawing programs, such as Adobe Illustrator, have features specifically for designing and creating Web graphics including versatile transparency capabilities and powerful object and layer effects, as well as other innovative features.

FIGURE 6-30

In a drawing a program, an image (top) is made up of many different components (bottom); each is independent and must be edited individually

Grouped

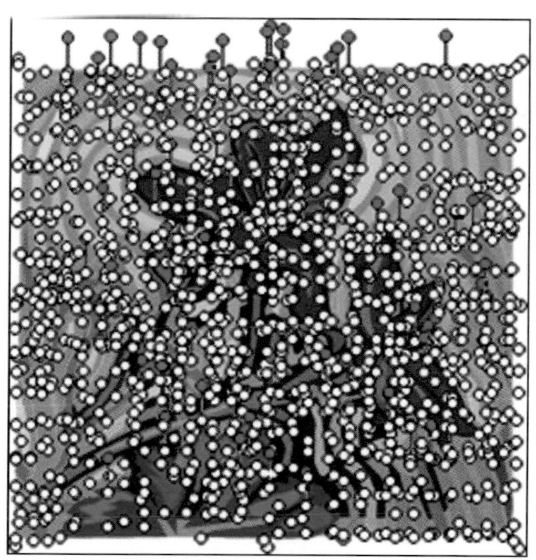

Ungrouped

3-D Modeling Programs

Three-dimensional objects help create a virtual world by adding depth to two-dimensional objects. **3-D modeling** programs (also called **rendering programs**) are used to create and manipulate 3-D images.

In creating 3-D objects, geometric forms or wireframe models serve as basic building blocks (see Figure 6-31). For example, cubes and cylinders are combined to form models. This wireframe model concept comes from clay modeling where artists first create a wireframe model to which they apply clay. With 3-D modeling programs, different surfaces or **textures** are applied or mapped to the models to give them shadows and provide special effects. After the model is created and a surface applied, the next step in most programs is to select a **perspective** (top, front, or side) and lighting from which the object is to be viewed.

After an object or a scene has been modeled in three dimensions and a perspective has been established, it must then be converted to an image that will be visible on a Web page. This conversion process is called **rendering**. Though 3-D objects created in modeling programs are quite impressive, rendering requires a great deal of processing power. Depending on the complexity of the image, it may take hours or even days to render a 3-D drawing.

Features of 3-D Modeling Programs

There are many software programs available that allow you to build 3-D objects, add colors and textures to these objects, arrange the objects in a scene, light the scene, and finally, render it. Among others, some of the common modeling programs used today are Maya, Softimage, 3D Studio Max, Poser, Bryce, Carrara, RenderMan, and LightWave 3D. A discussion of several common features found in 3-D modeling programs follows.

FIGURE 6-31
Different surfaces and textures will be applied to this wireframe model to make it appear lifelike

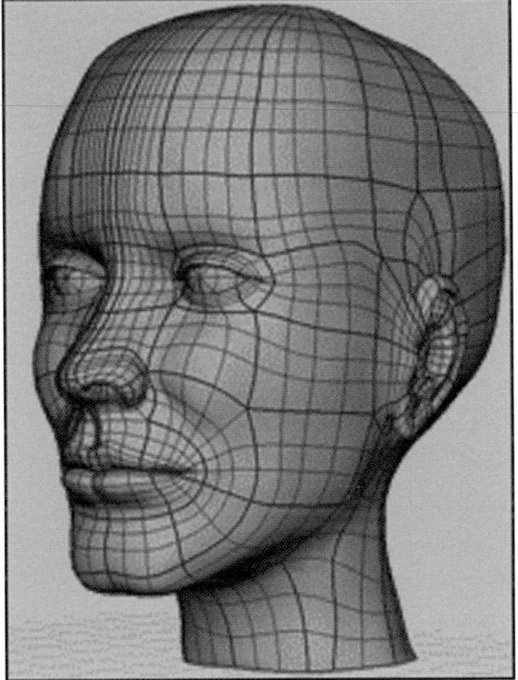

Modeling. **Modeling** is the process of creating an object to place in a scene. There are three different ways to model an object. You can use primitive objects (see Figure 6-32), which are 3-D geometric figures, such as cones, spheres, and cylinders. You can design your own free-form objects with the drawing tools. Or, you can create text objects, which are blocks of 3-D type.

Arranging objects. Arranging objects is the process of positioning and orienting them. As you can imagine, arranging objects is very important when you are trying to create a realistic 3-D scene. An object's spatial relationship to other objects is particularly important. This means that resizing objects as they change position may also be necessary.

Shading. The process of assigning surface properties such as color, texture, and finish to an object is called **shading**. Shading determines whether an object appears rough or smooth, shiny or dull, transparent or opaque (see Figure 6-33). Trying different shading features is generally a simple drag-and-drop process. Two-dimensional images can also be used as a texture. If done well, these images can give your objects unparalleled realism. For example, you can use a scanned photograph or illustration as a texture map. This is helpful because many complex real-world surfaces are difficult or nearly impossible to design even with today's sophisticated tools. By combining multiple surface attributes, you can create objects that simulate complex materials such as hammered gold, polished wood, or rough granite.

FIGURE 6-32

Primitive objects, such as cones, spheres, and cylinders, can be used to model an object

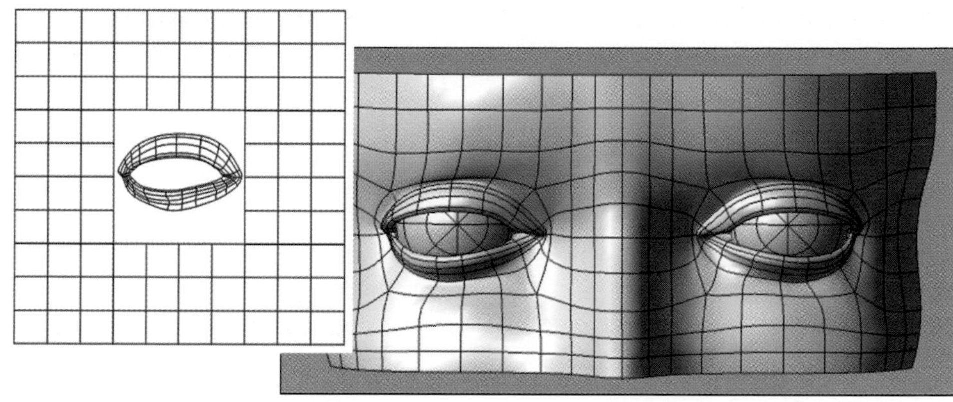

FIGURE 6-33

Surface attributes can be applied to the entire object or to parts of an object

To apply shading to a limited area on the surface of an object, you can use 3-D paint tools that allow you to paint shapes directly on the surface of an object. The 3-D paint tools are not limited to painting with color, you can load your brush with gold, marble, or concrete and apply color, reflection, transparency, and other shading attributes. Once these shapes have been painted, they can also be moved, resized, or layered.

Lighting and camera angle. Setting lighting and camera orientation is important in establishing a perspective and setting the mood of a scene. Lighting conditions are important in creating high-quality 3-D objects. The exact scene rendered under different light can create an entirely different result. Different types of lights are supported in most 3-D modeling programs. As shown in Figure 6-34, using different types of lights creates differences in the appearance of a 3-D object.

FIGURE 6-34
Different types of lights and lighting effects are supported in most 3-D modeling programs

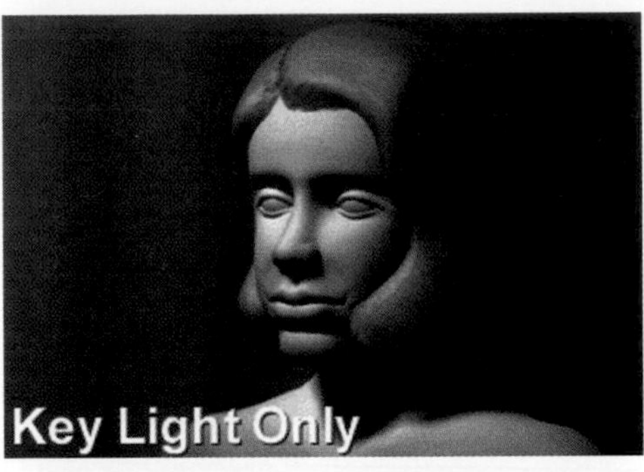

Using only a key light, the subject's hair and face are in dark shadows.

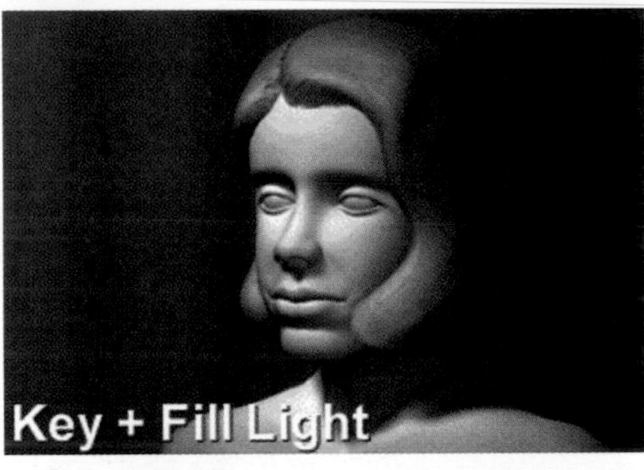

By adding a fill light, the subject's face, hair, and neck have noticeably fewer shadows.

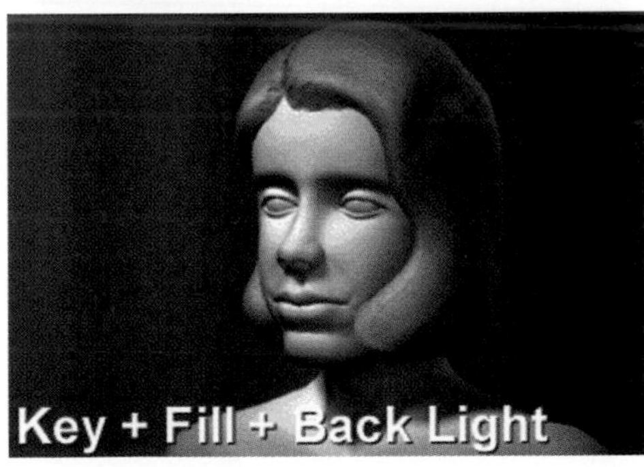

The inclusion of a back light creates a glow around the back of the subject's hair and neck.

The position and orientation of a camera is also important in establishing a perspective. Camera angles provide viewpoints. As you work and build the scene, several cameras can be placed at different locations. By switching between the cameras, you can see alternate perspectives of your object or scene.

Rendering. Rendering is the process of capturing a view of a 3-D scene and saving it as a 2-D image. When a scene is rendered, all of the forms, colors, and textures of all objects, as well as the lights and surfaces, are analyzed and converted to a 2-D image, as shown in Figure 6-35.

If you want to see a 2-D object created from a drawing program from another side, you must redraw it. With 3-D scenes, you can see different views by changing the lighting and the camera angles and re-rendering the scene based on the new settings. The original scene is a separate file and is stored in a different format than the rendered scenes. Rendering produces a 2-D, photorealistic, bitmapped image of a scene. Therefore, in order to open an image in another program, such as an image editing program, it must be rendered first.

FIGURE 6-35
The vector model for this image was drawn with a 3-D modeling program; the computer then rendered a realistic picture of the model by tracing the course of theoretical rays of light

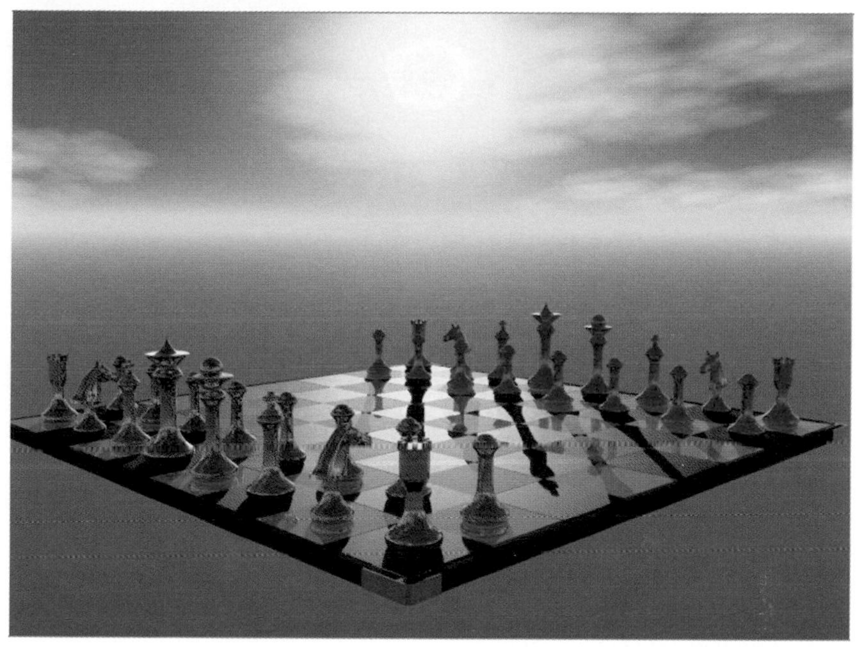

Image Editing Programs

Image editing programs allow you to manipulate digitized images using a variety of features that combine painting, editing, and other image composition tools. There are several good image editing programs from which to choose. Adobe Photoshop, which is the leader and industry standard, is comprehensive, versatile, and accurate. It is used by graphic artists, photographers, and illustrators, and can be used to work with almost any kind of graphic file format.

FIGURE 6-36

Use the Crop tool to remove unwanted or unnecessary areas of an image

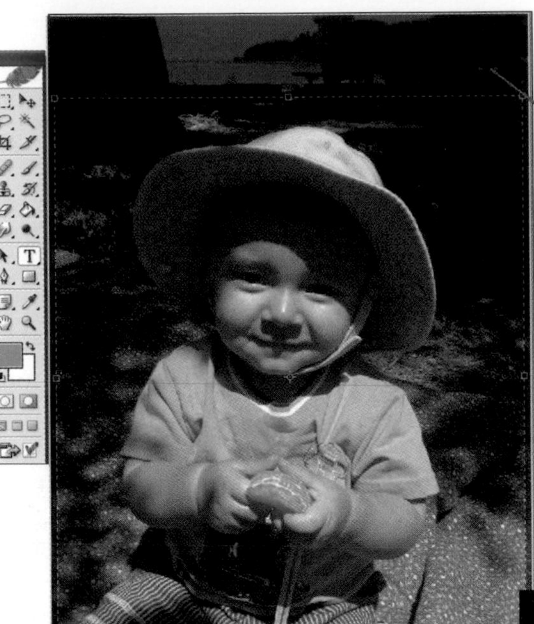

Unwanted area cropped from image

In the cropped image, unwanted areas are removed and the subject becomes the focus.

Features of Image Editing Programs

A discussion of some predominant features available in Photoshop and most image editing programs follows.

Cropping. Because image editing programs are used extensively to manipulate photographs, one of the first tasks you may encounter is the need to remove or **crop** areas of a photograph you do not wish to include on a Web page. See Figure 6-36. In addition to removing items that you do not want in the photograph, cropping will also contribute to a smaller file size. The crop tool in the tool palette makes it easy for the designer to select a section of an image he or she wants to keep and remove the rest of the image.

Brightness, contrast, and color correction. Slider controls allow you to adjust the brightness and contrast of an image, as shown in Figure 6-37. As you use the slider, you can preview the change and establish just the effect you are trying to achieve. Because it is rare that an image you scan will appear on your screen with the same color values as the original, you can also adjust the color using color sliders; or you can completely change the colors in an image.

Layers. Another wonderful feature of image editing programs is the ability to add **layers**. Layers are different levels in a document. Every Photoshop document contains one or more layers. When you start a new file, it contains a background layer. Each new layer that is added is transparent until pixel values (artwork, text, images) are added to it. On each layer, you can draw, paste images, or reposition artwork without affecting the pixels on the other layers.

FIGURE 6-37
Use the sliders to adjust the color balance

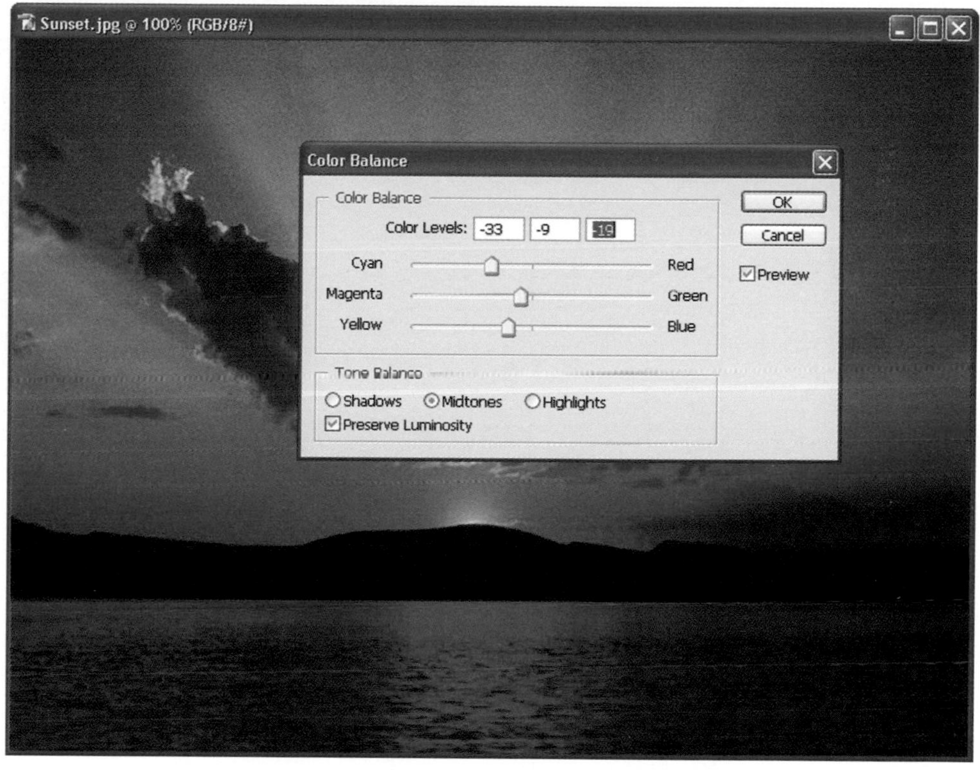

Filters. **Filters** are special effects applied to an image or part of an image. Filters can be applied to an entire image or to a selected area of an image. Filters can be used to blur or sharpen an image, create a mosaic effect, or distort the image. Filters are available with the program or additional filters can be purchased from third-party vendors. Within Photoshop there are a number of different types of filters each with a number of settings. As shown in Figure 6-38, a dialog box allows you to preview the result of the filter before you apply it.

File format conversion. Though there are programs designed specifically to convert graphic files from one format to another, image editing programs are also quite good at doing this. For example, if a file is in a **Tagged Image File Format (TIFF)**, and you need to use it on a Web page that supports **Graphics Interchange Format (GIF)** or **Joint Photographic Experts Group (JPEG)** files, you can open the TIFF file in an image editing program and save it as a GIF or JPEG file. In other words, if you need a file in a particular format, Photoshop and other image editing programs have features that will enable you to open the file and save it in the desired format.

FIGURE 6-38
Applying an artistic filter to this photograph makes it look like a painting

Enhancement Programs

Many third-party developers create **plug-ins** or add-on features that enhance the capabilities of painting, drawing, 3-D modeling, and image editing programs. For example, there are programs that expand the number of filters available in Adobe Photoshop. As you learn to use different graphics programs, you will probably want to experiment with some of their plug-ins as well.

In addition to plug-ins, Adobe and Macromedia have also developed programs specifically for working with Web graphics and Web animation. **Macromedia Fireworks** allows you to work with graphics and makes creating Web animations, buttons, and page compositions quick and easy. In addition, it is a superior program for **optimizing** images for the Web. Optimizing is the process of making the image file sizes as small as possible for quick download via the Web. Similarly, Adobe has a product called **ImageReady** that looks and feels like Photoshop but is specifically designed for producing and optimizing screen-based images and animation for the Web. As shown in Figure 6-39, there are different settings within the program that enable you to tweak the file format, amount of compression, and number of colors used in order to make your image as small as possible while maintaining adequate quality to project a professional image.

FIGURE 6-39

Adobe ImageReady offers different settings that enable you to reduce the size of an image file while still maintaining its quality

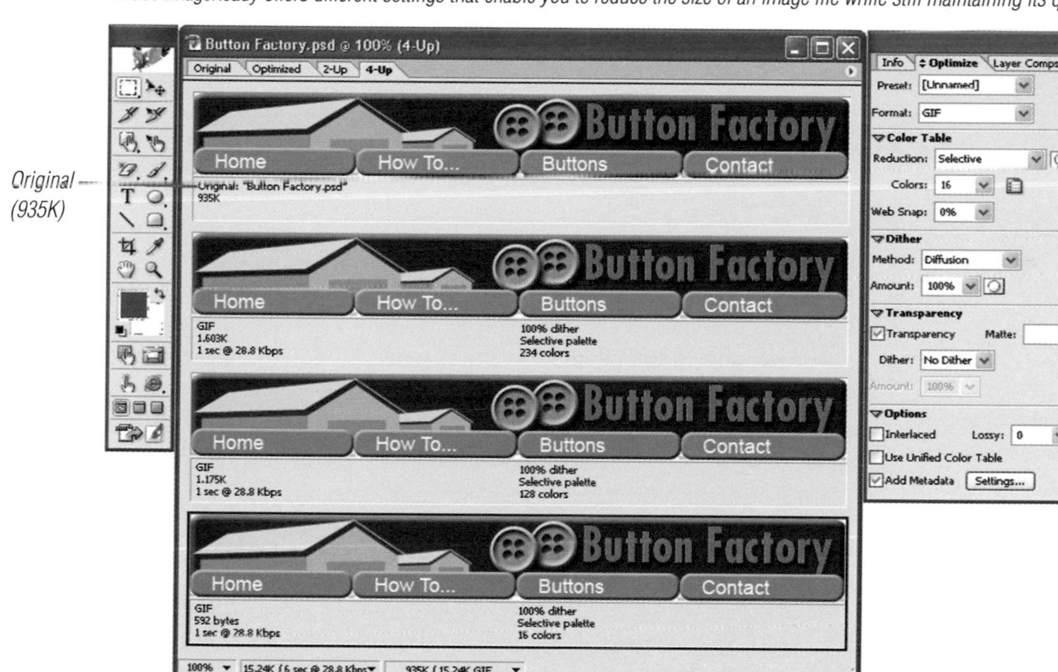

CONCEPT 5

DISCUSS WEB GRAPHIC File Formats

What You'll Learn

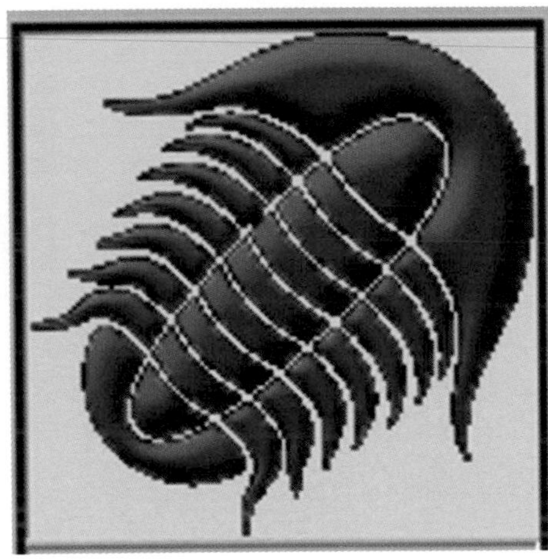

In this lesson, you will learn about the different Web graphic file formats - GIF, JPEG, and PNG. You will also understand which types of images are best saved in each of these file formats.

Graphic images may be stored in a variety of file formats. In choosing a format, you should consider how and where the image will be used. The Web limits the graphic file format choices to those currently supported by the most popular browsers, as discussed next. Even within these file formats, however, different types of formats are more appropriately designed for different types of images.

GIF (Graphics Interchange Format)

The Graphics Interchange Format (GIF) was created by CompuServe and is sometimes listed as CompuServe GIF. In the early 1990s, the original designers of the World Wide Web adopted the GIF format for its efficiency and widespread familiarity. It is one of the standard formats supported by Web browsers without the need for plug-ins. This format is generally best for solid color images rather than continuous-tone images. Today many images on the Web use the GIF format.

The GIF format provides a method for storing bitmaps on the Web. This format only supports up to 256 colors meaning GIF files are limited to an 8-bit color palette, which helps to keep files sizes at a minimum. The GIF format also supports **interlacing**. GIFs that include interlacing appear blurry and sharpen as they are downloaded. Interlacing enables users to see a complete, albeit, blurry image without having to wait for the entire image to download. The conventional (non-interlaced) GIF graphic downloads one line of pixels at a time. In interlaced GIF files, the image data is stored in a format that allows the browser to begin to build a low-resolution version of the full-sized GIF on the screen while the file is still downloading. The "fuzzy-to-sharp" effect of interlacing is visually appealing, but the most important benefit of interlacing is that it gives the reader a quick preview of the full area of the picture. Interlaced graphics are not faster to load than non-interlaced graphics, they just look as if they download faster because the rough preview comes up faster.

There are variations of the GIF file format that add support for transparency and animation. You may see references to the different GIF formats as "GIF87a"or "GIF89a," which are also respectively referred to as transparent GIF and animated GIF. Transparency is used to create irregularly shaped graphics by allowing designers to set a background color to transparent so that the image does not appear with a rectangular background, as shown in Figure 6-40. Unfortunately, the transparent property in the GIF format is not selective. In other words, if you make a color transparent, every pixel in the graphic that shares that same color will become transparent. This can lead to unexpected and undesirable results when a color is used both in the background and in other places of the graphic. Animated GIFs are a single file in which multiple images are stored. When the animated GIF is viewed on the Web, the multiple images are played back one at a time. This creates the illusion of motion. To create the illusion of motion, transparency is necessary.

In summary, the advantages of the GIF format include the following:

- All Web browsers support the GIF file format without plug-ins.
- Images that consist primarily of solid color look best and are smallest when saved in the GIF file format.
- GIF supports interlacing, transparency, and animation.

FIGURE 6-40

Transparent GIFs allow irregularly shaped images on a Web page to drop the rectangular backgrounds that contain them

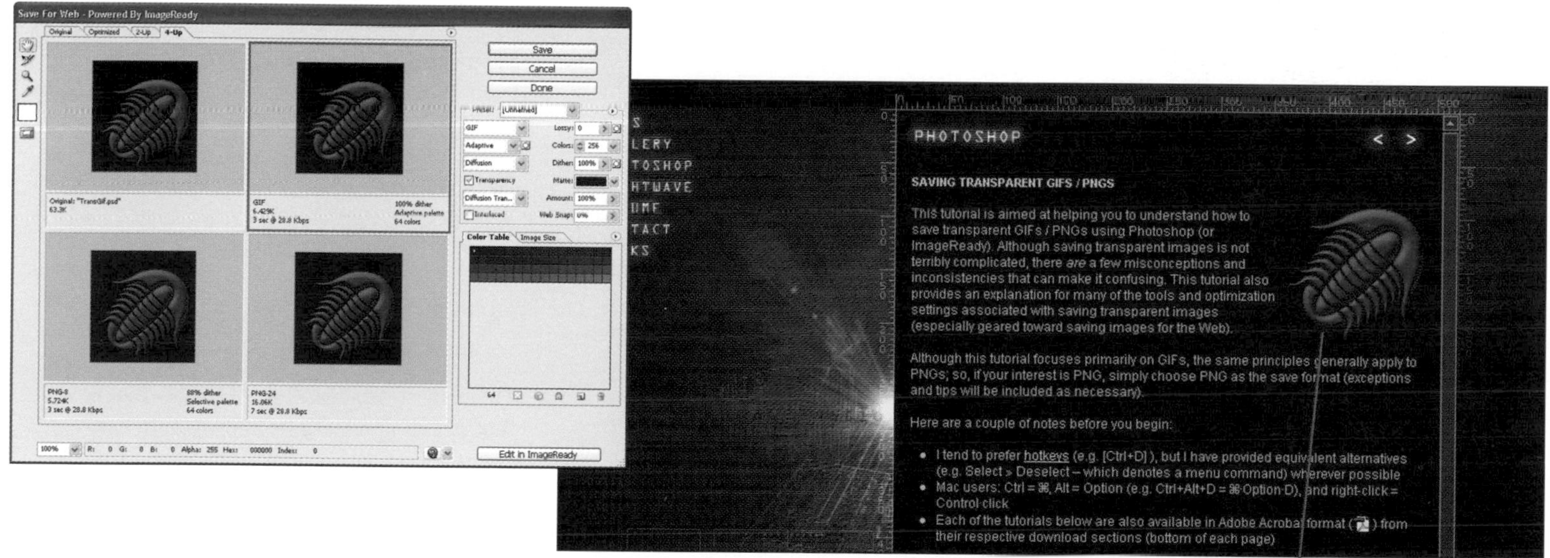

Transparent GIF on Web page

JPEG (Joint Photographic Experts Group)

Another graphic file format commonly used on the Web is the Joint Photographic Experts Group (JPEG) format. Unlike the GIF format that is limited to a maximum of 256 colors, the JPEG format supports millions of colors (24-bit). This format is best for continuous-tone images, such as photographs and images, in which color fidelity cannot be compromised.

JPEG uses a sophisticated mathematical model to produce a sliding scale of graphic compression that enables you to choose the degree of compression you wish to apply to the image. Essentially, you are choosing the size and image quality. The more you compress a JPEG image, the more you degrade the image quality (see Figure 6-41). The JPEG file format can achieve incredible compression ratios; graphics can be reduced to a file size that is as much as 100 times smaller than the original file. To create such a compact file, lossy compression is used. As you will recall, this means that the algorithm discards "unnecessary" data as it compresses the image. Once you compress an image as a JPEG, you have lost data and can never recover it again. Therefore, you should always save an uncompressed original file of your graphic.

A form of JPEG file called a **progressive JPEG** gives JPEG graphics the same gradual image display seen in interlaced GIFs. Like interlaced GIFs, progressive JPEG images offer a quicker preview to the user. JPEG images are rectangular because transparency is not available in this format.

In summary, the advantages of the JPEG format include the following:

- All Web browsers support the JPEG file format without plug-ins.
- Photographs and continuous-tone images look best and are generally smallest when saved in the JPEG file format.
- Huge lossy compression ratios are possible.
- JPEG supports millions of colors (24-bit).
- Progressive JPEGs are available.

PNG (Portable Network Graphics)

PNG is one of the most flexible formats on the Web. Unlike GIF or JPEG, the PNG file format supports a number of different color depths including 256 colors (8-bit) as well as millions of colors (24-bit or 32-bit). PNG uses compression to create small file sizes.

The PNG file format supports variable transparency that allows you to store up to 256 different levels of partial transparency. PNG also supports interlacing. PNG's interlacing method is conceptually similar to GIF interlacing and visually similar to progressive JPEG, which means that embedded text in an image is typically readable about twice as fast in a PNG image as it is in a GIF image.

The PNG file format has one more advantage over GIF and JPEG—the capacity for **gamma correction**. Due to differences in **gamma settings**, there is a difference between the display of images on different platforms. For example, images on a PC tend to look darker than those same images on a Macintosh computer. Gamma correction refers to the ability to correct for differences in how computer monitors interpret color.

In summary, the advantages of the PNG format include the following:

- PNG supports a number of different color depths.
- PNG uses compression to obtain small file sizes.
- PNG supports variable transparency and interlacing.
- PNG contains the capacity to correct for differences in gamma settings.

The biggest disadvantage of this format is that not all applications allow you to easily create PNG files and not all browsers support this file format without plug-ins.

FIGURE 6-41
Varying amounts of compression can be applied to a JPEG image

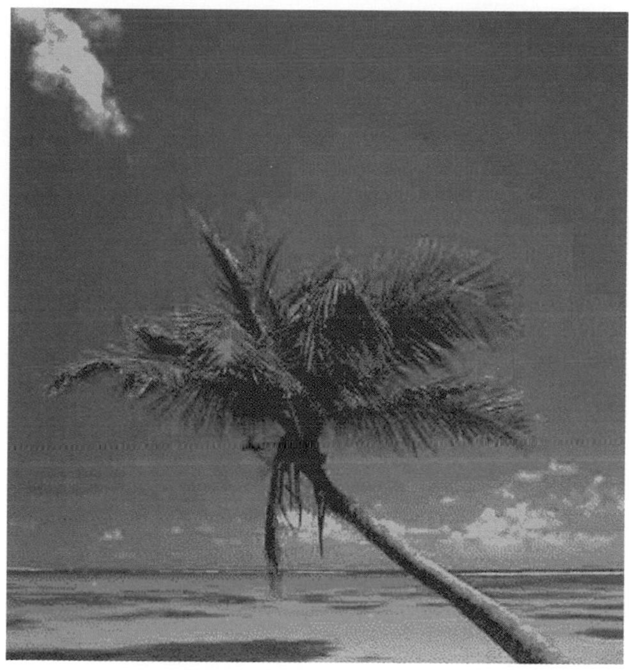

JPEG Image–low quality, high compression
(notice the banding in the sky and around the tree)

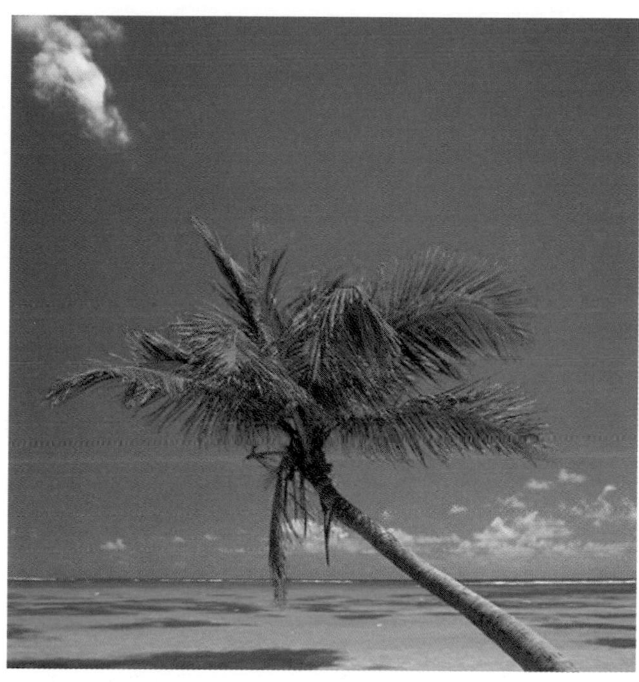

JPEG Image–high quality, low compression
(notice how much smoother the image appears)

SUMMARY

Digitizing is the process of converting images into a format that the computer can recognize and manipulate. **Scanners** and **slide scanners** digitize already developed photographs, drawings, and slides. **Digital cameras** and **digital video cameras** capture still images and frames of video in a digital format.

Service providers can process your film and save the images in digital format to a **Photo CD**. **Commercial image providers** or **stock photography houses** provide access to **stock photography**. Like stock photography, **clip art**, collections of drawings, and illustrations, are also available for a fee or free if they are within the **public domain**. You can also use software together with a **stylus** and a **digitizing tablet** or **graphics tablet** to create your own original artwork.

When you include graphics and other multimedia elements on your Web pages, it is important to understand **copyright law**. The **1976 Federal Copyright Act** and the **Digital Millennium Copyright Act of 1998** clarify copyright law. If your use of the piece does not fall under the exclusions of **fair use** or the piece is not clearly in the public domain, always get permission from the artist, publisher, or owner of the piece.

Drawings and **line art** consist of flat colors while **continuous-tone images** offer tonal variations in either **grayscale** or color. Images can be either **two-dimensional** or **three-dimensional** and all graphics can serve as **hypergraphics**. **Image maps** are hypergraphics that consist of a single graphic with multiple hotspots.

Image quality is determined by an image's **color** and image resolution. The colors that make up the image are referenced to a **palette**. The fixed palette shared by most browsers contains 216 common colors and is called the **Web-safe** or **browser-safe color palette**. If you use this palette you do not have to worry about **banding** or **dithering** when your image is displayed on the user's computer. **Image resolution** is the amount of information stored for each image or the number of pixels making up the image. **Compression** is an algorithm used to create smaller file sizes. There are two types of compression, **lossless** and **lossy**.

Programs used to create or modify two-dimensional and three-dimensional images are called **graphics programs** and include **drawing**, **paint,** and **image editing programs.** Paint programs are used to create bitmapped graphics, which consist of pixels mapped to a **bitmap**. Drawing programs are used to create vector graphics. Both of these programs make extensive use of **tool palettes**. Bitmapped graphics are also called **raster graphics**, and the process of converting a vector graphic to a raster graphic is called **rasterizing**. Image editing programs allow you to manipulate images using a variety of features that combine painting, editing, and other image composition tools. Images can be **cropped**. Color, brightness, and contrast can be adjusted. **Filters** and **layers** can be applied to create special effects.

Programs that allow you to create or modify three-dimensional images are called **3-D modeling programs**. 3-D modeling programs are used to create and manipulate 3-D images. **Textures** are applied to wireframe models. This process is called **shading**. After the objects have been arranged and after lighting and a **perspective** have been set, the scene must be **rendered**.

Web graphic images may be stored in several different file formats. The **Graphic Interchange Format (GIF)** format supports 256 colors, transparency, and interlacing. The **Joint Photographic Experts Group** (**JPEG**) format uses lossy compression and supports millions of colors. **Progressive JPEGs** are also an option. The **Portable Network Graphics (PNG)** format supports both 8-bit and 32-bit color. It also offers variable transparency and interlacing as well as **gamma correction** capabilities, which helps to eliminate some of the color discrepancy that often occurs from one operating system to the next as a result of different **gamma settings**.

KEY TERMS

1976 Federal Copyright Act
3-D modeling program
banding
Bézier curve
bit
bitmap
bitmapped image
browser-safe color palette
clip art
color resolution
commercial image provider
compression
continuous-tone image
copyright
copyright law
crop
digital camera
Digital Millennium Copyright Act of 1998
digital video camera
digitizing
digitizing tablet
dithering
drawing program
fair use
filters
gamma correction
gamma settings
Graphics Interchange Format (GIF)
gradient fill
graphics program
graphics tablet
grayscale image
hypergraphic
image editing program
image map
image resolution
interlacing
jaggies
Joint Photographic Experts Group (JPEG)
layers
line art
lossless compression
lossy compression
Macromedia Fireworks
Macromedia FreeHand
mapping software
modeling
morphing
optimizing
paint program
palette
perspective
Photo CD
pixel
plug-ins
Portable Network Graphics (PNG)
progressive JPEG
public domain
raster graphic
rasterize
refresh rate
rendering
rendering program
scanner
shading
slide scanner
staircasing
stock photography
stock photography house
stylus
Tagged Image File Format (TIFF)
texture
three-dimensional (3-D)
tool palette
transparency
two-dimensional (2-D)
ungroup
vector graphic
Web-safe color palette

MATCHING QUESTIONS/DISCUSSION QUESTIONS

Match each term with the sentence that best describes it.

a. color resolution	**b.** digitizing	**c.** filters
d. hypergraphics	**e.** image map	**f.** image resolution
g. JPEG	**h.** morphing	**i.** optimizing
j. plug-ins	**k.** PNG	**l.** rasterizing
m. refresh rate	**n.** rendering	**o.** shading

_____ **1.** Measures the number of bits of stored information per pixel or how many tones or colors every pixel in a bitmap can have.

_____ **2.** The process of assigning surface properties, such as color, texture, and finish to an object.

_____ **3.** The process of converting images into a format that the computer can recognize and manipulate.

_____ **4.** The amount of information stored for each image.

_____ **5.** Web graphic file format that supports variable transparency and gamma correction.

_____ **6.** Graphic that contains more than one hotspot.

_____ **7.** The process of capturing a view of a three-dimensional object or scene and saving it as a two-dimensional image.

_____ **8.** Web graphic file format that is best used for continuous-tone images, such as photographs.

_____ **9.** The process of converting a vector image to pixels or a bitmapped file format.

_____ **10.** Clickable graphics that allow you to link to other locations within the same Web site or outside of it.

_____ **11.** Add-on features that enhance the capabilities of programs.

_____ **12.** Special effects applied to an image or part of an image.

_____ **13.** The process of the entire screen being redrawn each time items on it change.

_____ **14.** The process of making the image file sizes as small as possible for quick download via the Web.

_____ **15.** Blending one object into another.

Answer each question either in writing or in a class discussion as directed by your instructor.

1. What are three different technologies used to capture digital images? How are those three technologies different?
2. What is the primary difference between paint programs and drawing programs? How are bitmapped graphics different from vector graphics?
3. How does staircasing or jaggies occur? What can be done to prevent this?
4. What is the difference between lossy and lossless compression? What are the advantages and disadvantages of each?
5. Name the three most common Web graphic file formats. Which file format is best suited for each kind of image?

DESIGN PROJECT

Working with Graphics

1. Working with graphics using Adobe Illustrator
2. Working with graphics using Adobe Photoshop
3. Inserting graphics into a Web page using Macromedia Dreamweaver

Introduction

This is a continuation of the Design Project in Chapter 5.

The client The Inn at Birch Bay has reviewed the Web pages and has asked that additional content be provided on the Tour page. They would like the following:

- A single logo to appear on each page
- A photograph of the Inn on the home page
- A new background color
- Removal of the text background color

You have been asked to modify the tour.htm and homepage.htm Web pages. The WebsByCT multimedia development team has decided that this project would be ideal for you to learn the basics of a drawing program and an image editing program, and to work with the XHTML coding needed to position graphics on a Web page. To complete the lessons in this design project, you will be using Adobe Illustrator to create a logo for the Inn and Adobe Photoshop to enhance a photograph of the Inn. Then you will use Macromedia Dreamweaver to insert the images and make the changes to the Web pages.

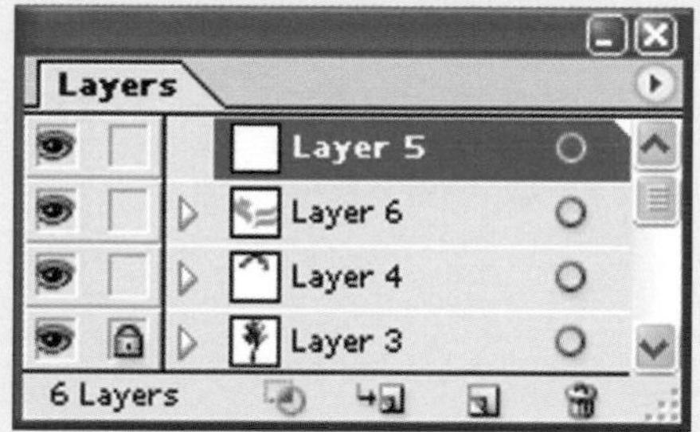
Layers
Layer 5
Layer 6
Layer 4
Layer 3
6 Layers

Character
Paragraph
Arial
Regular
36 pt
(Auto)
Metrics
0
100%
100%
0 pt
Color:
English: USA
Sharp

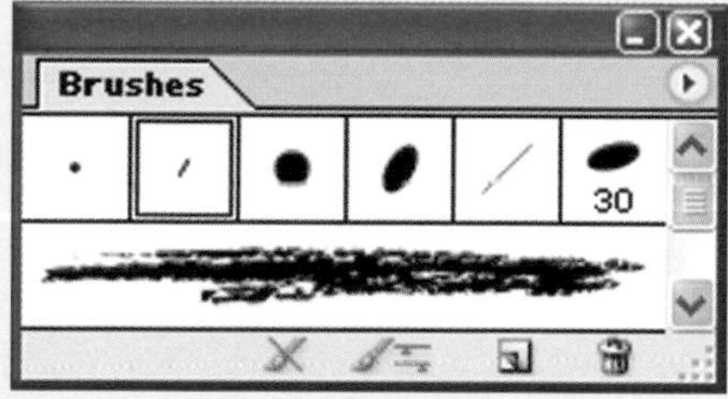
Brushes
30

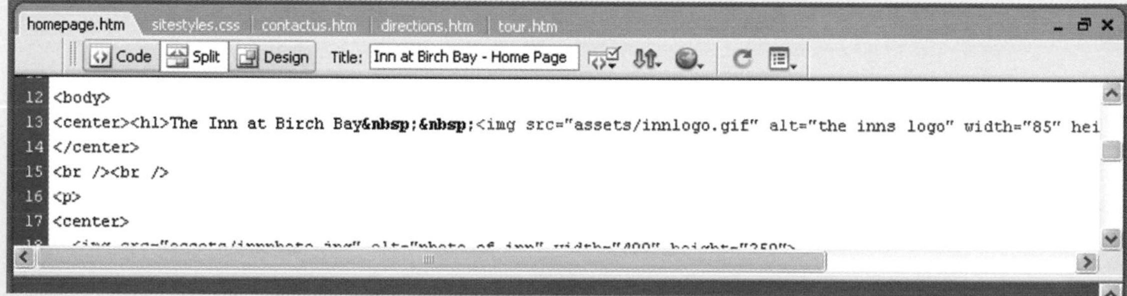
homepage.htm
sitestyles.css
contactus.htm
directions.htm
tour.htm
Code
Split
Design
Title:
Inn at Birch Bay - Home Page
<body>
<center><h1>The Inn at Birch Bay <img src="assets/innlogo.gif" alt="the inns logo" width="85" hei
</center>

<p>
<center>

LESSON 1

WORKING WITH GRAPHICS
Using Adobe Illustrator

What You'll Do

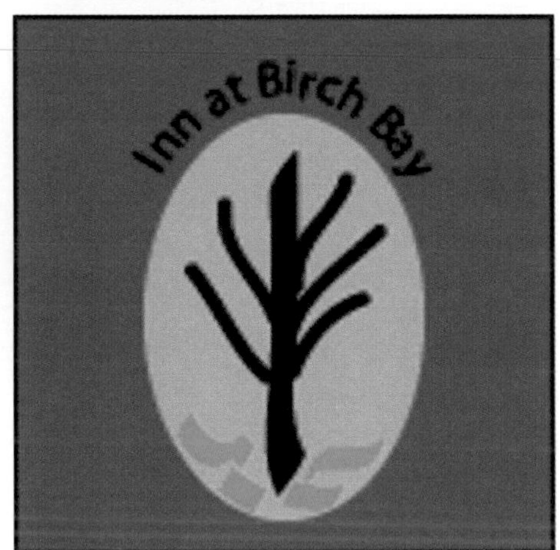

In this lesson, you will learn how to use a drawing program, Adobe Illustrator, to create and enhance an image that will be inserted into Web pages. You will begin by studying the Illustrator workspace and some of the basic tools and features available in the program. Then you will use these tools to draw and edit an image.

The Adobe Illustrator Workspace

Adobe Illustrator originated as an illustration tool that allowed graphic artists to create high-quality images used for print. Therefore, the workspace uses tools and terms similar to those used in the art world, including artboard, brushes, and palettes. Images are often made up of several parts, such as a background color, text, and various shapes. Illustrator refers to these parts as "objects" and the file that is saved as a "document". Figure 6-42 shows the Illustrator window and identifies several important components including the Artboard, which is the area used to create and edit an image.

Toolbox

The Toolbox is the palette containing the tools used to create, select, and edit images. Some of the basic tools and buttons in the Toolbox are:

Selection tool : Used to select and move objects

Type tool : Used to type and modify text

Rectangle tool : Used to draw rectangles

Paintbrush tool : Used to draw images

Zoom tool : Used to zoom in and out when viewing images

Fill button : Used to specify the fill color for an object

Stroke button : Used to specify the stroke color for an object

Pointing to a tool in the Toolbox displays its name. Some of the tools are hidden. To reveal them you point to another tool, then click and hold the mouse button. For example, the Ellipse tool can be displayed by clicking and holding the Rectangle tool.

QUICKTIP

Pay particular attention to which tool is selected before carrying out any action. When a tool is selected its icon in the Toolbox is depressed and the pointer symbol may change.

Palettes

Palettes are panels that are used to edit and manipulate objects as well as provide information about selected objects. The Window menu on the menu bar displays a list of palette names. A check mark next to the name indicates the palette is currently displayed in the workspace. You click a name in the menu to add the palette to or remove it from the workspace. Once the palette is in the workspace you can move it around by dragging the title bar. As you carry out certain actions in Illustrator, additional palettes will appear on the workspace. For example, when you click on the Fill button, the Color palette appears.

QUICKTIP

Limit the palettes to those that are currently being used so your workspace is less cluttered.

Layers

One of the most useful features in any graphics program is layers. As you create an image you actually create objects that are stacked. You may start with a background color, then add an oval shape, and then add some text. Each object can be independent

FIGURE 6-42

The Adobe Illustrator window

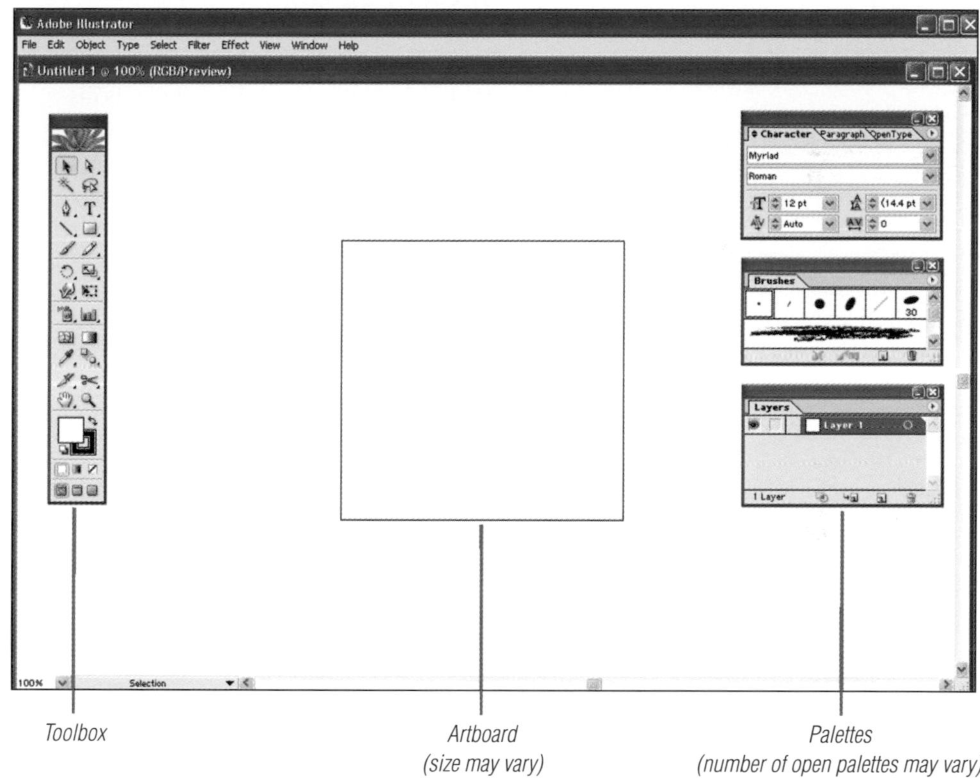

of the others so that they are easier to edit. Each object is placed on its own layer allowing it to be selected, hidden, locked, and its order changed. The Layers palette displays the layers and provides a thumbnail of the object. Clicking a layer selects the object on the Artboard.

QUICKTIP

Be sure to select the appropriate layer when you want to edit an object. Naming layers helps to identify which objects have been placed on them.

Vector Graphics

The images created in Illustrator are vector graphics that are described with lines and curves. Vector graphics consist of anchor points and line segments that together make up a path as shown in Figure 6-43. The anchor points can be moved to alter the drawing. When the anchor points are visible the object is selected and any changes, such as choosing a different color, will affect the selected object.

Selecting and Deselecting an Area of an Object

When an object on the Artboard has been selected (by clicking it with the Selection tool), a bounding box with handles is displayed around the object. The handles can be dragged to reshape the object and any actions, such as choosing a color using the Fill button, may affect the selected object. To deselect an object, click Select from the menu bar, then click Deselect.

FIGURE 6-43

A vector graphic showing the path and anchor points

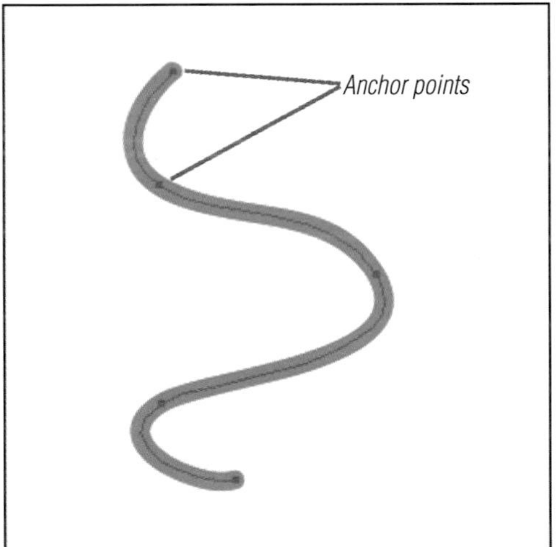

Undo and Redo Features

Illustrator provides two commands within the Edit menu that allow you to undo a step. The Undo command will undo the most recent action up to as many times as your computer memory allows and the Redo command will redo the most recent undo action.

QUICKTIP

You will find these to be among the most useful commands.

Working with Colors

As you are creating an image you will need to specify colors for various objects. There are two buttons that allow you to select a color. Each button applies the color to different types of objects. The Fill button is used to specify the fill color for a closed-shape object such as a rectangle or circle. The Stroke button is used to specify the stroke color for an object such as a line or text. The buttons are located on the Toolbox and their color changes to reflect selected color. There is a None button that you can click to indicate no color is to be used for the color button currently selected. When you double-click the Fill or Stroke button, the Color Picker dialog box appears allowing you to specify a color as shown in Figure 6-44. You can specify a color by clicking the color palette or by entering values for the various color schemes, such as RGB (red, green, blue). If you know the six-character hexadecimal value for a color you can enter it into the # box. For example, the hexadecimal value for an aqua color is #00CCFF.

File Formats

The Adobe Illustrator native file format is ai. As you work with Illustrator, you can save your files in the ai format. When you have completed your edits to the file, you can use the Save for Web command to save the image in a file format such as GIF, JPEG, or PNG.

Creating the Completed Logo for the Inn at Birch Bay

The completed logo is made up of several objects including a background color, a filled oval, a tree with branches, and text. Each of these objects will be created on its own layer. As you work you will be saving the document as an Illustrator file with the filename innlogo.ai. The file will be saved into an images folder on your hard drive. When you have completed the logo, you will save it to the assets folder in the InnWebsiteDW folder so it can be inserted into the Web pages.

QUICKTIP

The exercises in this chapter were created with the screen resolution set at 1024 x 768. If your computer's screen resolution has a different setting, the figures in the book may appear different. You may want to verify the screen resolution on your computer and set it to 1024 x 768, if necessary.

FIGURE 6-44
The Color Picker dialog box

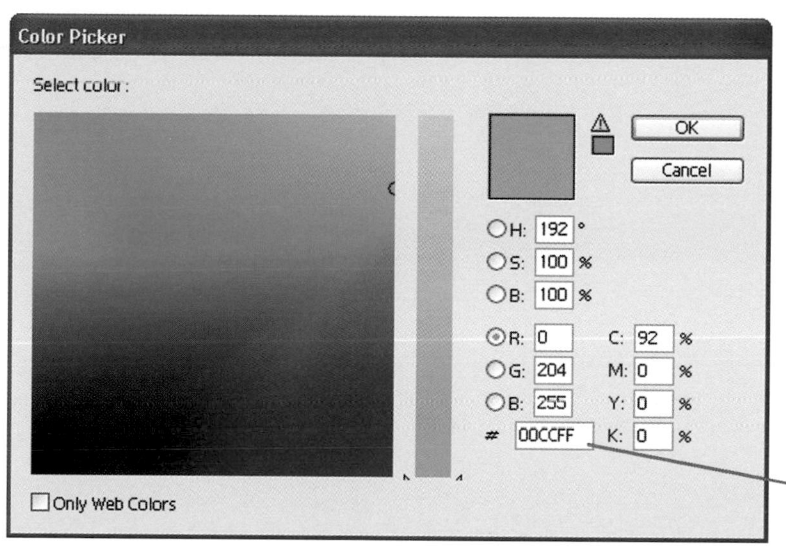

Start Illustrator and customize the work area

1. Start **Illustrator**. If a What's New in Illustrator window appears, click the Close button.
2. Click **Window** on the menu bar, verify **Tools** is selected, point to **Type**, then click **Character,** if necessary, to select it.
3. Click **Window** on the menu bar, then click **Brushes**, if necessary, to select it.
4. Click **Window** on the menu bar, then click **Layers**, if necessary, to select it.
5. Click **Window** on the menu bar, then deselect all other selected palettes you want to close by clicking each palette name that has a check mark next to it.

   TIP Closing one palette may close other related palettes as well.
6. Drag each palette using the palette title bar to the side of the workspace area as shown in Figure 6-45.

You started Illustrator and customized the workspace.

FIGURE 6-45
The workspace with selected palettes displayed

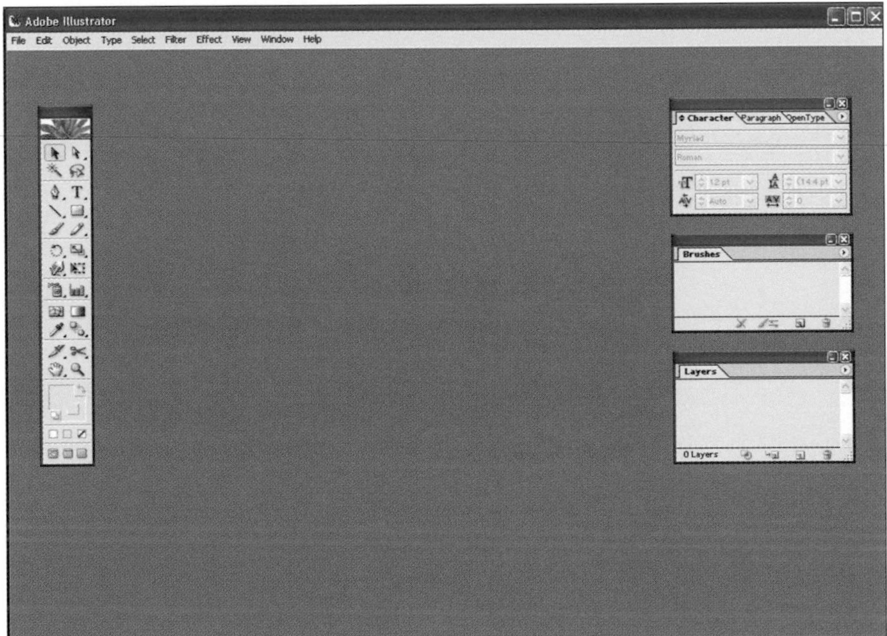

FIGURE 6-46

The completed New Document dialog box

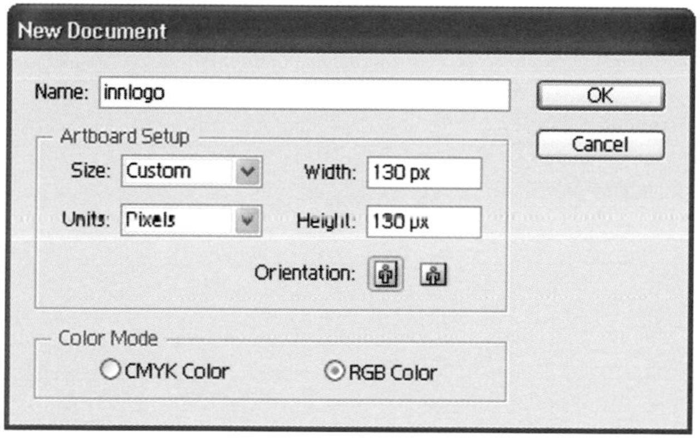

Start a new document and save it

1. Click **File** on the menu bar, then click **New**.
2. Type **innlogo** for the name, click the **RGB Color option button** to select it, change the Units to Pixels if necessary, then change the dimensions to **130 px** for the width and **130 px** for height as shown in Figure 6-46.
3. Click **OK** to accept the changes to the dialog box.
4. Click **View** on the menu bar, then click **Actual Size**.
5. Create a folder on your hard drive named **images**.
6. Return to Illustrator, click **File** on the menu bar, click **Save as**, then save the document to the images folder with the filename **innlogo.ai**.
7. Click **OK** when the Illustrator Options dialog box appears.

You started a new document and saved it.

Draw shapes and fill them with colors

1. Click the **Stroke button** in the Toolbox, then click the **None button**.
2. Double-click the **Fill button** in the Toolbox to open the Color Picker, delete the entry inside the # box, type **6666CC**, then click **OK**.

(continued)

3. Click the **Rectangle tool** in the Toolbox.
4. Click the Artboard, hold the mouse button, drag to the lower-right to create a rectangle as shown in Figure 6-47, then release the mouse button.

   You will size the image later so you do not need to match the size exactly.
5. Click **Select** on the menu bar, then click **Deselect** to deselect the rectangle.
6. Drag the **Color palette** to reveal the Layers palette, if necessary.

   When you selected the Fill color on the Toolbox, the Color palette was displayed in the workspace.
7. Double-click **Layer 1** in the Layers palette, type **background**, then click **OK**.
8. Click the **Create New Layer button** on the Layers palette, double-click **Layer 2** in the Layers palette, type **oval**, then click **OK**.
9. Double-click the **Fill button** in the Toolbox, delete the entry inside the # box, type **COCOCO**, then click **OK**.
10. Point to the **Rectangle tool** in the Toolbox, click and hold the mouse button until the **Ellipse tool** appears, then point to it and release the mouse button.
11. Click the Artboard and drag to create the oval as shown in Figure 6-48.
12. Draw the **oval** as shown in Figure 6-48, click **Select** on the menu bar, then click **Deselect**.
13. Save the document.

You drew a rectangle and oval and filled them with colors.

FIGURE 6-47
Drawing a rectangle

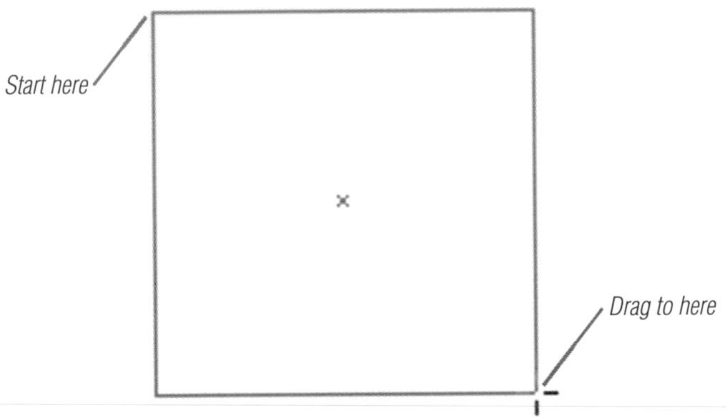

Start here

Drag to here

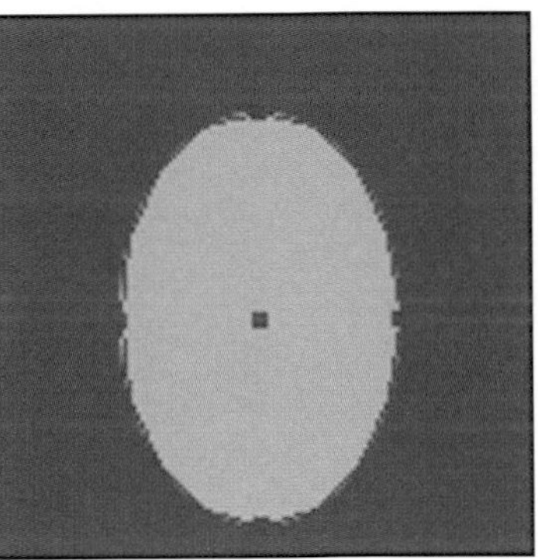

FIGURE 6-48
The completed oval

FIGURE 6-49
Selecting the 6 pt flat option for the Paintbrush tool

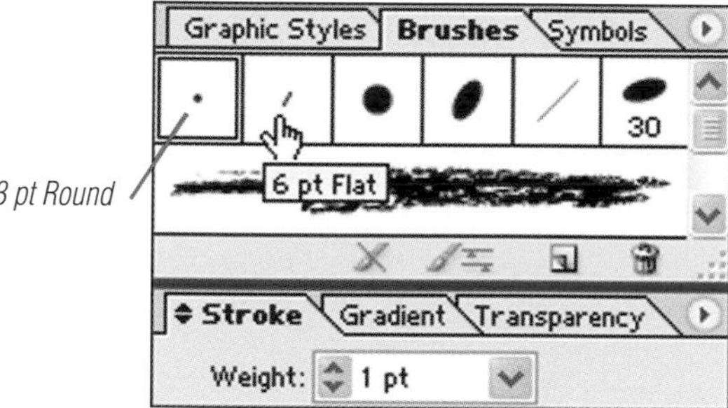

FIGURE 6-50
The trunk of the tree

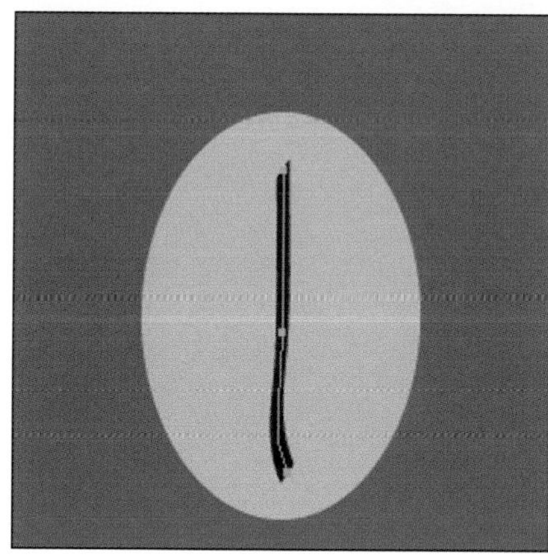

FIGURE 6-51
Changing the stroke weight

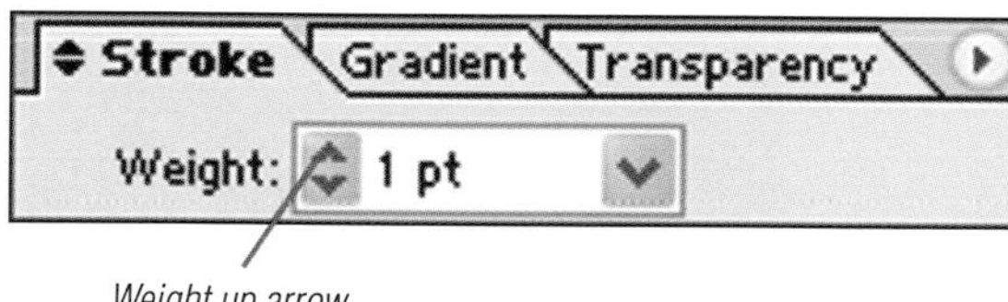

Draw freeform shapes

1. Click the **Zoom tool** in the Toolbox, point to the middle of the oval, then **click twice** to zoom in on the image.
2. Click the **Create New Layer button** on the Layers palette, double-click **Layer 3** in the Layers palette, type **tree**, then click **OK**.
3. Click the **Fill button** , then click the **None button** .
4. Double-click the **Stroke button** , verify **000000** is displayed in the # box, then click **OK**.
5. Click the **Paintbrush tool** in the Toolbox, then click the **6 pt flat** option in the Brushes palette as shown in Figure 6-49.

   TIP The Brushes palette may be hidden under other palettes. If so, you can drag the other palettes to another location in the workspace to reveal the Brushes palette.
6. **Draw** the trunk of the tree to approximate the one shown in Figure 6-50.
7. Open the Stroke palette if necessary, then with the line selected, click the **up arrow** in the Weight box as shown in Figure 6-51 to select **2 pt**.
8. **Hold down [Shift]** and **[Ctrl]**, then press **A** to deselect the line (PC) or **[command] [shift] A** (Mac).

(continued)

9. Click the **3 pt Round** option in the Brushes palette, then continue drawing the tree using short strokes and deselecting each line after drawing it.

   TIP Use the Undo command in the Edit menu when you want to undo an action.

   TIP If you want to delete a layer and start again, you can highlight the layer name in the Layers palette and click the Delete Selection button in the Layers palette.

   Your image should resemble Figure 6-52.

10. Click the **Create New Layer button** on the Layers palette, double-click **Layer 4** in the Layers palette, type **water**, then click **OK**.
11. Double-click the **Stroke button**, delete the entry inside the # box, type **00CCFF**, then click **OK**.
12. Use the **Paintbrush tool** and the **6 pt Flat option** to create the lines for the water as shown in Figure 6-53.
13. Save the document.

You drew freehand shapes using the Paintbrush tool.

FIGURE 6-52
The completed tree

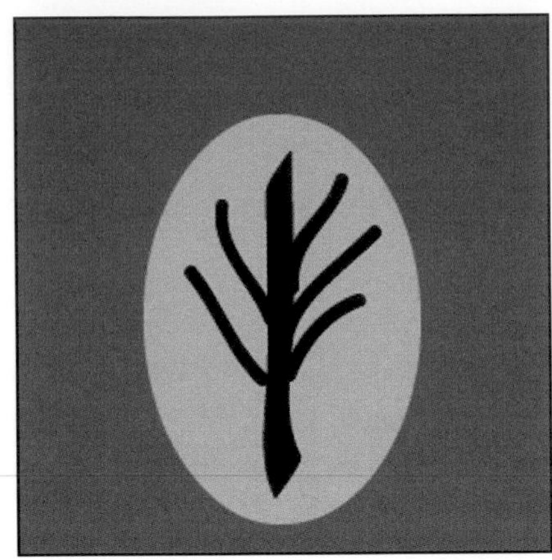

FIGURE 6-53
The completed lines for the water

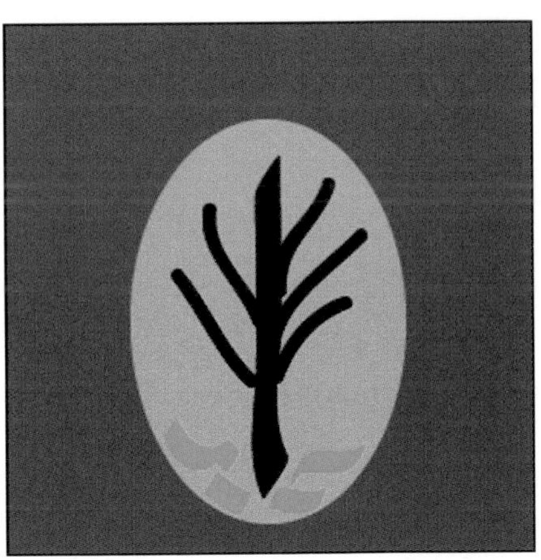

FIGURE 6-54
Drawing the oval outline

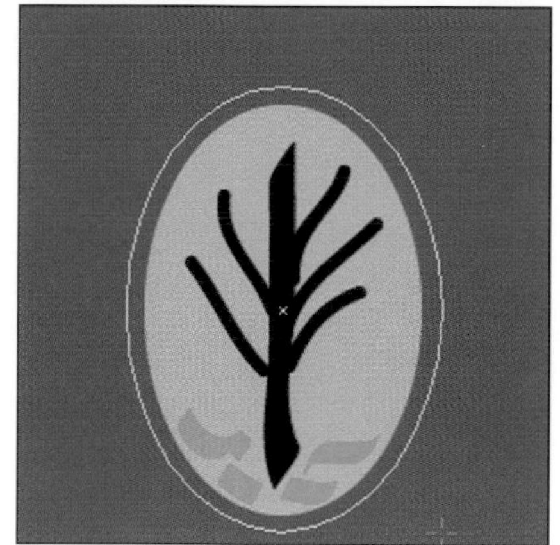

FIGURE 6-55
The font type down arrow in the Character palette

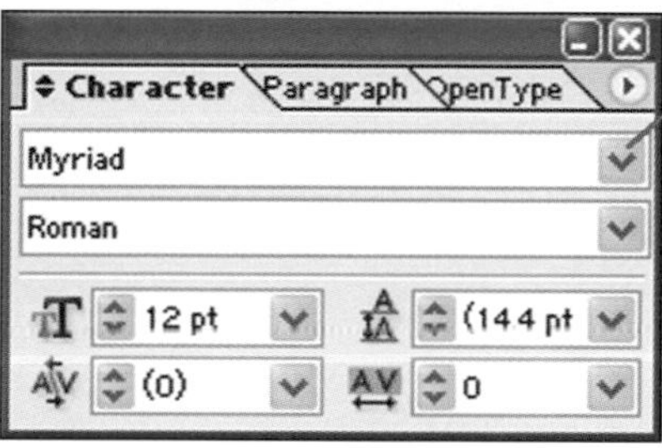

FIGURE 6-56
Positioning the insertion point

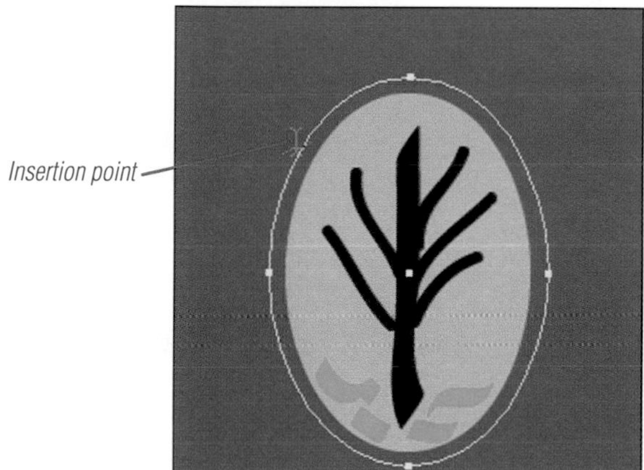

Add text along a path

1. Click the **Create New Layer button** on the Layers palette, double-click **Layer 5** in the Layers palette, type **text**, then click **OK**.
2. Click the **Stroke button**, then click the **None button**.
3. Click the **Ellipse tool**, then draw an oval outline slightly larger than the filled oval as shown in Figure 6-54.

   TIP When an image is selected, you can use the arrow keys on the keyboard to position it.

4. Click the **down arrow** for the font type in the Character palette as shown in Figure 6-55, then select **Arial** (PC) or point to **Arial**, then click **Regular** (Mac).
5. Verify that the point size is set to 12.
6. Point to the **Type tool** T. in the Toolbox, hold down the mouse button, point to **Type on a Path Tool**, then release the mouse button.
7. Position the insertion point as shown in Figure 6-56, click, then type **Inn at Birch Bay**.
8. Save the document.

You added text along a path.

Resize an image

1. Click the **Zoom tool** in the Toolbox, point to the middle of the image, **hold down [Alt],** then click **twice** to display the image at 100% size.
2. Click the **Selection Tool**, click **Select** on the menu bar, then click **All**.
3. Click the **Free Transform tool** in the Toolbox.
4. Point to the upper-right corner handle as shown in Figure 6-57.
5. Hold down the mouse button and drag the handle to approximate Figure 6-58.

   Because these are vector drawings, they resize without altering the quality of the image. You will size the image precisely in the next lesson.
6. Click **Select** on the menu bar, then click **Deselect**.
7. Save the document.

You resized an image.

FIGURE 6-57
Pointing to the handle

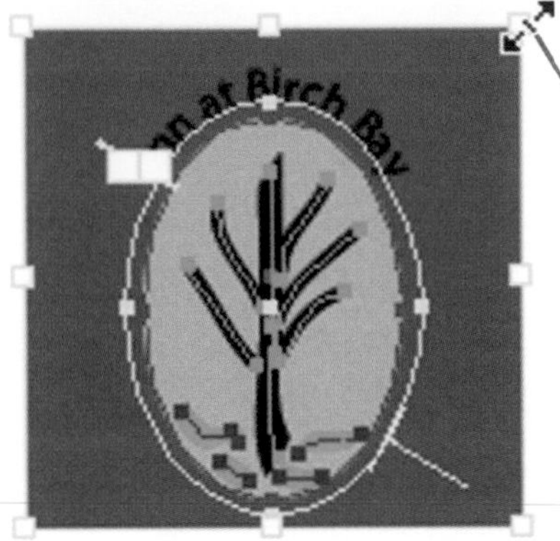

Insertion point on sizing handle

FIGURE 6-58
The resized image

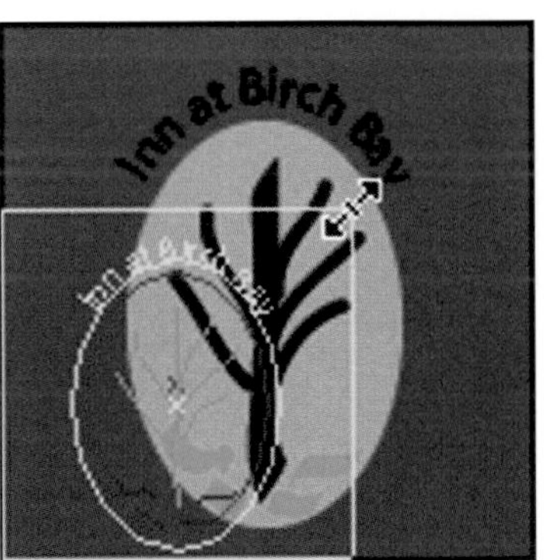

FIGURE 6-59
The Save for Web dialog box

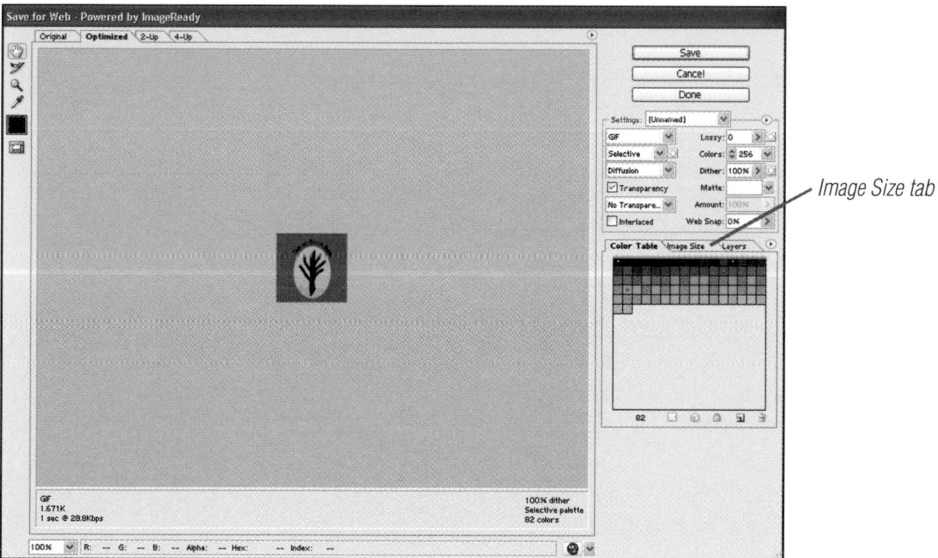

Save an image for the Web

1. Click **File** on the menu bar, then click **Save for Web**.

   The Save for Web dialog box appears as shown in Figure 6-59.

   This dialog box allows you to change several settings such as the file type (GIF, JPEG, PNG, SWF) and amount of compression. It also displays a Color Table displaying the colors used for the image and a tab to display the image size. This provides another way to resize the image.
2. Click the **Image Size tab**, verify Constrain Proportions is checked.
3. Change the width to **85** pixels if that is not the current width setting, then click **Apply**.
4. Verify that **GIF** is specified in the settings, then click **Save**.
5. Navigate to the assets folder in the InnWebsiteDW folder.
6. Save the document with the filename **innlogo.gif**.

You saved the image for the Web.

LESSON 2

WORKING WITH GRAPHICS USING Adobe Photoshop

What You'll Do

In this lesson, you will learn how to use an image editing program, Adobe Photoshop, to enhance an image that will be inserted into a Web page. You will begin by studying the Photoshop workspace and some of the basic tools and features available in the program. Then you will use these to edit a photograph and prepare it for use on the home page of the Inn at Birch Bay Web site.

The Adobe Photoshop Workspace

Adobe Photoshop is the industry standard in digital image editing. As such, the program has an extensive array of tools and features. Adobe Illustrator and Adobe Photoshop were designed to work together, the former for image creation and the latter for image editing. Therefore, they have similar components and workspace features. However, some of the components are not named the same. For example, the Paintbrush tool in Illustrator is called the Brush tool in Photoshop. Palettes and layers work in similar ways in both programs. Figure 6-60 shows the Adobe Photoshop window and identifies several important components. Notice the Active image area is the area used to create and edit an image.

Toolbox

The Toolbox is the palette containing the tools used to create, select, and edit images. Some of the basic tools and buttons in the Toolbox are:

Rectangular Marquee tool: Used to select objects or parts of objects

Crop tool: Used to select an area that will be cropped out of an image

Move tool: Used to move a selected object

Horizontal Type tool T: Used to type and modify text

Rectangle tool: Used to draw rectangles

Brush tool: Used to draw images

Zoom tool : Used to zoom in and out when viewing images

Set Foreground Color button : Used for paint, fill, and stroke selections

Set Background Color button : Used to make gradient fills and fill in the erased areas of an image

Note: The Set Foreground Color button and the Set Background Color button overlap. The Set Foreground Color button is on top and the Set Background Color button is on the bottom.

Pointing to a tool in the Toolbox displays its name. Some of the tools are hidden. To reveal them, point to another tool, then click and hold down the mouse until the new tool icon appears. For example, the Ellipse tool can be displayed by clicking and holding the Rectangle tool.

QUICKTIP

Pay particular attention to which tool is selected before carrying out any action. When a tool is selected its icon in the Toolbox is depressed and the pointer symbol may change.

FIGURE 6-60

The Adobe Photoshop window

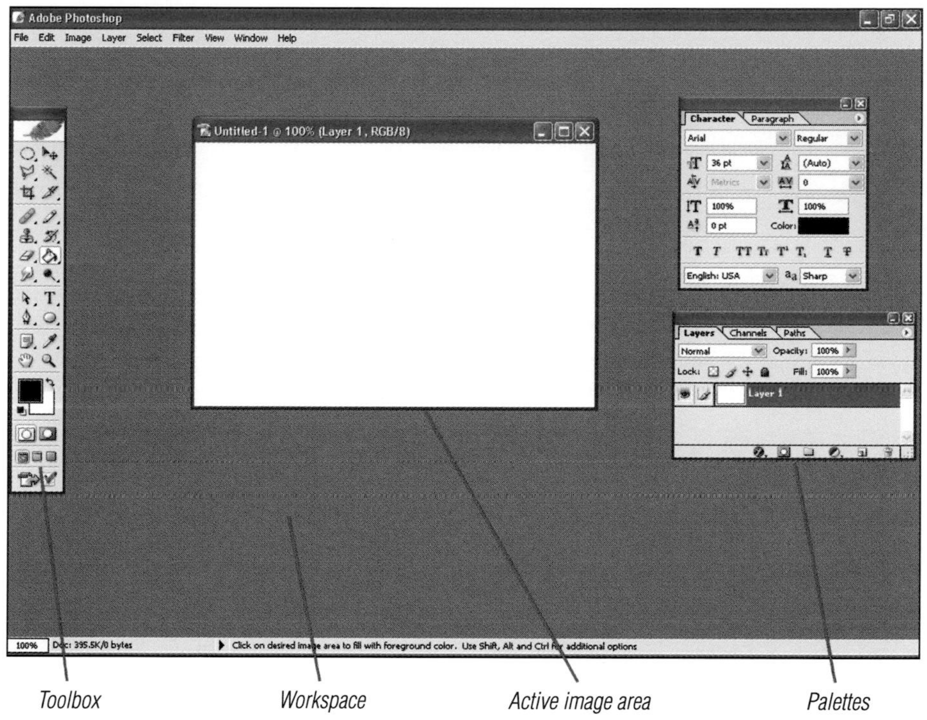

Filters and Layer Styles

Photoshop provides several ways to apply special effects to an image including Filters and Layer Styles. You can change the appearance of an image by applying filters.

For example, you can apply a watercolor filter to a photograph and have it appear as a watercolor painting. Also, you can apply special effects, such as a drop shadow, to an image by using the Layer Styles feature.

Selecting and Deselecting an Area of an Object

When an object or part of an object has been selected (by using one of the selection tools), a moving dotted line surrounds the image. Actions that follow may affect the selected area. To deselect an area, click Select from the menu bar, then click Deselect.

Undo and Redo Features

Photoshop provides four commands within the Edit menu that allow you to undo a step or series of steps. The Undo command will undo the most recent action, and the Step Backward command will undo a series of actions. The Redo command allows you to redo the most recent undo action and the Step Forward command allows you to redo a series of actions that have been undone.

> **QUICKTIP**
>
> You will find these commands to be among the most useful commands.

File Formats

The Adobe Photoshop native file format is psd. As you work with Photoshop you can save your files in the psd format. When you have completed your edits to the file you can use the Save for Web command to save the image in a file format such as JPEG, GIF, or PNG.

Creating the Completed Photo for the Inn at Birch Bay

In order to create the completed photo for the home page you will work with two files and merge them into one. You will start by creating a new Photoshop file that will serve as the background for the photo image. You will name it innphoto.psd and save it to the images folder on your hard drive. Next, you will open a photograph (innphoto-original.jpg) of the inn, crop it, and then copy it to the innphoto.psd image. Then you will make several changes to enhance the image and save it for use on the Web as a JPEG file format with the file-name innphoto.jpg. This file will be saved to the assets folder in the InnWebsiteDW folder so it can be inserted into the Web home page.

FIGURE 6-61
The completed New dialog box

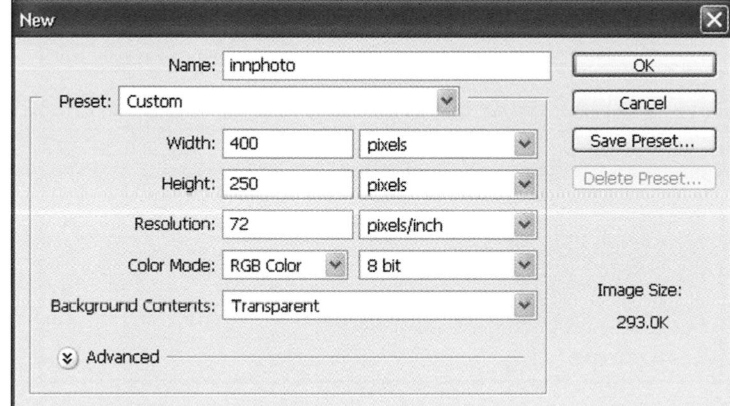

Start Photoshop and start a new file

1. Start **Photoshop**. If the Welcome Screen appears, click **Close**.
2. Click **Window** on the menu bar, click the following palette names to open them: **Character**, **Layers**, **Tools**, then click any other currently active palette names to close them.

   Note: A check mark next to a palette name means it is open.
3. Click **File** on the menu bar, then click **New**.
4. Complete the dialog box to resemble Figure 6-61 by entering the following:

   Name: innphoto

   Width: 400 pixels

   Height: 250 pixels

   Color Mode: RGB Color
5. Click **OK** to continue.
6. Click **File** on the menu bar, click **Save As**, then save the document to the images folder with the filename **innphoto.psd**.

   Note: When saving the file you may need to change the file format to Photoshop (*PSD...) in the Format box in the Save As dialog box.
7. If the Photoshop Format Options dialog box opens, click **OK**.

You started Photoshop, customized the workspace, opened, and then saved a new file.

Apply a background color

1. Click the **Set foreground color icon** in the Toolbox.
2. Delete the entry inside the # box, **type 6666CC** as shown in Figure 6-62, then click **OK**.
3. Point to the **Gradient tool** in the Toolbox, hold down the mouse button until the **Paint Bucket Tool** appears, then point to it and release the mouse button.

   Note: the **Paint Bucket tool** may already be displayed without pointing to the **Gradient tool**.
4. Point to the image, then **click** to change the color.
5. Double-click **Layer 1** in the Layers palette, type **background**, then press **[Enter]** (PC) or **[return]** (Mac).
6. Save the file.
7. If the Format Options dialog box opens, click **OK**.

You applied a background color to a new image.

FIGURE 6-62
The completed Color Picker dialog box

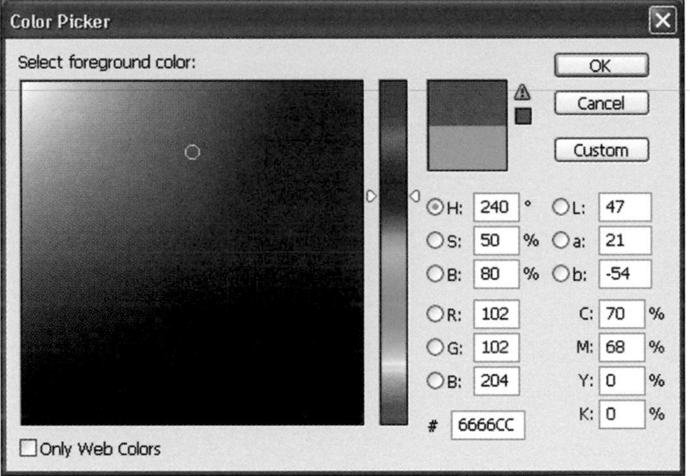

FIGURE 6-63
Positioning the pointer

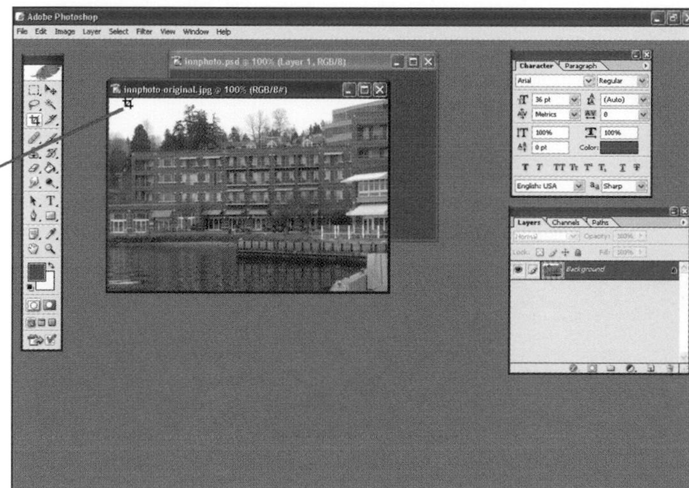

Crop tool pointer

FIGURE 6-64
The crop selection

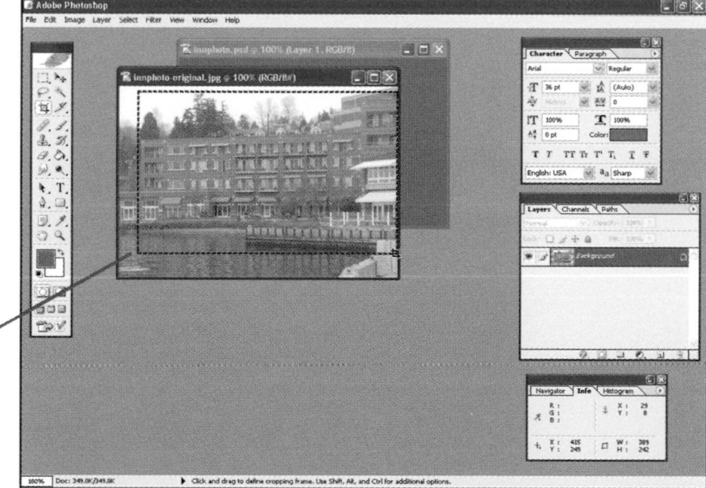

Your crop outline will be a dotted black line

Open an existing file and crop the image

1. Click **File** on the menu bar, click **Open**, navigate to the folder containing the files for this lesson, then open **innphoto-original.jpg**.
2. Click **File** on the menu bar, click **Save As**, then save the file to the images folder with the filename **innphoto-original.jpg**.
3. When the JPEG Options dialog box opens, click **OK**.
4. Click the **Crop tool** in the Toolbox.
5. Position the pointer as shown in Figure 6-63.
6. Hold down the mouse button, drag the pointer to approximate the rectangle shown in Figure 6-64, then release the mouse button.

   TIP You can drag the handles to resize the selection. If you want to remove the crop selection, click the Crop tool, then click Don't Crop.
7. Click **Image** in the menu bar, then click **Crop**.
8. Click **File** on the menu bar, click **Save As**, then save the file to the images folder with the filename **innphoto-cropped.jpg**.
9. When the JPEG Options dialog box opens, click **OK**.

You cropped an image.

Copy an image

1. Click **Select** on the menu bar, then click **All**.
2. Click **Edit** on the menu bar, then click **Copy**.
3. Click the **Close button** in the innphoto-cropped.jpg window as shown in Figure 6-65. The Close button is on the left on a Mac.
4. With the innphoto.psd window displayed, click **Layer** on the menu bar, point to **New**, then click **Layer**.
5. Type **photo** in the Name box, then click **OK**.
6. Click **Edit** on the menu bar, then click **Paste**.
7. Save the file.

You copied one image to a layer of another image.

Change the contrast setting for an image

1. Verify that the photo layer is selected in the Layers palette, click **Image** on the menu bar, point to **Adjustments**, then click **Brightness/Contrast**.

   The Brightness/Contrast dialog box appears allowing you to make changes in these settings.
2. Drag the sliders for both of these settings to see how they change the image.

   Note: The Preview check box must be selected in order to see the changes made in the dialog box.
3. Set the Brightness to **0** and the Contrast to **+37** as shown in Figure 6-66.
4. Click **OK** to return to the file.
5. Save the file.

You changed the contrast setting for an image.

FIGURE 6-65
The Close button

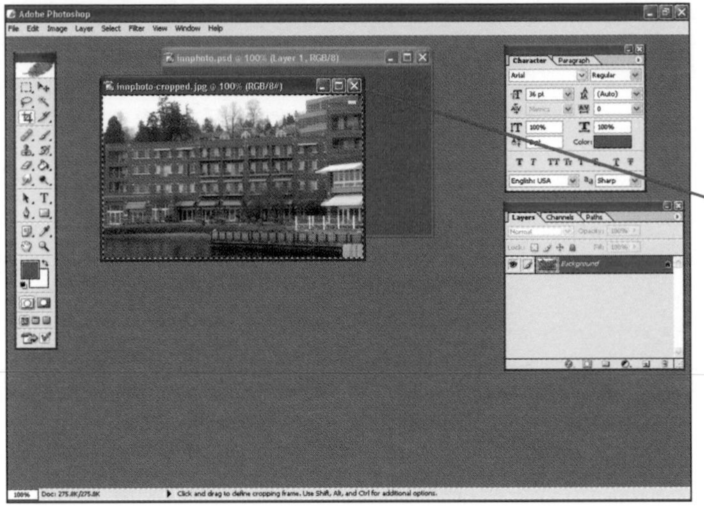

FIGURE 6-66
The completed Brightness/Contrast dialog box

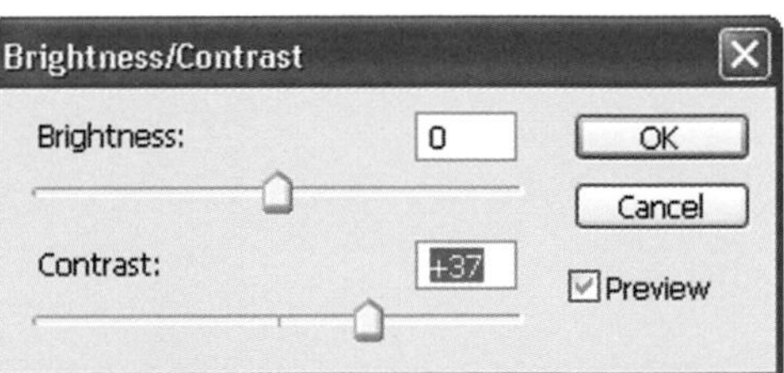

FIGURE 6-67

The completed Layer Style dialog box

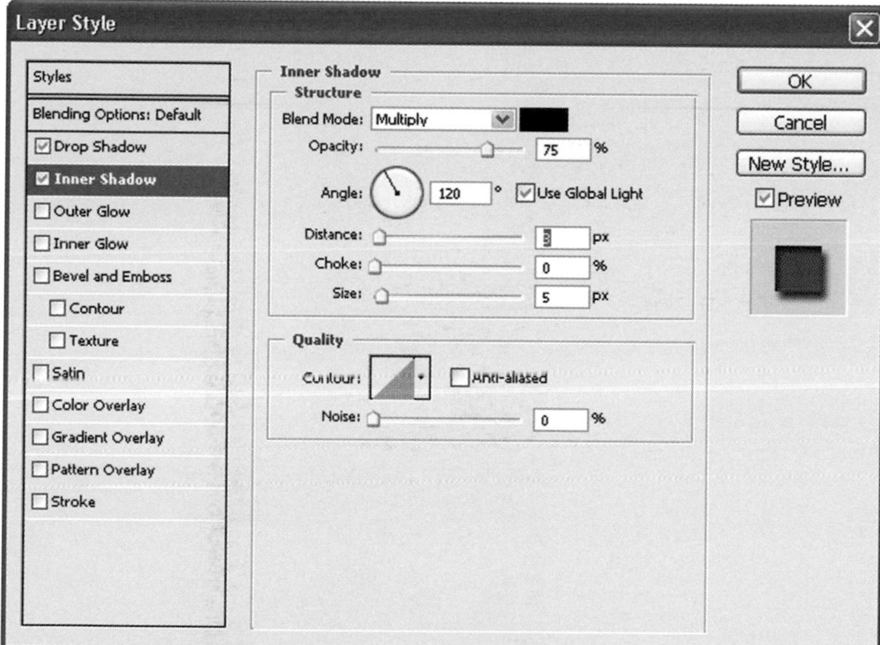

Add special effects

1. Verify that the photo layer is selected in the Layers palette, then click **Layer** on the menu bar.
2. Point to **Layer Style**, then click **Drop Shadow**.

   The Layer Style dialog box appears allowing you to apply various effects to the image. The Drop Shadow option is selected and there is a thumbnail image of the effect in the Preview window. Currently the Distance setting (how far the shadow falls from the image) is set to 5 pixels. You can move the slider to see the effect with different settings.
3. Drag the Distance slider to **30**, view the effect in the Preview window, then drag the slider to **6**.
4. Click **Inner Shadow**, move the Distance slider to **3** as shown in Figure 6-67, then click **OK**.

   TIP You can type a value rather than moving the slider.
5. Save the file.

You added a drop shadow and inner shadow to an image.

Add text to an image

1. Click the **Set Foreground color icon** in the Toolbox.
2. Delete the entry inside the # box, type **00CCFF**, then click **OK**.
3. Click **Layer** on the menu bar, point to **New**, then click **Layer**.
4. Type **text** in the Name box, then click **OK**.
5. Click the **Horizontal Type Tool** in the toolbar, click the **down list arrow** in the Set the font size box in the Character palette, then click **36 pt** as shown in Figure 6-68.
6. Verify **Arial** is the selected font in the Character palette.
7. Point near the top of the image, **click** to place the insertion point, then type **Welcome**.
8. Click **Layer** on the menu bar, point to **Layer Style**, then click **Bevel and Emboss**.
9. Click **OK** in the Layer Style dialog box.
10. Click the **Move tool** in the Toolbox, point to the **text**, hold down the mouse button, then drag the text to position it at the center top of the image as shown in Figure 6-69.
11. Save the file.

You added text to the image and applied a style to the text.

FIGURE 6-68
Specifying a font size in the Character palette

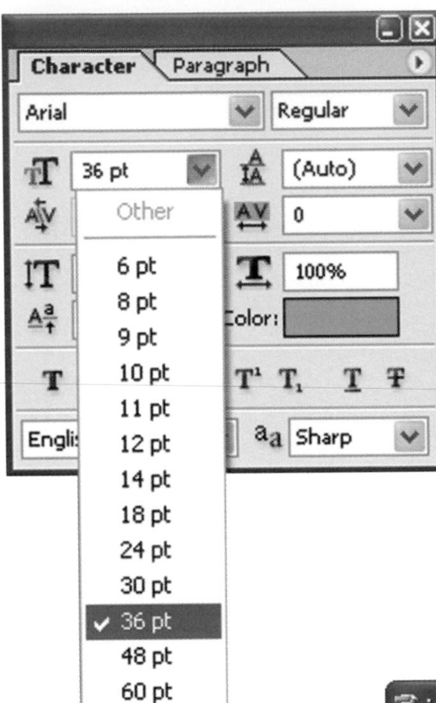

FIGURE 6-69
Text centered on image

FIGURE 6-70

The completed Save for Web dialog box

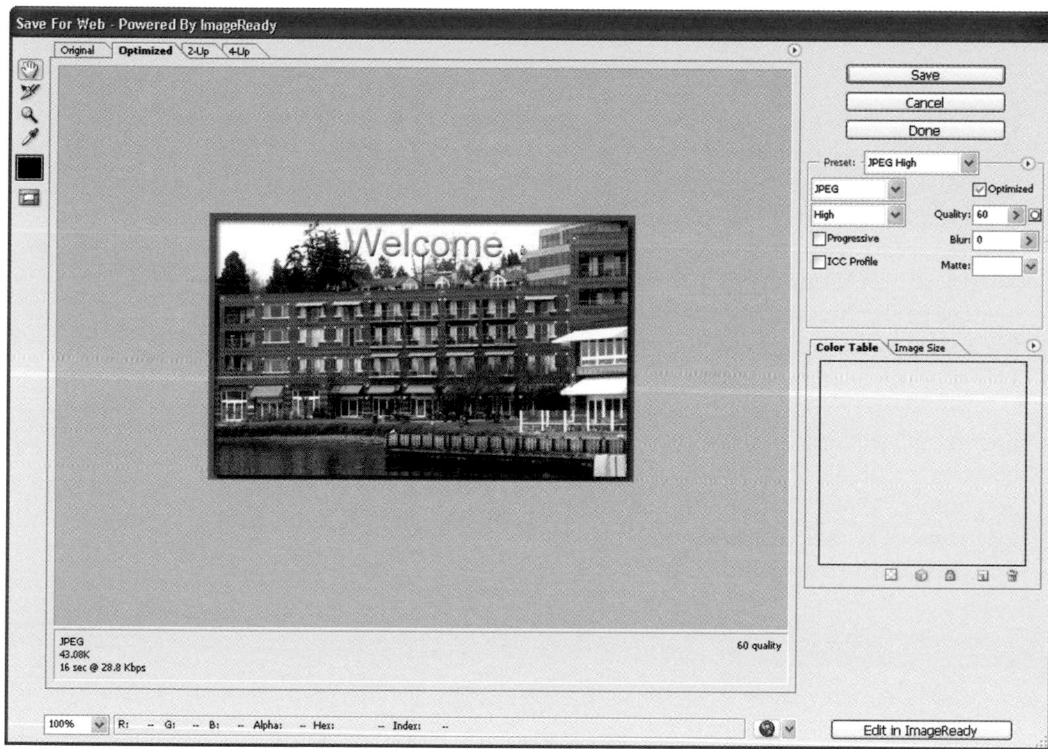

Save an image for the Web

1. Click **File** on the menu bar, then click **Save for Web**.
2. Complete the dialog box to resemble Figure 6-70.

   Notice that the file will be saved in a JPEG file format.
3. Click **Save**.
4. Navigate to the assets folder in the InnWebsiteDW folder.
5. Save the document with the filename **innphoto.jpg**.

You saved the image for the Web.

LESSON 3

ADDING GRAPHICS TO A WEB SITE
Using Macromedia Dreamweaver

What You'll Do

In this lesson, you will learn how to use Macromedia Dreamweaver to insert images into a Web page, align them to text, insert spacing between images and text, and specify alternate text.

Inserting Images, Adding Spacing, and Aligning

Currently, there are two image placeholders in the Inn at Birch Bay home page. Now that you have the logo and photo, you can delete the placeholders and insert the new images by dragging them from the Files panel to the desired location on the Web page. Because there are size differences between the placeholders and the images, you will need to add spaces between the heading text and the logo. You cannot simply press the spacebar to insert spaces because browsers compress extra spaces. However, you can add spaces using the code   (a non-breaking space). The   code (one for each space desired) can be typed directly into the XHTML code using the Split view.

Also, you will need to realign the logo and the text heading using the align attribute of the <img src> tag. There are several options for aligning text and images including texttop (aligns the top of the image with the top of the text); absmiddle (aligns the absolute middle of the image with the absolute middle of the text); and absbottom (aligns the absolute bottom of the image with the absolute bottom of the text). These are shown in Figure 6-71.

Alternate Text

In some cases an image may not be accessible either because of technical problems or a viewer's disability. Alternate text will display if the image is not accessible and, using certain browsers, can be output in an audio form. Using alternate text makes the contents of the Web page more accessible to those who are visually impaired. You specify alternate text using the alt attribute of the <img src> tag. Dreamweaver makes the process easy. You click an image to select it, then you type the alternate text in a box in the Property inspector. In XHTML Web pages, every image must have alternate text.

Before inserting the new images, you will edit the style sheet to make changes in the home page requested by the client. These include a new background color, removal of the text background color, and increasing the size of the navigation text. You will also be changing the color of the marquee text.

FIGURE 6-71
Aligning text and images

This is texttop alignment 

This is absmiddle alignment 

This is absbottom alignment 

Edit a style sheet

1. Start **Dreamweaver MX 2004**, display the InnWebSiteDW folder in the Files panel.
2. Double-click **homepage.htm** in the Files panel to open it.
3. Double-click the **sitestyles.css** file in the Files panel.
4. Select **50px** in the h1 tag, press **[Delete]**, then type **60px; text-align:center**.
5. Select **background-color:#C0C0C0** in the <h3> tag, press **[Delete]**, then type **font-size:24px; text-align:center**.
6. Select **00FF** in the body tag, press **[Delete]**, then type **66CC** as shown in Figure 6-72.
7. Save the document, then click **homepage.htm** just to the left of sitestyles.css at the top of the workspace window.
8. Preview the homepage.htm document in a browser, then return to the Dreamweaver document window.

You edited a style sheet.

FIGURE 6-72
The completed style sheet

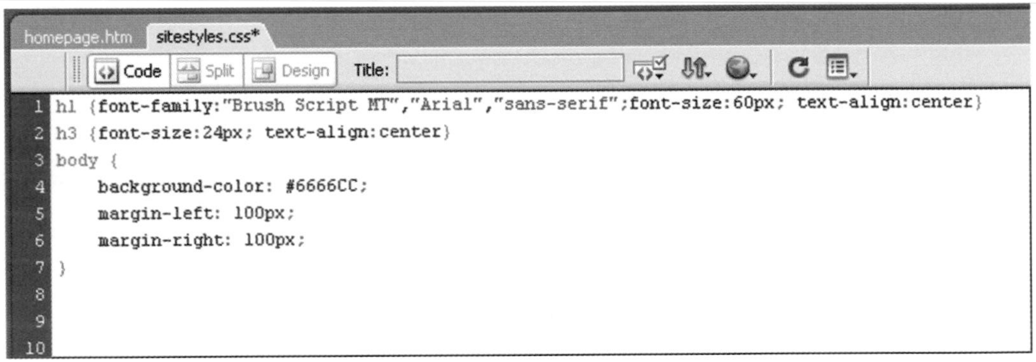

homepage.htm sitestyles.css*
Code Split Design Title:

```
h1 {font-family:"Brush Script MT","Arial","sans-serif";font-size:60px; text-align:center}
h3 {font-size:24px; text-align:center}
body {
    background-color: #6666CC;
    margin-left: 100px;
    margin-right: 100px;
}
```

Change headings and text color

1. Double-click **contactus.htm** in the Files panel, select the text **Contact us** at the top of the document, then type **Contact us Anytime**.
2. Save the document, preview it in a browser, then return to Dreamweaver.

(continued)

3. Double-click **directions.htm** in the Files panel, select the text **Directions**, then type **Directions to the Inn**.
4. Save the document, preview it in a browser, then return to Dreamweaver.
5. Double-click **tour.htm** in the Files panel, select the text **Tour**, then type **Tour our Facility**.
6. Select the marquee text **Our new Conference Center is now open!**.
7. Select the entry in the Text Color box in the Property inspector as shown in Figure 6-73.
8. Press **[Delete]**, type **#00CCFF**, then press **[Enter]** (PC) or **[return]** (Mac).
9. Save the document, preview it in a browser, then return to Dreamweaver.

You changed headings and text color.

FIGURE 6-73

The Text Color box in the Property inspector

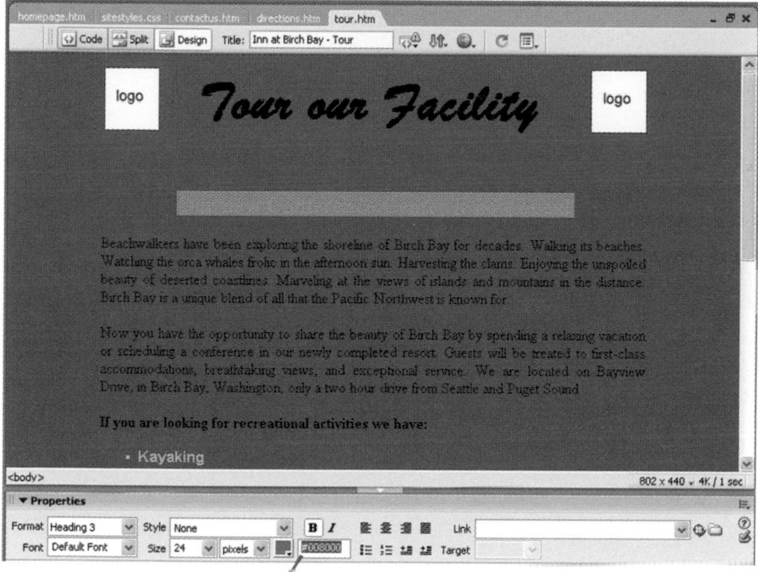

Replace images in a Web page

1. Display the **homepage.htm** document.
2. Click the left side **logo placeholder image** to select it, then press **[Delete]**.
3. Click the right side **logo placeholder image** to select it, then press **[Delete]**.
4. Drag the **innlogo.gif icon** from the assets folder in the Files panel to the right side of the heading **The Inn at Birch Bay** as shown in Figure 6-74.
5. Right-click (PC) or Ctrl-click (Mac) the **image**, point to **Align**, then click **Absolute Middle**.

(continued)

FIGURE 6-74

Positioning the innlogo.gif image

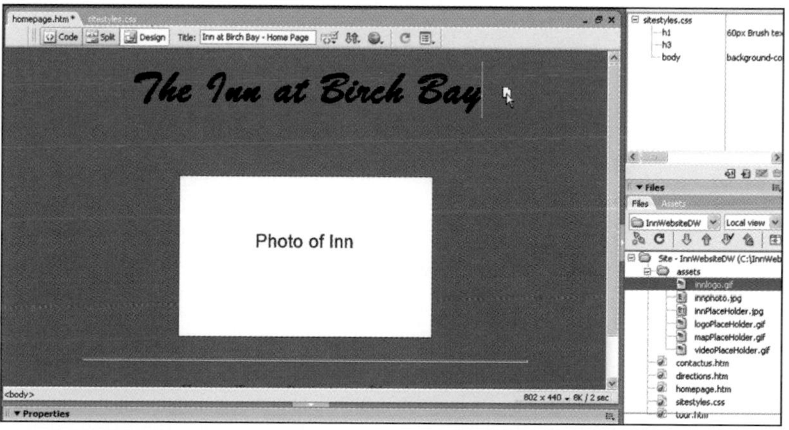

6. Click the Photo of Inn placeholder, press **[Delete]**, then drag the **innphoto.jpg** to the horizontal middle of the document as shown in Figure 6-75.
7. Save the document, preview it in a browser, then return to Dreamweaver.

   In some browsers, the font may not appear as it does in the figure.
8. Complete steps 1 through 5 for contactus.htm, directions.htm, and tour.htm, save each file as they are completed.

You replaced the logo placeholders with another image.

FIGURE 6-75

Positioning the innphoto.jpg image

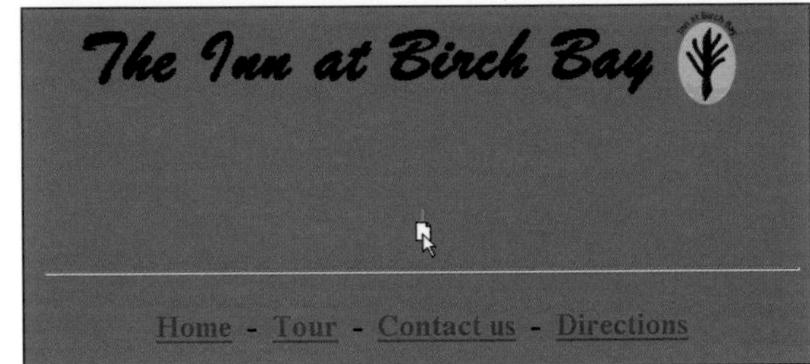

Add <alt> tags

1. Display the homepage.htm document.
2. Click the logo image to select it, click in the Alt box in the Property inspector.
3. Type **the inn's logo** as shown in Figure 6-76, then press **[Enter]** (PC) or **[return]** (Mac).
4. Click the **photo**, click in the Alt box in the Property inspector.
5. Type **photo of inn**, then press **[Enter]** (PC) or **[return]** (Mac).
6. Save the document, then view it in a browser.
7. Point to the logo, wait, notice the text that appears, then return to Dreamweaver.
8. Repeat steps 1 through 3 for contactus.htm, directions.htm, and tours.htm, saving the document each time.

You added <alt> tags for the images on the Web pages.

FIGURE 6-76

The completed Alt box entry

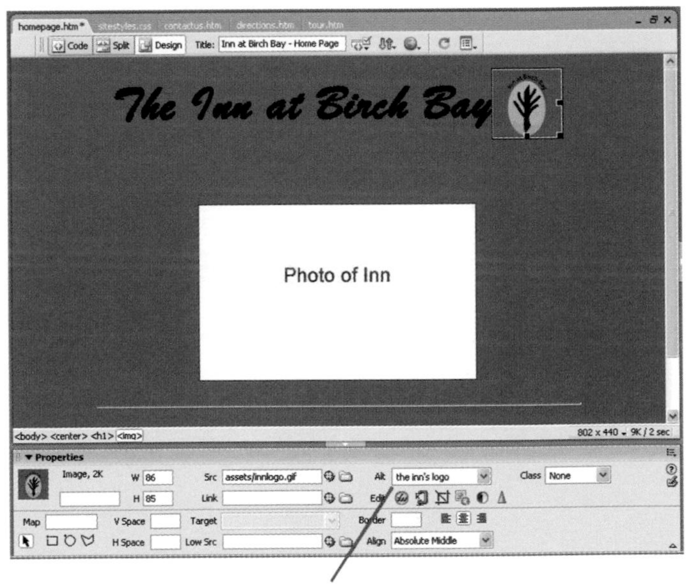

FIGURE 6-77
Positioning the pointer

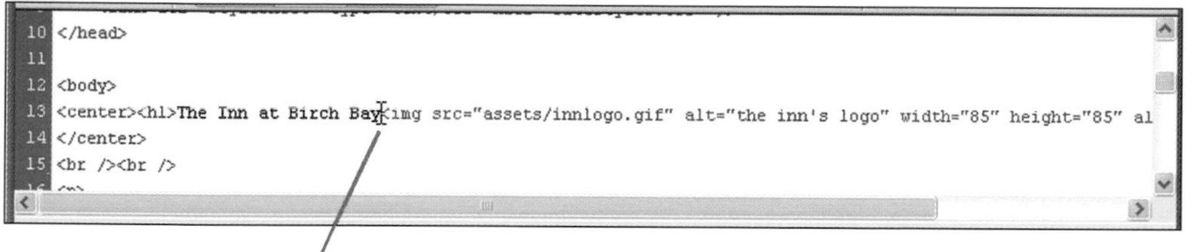

Insertion point

FIGURE 6-78
The completed entry

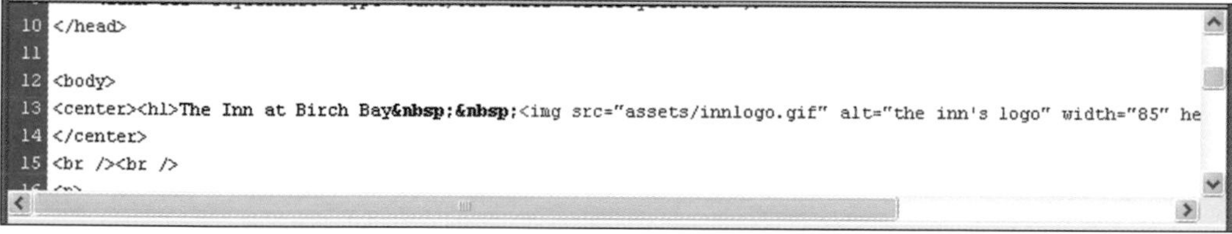

Add spacing to a Web page

1. Display the homepage.htm document.
2. Point to just after Bay, then click to set the insertion point.
3. Click the **Split button** [Split] to view the code.
4. Point to between Bay and <img, as shown in Figure 6-77, then click to set the insertion line.
5. Type ** ** as shown in Figure 6-78, then click the document window.

   TIP Make sure you are typing in the Code view window, not in the document window. Also, be sure to type the text exactly as shown, including the semicolons.

6. Preview the homepage.htm document in a browser, then return to the Dreamweaver document window.
7. Save the document.

You added spaces between text and an image.

PROJECT BUILDER 1

You are an intern with a company that develops Web sites for clients. During your internship training you learned how important images are in the development of Web pages. One of the most important considerations when using images is the target audience. The variance in images is evident in different Web sites that target businesses, adults, and children. Figure 6-79 shows two Web sites using graphics. You have been asked to write a report that compares how graphics are used on Web sites that have different target audiences.

1. Connect to the Internet, and go to *www.course.com*, navigate to the page for this book, click the Student Online Companion link, then click the link for this chapter.
2. Navigate through each Web site (there are two) and study the use of graphics for the Web pages for each Web site (see Figure 6-79).
3. Open a document in a word processor, save the file as **Ch6pb1**, create a table with these column heads: Topic, Web site 1, Web site 2, then create one row for each topic that follows:
    a. Target audience and rationale for that audience
    b. Type of images (photographs and drawings)
    c. The mood created with various graphics (serious, fun, formal, informal, and so on)
    d. The use of alternate text (Note: you can view the Web page source code and search for "alt")
    e. Relative amount of space dedicated to images versus text on a Web page
    f. Linked images (are images used to link to other pages or URLs?)
4. Compare the Web pages using the topics listed in your table, record your findings in your table.

One Step Beyond

5. Do you think the use of graphics was appropriate for each target audience? Why, or why not?
6. What recommendations would you make to improve the use of graphics and why?

Two Steps Beyond

7. Conduct a Web search for two online stock photo companies.
8. Choose one subject and search for images available on the sites.
9. Write a summary of each site and include the following in the summary:
    a. The name and URLs for each company
    b. The approximate number of photos available for the chosen subject
    c. Ease of finding the desired photo
    d. Approximate cost of photos
    e. How photos are distributed
    f. What safeguards does each site have for preventing the copying of an image from the site?
    g. File formats that are available
    h. The terms of use (what is allowed and what is forbidden)
    i. Which site would you evaluate as better and why?

FIGURE 6-79
Two Web sites using graphics

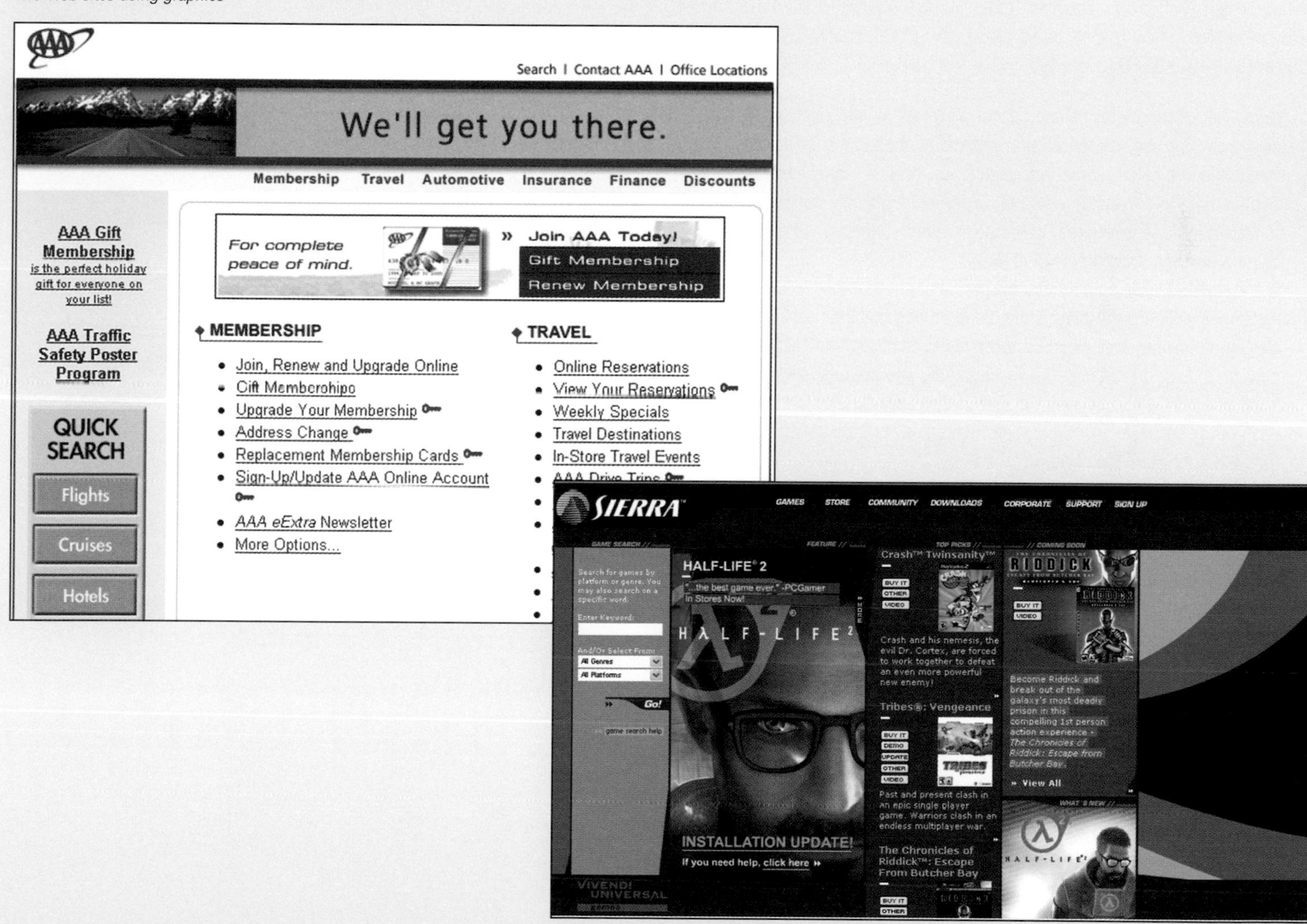

PROJECT BUILDER 2

You have been studying Web development. You decide it would be useful to apply various graphic features to a portfolio Web site. Complete the following steps to create two Web pages similar to the ones shown in Figure 6-80.

1. Using Adobe Illustrator develop three drawings of your choice. Use the freeform tools such as the Paintbrush and shape tools such as the Rectangle and Ellipse tools. Add text, if appropriate. Apply various colors and features to enhance the image. Experiment with the various options in Illustrator. Use layers for each of the separate objects and name the layers. Save the drawings for the Web.
2. Using Adobe Photoshop enhance a personal photograph by applying various special effects (layer styles) and editing features such as cropping and resizing. Be sure to save the file in its original format before altering it. Experiment with the various tools and options in Photoshop such as brightness and contrast. Add text, if appropriate. Use layers for each of the separate objects and name the layers. Save the photo as a .psd file, then save the photo for the Web.

One Step Beyond

3. Using Dreamweaver, open mysitech6.htm and edit as follows.
   a. Insert the Photoshop photo at a location of your choice.
   b. Add alternate text.
   c. Align the image as desired.
4. Save the document with the filename **mysitech6-homexx.htm** (where *xx* are your initials).

Two Steps Beyond

5. Create a second Web page named **Showcase** with the same formatting as the home page.
6. Insert the three Illustrator drawings, align them as desired, then add alternate text.
7. Link the two Web pages.
8. Save the document with the filename **mysitech6-showcasexx.htm** (where *xx* are your initials).

FIGURE 6-80
The Web pages with placeholders for images

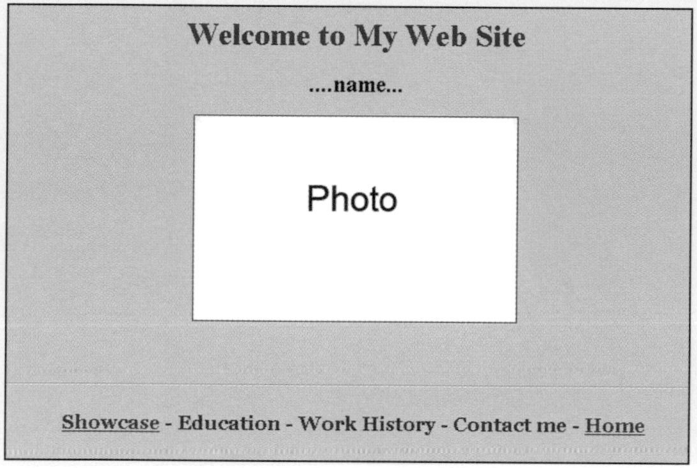

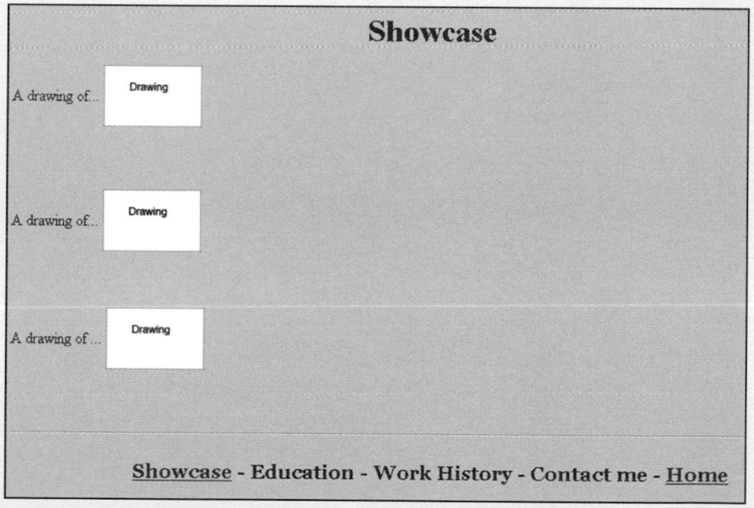

CAPSU
5
a.
7
50°
8
60°
9
70°
10

chapter 7

MULTIMEDIA ELEMENT—Animation

1. Discuss Using Animation on the Web
2. Examine the Methods for Creating Animation
3. Understand 3-D Animation, Special Effects, and VR
4. Explore Animation Software
5. Discuss Animation File Formats for the Web

chapter 7 MULTIMEDIA ELEMENT—Animation

Animation is part of our daily lives and has been for years. Animation is simply a moving or changing graphic image. See Figure 7-1. The perception of motion in an animation is an illusion. The computer is used to display a series of still images fast enough to create movement on the screen or to trick our eyes into believing that this series of still images is actually in motion. The virtual world created by animated objects has physical properties including height, width, depth, and time.

More than 50 years ago, Walt Disney was creating animated objects and characters, such as Mickey Mouse, that were making movie-goers laugh and cry. Others have joined Disney, and today, realistic animation is all around us. Entertainment in general and children's entertainment in particular rely heavily on animation, but animation can also be extremely effective in education and training as well as in advertising and e-commerce. Although animation was founded by the entertainment industry, it certainly is not restricted to video games, television, or movies. Animation plays a significant role in entertainment (providing action and realism), in education (providing visualization and demonstration), and in advertising (providing interest and stimulation).

The need for movement on a page depends on the purpose and content of the page. Animation may not be appropriate for a multimedia Web site for a financial institution, while an entertainment site might obviously benefit from such movement. Multimedia Web sites advertising creative services such as graphic design and marketing may want to include animation as a means of showcasing their creativity.

When used appropriately, animation can be an integral part of a Web site. It can add a great deal to the overall quality and content of a Web site. Animation usually grabs the user's attention more than some of the other multimedia elements, but if animation is done improperly, it can be distracting. There are things to consider before you decide to include animation on a multimedia Web page. You need to know if it will add value to the page or detract from the page. There are also certain rules to keep in mind when adding animation to a Web page.

Too much of a good thing can backfire. Animated banner ads or company logos can become very irritating if they are continually blinking or moving while a user is trying to read content or locate information. Of course the company does not intend to alienate the user with the animation, but that is often what happens. The same is true if the animation has no real value. Drawing attention to something of no use is an example of an ineffective and even negative application of animation.

An **animation specialist** is responsible for creating the animation on a Web site. Planning is important in ensuring that the animation is appropriate and well conceived. The storyboards and other planning documents used in designing animations must be consistent with the purpose and target audience of the Web site. The storyboards help the animation specialist visualize the multimedia Web site and work out problems before the animation is developed. This keeps the creative process from being halted in order to work out a problem that should have been resolved before production began. For example, the animation specialist needs scripts if the animation includes characters so that the dialogue is tailored to the target audience.

If the Web site is interactive, the animation specialist will need to refer to flowcharts. The animation specialist must design animated characters and objects that change as a result of a change in mood or tone within the Web site. In other words, as the user makes choices, the outcomes are different. Obviously, the animated characters and objects must correctly reflect this outcome. For example, in a training Web site, a character might be designed to jump for joy if the user chooses the correct answer. However, if the user responds incorrectly, the character should reflect this mood, perhaps by hanging its head and looking dejected.

There are a number of different software programs available to assist the animation specialist in designing effective animation for a Web site. In addition to designing appropriate animation for the project, the animation specialist also needs to optimize the files so that they are quick to download, and functional, and in an animation file format that is widely supported by all of the major Web browsers. Consequently, the animation specialist must have technical skills as well as design savvy. As a specialist, the animator needs to understand how to develop for high-end systems as well as for those systems that might be found in the average user's home or office.

FIGURE 7-1

To create the illusion of animation, a series of still images is displayed fast enough so the viewer believes the images are moving

DISCUSS USING ANIMATION on the Web

What You'll Learn

In this lesson, you will learn that animation is used in multimedia Web sites for education and training, entertainment and games, and advertising and e-commerce. You will also learn guidelines to help use animation effectively while conserving computer resources.

In order to understand the guidelines for using animation on the Web, you first need to look at animation and how it is currently used on the Web. Due to some key technologies that have become more sophisticated, user-friendly, and powerful, animation is very common on the Web and will continue to grow more prominent as technologies evolve. Animation can be used to achieve a variety of different effects. Animation is an excellent way to increase the appeal of a Web site and to help ensure return visits.

Animations can be as simple as blinking text, marquee-like scrolling headlines, rotating logos, animated icons, Web buttons, and 2-D action figures. Simple, premade animations are available on the Web (see Figure 7-2) for a fee or for free. Within a multimedia Web site, there are many opportunities for adding animation. Objects and characters of all types have the potential to be animated. An animated children's story designed to teach children about the importance of recycling might have fairly simplistic animation such as a talking recycle bin. On the other end of the spectrum, it is now possible to create full-length animated feature films with extremely complex animation and fully developed, life-like human characters. Shorts and trailers of these animated files have made their way onto the Web as have complex 3-D virtual reality environments with user control.

FIGURE 7-2

Simple animations including animated icons, Web buttons, and 2-D action figures are available commercially

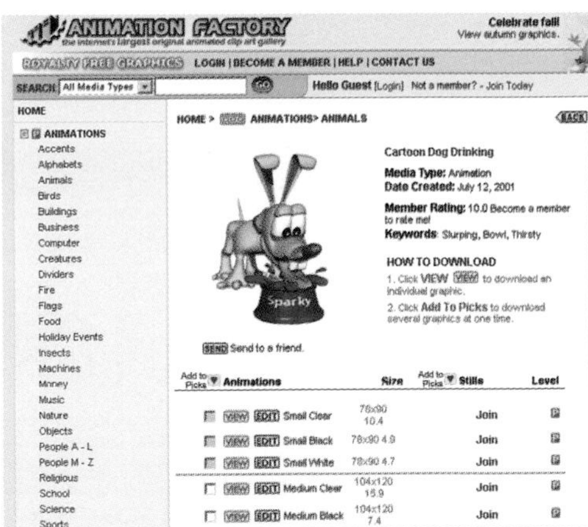

Animation has been used in Web-based training programs where animated illustrations demonstrate the correct way to assemble parts, adjust controls, or even perform surgery. Web sites with animation also provide an effective way to teach other applied and hands-on skills. For example, musicians can learn to play instruments; athletes can learn the proper methods and techniques in sports, such as football, inline skating, tai chi, and yoga.

QUICKTIP

After learning concepts with the help of animation, some Web sites offer credit or certification upon completion of a test.

In many contexts, animation is a superior choice over video because video represents real life and real life is sometimes too complex for words. Complex concepts can be explained by simplifying them and using animation to visualize each concept. For example, if a mechanic needs to be trained on the hydraulic system for the landing gear of a jet plane, an animation might be used to provide information on the flow of hydraulic fluid through the system by providing a simulation of the process and a dramatization of how pressure is created during the process (see Figure 7-3). Animation is often a better instructional tool than video because it is simple and easy to understand. It can also be better than video because it is generally more cost-effective and creates smaller files for quicker downloads.

Although delivering technical training via the Web is more common, Web sites can also be effective in teaching soft skills, such as human relations and communications. For example, employees involved in international business who lack knowledge of cultural differences could receive training from an animated cultural guru who might explain body language and customs. Web sites like this are useful not only for new employees but also as retraining for employees who have been with the company for some time.

FIGURE 7-3

Animation is used in educational and training Web sites to teach skills and concepts, animation (left) is used to show the effect (right) of applying force to the left piston

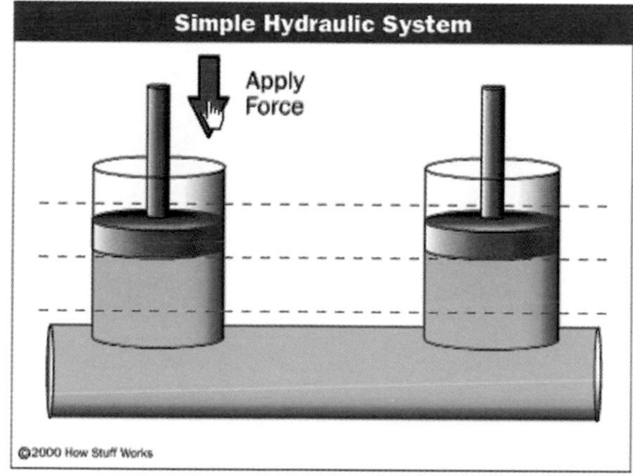

A simple hydraulic system consisting of two pistons and an oil-filled pipe connecting them. Click on the red arrow to see the animation.

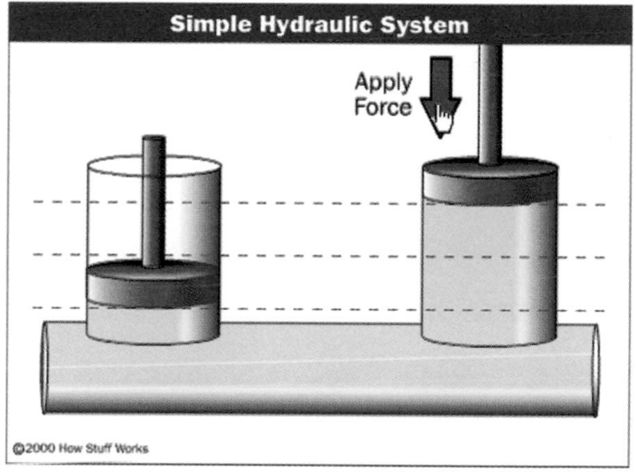

A simple hydraulic system consisting of two pistons and an oil-filled pipe connecting them. Click on the red arrow to see the animation.

Web-based training is not limited to business and industry. Comparable programs are also available in education, and animation can be particularly effective in teaching children. Many Web sites use animation geared toward entertaining kids as they learn. Like the PBS Kid's Web site shown in Figure 7-4, many of these Web sites are incredibly creative and well done. On the Web, you will find everything from spelling and foreign language programs for grade school children to Web sites that prepare high school students for college entrance exams such as the SAT or ACT. You will even find Web sites for college students who are preparing for a career including online animated counselors who use animated demonstrations to teach future counselors effective and ineffective ways of working with clients.

People of all ages and from different backgrounds enjoy playing games on the Web. To take advantage of this, nearly all entertainment Web sites use animation in one way or another. Animated characters encounter animated objects in animated worlds, such as the games like those on the Looney Tunes Web site (see Figure 7-5). Animated games are designed so that users can play alone against the computer or log in and play unknown users, friends, or family members across the country or around the world.

Animation grabs attention, and businesses want your attention. They want to get you to their Web site and keep you there until you buy their products or services. Because of technologies like Macromedia Flash, Web pages running animations with small file sizes abound on the Web today. They are quick to load and effective at producing the desired result, for example prompting a viewer to order a product or complete a survey. Animated buttons, banners, text, and characters are used for advertising and information. At some sites, these animated art forms themselves are the reason viewers choose to visit. Because animation grabs attention, it is commonly found on Web

FIGURE 7-4

Animation can be used in education to entertain and teach, for example, on this Web page, animation is used to draw attention to what the goldfish is thinking about, in this case "frog;" the student is challenged to find the object that rhymes with "frog"

FIGURE 7-5

Web-based computer games include animated characters and objects, for example, when visitors first arrive at this Web page, animation is used to grab attention and draw users into the game

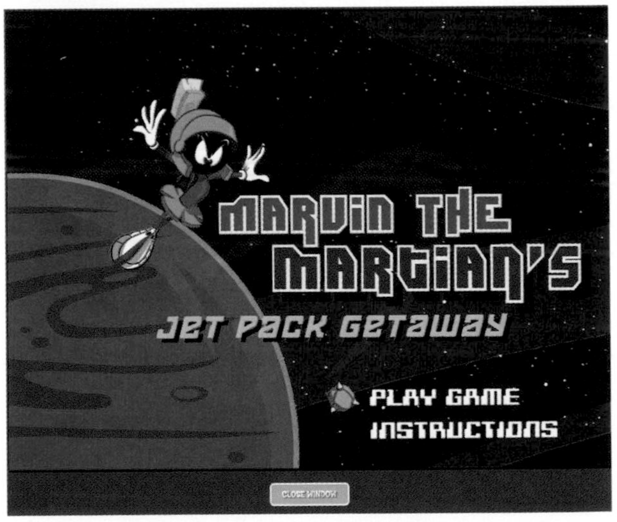

pages as an introduction to the site as well as for advertising banners and navigational directions.

Well-designed and effective animations can be cute and informative. On the other hand, if the animation is poorly designed and poorly incorporated into a Web page, it can be annoying and downright detrimental to the site. The bottom line is that you must design animation that is appropriate to the application and geared toward the users of the site. To accomplish a well-designed animation, be sure to thoroughly examine the scripts and storyboards. Then use the guidelines that follow to help ensure that animation is effective, not annoying.

- Consider the purpose of the Web site and make sure the animation adds to the project by gaining the user's attention or creating a more thorough understanding of a concept. Animations should impact not detract from the ideas presented.
- Determine how much animation to use, what objects should be animated, and how long the animation should run. These factors will vary depending on the intent of the site.
- Realize that moving objects draw attention. Make sure you animate what you want your users to notice. If you animate something else, users will be distracted from the content you are actually trying to emphasize.
- Make sure the animation is appropriate to the mood and content of the application.
- Do not use too many animated objects per page. If you use too much animation, users do not know where to focus and they become overwhelmed and annoyed.
- Animation that does the same thing over and over is also annoying. If possible, keep the animation changing or stop the animation by limiting the number of cycles or loops.
- Use transitions and special effects that help communicate your message, but do not get overzealous and add too many.
- Make sure your animation loads quickly. The importance of a Web page that downloads quickly cannot be overstated. The bottom line: users will not wait! Your animation is completely wasted if your viewers never see it because they do not have the patience to wait for it to download.

DESIGNTIP Planning

- Successful animation is based on knowing what, when, and how much to animate.
- Plan your animation by following scripts, storyboards, and flowcharts.
- Keep transitions between frames smooth to prevent flicker, which occurs when the still images become obvious and the illusion of animation is lost.
- Plan only one animation per page; too many distracting animations will confuse the user, who will not know where to focus.

DESIGNTIP Save Computer Resources

When you design animation, you also need to take into account the computer resources that will be used to run the animations. A few guidelines on how to save computer resources follow:

- Limit the number of animations running at the same time. More animated objects require more memory.
- Keep animated objects to a relatively small size. One way to minimize the file size is to keep the color depth low.
- Keep the sequence of recorded images at a rate that is as low as possible, yet high enough to maintain the illusion of motion.

CONCEPT 2

EXAMINE THE METHODS for Creating Animation

What You'll Learn

In this lesson, you will learn about the different methods used to create animation including frame-based, path-based, and program-based animation.

The process used to create animated objects continues to change. If you have seen an animated feature film lately, you are probably well aware of how sophisticated big-screen movie animation has become. Even on the Web, you find a range of animation, from very simple to very complex, high-caliber animation involving the use of high-end computer technology and sophisticated software.

Digital animation is based on the **flipbook approach**, which is when a sequence of slightly different visual images is compressed and then played back to convey a sense of motion. In other words, animation is a series of still images played back fast enough to trick our minds into believing that there is movement. The flipbook approach can be demonstrated by drawing a ball on an index card, then drawing the same ball on a second index card in a slightly different location. Then repeat this with many index cards. If you hold the edge of the stack of index cards and fan or flip the cards, the ball will appear to move.

2-D images are flat. By changing the position or location of the image and then recording this change and replaying the entire sequence of changes, the 2-D image appears to be animated. You can convert a 2-D image into a 3-D image by adding texture and shading. This creates the illusion of depth even on a flat surface. Animating 3-D objects is more complicated than animating 2-D objects. Unlike working with When animating 3-D images, relative space must also be considered (see Figure 7-6).

There are two rates used to measure animation. The **sampling rate** is the number of different images that occur per second. In other words, the sampling rate refers to the number of images captured and available to be used in an animation. The **playback rate** is the number of frames displayed per second when the animation is being viewed. Both the sampling rate and playback rate work together to create high-quality animation. The sampling rate and the playback rate can be, and often are, different. Obviously, the playback rate cannot be higher than the sampling rate, and a higher sampling rate will generally result in a higher-quality animation.

The complexity of the animation as well as bandwidth and the hardware of the computers delivering and used for viewing the animation all help determine the speed at which animation plays. To create the illusion of motion effectively, the playback rate of animation must be between 24 and 30 frames per second at full-motion video standards. On the Web, the standard is generally 12 to 15 frames per second. Anything less than 12 frames per second, however, creates a jerky motion as the eye detects the changes from one frame to the next. When the illusion of motion fails and the animation appears as a rapid sequence of still images instead of a fluid object in motion, the animation is said to **flicker**.

Frame-based Animation

Frame-based animation is also called **cel animation**. The term "**cel**" comes from the word *celluloid*, which is a clear sheet material on which images are drawn by movie animators. The celluloid images are then placed on a stationary background. The background remains fixed as the object changes from frame to frame (see Figure 7-7). You can have more than one object move against a fixed background. Computer-based cel animation is based on changes that occur from one frame to the next, which gives the illusion of movement.

FIGURE 7-6
3-D animated images must create the illusion of depth

On this Web page, animation is used to move the vessel up the stream and to make the vessel look smaller as it moves into the distance

FIGURE 7-7
Example of cel animation

The concept behind animation is the same whether the computer generates the animation or is created by hand. Prior to computer-generated animation, artists drew each of the cels or frames needed to create the illusion of movement. These artists were called **tweeners**. Drawing each frame manually is an incredibly labor-intensive and time-consuming process. Today the computer automatically draws the between frames. This process is called **tweening**. To use tweening, the animator must create **keyframes**. Each keyframe is unique and illustrates a key event in the timeline of the animation. The animator then uses tweening, the process of filling in the frames between the keyframes, to generate new frames based on the differences calculated from one keyframe to the next. The difference between one keyframe and the next keyframe could be the result of a new position, color, shape, or any number of other characteristics or combinations of characteristics. With computer-generated animation, the computer program generates the between frames that make the animation appear fluid. In order for animation to be effective, it must create the illusion of natural movement. This requires frames running at least 12 frames per second; a more professional look requires a rate of 24 to 30 frames per second.

Morphing is a special technique that uses frames to create the illusion of one object changing into another (see Figure 7-8). Morphing is quite common on television and in the movies. Morphing is useful in showing not only how two images blend together, but also how an image might change over time. Morphing on the Web is generally created using a process referred to as **shape tweening**. Again, keyframes are created by the animator and the computer generates the between frames. By displaying a series of frames that create a smooth transition, it appears that one shape actually becomes another.

Tweening and morphing are quite time-consuming when done manually, however special computer software has been developed for creating frame-based animation. Theoretically, frame-based animation on the computer uses basically the same technique employed by tweeners. However, with the help of the computer, drawings can be reused and altered. This means keyframes can be created and modified in a much shorter time period because between frames can be created automatically.

QUICKTIP

Because writing code is time-consuming as well as challenging, animation specialists often refer to resources such as users' groups and online journals, which provide assistance for programmers at all levels.

FIGURE 7-8

Morphing makes it appear as if one object actually evolves into another

Path-based Animation

Path-based animation is also called **vector animation**. This type of animation creates animated objects by following an object's transition over a line or vector (see Figure 7-9). Specifically, it tracks the beginning, direction, and length that an object travels along a predetermined path. The path the line takes could be a straight line or it could include any number of curves. With path-based animation, the artist creates only one object and a path. **Motion tweening** is used to fill in the frames as the object moves along the path. For this reason, path-based animation is often easier to create as compared to frame-based animation because you need only one object instead of several objects.

Computational animation allows an object to be moved across a screen by varying its x- and y-coordinates. Changing the x-coordinate changes the object's horizontal position; changing the y-coordinate changes the object's vertical position. This method is similar to path-based animation; however, instead of specifying a path for the object to travel, you vary its position based on axes.

If you are using a software program to create animation instead of writing the programming code yourself, the software program is actually generating x- and y-coordinates for the object. The computer program manipulates the object by drawing the frames as the object travels along the path. The animation specialist simply creates the path by dragging the pointer around the screen or by pointing to different locations on the screen and clicking the mouse button. Tweening can also be used to create this path. The animation specialist would set the object's beginning position on one frame and its ending position on another frame. The software program would then fill in the intervening frames.

Most programs allow you to combine frame-based and path-based animation. Typically, the animated object is created using frame-based techniques, then it is moved along a path using path-based animation.

Program- or Script-based Animation

Program-based or **script-based animation** involves the use of programming and scripting languages to create animation. Through the use of a sometimes-elaborate set of commands, frames can be substituted for other frames thus creating a sequence of movement or animation. Program-based and script-based animations are often more flexible than those created using the other methods because they can be very easily modified to use new images and objects.

FIGURE 7-9
With path-based animation, the computer program manipulates the object by drawing the frames along the path that the object follows

CONCEPT 3

UNDERSTAND 3-D ANIMATION, Special Effects, and VR

What You'll Learn

In this lesson, you will learn about 3-D animation, special animation effects, and virtual reality (VR).

While 2-D animation can be effective in enhancing a multimedia Web site, 3-D animation takes the entire multimedia experience to another level. 3-D animation is the foundation of many multimedia games and adventure Web sites. By creating the illusion of a 3-D world, 3-D animation brings users into the setting as participants, not just as spectators. However, creating 3-D animation is considerably more complex than creating 2-D animation for the same reason creating 3-D images is more complex than creating 2-D images. 3-D animation involves two additional steps—modeling and rendering.

As you will recall from Chapter 6, modeling is the process of creating the wireframe or structure of 3-D objects and scenes. Various views of an object (top, side, cross-section) are drawn by setting points on a grid or polygon mesh (see Figure 7-10). These views are then used to define the object's 3-D shape.

Animating 3-D images and objects may involve frame-based, cell-based, or program-based animation to change the object's shape or position. In addition, however, lighting and perspective as well as camera angle must be considered. Changing these features and the camera angle assists in creating the illusion of animation in a 3-D world.

Rendering is the final step in creating 3-D animation. It involves giving objects attributes such as colors, surface textures, and opacity. Figure 7-11 shows an image that has been rendered. Rendering is a time-intensive use of computer resources. For this reason, animation specialists may initially render the animation using a quick, low-resolution process as a test. They will then analyze the test and make adjustments accordingly. Once they are satisfied, they will use a slower, higher-resolution process to render the final animation.

FIGURE 7-10
3-D modeling process

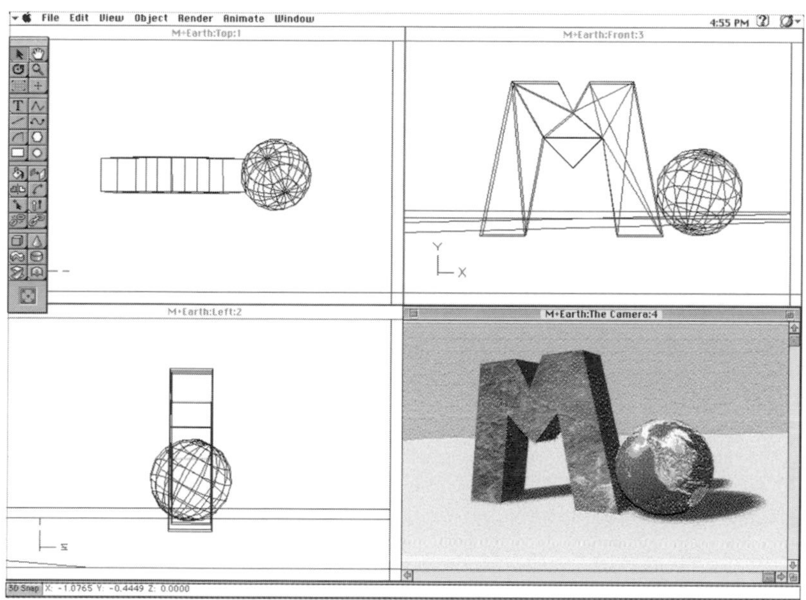

FIGURE 7-11
Results of a rendering process in a 3-D animation

Special Animation Effects

Special **animation effects**, such as those discussed next, allow you to create interesting effects.

Onion skinning allows you to create new images by tracing over an existing image. It is a particularly useful technique when you are creating parallel animation in which part of an image remains static while another portion of the image changes. For example, you may want the head of the image to remain static while the facial features change.

Trail effect is when the image from the previous frame is not completely erased so that it appears in the new frame. In other words, a trail of the image remains. This is particularly effective when images would remain visible; for example, you might use the trail effect to animate footprints in the snow.

A **film loop** consists of a series of animated frames looped to play over and over again. Although film loops can improve the performance of animation by helping you create a smaller file, they have to be done well or they can become annoying when they loop over and over again.

Warping is similar to morphing, however, instead of using two different images as is done with morphing, when an image is warped, a single image is used. Warping allows you to distort part of an image. For example, you could warp a facial feature to change a frown into a smile (see Figure 7-12).

FIGURE 7-12
Software can be used to distort or warp an image to create a special animation effect

Virtual Reality

Virtual reality (VR) is used to describe 3-D scenes on the Web that surround the user so that he or she becomes part of the experience. The term *virtual reality (VR)* has been used to describe various types of applications, some of which are more experiential than others. Using VR, Web developers are able to create 3-D objects that users can manipulate with a pointing device such as a mouse, trackball, or joystick.

Virtual reality originated with the military where it is still used for simulations. Today, VR is often encountered in electronic games. Many multimedia Web sites can be used to create an artificial environment complete with 3-D images that can be explored and manipulated. The reality of this artificial environment is dependent on the hardware and software used to create and play it. The hardware and software also determine how much users can interact with the environment. In order to make the experience more lifelike, experts are currently researching the inclusion of smell and touch in this environment.

There are many practical applications of virtual reality. For example, VR has been used effectively by architects to create Web-based models of buildings that clients can "walk through" before construction begins. Using VR, clients get a much better sense of what the building will look and feel like before they spend hundreds of thousands of dollars on construction. Similar applications have spilled over into the automobile-, airplane-, and boat-manufacturing industries. Sea Ray offers virtual tours of most of its yachts. You can see an example of the aft stateroom of the 460 Sundancer in Figure 7-13. A viewer visiting this site could use the pointer to move through the stateroom, seeing it from different angles. VR is found increasingly at e-commerce Web sites so potential customers can gather additional information about a product before purchasing it, for example, seeing all sides of a table or trying clothes on virtual models.

FIGURE 7-13

A virtual tour of a product, such as the yacht shown here, is possible using VR on the Web

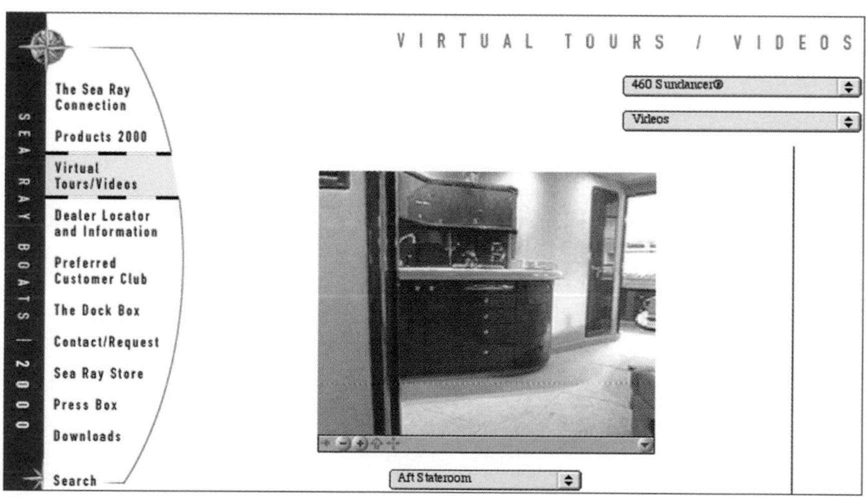

CONCEPT 4

EXPLORE ANIMATION
Software

What You'll Learn

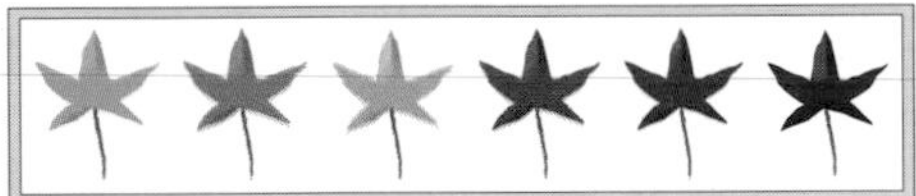

In this lesson, you will learn about the different software programs developed by Macromedia and Adobe to create animation for the Web. Shareware programs will also be discussed.

Just as clip art can be purchased or downloaded from the Internet, animated graphics can also be purchased on CD or downloaded from the Internet. Although more and more premade animated graphics are available, you may find that you need to create your own animated image to achieve the desired effect. If you do decide to create your own animated graphic, you may need several pieces of software to do it.

Depending on the program you plan to use as well as the type of animation you wish to create, you may need to create the series of still images used to generate the animation (see Figure 7-14). Unless the images you wish to animate already exist, the first tool you may need is graphics software or equipment to capture images. To create an animated image, each graphic image is modified slightly and then played back in rapid sequence. Using this technique, the graphic appears to change or move. Graphics software is needed to create the image or images, and animation software is needed to animate the image or images once they are created.

There are many software programs that can be used to create animation for the Web. As mentioned previously, the animation process can be achieved through the use of software, programming languages, or a combination of the two. Of course, there are also software programs that allow you to create and modify objects and images as well as animate them. You can use almost any commercial graphics program, which would include virtually every drawing, paint, and modeling program. After you have captured or created your image, you may need to edit the image with an image editing program. This program may be the same software used to capture or create the image, or it might be something different. Among other things, a good image editing utility should offer you the ability to resize the object, apply different design aspects to various parts of the image, and modify the object using paint or drawing tools. Many programs come with special effects, filters, and the ability to manipulate the color depth and image resolution of each image individually.

> **QUICKTIP**
>
> There are many ways to create animation. Knowing the tools and having several tools available for use will help you to be productive and creative.

After your graphics have been captured, created, and edited to your satisfaction, you will need to animate them. Programs specifically designed to create animation for the Web are available. These programs range from simple to complex. Many of them share common features including a **compiling engine** that allows you to **compile** still images into animated objects. Compiling is the process of generating a single file from multiple files. Most of these animation packages will also include a **codec** (compressor/decompressor). The codec enables you to choose the amount of compression as well as the type of compression used.

Macromedia

Macromedia has long been a leader in the world of multimedia, and when the possibilities of developing multimedia for the Web began to surface, Macromedia was at the forefront in developing products to make it all happen. Today Macromedia continues to spur the growth of Web-based multimedia by making it possible for Web designers and developers to create engaging and effective Web sites that include animation. Macromedia has made it easy for professional Web developers and designers to use and integrate programs such as Macromedia Dreamweaver, Macromedia Fireworks, and Macromedia Flash to build high-impact, interactive sites that deliver rich media and full-motion animation.

FIGURE 7-14

Animation can be used to show the changing color of leaves from spring to fall by slightly changing the color in each leaf

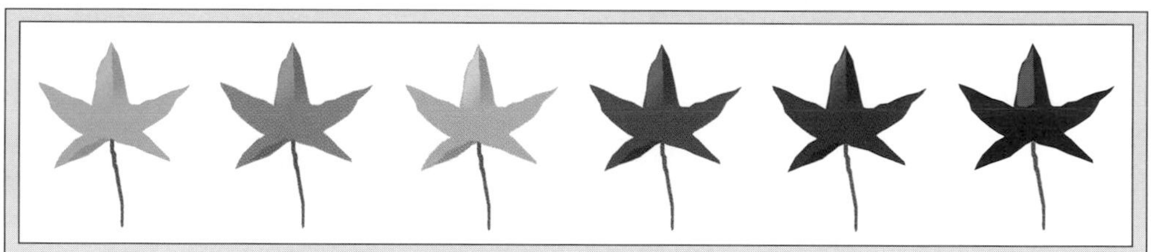

Fireworks

As discussed in Chapter 6, Macromedia Fireworks is a solution for professional Web graphics design and production. This tool also includes features that allow developers and designers to quickly and easily create animations.

Macromedia Fireworks combines both bitmap- and vector-editing tools within a single environment. As shown in Figure 7-15, Macromedia Fireworks includes autoshapes that make it easy to create simple and complex images for animations. In addition, Macromedia Fireworks allows you to import files from digital cameras, scanners, and other graphics applications. Upon import, everything remains editable until you are ready to convert the completed piece to an animation. Macromedia Fireworks uses a frame-based environment that allows you to create and optimize animations using features such as tweening and onion skinning.

Macromedia Fireworks includes special effect features, including those shown in Figure 7-16. It also makes it possible to include JavaScript code through the use of **behaviors**, which are ready-made scripts. This makes it easy to create animated rollover buttons and image maps. In addition, you can preview your animations within the program, so you do not have to access your Web browser in order to preview an animation.

FIGURE 7-15
Macromedia Fireworks includes autoshapes that can be animated

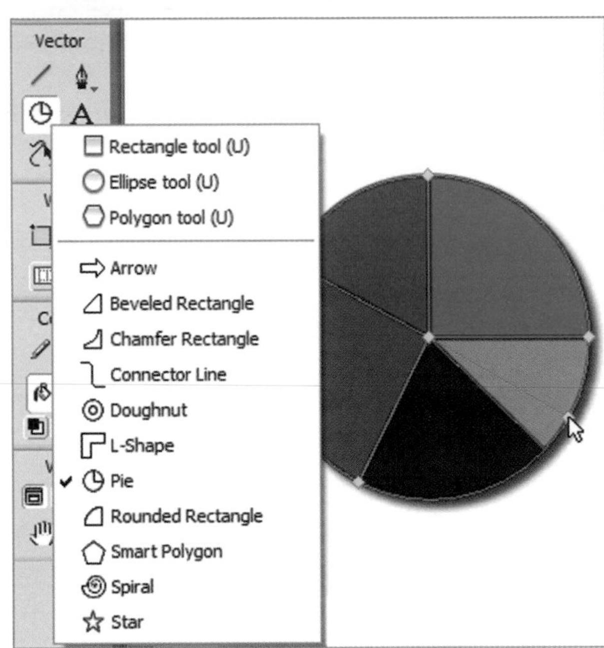

FIGURE 7-16
Macromedia Fireworks includes motion blur effects to create the illusion of motion

Macromedia Flash

Macromedia Flash is an excellent choice for producing and delivering gorgeous high-impact Web animation with resounding musical tracks and sound effects. The vast majority of animations seen on the Web are created using Macromedia Flash. You can right-click on an animation and if "About Macromedia Flash Player" is displayed in a pop-up menu, the animation was probably created in Macromedia Flash (see Figure 7-17).

Unlike many animation tools that only allow you to work with bitmapped graphics, Macromedia Flash allows you to work with vector graphics to create incredibly smooth, compact animation. Using the drawing tools in Macromedia Flash, you can create an array of brilliant effects or you can import artwork from drawing programs such as Adobe Illustrator and Macromedia FreeHand. Macromedia Flash also allows you to integrate high-quality, compressed, streaming audio into your animations. This means you can author longer animations with both voiceovers and background music while still keeping your file sizes small enough to deliver over low-bandwidth connections.

QUICKTIP

Files created with Macromedia Flash are dependent on the Macromedia Flash Player to be viewed. This is not much of a problem because the **Macromedia Flash Player** is free, readily available for download, and has been widely distributed.

FIGURE 7-17

Macromedia Flash is an excellent solution for creating high-impact Web animations

Macromedia Flash uses a **timeline** for the development and control of the animation. In Macromedia Flash, animation can be created using either motion tweening for creating path-based animation or shape tweening for morphed effects (see Figure 7-18).

Like Macromedia Fireworks, Macromedia Flash includes behaviors (see Figure 7-19), which are written using Macromedia Flash's built-in scripting language **ActionScript**. Behaviors enable Web developers to create customizable and engaging interactivity without writing complex code. Media elements in Macromedia Flash are stored in a **library**. Macromedia Flash supports a wide spectrum of file formats for both import and export.

FIGURE 7-18

Using a simple drop-down list box, Macromedia Flash users can choose either shape or motion tweening

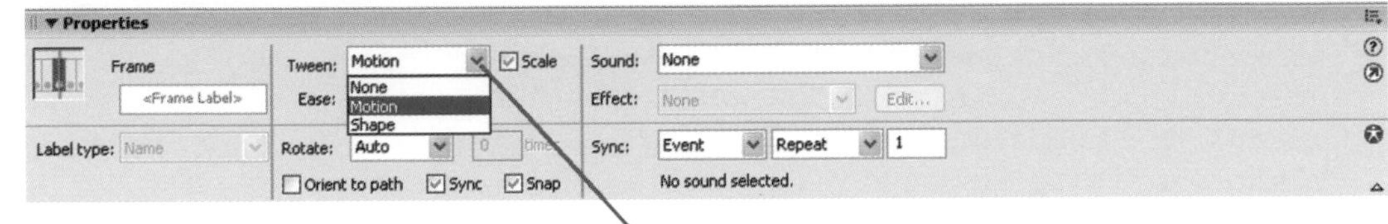

FIGURE 7-19

In Macromedia Flash, behaviors reduce the need to script simple tasks, such as controlling a movie clip

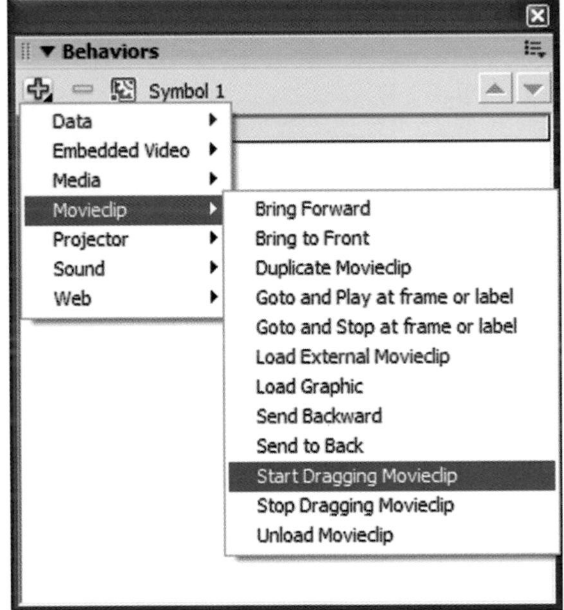

To ensure consistency across platforms and browsers, Macromedia Flash includes a one-step publishing feature (see Figure 7-20) that exports file formats and writes the code to include newly generated files in a completed Web page. In addition, all of the Macromedia products are highly integrated, which means you can directly import and export Macromedia formats from one program to another.

Adobe

Although Adobe has been a leader in the graphics industry for quite some time, it is relatively new to the world of Web animation. Like Macromedia, Adobe continues to develop high-quality Web-based software for creating animation for the Web. All of Adobe's programs are also integrated, making it easy to work between and across all of its products. The Adobe program created specifically for creating and optimizing images for the Web and building high-impact, full-motion animation is Adobe ImageReady.

Adobe ImageReady

Adobe ImageReady is packaged with Adobe Photoshop and is specifically designed for the production of superior Web graphics and animation. Adobe ImageReady allows developers to create interactive rollover effects without writing

FIGURE 7-20

One-step publishing exports the file and writes the code for the Web page at the same time

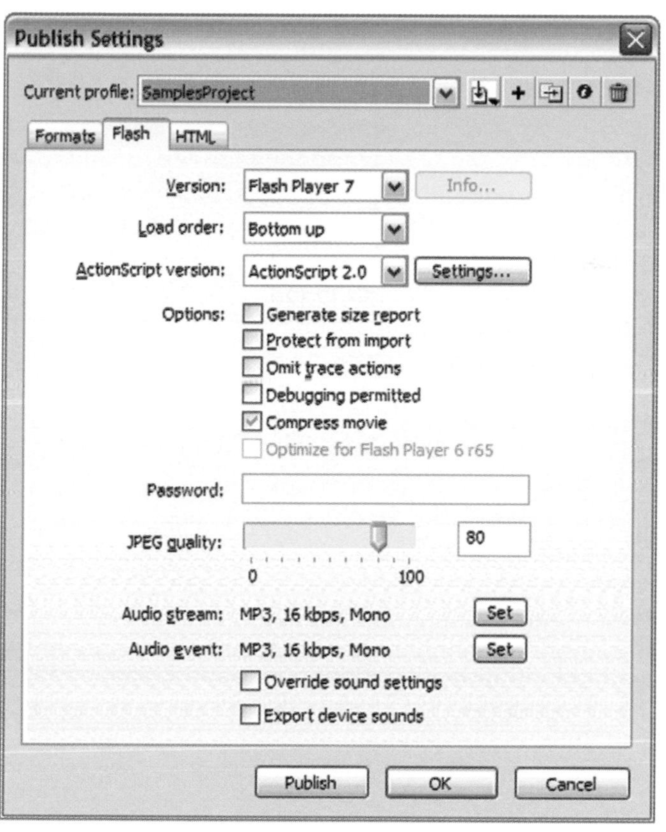

a single line of JavaScript code. By just slicing an image and associating rollover behaviors to the different slices of the image, you can make a specific area of an image change when you click, press, or roll over the area with your pointer. For example, you could create a single-image navigation bar with multiple slices representing different links to different pages of a Web site. Rollovers may be applied to each slice of the image, which would cause the selected slice to change thereby indicating that a page was active.

To create animation in Adobe ImageReady, you open a multilayered Adobe Photoshop or Illustrator file and then create new frames or edit the layers in Adobe ImageReady. Each layer becomes a separate object or frame within the animation. Some changes to the layers are reflected in each frame. For example, if you hide, show, or move a layer, the change is immediately shown in the respective frame. Changes to the opacity of the layer or the application of special effects also affect each frame. You can then use the **animation palette** to preview and set playback options for the animation. There is also a tween feature (see Figure 7-21) that allows you to create smooth transitions between frames automatically.

FIGURE 7-21

Adobe ImageReady's tween feature is used to generate the between frames from one keyframe to the next

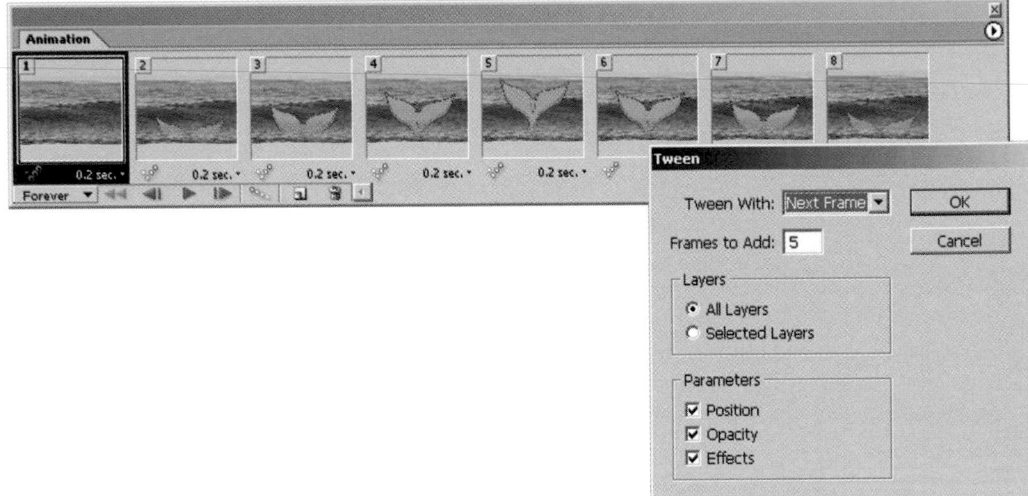

The optimization features (see Figure 7-22) allow you to use ImageReady to produce high-quality graphics and animations with the smallest possible file sizes. You can compare original images side-by-side with optimized versions. Panels allow you to work in 2-up and 4-up views so that you can analyze files with different compression settings while comparing quality, file size, and download time. This feature gives you unparalleled precision in your efforts to create high-quality Web graphics. In addition, you can apply compression to create files as much as 10 to 50 percent smaller than the original files.

Shareware

Shareware programs are distributed based on the honor system. They are sometimes free of charge, although there might be a small fee for delivery. In addition, the developer usually requests that you pay a small fee if you like the program and use it regularly. There are high-quality shareware programs available for creating Web animation. These programs range in price as well as functionality. For a minimal fee, you often get programs that include wizards to assemble your original graphics effortlessly, which helps you create sophisticated animations in no time. You can create animated banners and signs, apply special effects such as transitions and spins, or rotate, crop, color-adjust, and resize all or part of an animation. Use your favorite search engine and the search phrase "animation shareware programs" to find out more about these programs.

FIGURE 7-22
After the animation is complete, it should be optimized using ImageReady's optimization features

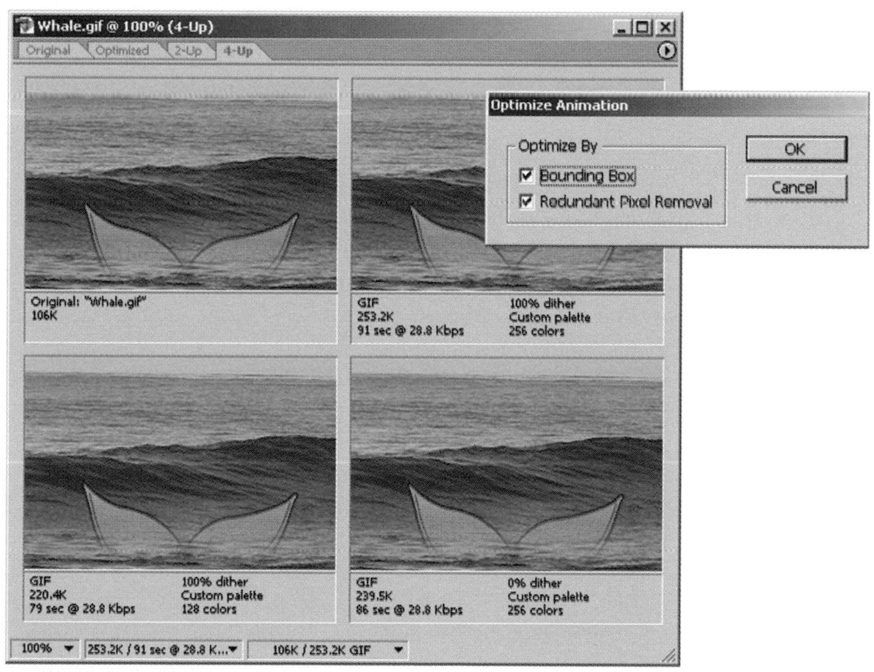

CONCEPT 5

DISCUSS ANIMATION FILE Formats for the Web

What You'll Learn

In this lesson, you will learn about the different animation file formats commonly used on Web pages including animated GIF, SWF, MOV, MPEG, AVI, and MNG.

Animation files for the Web may be saved in a number of different file formats. In choosing a format, you should consider how and where the animation will be used. When preparing animation for the Web, choose a format that is supported by the most popular Web browsers.

Animated GIF

Animated GIFs are a special kind of GIF file known as **GIF89a**. The GIF89a format can be used to create animated 2-D and 3-D images for Web pages. Animated GIFs are a very popular format for storing quick and simple animations such as cartoon faces that change expressions. An animated GIF file stores multiple images as separate blocks within one single GIF file. Consequently, animated GIFs are also called multiblock GIFs. When the animated GIF is viewed on the Web, the multiple images are **streamed**, or played back one at a time. This creates the illusion of motion. Animated GIFs are very efficient because the viewer does not have to wait for the entire GIF to be downloaded before it begins running on the Web page. Animated GIFs require no plug-ins or players and are supported by all major browsers. You can include animated GIFs in Web pages without being concerned about compatibility or user accessibility.

SWF

The **SWF** (pronounced "swiff") file format was designed from the ground up to efficiently deliver graphics and animation over the Web. It is a compressed Macromedia Flash file type. However, most programs allow you to export files in a SWF format, which is an indication of how the SWF format has become a standard file format for animation on the Web. Macromedia Flash files are designed to be rendered very quickly and at a very high quality. Because SWF files are small and support streaming, they can be delivered over a network with limited bandwidth. This file format is for viewing only. The content of the SWF file cannot be edited. In order to view SWF files, the Macromedia Flash Player must be installed on the user's computer.

QuickTime (MOV)

QuickTime (MOV) is Apple's animation and movie file format. QuickTime animation is non–platform specific. You will find QuickTime files running on Macs and PCs as well as most other platforms. QuickTime files can be either downloaded or streamed for quicker viewing. The QuickTime file format is among the most convenient and powerful formats for storing animation. Like many of the other animation file formats already mentioned, QuickTime files are viewed with a player. The QuickTime player is free, available for download (see Figure 7-23), and will display and play a multitude of different file formats. Because the QuickTime player has been widely distributed, most users will already have it available for viewing files that have been saved in the MOV format.

MPEG

Different types of **MPEG** files have developed and evolved through the work of the Moving Picture Experts Group who has created standards for interactive animation and video. MPEG is the name given to this entire family of standards used for coding audio-visual information (e.g., animation, movies, video, music) in a digital compressed format. The major advantage of MPEG files compared to other coding formats is that MPEG files tend to be much smaller and of much higher quality for the size. This is because MPEG uses very sophisticated compression techniques.

AVI

Another common animated file format is **AVI** or the Audio Video Interleave format. This is Microsoft's animation and movie file format for Windows. Although AVI files are native to Windows, other programs and players will also recognize and play them. This makes them a suitable, although not necessarily optimal, option for the Web. Though the quality of AVI files is adequate, AVI files do not offer some of the features and cross-platform compatibility found in some of the other formats. In addition, the compression available for AVI files is not as high as some of the other file formats, which means these files may take longer to download. Therefore, if you want your animation to reach the widest audience possible in the shortest amount of time, there are other file formats that are better suited for most Web animation than AVI. Conversion programs do exist that allow you to convert animation files from AVI to other formats.

MNG

MNG stands for Multiple Image Network Graphics. This file format is an outgrowth of the PNG graphics file format. Similar to an animated GIF, this file format stores multiple images that are then streamed for quick download and playback. Just as the PNG format offers advantages over the GIF format, the MNG file format offers many of the same advantages over an animated GIF or GIF89a file. It supports multiple levels of transparency, which permits subtle changes in opacity for the creation of animation that is more professional in appearance. It also offers platform-independent color correction so that animation will display accurately across multiple platforms. In addition, it sometimes offers better compression than the GIF89a format.

FIGURE 7-23

Media players, such as QuickTime and Macromedia Flash, are available to download for free

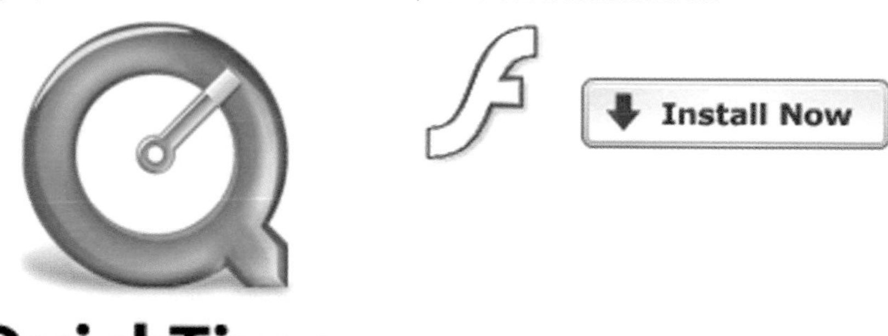

SUMMARY

Animation is a series of graphic images displayed fast enough to trick our eyes into believing there is movement. Today, creating animation involves sophisticated computer programs and technology. Animation is often a better choice than video in education and training because it can be used to simplify complex concepts. Of course, it continues to be used extensively on Web sites that are focused on entertainment and games as well as in advertising and e-commerce.

An animation specialist can use different methods to create animation for the Web. Most of these methods are based on the **flipbook approach** whereby a sequence of slightly different visual images is compressed and then played back to convey a sense of motion. There are two rates used to measure animation: the **sampling rate** and the **playback rate**. When the illusion of motion fails and the animation appears as a rapid sequence of still images instead of a fluid object in motion, the image is said to **flicker**.

Frame-based animation is also called **cel animation** because **cels** were once used by **tweeners** for drawing images. In creating animation for the Web, **keyframes** identify key events in the timeline. **Tweening** is used to fill in the frames between the keyframes. **Morphing**, or **shape tweening**, is a special technique that uses frames to create the illusion of one object changing into another. **Path-based animation**, or **vector animation**, creates animated objects by tracking the path that an object travels. **Motion tweening** is used to create frames as an object moves along a path. **Computational animation** allows an object to be moved by varying its x- and y-coordinates. Finally, **program-** or **script-based animation** uses programming and scripting languages to create or enable animation.

Special **animation effects** including **onion skinning**, **trail effects**, **film loops**, and **warping** are used to create interesting effects. **Virtual reality (VR)** is used to describe 3-D scenes on the Web.

Animation tools share common features including a **compiling engine** that **compiles** still images into animated objects. Some also include **codecs** that allow you to compress the files for the Web. Macromedia has taken a leadership role in developing multimedia and animation for the Web. Macromedia Fireworks combines both bitmap and vector-editing tools, uses a frame-based environment, includes **behaviors**, and converts a final series of images to an animated format. Macromedia Flash, another animation program, allows you to work with vector and bitmapped graphics. Macromedia Flash uses a **timeline** for the development and control of the animation and includes its own scripting language, **ActionScript**. Media elements in Macromedia Flash are stored in the **library**. Web animations created in Macromedia Flash require the **Macromedia Flash Player** in order to be viewed.

Adobe is another big player in the development of tools and software for creating Web animation. You can use ImageReady to produce high-quality graphics and animations with the smallest possible file sizes. An **animation palette** is used to preview and set playback options. There are also high-quality **shareware programs** available for creating Web animation. These programs range in price as well as functionality.

Different animation file formats serve different purposes on the Web. One of the simplest file formats is the **animated GIF** or **GIF89a** format, which creates small file sizes that are **streamed** as they are downloaded. The **AVI** format is native to the Windows environment, but can be recognized and played with other programs. The **MNG** format is an animated extension of the PNG graphic file format. **MPEG** files are based on a group of standards developed by the Moving Picture Experts Group. Due to advanced compression technology, these files tend to be small and high quality. **QuickTime (MOV)** is Apple's animation. The **SWF** file is the Macromedia Flash format.

KEY TERMS

ActionScript
animated GIF
animation
animation effect
animation palette
AVI
behavior
cel
cel animation
codec
compile
compiling engine
computational animation
film loop
flicker
flipbook approach
frame-based animation
GIF89a
keyframe
library
Macromedia Flash Player
MNG
morphing
motion tweening
MPEG
onion skinning
path-based animation
playback rate
program-based animation
QuickTime (MOV)
sampling rate
script-based animation
shape tweening
shareware program
streamed
SWF
timeline
trail effect
tweener
tweening
vector animation
virtual reality (VR)
warping

MATCHING QUESTIONS/DISCUSSION QUESTIONS

Match each term with the sentence that best describes it.

a. animation	**b.** compiling	**c.** flicker
d. flipbook	**e.** GIF89a	**f.** morphing
g. onion skinning	**h.** path-based	**i.** sampling rate
j. shape tweening	**k.** shareware	**l.** SWF
m. timeline	**n.** tweening	**o.** warping

_____ **1.** Digital animation is based on this approach, where a sequence of slightly different visual images is compressed and then played back to convey a sense of motion.

_____ **2.** The process of filling in the frames between the keyframes to make the animation appear fluid.

_____ **3.** The actual number of different images that occur per second.

_____ **4.** A moving graphic image.

_____ **5.** Software programs distributed on an honor system.

_____ **6.** This occurs when the illusion of motion fails.

_____ **7.** A special technique that uses frames to create the illusion of one object changing into another.

_____ **8.** This is another name for morphing.

_____ **9.** Process of generating a single file from multiple files.

_____ **10.** Type of animation that follows an object's transition over a line or vector.

_____ **11.** Effect that allows you to create a new image by tracing over an existing image.

_____ **12.** File format that requires the Macromedia Flash Player in order to be viewed.

_____ **13.** File format for an animated GIF that results in small file sizes.

_____ **14.** Feature within Macromedia Flash that enables the animation specialist to develop and control the animation.

_____ **15.** Special effect that enables you to distort a single image.

MATCHING QUESTIONS/DISCUSSION QUESTIONS

Answer each question either in writing or in a class discussion as directed by your instructor.

1. What are some of the different methods used to create animation? How would you describe each of these methods?
2. What are some of the key features found in Macromedia Fireworks and Flash?
3. What are some of the key features of Adobe ImageReady?
4. What are shareware programs?
5. What are some of the different animation file formats for the Web? What are some of the features of each of these file formats?

DESIGN PROJECT

Working with Animation

1. Start Macromedia Flash, customize the workspace, and work with graphics
2. Import graphics and convert a graphic to a symbol
3. Create buttons
4. Assign actions to buttons
5. Publish a Macromedia Flash movie and insert it into a Web page

Introduction

This is a continuation of the Design Project in Chapter 6.

The client The Inn at Birch Bay has reviewed the Web pages and has asked that an interactive map be provided on the Directions Web page. They have requested that the map be somewhat fanciful.

You have been asked to create the interaction with an animated map. The WebsByCT multimedia development team has decided that this project would be ideal for you to learn the basics of an animation program. To complete the lesson in this design project, you will be using Macromedia Flash to create a Macromedia Flash movie with animations. Then you will use Macromedia Dreamweaver to insert the movie into a Web page.

There are no precise naming conventions that are consistent from one animation program to another. Macromedia Flash uses terms defined as follows:

Document: Used to describe the file that is currently being worked on in Macromedia Flash. When working in Macromedia Flash there are commands such as Edit Document and Modify Document.

Movie: Generally synonymous with document. When working in Macromedia Flash there are commands such as Test Movie and Debug Movie. A loose distinction between documents and movies is that you work on documents, but you view, test, and publish movies.

Animation: Part(s) of the movie that is an actual animation.

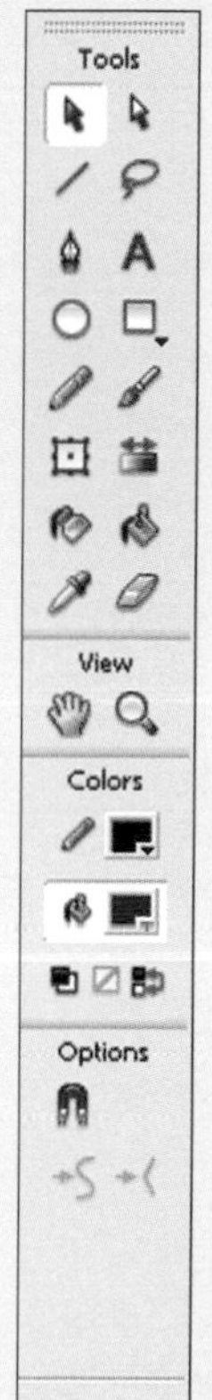
Tools
View
Colors
Options

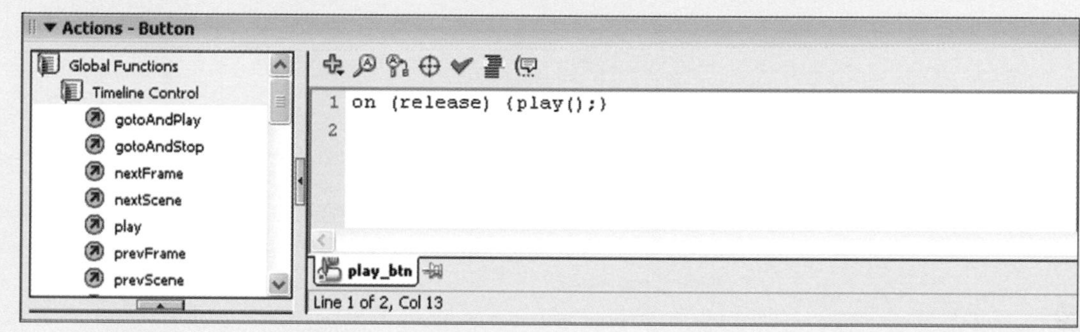
Actions - Button
Global Functions
Timeline Control
gotoAndPlay
gotoAndStop
nextFrame
nextScene
play
prevFrame
prevScene
1 on (release) {play();}
2
play_btn
Line 1 of 2, Col 13

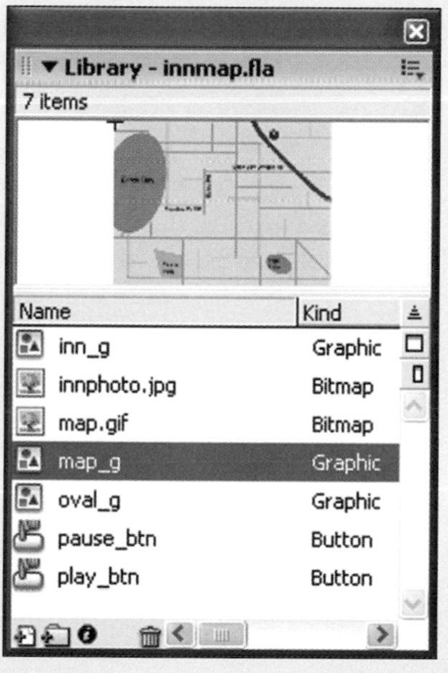
Library - innmap.fla
7 items
Name
Kind
inn_g Graphic
innphoto.jpg Bitmap
map.gif Bitmap
map_g Graphic
oval_g Graphic
pause_btn Button
play_btn Button

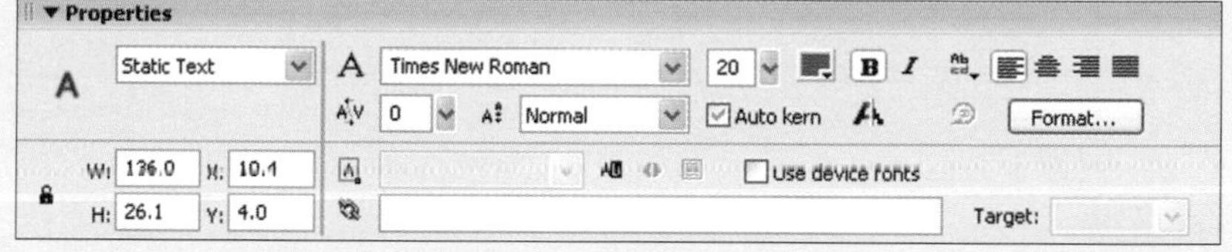
Properties
Static Text
Times New Roman
20
Normal
Auto kern
Format...
W: 136.0
X: 10.4
H: 26.1
Y: 4.0
Use device fonts
Target:

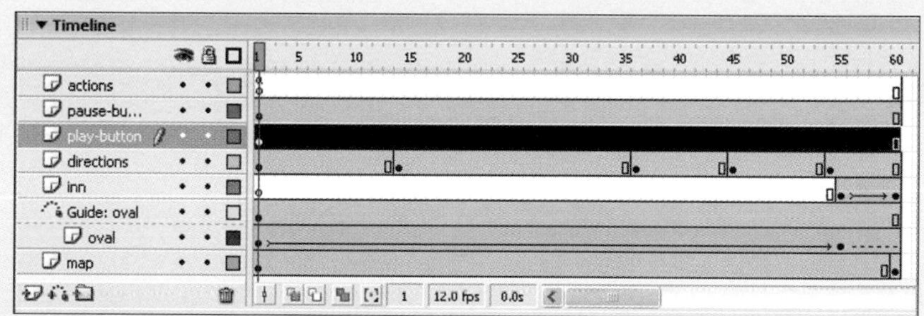
Timeline
actions
pause-bu...
play-button
directions
inn
Guide: oval
oval
map
12.0 fps
0.0s

LESSON 1

START MACROMEDIA FLASH, Customize the Workspace, and Work with Graphics

What You'll Do

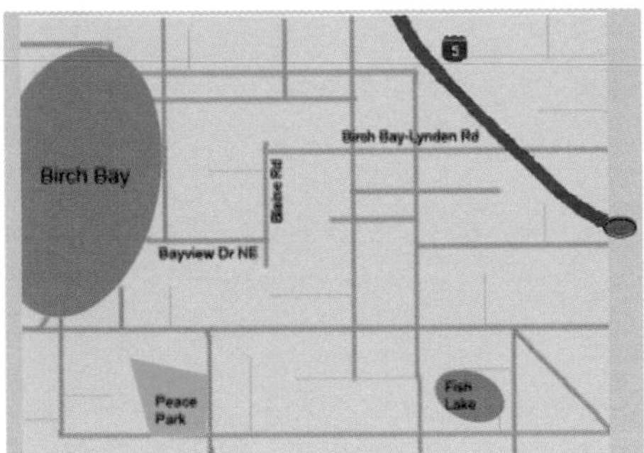

In this lesson, you will learn how to use a Web application and animation program, Macromedia Flash, to create a Macromedia Flash movie that contains interactive animations that will be inserted into a Web page. You will begin by studying the Macromedia Flash workspace and some of the basic tools and features available in the program. Next, you will open a new document, import graphics into Macromedia Flash, and use the drawing tools to create a graphic.

The Macromedia Flash Workspace

Macromedia Flash is a program that allows you to create compelling interactive experiences, primarily by using animation. Macromedia Flash has excellent drawing tools and tools for creating interactive controls, such as navigation buttons. As a developer, one of the most important things to do is to organize your workspace. That is, to decide what to have displayed on the development environment (workspace) and how to arrange the various tools and windows, called panels. Because Macromedia Flash is a powerful program with many tools, your workspace may become cluttered. Fortunately, it is easy to customize your workspace to display the tools and panels needed at any particular time.

The workspace in Macromedia Flash operates according to a movie metaphor: you create scenes on a stage; these scenes run in frames on a timeline. As you work with Macromedia Flash, you create a movie by rearranging objects (such as graphics and text) on the stage, and you animate the objects using the timeline. You play the movie on the stage, as you are working on it, by using the movie controls (start, stop, rewind, and so on). In addition, you can test a movie in a browser. When the movie is ready for distribution, you can export it as a Macromedia Flash Player movie, which viewers access using the Macromedia Flash Player.

When you start Macromedia Flash, three basic parts of the workspace are displayed, as shown in Figure 7-24: a main toolbar with menus and commands, a stage on which objects are placed, and a timeline used to organize and control the objects on the stage. In addition, one or more panels may be displayed. Panels are used when working with objects and features of the movie. The most commonly used panels are the Tools panels (also called the Toolbox), the Properties panel (also called the Property inspector), and the Library panel.

Stage

The **stage** contains all of the objects that are part of the movie and that will be seen by your viewers. It shows how the objects behave within the movie and how they interact with each other. You can resize the stage and change the background color applied to it. You can draw objects on or import objects to the stage and then edit and animate them.

Timeline

The **timeline** is used to organize and control the movie's contents by specifying when each object appears on the stage. The timeline is critical to the creation of movies because a movie is merely a series of still images that appear over time. The images are contained within frames, which are segments of the timeline. Frames in a Macromedia Flash movie are similar to frames in a regular motion picture. When a Macromedia Flash movie is played, a playhead moves from frame to frame in the timeline, causing the contents of each frame to appear on the stage in a linear sequence. The contents of a frame might be a single object as shown in Figure 7-25 or the contents might be many objects. The timeline indicates where you are at any time within the movie and allows you to insert, delete, select, and move frames. The timeline contains layers that are used to organize the objects on the stage and work with one object, independent of any others.

Layers

When you start a new document, the timeline has one layer named Layer 1. As you insert layers they are automatically named sequentially Layer 2, Layer 3, and so on. Renaming a layer helps you to keep track of which objects are on a layer. For example, you might name a layer *map* and then insert or draw a map on that layer.

FIGURE 7-24

The Macromedia Flash workspace

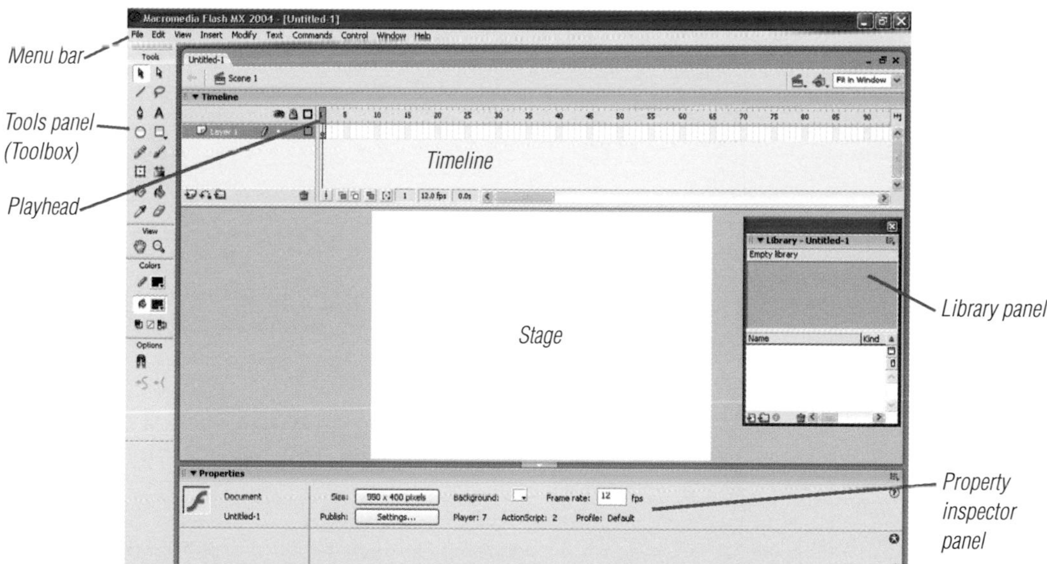

Keyframes

A keyframe is a frame on which you define a change in an animation. For example, if you have an animation that starts in Frame 20 and ends in Frame 50, you need to insert keyframes in both these frames. If later, you decide to make a change to the animation in Frame 35, you need to insert a keyframe in Frame 35 before making the change. Keyframes can be inserted into the timeline by using the Keyframe command from the Timeline option of the Insert menu. Also, you can right-click (PC) or Ctrl-Click (Mac) a frame and choose Insert Keyframe, or you can click a frame and press [F6]. Keyframes are automatically inserted into the first frame of every layer in the timeline.

Panels

Panels are used to view, organize, and modify objects and features in a movie. For example, the Property inspector is used to change the properties of an object, such as the fill color of a circle. The Property inspector is context sensitive so that if you are working with text it displays the appropriate options, such as font and font size. You can control which panels are displayed individually or you can choose to display panel sets (groups of panels). You can also make room in the workspace by collapsing panels so only their title bars display. Clicking the panel's name will alternately expand and collapse the panel. Right-clicking (PC) or Ctrl+clicking (Mac) the panel's name will display a menu that allows you to close the panel. As you work with Macromedia Flash, panels may appear based on actions you have taken.

Tools Panel

The Tools panel contains a set of tools used to draw and edit graphics and text. It is divided into four sections as shown in Figure 7-26.

Tools. Includes draw, paint, text, and selection tools, which are used to create lines, shapes, illustrations, and text. The selection tools are used to select objects so that they can be modified in a number of ways.

View. Includes the Zoom tool and the Hand tool, which are used to zoom in and out on parts of the stage and move the stage around the workspace, respectively.

Colors. Includes tools and icons used to change the stroke (border of an object) and fill (area inside an object) colors.

Options. Includes options for selected tools, such as allowing you to choose the size of the brush when using the Brush tool.

Regardless of how you decide to customize your workspace, the stage and timeline are always displayed. Usually, you display the Tools panel and one or more panels, such as the Property inspector and Library panels.

FIGURE 7-25

The playhead at Frame 5 of the timeline displays the content of Frame 5 on the stage

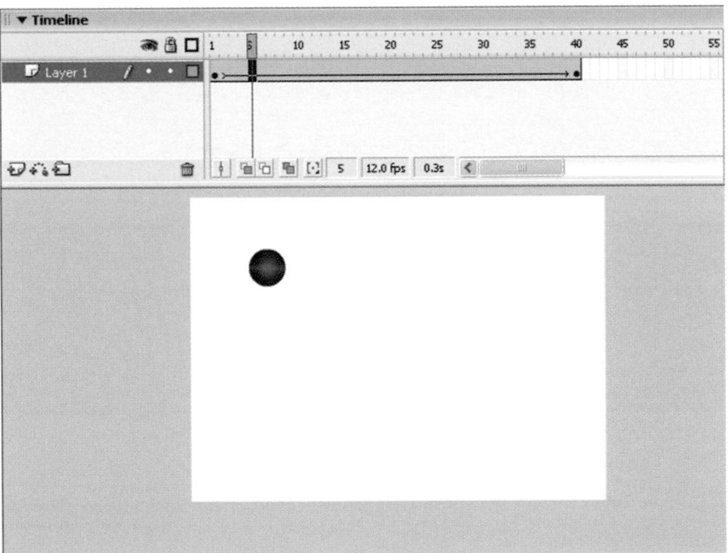

When you start a new Macromedia Flash document (movie), you can set the document properties, such as the size of the window (stage) the movie will play in, the background color, and the speed of the movie in frames per second. To increase the size of the stage so that the objects on the stage can be more easily edited, you can change the magnification setting using commands on the View menu.

Symbols

Macromedia Flash allows you to create a graphic (drawing) and then make unlimited copies. Macromedia Flash calls the original drawing a **symbol** and the copied drawings **instances**. Using instances of symbols helps to keep the movie's file size down. You can create your own symbols, or you can convert a graphic that has been imported to Macromedia Flash into a symbol. In addition to graphic symbols, you can create button symbols, which are explained in the next lesson. Macromedia Flash stores symbols and all the other objects used in a movie in the Library panel. You can import objects into the Library and you can drag an object from the Library to the stage.

Undo and Redo

The Undo [([Ctrl] + z) (PC)] or [(Command + z) (Mac)] and Redo [([Ctrl] + y) (PC)] or [(Command + y) (Mac)] commands in the Edit menu can be used to undo and redo up to 100 of the most recent actions. You will find these to be among the most useful Macromedia Flash commands.

FIGURE 7-26
The Tools panel

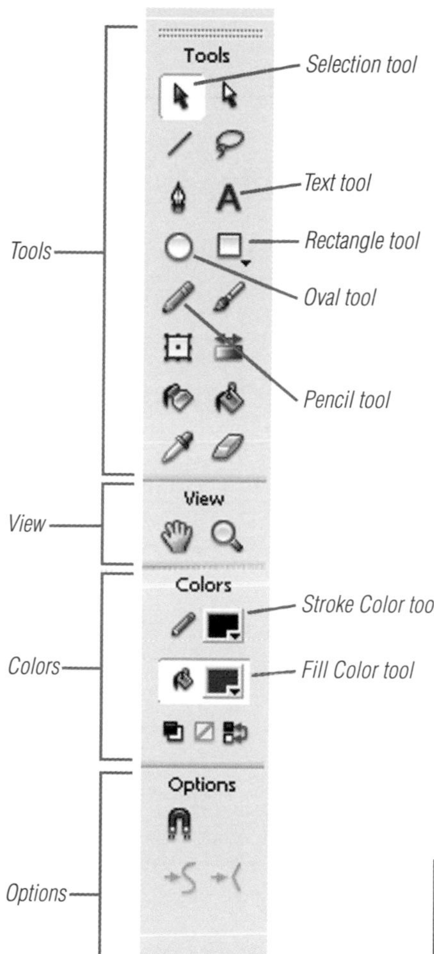

QUICKTIP

The exercises in this chapter were created with the screen resolution set at 1024 × 768. If your computer's screen resolution has a different setting, the figures in the book may appear different. You may want to verify the screen resolution on your computer and set it to 1024 × 768, if necessary.

Start Macromedia Flash and customize the workspace

1. Start **Macromedia Flash**, click **File** on the menu bar, click **New**, then click **OK** to open a new document.
2. Click **Window** on the menu bar, then click **Hide Panels**.
3. Click **Window** on the menu bar, then click **Properties** to open the Property inspector panel.
4. Repeat step 3 to open the **Timeline**, **Tools**, and **Library** panels.

   TIP The Timeline might already be open.
5. Click **Window** on the menu bar, point to **Toolbars**, verify **Edit Bar** is selected, then deselect any others, if necessary.
6. Click **View** on the menu bar, point to **Magnification**, then click **Fit in Window**.
7. Click the **Size button** [550 x 400 pixels] in the Property inspector panel, delete the entry in the width box, then type **400**.

   TIP If the Size button is not visible, then click the Selection tool.
8. Delete the entry in the height box, type **300**, then click **OK**.
9. Point to the blue bar at the top of the Library panel, click and hold, then drag the panel to the right side of the document window.
10. Verify that your screen resembles Figure 7-27.

    TIP Your screen might look slightly different if you have floating panels. Also, you many need to close panels that opened automatically.

You started Macromedia Flash and customized the workspace.

FIGURE 7-27
The workspace with selected panels displayed

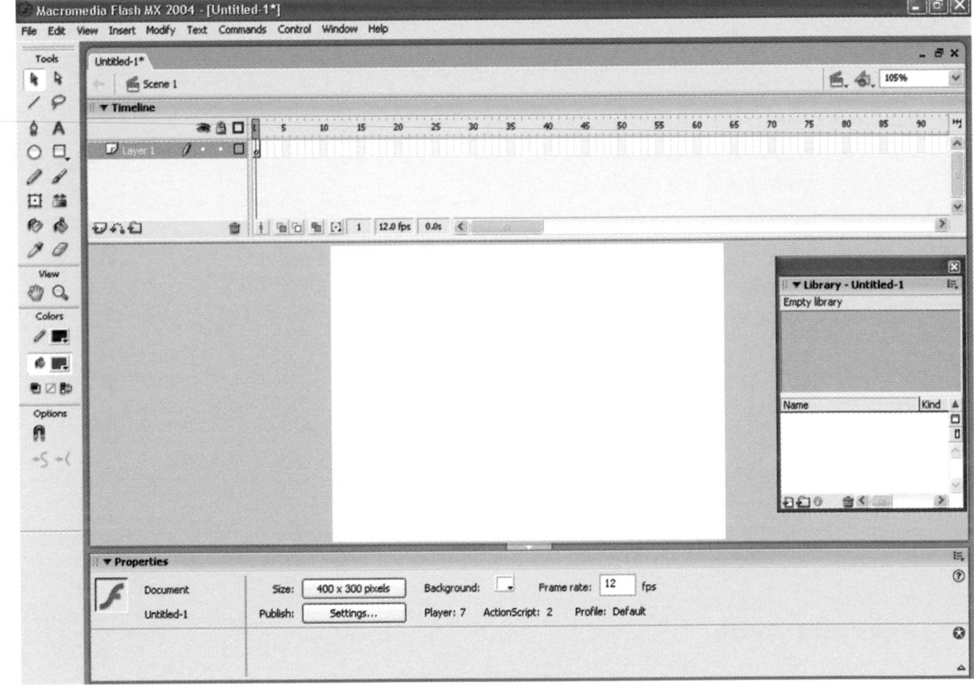

FIGURE 7-28

Dragging the object to the stage

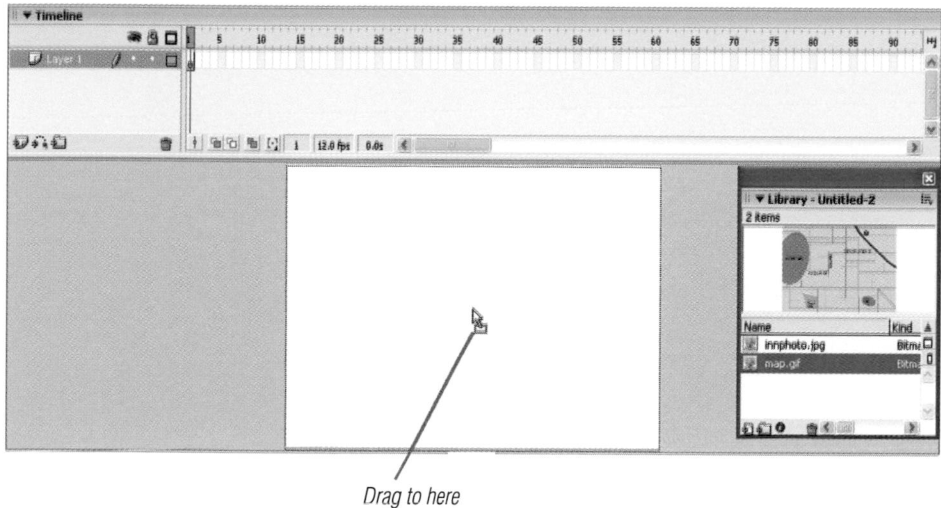

FIGURE 7-29

The completed Convert to Symbol dialog box

Import graphics and convert a graphic to a symbol

1. Click **File** on the menu bar, point to **Import**, then click **Import to Library**.
2. Navigate to the location of the files for this lesson, select **innphoto.jpg**, then click **Open** (PC) or **Import to Library** (Mac).
3. Click **File** on the menu bar, point to **Import**, then click **Import to Library**.
4. Navigate to the location of the files for this lesson, select **map.gif**, then click **Open** (PC) or **Import to Library** (Mac).
5. Click **Frame 1** of Layer 1 on the timeline.
6. Point to the **map.gif** icon in the Library panel, drag the map to the stage as shown in Figure 7-28, then release the mouse button.
7. Use the arrow keys on the keyboard to fit the map exactly over the stage.

   Pressing an arrow key moves the selected object one pixel in the direction of the key.
8. With the map selected, click **Modify** on the menu bar, then click **Convert to Symbol**.
9. Delete the entry in the Name box, type **map_g**, then click the **Graphic option button** in the Behavior list.
10. Verify that the dialog box resembles Figure 7-29, then click **OK**.
11. Double-click **Layer 1** on the Timeline, delete the entry, type **map**, then press **[Enter]** (PC) or **[return]** (Mac).

(continued)

12. Click **Frame 60** in the map layer, click **Insert** on the menu bar, point to **Timeline**, then click **Keyframe**.
13. Create a folder in the location where you are storing the files for this book with the name **directions**, then return to the Macromedia Flash document.
14. Click **File** on the menu bar, click **Save As**, then navigate to the directions folder, type the filename **innmap.fla**, then click **Save**.

You imported graphics and converted a graphic to a symbol.

Draw a graphic and convert it to a symbol

1. Click **Insert** on the menu bar, point to **Timeline**, then click **Layer**.
2. Double-click **Layer 2**, delete the entry, type **oval**, then press **[Enter]** (PC) or **[return]** (Mac).
3. Click the **Stroke Color button** on the Tools panel, then click the **black color** in the palette box.
4. Click the **Fill Color button** on the Tools panel, delete the hexadecimal entry, type **#996699**, then press **[Enter]** (PC) or **[return]** (Mac).

(continued)

FIGURE 7-30
Positioning the pointer

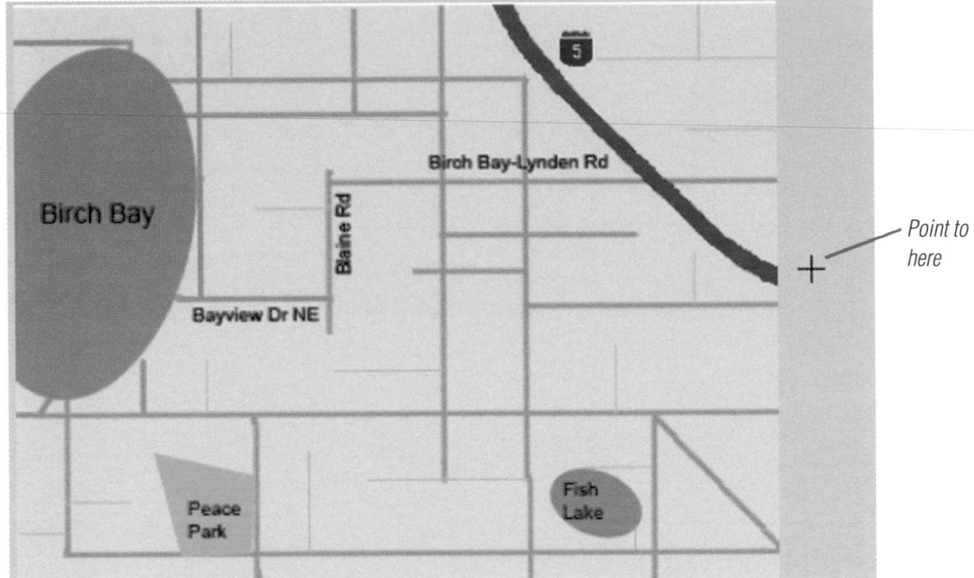

FIGURE 7-31
The completed oval

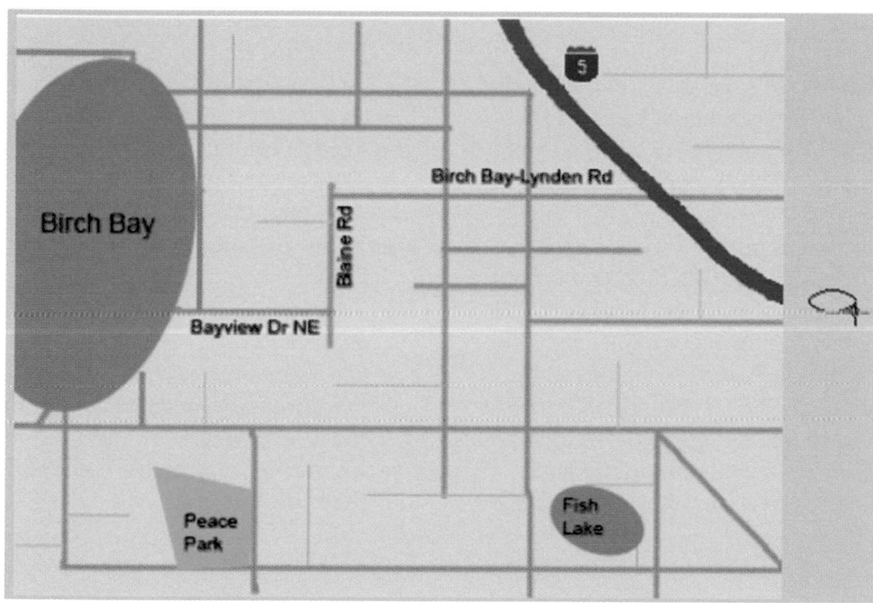

5. Click **Frame 1** on the oval layer.
6. Click the **Oval Tool button** ○ on the Tools panel, point to just off the stage as shown in Figure 7-30.
7. Drag the mouse to draw the oval as shown in Figure 7-31.
8. Click **Frame 1** of the oval layer to select the object.
9. With the oval selected, click **Modify** in the menu bar, then click **Convert to Symbol**.
10. Delete the entry in the Name box, type **oval_g**, verify **Graphic** is selected as the behavior, then click **OK**.
11. Click **File** on the menu bar, then click **Save**.

You drew an object using the Macromedia Flash drawing tools and converted it to a symbol.

LESSON 2

CREATE ANIMATIONS USING Macromedia Flash

What You'll Do

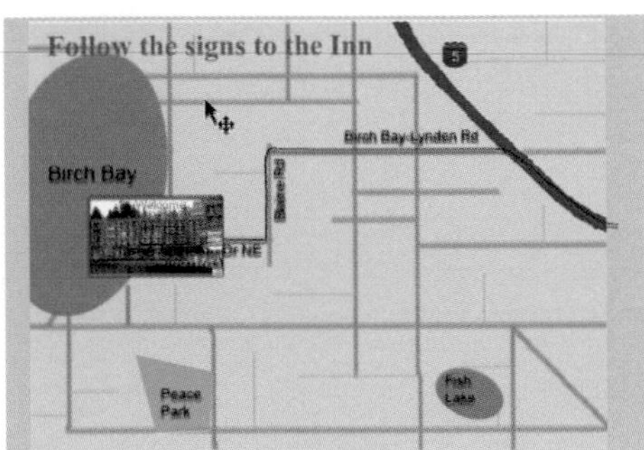

In this lesson, you will learn how to create a motion animation and apply a motion guide. Then you will create a zoom effect and add text to a Macromedia Flash movie.

Animations

Animations are a series of still images that are rapidly displayed in a linear sequence. One type of animation is a motion animation in which an object moves from one location on the screen to another location. In Macromedia Flash this can be done by positioning the object on (or off) the stage in one frame and changing its location in a subsequent frame. Then the Create Motion Tween command can be used to cause the program to fill in the in-between frames automatically as shown in Figure 7-32. When the animation is played, the object moves across the stage in a direct line from the beginning location to the ending location. If you do not want the object to move in a direct line you can create a path that the object follows. The process for creating a motion tween animation follows:

- Select the frame in the timeline where the animation will begin.
- Select the object on the stage to be animated.
- Select the Create Motion Tween command from the Timeline options in the Insert menu.
- Insert a keyframe in the frame where the animation ends.

- Move the object to a new location on or off the stage.
- Repeat each time the animation path changes, or you can alter the path of the object by inserting a Motion Guide layer and using the Pencil tool to draw a customized path that the object will follow.

Using the Motion Tween feature you can create an animation that zooms an object in or out. This is done by changing the size of the object in the beginning and ending frames of the animation. The process is to select a frame, place the object on the stage, then use the Free Transform tool to resize the object. Select another frame and use the Free Transform tool to resize the object again.

FIGURE 7-32
The in-between frames filled in using the Create Motion Tween command

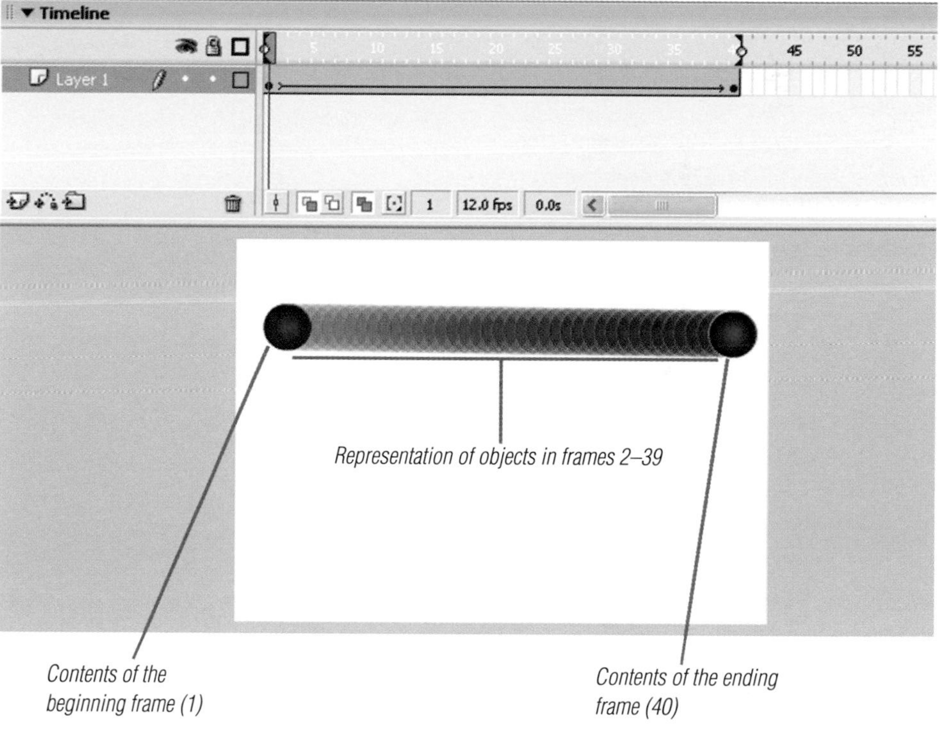

Create a motion guide and a motion tween

1. Click **oval** on the Timeline to select the layer if necessary, click **Insert** on the menu bar, point to **Timeline**, then click **Motion Guide**.
2. Click **Frame 1** on the Motion Guide layer to select the frame.
3. Click the **Pencil Tool button** on the Tools panel, point to the oval, hold down the mouse button, then draw the line shown in Figure 7-33.
4. Click **Frame 1** on the oval layer to select the frame.
5. Click **Insert** on the menu bar, point to **Timeline**, then click **Create Motion Tween**.
6. Click **Frame 55** on the oval layer, then press **[F6]** to insert a keyframe.
7. Click the **Selection Tool button** on the Tools panel, click the **oval** to select it, then drag the oval to the end of the path as shown in Figure 7-34.
8. Click **Frame 1** of the oval layer, then press **[Enter]** (PC) or **[return]** (Mac) to play the movie.
9. Click **Frame 1** of the oval layer.
10. Click **Properties** on the Property inspector panel to open the panel, if necessary, then click **Orient to path** in the Property inspector panel.
11. Press **[Enter]** (PC) or **[return]** (Mac) to play the movie.

(continued)

FIGURE 7-33
Drawing the guide path

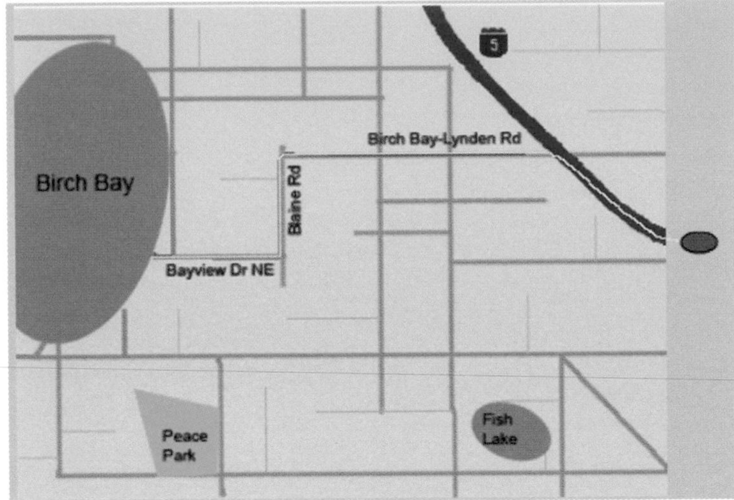

The line you draw will be black; the line is shown here in yellow so it is easier to see

FIGURE 7-34
Positioning the oval at the end of the path

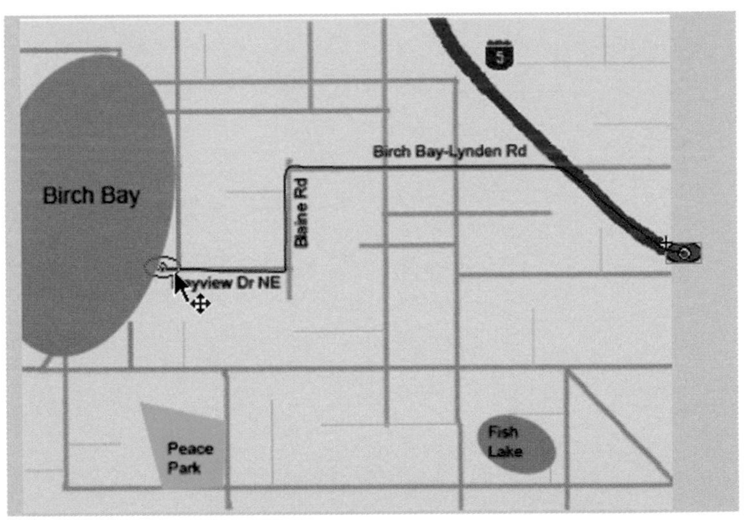

FIGURE 7-35
The diagonal double-arrow pointer

12. Save the document.

You created a motion guide and a motion tween animation.

Create a zoom effect

1. Click the **Guide:oval** layer to select it, click **Insert** on the menu bar, point to **Timeline**, then click **Layer**.
2. Double-click **Layer 4** in the timeline, delete the entry, type **inn**, then press **[Enter]** (PC) or **[return]** (Mac).

   Layer 3 is the Guide layer so the next number in the sequence is 4. Note: if you delete a layer, that layer's number is not repeated. For example, if you delete Layer 4, the next layer you insert would be named Layer 5. So, the layer numbers used in these steps may differ from those in your document.
3. Click **Frame 55** on the inn layer, then press **[F6]** to insert a keyframe.
4. Drag the **innphoto.jpg** from the Library panel to the stage.
5. Click **Modify** on the menu bar, then click **Convert to Symbol**.
6. Delete the entry in the Name box, type **inn_g**, verify **Graphic** is selected, then click **OK**.
7. Verify the graphic is selected on the stage, then click the **Free Transform Tool button** on the Tools panel.
8. Point to the upper-right corner handle until the pointer changes into a diagonal double-arrow as shown in Figure 7-35.

(continued)

9. Hold down **[Shift]**, drag the handle to the middle of the image until it resembles Figure 7-36, then release the mouse button.

   Holding down [Shift] while dragging the handle causes the shape of the image to shrink proportionally.

10. Use the **arrow keys** on the keyboard to position the object as shown in Figure 7-37.
11. Click **Insert** on the menu bar, point to **Timeline**, then click **Create Motion Tween**.
12. Click **Frame 60** on the inn layer, then press **[F6]** to insert a keyframe.
13. Point to the upper-right corner handle until the pointer changes into a diagonal double-arrow, hold down **[Shift]**, then drag the handle outward to enlarge the image as shown in Figure 7-38.
14. Press **[Enter]** (PC) or **[return]** (Mac) to play the movie.
15. Save the document.

You created a zoom effect.

Add text to the movie

1. Verify the inn layer is the active layer, click **Insert** on the menu bar, point to **Timeline**, then click **Layer**.
2. Double-click **Layer 5**, delete the entry, type **directions**, then press **[Enter]** (PC) or **[return]** (Mac).

(continued)

FIGURE 7-36
Dragging the handle to resize the object

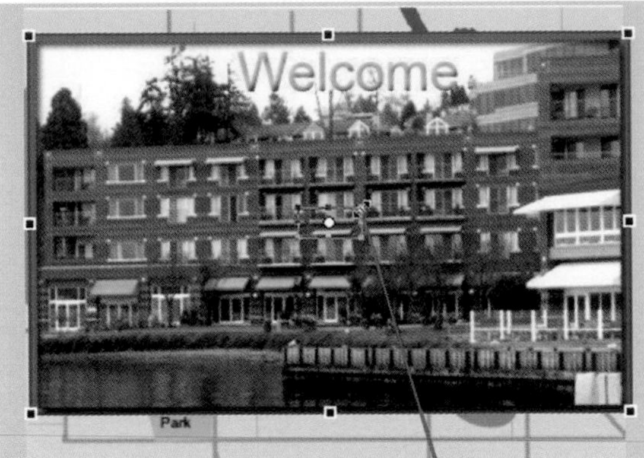

As you drag the corner, a rectangle shows the size; your rectangle outline will be black, it is shown here in red so it is easier to see

Drag to here

FIGURE 7-37
Positioning the object on the stage

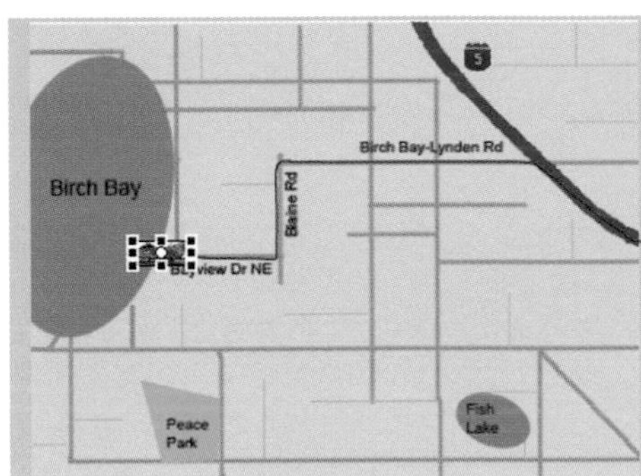

FIGURE 7-38
Dragging the handle to enlarge the object

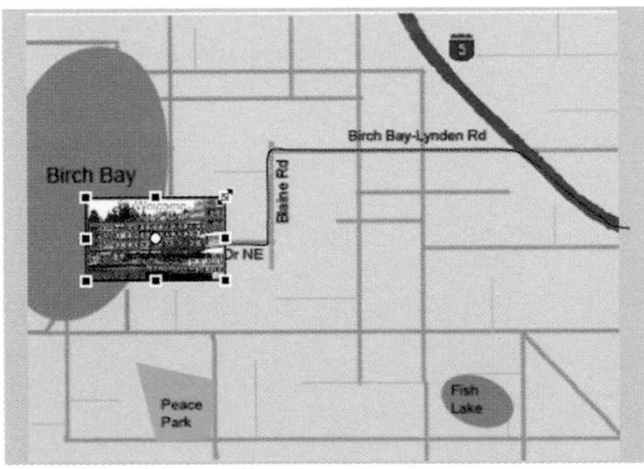

FIGURE 7-39
Positioning the pointer on the stage

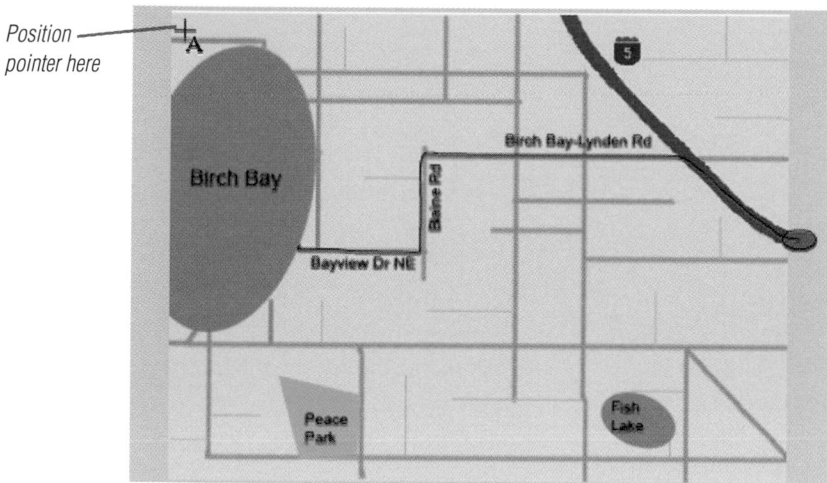

FIGURE 7-40
The completed text entry

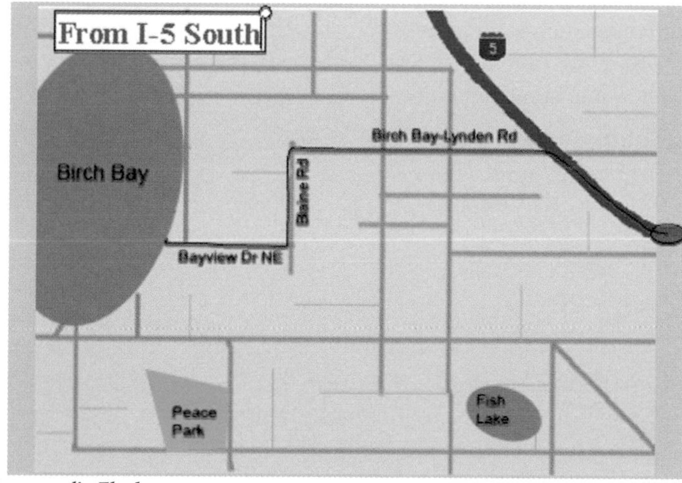

3. Click **Frame 1** of the directions layer, click the **Text Tool button** A on the Tools panel, position the pointer as shown in Figure 7-39, then click to insert a text box.
4. Click the **Font size down arrow** in the Property inspector, then drag the slider to **20**.
5. Type **From I-5 South** as shown in Figure 7-40.
6. Click **Frame 14** on the directions layer, then press **[F6]** to insert a keyframe.
7. Drag the pointer to highlight the text in the text box, press **[Delete]**, then type **Take Birch Bay-Lynden Rd West**.
8. Click **Frame 36** on the directions layer, then press **[F6]** to insert a keyframe.
9. Drag the pointer to highlight the text, press **[Delete]**, then type **Turn left onto Blaine Rd**.
10. Click **Frame 45** on the directions layer, then press **[F6]** to insert a keyframe.
11. Drag the pointer to highlight the text, press **[Delete]**, then type **Turn right onto Bayview Dr NE**.
12. Click **Frame 54** on the directions layer, then press **[F6]** to insert a keyframe.
13. Drag the pointer to highlight the text, press **[Delete]**, then type **Follow the signs to the Inn**.
14. Click **Frame** 1 on the directions layer, press **[Enter]** (PC) or **[return]** (Mac) to view the movie, then save the document.

You added text to a movie.

CREATE Buttons

What You'll Do

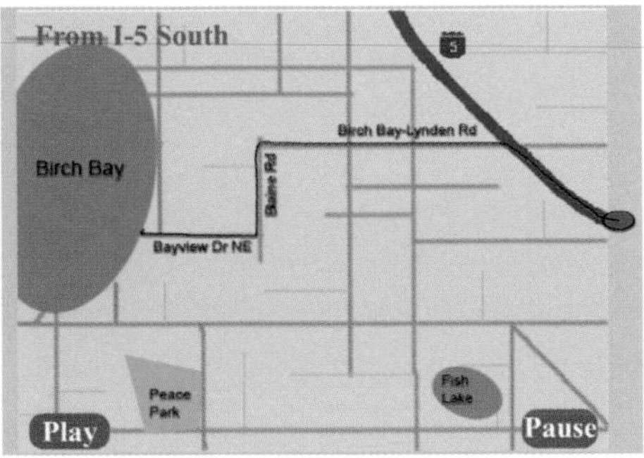

In this lesson, you will learn how to create buttons that will add interactivity to the Macromedia Flash movie. You will create two buttons, Play and Pause. When the viewer clicks the Play button the playhead in the timeline will start moving. When the viewer clicks the Pause button the playhead will stop.

Understanding Buttons

Button symbols are used to provide interactivity. When you click a button, an action occurs, such as starting an animation. Any object, including Macromedia Flash drawings, text blocks, and imported graphic images, can be made into buttons. Button symbols have four states: Up, Over, Down, and Hit. These states correspond to the use of the pointer and recognize that the user needs feedback when the pointer is over a button and when the button has been clicked. Often this is shown by a change (such as a different color) in the button. These four states are explained below and shown in Figure 7-41.

Up—Represents how the button appears when the pointer is not over it.

Over—Represents how the button appears when the pointer is over it.

Down—Represents how the button appears after the pointer clicks it.

Hit—Defines the area of the screen that responds to the click. In most cases, you will want the Hit state to be the same or similar to the Up state in location and size because the viewer anticipates that the entire button is clickable.

When you create a button symbol, Macromedia Flash automatically creates a new timeline. The timeline has only four frames, one for each state. The timeline does not play; it merely reacts to the pointer by displaying the appropriate button state and performing an action, such as stopping an animation.

The process for creating and previewing buttons follows.

- *Create a button symbol.* Start by drawing an object or selecting an object that has already been created and placed on the stage. Use the Convert to Symbol command on the Modify menu to convert the object to a button symbol and to enter a name for the button.
- *Edit the button symbol.* Start by selecting the button and choosing the Edit Symbols command from the Edit

menu. This displays the button timeline, shown in Figure 7-42, which allows you to work with the four button states. The Up state is the original button symbol that Macromedia Flash automatically places in Frame 1. You need to determine how the original object will change for the other states. To change the button for the Over state, click Frame 2 and insert a keyframe. This automatically places a copy of the button in Frame 1 into Frame 2. Then, alter the button so that it appears differently for the Over state. The same process is used for the Down state. For the Hit state, insert a keyframe at Frame 4 and then specify the area on the screen that responds to the pointer.

- *Return to the main timeline.* When you are finished editing a button, choose the Edit Document command on the Edit menu to return to the main timeline.
- *Preview the button.* By default, Macromedia Flash disables buttons so that you can work with them on the stage. You can preview a button by choosing the Enable Simple Buttons command on the Control menu. You can also click the Test Movie command on the Control menu to play the movie and test the buttons.

FIGURE 7-41
The four button states

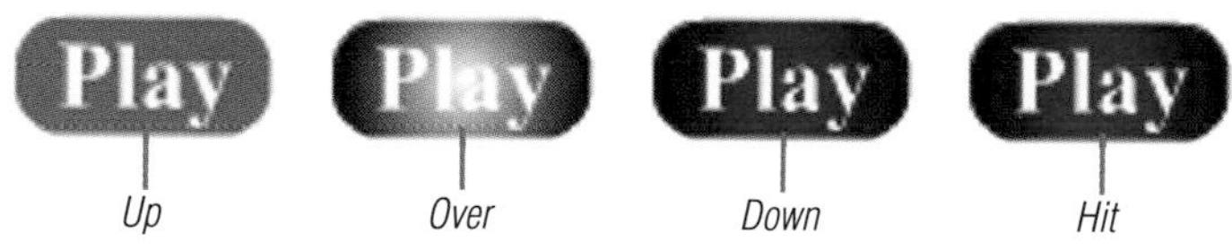

FIGURE 7-42
The button symbol timeline

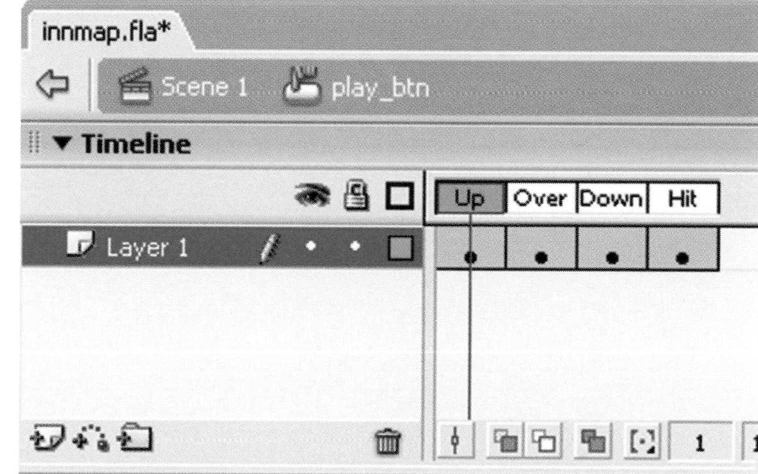

Create buttons

1. Click **directions** on the Timeline to select the layer, click **Insert** on the menu bar, point to **Timeline**, then click **Layer**.
2. Double-click **Layer 6**, delete the entry, type **play-button**, then press **[Enter]** (PC) or **[return]** (Mac).
3. Click **Frame 1** of the play-button layer.
4. Click the **Rectangle Tool button** on the Tools panel, click the **Round Rectangle Radius option button** near the bottom of the Tools panel, type **10** for the Corner radius, then click **OK**.
5. Click the **Stroke Color button** , then click the **None button** .

(continued)

FIGURE 7-43
Positioning the pointer

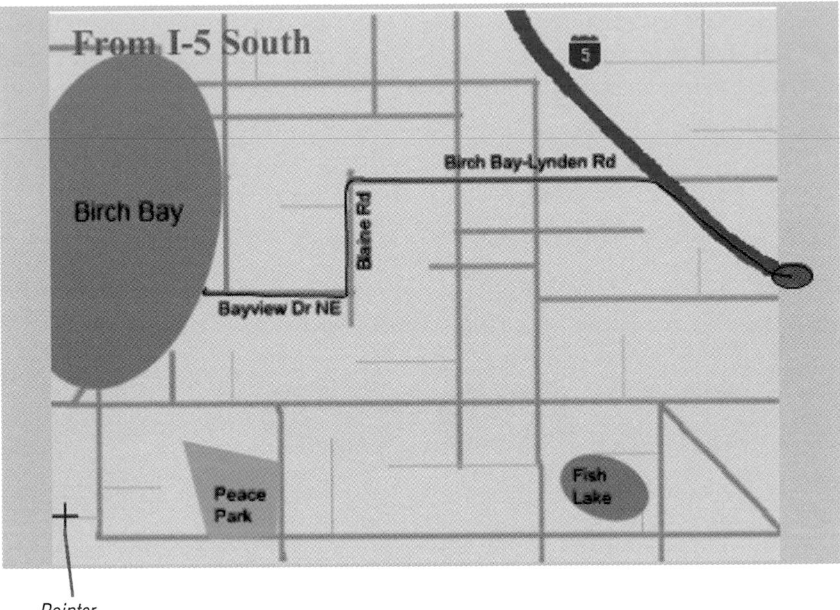

FIGURE 7-44
Rounded rectangle complete

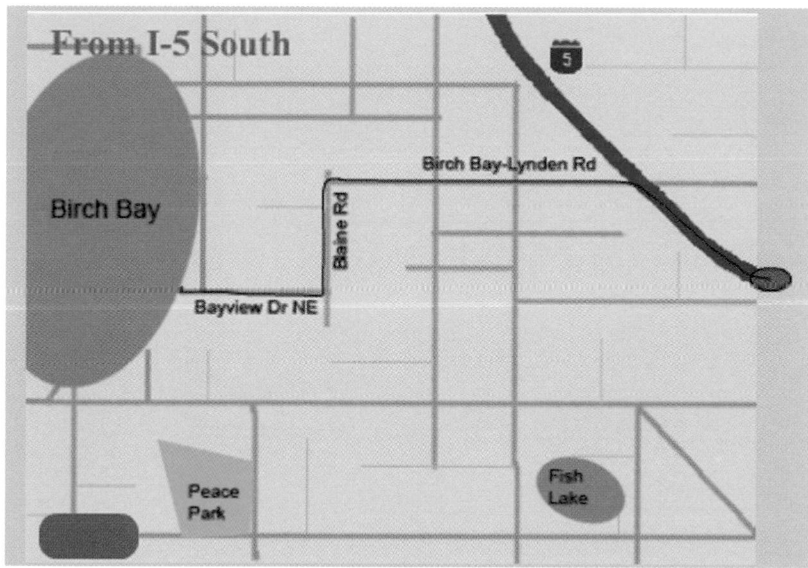

6. Point to the lower-left corner of the map as shown in Figure 7-43, then click and drag the pointer to draw the rounded rectangle shown in Figure 7-44.
7. Click the **Text Tool button** on the Tools panel, click the **Fill Color button**, then select the **white color**.
8. Point inside the rectangle, click to position the pointer, then type **Play**.
9. Click the **Selection Tool button** in the Tools panel, then use the **arrow keys** on the keyboard to center the text on the rectangle.
10. Click **Frame 1** of the play-button layer, then verify that the button is selected.
11. Click **Modify** on the menu bar, click **Convert to Symbol**, delete the entry in the name box, then type **play_btn**.
12. Click **Button** to select the behavior, then click **OK**.
13. Click the **play_btn** button in the Library panel to select it, click **Edit** in the menu bar, then click **Edit Symbols**.
14. Click the blank **Over** frame, then press **[F6]** to insert a keyframe.

(continued)

15. Click the **Fill Color Tool button** in the Tools panel, then click the **gray oval** near the bottom of the palette box as shown in Figure 7-45.

16. Click the blank **Down** frame, then press **[F6]** to insert a keyframe.

17. Click the **Fill Color Tool button** in the Tools panel, then click the **blue oval** near the bottom of the palette.

18. Click the blank **Hit** frame, then press **[F6]** to insert a keyframe.

    Because the Hit Frame defines only the location and size of the clickable area, if no changes in size or location are made (such as by drawing a smaller shape covering only a portion of the button), the Hit area and location are the same as the Up state.

19. Click **Edit** on the menu bar, then click **Edit Document**.

20. Click the **Fill Color Tool button** in the Tools panel, delete the entry in the hexadecimal box, type **#996699**, then press **[Enter]** (PC) or **[return]** (Mac).

(continued)

FIGURE 7-45
The gray oval in the palette box

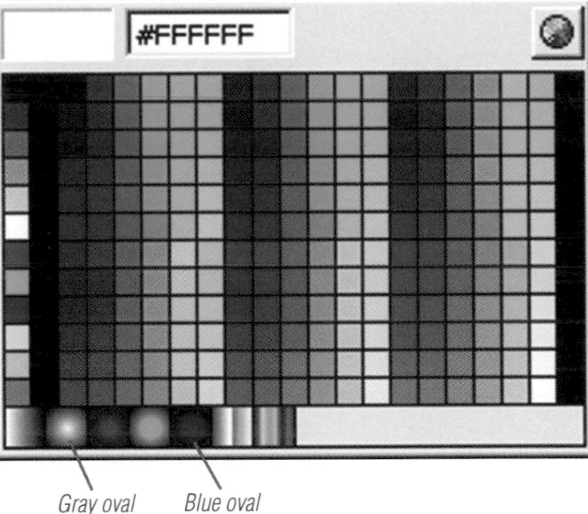

21. Verify the **play_button** layer is selected, click **Insert** on the menu bar, point to **Timeline**, then click **Layer**.

22. Double-click **Layer 7**, delete the entry, type **pause-button**, then press **[Enter]** (PC) or **[return]** (Mac).

23. Click **Frame 1** of the pause-button layer.

24. Repeat steps **4** through **19** to create a second button named pause_btn in the lower-right corner of the stage as shown in Figure 7-46.

25. Click **Control** on the menu bar, then click **Enable Simple Buttons**.

26. Point to the **Play** button on the stage and notice the color change.

27. Click the **Play** button on the stage and notice the color change.

28. Click the **Pause** button on the stage and notice the color change.

29. Click **Control** on the menu bar, then click **Enable Simple Buttons** to turn off the feature.

30. Save the document.

You created buttons and changed the colors for the over and down states.

FIGURE 7-46
The Pause button

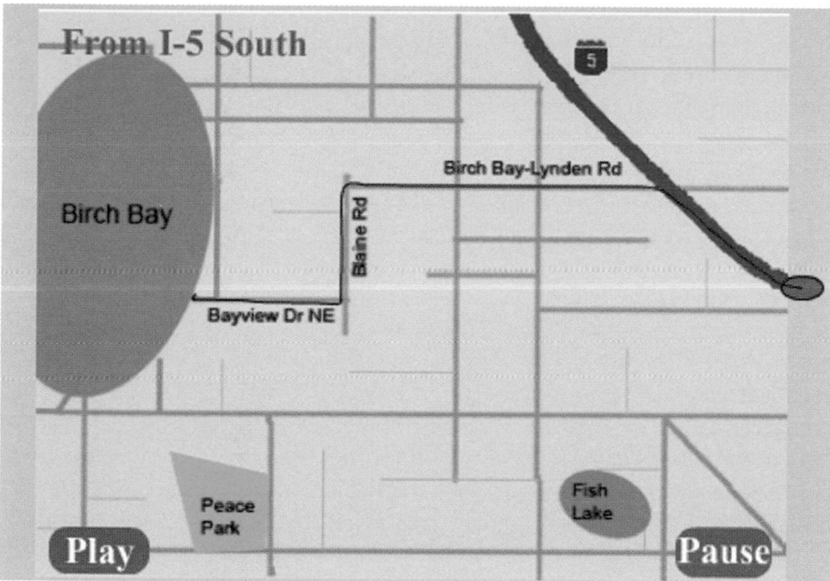

LESSON 4

ASSIGN ACTIONS TO Buttons and Frames

What You'll Do

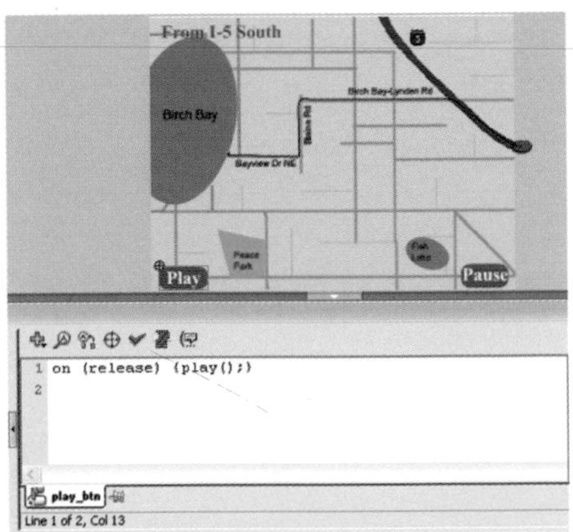

In this lesson, you will use ActionScript to assign actions to frames and buttons.

Understanding Actions

In a basic movie, Macromedia Flash plays the frames sequentially, repeating the movie without stopping for user input. However, in most cases, you want to provide users the ability to interact with the movie by allowing them to perform actions such as starting and stopping the movie or jumping to a specific frame. One way to provide user interaction is to assign an action to the Down state of a button. Then, whenever the user clicks the button, the action occurs. Macromedia Flash provides a scripting language, called ActionScript, that allows you to add actions to buttons and frames within a movie. For example, you can place a Stop action in Frame 1 of a movie to prevent the movie from automatically playing when a Web page is open in a browser. Then you could assign a Play action to a button that starts the movie when the user clicks the button.

ActionScript

A basic ActionScript involves an event (such as a mouse click) that triggers the script and causes some action to occur. Following is an example of ActionScript code:

```
on (release) {Play();}
```

In this example, the event is a mouse click (indicated by the word `release`), and the action is Play, which causes the movie's playback head to start moving.

This is simple code that is easy to follow. The Actions panel allows you to assign basic actions to frames and objects, such as buttons. Figure 7-47 shows the Actions panel displaying ActionScript code that indicates when the user clicks on the selected object (a button), the movie plays.

The process for assigning actions to buttons follows:

- Select the desired button on the stage.
- Display the Actions panel.
- Type the ActionScript code. (Note: For longer and more complex entries, Macromedia Flash provides several Action categories and pre-scripted code that makes it easier to complete an entry.)

Button actions respond to several mouse events such as press (user presses the mouse button) and release (user presses and releases the mouse button).

FIGURE 7-47

The Actions panel displaying an ActionScript code

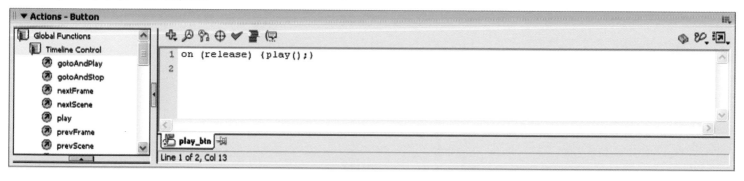

Assign actions to buttons

1. Click the **Play button** on the stage to select it.
2. Click **Window** on the menu bar, point to **Development Panels**, then click **Actions** to display the Actions panel.
3. With the insertion point on line 1 of the Actions panel, type **on (release) {play( );}** as shown in Figure 7-48, then press **[Enter]** (PC) or **[return]** (Mac).
4. Click the **Pause button** on the stage to select it.
5. Click the pointer on line 1 of the Actions panel, type **on (release) {stop ( );}**, then press **[Enter]** (PC) or **[return]** (Mac).
6. Save the document.
7. Click **File** in the menu bar, point to **Publish Preview**, then click **Default - (HTML)** to display the movie in a browser.

   Note: A message may appear indicating that you need to allow active content before being able to view the file in the browser.
8. View the movie and notice that it starts automatically and loops continuously.
9. Click the **Pause** button, then click the **Play** button.
10. **Close** the browser window, then return to the Macromedia Flash document.

You used the Actions panel to assign Play and Stop actions to buttons.

FIGURE 7-48

The completed entry in the Actions panel for the button action

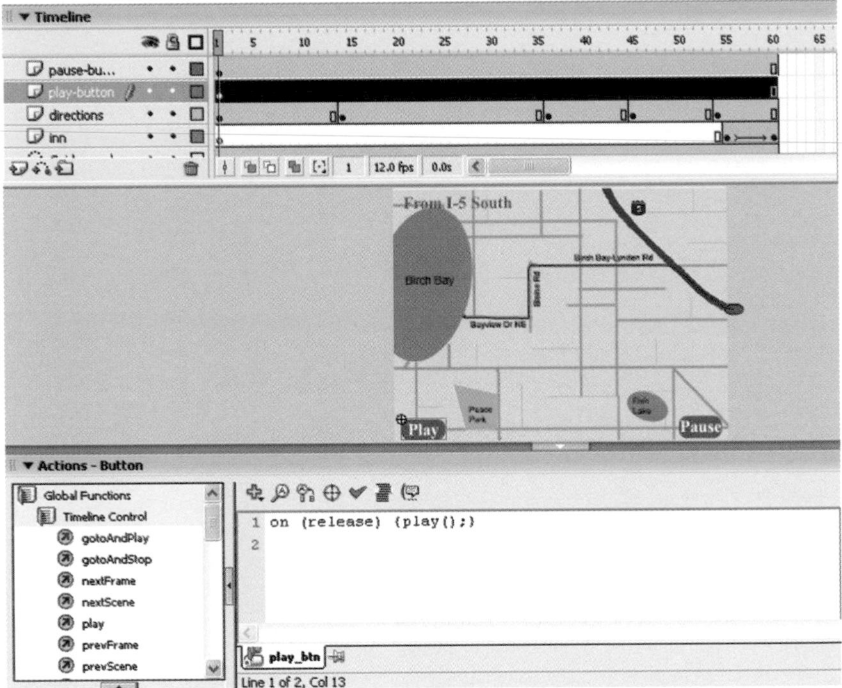

FIGURE 7-49
The completed entry in the Actions panel for the frame action

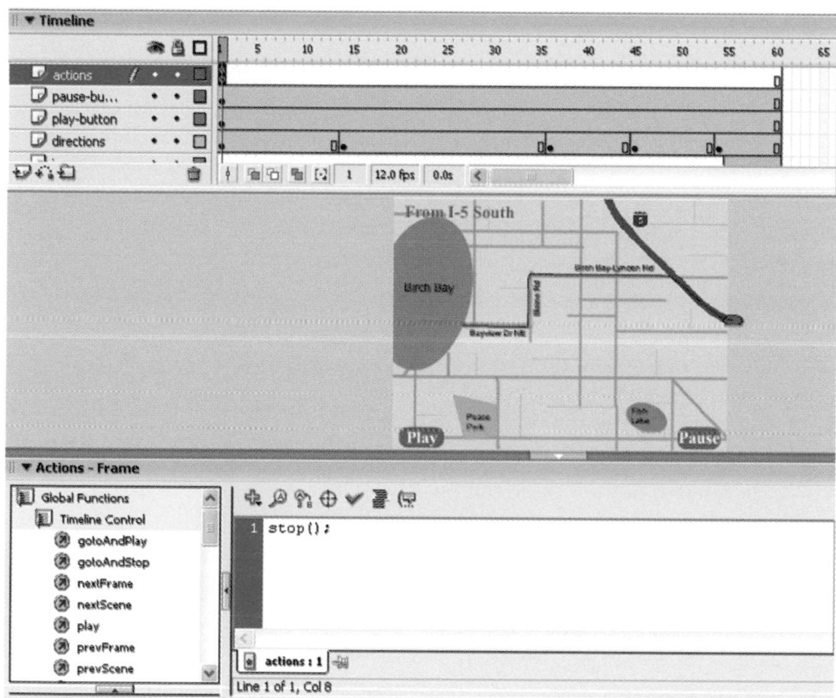

Assign an action to a frame

1. Verify that the pause-button layer is selected, click **Insert** on the menu bar, point to **Timeline**, then click **Layer**.
2. Double-click **Layer 8**, delete the entry, type **actions**, then press **[Enter]** (PC) or **[return]** (Mac).
3. Click **Frame 1** of the actions layer.
4. Position the insertion point on line 1 of the Actions panel, type **stop( );** as shown in Figure 7-49, then press **[Enter]** (PC) or **[return]** (Mac).
5. Click **Frame 60** of the actions layer, then press **[F6]** to insert a keyframe.
6. Position the insertion point on line 1 of the Actions panel, type **stop( );**, then press **[Enter]** (PC) or **[return]** (Mac).
7. Save the Macromedia Flash document.
8. Click **File** in the menu bar, point to **Publish Preview**, then click **Default - (HTML)** to display the movie in a browser.
9. Click the **Play** and **Pause** buttons several times.
10. **Close** the browser window, then return to the Macromedia Flash document.

You used the Actions panel to assign stop actions to frames.

LESSON 5

PUBLISH A MOVIE AND INSERT It into a Web Page

What You'll Do

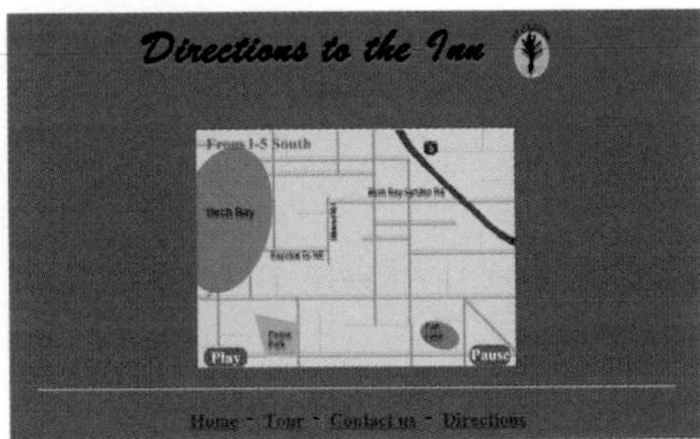

In this lesson, you will publish a Macromedia Flash movie and add a Macromedia Flash movie to a Web page.

When you create Macromedia Flash movies they are saved in a file format (.fla) that can be viewed only by those who have the Macromedia Flash program installed on their computers. Usually, Macromedia Flash movies are viewed on the Web as part of a Web site or directly from a viewer's computer using the Macromedia Flash Player. In order to view your Macromedia Flash movies on the Web, the movies must be changed to a Shockwave (.swf) file format. In addition, the HTML code that references the Shockwave file needs to be generated. Both of these can be done by using the publish feature of Macromedia Flash.

The process for publishing a Macromedia Flash movie is to create and save a movie, then select the Publish command from the File menu. You can specify various settings, such as dimensions for the window that the movie plays within the browser, before publishing a movie. Publishing a movie creates two files, an HTML file and a Shockwave file. Both of these files have the same name as the Macromedia Flash movie file, but with different file extensions:

.html—the HTML document

.swf—the Macromedia Shockwave file

The HTML document contains the code that is interpreted by a browser to display the movie on the Web and the code that specifies the Shockwave movie that is to be played.

The process for inserting a .swf file into a Web page using Dreamweaver is to save or copy the file to the appropriate folder so that the filename appears in the Files panel. Then drag the file icon from the Files panel to the desired location in the document window. Dragging the file icon into the document window inserts the HTML code associated with that file into the Dreamweaver file.

> **QUICKTIP**
>
> The process for inserting a file into an HTML document using a text editor is to copy the HTML code, generated by Macromedia Flash, to the HTML document.

HTML and Multimedia files

There are two HTML elements—embed and object—that are used to play certain types of multimedia files such as audio, video, and animation. Both should be used because different browsers recognize only one or the other. Figure 7-50 shows the innmap.swf code embedded into a Web page using Dreamweaver. You do not have to know how to write the code for the .swf file because it is created for you when you publish your Macromedia Flash movie. However, learning some basics about the code helps you understand how it can be changed, if desired.

<object classid...: Identifies the kind of object being embedded in the Web page— in this case a swflash object

<param name...: Identifies properties of the object, such as the "movie"— "innmap.swf"—and the quality— "high"

<embed src...: Identifies the file (innmap.swf) and its properties such as the quality— "high"— and the type— "shockwave-flash". In addition, the URL for the plugin is identified— "www.macromedia.com".

FIGURE 7-50

The HTML code that specifies the Shockwave movie that is to be played in the browser

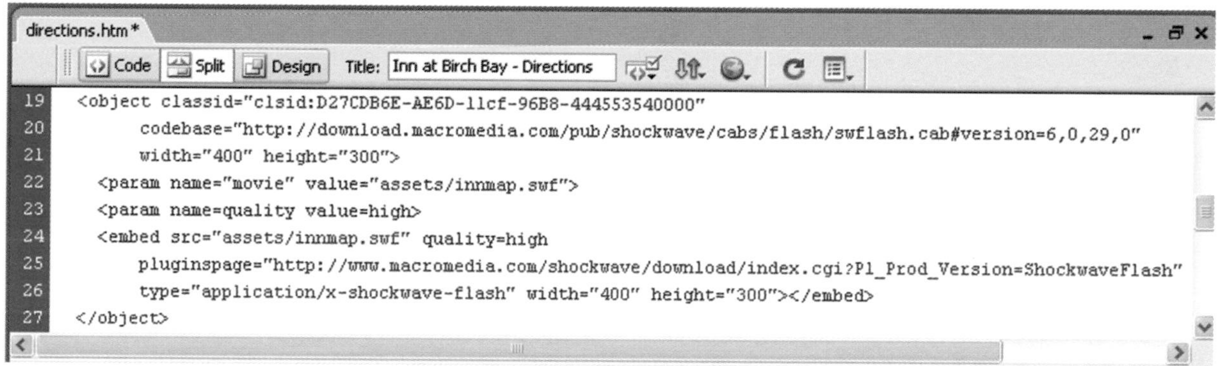

Publish a movie

1. Click **File** on the menu bar, then click **Publish Settings**.
2. Verify the Formats tab is selected in the Publish Settings dialog box.
3. Verify the Flash (.swf) and HTML (.html) options are selected.
4. Click **Publish**, then click **OK**.
5. Navigate to the directions folder.

   Notice that there are three files that start with the filename innmap (innmap.fla, the Macromedia Flash Document; innmap.swf, the shockwave file; and innmap.html, the HTML document), as shown in Figure 7-51.
6. Click **innmap.swf**, click **Edit** in the menu bar, then click **Copy**.
7. Navigate to the assets folder of the **InnWebsiteDW folder**.
8. Click **Edit** in the menu bar, then click **Paste**.

You published a movie and copied the .swf file to the Web site assets folder.

Insert a Macromedia Flash movie into a Web page

1. Start **Dreamweaver**, then display the **InnWebsiteDW folder** in the Files panel.
2. Double-click **directions.htm** in the Files panel to open the Web page in the document window.
3. Click the **Map placeholder** to select it, then press **[Delete]**.

(continued)

FIGURE 7-51
The folder with the three files

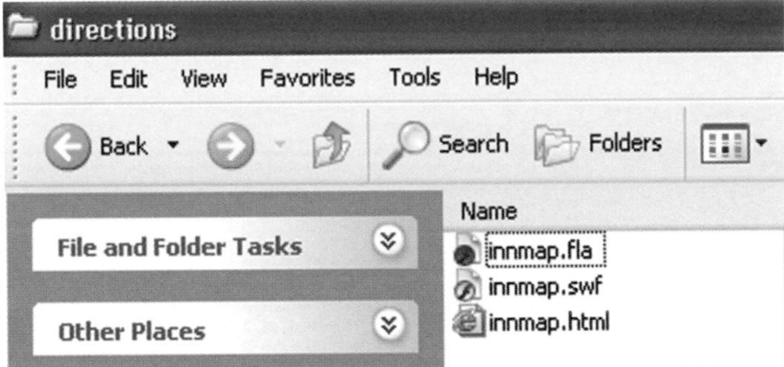

FIGURE 7-52
Dragging the icon to the document window

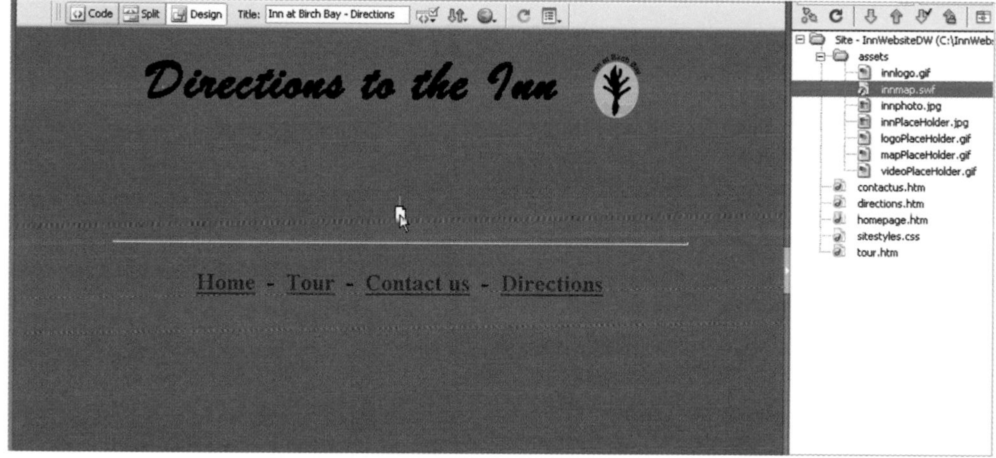

4. Expand the assets folder in the Files panel if necessary, then drag the **innmap.swf** icon from the Files panel to the document window as shown in Figure 7-52.

   A placeholder for the Macromedia Flash movie appears. The icon might look slightly different on a Mac. With the placeholder selected, you can play the movie using the Play button in the Property inspector.

5. Click the **Play button** [Play] in the Property inspector panel.
6. Click the **Play** and **Pause buttons** on the map several times.
7. Click the **Stop button** [Stop] in the Property inspector panel.
8. Save the document.
9. Press **[F12]** to view the Web page in a browser, then click the **Play** and **Pause buttons** on the map several times.
10. Close the browser window, then return to the Dreamweaver document.
11. Click the **Split button** [Split] at the top of the document window to display the code.

    Notice the object code has been inserted into the Web page XHTML code.

12. Click the **Design button** [Design] to hide the code.

You inserted a Macromedia Flash movie into a Web page.

PROJECT BUILDER 1

You are an intern with a company that develops Web sites for clients. During your internship training you learned how important animations can be to Web pages. One of the most important considerations when using animation in a Web site is the time it takes for the animation file to be downloaded to the viewer's computer. In an effort to address the needs of both those who have broadband and those who have dial-up Internet connections, some companies allow the viewer to choose between two versions of their sites as shown in Figure 7-53. The versions have similar content, however one version is multimedia-rich (animations, audio, video) and the other version is more graphics and text intensive.

1. Connect to the Internet, and go to *www.course.com*, navigate to the page for this book, click the Student Online Companion link, then click the link for this chapter.
2. Navigate through the Flash version of the site and then through the HTML version of the site.
3. Open a document in a word processor, save the file as **Ch7pb1**, create a table with these column heads: Topic, Flash version, and HTML version, then create one row for each topic that follows:
   a. Use of animation
   b. Use of audio
   c. Interactivity
   d. Controls provided
   e. Amount of time taken to load the pages
   f. Amount of text
   g. Use of color
4. Complete the table by comparing the Web pages based on the topics listed in your table.
5. List the type of Internet connection you are using (broadband or dial-up).

One Step Beyond

6. If you used a computer with a broadband connection to complete the previous exercise, then find a computer with a dial-up Internet connection and view the two versions again. If you used a computer with a dial-up connection to complete the previous exercise, find a computer with a broadband Internet connection and view the two versions again.
7. Do you think that the broadband version is more effective than the dial-up version. Why, or why not? Provide specific examples in your answer.

Two Steps Beyond

8. Conduct a Web search for two companies that provide stock animation clips.
9. Choose one subject and search for animations available on the sites.
10. Write a summary of each site and include the following in the summary:
    a. The name and URL for each company
    b. The approximate number of animation clips available for the chosen subject
    c. Ease of finding the desired animation
    d. Approximate cost of an animation clip
    e. How animations are distributed
    f. The terms of use (what is allowed and what is forbidden)
    g. Which site would you evaluate as better and why?

FIGURE 7-53
A choice between two versions of the Web site

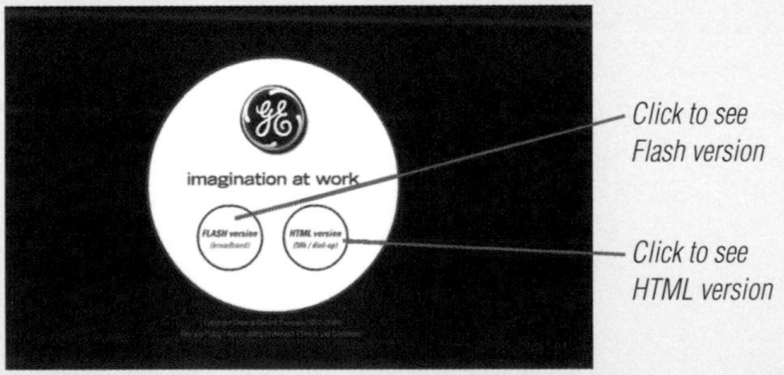

PROJECT BUILDER 2

You have been studying Web development. You decide it would be useful to develop an animation for a portfolio Web site. Complete the following steps to create animations and insert them into a Web page.

1. Using Macromedia Flash, develop two animations of your choice. Include the following in your animations:
   a. Text using the Text tool
   b. A drawing using the Flash drawing tools
   c. An imported graphic
   d. A path animation
   e. A zoom effect
   f. Buttons with ActionScript
   g. Frames with ActionScript
2. Follow these guidelines:
   a. Create a new layer for each object
   b. Name all layers
   c. Convert all graphics to symbols
   d. Have buttons change for each button state
   e. Create a folder named **Ch7files** that will hold the .fla, .swf, and .html files created using Flash
   f. Save the animations with the filename **myan1xx.fla** and **myan2xx.fla** (where *xx* are your initials)
   g. Publish each animation
   h. View the animations in a browser

One Step Beyond

3. Using Dreamweaver, open mysitech7-anim.htm (shown in Figure 7-54) and add the two animations to the Web page.
4. Play the animations within Dreamweaver.
5. Open the Web page in a browser and play the animations.
6. Save the document with the file name **mysitech7-anxx.htm** (where *xx* are your initials).

Two Steps Beyond

7. Use the Flash Help feature to search for Tweening Shapes.
8. Follow the instructions to create a shape tween animation.
9. Save the animation with the filename **shapetweenxx.fla** (where *xx* are your initials).
10. Publish the movie, then test it in a browser.

FIGURE 7-54
A Web page with placeholders for animations

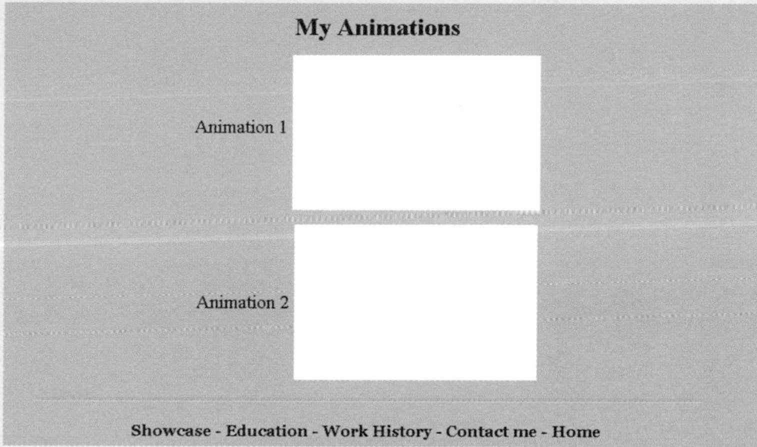

GREAT
ESTONIA
MOSKVA

chapter

8 MULTIMEDIA ELEMENT — Sound

1. Discuss the Use of Sound on the Web
2. Understand the Basic Principles of Sound
3. Examine Digital Audio Sources
4. Explore Digital Audio Software
5. Discover Audio File Formats for the Web

chapter 8 MULTIMEDIA ELEMENT — Sound

Introduction

In the early days of desktop computers, the only sound that you heard from a computer was a beep, which was often accompanied by an error message. Now an entire range of sounds can be played through a computer, including music, narration, sound effects, and original recordings of events such as a presidential speech or a rock concert. The element of sound can be important to achieving the goals of a multimedia Web site.

People acquire a great deal of knowledge and enjoyment through their sense of hearing. Sound adds another dimension to a multimedia Web site. If used well, it is an extremely powerful element that can stimulate emotional responses that would never be activated from text and graphics alone. Sound should be used selectively and appropriately whenever and wherever it will help convey the intended message or complement the purpose of the Web site.

Other than in the entertainment industry, many multimedia Web developers do not take advantage of this sense by incorporating sound into their Web sites. There are obvious reasons for this. If improperly created, sound files can take too much time to download. Many designers and users do not feel sound files are worth the wait. In general, people have been conditioned to expect good sound. Inappropriate or poor quality sound can detract from the site and be downright annoying to the user. Keep in mind that the decision of whether to use sound in a multimedia Web site is often a trade-off between cost, time, or effect. If you are in doubt as to whether or not you should or should not use sound on your Web site, you probably should not. It may do more harm than good.

On the other hand, if sound files are properly designed and incorporated into a Web page, they will be quick to load and they can significantly enhance a Web site by supplementing online presentations, images, animations, and video. It also sets the mood for the Web site and can add to the overall user experience. There are many Web sites that would be completely ineffective and dull if it were not for the addition of sound. Companies use sound to draw attention to their Web sites and market their products; developers search the Internet for sound files to use in other applications; educators deliver audio lectures in their online courses; musicians provide sample versions of their latest songs; and Web-based game developers use sound to enhance their entertainment sites. Sound can be used to enhance computer-based training on the Web. Appropriate narration can be used to augment the demonstration of correct techniques or procedures. Instructions are more likely to be followed if audio accompanies the written instructions. Sound can also be effectively used to provide feedback. For example, in a simulated experience, a buzzer noise may signal that the wrong choice has been selected.

Working with sound can be an intricate process. If you are working as part of a multimedia team on a larger project, an audio specialist has probably already been assigned to work with you. If not and the sound files you need are complicated, you may find it worthwhile to secure the services and skills of an audio specialist to assist you in developing the audio for your Web site.

Audio specialists are responsible for recording and processing the audio files used in a multimedia Web site (Figure 8-1). Working with the Web designers and developers on the project, they will ensure that the audio is correctly incorporated and appropriately configured for online delivery.

The services of the audio specialist are even more valuable to the project as the audio at the Web site gets more complicated. For example, when audio needs to be streamed or when multiple sounds from multiple sources have been incorporated into a single file that must be delivered across low bandwidth, it may be time to involve the audio specialist. Streaming audio means that the sound file will begin playing after part of the file is downloaded. In other words, the entire sound file does not have to be downloaded first before the sound begins to play.

Sound adds another dimension to a Web site and makes use of another sense. Sound can significantly enhance or destroy a user's online experience. To help ensure its effectiveness, it is important to incorporate sound files that are high quality, appropriate, and consistent with the goals of the multimedia Web site. This lesson examines how sound is produced and incorporated into a multimedia Web site.

FIGURE 8-1
The audio specialist is responsible for recording and processing the audio files for the Web-based multimedia application

CONCEPT 1

DISCUSS THE USE OF Sound on the Web

What You'll Learn

In this lesson, you will learn how sound files can be effectively incorporated into different types of multimedia Web sites following the basic design guidelines for including audio on a Web page.

As shown in Figure 8-2, the Web has made it very easy for users to purchase and download music files directly from online music stores. But the use of sound on the Web goes way beyond music sound files. It is the entertainment and game industry that has spurred the growth of computers with multimedia capabilities. Developers of multimedia games know the value of sound. Arcade games come complete with the sounds of tilting pinball machines and bumper pool. Online card and casino games use sounds to simulate the spinning of a roulette wheel, the shuffling of cards, and spewing coins from a slot machine. The sound of tornadoes, earthquakes, floods, firing guns, engines, and screeching tires can be heard throughout action games on the Web. Developers are always creating fun little animated creatures that make noises we have never heard before, and nearly all multimedia Web sites designed for entertainment have background music that sets the mood to light and cheery or dark and dreary.

An increasing number of Web pages include background music, narration, and sound effects, which means sound is becoming less of a novelty on multimedia Web sites. On the Web, recorded testimonials from customers are used to market and sell products and services. Interviews with political candidates are designed to sway votes. Options to have screen tips and text narrated are available. Beeps, squeaks, claps, and whistles are all quite common sound effects found throughout the Web.

On the Web, audio can either be synched with the occurrence of other objects in the production, or it can serve as a trigger when clicked. It can be used to get attention, to entertain, to give directions, to personalize an interface, or to convey an educational or persuasive message. But no matter how it is used, sound must keep users involved if it is to be effective. Providing controls (such as skip, pause, mute, volume adjustment, etc.) is an effective way of keeping users involved and motivated. If users do not have control over the sound, the sound may be lost as it blends in with the rest of the noises in the environment. Once lost, the sound becomes a useless element.

FIGURE 8-2

Users can preview, purchase, and download music files from online music stores such as iTunes and MP3.com

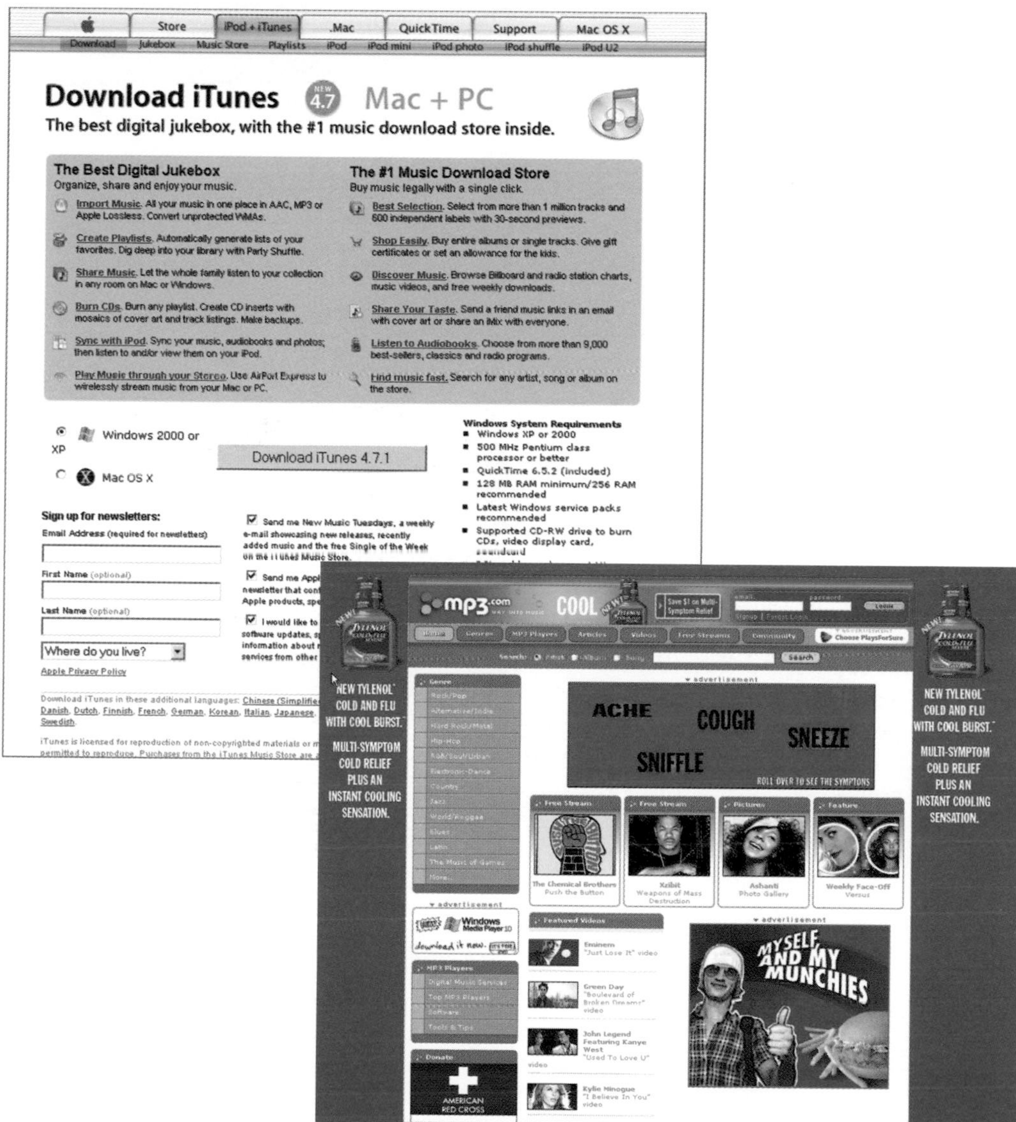

Like every other multimedia element, if you decide to incorporate sound into a multimedia Web site, you should have a reason for doing so (see Figure 8-3). For example, in education sound is used to accommodate auditory learners. Sound is imperative in teaching the correct pronunciation of words. And, as in computer-based training, sounds can provide feedback such as a buzzer when an incorrect answer is given. Sound can also be used to illustrate a concept. For example, a Web site geared toward assisting medical students in diagnosing disease could include the sounds of different types of breathing patterns, which signify different ailments.

In multimedia Web sites, sounds are either content sounds or ambient sounds. **Content sounds** furnish information. Narration and dialogue are content sounds. Music and other sounds can also be considered content sounds if they are part of the topic itself. For example, the sound of a motor would be content sound if it were used to distinguish among different engine problems.

FIGURE 8-3

Sound can be used for educational as well as entertainment purposes

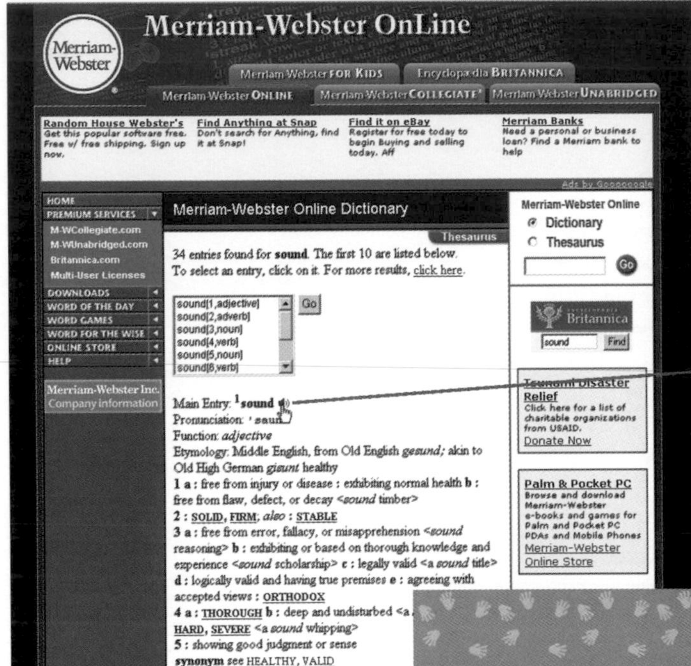

Some online dictionaries, such as the one shown here, offer a link to an audio file with the pronunciation of the entry

Click the speaker to hear the word pronounced

Some educational sites, such as the one shown here, provide links to audio files with songs

Ambient sounds include background sounds and special effects. **Ambient sounds** reinforce messages and set the mood. Music is a universal language that most people enjoy and appreciate. Special sound effects can reinforce or enliven a message. Classical music can be used in the background to set the mood for a Web site on literature and the arts while new age rhythms would be better for a multimedia Web site on the healing power of crystals. Many **splash screens** or intro pages use background music to set a mood for the Web site before the user even enters the site (see Figure 8-4).

FIGURE 8-4

The splash page of the Cleveland Institute of Music Web site uses a scrolling music score and background music to set the tone of the site before the user enters

DESIGNTIP Creating Effective Sound Files

- In order to maintain a sense of unity throughout the multimedia Web site, use the same style of music if multiple sound files are needed.
- Coordinate your sound files with the other graphic, animation, and video elements used on your Web pages.
- Keep the sound quality consistent throughout. Do not include low-resolution sound and high-resolution sound together at the same site.
- Record at a rate and resolution appropriate to the delivery mode of the site. Remember that even though 44 kHz, 16-bit sounds are higher-quality sounds, they also require greater storage capacity and can slow your Web site when they are downloaded or played.
- Use the same voice for narration and voiceovers, but different voices for different characters. If different characters are used within the site, the voice for each should be distinct. Remember to get signed releases before you use someone's recorded voice in your multimedia Web site.
- Optimize files for background music. Small file sizes begin to play quickly. Also, be sure to clearly label the size and type of audio files when you embed downloadable sound files on your Web pages. By labeling files, you enable users to choose only those files that are compatible with their systems and that they want to hear.
- If appropriate, provide a way to give the user some control over the audio. Consider allowing the user to skip a sound clip or adjust the volume. This issue is especially important if a musical introduction is played when the user first enters a Web site. The second time visiting the site, the user may not want to hear the musical introduction again.

CONCEPT 2

UNDERSTAND THE BASIC
Principles of Sound

What You'll Learn

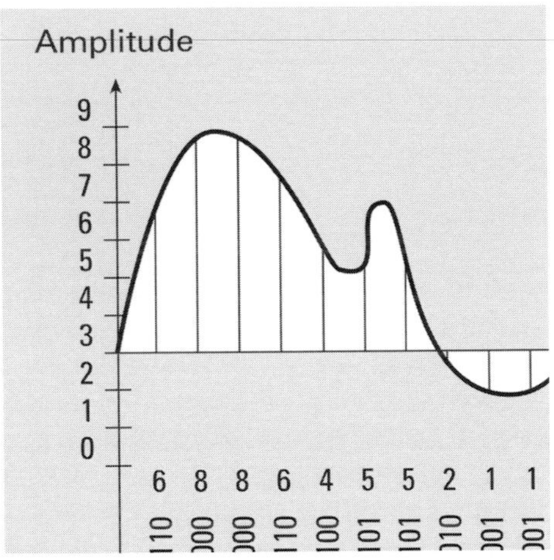

In this lesson, you will learn about analog and digital sound files. You will also learn about the factors that determine digital audio sound quality.

To understand the use of sound on multimedia Web sites, you need an understanding of the basic principles of sound. When you speak, vibrations, called **sound waves**, are created. These sound waves have a recurring pattern or an analog wave pattern called a **waveform**. All sounds have a waveform as shown in Figure 8-5. The waveform includes the frequency, the amplitude, and the harmonic content of the sound.

The **amplitude** is the distance between the valley and the peak of a waveform. The amplitude of a waveform determines its volume, which is measured in decibels. The higher the peak, the louder the sound. A **decibel (dB)** is the smallest variation in amplitude that can be detected by the human ear. The **frequency** is the number of peaks that occur in one second measured by the distance between the peaks. The frequency of a waveform determines its pitch. The greater the distance between peaks, the lower the sound. Frequency is measured in **hertz (Hz)**. A pattern that occurs every second is equal to one hertz. If the pattern recurs 1000 times in one second, it would be equal to 1000 Hz or 1 **kilohertz (kHz)**.

Analog sound is a continuous stream of sound waves. For sound to be included on a multimedia Web site, the sound waves must be converted from analog (sound waves) to digital (bits) form. Just as an image has to be digitized (converted to 1s and 0s) in order for the computer to recognize it, a sound must also be digitized. In other words, in order for the computer to recognize and manipulate the sound, the waveform must be converted to numbers. The process of converting an analog sound to numbers is called **digitizing** or **sound sampling**, in which every fraction of a second a sample of the sound is recorded in digital bits (see Figure 8-6). An analog sound that has been converted to numbers is called **digital audio**.

FIGURE 8-5
This analog wave pattern represents the volume and frequency of a sound

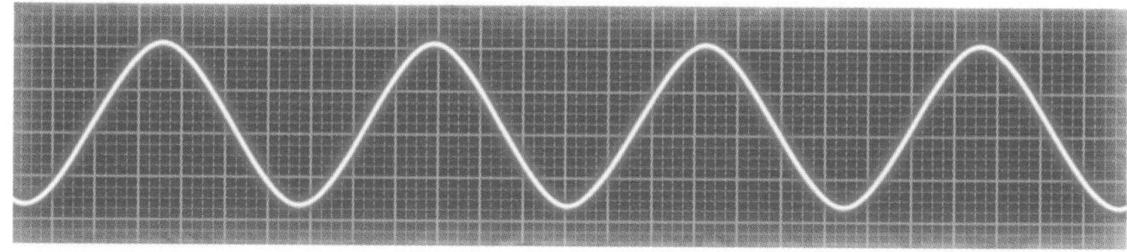

FIGURE 8-6
Sound sampling converts analog sound to digital audio—1s and 0s

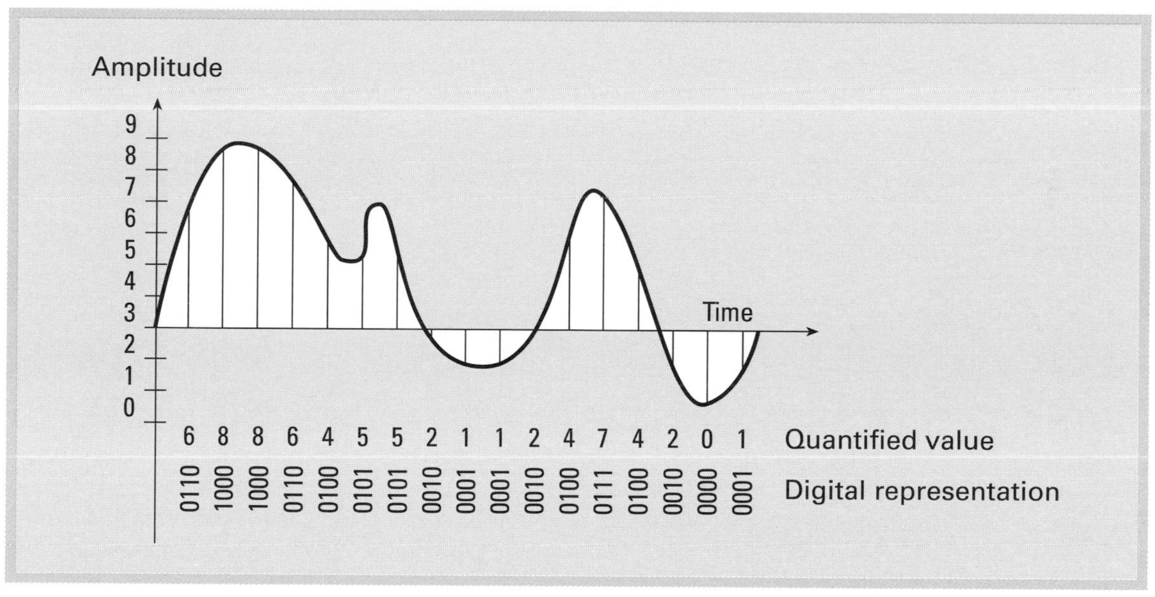

Sound Quality

Sound quality will affect the credibility and effectiveness of the Web site. Recording and playback environments and equipment have a huge impact on the quality of sound. There are several other factors that determine the quality of a sound including **sample rate**; **resolution**; whether the sound is **mono** or **stereo**; **downloaded**, or **streamed**; and the **compression** applied.

Sample Rate

The sample rate is the number of waveform samples per second or the number of times the sample is taken. The sampling rate is measured in kilohertz, with 11 kHz, 22 kHz, and 44 kHz being the most common sampling rates. A higher sampling rate produces a higher-quality sound. The disadvantage of using a higher sampling rate is that sound files with higher sampling rates are larger and therefore require greater storage capacity and take longer to download.

Resolution

Resolution is the number of binary bits processed for each sound wave. The resolution is sometimes referred to as the **sample size**. Like all digital data, sound that has been recorded by a computer is represented in bits, which represent the vibrations in the sound wave. As the number of bits used to sample the sound increases, the range and the quality of the sound also improves. When more bits are processed, the recording is smoother and purer, thus the sound is more realistic (see Figure 8-7). Because 16-bit recordings contain twice as much information as 8-bit recordings, they are higher quality. In addition, 16-bit recordings offer a dynamic range of 98 dB (decibels). This makes them superior to 8-bit recordings, which offer only 50 dB. Once again, there is a trade-off in recording sound with a higher resolution. A sound file with a higher resolution will be of a higher quality, but the file size will also be larger.

FIGURE 8-7
Rate and resolution affect the quality of a sound

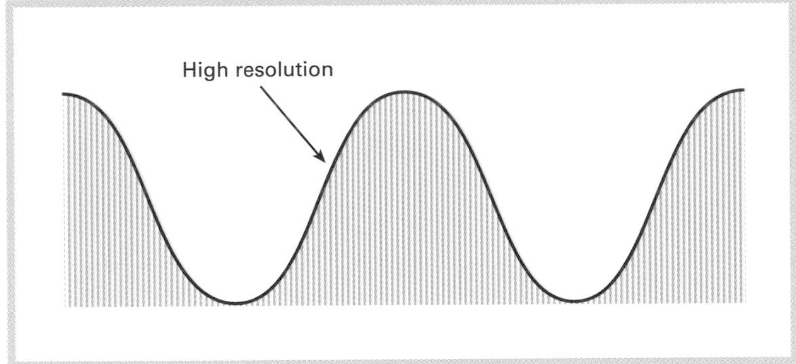

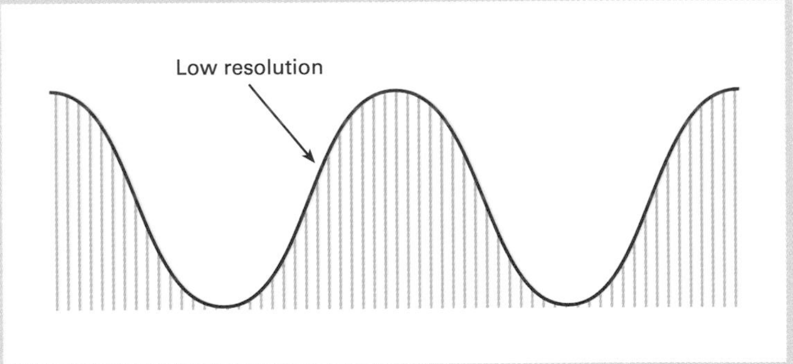

Mono versus Stereo Sound

Mono sounds are flat and unrealistic compared to stereo sounds, which are much more dynamic and lifelike. However, stereo sound files require twice the storage capacity of mono sound files. Therefore, on the Web where storage and transfer are major concerns, mono sound files are sometimes a more appropriate choice. For example, narration and voiceovers can effectively be saved in a mono format while music almost always must be recorded and saved in stereo.

Live sounds and music resonate and surround us. **Surround sound** or **3-D sound** attempts to create this same encompassing experience by inserting delays into the sound recording. These delays attempt to simulate the time it would take for sound waves to reach your ears if you were listening to a live sound or performance. In order for this to happen, multiple speakers are necessary, and a pair of front and rear speakers is preferable. To create virtual worlds, 3-D sound must be incorporated. As virtual reality becomes more and more sophisticated, the use of 3-D sound in virtual worlds will become more and more common.

Downloaded versus Streamed

Audio on the Web can either be downloaded or streamed. A downloaded audio file must be entirely saved to the user's computer before it can be played. In other words, the file cannot be heard until it is completely transferred from the server to the user's computer. Streaming is a more advanced process that allows the sound file to be played as it is downloading and before the entire file is transferred to the user's computer. Different file formats and technologies are available to support these two different methods of delivering sound via the Web. If you want your sound files to be streamed, your Web-hosting service must support streaming.

Compression

As discussed in previous chapters, **compression** is a technique that mathematically reduces the size of a file. A primary consideration when using sound files on the Web is file size. Compression is beneficial for storing and transferring sound files. Uncompressed audio files can be extremely large, requiring unacceptable playback time when delivered. For example, a 10-second recording of CD-quality audio in stereo would be nearly 2 MB in size and take as long as 30 seconds to download using a dial-up connection.

There are several different compression rates that can be applied to sound files. Different compression schemes are recommended for voiceovers, music, and audio files recorded and stored at different resolutions. In addition, different compression schemes are available for different file formats, and some file formats include the compression scheme within the format itself. Although there is no single standard for compressing and decompressing digital audio for the Web, the type of compression applied impacts the quality of the sound file as well as the file size.

CONCEPT 3

EXAMINE DIGITAL Audio Sources

What You'll Learn

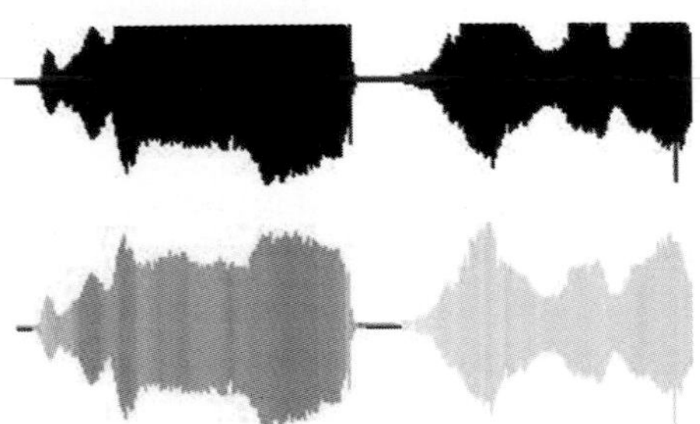

In this lesson, you will learn the sources of digital audio files including the steps involved in producing your own digital audio files.

There are many sources from which you can obtain digital sound for your multimedia Web site. Just as clip art gives you access to a variety of graphic art files, **clip audio** gives you access to prerecorded digital audio clips of music and sound effects. Audio can be purchased on CD or you can download it for free or for a fee from Web sites such as the one shown in Figure 8-8.

Music that has been recorded to compact disc is already in a digital format that can be included as background music or a melody on a multimedia Web site. Most of the sound on CDs has been sampled at almost 45,000 samples per second, which means that you can get very high-quality sound from a CD.

As always, be sure to carefully read the licensing agreements that come with clip audio. These agreements contain information about royalties and copyright. Although some of these digital audio files will undoubtedly be copyright protected, others will fall within the public domain. If you wish to use a piece from a music CD or download, be sure to get permission. If in doubt, assume that the audio file you wish to use is copyright protected and obtain permission and a release before you use it on your Web site.

Producing Digital Audio

In addition to using prerecorded audio files, you can also record, digitize, and process your own sound files. Obviously there is a trade-off in producing your own digital audio. Although you have ultimate control over the creation of the audio file, you also need the necessary equipment (see Figure 8-9), room and acoustics, sound editing and mixing software, and skills or trained professionals who know how to use all of these tools.

FIGURE 8-9

With the right equipment, you can produce your own digital audio files

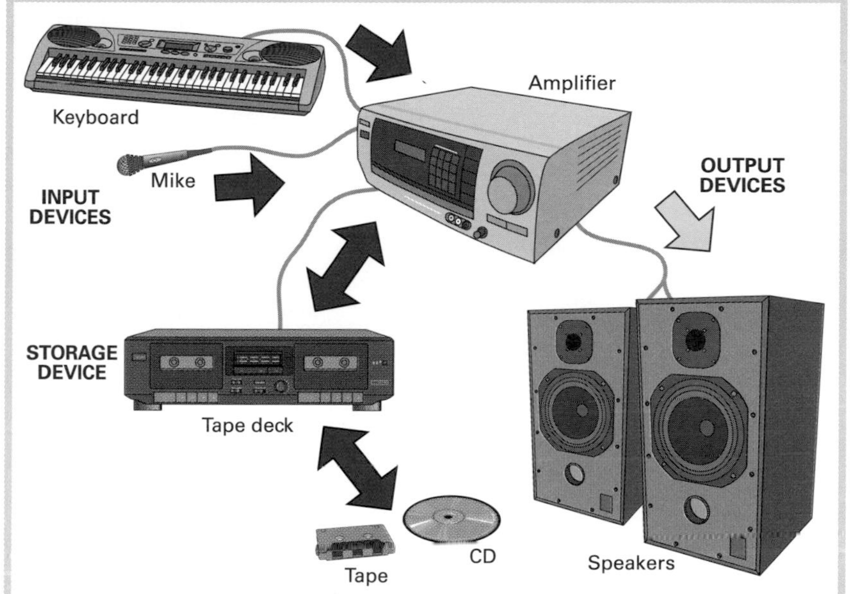

FIGURE 8-8

Audio clips can be downloaded for free or for a fee

FreeAudioClips.com

Audio Clip Search

all GO

Categories

- New Stuff
- Classic/Hard Rock
- Comedy Clips
- Country Music
- Disco/Dance
- Folk/Bluegrass
- Holidays
- Jazz/Blues
- Movies/TV
- Pop Music
- Sound Effects

Other Stuff To Do

Looking for awesome audio clips? Look no further! FreeAudioClips.com is loaded with tons of wav, midi and au files for your listening and downloading pleasure!

Select a category on the right and easily find what you're looking for. Or, use the quick "audio clip keyword search" to search through the database for that special sound clip!

CLICK This weeks top 10 downloads	
Ambience Night Sound In The Jungle	wav 30kb DL: 181
Austin Powers "Youve got mail, baby, yeah!"	wav 30kb DL: 174
Answering Machine Alien Conspiracy	wav 604kb DL: 168
Female Voice "You Are So Good Looking!"	wav 22k DL: 153
Female Voice "Oh ma God!"	wav 12kb DL: 153
Answering Machine Homer Simpson	wav 50kb DL: 153
Big Bopper "Helloooo baby!"	wav 24kb DL: 151

Planning

Proper planning is critical if sound is to be incorporated into a multimedia Web site. Regardless of whether you intend to use prerecorded audio or record your own, it is very important to plan what, when, where, and how sound will be incorporated into the Web site. First you must consider what content should be delivered via sound as well as the types of ambient sounds that will be used to set the mood or create a special effect. If the multimedia Web site is interactive, flowcharts should distinguish between which sounds are played as users make different choices. To plan the sound for your Web site you will need to rely heavily on the planning documents including flowcharts, storyboards, and scripts (see Figure 8-10).

To properly plan the inclusion of sound on a Web site, sound files should also be considered in the storyboarding phase. Storyboards should designate where sound will begin and end on the Web site. Detailed scripts are particularly important if voice-overs and narration are included at the Web site. Because there is a difference between the way words are heard and the way they are read, scripts should be written for listening rather than for reading. This involves using short, simple phrases and questions with familiar words and adequate pauses. Scripts should include details about narration and voice dialogues including what is said and how it is said.

Recording

Minimally, a sound card and software program are needed to digitize sound. A sound from an external source is sent to the sound card. The external source could be a tape, videotape, CD, or sound coming through a microphone. The sound card samples or digitizes the sound based on the sample rate (11, 22, or 44 kHz) and resolution (8- or 16-bit), and then produces the digital approximation of the analog signal. Settings provided in the software program analyze the sample rate and resolution values used by the sound card, and the audio specialist determines the final settings for the digital audio file.

Next to the original sound, the microphone, sound card, and other digitizing equipment are of utmost importance. Regardless of the quality of the original sound file, the true attributes of it are forever lost if the other audio-system components do not capture the full quality.

For simple recording projects such as narration, a microphone and computer can serve as the recording unit. **Microphones** translate analog signals into electrical impulses. Through the use of an **analog-to-digital converter (ADC)**, these impulses are converted to numbers that can be stored, understood, and manipulated by a microprocessor.

FIGURE 8-10

A script is used to identify all the sounds and dialogue used in a Web site

THE SOUND OF COFFEE

INTERIOR KITCHEN

CLOSEUP: Tap water filling carafe
SOUND EFFECT: Running water filling container

CLOSEUP: Measuring cup empties coffee into filter
SOUND EFFECT: Dry coffee filling filter

MEDIUM SHOT: Water-filled carafe moves toward filter; hits edge of sink; falls; breaks
SOUND EFFECT: Glass container hits object, (pause) shatters; water splashes

Coffee Cook: AAAaaarrrrrgggghhh!

The microphone is designed to precisely and correctly pick up and amplify incoming acoustic waves or harmonics and convert them to electrical signals. Depending on its sensitivity, the microphone will pick up the sound of someone's voice, sound from a musical instrument (see Figure 8-11), and any other sound that comes to it. Microphone sensitivity is directly related to how much feedback is around it, such as the shape of the room, the materials used, equalizers, and the position of the microphone.

QUICKTIP

When recording sound, be sure to consider the recording environment. Record in a soundproof room, or at the very least be sure to eliminate any unnecessary noise before you begin.

Narration, voiceovers, and interviews can be recorded directly into the computer. If music is included, a more complex system is needed. One way to transfer music or other sound into the computer is to use **digital audio tape (DAT) devices**. DAT devices convert analog sound into digital sound. These high-quality digital sounds are then stored in a digital format on digital audio tape (DAT). The DAT tape is then used to transfer the digital data (sounds) into the computer. Audio CDs that are made from DAT tape can also be used to transfer digital sounds into the computer. Other options for transferring digital sound into the computer include recording digital sounds directly from a synthesizer or using appropriate software to generate a digital audio file.

When you choose the settings at which to record sound for a multimedia Web site, you must consider your own system capabilities including storage and memory capacity, as well as the capabilities of the equipment on which your multimedia Web site might be delivered and viewed. The most common sampling rates are 11, 22, and 44 kHz. Most software programs and computer systems will support both mono and stereo recording and playback with an option for either an 8-bit or 16-bit sampling size or resolution.

The recording we have discussed thus far involves the use of waveform audio digitizers that convert sounds to a digital format by sampling the waveform thousands of times per second and then storing the file in a digital format. MIDI (Musical Instrument Digital Interface) offers another solution. MIDI is a standard format that was agreed on by the major manufacturers of musical instruments. The MIDI standard was established so musical instruments can communicate sound information with one another.

FIGURE 8-11

The right microphone is important in recording high-quality sound

To communicate, MIDI instruments have an "in" port and an "out" port that enable them to be connected to another MIDI-ready device such as a musical instrument or computer (see Figure 8-12). Some MIDI instruments also have a "through" port that allows several MIDI instruments to be daisy-chained, which means they are connected to one another in a series and able to communicate simultaneously. Today it is also possible to connect MIDI instruments directly to computers. This connection is possible through the use of an interface that translates messages between the computer and the MIDI instruments.

A MIDI file begins with an event, such as pressing a key on a MIDI keyboard. Information from this event, such as which key was pressed as well as how hard and how long it was pressed, is coded as a series of commands. This information is stored in a file, which can be sent from the computer to an instrument or device, such as a synthesizer or sound card, for playback. Because MIDI files contain instructions instead of the actual digitized sounds, they can be hundreds of times smaller than audio files. Working with MIDI requires specialized software and may require specialized equipment for recording and playback or a MIDI-compatible sound card.

To play music files that have been generated by digitally controlled musical equipment such as synthesizers and keyboards (MIDI files), your computer needs a MIDI synthesizer for the sound card. If a MIDI synthesizer is not available for your sound card, you will need external equipment, such as an electronic keyboard connected to your computer to play the MIDI file. The MIDI synthesizer probably will not sound as good as external equipment, but it is significantly less expensive.

FIGURE 8-12

A MIDI port is used to connect MIDI instruments to computers that also have a MIDI connector

MIDI out to MIDI in: the MIDI data from your musical instrument (for example, a keyboard) travels out of the instrument through the MIDI out port on the instrument to the MIDI in port of the computer's soundcard synthesizer. The soundcard then records what was played.

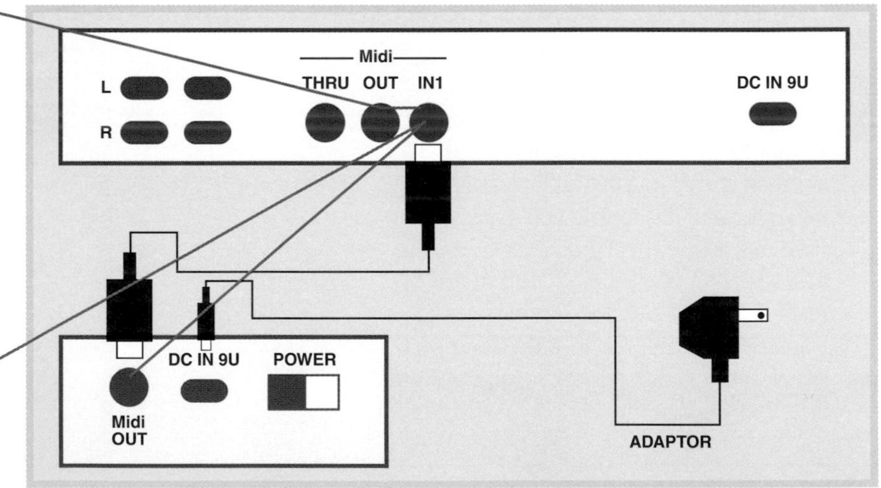

MIDI in to MIDI out: if you have an external synthesizer or would like to play a MIDI file from the computer to a MIDI-ready musical instrument, the MIDI data is sent out of the MIDI out port of the computer's soundcard to the MIDI in port of the synthesizer or musical instrument.

QUICKTIP

QuickTime, which is available as a free download, will play MIDI files.

Because a synthesizer is what reproduces the sound from the instructions in the MIDI file, sounds that cannot be reproduced by a synthesizer cannot be effectively stored in the MIDI format. For example, human voices and animal sounds are difficult to reproduce with a synthesizer, although advances in technology are making this more feasible. Also, the same MIDI file might sound different using different MIDI devices. The sound created by a MIDI file is not consistent across platforms and equipment. Therefore, MIDI files should be tested on a variety of different computer systems.

MIDI instruments make it possible and affordable for even novice musicians to import digital audio and music directly into the computer. If your musical talent is more highly developed, you can compose your own piece. Even if you are not musically inclined, keyboards and other instruments enable you to create thousands of special sound effects just by pressing a few buttons or depressing a few keys. If you are planning to create music for your multimedia Web sites by capturing sound directly from musical instruments, be sure your computer and the musical instruments you plan to connect it to are MIDI-ready.

Processing

At one time, sound recording and processing was an option only for those who could afford to purchase or rent expensive equipment and facilities. However, today's computers and synthesizers make it possible for the average person to produce high quality and relatively inexpensive recorded sound and music.

Once the sound has been sampled or digitized, it will probably need to be modified. Newer technologies, such as Comparisonics waveform displays, are available that allow audio specialists to see the sound file in color (see Figure 8-13), which conveys the frequency content of the audio data. This color coding can assist audio specialists in removing unwanted noise, pauses, and other mistakes. In addition, files may need to be trimmed. Fade-ins, fade-outs, background music, and special effects may need to be added. Pieces of sound files may need to be copied and moved or several sound files may need to be mixed and spliced together. All of this processing must be carefully completed to create sound that is appropriate and coordinated with the other media elements on the Web site.

FIGURE 8-13

Comparisonics waveform displays assist audio specialists in editing sound files

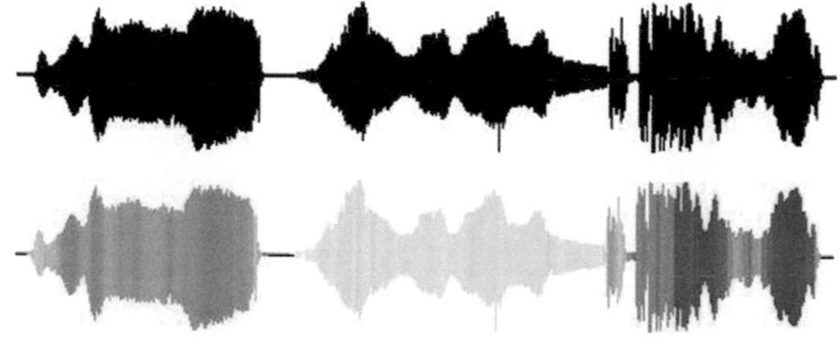

A cat (orange), a fly (lavender), and a rooster (red)

Using Comparisonics waveform displays, the audio specialist can quickly determine where within the waveform the sound changes from a cat, to a fly, to a rooster.

Assembling

Effectively incorporating sound into the Web site is very important. In fact, the success of Web audio depends not only on sampling the appropriate sound and effectively processing it, but also on correct timing and placement. Within the Web site the sound may be set up as a link (see Figure 8-14). In this example, the streaming sound file will begin playing as soon as the user clicks the link to the appropriate song.

> **QUICKTIP**
>
> When linking to sound files, it is a good idea to let your users know what to expect, including file type and size, such as "Song About a Rainbow" (30K .mp3).

Sound files can also be embedded in a Web page. This is the best technique to use if you want background music at your Web site. When a sound file is embedded it begins to load when the page loads and either plays automatically or a controller appears on the screen, which allows the user to control when or if the sound file will be played.

Sound can also be assembled directly into an animation or video clip that can then be embedded on the Web page. Animation software, such as Flash, allows developers to sync sound with the other media elements that have been created and then combine them into one cohesive element that can be included at the site.

SMPTE timecodes were developed by the Society of Motion Picture and Television Engineers for frame-accurate video and audio data. These timecodes help editors keep the different audio and video elements properly synchronized. By using professional SMPTE codes, beats of music can be set to match changes in video for all standard video frame rates.

Most authoring tools and animation programs allow you to import sound files by choosing import from the File command on the menu bar. You can select the sound file you wish to import, and it will appear in the program where it can generally be moved to an audio player or to a particular frame on a timeline. In some programs, special layers are reserved for voice and special sound effects, and others layers are used for background music. If two different sounds are placed in the same frame on different layers, the sounds will play at the same time. Be sure the volume is set so that the narration is heard over the background music. The appropriate volume should be set during the recording process, however many animation and authoring programs also allow you to make adjustments.

FIGURE 8-14

When the play button is clicked, the selected sound file plays

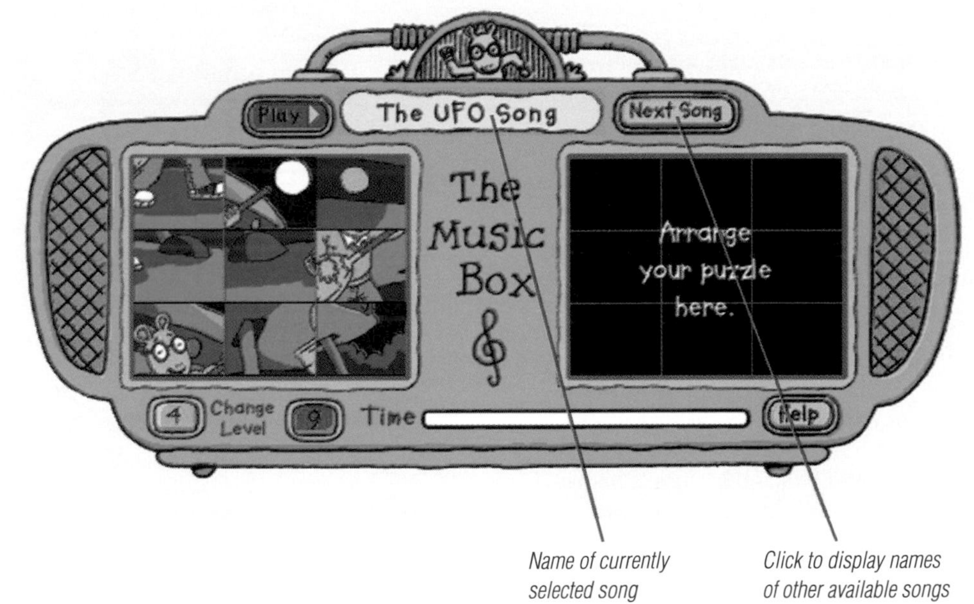

Delivering

Once a sound has been recorded, digitized, processed, and assembled into the Web pages of a site, it is ready to be delivered. In preparing the sound for delivery, consider the number of different sounds to be delivered, how they will be delivered, where they will be delivered, and to whom they will be delivered. In other words, the Web site may include one voice and some background music, or it may be a presentation with various different types of music, narration, and special effects. It may be delivered via a high-bandwidth intranet connection or to the global Internet community under possible low-bandwidth constraints.

To play sound on a computer system, the user will need a sound card and speakers or a headset. The digital audio file is sent through a **digital-to-analog converter (DAC)** so that it can be heard. Because the dynamic range of sound is dependent on the sound card, the delivery system varies from one computer to another when audio is included on the Web. Be sure to provide a controller on your Web site so that users have the ability to control what they want to hear, when they want to hear it, and at what volume it will be played (see Figure 8-15).

QUICKTIP

Know how your sound file will be delivered before you save it. A file sampled at 22 kHz will save disk space and is often adequate for the Web.

A high-quality sound system will help ensure that the sounds you have worked hard to create make the right impression. Unfortunately, there is no guarantee that the user visiting your Web site will have a high-quality sound system. As always, it is important to test your sounds under a variety of different conditions and possibilities.

In addition to hardware, many sound files delivered via the Web require players or helper applications to be heard. Many players come standard with the operating system or Web browser while others must be installed.

QUICKTIP

When incorporating sound into your Web site, accurately time narration so it occurs with the appropriate elements, keep background sounds at a volume that complements voices, and remove any unnecessary interruptions.

FIGURE 8-15

Sound files either play automatically or a controller is available that allows the user to control when they are played

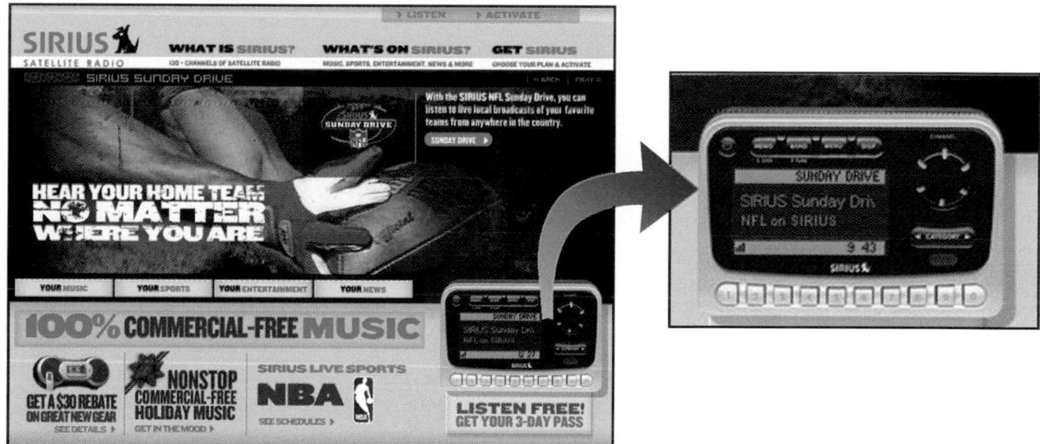

CONCEPT 4

EXPLORE DIGITAL
Audio Software

What You'll Learn

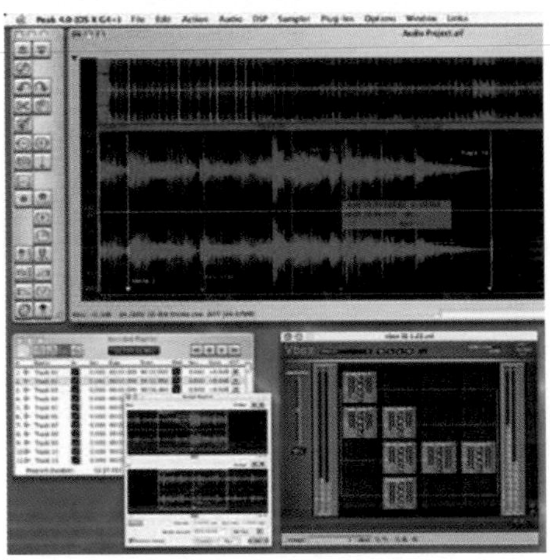

In this lesson, you will learn about some of the leading software programs for editing and mixing digital audio.

As seen in Figure 8-16, traditional sound studio equipment utilized to record, mix, and edit audio costs tens of thousands of dollars. With sound editing and mixing software, you can now produce your own sound files for much less money.

There are many different types of audio tools. Off-the-shelf recorders and converters that allow you to change the audio file format often come with your computer's operating system. If your audio authoring needs are more sophisticated, there are several excellent professional audio-authoring packages available. As is generally true with most software packages, there are a few companies that have become leaders in providing professional solutions. In the sound editing and mixing industry, two of these leaders are Bias and Sony. There are also a number of high-quality shareware packages worth mentioning, such as SoundEdit Pro, AudioEdit Deluxe, and ADC Sound Recorder.

FIGURE 8-16

Sound editing software is generally a much cheaper way to mix audio for a multimedia Web site than using traditional sound studio equipment

BIAS

Berkley Integrated Audio Software (BIAS) is a leader in developing solutions for sound editing and mixing. The company offers a number of different sound-editing products each of which serves a slightly different need and audience. These products include Peak and Deck. A brief discussion of Peak follows.

Peak

Peak is a leading digital audio editor for the Macintosh platform (see Figure 8-17). Peak is ideal for manipulating sound files. It touts the fastest and most intuitive waveform editing available on any platform. Using Peak you can modify many sound properties including volume, pitch, and tempo. Sounds modified with Peak can be imported into multimedia Web sites, animations, and authoring programs.

Peak supports a variety of file formats. It also enables you to digitally capture music and sound directly from CD and supports automated Redbook CD burning direct from the playlist as well as from any audio document window. RedBook is the international storage standard for compact disc audio. It allows audio segments on CDs to be addressed by minutes, seconds, and frames.

When first started, Peak opens with an empty, untitled window, a control palette, and a selection window. The Peak window includes a title bar, track information, measurements for time and amplitude, and a waveform area. At the bottom of the window is the transport window, which offers playback controls and high-precision meters.

Once a sound has been recorded or opened, the sound is displayed in the Peak window. In this window, time displays horizontally from left to right, while amplitude displays vertically from top to bottom. Portions of the sound file can be selected by dragging over the sound file or entering numbers into the value boxes. Once selected, portions of the file can be cut, copied, or otherwise modified.

FIGURE 8-17
Peak by Bias is a sound editing software program for the Macintosh platform

There are many special effects that can be applied to a sound file or a portion of a sound to emphasize a point, stimulate emotions, define space, and add realism. A description of some of the many sound effects available in Peak are presented in Figure 8-18. Although the possibilities for adding sound effects seem limitless, keep in mind that there are drawbacks to using sound effects, which include taking time to process and making your sound files bigger.

Sony

Sony is a leading developer and marketer of digital media and Internet software tools. Sony has developed several software solutions that enable consumers to create and capture audio, edit the content, and deliver it via the Web. Among others, Sony's digital audio tools include the award-winning Sound Forge, Vegas, and ACID.

Sound Forge

Sound Forge is similar to Peak, however Sound Forge is designed for the Windows platform. Sound Forge provides a great introduction to digital audio editing software. Its powerful audio processing tools allow you to create high-quality audio for your Web sites. You can record your own audio and then enhance it with different effects and processes. Sound Forge offers an easy-to-use interface and intuitive features. You can even use it to open and save files in a number of different audio formats and to create streaming audio content.

Sound Forge offers many of the same editing features available in Peak. When you start Sound Forge, the data window (as shown in Figure 8-19) opens, which is where you will edit your sound files. In addition to the data window, the main screen also includes the typical program title bar, menu bar, and status bar. The standard toolbar provides quick access to many commonly used commands and the transport toolbar provides controllers, such as record, play, rewind, and fast forward among others.

FIGURE 8-18
Examples of sound effects

Sound effect	Description
Fades	You can set the file to fade in and out. Fade sound effects are effective in providing a professional transition from one sound to another. Generally, fade in is applied at the beginning of the sound file and fade out is applied at the end.
Envelopes	You can apply the envelope sound effect to stereo files. The envelope sound effect transitions the sound from the left speaker to the right speaker or from a rear speaker to a front speaker.
Equalizer	By using the equalizer sound effect, you can control the bass and treble as well as emphasize and stretch frequencies.
Echo and reverberation	The echo and reverberation sound effects make audio files sound as if they were recorded in a stadium, a concert hall, or even outer space.
Pitch shift	The pitch shift sound effect allows you to actually change the sound. It is particularly effective in altering a voice so that it sounds entirely different from the original.
Normalize	The normalize sound effect amplifies a sound file to its maximum value without distorting the sound.
Backward	The backward sound effect allows you to play a sound file backward.
Tempo	The tempo sound effect changes the tempo or speed at which the sound file plays.

When you set up a new data window, you can choose from several options. You can set the quality of the sound file including the sample rate, the resolution or sample size, and whether you want the sound file to be mono or stereo. Once you have set up the new data window, you can record or sample sound. You can record new data or record over existing data. You can record from CD, microphone, LP, tape, or musical instrument. Before you begin recording you can check the level of your input source. Colored meters light up to indicate the recording volume of the input device.

The edit operations used most often include cut, copy, paste, delete, trim/crop, and mix. Mixing allows you to combine two sounds together into one. This feature makes the creation of complex sound effects fast and simple. In the mix dialog box you can even control the volume for the two sound files being mixed. After processing, the sound files can be mixed down to create a stereo file that contains preset volume or you can apply a full range of effects (see Figure 8-20), including distortion, fade in/out, remove noise, pan, pitch bend, reverb, smooth/enhance, and time compress/expand. And of course you have access to unlimited Undo and Redo features so that you can revert your audio files to any previously edited stage. Sound Forge even allows you to synchronize a music file to a video clip.

FIGURE 8-19

The data window in Sound Forge

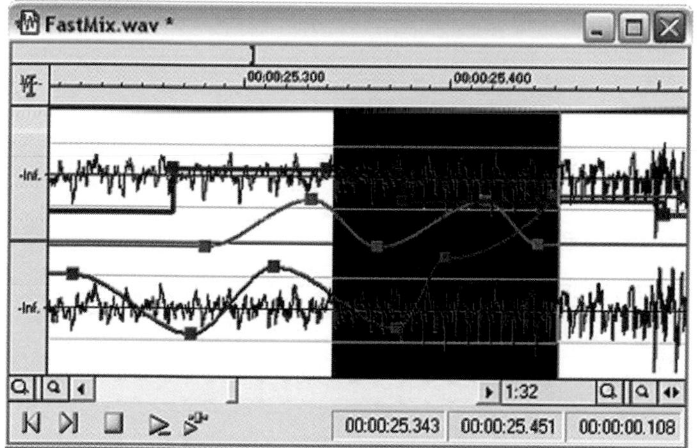

FIGURE 8-20

Sound Forge offers many different digital audio effects and processes

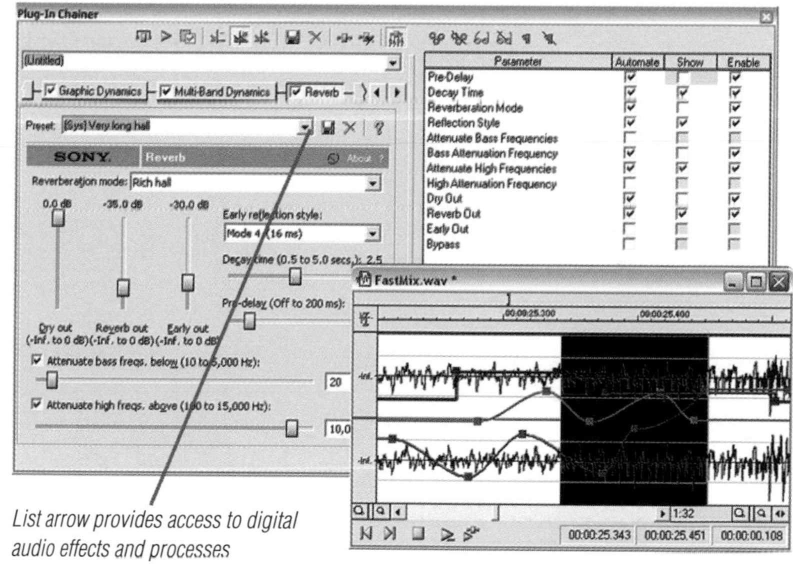

Vegas

If you are interested in multitrack recording and complex audio arrangement, Vegas is the tool you need. Vegas gives you frame-by-frame audio and video synchronization (see Figure 8-21) to produce high-quality streaming media. Unlike Sound Forge, which allows you to work with only a single track for recording, playing, editing, and mixing sound files, Vegas offers simple drag-and-drop operations that allow you to precisely and visually align, cut, paste, move, and crossfade audio events on multiple tracks or synchronize it with video. It also gives multimedia Web developers the ability to add URL captions and markers that automatically synchronize Web pages with media files.

ACID

ACID by Sony (see Figure 8-22) is music production software that offers musicians and media professionals the freedom to create custom music. It includes a library of professionally recorded loops that ACID can match to the tempos of your own music. It offers an unlimited number of tracks as well as the ability to adjust the volume, pan, and effects for each track. In addition, you can preview the effects before actually applying them. ACID is also MIDI-compatible. It supports MIDI files and software. You can use it to modify sounds created from MIDI instruments, including synthesizers and keyboards, or create your own MIDI files.

Examples of Other Software

There are hundreds of other programs on the market for sound production and editing. These programs range in price as well as functionality. Two, Digidesign Pro Tools and Adobe Audition, are discussed next.

Digidesign Pro Tools

Digidesign is a division of Avid. It is the world's leading nonlinear audio editing workstation and solutions manufacturer. Digidesign has developed state-of-the-art solutions for complete audio development for movies, multimedia, and the Web. Digidesign's Pro Tools is the most powerful and popular high-end audio solution on the market. Digidesign's Pro Tools is a complete, cross-platform package of hardware and software tools for every step in the creative media process. There are tools available for synthesizing, sampling, recording, editing, mixing, mastering, and distributing. Although more commonly used in the movie industry, this package is also widely touted by multimedia professionals including Web professionals.

Adobe Audition

Adobe Audition, formerly Cool Edit, is a digital audio software package that is comprehensive, yet easy to learn. It includes extensive top-quality digital effects and it can mix multiple tracks. Once you have recorded or loaded a file, you can cut, paste, and move audio around just as you do in any other sound editing package. It supports a variety of file formats and offers powerful analysis tools. You can examine the frequency components and other details about your audio.

FIGURE 8-21
Use Vegas to edit multiple tracks, including synchronizing audio tracks with video tracks

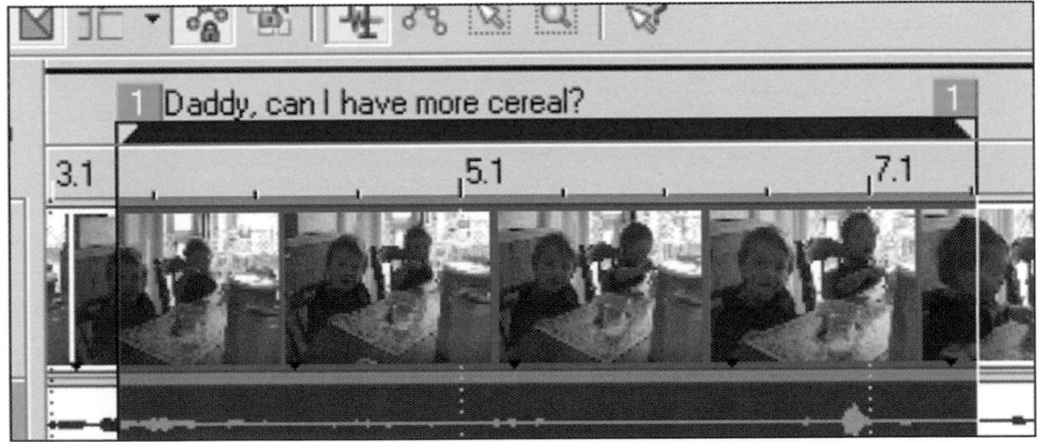

FIGURE 8-22
ACID is music production software by Sony

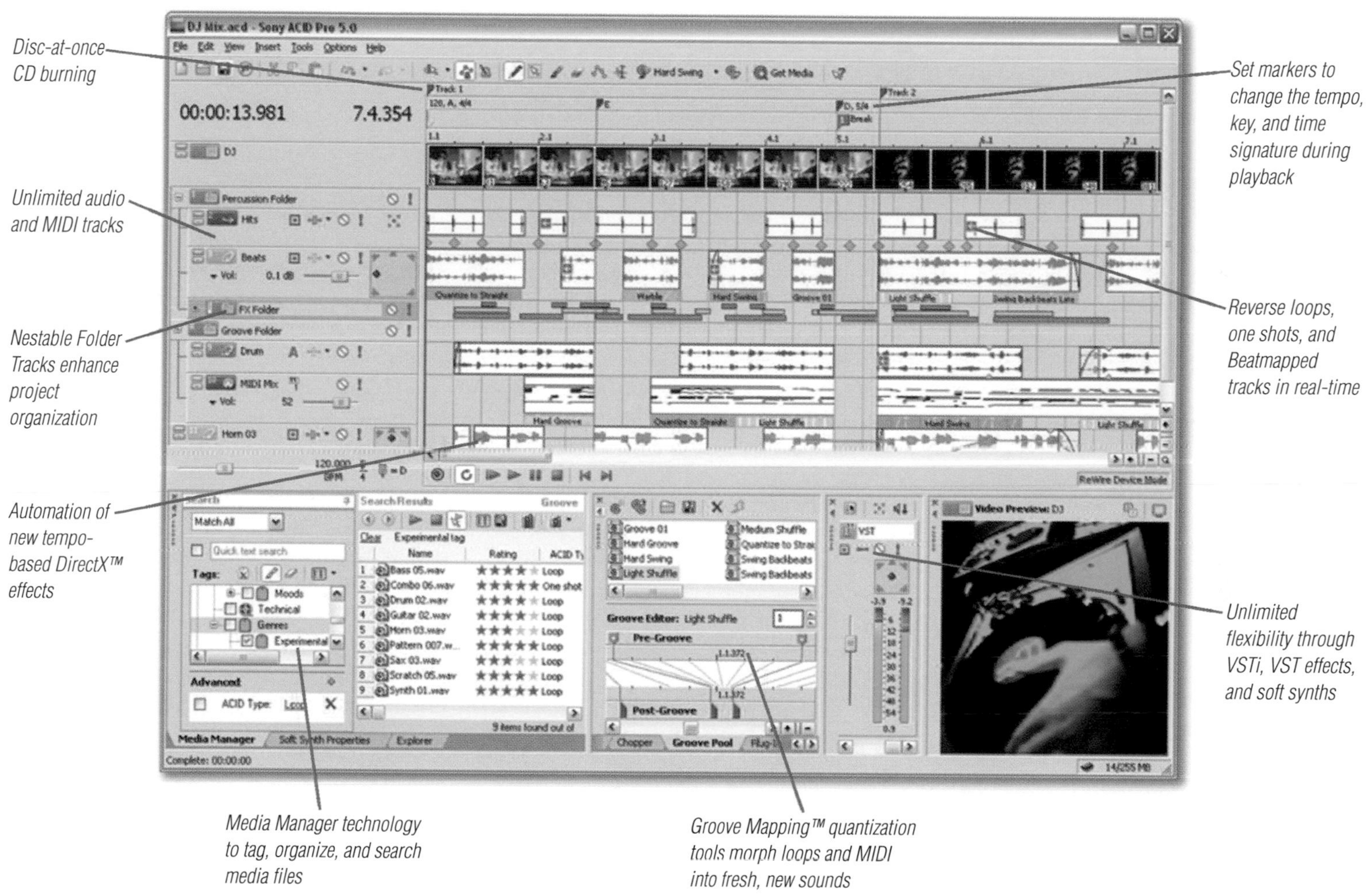

Disc-at-once CD burning
Unlimited audio and MIDI tracks
Nestable Folder Tracks enhance project organization
Automation of new tempo-based DirectX™ effects
Set markers to change the tempo, key, and time signature during playback
Reverse loops, one shots, and Beatmapped tracks in real-time
Unlimited flexibility through VSTi, VST effects, and soft synths
Media Manager technology to tag, organize, and search media files
Groove Mapping™ quantization tools morph loops and MIDI into fresh, new sounds

CONCEPT 5

DISCOVER AUDIO FILE FORMATS for the Web

What You'll Learn

In this lesson, you will learn about the common digital audio file formats used on multimedia Web sites.

Just as there are a variety of graphic and animation formats, there are also different audio file formats. All three media players QuickTime, RealPlayer, and Windows Media Player are equipped to open and display most popular audio file formats and possess the ability to play live streaming audio. All three players provide equally good audio quality. However, in the final analysis, QuickTime and RealPlayer are probably the best choices for streaming media in terms of their ability to support a variety of different media file formats. Figure 8-23 lists the audio file formats supported by each player at the time of this writing.

AAC

AAC (Advanced Audio Coding) is at the core of the MPEG-4 specification and is the new audio format of choice for Internet, wireless, and digital broadcast arenas. AAC provides audio encoding that compresses much more efficiently than older formats such as MP3, yet delivers quality rivaling that of uncompressed CD audio. AAC takes full advantage of advances in perceptual audio coding and compression, resulting in higher-quality output at lower data rates, allowing even dial-up users access to quality sound.

AIFF

AIFF or **AIF (Audio Interchange File Format**) is Apple's Macintosh waveform format. However, it is also supported on Windows and Unix machines. The AIFF format supports a large number of sampling rates up to 32 bits.

AU

AU (Audio/Basic) is the Sun audio format. It was developed by Sun Microsystems to be used on Unix, NeXT, and Sun Sparc workstations. It is a 16-bit compressed audio format that is fairly prevalent on the Web because it plays on a wide number of platforms. Most browsers contain internal support for AU playback.

EA

EA (Emblaze Audio) is a sound format developed specifically for the Internet by GEO for its Emblaze products. It uses a revolutionary compression scheme that takes an audio file and shrinks it down up to one-fiftieth of its original size. This format also uses Java, a programming language, to play back the file without plug-ins, and streams the audio so that you start to hear the file before the file is completely downloaded.

MIDI

MIDI (Musical Instrument Digital Interface) is the internationally accepted file format for storing MIDI data. MIDI files have a .mid or .midi extension. The MIDI format is used to represent electronic music produced by a MIDI device (e.g., a synthesizer, sequencer, electronic keyboard, or drum machine). This format provides instructions on how to replay music; it does not actually record the waveform. In other words, there are MIDI codes for making notes loud or soft, turning them off or on, and changing their tone. MIDI is not music; it is instructions. For this reason, MIDI clips offer smaller file sizes than most other audio file formats. Because MIDI files are small and efficient, they are fairly common on the Web.

FIGURE 8-23

A sampling of Web-based audio file formats played by the three most common players—QuickTime, Windows Media Player, and RealPlayer

Player	Audio File Formats Supported
QuickTime	• AAC • AIFF • AU • MIDI • MOV • MP3 • RA, RAM, RM • SWF • WAV • WMA
Windows Media Player	• AIFF • AU • MIDI • MOV • MP3 • RA, RAM, RM • WAV • WMA
RealPlayer	• AIFF • AU • MIDI • MOV • MP3 • RA, RAM, RM • SWF • WAV • WMA

MP3

MP3 (Moving Picture Experts Group (MPEG)—Audio Layer 3) is an open standard technology that uses file compression to create near-CD quality audio files that are small enough to be distributed via the Web. The MP3 format offers compression up to a factor of 14:1. Using MP3 compression, a typical 600 MB audio CD can be turned into a 50 MB MP3 collection. The compression scheme looks at samples of audio data and removes noise and redundant information not closely associated with the data recognized as "real music." The result is a close reproduction whose differences would be detected only by an incredibly sophisticated ear. In addition, through the process of "streaming," users can download MP3 files in segments and listen to them as they are downloaded. This is the most common file format and data reduction scheme for delivering audio on the Web. These files are high quality yet small and quick to load. In addition, this file type supports streaming.

QuickTime (MOV)

QuickTime (MOV) is another Apple file format. Although QuickTime files are most often used for animation and video, you can store audio alone in this file format. Because QuickTime files are platform independent and among the most convenient and powerful formats for storing data, this is a fine choice for storing audio with or without animation and video. Although QuickTime files require the QuickTime player to be heard, this player has been widely distributed and most users will already have access to it.

Real (RA, RAM, RM)

RealNetworks has been a leader in both developing and acquiring the latest in cutting-edge streaming media technologies. The current Real formats **(RA, RAM, RM)** offer excellent compression and incredibly popular and widespread support for streaming audio on the Internet. Like many of the media elements discussed thus far, Real files require a plug-in or player to be heard. RealPlayer can be downloaded and installed for free.

SWF

SWF is a compressed Macromedia Flash or Shockwave Flash file type that is designed for animation. Because SWF files are quite small and they support streaming, they can also be used for delivering audio alone. The content of SWF files cannot be edited and the Flash player is needed to listen to these files.

WAV

WAV is the Waveform format. It is a commonly used and supported format on the Windows platform. Developed by Microsoft, the Wave format is a subset of RIFF. RIFF is capable of sampling rates of 8- and 16-bits. When developing sound for the Internet, it is important to make sure you use the encoding method that the player you are recommending supports. Because the QuickTime player will also play WAV files, it can be used to deliver audio via the Web.

WMA

WMA (Windows Media Audio) offers a powerful compression technology for delivering audio and video quality at any bit rate, with features designed to provide superior quality at dial-up rates, as well as home-theater-like experiences over broadband connections or for download and play. Windows Media Audio codecs are automatically downloaded by the Windows Media Player.

Several popular players are shown in Figure 8-24. These players are either installed with an operating system or a browser, or downloaded via the Web for free.

FIGURE 8-24
Many sound file formats require players to be heard

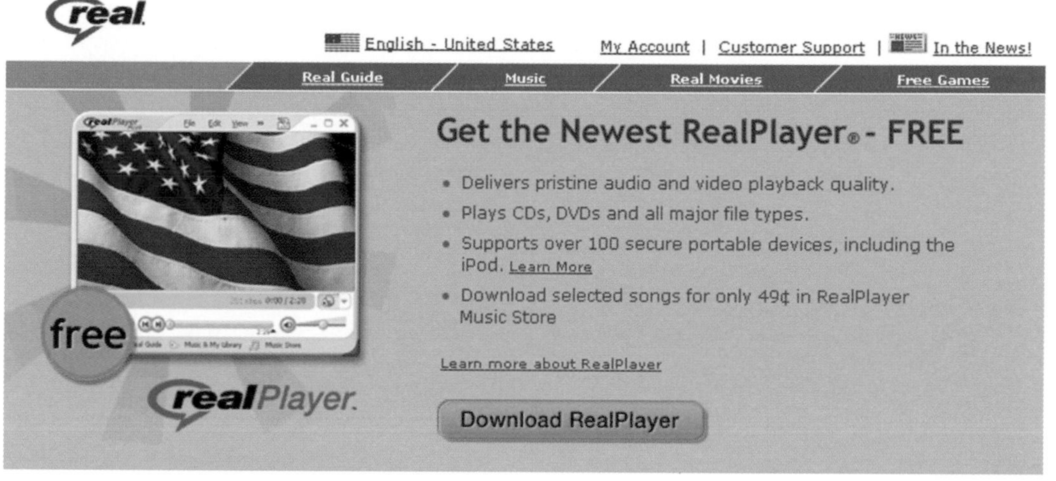

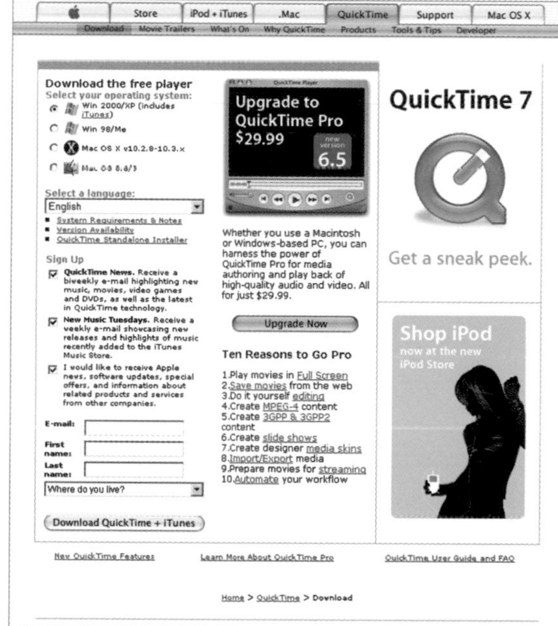

SUMMARY

Sound can be an extremely powerful element on a Web site. It can be used to get attention, to entertain, to give directions, to personalize an interface, or to convey an educational or persuasive message. Sound can be effectively added to Web sites, such as those designed for computer-based training and education, advertising, e-commerce, as well as entertainment and games. To ensure the effectiveness of sound files on a multimedia Web site, it is important to follow general design guidelines for incorporating sounds files that are high quality and consistent with the goals of the project.

Sounds are classified as either **content sounds** that supply information or **ambient sounds**, such as background music, that set the mood. Audio specialists are responsible for recording and processing the audio files used in **splash screens** and on other pages of a multimedia Web site.

Vibrations created by sound are called **sound waves**. The recurring pattern in a sound wave is a **waveform**. The **amplitude**, the distance between the valley and the peak of the waveform, determines the volume of the sound. A **decibel (dB)** is the smallest variation in amplitude that can be detected by the human ear. The **frequency**, the number of peaks that occur in one second, determines its pitch, which is measured in **hertz (Hz)**, most commonly **kilohertz (kHz)**. To be understood and edited by the computer, **analog sounds** must be **sampled** or **digitized** to convert the sound to **digital audio**.

Sound quality affects the credibility and effectiveness of the Web site. Recording, playback environment, and equipment have an impact on the quality of sound. Several other factors also influence sound quality. The **sample rate** is the number of waveform samples per second. A higher sampling rate produces a higher-quality sound. **Resolution** or **sample size** is the number of binary bits processed for each sound wave. As the number of bits used to sample the sound increases, the range and the quality of the sound also improves. **Compression** is useful for storing and transferring sound files. **Mono sounds** are flat and unrealistic compared to **stereo sounds**, which are much more dynamic and lifelike. **Surround sound** or **3-D sound** attempts to create an encompassing experience by inserting delays into the sound recording. In general, as the quality of the sound file increases, so does the size of the file.

On the Web, audio is either **downloaded** or **streamed.** Downloaded audio files must be saved entirely to the user's computer before they can be played. Streaming is a more advanced process that allows the sound to be played as it is downloaded.

Sources from which you can obtain digital sound include **clip audio** and CD audio or you can create your own sound files. Producing your own sound files involves planning, recording, processing, assembling, and delivering the sound files. **Microphones** use an **analog-to-digital converter (ADC)** that translates analog signals into electrical impulses. Analog sounds can also be converted to digital sounds from **digital audio tape (DAT)**. **MIDI (Musical Instrument Digital Interface)** enables recording to occur directly into the computer from a musical instrument. Once the digitized sound is in the computer, it will need to be processed, assembled, and delivered. To convert the digital sound back to an analog format, a **digital-to-analog converter (DAC)** is used.

Different software programs are available for recording and processing digital sound. Bias has developed Peak, which supports Redbook CD burning, and Deck for the Macintosh platform. Sony offers a number of solutions including Sound Forge for single-track editing. This program also supports **SMPTE** timecode, Vegas for multi-track editing and ACID for original music production. Digidesign, a division of Avid, offers an even more comprehensive set of tools, Pro Tools, for complete audio development. Adobe also has a sound editing application called Audition.

There are many different types of digital audio file formats including **AAC**, **AIFF**, **AU**, **EA**, **MIDI**, **MP3**, **RA**, **RAM**, **RM**, **SWF**, **WAV**, and **WMA**. Before choosing a file format you should investigate and experiment with the various options. Most of the file formats store a digitized version of a waveform file. The MIDI format does not. A MIDI file is not a recorded sound file, but instructions that dictate how the sound file is replayed on the user's computer.

Many Web-based audio formats require a player to be heard by the user. The three most common players—Windows Media Player, RealPlayer, and QuickTime—are free and widely distributed.

KEY TERMS

3-D sound
AAC
AIFF
ambient sound
amplitude
analog sound
analog-to-digital converter (ADC)
AU
clip audio
compression
content sound
decibel (dB)
digital audio
digital audio tape (DAT)
digital-to-analog converter (DAC)
digitizing
downloaded
EA
frequency
hertz (Hz)
kilohertz (kHz)
microphone
MIDI
mono sound
MOV
MP3
RA
RAM
resolution
RM
sample rate
sample size
SMPTE
sound sampling
sound wave
splash screen
stereo sound
streamed
surround sound
SWF
WAV
waveform
WMA

MATCHING QUESTIONS/DISCUSSION QUESTIONS

Match each term with the sentence that best describes it.

a. ambient	**b.** amplitude	**c.** analog sound
d. clip audio	**e.** compression	**f.** decibel
g. digital sounds	**h.** frequency	**i.** hertz (Hz)
j. Redbook	**k.** resolution	**l.** sample rate
m. sound sampling	**n.** streaming	**o.** waveform

_____ **1.** The distance between the valley and the peak of a waveform.

_____ **2.** The number of peaks that occur in one second.

_____ **3.** This is a continuous stream of sound waves.

_____ **4.** The smallest variation in amplitude that can be detected by the human ear.

_____ **5.** Prerecorded digital audio clips of music and sound effects.

_____ **6.** The number of waveform samples per second.

_____ **7.** A technique that mathematically reduces the size of a file.

_____ **8.** Advanced process that allows the sound to be played as it is downloading and before the entire file is transferred to the user's computer.

_____ **9.** Analog sounds that have been converted to numbers.

_____ **10.** The number of binary bits processed for each measurement.

_____ **11.** Sounds that reinforce messages and set the mood.

_____ **12.** The international storage standard for compact disc audio.

_____ **13.** Measurement used for frequency.

_____ **14.** Process of converting an analog sound to a digital sound; also called digitizing.

_____ **15.** The recurring pattern of an analog sound file.

Answer each question either in writing or in a class discussion as directed by your instructor.

1. How do content sounds differ from ambient sounds? When are music and special sound effects considered content sound?
2. What factors determine the quality of the sound file?
3. Why is it not always best to use the highest sampling rate and highest resolution when recording sound files?
4. Why is a high-quality microphone important when you are recording sound for a multimedia Web site?
5. If you are developing sound for a Web site, which sound file format should you use? Why?

DESIGN PROJECT

Working with Sound

1. Add sound to an animation
2. Edit sounds
3. Compress sound files
4. Add sound to a button

This is a continuation of the Design Project in Chapter 7.

The client, The Inn at Birch Bay, has reviewed the Web pages and has asked that sounds be added to the site.

The WebsByCT multimedia development team has decided that this project would be ideal for you to learn the basics of working with sound. To complete the lessons in this design project, you will be using Macromedia Flash to add background sound to the animated map and the sound of a click to the Play and Pause buttons. Then you will use Macromedia Dreamweaver to insert the new animation with sound into a Web page.

Sounds can be an important part of an interactive Web experience, and Macromedia Flash makes it easy to incorporate sounds into a movie. In addition, Macromedia Flash provides some basic editing features that allow you to add sound effects, such as fade-ins and fade-outs, edit sounds by trimming the sound waveform, and fluctuate the volume for various segments of the sound. In addition, you can choose from various compression options to optimize the trade-off between sound quality and file size. When working with sounds you begin by importing a sound file into the document Library panel. Macromedia Flash can import several popular file formats including the following:

- Waveform Audio File (.wav)
- Audio Interchanges File (.aif)
- MPEG-1 Audio level 3 (.mp3)
- Sound only QuickTime movies (.mov)
- SunAu (.au)

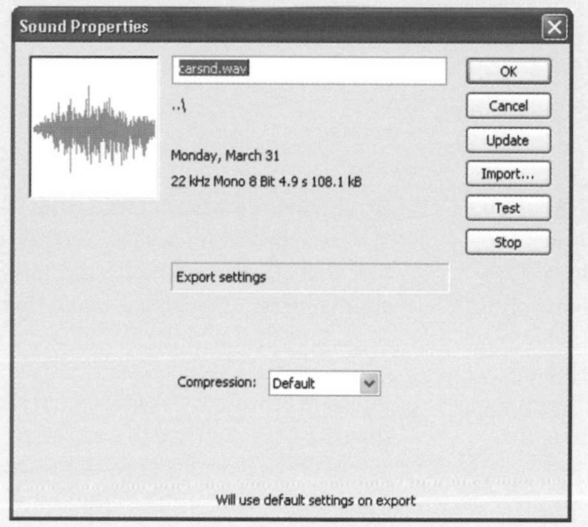
Sound Properties
carsnd.wav
..\
Monday, March 31
22 kHz Mono 8 Bit 4.9 s 108.1 kB
OK
Cancel
Update
Import...
Test
Stop
Export settings
Compression: Default
Will use default settings on export

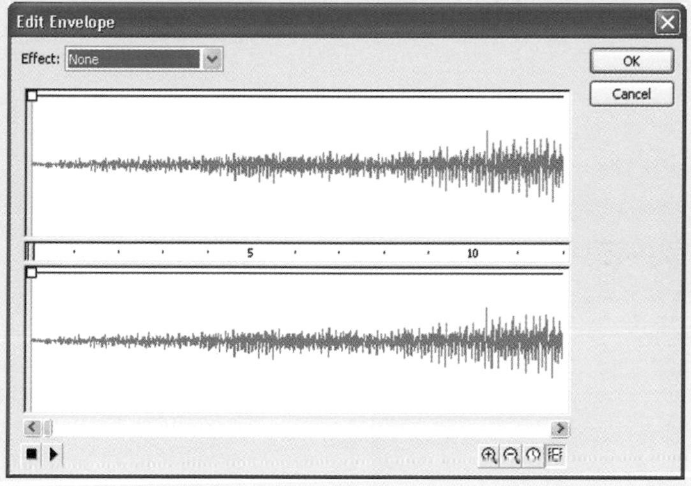
Edit Envelope
Effect: None
OK
Cancel
5
10

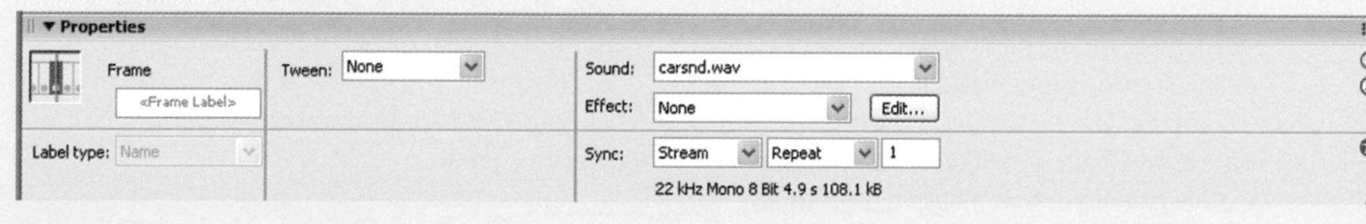
Properties
Frame
<Frame Label>
Tween: None
Sound: carsnd.wav
Effect: None
Edit...
Label type: Name
Sync: Stream
Repeat
1
22 kHz Mono 8 Bit 4.9 s 108.1 kB

Library - innmap.fla
9 items
Name
Kind
carsnd.wav
click.wav
inn_g
innphoto.jpg

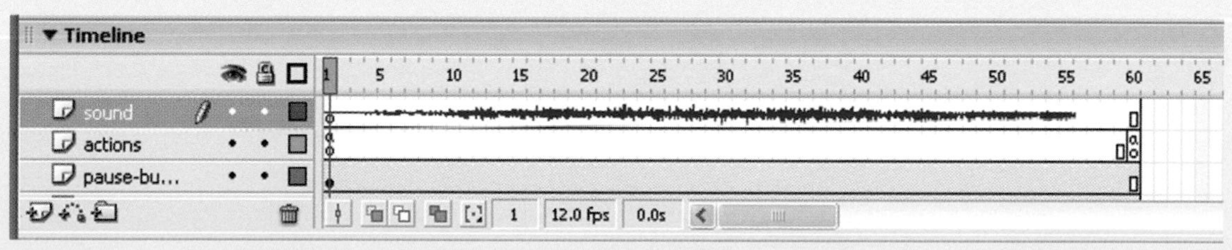
Timeline
sound
actions
pause-bu...
1
12.0 fps
0.0s

LESSON 1

ADD SOUND TO an Animation

What You'll Do

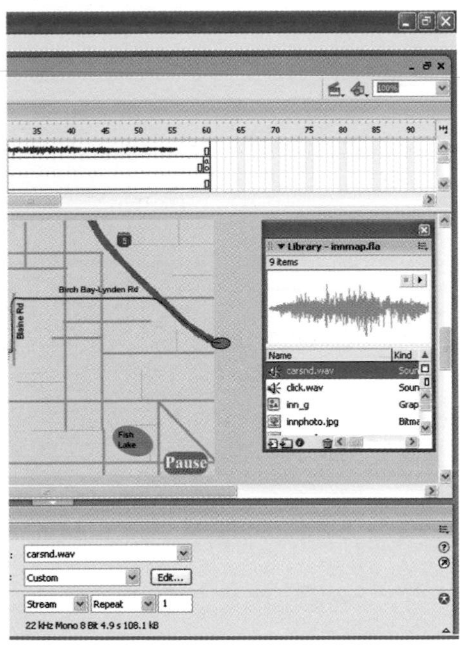

In this lesson, you will learn how to import sounds into the Library panel of a Macromedia Flash movie and add a background sound to an animation. You will begin by studying how sounds can be used in Macromedia Flash.

Macromedia Flash and Sounds

Macromedia Flash allows you to add sounds to objects, such as a button, or to the timeline as a background sound or a narration. When you want a sound to play in the background, you add a layer, insert a keyframe in the timeline where you want the sound to begin, and either drag the sound file from the Files panel to the stage or choose the sound file in the Property inspector. Sounds are represented on the timeline by a waveform, as shown in Figure 8-25, and will extend only to the last keyframe in the movie. If the duration of the sound is longer than the duration of the movie, the sound will continue playing unless you have provided controls or specified actions, such as a stop action in an ending frame.

Synchronization Options

Macromedia Flash provides a stream feature that allows a sound to start playing as your computer downloads it and then stops the playing of the sound at the end of the movie. This is useful when delivering sound through the Internet because the user does not have to wait for an entire sound file to download before the sound is played. In addition, streaming sounds allow you to synchronize animation and audio. If the computer playing a movie is slow, Macromedia Flash will skip frames of an animation in order to maintain synchronization. You set the sound to stream using the Sync option in the Property inspector panel.

Adding Sound Effects

Macromedia Flash also includes the following effects that you can apply to your sound:

- Left Channel will play the sound only in the left channel or speaker.
- Right Channel will play the sound only in the right channel or speaker.
- Fade Left to Right gradually shifts the sound from the left channel to the right channel over the duration of the sound.
- Fade Right to Left gradually shifts the sound from the right channel to the left channel over the duration of the sound.
- Fade In ramps up the volume of the sound as it begins to play.
- Fade Out diminishes the volume of the sound as it ends.

The Property inspector of the frame to which your sound is attached and the Edit Envelope dialog box for the sound can both be used for setting these effects. If your volume needs are not met by Fade In or Fade out, use the Custom option to create your own volume variations. This option provides you with a graphic representation of the volume across the duration of the sound that you can modify according to your needs.

FIGURE 8-25

The waveform representing a sound

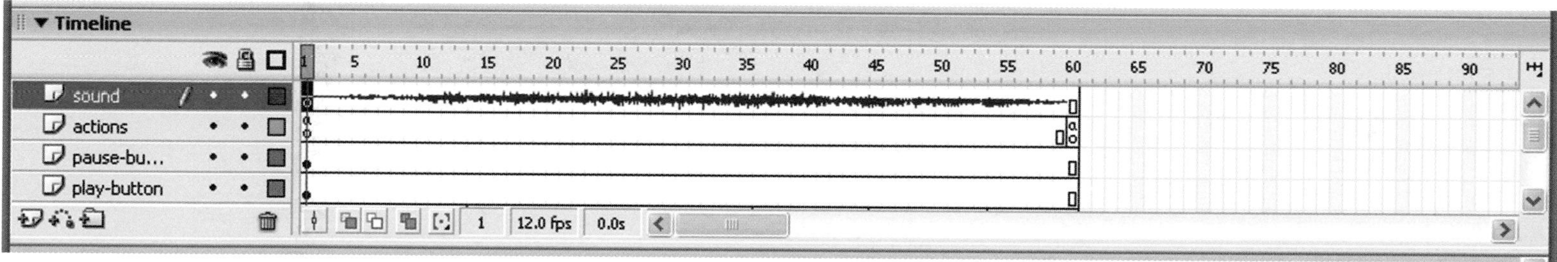

Add sound to an animation

1. Start Macromedia **Flash**, then open **innmap.fla** from the directions folder you created in the previous chapter.
2. Click **File** on the menu bar, point to **Import**, then click **Import to Library**.
3. Navigate to the location of the files for this lesson, select **carsnd.wav**, then click **Open** (PC) or **Import to Library** (Mac).
4. Click **File** on the menu bar, point to **Import**, then click **Import to Library**.
5. Navigate to the location of the files for this lesson, select **click.wav**, then click **Open** (PC) or **Import to Library** (Mac).
6. Click **actions** in the actions layer to select it.
7. Click **Insert** on the menu bar, point to **Timeline**, then click **Layer**.
8. Double-click **Layer 9**, delete the entry, type **sound**, then press **[Enter]** (PC) or **[return]** (Mac).

   Note: Your layer number may be different.
9. Click **Frame 1** of the sound layer.
10. Click the **down list arrow** for the Sound box in the Property inspector, then click **carsnd.wav** as shown in Figure 8-26.

    The sound waveform is displayed in the sound layer beginning in Frame 1.
11. Press **[Enter]** (PC) or **[return]** (Mac) to play the movie and hear the sound.

    Note: Mac users may need to click Frame 1 on the sound layer, and then press [return].
12. Save the document.

You added sound to an animation.

FIGURE 8-26

The Sound option in the Property inspector

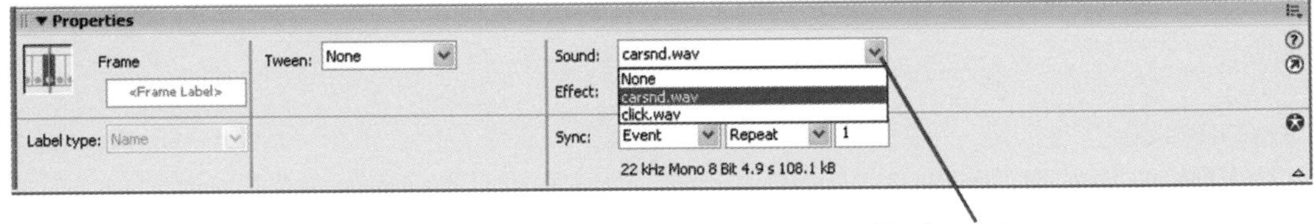

FIGURE 8-27

The completed Property inspector panel

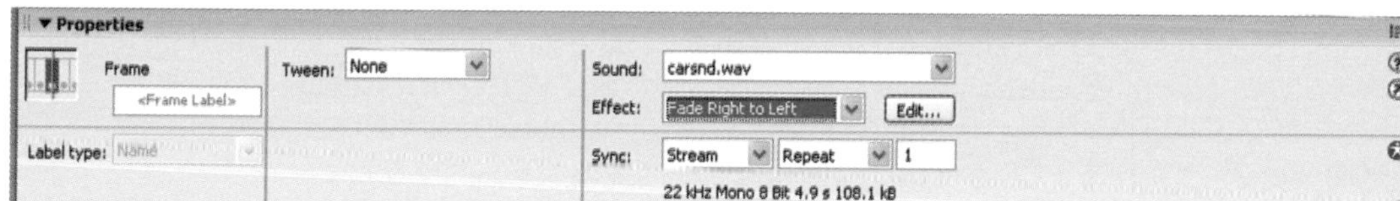

Apply a sound effect

1. Click **Frame 1** of the sound layer.
2. Click the **down list arrow** for the Sync box in the Property inspector, then click **Stream**.
3. Click the **down list arrow** for the Effect box in the Property inspector, then click **Fade Right to Left**.

   The Fade Right to Left will gradually change the sound output from the right speaker to the left speaker. This will give the impression of the sound playing in sync with the moving oval.
4. Verify the Repeat option in the Property inspector is set to **1**.
5. Verify your Property inspector panel resembles Figure 8-27.
6. **Save** the document.
7. Click **File** in the menu bar, point to **Publish Preview**, then click **Default – (HTML)**.
8. Click **Play** to start the movie and notice how the sound changes from one speaker to another.

   Note: If you have installed Windows XP Service Pack 2, you might need to allow blocked content to view the preview. To allow blocked content, click the Internet Security bar, and then select Allow Blocked Content.
9. Close the browser, then return to the Macromedia Flash document.

You applied a fade sound effect.

LESSON 2

EDIT Sounds

What You'll Do

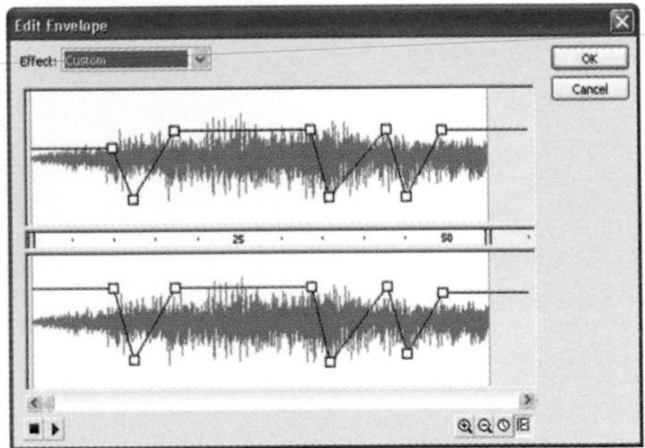

In this lesson, you will learn how to edit sounds including trimming the waveform and adjusting the volume using the Edit Envelope feature.

Editing Sound in Macromedia Flash

Macromedia Flash includes some basic editing features to use on sounds you have imported. A discussion of some of the ways you can edit sounds using the Edit Envelope dialog box shown in Figure 8-28 follows:

a. You can trim the length of a sound file by dragging the Trim buttons in from either end of the waveform. This reduces the length of the waveform, by eliminating either or both ends of the sound.

b. You can adjust the volume for selected segments of the sound. The Edit Envelope dialog box is divided into two channels, top and bottom (corresponding to your speakers, left and right respectively). The handles (up to eight per sound), are used to adjust the volume of different segments of the sound. In Figure 8-29 the volume begins at a middle setting, then decreases about Frame 10 reaching a low level at about Frame 12, then starts increasing again. You can drag the handles to change the volume as desired. You can use up to eight handles. New handles are displayed by clicking the line, and handles can be removed by dragging them to the center of the Edit Envelope dialog box.

The Play Sound button at the bottom-left corner of the Edit Envelope dialog box allows you to preview the changes. You can switch the units in the center of the dialog box to display as seconds or as frames. This helps when you need to make frame-by-frame adjustments to a waveform.

FIGURE 8-28
The Edit Envelope dialog box

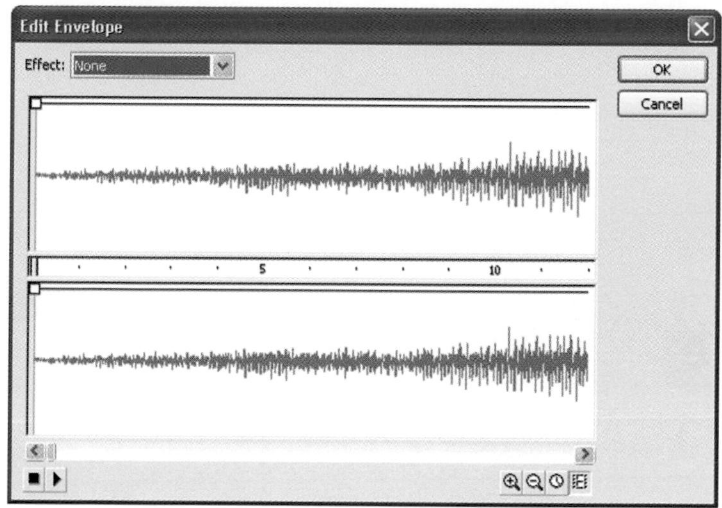

FIGURE 8-29
Setting the handles to adjust the volume

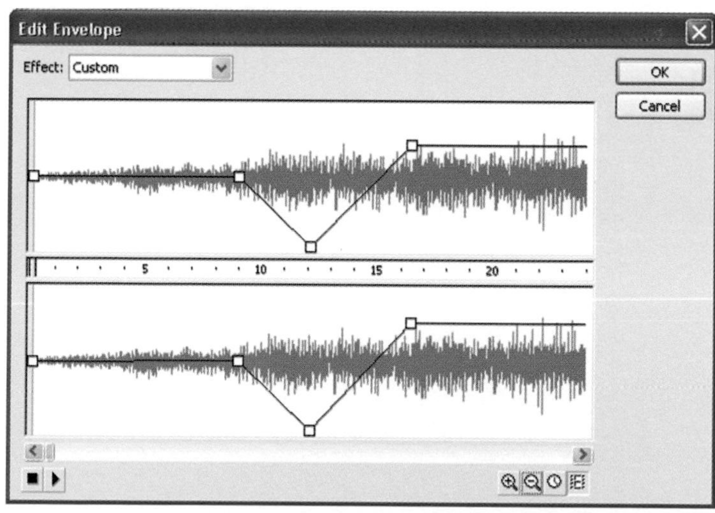

Trim a sound clip

1. Click **Frame 1** on the sound layer.
2. Click **Edit** in the Property inspector.
3. Click the **Frames button** in the Edit Envelope dialog box, if necessary, to set the view to frames.
4. Click the **Zoom out button** twice to display all 60 frames of the movie.

   The Edit Envelope dialog box displays the two channels and the results of applying the Fade Right to Left effect. Notice the diagonal line in the bottom channel (right speaker) starts high and ends low, indicating that the sound in this channel will be at the loudest level in Frame 1 and will fade to no sound in Frame 60. Conversely, the line in the top channel (left speaker) starts low and ends high, indicating that the sound in this channel will be absent in Frame 1 and will increase to the loudest level in Frame 60.
5. Click the **Play Sound button** in the Edit Envelope dialog box to play the sound.
6. Drag the **Trim** button in the Edit Envelope dialog box from Frame 60 to Frame 55 as shown in Figure 8-30.

   Frame 55 is where the inn photo first appears, so the sound can end at this frame.
7. Click **OK**.

(continued)

FIGURE 8-30
Dragging the Trim button

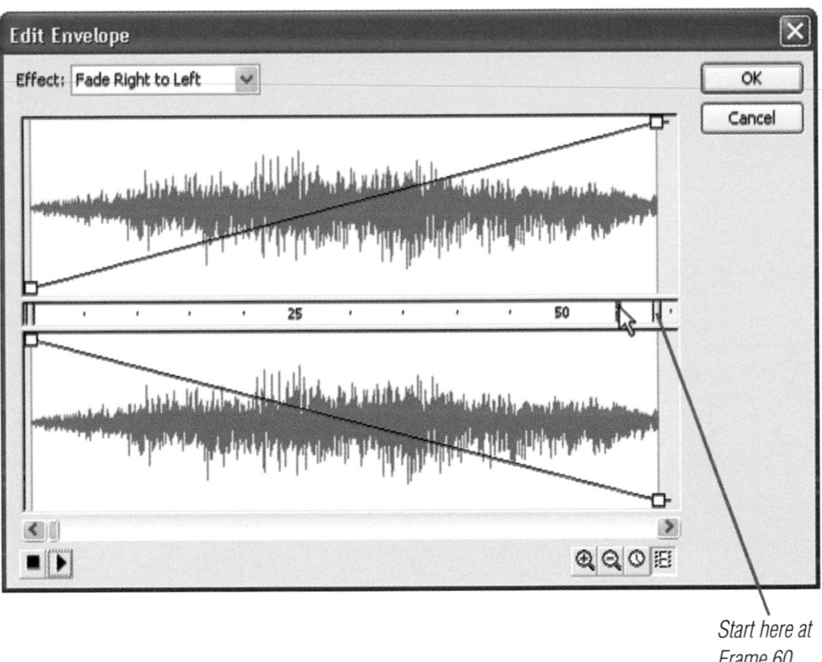

FIGURE 8-31

Dragging a handle

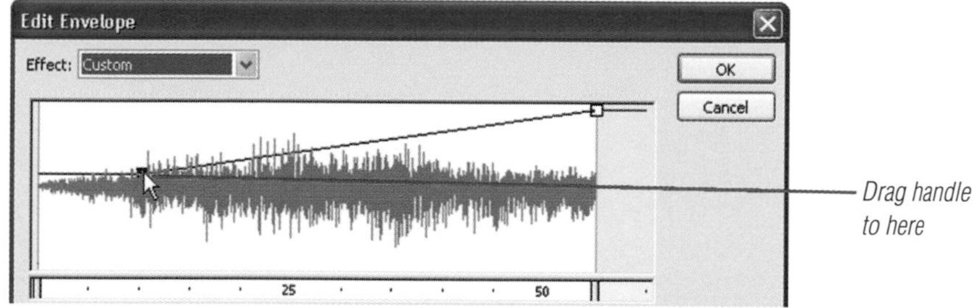

FIGURE 8-32

Adding a handle and dragging it to a new position

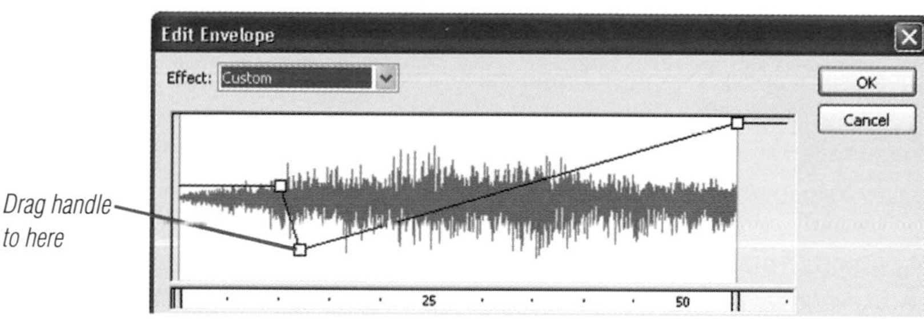

FIGURE 8-33

The completed Edit Envelope dialog box

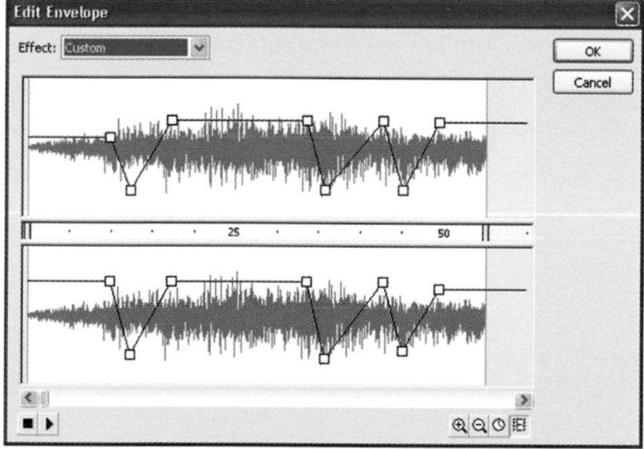

8. Save the document, preview the movie in a browser and then click the **Play button** to test it, then return to the Macromedia Flash document.

You used the Edit Envelope dialog box to trim a sound waveform.

Edit a sound

1. Click **Frame 1** on the sound layer.
2. Click **Edit** in the Property inspector.
3. Verify the Frames view is displayed and all 55 frames of the waveform are displayed.
4. Drag the **handle** in the bottom-left corner of the top channel to the position shown in Figure 8-31.
5. Click the line to the right of the handle to display another handle, then **drag** it to the position shown in Figure 8-32.
6. Continue to click the line in the top channel to display handles and **drag** them to duplicate Figure 8-33, then repeat by dragging handles in the bottom channel.
7. Click the **Play Sound button** ▶ in the Edit Envelope dialog box to play the sound.

   Adjusting the lines will cause the volume to adjust in synch with the curves on the animation. This gives the impression that the oval object is slowing down at each curve.
8. Click **OK**, then save the document.
9. Play the movie in a browser, then return to the Macromedia Flash document.

You used the Edit Envelope dialog box to trim a sound waveform.

LESSON 3

COMPRESS SOUND Files

What You'll Do

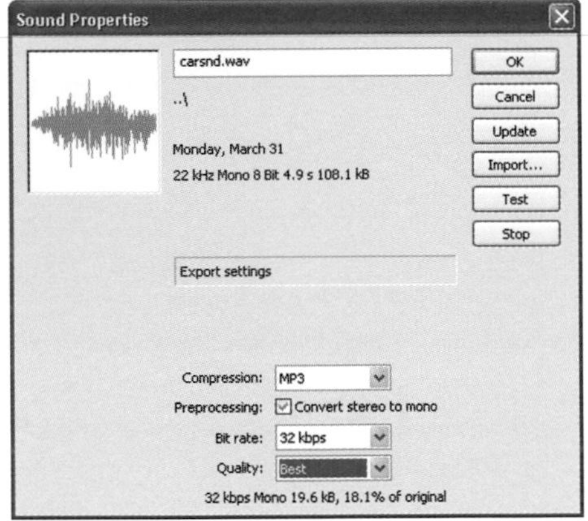

In this lesson, you will learn how to compress a sound file in order to reduce the size of a published movie.

Understanding Compression Options

Adding sound to a movie can increase the file size of the published movie. Macromedia Flash includes a number of options for compressing or reducing the sampling rate of sounds. Depending on the options you choose there may be a trade-off in the quality of the sound. Be sure to test your exported movies so that any trade-offs are acceptable. The Sound Properties dialog box, shown in Figure 8-34, is used to select compression options. Macromedia Flash includes the following compression options:

ADPCM (Adaptive Differential Pulse Code Modulation)
This option is best for short sounds, such as those used for buttons or accents. When you select this option, you can also set whether the sound is converted from stereo to mono (which will reduce the file size), a sampling rate (a lower sampling rate degrades sound quality but reduces file size), and number of bits (again, a lower bit rate reduces both sound quality and file size).

MP3 (MPEG-1 Audio Layer 3)
This option is used primarily for music and longer streaming sounds, but can also be applied to speech. When you select this option, you can also select a bit rate (20 kbps or higher is recommended for music), whether the sound is converted from stereo to mono, and an option for compression speed/sound quality (the Fast option increases download speed for Web delivery, although it may result in poorer sound quality).

Raw
This option exports a sound with no compression, although you can select to convert stereo to mono and a sampling rate.

Speech compression
This option is best for voiceovers and other speech. It does not work well for music. You can set a sampling rate with this option.

By default, Macromedia Flash uses MP3 16-bit mono compression.

FIGURE 8-34
The file size information before compression

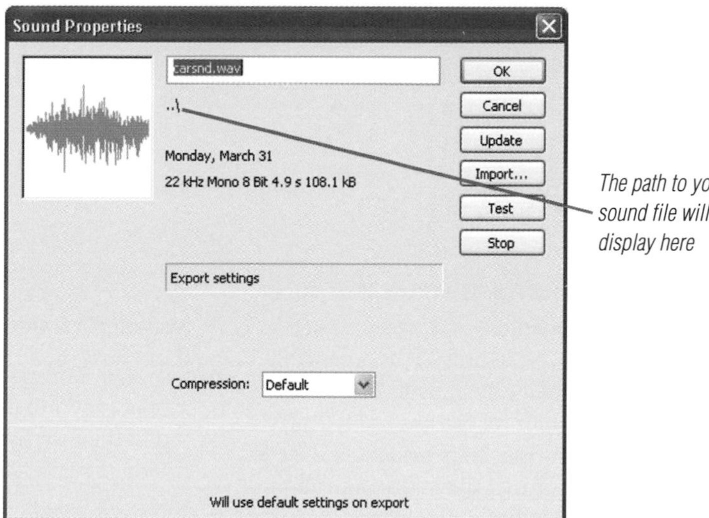

FIGURE 8-35
The file size information after compression

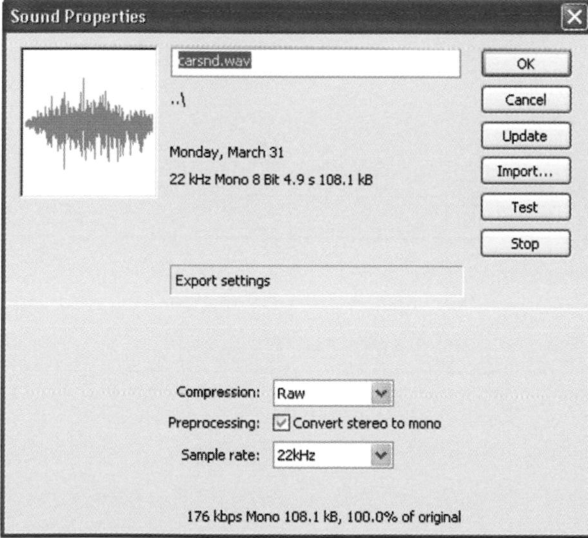

Compress a sound file

1. Right-click (PC) or Ctrl-click (Mac) **carsnd.wav** in the Library panel, then click **Properties**.
2. Click the **down list arrow** for the Compression option, then click **Raw**.
3. Verify Convert stereo to mono is checked and the Sample rate is 22kHz.

   The carsnd.wav file size when imported was approximately 108 kB. Notice the information at the bottom of the dialog box (shown in Figure 8-34) indicates that with the current settings the expected size of the file at output is 108 kB. This is because the Raw option does not compress the file.
4. Click the **down list arrow** for the Compression option, then click **MP3**.
5. Click the **down list arrow** for the Bit rate option, then click **32 kbps**.
6. Click the **down list arrow** for the Quality option, then **Best**.
7. Verify your Sound Properties dialog box resembles Figure 8-35.

   Notice the information at the bottom of the dialog box now indicates that with the current settings the expected size of the file at output is 19.6 kB, or 18.1% of the original. These compression settings have reduced the output file size by 82%.
8. Click the **Test button** to listen to how the file sounds with these settings.
9. Click the **Update button**, then click **OK**.
10. Save the document.

You compressed a sound file.

LESSON 4

ADD SOUND TO a Button

What You'll Do

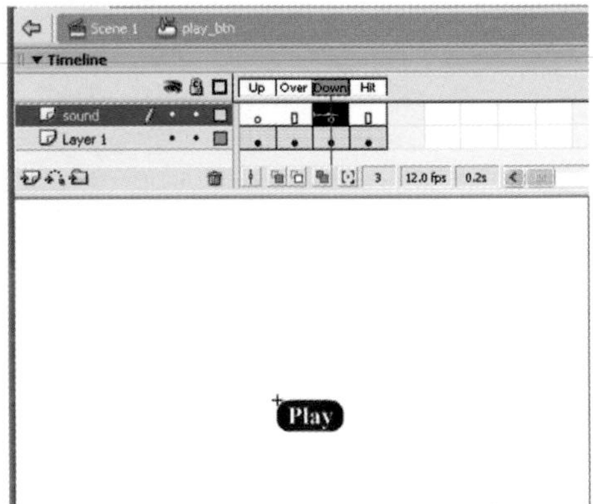

In this lesson, you will learn how to add sound to a button.

Understanding Button Sounds

In an earlier chapter you created a Play and Pause button to provide user control over the playing of the movie. You changed the color for the Over and Down states of the buttons to provide visual feedback to the user that they were pointing to a button or had clicked the button. You can also provide auditory feedback by assigning a sound to a button when the user clicks it.

To add sound to a button, display the button in the Edit Symbol window, add a new layer and name that layer sound, then insert the sound in the sound layer's Down Frame as shown in Figure 8-36.

FIGURE 8-36

The Edit Symbol timeline with a sound added

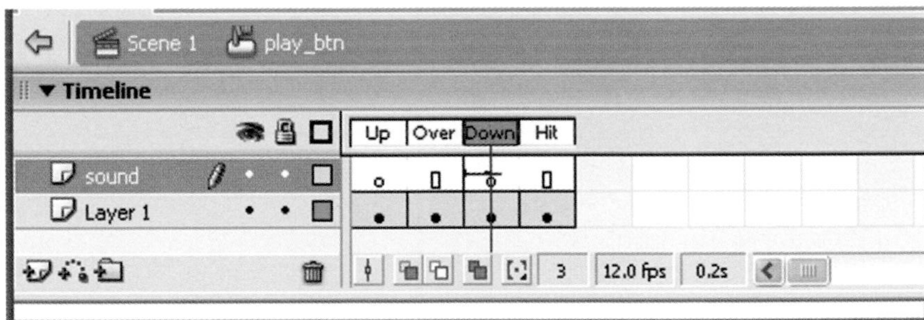

FIGURE 8-37

Dragging the click.wav icon to a spot adjacent to the button

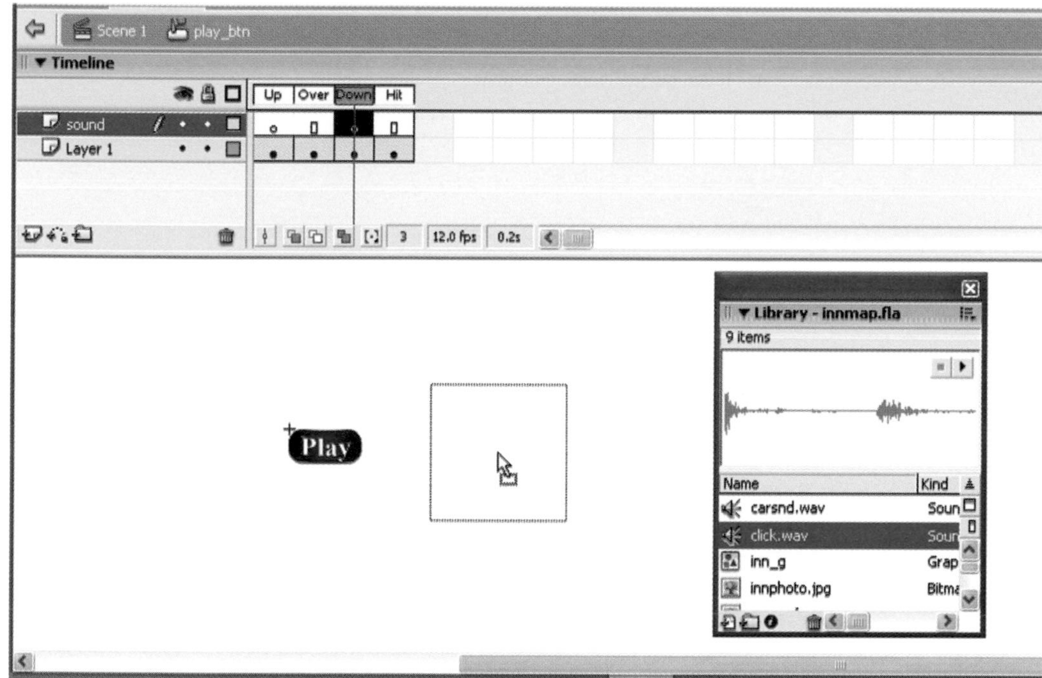

Add sound to a button

1. Right-click (PC) or Ctrl-click (Mac) the **Play button** in the Library, then select **Edit**.
2. Click **Insert** on the menu bar, point to **Timeline**, then click **Layer**.
3. Rename the new layer **sound** as shown in Figure 8-37, then press **[Enter]** (PC) or **[return]** (Mac).
4. Click the **Down Frame** in the sound layer, then press **[F6]** to insert a keyframe.
5. Drag the **click.wav** icon from the Library panel to the stage, adjacent to the button as shown in Figure 8-37.

   Notice the waveform in the Down Frame of the sound layer.
6. If necessary, click the **Down Frame** in the sound layer to select it.
7. Click the **down list arrow** for the Sync box in the Property inspector panel, then click **Event**.
8. Click **Edit** in the menu bar, then click **Edit Document**.
9. Click **Control** in the menu bar, then click **Enable Simple Buttons**.
10. Click the **Play button**.
11. Repeat steps 1 through 8 for the **Pause button**.
12. Click **Control** in the menu bar, then click **Enable Simple Buttons** to turn off the feature.
13. Save the document.

(continued)

14. Display the movie in a browser (see Figure 8-38), test the movie, then close the browser.
15. Click **File** on the menu bar, then click **Publish** to create the .swf file needed for the Web page.

You added sound to buttons.

Test sounds on a Web page

1. Copy the innmap.swf file from the directions folder to the assets folder of the **InnWebsiteDW** folder.

   This replaces the previous innmap.swf file with the one that has the sounds.
2. Start **Dreamweaver**, then open the **InnWebsiteDW** site in the Files panel.
3. Double-click **directions.htm** to display it in the document window.

   Your filename might use the .html extension.
4. Click the **Flash placeholder** in the Document window, then press **[Delete]**.
5. Click **Insert** on the menu bar, point to **Media**, then click **Flash**.
6. Save changes if prompted to do so.

(continued)

FIGURE 8-38
Movie displayed in a browser

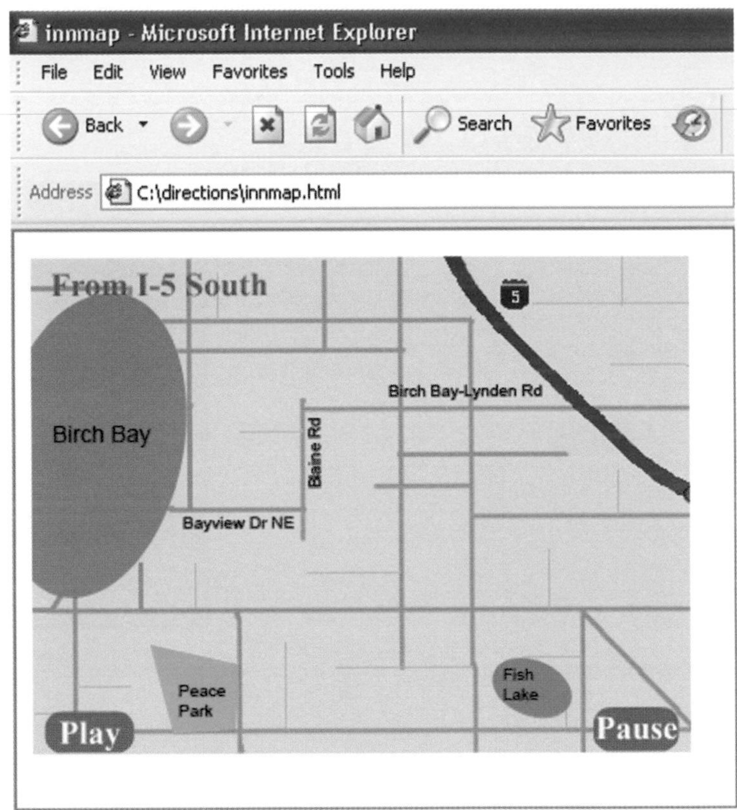

FIGURE 8-39
Selecting the innmap.swf file

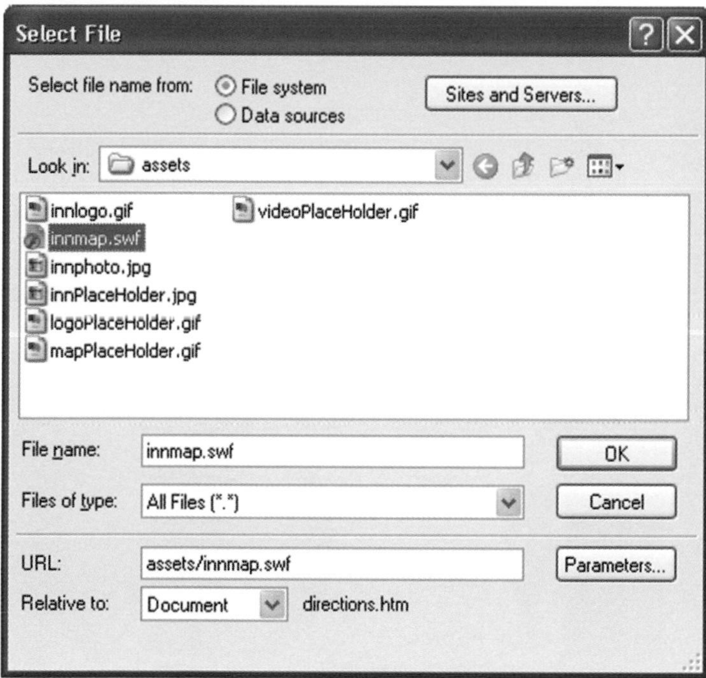

7. Verify the assets folder is open, select **innmap.swf** from the Select File dialog box as shown in Figure 8-39, then click **OK** (PC) or **Choose** (Mac).

   When you published the innmap.fla file earlier, the .swf file was created. The .swf file is inserted into the Web page because, unlike the .fla file, a browser can display it.

8. Save the directions.htm document if necessary.
9. Click **File** in the menu bar, point to **Preview in Browser**, then click **iexplore** (PC) or **Internet Explorer** (Mac).
10. Click **Play**, then click **Pause** to test the button sounds.
11. Click **Play** to test the background sound.
12. Close the browser, then return to Dreamweaver.

You tested the sounds in the Web page.

PROJECT BUILDER 1

You are an intern with a company that develops Web sites for clients. During your internship training you learned how important sound can be to Web pages. You have decided to study how other Web sites use sound.

1. Connect to the Internet, go to *www.course.com*, navigate to the page for this book, click the Student Online Companion link, then click the link for this chapter.
2. Navigate through the site (see Figure 8-40) and note the use of sound and sound controls.
3. Open a document in a word processor, save the file as **Ch8pb1**, create a table with the column headings **Sounds**, **When does the sound occur?**, and **How would you describe the sound?**, and the following row headings:
   - Background
   - Button
   - Narration
   - Other
4. Complete the table by comparing the Web pages based on the sounds listed in your table.

One Step Beyond

5. What audio controls are provided, if any?
6. Do you think the use of sound was beneficial to the site? Why, or why not?
7. What improvement would you suggest for use of sound in the site?

Two Steps Beyond

8. Conduct a Web search for two companies that provide clip audio.
9. Choose one subject and search for sounds available on the sites.
10. Write a summary of each site and include the following in the summary:
    a. The name and URL for each company
    b. The approximate number of audio clips available for the chosen subject
    c. Ease of finding the desired audio clip
    d. Approximate cost of an audio clip
    e. How audio clips are distributed
    f. The terms of use (what is allowed and what is forbidden?)
    g. Which site would you evaluate as better and why?

FIGURE 8-40
The use of sound on a Web site

PROJECT BUILDER 2

You have been studying Web development. You decide it would be useful to add sound to a Web page for a portfolio Web site. Complete the following steps to develop a Macromedia Flash movie with sounds and to insert the movie into a Web page.

1. Using Macromedia Flash develop a movie of your choice. Include the following in your movie:
   a. A background sound
   b. A Play button that starts the playing of the sound
   c. A Pause button that stops the playing of the sound
   d. A button sound (of your choice)
   e. Compression settings for the background sound
2. Follow these guidelines:
   a. Create a new layer for each object and sound
   b. Create an action layer
   c. Name all layers
   d. Convert the button symbols with appropriate button symbol names
   e. Have buttons change for each button state
   f. Create a folder named **ch8files** that will hold the .fla, .swf, and .html files created using Macromedia Flash
   g. Save the movie with the filename **mysndxx.fla** (where *xx* are your initials)
   h. Publish the movie
   i. View the movie in a browser

One Step Beyond

3. Using Dreamweaver, open mysitech8-snd.htm (shown in Figure 8-41) and add the .swf file to the Web page.

The background color of your Web page may be white.

4. Play the movie within Dreamweaver.
5. Open the Web page in a browser and play the movie.
6. Test the sounds.
7. Save the document with the filename **mysitech8-sndxx.htm** (where *xx* are your initials).

Two Steps Beyond

8. Create a third button named **Rewind** and have it cause the playhead to go to Frame 1 of the movie when the button is clicked. Hint: use the following ActionScript for the button:

```
on(release){gotoAndStop(1);}
```

9. Save the movie with the filename **mysndTwoxx.fla** (where *xx* are your initials).
10. Publish the movie and then test it in a browser.

FIGURE 8-41
A Web page to which sound will be added

My Sample Sound
Showcase - Education - Work History - Contact me - Home

PAN AMERICAN WORLD AIRWAY
PAA
DOUGLAS

chapter 9

MULTIMEDIA ELEMENT—Video

1. Discuss the Use of Video on the Web
2. Discuss the Different Types of Video
3. Analyze the Factors That Determine Video Quality
4. Examine Digital Video Sources and Production
5. Explore Video Editing Software
6. Discover Digital Video File Formats and Codecs for the Web

chapter 9 MULTIMEDIA ELEMENT— Video

Introduction

We are bombarded with visual images designed to communicate messages—to inform, persuade, or engage our emotions. Video images are combined to convey a desired message just as words are used to create sentences, paragraphs, and stories. The trick is to communicate what you set out to communicate. Video provides the power to communicate with motion and sound. It serves as a rich resource on the Web. It provides a level of realism not possible with animation or still images. Video is multimedia, and as technology improves, it is becoming more and more common on Web sites.

In the past, video editing equipment was too costly for the average person to purchase. Consequently, producing video used to be limited to professional video production studios. Today, video technology has become more affordable. With the introduction of desktop tools and several other new technologies, users have everything they need to manipulate video and create high-quality images at a fraction of the cost of professional equipment. Video cameras are commonplace and digital video (DV) is a standard format. The production tools that are widely available to individuals today give you the creative power to tell stories through video.

Video can stimulate emotions, convey messages, provide instructions, demonstrate techniques, and relate experiences. Consider the following scenario: You are developing a multimedia Web site on the civil rights movement in the United States. You want to include excerpts from Martin Luther King, Jr.'s "I have a dream. . . ." speech. On the Web site, you could include any or all of the following: part of the speech typed out; a photo of Martin Luther King, Jr., an audio excerpt of the speech, or a video excerpt of the speech. Users viewing the video would definitely recognize the impact of seeing the actual event rather than just reading about it or listening to it.

Incorporating video into a multimedia Web site requires planning and attention to detail. Lack of planning often results in poor-quality video. When planning the use of video on the Web, alternatives such as animation or still images with sound should be explored. These alternatives will provide smaller file sizes and quicker download times; they may also reduce costs and development time. As always, balance is important. You should use video if, when, and where it is appropriate. If you determine that the use of video is the best way to convey a concept or achieve the desired effect on a multimedia Web site, you can use ready-made video clips or you can produce your own digital video clips. Because the inclusion of video on Web pages requires broader bandwidth, powerful processors, and large amounts of storage, you should never use video if it does not add to the site. In addition, you should allow users to decide if they wish to view the video. As bandwidth continues to become less of a concern and compression techniques continue to improve, video will become a more common multimedia element on Web sites.

Because working with video can be a complicated and tricky endeavor, you may find it worthwhile to hire a video specialist, such as a videographer or a video editor. Like professional photographers, videographers are skilled in the art of video recording (see Figure 9-1). These professionals know which elements to include in video footage. They are also skilled at setting up the location, camera angle, and lighting conditions. Videographers with experience working on multimedia projects or designing video for the computer should also know how to set all of these conditions to design video footage that is appropriate for computer viewing and Web delivery. Many videographers freelance. If you do not feel qualified to capture professional-quality video, it may be worth your time and money to hire a skilled videographer to help you obtain the video footage you need for your Web site.

Video editors are responsible for working with Web designers, developers, and videographers to assist with the recording and processing of digital video files to be used on the Web site. They also ensure that the video is correctly incorporated into the Web site.

There are a number of different consumer and professional software programs available for editing video footage, creating movies, and thereby conveying a message or telling a story. At the consumer level, some of these programs are free and offer a very intuitive interface that enables the user to start creating movies for the Web almost immediately. Obviously, more serious video work requires more sophisticated software. On the high end, these systems may even include additional hardware to assist in real-time editing.

Once the video is complete, it can be exported in a wide range of Web formats using a number of different compression schemes designed to make the file small for easier online delivery. When viewed on the Web, most of these videos will require a player that can be downloaded for free.

FIGURE 9-1

Professional videographers are skilled at setting up the location, lighting, and camera angle for shooting video footage

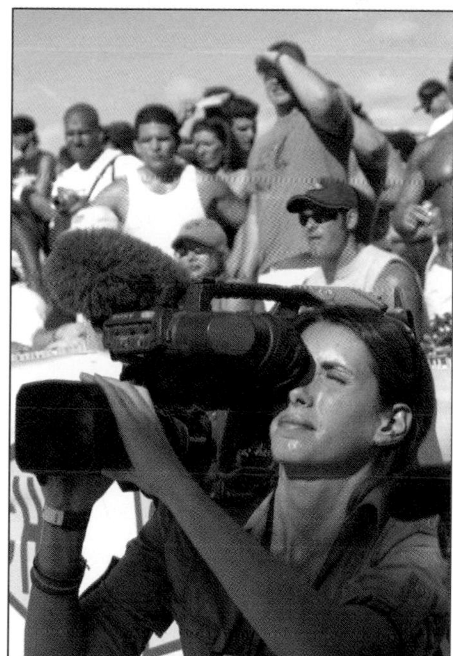

CONCEPT 1

DISCUSS THE USE OF Video on the Web

What You'll Learn

In this lesson, you will learn that different types of Web sites can incorporate video effectively. You will also learn about basic design guidelines for including video on a Web page.

Video is effective because multiple senses are involved and this enhances learning. Video can be extremely effective in online training programs. With video, both action and narration can be used to demonstrate correct techniques or procedures. Many companies have been using video for quite some time to train and retrain their employees. Larger companies can provide comprehensive video training programs and interactive employee orientations online. These Web sites cover aspects such as company history, goals, procedures, products, and other information. These applications save companies with a large employee base thousands of dollars in time-consuming, resource-intensive training, and orientation.

Video demonstrations of complex procedures and equipment are now available on the Web. User-friendly interfaces permit users to watch a video on installation, maintenance, or repair of equipment. This is a particularly cost-effective method of setting up and maintaining equipment that is shipped to distant or remote locations where it would be difficult or cost prohibitive to send repair personnel should a piece of equipment break down. In addition, these videos can be quickly updated as the technology changes.

Like computer-based training, video has long been used in education because it accommodates different learning styles. Video is particularly effective in reinforcing important points, illustrating difficult concepts, demonstrating processes, and teaching skills. For example, a Web site designed to improve golf skills could incorporate video to demonstrate proper golf swings (see Figure 9-2) . By selecting slight changes in grip, follow through, or stance, students could see a video demonstrating the effect slight changes in any or all of these areas have on the loft of the ball. External factors such as wind conditions and type of grass could also be included. In this golf example, students not only hear and see what happens, they are also involved in selecting choices that impact the outcome. Giving learners some control helps keep them involved and motivated.

Television has demonstrated how effective video can be in advertising and marketing. More and more Web sites are being created to sell products and services. The Web site shown in Figure 9-3 uses a video of the medical procedure to market laser eye surgery. Video has been incorporated into airline Web sites in an effort to encourage users to return to the skies. Because of its visual appeal, it is also effective in online advertising of real estate and vacation getaways. Of course, most sporting event Web sites, such as espn.com, include video footage.

Bandwidth measures the amount of data that can flow over a channel on a network. More and more Web pages include video, and if bandwidth were not a deterrent, nearly all Web pages designed to market and sell products and services would probably include video. Video and entertainment are almost synonymous. Web sites designed to entertain are more likely to include video clips than are other types of sites. Movie trailers and shorts are prolific on the Web. Many bands are now including video footage of live concerts or work in recording studios in addition to including traditional text, graphics, and sound on their multimedia Web sites. Games distributed via the Web often include short video clips that describe the purpose or mission of the game before the user begins.

FIGURE 9-2
A video clip would provide instruction to help users improve their golf game

FIGURE 9-3
This online video clip provides users with information on laser eye surgery

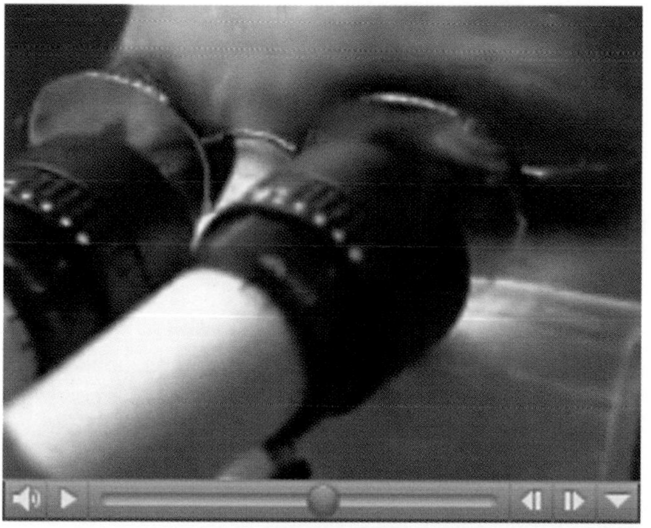

CONCEPT 2

DISCUSS THE DIFFERENT Types of Video

What You'll Learn

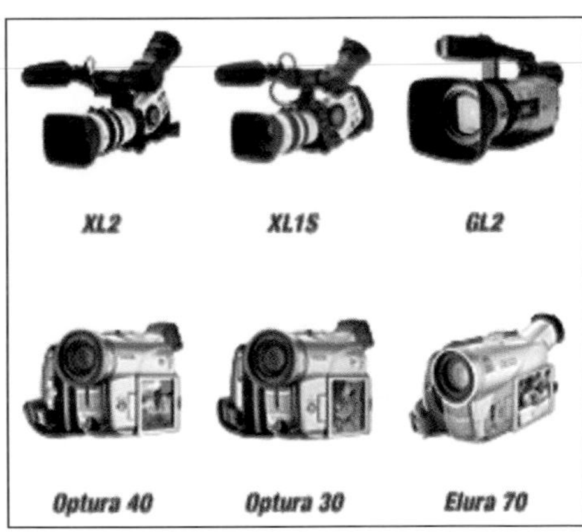

In this lesson, you will learn the difference between analog and digital video and the origins of these two types of video.

There are two different types of video—analog and digital. Although digital video is becoming more and more common, analog video still has a strong position in the world of video editing.

Analog Video

Analog video is generally linear, which means it has a beginning, a middle, and an end. It is recorded as a signal. Analog video is still used because there are a number of existing video clips already stored in an analog format on videotape and there is an abundance of equipment currently available for recording and playing analog video. Because videotape is linear, you must either fast-forward or rewind to get to the video segment you are interested in viewing or digitizing. This can be time consuming. It can also be difficult to get the tape to stop at just the right video frame. **Videodiscs** or **laser discs** also use analog technology, however, unlike videotape, they do provide a random access feature. Videodiscs allow you to access any segment of video without having to fast-forward or rewind to that segment in a linear fashion. This makes using videodisc faster and more accurate than videotape.

Before analog video can be used in a multimedia Web site, it must be converted to a digital format. **Video capture cards** are used to convert analog video to a digital format (see Figure 9-4). Video capture cards are generally placed into an open expansion slot on the main board of the computer. They may also be connected to an external port on the outside of the system unit. In addition, some computer systems come with video capture capabilities already included. Once installed, video capture cards allow you to connect a camcorder, VCR, TV, or live feed to the computer. Special software allows the images to be stored as graphic files or compressed as full-motion video clips. Once stored as a graphic file or full-motion video clip, special video editing software can be used to edit the file. Though low-quality cards can be purchased for less than fifty dollars, you should expect to pay a few hundred to thousands of dollars for an average to upper-end video capture card. Different video capture cards come with different compression technology, an important consideration because the compression technology reduces file size for improved transfer and easier storage.

The analog formats include the following:

VHS is the most common video format found in the consumer market. The biggest advantage to using VHS is the abundance of tapes and VCRs. Due to the low quality of this format, however, VHS is not really a usable format for video editing.

S-VHS is a higher quality format than VHS, but slightly lower quality than Hi-8. This format can be used for video editing. Provided you have the right computer setup including a video capture card, your computer can digitize data transferred directly from S-VHS tapes into your computer.

Hi-8 is the highest quality analog video format found in the consumer market. Tapes from this format are smaller than VHS and S-VHS. For video editing, this format is superior to VHS and S-VHS.

Betacam SP is a high-quality, analog video format used in professional video editing. Betacam SP offers a much higher resolution than the other analog formats. It is an almost universally accepted format for analog video.

FIGURE 9-4

A computer uses a video capture card to capture and convert analog video from a VCR or camcorder into a digital format

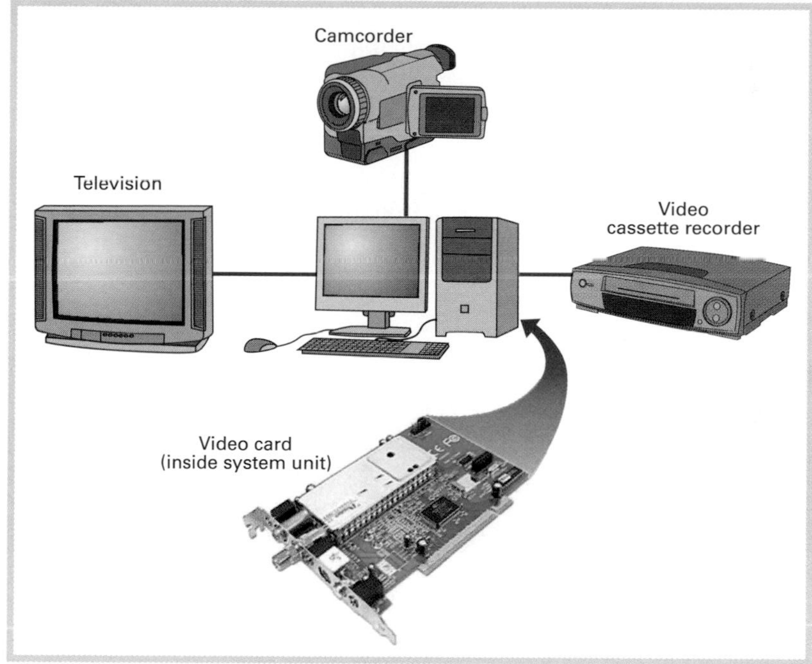

Digital Video

Digital video is video that is already in a digital format. Most major video camera manufacturers have introduced digital video camcorders based on the **DV standard**, an international standard created by a consortium of 10 companies for storing digital video. These DV cameras use a tape that stores the video and sound in a digital format. With the right adapters, hardware, and software, **digital video cameras** (see Figure 9-5) can be used to obtain full-motion images in a digital format. While regular camcorders store video in an analog format, digital video cameras store images as digital data.

The video data captured using a DV camera can be transferred to the computer using a high-speed connector called **FireWire** (also known as **IEEE 1394**). FireWire or IEEE-1394 is a Sony-supported standard that was developed by Apple Computer. FireWire has been adopted by multimedia professionals as the transmission standard for digital video. The availability of FireWire connectors on personal computers means that users will be able to transfer digital video captured with digital video cameras directly into their computers.

Because the video is already in a digital format and it is transferred through a digital connector, there is virtually no loss of image or sound quality—every copy is identical to the original. In other words, no imperfections in the signal are introduced. There is little or no degradation in quality when transferring the data into the computer because there is no conversion process.

Digital formats include the following:

> **D1**, **D2**, and **D3** are three common digital formats. D1 is not suitable for video. Professional video editors and television studios use D2 and D3 formats.
>
> **DV** is Sony's digital video recording format that has been set as the standard by the major producers of digital video camera technologies. DV offers smaller ¼-inch tapes while delivering higher quality images than Betacam SP.

DVD (**Digital Versatile Disc**, also called **Digital Video Disc**) can be used to store digital video. DVDs have tremendous storage capacity ranging from 4.7 GB to 17 GB (see Figure 9-6). DVDs can store up to four hours of digital video. In addition, the quality of video on DVD is clear and sharp.

FIGURE 9-5
Digital video cameras store video as digital data

FIGURE 9-6
A DVD offers significantly greater storage capacity than a CD

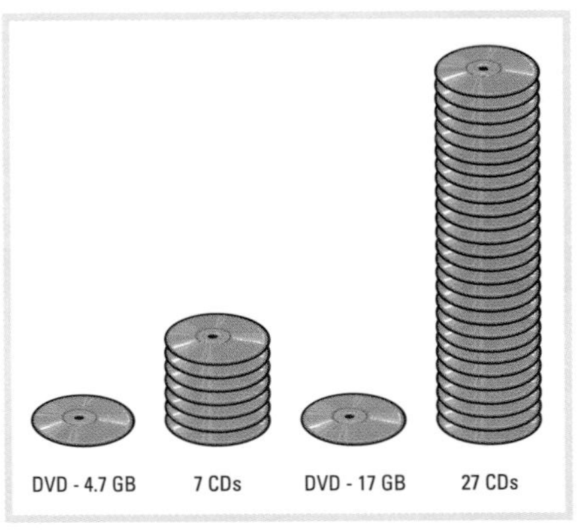

Guidelines for Using Video on the Web

Video can be both stimulating and informative. You should use it when and where it is appropriate. However, because the inclusion of video in Web sites requires significant bandwidth, powerful processors, and large amounts of storage, you should never use video if it does not add to the site.

If video is important to your site, it is worth your time and patience to properly design it to be high quality, appropriate for the mode of delivery, and consistent with the other media elements and goals of the application. Record and capture clean, high-quality video.

Plan accordingly. Keep your audience and the method of delivery in mind when you design video for a Web page. Your time will be wasted if only a few people have the ability to benefit from what you've created because they don't have the equipment to use it. Keep your video files at an appropriate size so they can be played on standard equipment if you plan to distribute your Web site to a wider audience.

Keep the video quality consistent throughout. Don't include poor-quality video footage and high-quality footage within the same site. Also, make sure the video is consistent with the other elements on the Web page.

Remember that in most cases, when the video is displayed on the computer monitor, it will probably take up about one-quarter or one-half of the computer screen. Appropriately adjust the recording and processing of your video based on this smaller screen size.

Not only should your video be consistent in quality with the other video on the Web site, it should also be consistent in content with the rest of the multimedia elements. In other words, stylistic unity should be created with the elements. They should work together to create a theme and enhance the content of the Web site. When you include video on your Web pages, keep the following guidelines in mind:

- Make sure the sound or music and the video match or complement one another.
- Use high-quality video footage that lends credibility and a professional feel to your Web site.
- Use different characters to add interest to the video clip, but don't use so many that your users get lost.
- Coordinate your video files to complement the graphic, animation, and sound elements used on the Web site.
- Do not overuse transitions.
- Trim footage that is excessive, boring, or inconsistent with your purpose.
- Properly place and time video clips so that they are consistent with the other media content.

QUICKTIP

If your computer system and processor are slow and sluggish when working with high-resolution video clips, work with lower-resolution clips. When you are ready to make the actual movie, revert to the higher-resolution video clips for output.

CONCEPT 3

ANALYZE THE FACTORS THAT Determine Video Quality

What You'll Learn

In this lesson, you will learn how frame rate and resolution determine the quality of digital video.

Several of the same factors that affect the quality of still images and animation also determine the quality of video. In order to transfer video clips between software programs, the video editing industry has established systems of measurement that address quality issues. If you wish to effectively work with video, it is important that you also understand the standard systems of measurement—frame rate and resolution.

Frame Rate

Life is a continuous flow of events. When we work with video, we are freezing moments along this continuum. Video is a sequence of individual images or frames displayed fast enough to create the illusion of motion, which tricks the brain into thinking still images are moving (see Figure 9-7).

In order to make this happen, we have to measure time in frames rather than hours, minutes, and seconds, which are generally not precise enough for video editing. There are actually two different frame rates, the **source frame rate** is the speed at which the video is recorded and the **playback frame rate** is the speed at which individual frames

FIGURE 9-7
When displayed fast enough, this sequence of images tricks the brain into thinking there is motion

display. For smooth and consistent playback, the source frame rate and the playback frame rate should be identical. If this is not possible, the playback frame rate must display at a rate that is fast enough to appear continuous. Generally, this must be somewhere between 15 to 30 **frames per second (fps)**. Frames displayed at a slower rate appear choppy.

Resolution

Factors that determine the **resolution** of video include aspect ratio, frame size, and bit depth. **Aspect ratio** is the ratio of width to height in the dimensions of a frame. For example, frames with a 4:3 aspect ratio would appear as shown in Figure 9-8. The **frame size** for playing video is expressed in horizontal and vertical pixel dimensions such as 800 by 600 pixels. A frame at 800 by 600 contains 480,000 pixels. **Bit depth** is the number of bits used to describe the color of a single pixel. The higher the bit depth, the more colors the image can contain. Obviously, this allows for more precise color reproduction and higher quality images.

The same guidelines that apply to determining the resolution of any multimedia element also apply to video. That is, the higher the resolution, the larger the size of the file. As always, there is a trade-off between high resolution, high-quality elements, and file size. You must experiment to find an acceptable balance.

In addition to frame rate and resolution, bandwidth, processor speed, memory, and monitor size are important considerations for Web-based video delivery. These factors are difficult to assess if your goal is to deliver video to the Internet community, so be sure to always test your video on different computer systems.

FIGURE 9-8
Aspect ratio is the ratio of width to height in the dimensions of a frame

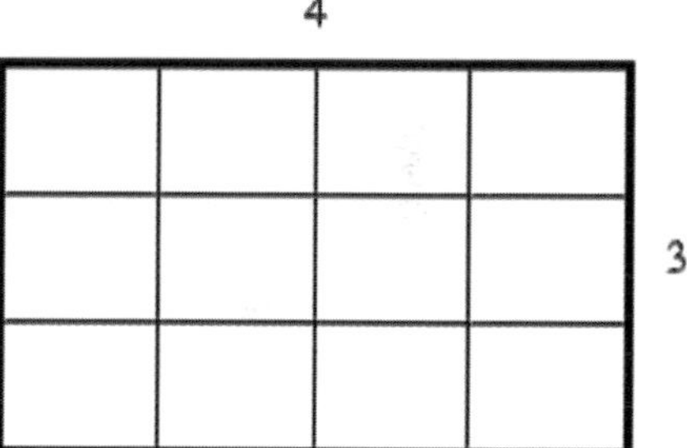

Video Standards

Frame rates vary because there are different video standards used throughout the broadcast world. **NTSC** stands for National Television Systems Committee. According to the standard established by this organization, video signals have a rate of about 30 fps (29.97 to be exact) and a single frame of video consists of 525 horizontal lines. The television and video industries in the United States and Japan have adopted the NTSC standard. **PAL** stands for Phase Alternating Line. According to this standard, video signals have a frame rate of 25 fps and a single frame of video consists of 625 horizontal lines. PAL is the most common television and video standard in Europe, South Africa, the United Kingdom, and Australia. **SECAM** stands for Sequential Color with Memory. Unlike NTSC and PAL, SECAM measures the speed of video in Hertz rather than in frames. The standard speed is 50 Hz with 625 horizontal lines per screen. SECAM is used in France, Russia, and several other countries. **HDTV** stands for High Definition Television. This video standard supports a resolution of 1,200 horizontal lines with an aspect ratio (length: width) of 16:9. Japan, Europe, and the United States have all developed different standards for HDTV.

When you are preparing video for Web delivery, these standards are not applicable. However, because these frame rates are generally available as options in your video editing programs, it is probably wise for you to have a general understanding of what they mean even though they are not entirely useful when your goal is to create video for the Web.

CONCEPT 4

EXAMINE DIGITAL VIDEO
Sources and Production

What You'll Learn

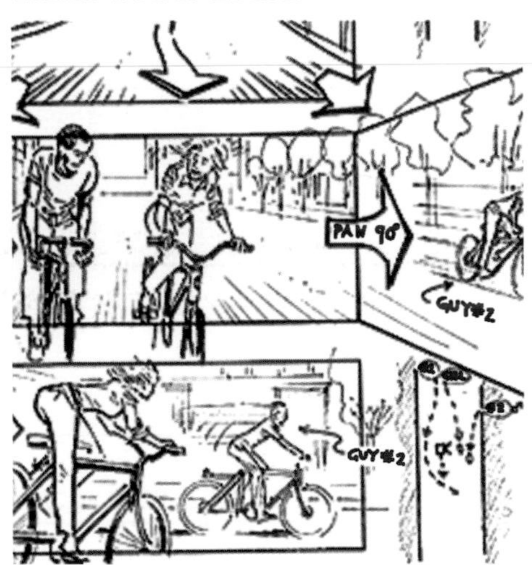

In this lesson, you will learn about the sources of digital video files and will understand the steps involved in pre-production, production, and post-production.

In order to work with digital video, you need to acquire the video and then manipulate it. You need to understand sources for digital video, as well as the production process, which includes three phases: pre-production, production, and post-production.

Video Sources

When you work with video for multimedia Web sites, you will work either with video you have recorded or **stock video footage** acquired from a third party, such as a freelance videographer or stock videography company (see Figure 9-9). Video footage may be available in either an analog or a digital format. Obviously, it will be easier to work with it if it is already in a digital format; however, you can digitize analog footage provided you have access to the proper equipment.

After you find the stock video footage or **clip video** for your project, be sure to carefully check the applicable licensing agreements. The footage may or may not be royalty free. Even if it is royalty free, it is still copyright protected. Read all licensing agreements and releases carefully before you agree to the terms. After signing, be sure to document everything and correctly follow the terms of the agreement.

FIGURE 9-9
Stock footage or clip video is becoming increasingly available online or on disc

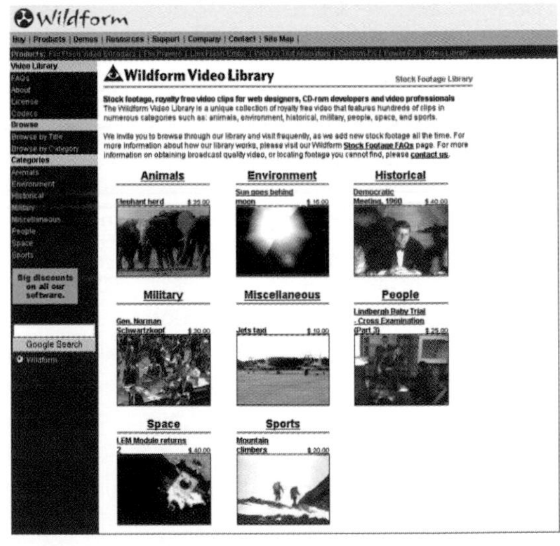

Though you can use some video royalty free in any Web site you create, with others, you will need to pay the creator a royalty for each page on which the video is used. Do not take chances. If you wish to use video footage within your Web site, always get permission from the videographer, publisher, or owner of the footage.

Video footage is not quite as abundant as stock photography nor is it as inexpensive. It is sometimes difficult to find video footage of what you want and need for your Web site. If you cannot find the video footage you want and need from a third party, or if you do not want to pay the royalties and cannot agree to the licensing agreement specified, you may want to hire a professional videographer to shoot the footage for you. The other option is to record your own video provided you have the equipment, skills, experience, and artistic talent to shoot professional footage.

Video Production

Pre-Production

Before you include video on a multimedia Web site, you should plan what, when, where, and how it will be incorporated into the Web site. Pre-production involves visualizing and sketching each scene on a storyboard, writing the scripts, and creating a production schedule. Throughout these stages, it is important that you always keep your audience in mind. First you must consider what pieces of the Web site content could be effectively delivered as video and when they should play. Next, you should include this information in the planning documents for the project. As seen in Figure 9-10, storyboards designate what each frame of video will look like. They provide a sketch and information about each frame of video footage. Storyboards should also specify where video footage will begin and end on the multimedia Web site.

The scripts are very important because they serve as the story that will be told with the video camera. The scripts include details about the narration, voiceovers, dialogs, sound effects, actors, scenes, and video footage that will be used on a multimedia Web site. Because video footage will also include audio, scripts should be written for listening rather than reading. If actors are involved, each should have a separate and detailed script. Flowcharts are needed if the Web site is interactive. The flowchart specifies where video will be included based on choices selected by the user.

FIGURE 9-10
Storyboards provide a sketch of each frame of video footage

Production

During production the video footage is acquired, recorded, and digitized if the original video footage is not already in a digital form. If you have already acquired video footage in a digital format from a stock videography company or videographer, the next step is simply to import the footage into your video editing program. If you are shooting your own video footage, be sure to plan accordingly so that production progresses as scheduled.

Always remember that video is copyright protected. If you intend to use someone else's video footage on your Web site, be sure to get permission and carefully read the licensing agreement. Even self-recorded video footage of artistic works may be copyright protected. In other words, if you videotape a choreographed dance or a play, you may need to get permission from the choreographer or playwright before you can use the footage even though you taped the video yourself. Films, television programs, motion picture videos, documentaries, and other commercially prepared video are also copyright protected. Also, if your video footage includes people, whether they were just passing by or scripted into your application as actors, interviewees, or narrators, you must have their permission through a signed release if you wish to use them in your multimedia project.

Provided your video equipment is properly connected to your computer and you have access to the appropriate software, you can capture or digitize your video from a live feed, a laser disc player, DVD, VCR, as well as analog or digital video cameras. Once the video footage has been recorded and captured, it is time to import the clips into your video editing program (see Figure 9-11).

FIGURE 9-11
Digital video clips are easily imported into video editing programs

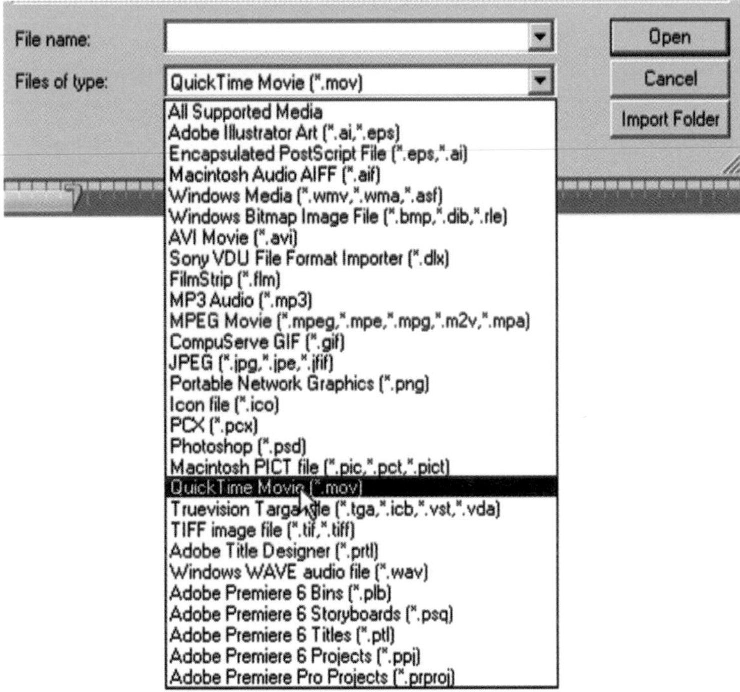

QUICKTIP

You should plan your videotaping in advance.

- Prepare the location
- Check your equipment
- Confirm appointments with actors and other key personnel

Before you begin recording you need to specify settings such as frame size, compression format, resolution, and output filetype. Many programs include presets (see Figure 9-12) that allow you to choose default settings from a list of options in case you are not comfortable setting all of these on your own. However, the more you know about the settings, the more control you will have over the recording process.

QUICKTIP

The video window on the Web is relatively small. You will get better results by recording close-ups and avoiding long shots of distant landscapes that will be lost in a small frame.

FIGURE 9-12

The New Project dialog box in Adobe Premiere allows you to choose preset or custom settings

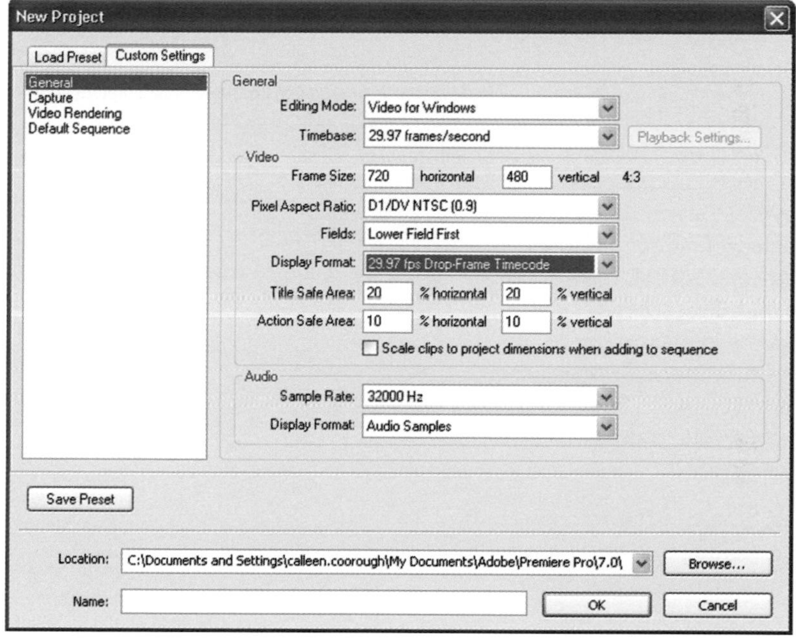

Post-Production

After you have captured the video you are ready to process it. In other words, you may need to trim it, splice it, add special effects and transitions, overlay titles and text, or even add additional sound tracks. There are many tools available to help you raise raw video footage from an amateur to a professional level. In most video editing programs, several different tracks are used to store video information (see Figure 9-13). There are also tracks that store the visual images while other tracks are reserved for the audio clips.

FIGURE 9-13

In most video editing programs, tracks, such as the ones shown, are used to store video and audio clips

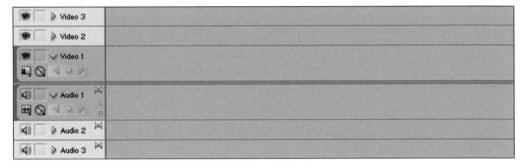

The timecode track is used to synchronize all of the components. The standard time code is called **SMPTE** because it was developed by the Society of Motion Picture and Television Engineers. SMPTE measures video in hours, minutes, seconds, and frames. This system of measurement enables video editors and audio specialists to synchronize voice, music, and sound effects to the appropriate frames of video based on the frame rate.

One of the most time-consuming aspects of working with digital video on a computer is rendering visual effects. Video editors often have to limit their use of motion, transitions, and filters because of the lengthy rendering times that these effects can require. Hardware vendors such as Pinnacle Systems have created video boards that can accelerate the rendering of many of these effects, often performing them in real-time.

After your video has been successfully recorded, digitized, and processed it is ready to be incorporated into your Web site. The success of the video clip on the Web site depends not only on effective processing but also on correct placement within the Web site. Video on the Web can either be downloaded or streamed. Downloadable video files such as those shown in Figure 9-14 are stored on the user's computer before they are played. Streaming video is a more advanced process that allows the video to be played as it is downloading.

The delivery quality of video on the Web is as dependent on the delivery equipment as it is on the recording and processing equipment. Even if the video appears to be of superior quality running on your computer, it may be ineffective when played on the end-user's equipment. When planning for delivery, consider the potential delivery system and the intended audience before you begin. If you plan to stream the video from the server, you will need to post your Web site with a Web hosting company that supports streaming. In most cases, the hardware and software needed to stream video files must be purchased even though users can download and install the players to view streaming media for free.

FIGURE 9-14
For a user to view one of these videos, it must be downloaded and stored on the user's computer first

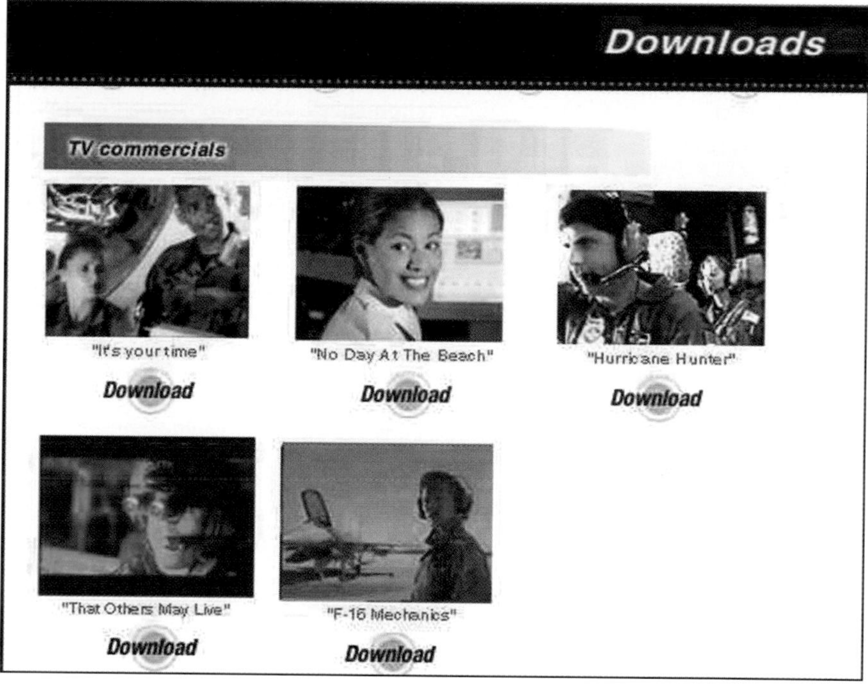

CONCEPT 5

EXPLORE VIDEO
Editing Software

What You'll Learn

In this lesson, you will learn about some of the industry-leading software programs for editing and compositing digital video.

High-speed, always-on, broadband Web access has changed the way people interact with their computers. Today, there are millions of streaming media–enabled computers capable of delivering video on the Web. Several affordable software applications available for editing and compositing digital video make this possible. Compositing is a special-effects technique that involves layering several different clips of video over each other.

Web designers and developers can use video editing tools to digitize motion graphics and put messages and stories on the Web. Adobe, Avid, and Apple are three well-known companies offering mid-range and high-end desktop video editing packages for both the consumer and professional markets.

Adobe

Adobe has provided consumers and professionals with several award-winning software solutions for editing and compositing video for the Web. These dynamic media tools enable designers and developers to tell stories with moving pictures and sound.

Premiere

Adobe Premiere is an affordable, highly rated, non-linear, video-editing program. Using Adobe Premiere, you can capture, edit, and incorporate video into your multimedia Web site. Premiere allows you to bring your ideas to life by combining video, audio, animation, and still images without the need for special-effects hardware or expensive production services. You can even create still images from video. Adobe Premiere also offers extensive recording and processing capabilities. A discussion of some of the key features found in Adobe Premiere follows.

One reason Adobe Premiere is so highly rated is that it is based on an **open architecture**. This means that Adobe Premiere was designed to be compatible with numerous software programs, extensions, and file formats. This open architecture increases the functionality of Adobe Premiere and allows third-party developers to create software that extends Adobe Premiere's capabilities. Adobe Premiere supports all of the most commonly used digital video file formats as well as multiple still image and digital audio file formats.

In Adobe Premiere, documents or files are referred to as projects. Before you begin a new project, you need to specify several settings from the presets or custom dialog box. Any of these presets can be changed later. Adobe Premiere allows you to arrange video clips linearly and instantly edit them non-linearly. The media files are not actually included in the project file as this can make the project file too large and cumbersome. Instead, imported files are referenced from the project window (see Figure 9-15). When working with many files as part of a large project, you will probably want to group your files into a single folder. Other options that will help you organize your files include the ability to apply labels and comments to your files and sort by these options or the filename.

In Adobe Premiere, you use the Timeline (see Figure 9-16) to assemble, synchronize, and edit your files. The Timeline includes multiple video and audio tracks. It also includes built-in tools, such as the Razor tool for trimming unwanted frames from your video clips (see Figure 9-17). When you drag a video clip to the Timeline, the audio that accompanies the clip is automatically placed in the corresponding audio track. By using **nondestructive editing**, Premiere preserves your original video clips just in case you make a mistake, change

FIGURE 9-15

The Adobe Premiere Project window references the different files that will be used to create the movie

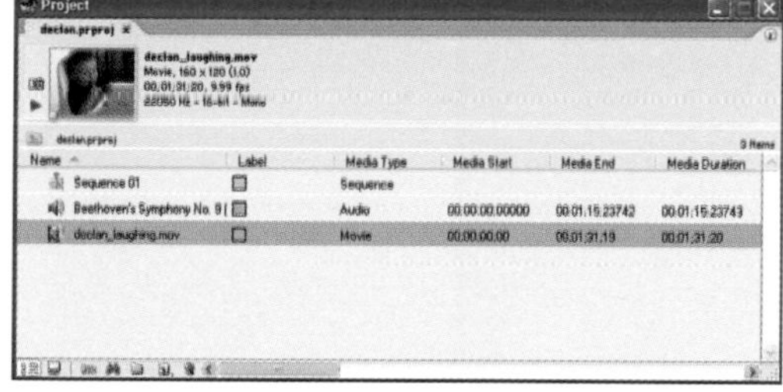

FIGURE 9-16

Use the Timeline to assemble and edit your clips non-linearly

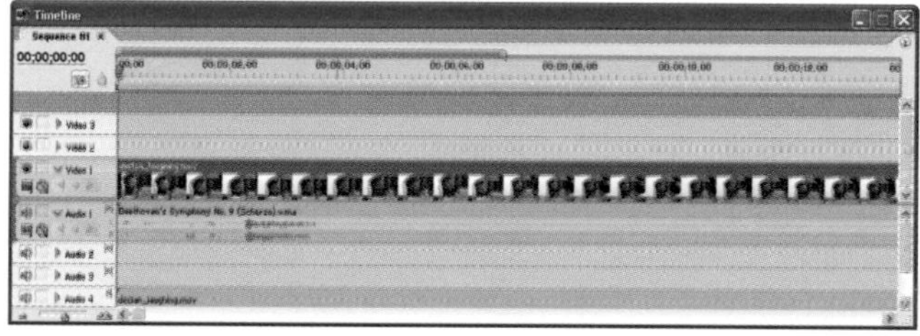

FIGURE 9-17

Built-in tools make editing quick and easy

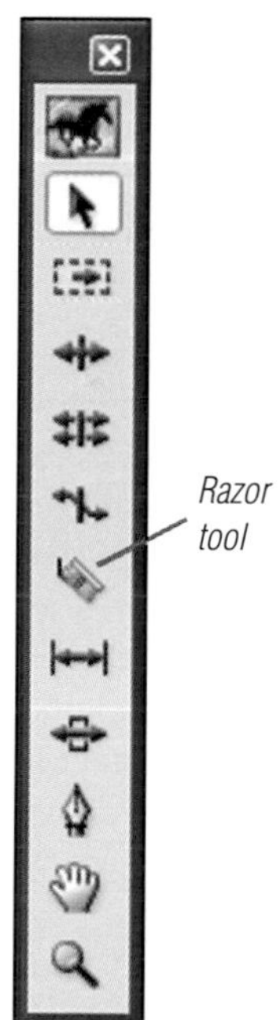

your mind, or wish to use them in another application.

Premiere includes some rather sophisticated sound editing features including the ability to apply special effects and transitions to both audio and video clips as shown in Figure 9-18. Premiere offers traditional special effects such as wipes, dissolves, spins, and filters.

You can create text with smooth edges, gradient fills, soft shadows, and transparent backgrounds. Text effects including transparent letters can be used for titles and subtitles. You can even create animated titles. In addition, you can design shapes and patterns for transitions and apply motion paths such as twisting, zooming, rotation, and distortion. You can add multiple layers and animated filters. You can add an unlimited number of keyframes to animate any attribute in any layer down to thousandths of a pixel.

Plug-in filters and special effects available from other Adobe products such as Adobe Photoshop as well as from third-party developers extend your creative options by allowing you to change the color, brightness, and contrast. You can also apply blurs, distortions, and morphing effects. Built-in and third-party audio processing filters are also available to enhance and change audio characteristics.

FIGURE 9-18
The Effects window provides special effects and transitions that can be applied to both audio and video clips

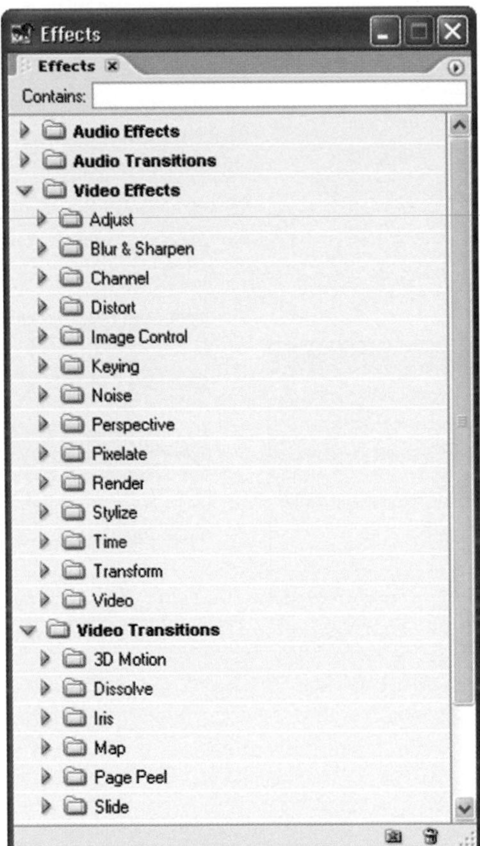

QUICKTIP

The best transitions are transparent to the user. Try to make your transitions appropriate and consistent with the rest of the Web site.

At any time you can use the monitor window to preview the source of a single video clip or all of the clips currently in the Timeline. Remember that each additional track you include will require additional storage and computer processing power. After you have captured and edited your movie to your liking, you can export it (see Figure 9-19) and set a variety of different output options including resolution, frame rate, frame size, file format, audio settings, and codec.

Adobe After Effects

Adobe After Effects is a compositing software program full of tools that can help you create special effects for Adobe Premiere projects. With Adobe After Effects, you can use unlimited layers of both moving and still images. In addition, special effects and animation can be applied to each layer. With Adobe After Effects you can combine an unlimited number of layers from files imported from a variety of other graphics and animation programs. You can mix multiple file resolutions and layer graphics to create full-screen video. Once this composite of layers has been created, Adobe After Effects gives you precise control over adjusting every aspect.

FIGURE 9-19

Adobe Premiere allows you to export your final movie to a number of different file formats

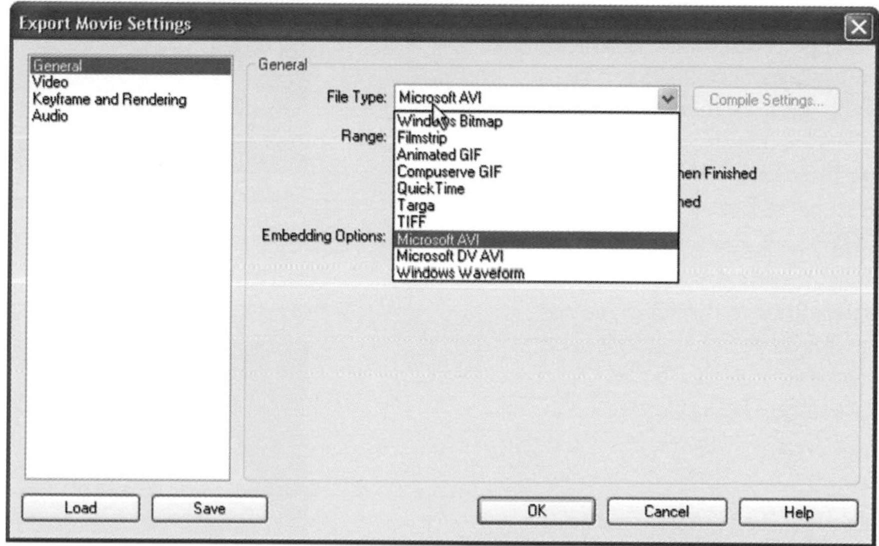

Tools are available that allow you to draw animation paths, record the velocity of these paths, and create high-quality mattes to produce effects such as glass and water. Special effects can also be applied to quickly animate still images and text. Samples of some text animation presets that are available are seen in Figure 9-20. There are many other special effects including lightning, scatter, ripple, bulge, and wave warp. In Adobe After Effects, the number of effects seems endless because of the precise and powerful tools available. In addition, multiple special effects can be applied to each layer. Figure 9-21 shows different effects applied to one clip so you can compare the effects.

QUICKTIP

Pay close attention to the mix of your piece. Special effects, filters, and transitions individually only last a few seconds. It is not the individual components of a video but how the entire piece is edited and composited that makes a lasting impression.

Apple

From simple to high end, Apple's video editing packages capture the creative spirit in consumers and professionals. Providing a product for almost anyone interested in entering the video industry at any level, Apple continues to maintain its leadership position in the video editing marketplace.

FIGURE 9-20
Samples of the more than 250 text animation presets

Raining Characters In

360 Loop

Chaotic

Squeeze

FIGURE 9-21
Different effects applied to the same clip

Particle World

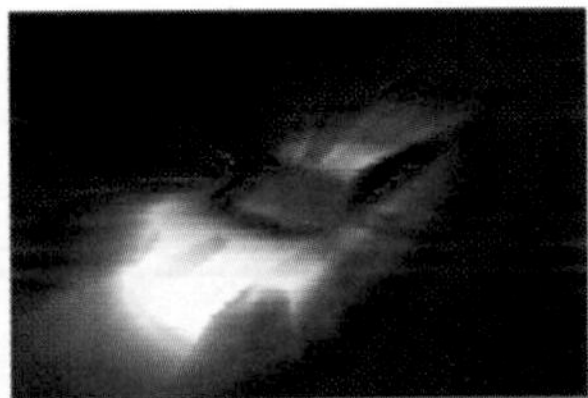

Light Burst

Light Rays

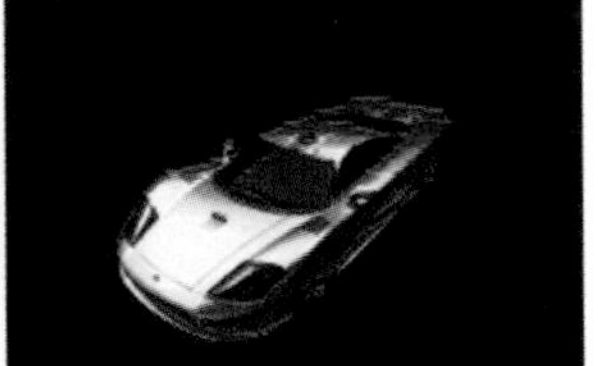

Tonar

QuickTime Pro

QuickTime by Apple actually serves many different purposes. As already discussed in previous chapters, QuickTime is a file format. It is also a player that plays not only QuickTime files, but a variety of other file types as well. In addition, Apple offers QuickTime Pro, which is a software-based, video-editing system. It is an engine that allows you to edit video on the computer without using additional hardware. QuickTime Pro is an excellent engine for working with most multimedia files, but it is particularly well suited for video.

QuickTime Pro provides a comprehensive, flexible, and integrated set of media services to creators and developers working with video. Because there is no upper limit on the frame rate of a QuickTime movie, it is an ideal format for high frame rate animations and it supports digital video standards, which enable even higher frame rates. QuickTime Pro can also handle and produce cross-platform video. With QuickTime Pro you can work with a variety of different audio, video, and image formats. You can use it to create Web-ready audio and video, enhance your movies with filters and special effects, and then export them to more than a dozen standard file formats. You can even create streaming movies with QuickTime Pro and take advantage of high-end compression technologies.

iMovie

iMovie is another video-editing package (see Figure 9-22). Using familiar drag and drop, copy, cut, and paste functions, you can use iMovie to trim unwanted footage and to arrange your video clips in any sequence. You can cut, copy, and paste clips or parts of a clip, as well as reorder and shuffle your video clips along the Timeline. You can also trim video clips to remove unwanted footage. You can keep your material in sync as you edit by locking audio clips to specific frames of video. You can also place audio at a precise location in your movie using markers for flexible music and sound editing. Editing tools within iMovie are simple and intuitive.

FIGURE 9-22
iMovie is another video editing solution by Apple

Once you have selected the clips for your video, you can add transitions, such as dissolves and fades between scenes. There are also multitudes of special effects available to further enhance your video clips.

Final Cut Pro

Final Cut Pro is a feature-rich, non-linear, video-editing application by Apple. Final Cut lets you create videos using interactive editing and compositing tools together with a host of special effects capabilities. In addition to a comprehensive set of tools, it offers built-in support for third-party plug-ins such as Adobe After Effects filters. In many respects, Final Cut combines the best features of several products into one package.

Using Final Cut Pro (see Figure 9-23) you can take full advantage of extensive text features and create innovative, professional-quality, fully animated titles. Trimming tools enable you to precisely edit video footage. You can even change the playback speed of a clip without rendering. A database tracks the relationship between your original video and audio clips. The database provides a vital link between your original footage and your edited footage.

With Final Cut Pro, it is easy to ensure that video and audio stay in sync during the editing process because the software automatically detects when an audio track is moved out of synchronization with its corresponding video. When this occurs, the software provides a visual warning and an easy way to slip and slide a clip back in sync. Final Cut Pro can even track and fix the synchronization when one audio clip is associated with multiple video clips, such as when the video cuts back and forth between an announcer and images of what the announcer is discussing.

FIGURE 9-23

Final Cut panels offer quick access to multiple features while using very little screen real estate

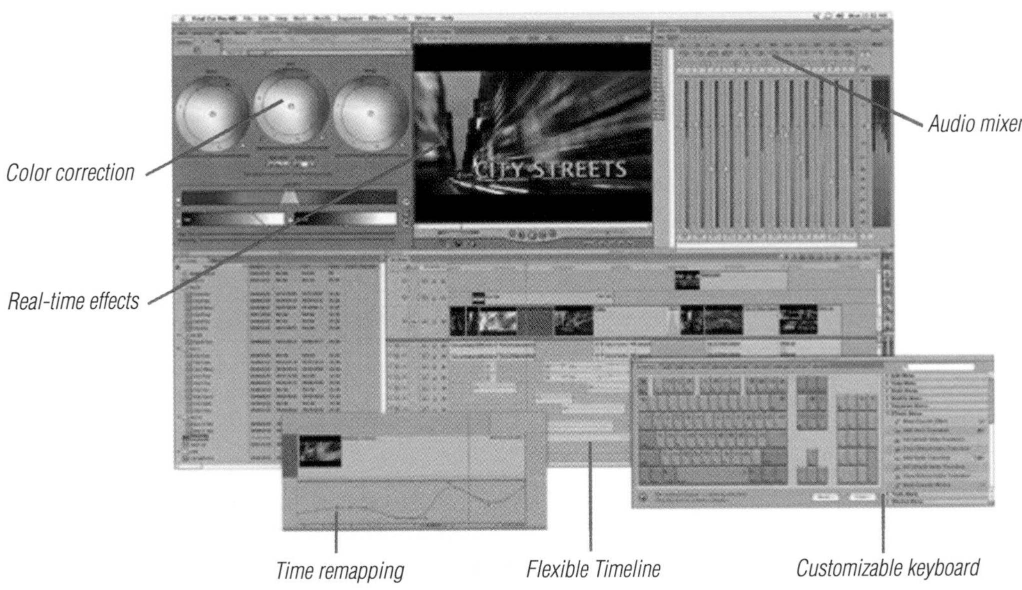

Avid

Avid is another premier provider of digital tools for film, video, audio, and broadcast (see Figure 9-24). The company has been and continues to be a major worldwide driving force behind the widespread acceptance of high-end, computer-based, digital technology.

Avid offers a number of creative tools that enable designers and developers from around the world to share stories through video. From Avid Xpress software to Avid Media Composer systems, there are a number of tools used to create countless award-winning feature films, television shows, and trailers and shorts for Web-based delivery.

Xpress

Avid offers several powerful audio and video editing tools that are based on an intuitive easy-to-use interface. Avid Xpress is a complete video-editing system. It features a full set of high-performance built-in features for editing video, managing audio, creating real-time effects and titles, adding graphics, compositing, and working seamlessly with third-party applications.

Media Composer

On the high-end, the Avid Media Composer family is the worldwide standard for editing video, primarily for television and film, but also for the Web. The newer products hold great promise for networking collaboration as well. Avid Media Composer systems with accelerator boards deliver unprecedented performance, image quality, and workflow. They offer a dynamic combination of software and hardware that provides an integrated network of editing and compositing solutions.

Windows Movie Maker

Windows Movie Maker can be downloaded for free from Microsoft. This video editing program is easy to use, yet provides many powerful capabilities that enable you to capture and edit video footage. Using a few simple and intuitive drag-and-drop features, you can quickly create a movie for delivery via the Web.

Regardless of which software program you choose, the process for editing and compositing video for the Web is essentially the same:

1. Acquire the content (video footage, audio clips, and still images)
2. Capture and import the content into the video-editing program
3. Edit the video clips
4. Assemble the clips onto a video track
5. Add transitions such as dissolves
6. Add filters and effects such as lighting
7. Add text titles
8. Add audio
9. Compress the movie
10. Export the movie in a Web file format

FIGURE 9-24
Avid is a premier provider of digital tools for video editing and compositing

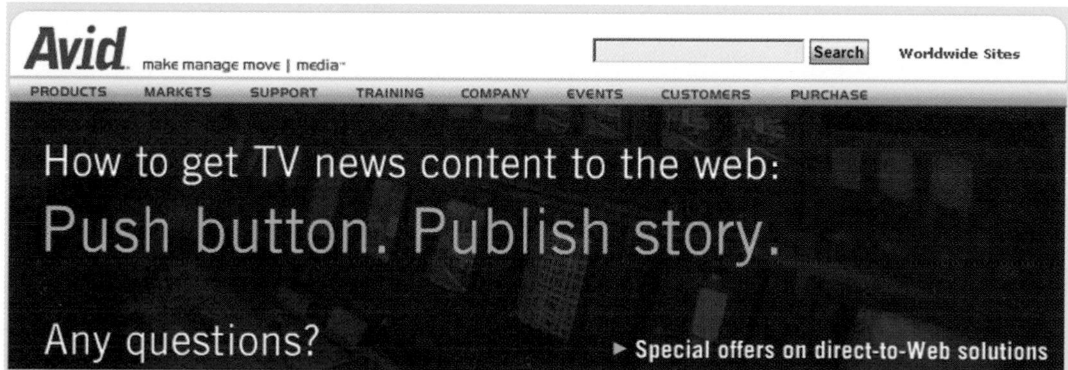

CONCEPT 6

DISCOVER DIGITAL VIDEO FILE
Formats and Codecs for the Web

What You'll Learn

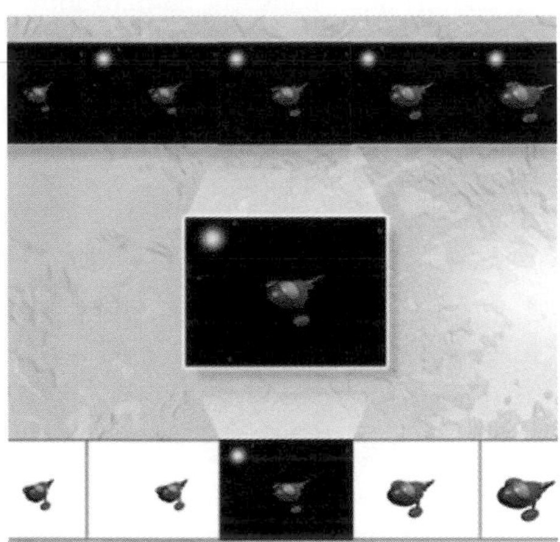

In this lesson, you will learn about the common digital video file formats and codecs used on multimedia Web sites.

There are different digital video file formats just as there are different graphic and sound file formats.

ASF (Advanced Streaming Format)

The **ASF (Advanced Streaming Format)** stores audio and video information, and it is specially designed to run on networks like the Internet. This file format is a highly flexible and compressed format that contains streaming audio, video, slide shows, and synchronized events. When you use .asf files, content is delivered to you as a continuous flow of data; you experience little wait time before playback begins. The file can be unlimited in length and can run over Internet bandwidths.

AVI (Audio Video Interleave)

AVI (Audio Video Interleave) is by Microsoft. An .avi file is really a Resource Interchange File Format (RIFF) file. RIFF is a Microsoft standard. Video for Windows is built in to the Windows environment. This means that any .avi movie will play on a Windows-based PC automatically, assuming the multimedia components of the operating system have been properly installed and the proper codec is available for decompressing the file. Other players, including QuickTime, will also play .avi files, making this format acceptable for delivering video via the Web.

MPEG (Motion Picture Experts Group)

MPEG (Motion Picture Experts Group). The MPEG video standard was developed to provide a format for delivering digital media to the consumer market. Because MPEG provides high-quality video and relatively low data rates, it has been successful in many markets and has emerged as a digital video standard. This is true not only in the United States, but also for most of the world. MPEG has defined several standards for storing audio and video. Original MPEG files had to be decoded with hardware, however, with the advances in processor technologies, it is now feasible to decode these files with software alone.

The new revolution in digital media is MPEG-4. Hundreds of researchers around the world contributed to MPEG-4, which was finalized in 1998 and became an international standard in 2000. It is the global multimedia standard, delivering professional-quality audio and video streams over a wide range of bandwidths, from cell phone to broadband and beyond.

MOV (QuickTime)

Apple has specified its own file format called **MOV (QuickTime)**. The QuickTime file format is among the most convenient and powerful formats for storing common digital media types such as audio and video. The QuickTime .mov file format is also able to store numerous video channels. This is essential for supporting real-time rendering of transitions and special effects. In addition, QuickTime files are platform neutral, open, and extensible.

Because QuickTime files work on any computing platform with a variety of different software, this file format continues to be a good option for distributing video on the Web. In fact, the QuickTime format has become a widely adopted format for publishing digital video on the Internet. To be viewed, the QuickTime player must be installed on the user's computer.

Video Delivery and File Size

To include video on a multimedia Web site, the file size must be small enough to be delivered effectively. The size of the file can be reduced by experimenting with file formats, making the frames smaller, reducing the frame rate, dropping the number of colors, and applying compression.

RM (RealMedia)

RM (RealMedia) is the leader in streaming media technologies. The Real formats offer excellent compression and incredibly popular and widespread support for streaming video on the Web. Like many of the media elements discussed thus far, Real files require a plug-in or player to be heard. RealPlayer can be downloaded and installed for free.

WMV (Windows Media File with Audio and/or Video)

The **WMV (Windows Media File)** is proprietary to the Windows operating system and is used by Windows MovieMaker. Video projects created using Windows MovieMaker use the .wmv filename extension. You can use a .wmv file either to download and play files or to stream content. The .wmv file format is similar to the .asf file format.

Codecs

Digital video files are huge! The **data transfer rate (dtr)** is the time it takes for the video to be transferred from the processor and displayed on the monitor. Different delivery systems offer different data transfer rates. Even within the same storage medium, data transfer rates vary depending on technologies such as bus structures and bandwidth. If the data transfer rate is too slow, the video will be choppy.

To be effectively delivered, video must fit on the delivery medium used to store it, and it must be accessed from this storage medium fast enough to trick our eyes into believing that it is really in motion. Even with broadband access and streaming technologies, delivering video on the Web is a challenge. One way to improve the data transfer rate and reduce the amount of storage space that video files consume is to compress them. Compression reduces the size of the video file. With some compression schemes, image quality is lost. However, these minor losses in quality are usually worth the benefits. In addition to improving data transfer and reducing file size, by compressing the files, the processor does not have to work as hard to display the video on the monitor. When the video is played back, the processor decompresses the file.

The compression/decompression algorithms used to compress data are called **codecs**. Depending on the codec used and the ratio employed, compressed video files can be significantly smaller than uncompressed video files. Working with digital video can be confusing because there are dozens of different compression schemes to choose from. Some of these compression formats are hardware-based while most use software-based playback engines. A brief discussion of some common codecs follows.

Compression Technology

One second of high-resolution, full-screen, uncompressed digital video with audio can require upwards of 30 MB of storage. This means that the average CD-ROM, which holds about 650 MB of data, can store about 25 seconds of uncompressed digital video. Though DVDs offer greater storage capacities, they still cannot begin to touch the storage needs of full-motion video in an uncompressed format.

The **Animation codec** was developed to compress and play QuickTime animated movies. It uses Run Length Encoding (RLE), which is great for sequencing single-color frames such as cartoons, but it is not a very good choice for compressing real video clips.

Apple Cinepak is a compression scheme that works well for CD-ROM video delivery and is acceptable for Web delivery as well because it is cross-platform. The Cinepak codec offers excellent image quality for thousands or millions of colors. The playback time is also very fast.

Indeo is Intel's compression scheme. Indeo is more common on Windows than the Mac. It is superior to Cinepak in resolution, however, it is inferior to Cinepak with regard to smoothness and compression ratio.

MPEG looks for changes in the image from frame to frame. Figure 9-25 shows, in a simplified way, how this process works. Key frames are identified every few frames, and the changes that occur from key frame to key frame are recorded.

The **Sorenson** codec is useful for compressing 24-bit video intended for CD or the Web. This codec offers high quality and fast data transfer. It offers better picture quality and smaller files than Cinepak.

DVI (digital video interleave) is Intel's proprietary compression technology. DVI is capable of reducing the size of the file while maintaining image quality.

On the Web, video will most often be displayed using one of three players: Windows Media Player, QuickTime Player, or RealPlayer. All of these players support most of the common video formats and allow users to control video using features such as play, pause/stop, rewind, and fast forward. These controllers enable users to control volume and view video non-linearly.

FIGURE 9-25
Video compression process

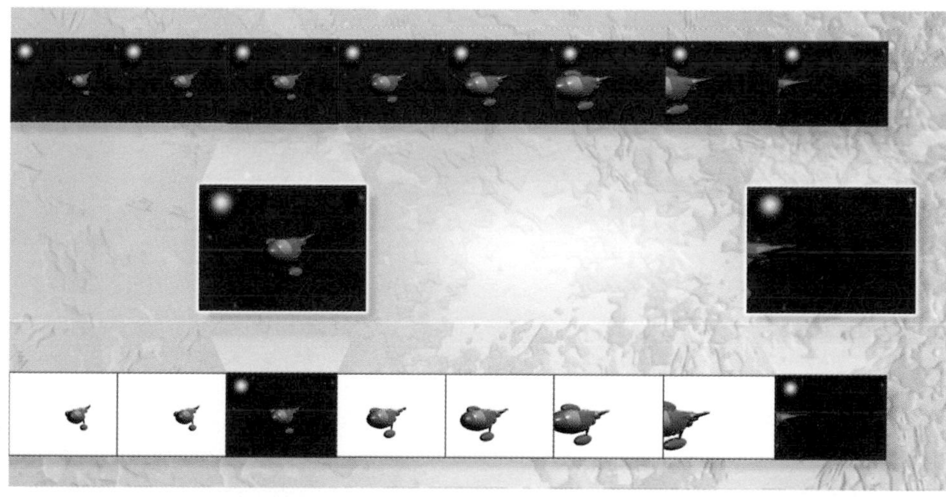

SUMMARY

Video provides the power to communicate with motion and sound and serves as a rich resource on the Web. Video editing technology is now affordable, making it possible for consumers and professionals to put their video stories on the Web.

Video can stimulate emotions, convey messages, provide instructions, demonstrate techniques, and relate experiences. Consequently, it has wide appeal and varied use on Web pages designed to educate, sell, and entertain. Because working with video can be a very intricate process, it may be necessary to hire video specialists, including videographers who are skilled in the art of shooting video as well as video editors who are able to edit and composite the final clips.

Analog video, such as video footage on videotape and **videodisc** or **laser disc**, must be digitized or converted to a digital format before the computer can understand and manipulate it. Common analog formats include **VHS, S-VHS, Hi-8**, and **Betacam SP**.

Video capture cards are needed to convert analog video to a digital format. **Digital video (DV)** is video that is already in a format that is recognizable by the computer. **Digital video cameras**, which are usually based on **DV standards**, store digital video that can be directly transferred to the computer using a high-speed connector called **FireWire** or **IEEE-1394**. Common digital formats include **D1, D2, D3**, and **DV**. **DVDs** (**digtal versatile discs**, also called **digital video discs**) can be used to store digital video.

The quality of a video clip is based on several factors, including frame rate and frame size. The **source frame rate** is the speed at which individual frames are recorded and the **playback frame rate** is the speed at which individual frames display. The smoothness of a video clip is determined by the frame rate, which on the Web must be between 15 and 30 **frames per second (fps)** in order to appear continuous. Frame rates vary because there are different video standards used throughout the world. The most common video standards are **NTSC**, **PAL**,

SECAM, and **HDTV**. Bandwidth, processor speed, memory, and monitor size and resolution are more important and applicable than these standards when developing video for the Web. **Resolution** is another factor. It is based on the **aspect ratio** of the frame as well as the **frame size** and **bit depth**.

Clip video and other **stock video footage** options are available. If you choose to use these options, be sure to follow all licensing agreements and copyright restrictions. If you decide to shoot, capture, and produce your own video, follow the pre-production, production, and post-production guidelines to ensure that your video clips use **SMPTE** standard timecode and that they are appropriate and effective.

Today, there are several affordable software programs available for editing and compositing digital video. Adobe, Avid, and Apple are three of the most well-known companies offering mid-range and high-end desktop video editing packages for both the consumer and professional markets. You can use these software tools to process your video once it has been captured. Using these various programs you can add special effects and transitions, overlay titles and text, and even add additional sound tracks. The Adobe products are known for their **open architecture** and **nondestructive editing** features.

There are different digital video file formats just as there are different graphic and sound file formats. Some of the most common include **ASF, AVI, MPEG, MOV, RM,** and **WMV**. Digital video files are huge. Compression reduces the video file size and improves the **data transfer rate (dtr)**. The compression/decompression algorithms used to compress data are called **codecs**. Different file formats support different codecs. Some of the most common video codecs include **Animation**, **Apple Cinepak**, **Indeo**, MPEG, **Sorenson**, and **DVI**.

KEY TERMS

analog video
animation codec
Apple Cinepak
ASF (Advanced Streaming Format)
aspect ratio
AVI (Audio Video Interleave)
Betacam SP
bit depth
clip video
codec
data transfer rate (dtr)
digital video
digital video camera
D1
D2
D3
DV
DVD (digital versatile disc, digital video disc)
DVI (digital versatile interleave)
DV standard
FireWire
frame size
frames per second (fps)
HDTV
Hi-8
IEEE-1394
Indeo
laser disc
MOV (QuickTime)
MPEG
nondestructive editing
NTSC
open architecture
PAL
playback frame rate
resolution
RM (RealMedia)
SECAM
SMPTE
Sorenson
source frame rate
stock video footage
S-VHS
VHS
video capture card
videodisc
WMV (Windows Media File)

MATCHING QUESTIONS/DISCUSSION QUESTIONS

Match each term with the sentence that best describes it.

a. Adobe Premiere	**b.** aspect ratio	**c.** bit depth
d. codec	**e.** data transfer rate	**f.** Hi-8
g. nondestructive editing	**h.** open architecture	**i.** playback frame rate
j. resolution	**k.** SMPTE	**l.** source frame rate
m. stock video footage	**n.** video capture cards	**o.** videodisc

_____ **1.** Hardware that allows you to convert analog video to digital video.

_____ **2.** The time it takes for the video to be transferred from the processor and displayed on the monitor.

_____ **3.** The speed at which individual frames display, measured in frames per second (fps).

_____ **4.** This is the time code that measures video in hours, minutes, seconds, and frames.

_____ **5.** Analog technology that provides a random access feature to video footage.

_____ **6.** Term used to refer to the way in which Adobe Premiere preserves original video clips in case you make a mistake, change your mind, or wish to use them in another application.

_____ **7.** The speed at which the video is recorded.

_____ **8.** Video footage acquired from a third party such as a freelance videographer or stock videography company.

_____ **9.** An affordable, highly rated, non-linear, video-editing program.

_____ **10.** This means the program is designed to be compatible with numerous software programs, extensions, and file formats.

_____ **11.** This measure of video quality is determined by aspect ratio, frame size, and bit depth.

_____ **12.** A compression/decompression algorithm used to compress data.

_____ **13.** The number of bits used to describe the color of a single pixel.

_____ **14.** The highest quality videotape format found in the consumer market.

_____ **15.** The ratio of width to height in a frame of video.

Answer each question either in writing or in a class discussion as directed by your instructor.

1. What is the difference between analog and digital video? How do you digitize analog video?
2. What factors determine the quality of the video file?
3. How do copyright laws affect the use of video on the Web?
4. What are some key features of Adobe Premiere?
5. What are codecs? What are some of the more common codecs used with digital video files?

DESIGN PROJECT

Working with Video—Windows Users

1. Organize the Collections Folders and Import Files
2. Assemble and Edit a Movie
3. Add Transitions, Effects, Titles, and Sound to a Movie
4. Save a Movie and Add It to a Web Page

This is a continuation of the Design Project in Chapter 8.

The client The Inn at Birch Bay has reviewed the Web pages and has asked that a video be added to the site.

The WebsByCT multimedia development team has decided that this project would be ideal for you to learn the basics of working with video. To complete the lessons in this design project, you will be using Windows Movie Maker 2 to develop a video. (If you are using a Macintosh, skip to Working with Video—Macintosh Users.) Then you will use Macromedia Dreamweaver MX 2004 to insert the new video into a Web page.

Video can be an important part of an interactive Web experience and Windows Movie Maker 2 provides an easy-to-use tool for creating video. The program allows you to import video clips, graphic images, and audio clips that can be assembled and edited. Then transitions, special effects, narrations, text titles, and credits can be added. As you are creating a movie, everything is stored in a project file. The project file is not the finished movie, but rather a file that contains the arrangement and timing information of the video and audio clips, pictures, transitions, effects, and titles that are used in the movie. When a project is saved, a .mswmm filename extension is used. Only Windows Movie Maker can open and edit a .mswmm file. A .mswmm file cannot be added to a Web page, however, a .mswmm file can be saved as a .wmv file, which can be added to a Web page.

After completing a project you can choose various settings for saving it as a movie, including saving to your computer, to a recordable CD, or as an e-mail attachment. In addition, you can specify settings that will affect the quality and file size of the movie. For example, choosing Video for broadband (512 Kbps) results in a movie with a bit rate of 512 and file size of 1.5 MB; the same movie with Video for broadband (150 Kbps) results in a bit rate of 150 and a file size of 437 KB. A higher bit rate results in higher-quality video with smoother motion. However, as the bit rate increases, so does the video file size. A .wmv file name extension is used when saving a movie that you want to add to a Web page.

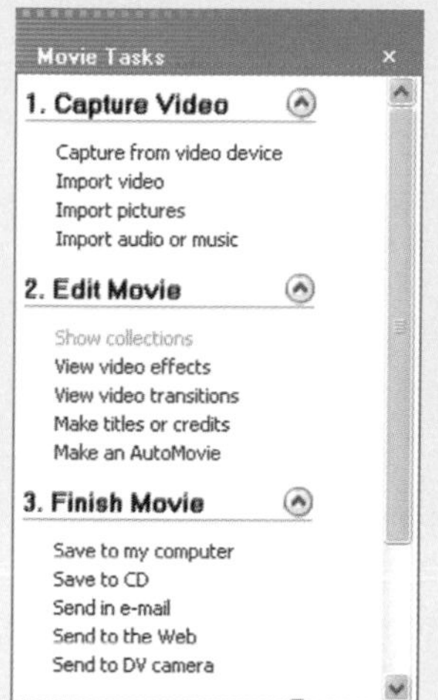
Movie Tasks
1. Capture Video
Capture from video device
Import video
Import pictures
Import audio or music
2. Edit Movie
Show collections
View video effects
View video transitions
Make titles or credits
Make an AutoMovie
3. Finish Movie
Save to my computer
Save to CD
Send in e-mail
Send to the Web
Send to DV camera

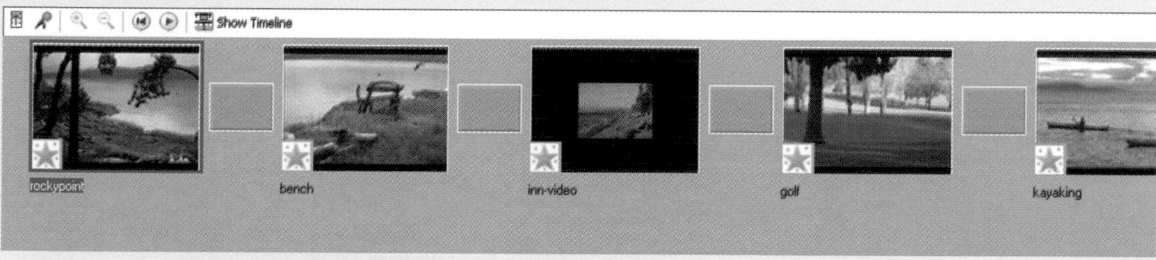
Show Timeline
rockypoint
bench
inn-video
golf
kayaking

Collections
Video Effects
Video Transitions
Collections
inn-video
otherFiles

Timeline: rockypoint
Rocky Point
Paused
0:00:00.87 / 0:00:43.87

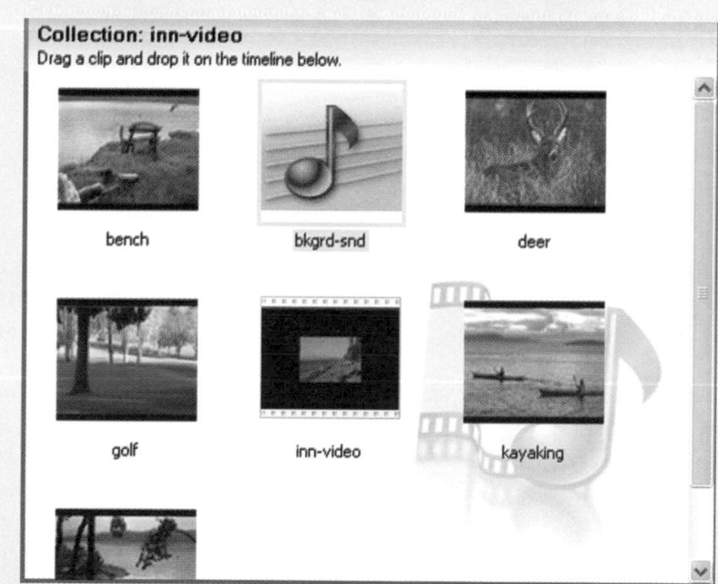
Collection: inn-video
Drag a clip and drop it on the timeline below.
bench
bkgrd-snd
deer
golf
inn-video
kayaking

LESSON 1

ORGANIZE THE COLLECTIONS

Folders and Import Files

What You'll Do

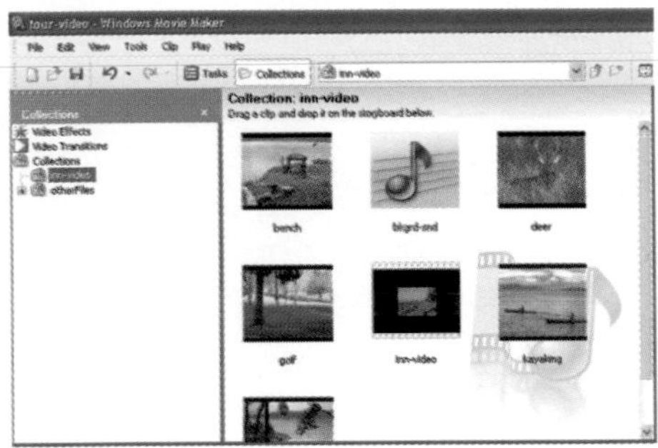

In this lesson, you will learn how to organize the Collections pane and how to import files.

The Windows Movie Maker Workspace

A description of the main components of the Windows Movie Maker 2 workspace as shown in Figure 9-26 follows:

Menu bar—Provides commands used when performing tasks in Windows Movie Maker.

Toolbar—Provides shortcuts to the most commonly performed tasks.

Panes—There are three panes that provide the features and hold the content you work with: Collections, Contents, and Movie Tasks (not shown in figure).

Collections pane—Lists your collections, which can be video clips, sound clips, and pictures that are available to be included in your movie. You can have more than one collection. The files for each collection can be organized in folders. As you create collections, the folders containing the collections are displayed in an alphabetical list in the pane. When you open a collection from the list, its contents (video clips, sound clips, and pictures) are displayed in the Contents pane as thumbnails.

Contents pane—Displays the clips and pictures of the currently selected collection. You can drag clips and pictures from the Contents pane to the Storyboard/Timeline to make a movie. A clip or picture represents the original source file but it is not the source file. If you make changes to a clip in a collection, such as trimming it, the changes do not affect the source file. In addition to displaying clips and pictures, the Contents pane displays thumbnails of transitions and effects that can be added to the movie.

Movie Tasks pane—Displays options for performing the following tasks depending on where you are in the movie making process:

Capture Video: Provides options for capturing your own video clips or importing existing video and audio clips, as well as pictures.

Edit Movie: Provides options for editing video and audio clips, as well as adding effects, transitions, titles, and credits.

FIGURE 9-26

The Windows Movie Maker 2 workspace

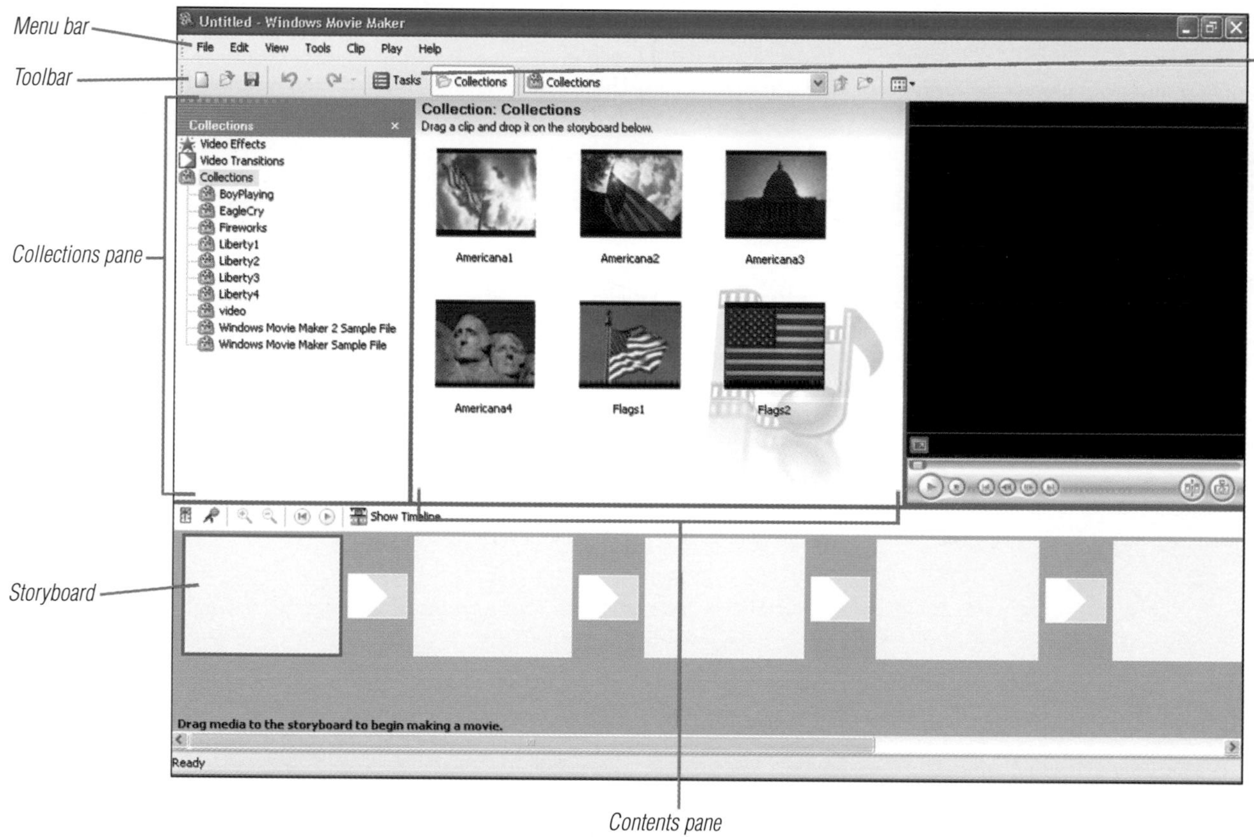

Finish Movie: Provides options for saving your final movie, such as to your computer or to a recordable CD.
Movie Making Tips: Provides help for completing common tasks in Windows Movie Maker.

As you work with Windows Movie Maker you will need to switch between the Collections view and the Movie Tasks view. This is done using the View option on the menu bar, or the Tasks and Collections buttons on the toolbar.

Storyboard/Timeline—The Storyboard and Timeline are used to assemble your movie assets and edit movie clips.

Monitor—The monitor is used to playback the movie as it is being developed.

Organizing the Assets for Your Project

Your first task will be to organize the assets for your project in the Collections pane, as shown in Figure 9-27. You will create two folders, inn-video and otherFiles. The otherFiles folder will hold all of the assets that come with Windows Movie Maker, such as EagleCry and Liberty1. After creating the otherFiles folder, you will drag each of the files to it. You will not be using these assets. The inn-video folder will hold all of the assets you will use for your project.

By default Windows Movie Maker creates a collection folder for each video clip that is imported to the Collections pane. You can add other files to a collection folder so that all of the project assets are in one folder. When you import a file (such as an .avi or .jpg) a thumbnail is displayed in the Contents pane. This thumbnail is not a copy of the source file, but rather provides a reference to it. Therefore, do not move, rename, or delete the original source files.

Undo and Redo

The Undo ([Ctrl] + z) and Redo ([Ctrl] + y) commands in the Edit menu can be used to undo and redo the last action. You will find these to be among the most useful Windows Movie Maker commands. If you want to undo or redo multiple actions at one time, you can use the Undo and Redo buttons on the toolbar.

QUICKTIP

The exercises in this chapter were created with the screen resolution set at 1024 x 768. If your computer's screen resolution has a different setting, the figures in the book may appear different. You may want to verify the screen resolution on your computer and set it to 1024 x 768, if necessary.

FIGURE 9-27

Organizing the assets for your project

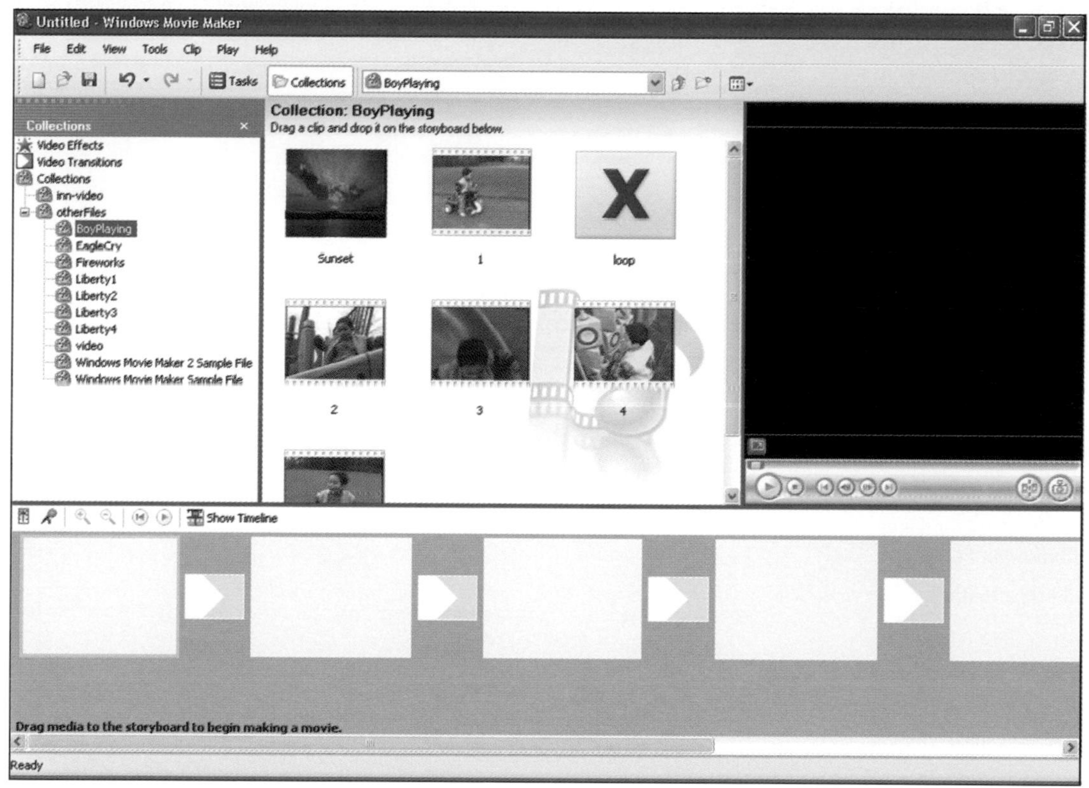

Organize the Collections folders and import files

1. Create a folder named **innMovieProject**, in the location where you will be saving the movie project.

   This folder is not part of the Movie Maker 2 Collections folders. Rather, it is used to save your project.
2. Start **Windows Movie Maker 2**.
3. Click **View** on the menu bar to display the View options, then select options so your View menu matches Figure 9-28.

   Note: Figure 9-28 shows the Contents pane with several clips and pictures. You may have other clips and pictures or none at all displayed on your computer. If the Contents pane is empty, skip to step 8. If you skip to step 8, you will not create the otherFiles folder, and your screens will be slightly different from the figures.
4. Click the **Collections folder** in the Collections pane, click **Tools** on the menu bar, then click **New Collection Folder**.
5. Type **otherFiles**, then press **[Enter].**
6. Drag each of the items in the Contents pane to the **otherFiles folder** so that it resembles Figure 9-29.
7. Click the **minus sign** next to the otherFiles folder to collapse the folder.
8. Click the **Collections folder** in the Collections pane, click **File** on the menu bar, then click **Import into Collections**.

(continued)

FIGURE 9-28
The View menu options

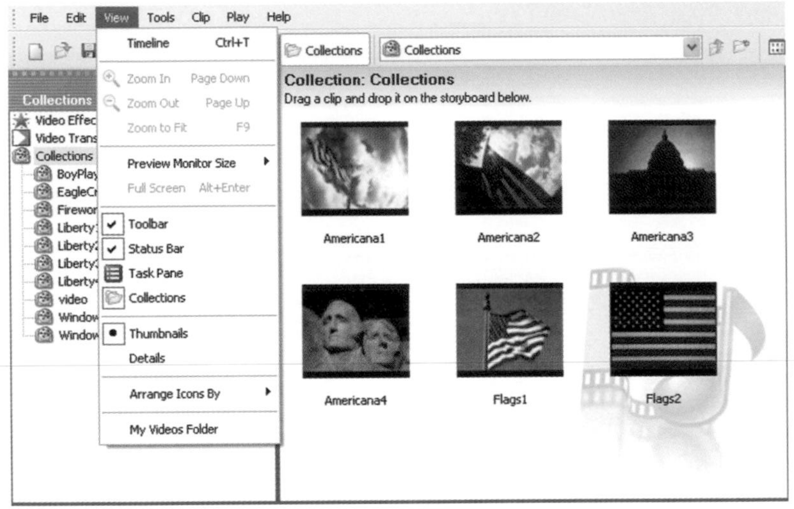

FIGURE 9-29
The otherFiles folder after dragging the items to it

FIGURE 9-30

The Contents pane displaying thumbnails of the imported files

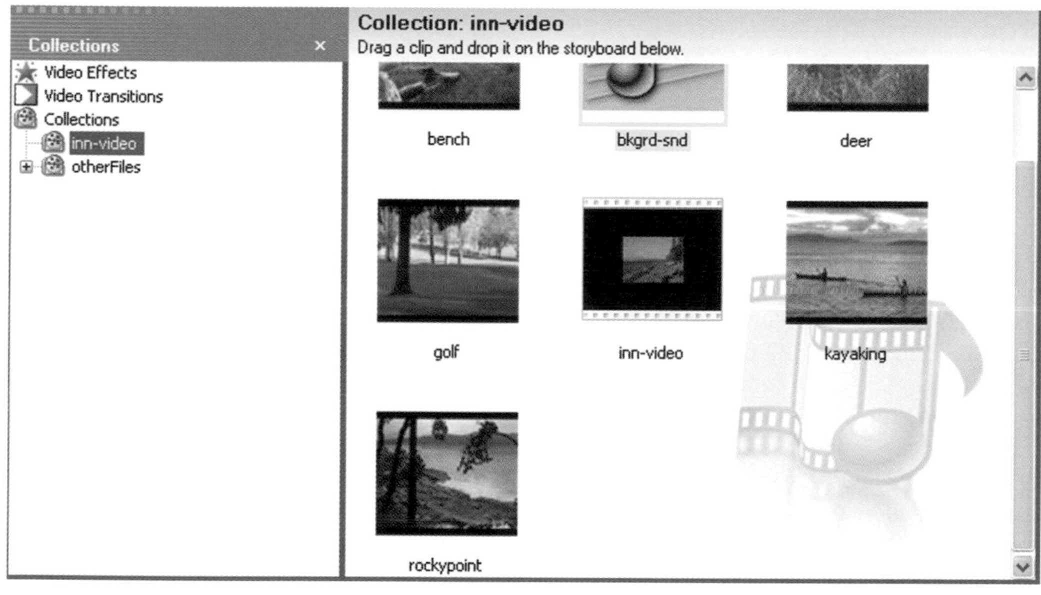

9. Navigate to the folder containing the files for this chapter, click **inn-video.avi**, then click **Import**.

   When you import a video file (inn-video.avi), a new collection (inn-video) is created. Later you will add the pictures to this collection so that all of the assets for the movie are in one collection.

10. Click the **inn-video folder** in the Collections pane, click **File** on the menu bar, then click **Import into Collections**.

11. Click **bench.jpg**, hold down **[Ctrl]**, click **bkgrd-snd.wav, deer.jpg, golf.jpg, kayaking.jpg** and **rockypoint.jpg** to select them, then click **Import**.

    After clicking Import, thumbnails of the files are displayed in the Contents pane as shown in Figure 9-30.

12. Click **File** on the menu bar, click **Save Project As**, then navigate to the **innMovieProject** folder and save the project as **tour-video.mswmm**.

You added a Collections folder, imported files, and saved the project.

LESSON 2

ASSEMBLE AND Edit a Movie

What You'll Do

In this lesson, you will learn how to assemble a movie and edit a video clip.

Storyboard/Timeline Views

The area where you assemble and edit your movie is displayed in two views, the Storyboard and the Timeline. You switch between these two views when making a movie.

The Storyboard

The Storyboard is best used to assemble the assets of your movie and to add transitions and effects. You simply drag each file, transition, or effect from the Contents pane to the Storyboard in the sequence that it will play in the movie. The Storyboard displays thumbnails of the assets you choose to have in your movie such as video clips, pictures, and transitions, as shown in Figure 9-31. You can rearrange the assets by dragging them to another location on the Storyboard and you can delete them by using the Delete command from the Edit menu. The Timeline can also be used to assemble the assets in your movie.

The Timeline

The Timeline is used to change the duration an asset is displayed in a movie. For example, if you would like a picture to be displayed for four seconds, you drag a handle on a thumbnail on the Timeline to adjust the length of time the picture is displayed in the movie. The Timeline is also used to trim video and audio clips and text titles. The Timeline is calibrated in hours, minutes, seconds, and hundredths of a second, which are displayed as h:mm:ss.hs. You can change the view so that more or less of the Timeline is displayed using the Zoom Timeline In and Zoom Timeline Out buttons on the Timeline or the equivalent commands in the View menu.

The Timeline displays the following tracks to indicate the assets you have added to your movie. These are shown in Figure 9-32.

Video track—Displays the video clips and pictures added to the movie, as well as their filenames. You can trim a video clip from either end by dragging a trim handle inward, and you can adjust the duration a picture is displayed by dragging an end trim handle.

Transition track—Displays the transitions you have added to the movie, as well as their filenames. You can drag the start trim handle that appears when the transition is selected to increase or decrease its duration.

Audio track—Displays the audio that is associated with a video clip. Deleting the audio will delete the associated video clip.

Audio/Music track—Displays audio clips you have added to the movie. You can add video clips to this track if you want the audio, but not the video, to play in your movie.

Title Overlay track—Displays the titles and credits that you add to this track. You can add multiple titles to this track at different points in your movie. The titles overlay the video that is displayed. You can drag the start or end trim handle that appears when the title is selected to increase or decrease its duration.

You can change the view so that all the tracks are displayed or only the Video, Audio/Music, and Title Overlay tracks are displayed.

FIGURE 9-31
The Storyboard with thumbnails

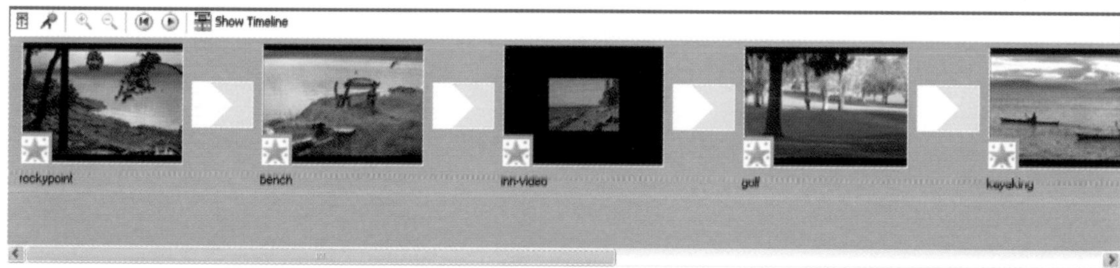

FIGURE 9-32
The Timeline tracks

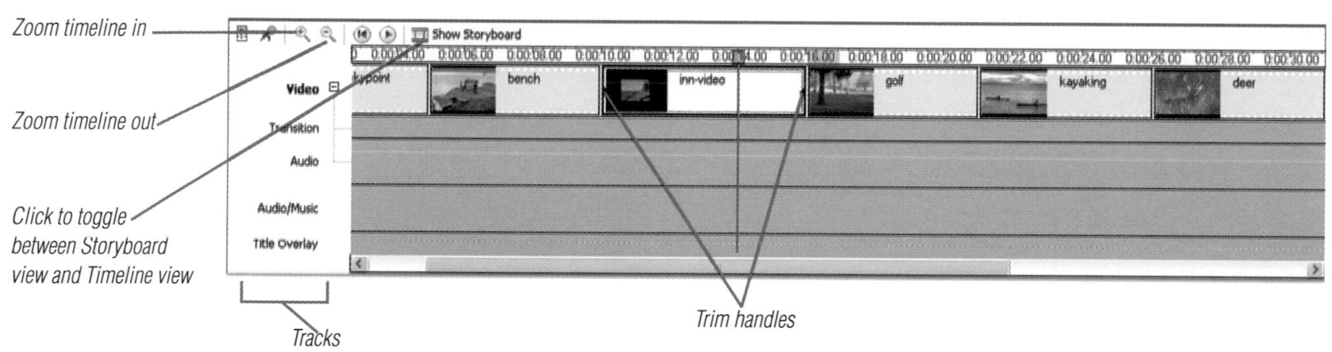

Assemble the movie

1. Verify the Storyboard view is displayed.
2. Click **Tools** on the menu bar, click **Options**, then click the **Advanced tab**.
3. Click the **up** or **down list arrow** for the Picture duration to set the amount of time that each picture will be displayed to **5 seconds**, then click **OK**.
4. Drag the **rockypoint picture** to the first placeholder in the Storyboard as shown in Figure 9-33.
5. Drag the **bench picture** to the second placeholder in the Storyboard.
6. Drag the **inn-video clip** to the third placeholder in the Storyboard.
7. Drag the **golf picture** to the fourth placeholder in the Storyboard.
8. Drag the **kayaking picture** to the fifth placeholder in the Storyboard.
9. Drag the **scroll button** on the bottom of the Storyboard to the right to display the sixth placeholder, then drag the **deer picture** to the placeholder.
10. Click the **Stop button** on the monitor controls as shown in Figure 9-34.

    The Stop button rewinds the movie.
11. Click the **Play button** on the monitor controls, then watch the movie on the monitor.
12. Click **File** on the menu bar, then click **Save Project**.

You used the Storyboard to assemble a movie and play it.

FIGURE 9-33
Dragging a picture to the Storyboard

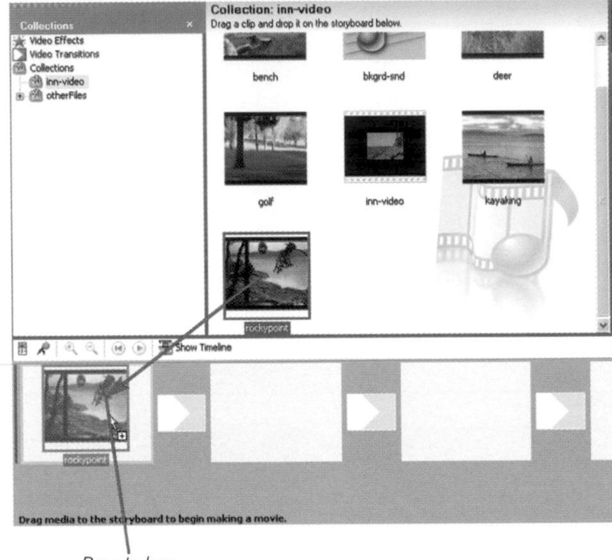

FIGURE 9-34
The Stop button on the monitor

FIGURE 9-35
The double-headed arrow

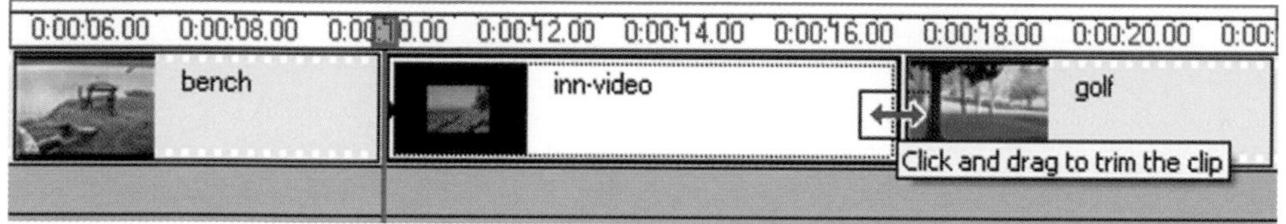

FIGURE 9-36
Trimming the video clip

Edit a video clip

1. Click **View** on the menu bar, then click **Timeline**.
2. Click the **Zoom Timeline In button** twice to enlarge the thumbnails displayed on the Timeline.
3. Drag the **scroll button** at the bottom of the Timeline to the left to display the beginning of the movie.
4. Click the **inn-video clip** on the Timeline.
5. Point to the end of the clip to display the double-headed arrow as shown in Figure 9-35.
6. Drag the arrow back to about the **16 second mark** as shown in Figure 9-36.
7. Click the **Stop button** on the monitor to rewind the movie, then click the **Play button**.
8. Save the project.

You edited a video clip by trimming it.

LESSON 3

ADD TRANSITIONS, EFFECTS, TITLES, and Sound to a Movie

What You'll Do

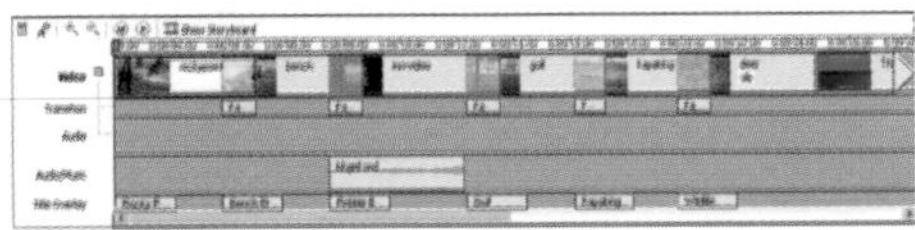

In this lesson, you will learn how to add transitions, effects, titles, and sound to a movie.

Transitions

The movie you are creating has a video clip and several pictures. Windows Movie Maker 2 allows you to insert transitions, such as wipes and fade-ins, between these assets. Transitions add interest and unity to the movie because they help the assets appear more like a continuous motion picture than a series of still pictures. To add transitions to a movie, you must display Video Transitions in the Contents pane, and then drag each transition to the desired location on the Transitions track on the Timeline or to the area between two assets on the Storyboard. They appear as thumbnails on the Storyboard and as labels on the Timeline as shown in Figure 9-37. You can delete a transition by selecting it and pressing [Delete].

Effects

In addition to transitions, you can apply effects to a video clip or picture. Effects can be very radical, such as displaying a photograph as a watercolor or displaying a video clip with an aged appearance; or, they can be a simple zoom in effect. To add effects to a clip or picture, you must display Video Effects in the Contents pane, and then drag each effect to the desired location on the Transitions track on the Timeline or to a picture or video clip on the Storyboard. A colored star on the Storyboard or the Timeline indicates that an effect has been applied to that picture or video. When you point to a star, its name is displayed. You can delete an effect by selecting it and pressing [Delete].

Titles

Titles are text that you add to the movie. Titles can be added at the beginning or ending of a movie; before or after a video clip or picture; or superimposed on a clip or picture. In addition to specifying the text and its location, you can indicate how the text animates (such as flying in, scrolling, flashing, and so on), and you can specify a font, font color, type size, alignment, and amount of transparency. To add a title or credits, you must select a video clip or picture, choose Make titles or credits from the Movie Tasks pane, and follow the prompts to complete the title. You can use the Storyboard view or the Timeline view to complete a title. However, if you have overlaid a title on a clip or picture in Storyboard view, Windows Movie Maker 2 switches you to Timeline view. Credits are text displayed at the end of the movie. You can animate the text and change its font attributes. The Credits feature can be used for displaying any type of text, such as an ending for the movie.

Sound

Windows Movie Maker 2 provides an Audio/Music track in the Timeline view that allows you to add a narration as well as sounds, such as background music, to your movie. These audio clips can be edited (e.g., trimmed), the volume can be adjusted, and audio effects (fade in and fade out) can be specified. To add audio, you must drag the audio clip from the Contents pane to the desired location on the Timeline.

FIGURE 9-37
The Storyboard and Timeline with the same transitions

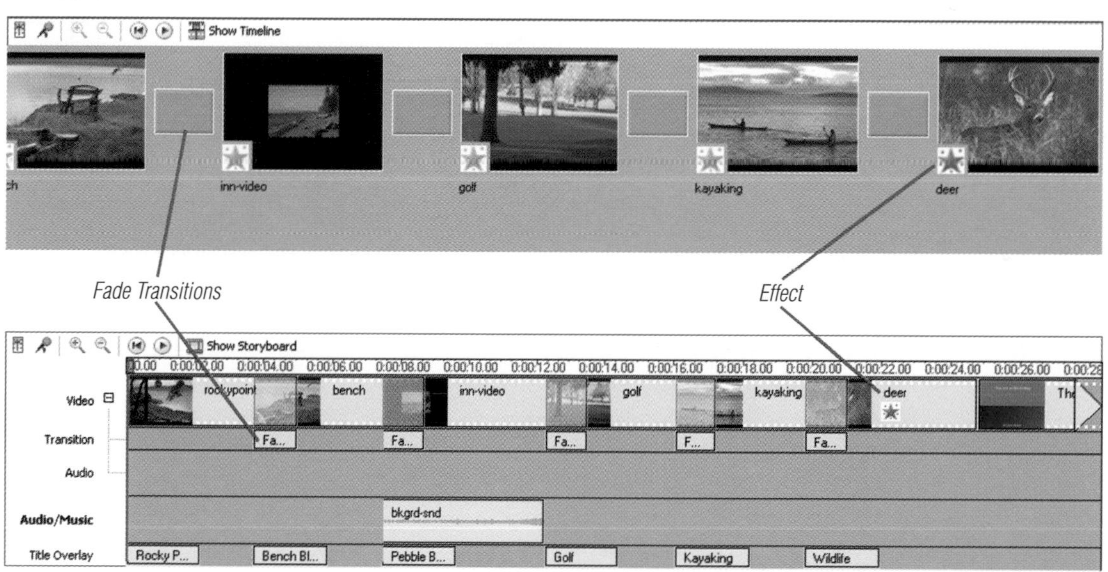

Add transitions to a movie

1. Click **View** on the menu bar, then click **Storyboard**.
2. Click **View** on the menu bar, then click **Task Pane**. If necessary, click the **down arrow** next to Edit Movie to expand its options.
3. Click **View video transitions** in the Movie Tasks pane.
4. Drag the **scroll button** on the scroll bar in the Contents pane down to display the **Fade transition**.
5. Drag the **scroll button** on the scrollbar in the Storyboard to the left to display the rockypoint picture.
6. Drag the **Fade transition** to between the rockypoint picture and the bench picture as shown in Figure 9-38.
7. Drag the **Fade transition** to between the bench picture and the inn-video clip.
8. Continue to drag the **Fade transition** so it is placed between each of the other movie elements.
9. Click the **Stop button** on the monitor, then click the **Play button**.
10. Save the project.

You added transitions to the movie.

Add an effect to a movie

1. Verify the Storyboard is displayed.
2. Drag the **scroll button** to the right as needed so that the deer picture is displayed.

(continued)

FIGURE 9-38
Dragging a transition to the Storyboard

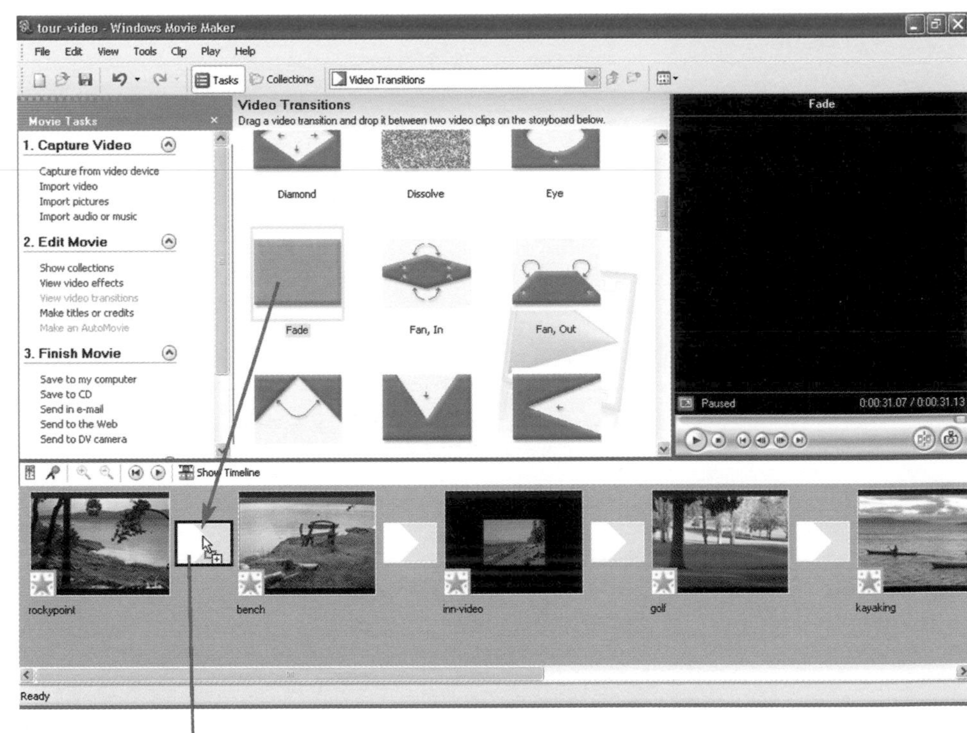

FIGURE 9-39
Dragging the Ease In effect to the Storyboard

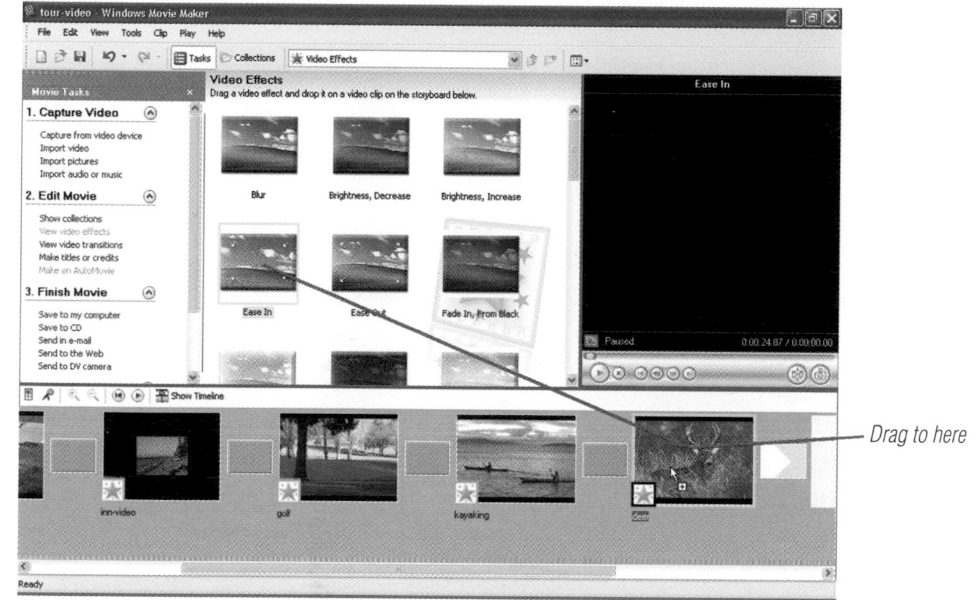

FIGURE 9-40
Trimming the title

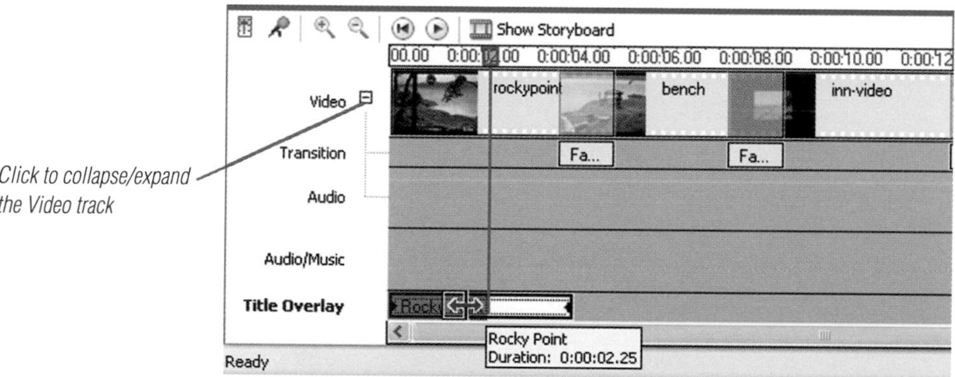

3. Click **View video effects** in the Movie Tasks pane.
4. Drag the **Ease In** effect to the deer picture as shown in Figure 9-39.
5. Click the **Stop button** on the monitor, then click the **Play button**.
6. Save the project.

You added an effect to the movie.

Add titles to a movie

1. Drag the **scroll button** to the left as needed to display the rockypoint picture, then click to select the **rockypoint picture**.
2. Click **Make titles or credits** in the Movie Tasks pane, then click **title on the selected clip**.
3. Type **Rocky Point**, then click **Change the title animation**.
4. Scroll the list to display **Fade, Slow Zoom**, click it, then click **Done, add title to movie**.
5. When the message appears, read it, then click **OK**.
6. Click the **Rocky Point title** in the Title Overlay track, position the double-headed arrow over the right end of the title, then **drag** to the left to trim the title length as shown in Figure 9-40.
7. Rewind and play the movie, then return to the Storyboard view.
8. Click the **bench picture**, click **Make titles or credits** in the Movie Tasks pane, then click **title on the selected clip**.

(continued)

9. Type **Bench Bluff**, then click **Done, add title to movie**.
10. When the message appears, click **OK**.
11. Click the **Bench Bluff title** on the Timeline, position the double-headed arrow [↔] over the right end, then **drag** to the left as far as possible to trim the title.
12. Rewind and play the movie, then return to the Storyboard view.
13. Repeat steps 8 through 11 for the remaining video clip and pictures using the following titles: **Pebble Beach**, **Golf**, **Kayaking**, **Wildlife**, then rewind and play the movie.
14. Save the project.

You added titles to the movie and trimmed them.

Add text to a movie

1. Display the Storyboard view.
2. Drag the **scroll button** on the Storyboard to the right to display the end of the movie, then click the empty placeholder after the deer picture.
3. Click **Make titles or credits** in the Movie Tasks pane, then click **credits at the end**.

   The Credits feature will be used to display text at the end of the movie.
4. Type **The Inn at Birch Bay** as shown in Figure 9-41.
5. Press **[Tab]**, then type **Get away!**.
6. Press **[Tab]** twice, then type **Get active!**.
7. Press **[Tab]** twice, then type **or just relax!**.

   Notice the monitor displays a preview of the credit text.

(continued)

FIGURE 9-41
Typing a heading for the credits

Enter Text for Title
Click 'Done' to add the title to the movie.

The Inn at Birch Bay

Done, add title to movie
Cancel

More options:
Change the title animation
Change the text font and color

FIGURE 9-42
Selecting a color from the color palette

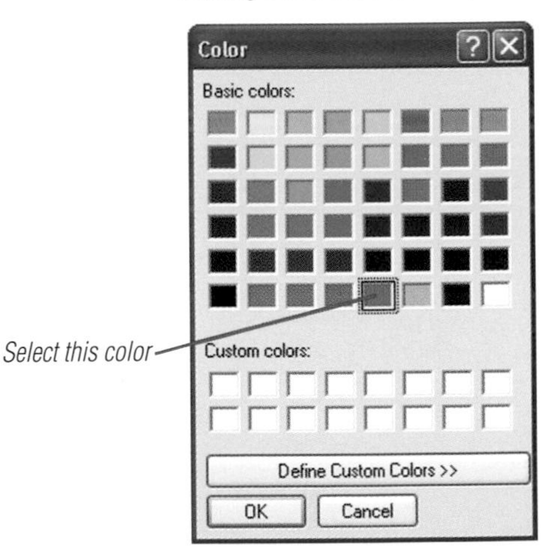

FIGURE 9-43

Dragging the sound file to the Timeline

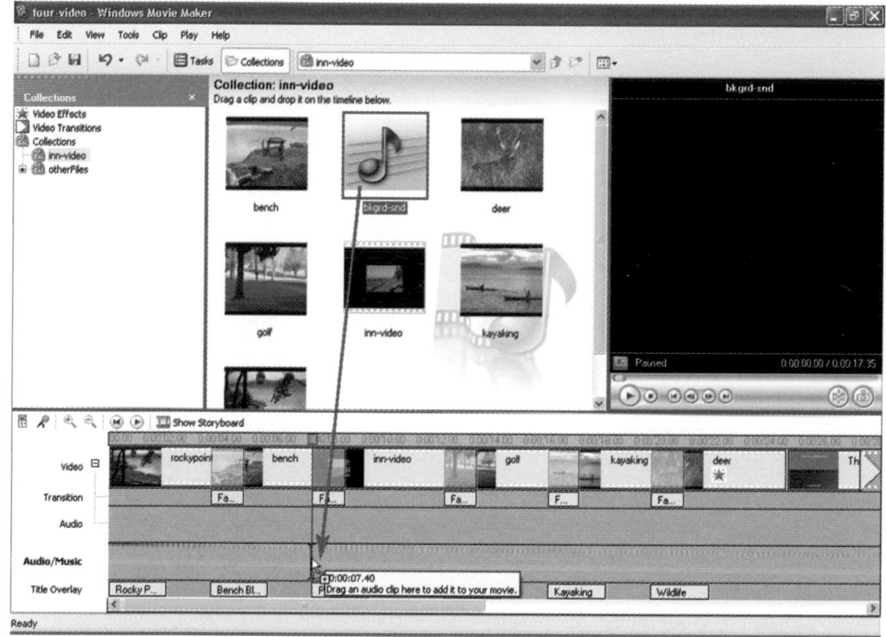

FIGURE 9-44

Trimming the sound file

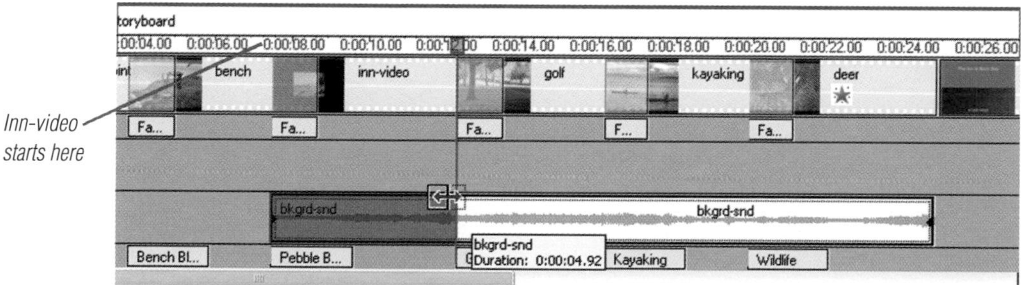

8. Select **The Inn at Birch Bay**, then click **Change the text font and color**.
9. Click the **color icon** , click the **teal color** shown in Figure 9-42, then click **OK**.
10. Click **Change the title animation**, scroll to the bottom of the list, then click **Credits:Video Top**.
11. Click **Done, add title to movie**.
12. Rewind and play the movie, then save the project.

You added text to the movie.

Add sound to a movie

1. Click **View** on the menu bar, then click **Timeline**.
2. Click **View** on the menu bar, then click **Collections**.
3. Click the **inn-video folder** in the Collections pane.
4. Click the **inn-video folder** on the Timeline.
5. Drag the **bkgrd-snd thumbnail** to the Audio/Music track of the Timeline and align it with the inn-video clip as shown in Figure 9-43.
6. Position the double-headed arrow on the right end of the sound file, then drag to the left to trim the sound file to the size of the clip as shown in Figure 9-44.
7. Right-click the sound file on the Timeline, then click **Fade Out**.
8. Rewind the movie, then play the movie.
9. Save the project.

You added a background sound to the movie.

LESSON 4

SAVE A MOVIE AND ADD It to a Web Page

What You'll Do

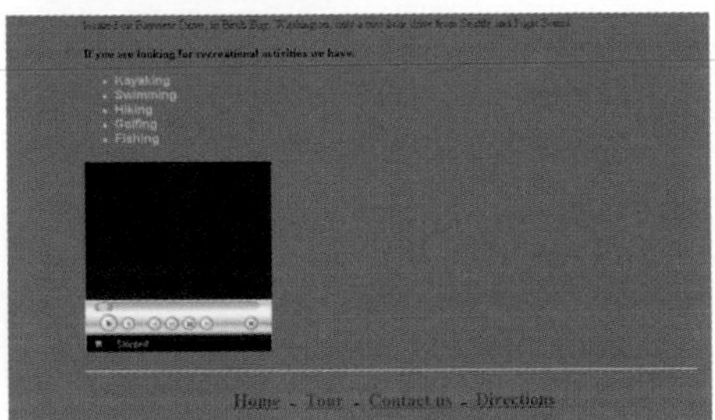

In this lesson, you will learn how to save a project as a movie and add a movie to a Web page.

Saving a Movie

Until now you have been working with a Windows Movie Maker 2 project. A project contains all of the assets, timing information, transitions, video effects, and so on that you have specified in your movie. The important thing about a project is that you can save it, make changes, and then save it again using Windows Movie Maker 2. You cannot, however, use a project file in a Web page. You must save the project as a movie using the Save Movie Wizard. Windows Movie Maker 2 provides several options based on what you want to do with the movie. These include saving it to your computer, saving to a recordable CD, and saving it as an attachment for e-mailing. In addition, you can choose from several settings that help you tailor the movie to your target audience. These include options for file type, bit rate, and frames per second. To save a project as a movie, you must choose Save Movie File from the File menu, then follow the prompts using the Save Movie Wizard. Movies are saved with a .wmv filename extension, which allows them to be viewed in a browser using a media player.

Adding a Movie to a Web Page

The process for adding a movie to a Web page is similar to adding .swf files. There are two HTML elements—object and embed—that are used to play certain types of multimedia files such as audio, video, and animation. Both should be used because different browsers recognize only one or the other. Figure 9-45 shows the code used to play the tour-video.wmv file.

<object id...: identifies the kind of object being embedded in the Web page

<param name...: identifies properties of the object, such as the filename — "tour-video.wmv"—and whether to show the video controls — "true" (yes)

<embed src...: identifies the file — "tour-video.wmv"—and its properties such as the width and height and whether to show the controls (1 is true). In addition, the URL for the plug-in needed to view the video in a browser is identified — "http://www.microsoft.com/Windows/MediaPlayer/"

Macromedia Dreamweaver provides another way to add a movie to a Web page. You can type text into a Web page, and then create a link between the typed text and the source file that causes the movie to play when the text is clicked.

FIGURE 9-45
The html code used to play a video file

```
<object id="MediaPlayer1" width="240" height="252"
        classid="CLSID:22D6F312-B0F6-11D0-94AB-0080C74C7E95"
             codebase="http://activex.microsoft.com/activex/
             controls/mplayer/en/nsmp2inf.cab#version=6,4,5,715"
        type="application/x-oleobject">
  <param name="autostart" value="false">
  <param name="filename" value="assets/tour-video.wmv">
  <param name="showcontrols" value="true">
  <param name="ShowStatusBar" value="true">
  <embed
        src="assets/tour-video.wmv"
        width="240"
        height="252"
        autostart="0" type="application/x-mplayer2"
        pluginspage="http://www.microsoft.com/Windows/MediaPlayer/"
        showcontrols="1"
        showstatusbar="1">
  </embed>
</object>
```

Save a movie file

1. Click **File** on the menu bar, then click **Save Movie File**.
2. Verify **My computer** is selected as the Movie location, then click **Next**.
3. Type **tour-video** for the filename if necessary, click **Browse**, navigate to the **innMovieProject folder**, select it and click **OK**, then click **Next**.
4. Study the Movie Setting dialog box and note the bit rate and estimated file size, then click **Show more choices** to expand the options if necessary.
5. Click the **Other settings option button**, then click the **Other settings down list arrow**.
6. Click **High quality video (large)** as shown in Figure 9-46, then click **Next**.
7. When the saving movie process is complete, verify the Play movie when I click Finish option is selected, then click **Finish**.
8. View the movie in the media player, click **Yes** to install a codec if prompted to do so, then close the player.

You saved a movie with selected settings.

FIGURE 9-46
Selecting the movie settings

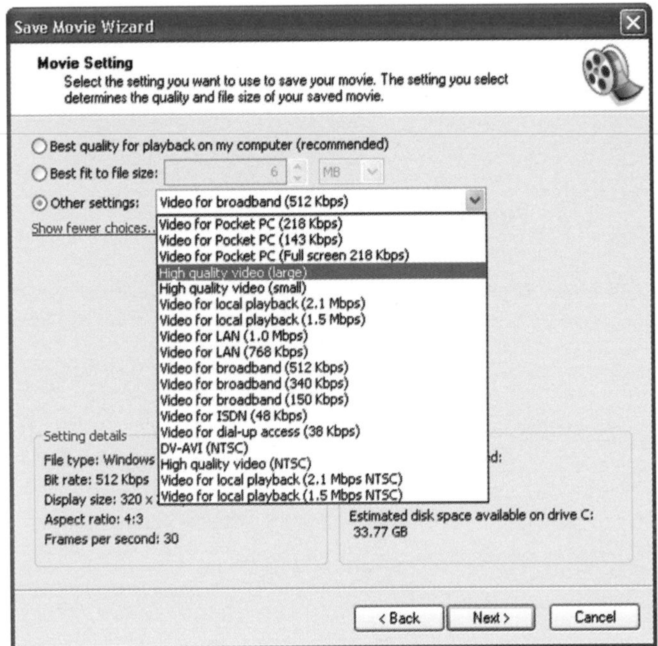

FIGURE 9-47

Dragging the icon to the Link box

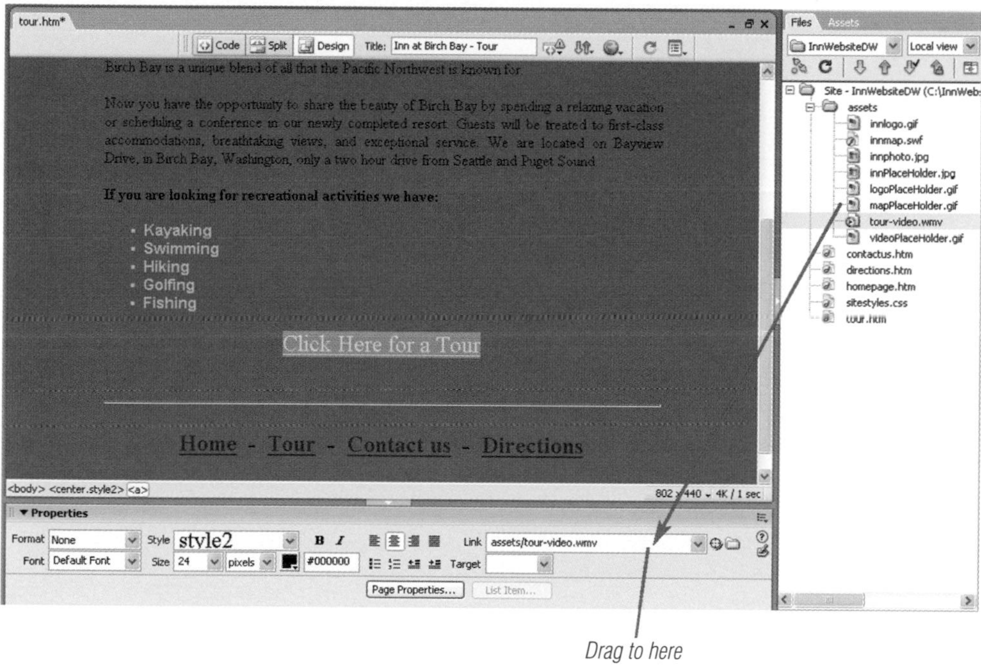

Link a movie to a Web page

1. Copy the **tour-video.wmv file** from the innMovieProject folder to the assets folder of the InnWebsiteDW folder.
2. Start **Dreamweaver**, then display the **InnWebsiteDW site** in the Files panel.
3. Double-click **tour.htm** in the Files panel to open the Web page in the document window.
4. Scroll the document window to display the **Video placeholder**, click to select the **Video placeholder**, then press **[Delete]**.
5. Type **Click Here for a Tour**.
6. Select **Click Here for a Tour**, then use the Property inspector to change the font color to **black** and the size to **24**.
7. Verify **Click Here for a Tour** is selected, then drag the **tour-video.wmv** icon from the assets folder in the Files panel to the Link box as shown in Figure 9-47.

   This creates a link between the Click Here for a Tour text and the tour-video.wmv movie.
8. Return to the Dreamweaver document, then save the document.
9. Press **[F12]** to view the Web page in a browser, then click the **Click Here for a Tour** text.
10. View the movie, click **Yes** to install a codec if prompted to do so, close the media player, then close the browser window.

You added a .wmv movie file to a Web page and linked it to text.

Embed a movie into a Web page

1. Click **File** on the menu bar, click **Save As**, type **tour-embed.htm**, then click **Save**.
2. Select the **Click Here for a Tour** text, then press **[Delete]**.
3. Navigate to the folder containing the files for this chapter, then open **video-code.txt**.
4. Copy the text, then display the Dreamweaver document.
5. Click the **Split button** [Split] on the Document toolbar.
6. Click to position the insertion point after the </center> tag as shown in Figure 9-48.

   Note: Your code may display differently. If so, click to position the insertion point before the <hr> tag.
7. Press **[Enter]**.

(continued)

FIGURE 9-48
Positioning the pointer

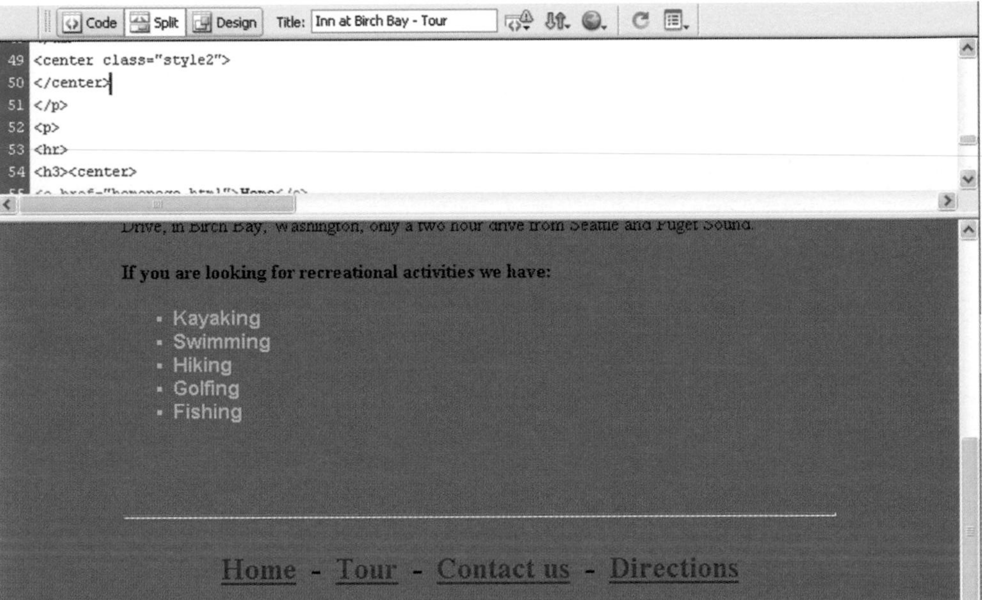

FIGURE 9-49

Movie displayed in a browser window

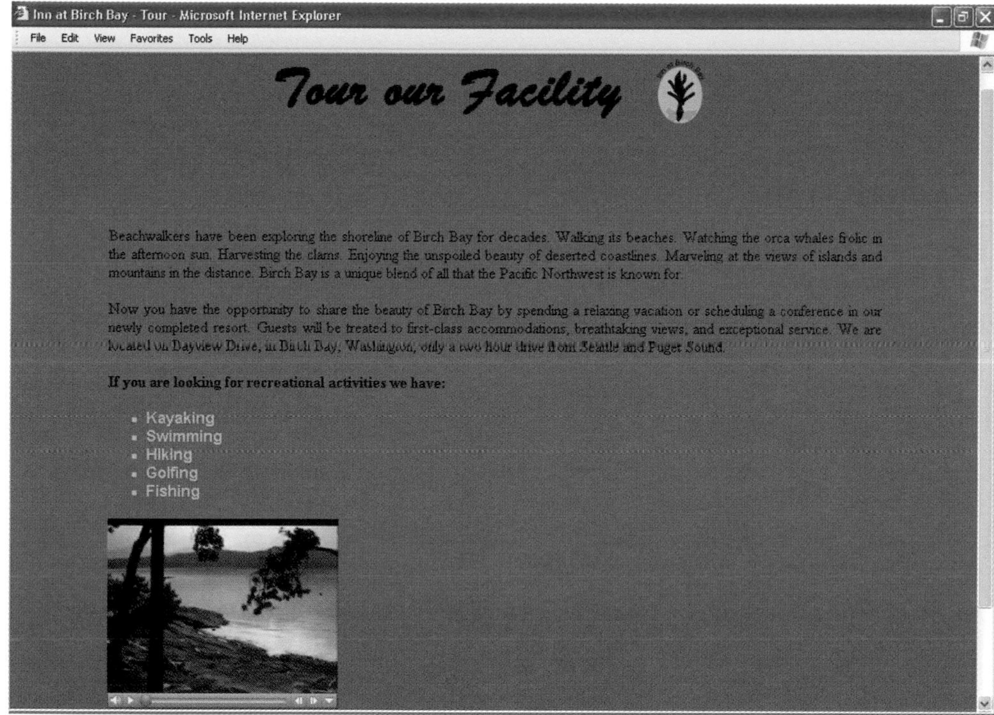

8. Click **Edit** on the menu bar, then click **Paste**.
9. Click the **Design button** [Design] on the Document toolbar to close the split window.
10. Save the document.
11. Press **[F12]** to view the Web page in a browser (see Figure 9-49), then play the movie and click **Yes** to install a codec if prompted to do so.

    Note: If you are running Windows XP with SP2, you may have to click Allow blocked content on the Internet.
12. Close the browser window, return to the Dreamweaver document.

You embedded a .wmv movie file into a Web page.

DESIGN PROJECT

Working with Video—Macintosh Users

1. Start a Project and Import Files
2. Assemble and Edit a Movie
3. Add Transitions, Effects, Titles, and Sound to a Movie
4. Save a Movie and Add It to a Web Page

This is a continuation of the Design Project in Chapter 8.

The client The Inn at Birch Bay has reviewed the Web pages and has asked that a video be added to the site.

The WebsByCT multimedia development team has decided that this project would be ideal for you to learn the basics of working with video. To complete the lessons in this design project, you will be using iMovie 3 to develop a video. Then you will use Macromedia Dreamweaver MX 2004 to insert the new video into a Web page.

Video can be an important part of an interactive Web experience and iMovie provides an easy-to-use tool for creating video. The program allows you to import video clips, graphic images, and audio clips that can be assembled and edited. Then transitions, special effects, narrations, and text titles can be added. As you are creating a movie everything is stored in a project file. The project file is not the finished movie, but rather a file that contains the arrangement and timing information of the video and audio clips, pictures, transitions, effects, and titles that have been added to the project as the movie is being assembled. Only iMovie can open and edit an iMovie project file. An iMovie file cannot be added to a Web page. However, after completing a project you can choose various settings for saving it as a movie, including saving in a QuickTime file format that is optimized for the Web.

Note: File names may appear as all capital letters (BENCH.JPG) or all lowercase letters (rockypoint.jpg). Either format is acceptable.

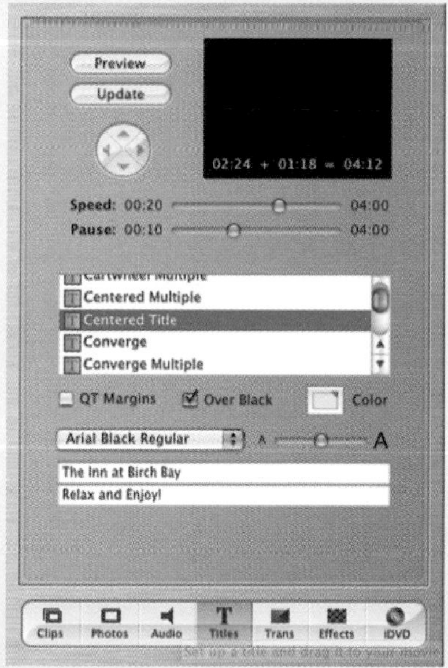

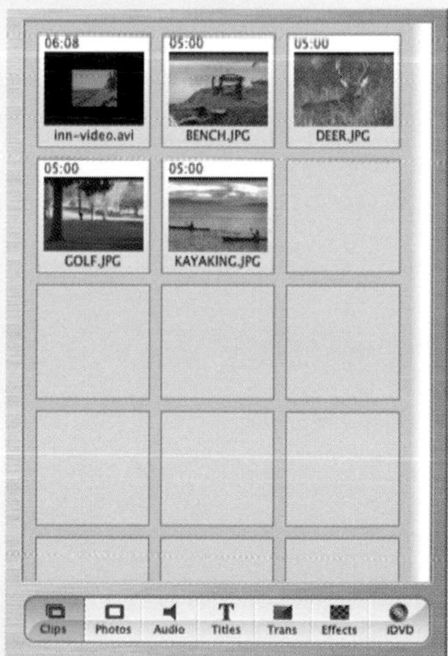

LESSON 1

START A PROJECT AND Import Files

What You'll Do

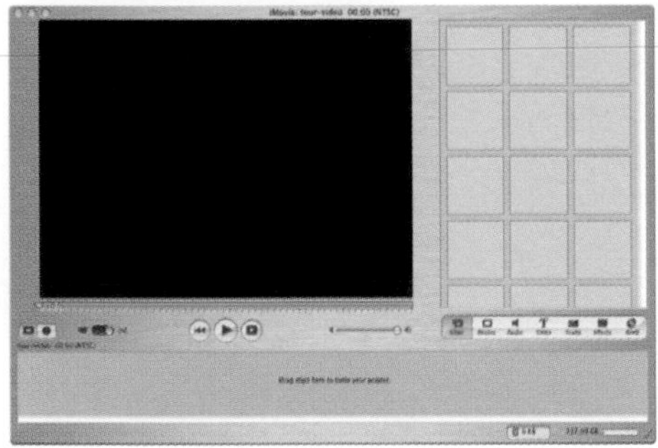

In this lesson, you will learn how to start a project and import files.

The iMovie Workspace

A description of the main components of the iMovie workspace as shown in Figure 9-50 follows:

Menu bar—Provides commands used when performing tasks in iMovie.

Clips pane—Displays the video clips and pictures that are used in the project.

Clip Viewer—Displays thumbnails of the video clips and pictures as you assemble them in sequential order to create the movie.

Monitor—Used to playback the movie as it is being developed. It can also be used to edit video clips by trimming and cropping them.

Undo and Redo

The Undo (Command + z) and Redo (Shift + Command + y) commands in the Edit menu can be used to undo and redo up to 10 actions. You will find these to be among the most useful iMovie commands.

Note: Your screen resolution must be set to 1024 × 768 or better to use iMovie.

Getting Started

Your first tasks will be to create a folder that will be used to store the completed project file and its support files, then you will start a new project and import the video file and photographs that will be used to create the movie.

FIGURE 9-50
The iMovie workspace

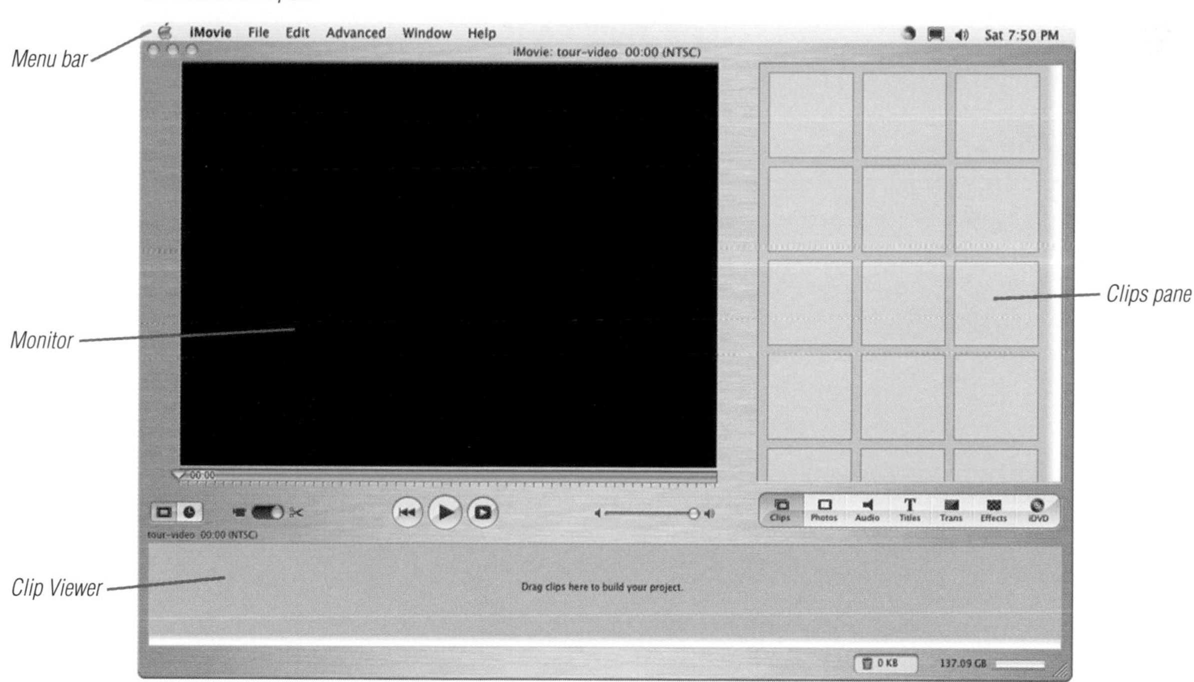

Start a project and import files

1. Create a folder named **innMovieProject** on the desktop.
2. Launch **iMovie**, then when the iMovie introduction screen appears click **Create Project**.

   If the iMovie introduction screen does not appear, click File in the menu bar, then click New Project.
3. Type **tour-video** for the Save As filename, then click the **down list arrow** to expand the dialog box, if necessary.
4. Click **Desktop**, click **innMovieProject**, then click **Save**.
5. Verify the **Clip Viewer button** and the **Edit Mode button** are selected as shown in Figure 9-51.
6. Click **File** on the menu bar, then click **Import**.

(continued)

FIGURE 9-51
Clip Viewer and Edit Mode buttons

FIGURE 9-52
Selecting the .jpg files

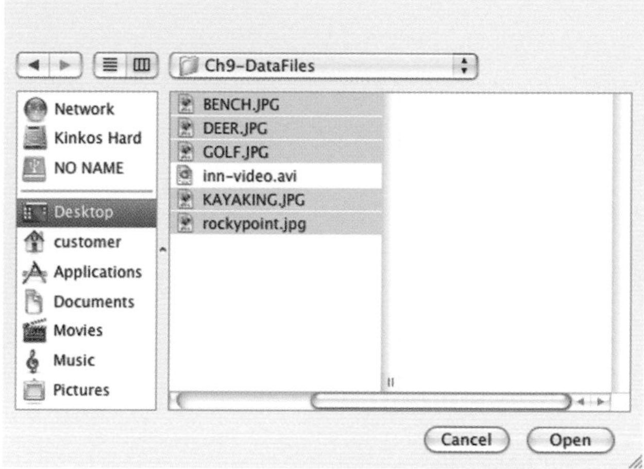

Thumbnails displayed in the Clips pane

7. Navigate to the folder containing the files for this chapter if necessary, click **inn-video.avi**, then click **Open**.
8. Click **File**, **Import**, and navigate to the folder containing the files for this chapter, hold down **[command]**, then click each .jpg file to select all the files as shown in Figure 9-52 (top).
9. Click **Open**.

   The import process may take a few minutes. When done, thumbnails of the files are displayed in the Clips pane as shown in Figure 9-52 (bottom).
10. Click **File** on the menu bar, then click **Save Project**.

    Note: A dialog box may appear indicating that the movie is being rendered.

You created a project, imported files, and saved the project.

LESSON 2

ASSEMBLE AND Edit a Movie

What You'll Do

In this lesson, you will learn how to assemble a movie and edit a video clip.

Clip/Timeline Views

You assemble and edit your movie in either of two views: the Clip Viewer view or the Timeline Viewer view. You use the Clips View button and the Timeline View button to switch between these two views.

The Clip Viewer

The Clip Viewer is used to assemble the assets of your movie and to add transitions and effects. You simply drag the desired files, transitions, and effects from the Clips pane to the Clips Viewer in the sequence that they will play in the movie. The Clips Viewer displays thumbnails of the assets you choose to have in your movie such as video clips, pictures, and titles as shown in Figure 9-53. You can rearrange the assets by dragging them to another location in the Clips Viewer, and you can delete them by using the [delete] key.

The Timeline Viewer

The Timeline Viewer can also be used to assemble the assets in your movie. However, instead of showing thumbnails, it displays the assets along a timeline that provides information on the length of the various clips and pictures. This allows you to change the duration an asset is displayed in the movie by trimming or cropping it. The Timeline Viewer provides an audio track for adding and editing sounds, as well as for synchronizing them with the other parts of the movie.

FIGURE 9-53
The Clip Viewer with thumbnails

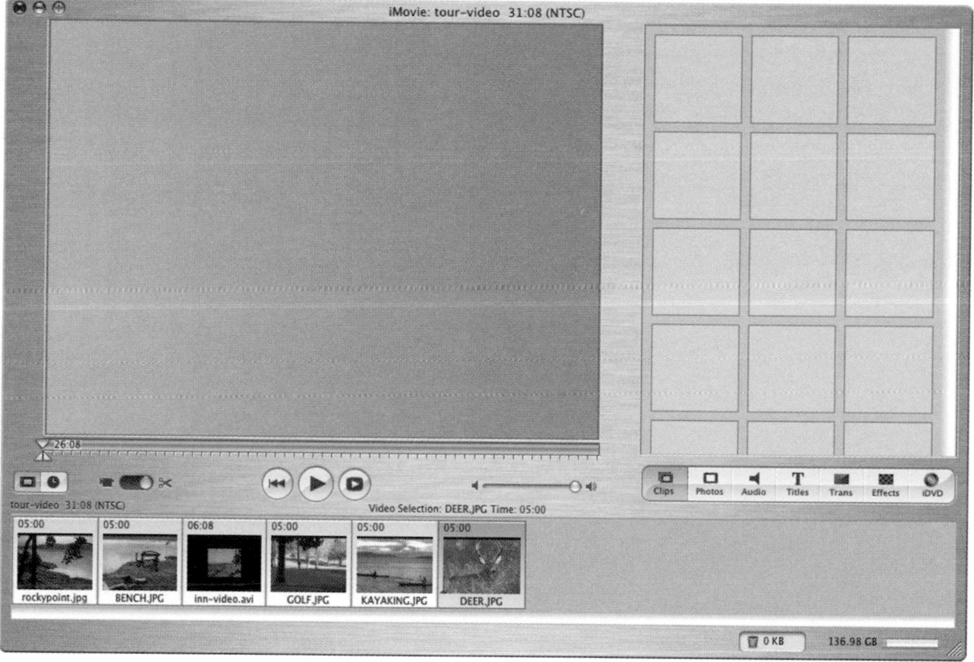

Assemble the movie

1. Click the **rockypoint picture** in the Clip pane to select it.
2. Drag the **rockypoint picture** to the Clip Viewer as shown in Figure 9-54.
3. Drag the **bench picture** so it is adjacent to the rockypoint picture.
4. Drag the **inn-video clip** so it is adjacent to the bench picture.
5. Continue to drag the pictures to the Clip Viewer in this order: **golf**, **kayaking**, **deer** so that your screen resembles Figure 9-55.
6. Click the **Rewind button** on the monitor controls, then click the **Play button** to view the movie.
7. Click **File** on the menu bar, then click **Save Project**.

You used the Clip Viewer to assemble a movie, and then viewed the movie on the monitor.

FIGURE 9-54
Dragging a picture to the Clip Viewer

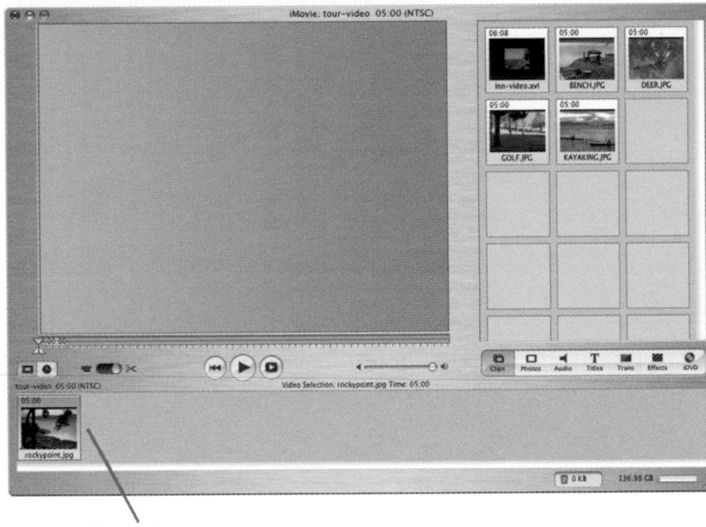

FIGURE 9-55
The Clip Viewer with all the pictures and the video clip

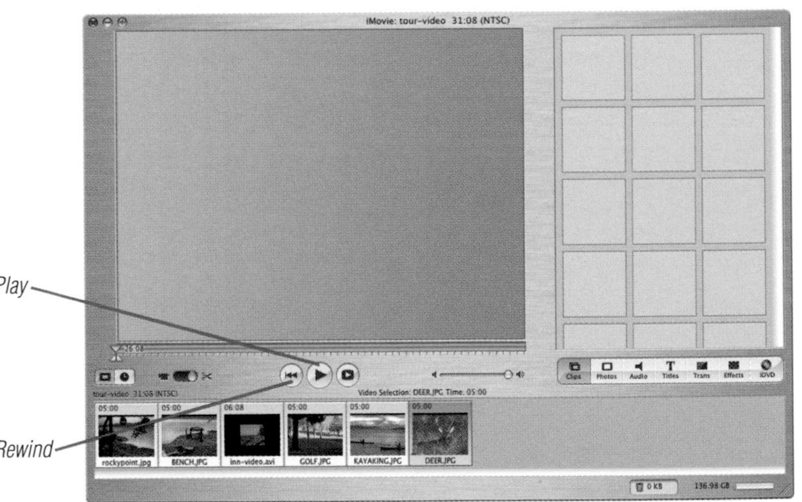

Edit a video clip

1. Click the **inn-video clip** in the Clip Viewer to select it.
2. Drag the **right marker** to about the 16:00 mark as shown in Figure 9-56.

   The yellow bar indicates the selected part of the clip.
3. Click **Edit** in the menu bar, then click **Crop**.

   The clip is shorter now, but the selected part of the clip remains.
4. Click the **Rewind button**, then click the **Play button** to view the movie.
5. Save the project.

You edited a video clip by cropping it.

FIGURE 9-56
Dragging the marker

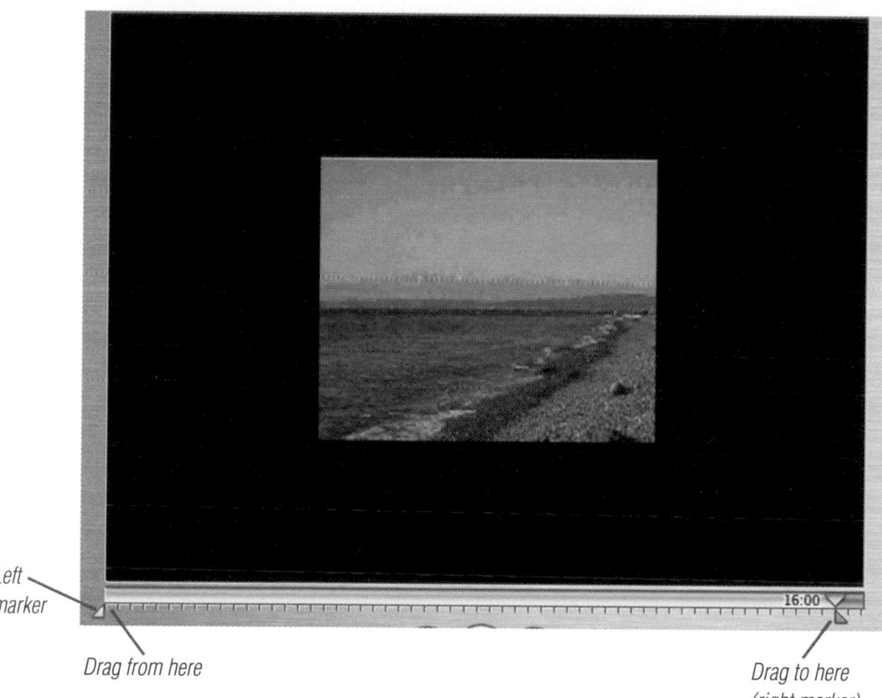

Left marker

Drag from here

Drag to here (right marker)

LESSON 3

ADD TRANSITIONS, EFFECTS, TITLES, and Sound to a Movie

What You'll Do

In this lesson, you will learn how to add transitions, effects, titles, and sounds to a movie.

Transitions

The movie you are creating has a video clip and several pictures. iMovie allows you to insert transitions, such as wipes and fade-ins, between assets. Transitions add interest and unity to the movie by having it appear more like a continuous motion picture than a series of still pictures. To add transitions, you must display the list of transitions in the Clips pane, and then drag the selected transition to the desired location on the Clip Viewer or the Timeline Viewer. Transitions appear as icons on the Clip Viewer as shown in Figure 9-57. You can delete a transition by selecting it and pressing [delete].

Effects

In addition to transitions, you can apply effects to a video clip or picture. Effects can be very radical such as displaying a video clip with an aged appearance or simple such as changing the contrast in a photograph. To add an effect, you must select an asset in the Clip Viewer, select an effect from a list in the Clips pane, and then click the Apply button.

Titles

Titles are text that you add to the movie. Titles can be added at the beginning or ending of a movie, before or after a video clip or picture, or superimposed on a clip or picture. In addition to specifying the text and its location, you can indicate how the text animates (such as scrolling or flying in), and you can specify a font, font color, and type size. To add text, you must select a video clip or picture in the Clip Viewer, display the Titles option, and type the desired text. Then you choose how the text will appear, such as centered, and drag the choice to before the selected video clip or picture.

Sound

iMovie provides an audio track on the Timeline Viewer that allows you to add narration as well as sounds, such as background music, to your movie. These audio clips can be edited (e.g., trimmed, volume adjusted, fade-in effects added, and so on), and synchronized to other parts of the movie, such as video clips or pictures. To add audio, you must drag the audio clip from the Clips pane to the desired location on the Timeline Viewer audio track.

FIGURE 9-57
The Clip Viewer with transition icons

Add transitions and an effect to a movie

1. Click the **bench picture** in the Clip Viewer, then click the **Trans button** under the Clips pane.
2. Click **Fade in,** then watch the preview.
3. Drag **Fade in** to the beginning of the bench picture as shown in Figure 9-58.
4. Drag **Fade in** to the beginning of the inn-video clip.
5. Repeat **step 4** for the remaining three pictures.
6. Click the **deer picture** in the Clip Viewer, then click the **Effects button**.
7. Click **Fog** in the Effects list, view the effect in the preview window, then click **Apply**.
8. If a message appears indicating that a transition must be re-rendered, click OK.

   You may need to wait a few minutes for the effect to render. Notice the red status bar on the deer image in the Clip Viewer.
9. Rewind and play the movie, and notice the transitions and effect.
10. Save the project.

You added transitions and an effect to the movie.

FIGURE 9-58

Dragging a transition to the Clip Viewer

FIGURE 9-59

Entering a title in the text box

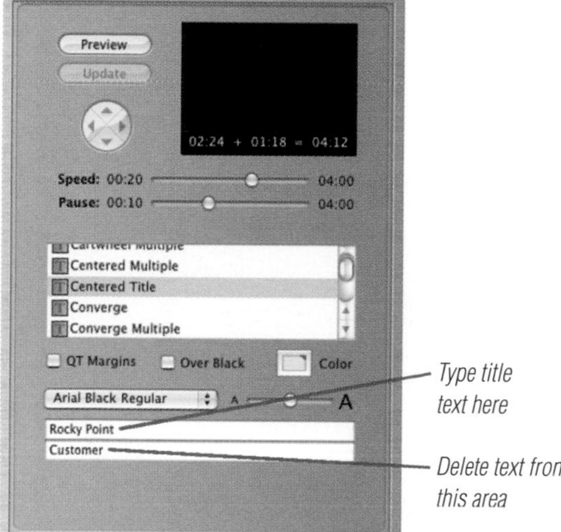

FIGURE 9-60

Dragging a title to the Clip Viewer

Add titles to a movie

1. Click the **rockypoint picture** on the Clip Viewer, then click the **Titles button** under the Clips pane.
2. Drag the **scroll button** to display Centered Title, then click **Centered Title**.

   Note: You may need to click Centered, then click Centered Title.
3. Select the **text** in the top text box, press **[delete]**, then type **Rocky Point** as shown in Figure 9-59.
4. Select the **text** in the bottom text box, then press **[delete]**.
5. Verify the **Over Black** option is not selected, then click the **Preview button** to view the title.
6. Drag **Centered Title** to the left of the rocky-point picture as shown in Figure 9-60.

   Another thumbnail of the picture (displaying the title) will be added to the Clip Viewer.
7. Click the **bench picture** in the Clip Viewer, verify **Centered Title** is still selected, select **Rocky Point** in the top text box, press **[delete]**, then type **Bench Bluff**.
8. Drag **Centered Title** to the left of the bench picture.

   When you add a title, the transition icons are no longer visible.
9. Repeat steps 7 and 8 for the remaining video clip and pictures using the following titles: **Pebble Beach**, **Golf**, **Kayaking**, **Wildlife**.
10. Click **Over Black** to select it.

(continued)

11. Type **The Inn at Birch Bay** in the top text box, then type **Relax and Enjoy!** in the bottom text box.
12. Drag the **scroll button** at the bottom of the Clip Viewer to display the last picture.
13. Drag **Centered Title** to the right of the last picture as shown in Figure 9-61.
14. Rewind and play the movie, then save the project.

You added titles to the movie.

Add audio in a movie

1. Click the **Timeline button** to display the Timeline Viewer.
2. Click the **Audio button** in the Clips pane.
3. If necessary, press and hold the **list arrow** for the Audio Source Selector, point to **iMovie Sound Effects**, then release the mouse button to display a list of sound effects, as shown in Figure 9-62.

   Note: You may need to expand the Skywalker Sound Effects.

(continued)

FIGURE 9-61

Dragging a title to the end of the Clip Viewer

FIGURE 9-62

The Audio Source Selector list arrow

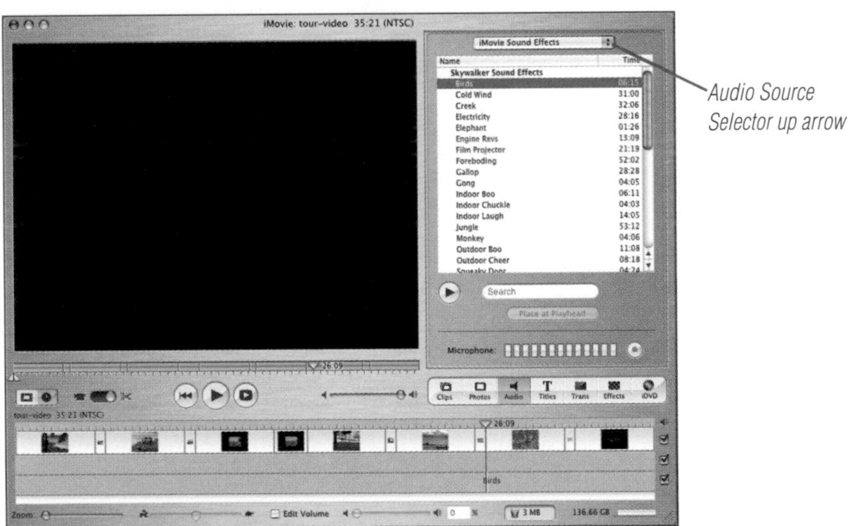

FIGURE 9-63

Dragging the sound effect to the Timeline Viewer

FIGURE 9-64

Trimming the sound file

4. Drag **Birds** to the audio track on the Timeline Viewer as shown in Figure 9-63.
5. Drag the **right arrow** on the Birds sound effect to the left as shown in Figure 9-64.

   This will trim the sound so that it synchronizes with the picture.
6. Rewind the movie, then play the movie.
7. Save the project.

You added a background sound to one clip in the movie.

LESSON 4

SAVE A MOVIE AND ADD It to a Web Page

What You'll Do

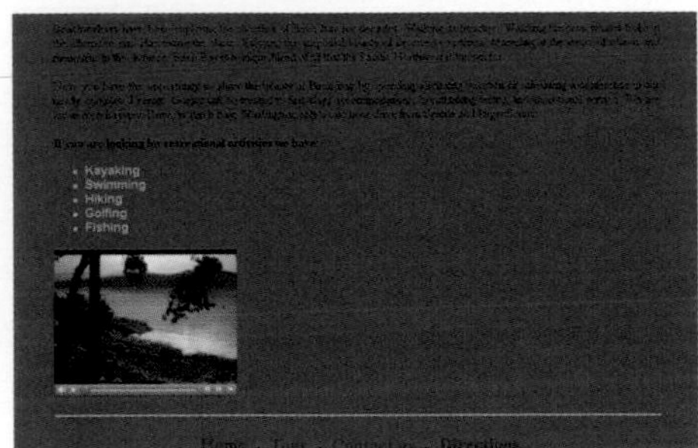

In this lesson, you will learn how to save a movie and add a movie to a Web page.

Saving a Movie

Until now you have been working with an iMovie project. A project contains all of the assets, timing information, transitions, video effects, and so on that you have specified for your movie. The important thing about a project is that you can save it, make changes, and save it again using iMovie. You cannot, however, use a project file in a Web page. You must export the project and save it as a movie file. iMovie provides several options based on what you want to do with the movie. These include optimizing the file for the Web, e-mail, streaming video, and full-quality video. If you choose the QuickTime option, movies are saved with a .mov filename extension, which allows them to be viewed in a browser using a media player.

Adding a Movie to a Web Page

The process for adding a movie to a Web page is similar to adding .swf files. There are two HTML elements—object and embed—that are used to play certain types of multimedia files such as audio, video, and animation. Both should be used because different browsers recognize only one or the other. Figure 9-65 shows the code used to play the tour-video.mov file. Tour-video.mov is the filename you will use when saving the movie.

<object classid...: identifies the kind of object being embedded in the Web page

<param name...: identifies properties of the object, such as the filename—"tour-video.mov"—and whether to show the video controls—"true" (yes)

<embed src...: identifies the file—"tour-video.mov"—its properties such as the width and height, and whether to show the controls. In addition, the URL for the plug-in is identified—"http://www.apple.com/quicktime/download"

Macromedia Dreamweaver provides another way to add a movie to a Web page. You can type text into a Web page, then create a link between the text and the movie that causes the movie to play when the text is clicked.

FIGURE 9-65

The html code used to play a video file

```
<object classid="clsid:02bf25d5-8c17-4b23-bc80-d3488abddc6b" width="240"height="196"
        codebase="http://www.apple.com/qtactivex/qtplugin.cab">
        <param name="src" value="tour-video.mov">
        <param name="autoplay" value="false">
        <param name="controller" value="true">
   <embed src="tour-video.mov" width="240" height="196" autoplay="false"
        controller="true" pluginspage="http://www.apple.com/quicktime/download/">
   </embed>
</object>
```

Save a movie file

1. Click **File** on the menu bar, then click **Export (Share)**.
2. Click the **down arrow** in the Export (Share) box, then click **To QuickTime**.
3. Click the **down arrow** in the Formats box, click **Web**, then click **Export (Share)**.
4. Verify **tour-video** is displayed for the Save As filename, then click the **down arrow** for the Save As box to expand the box, if necessary.
5. Click **Desktop**, then click **innMovieProject** so that your screen resembles Figure 9-66.

   Note: Your folder structure and folder names may vary from Figure 9-66.
6. Click **Save**.

   Depending on the processing speed of the computer the export process may take several minutes.
7. When the movie has been saved, open it with the **QuickTime Player** and view the movie, then close the player.

You saved a movie with selected settings.

FIGURE 9-66
Completing the Save As dialog box

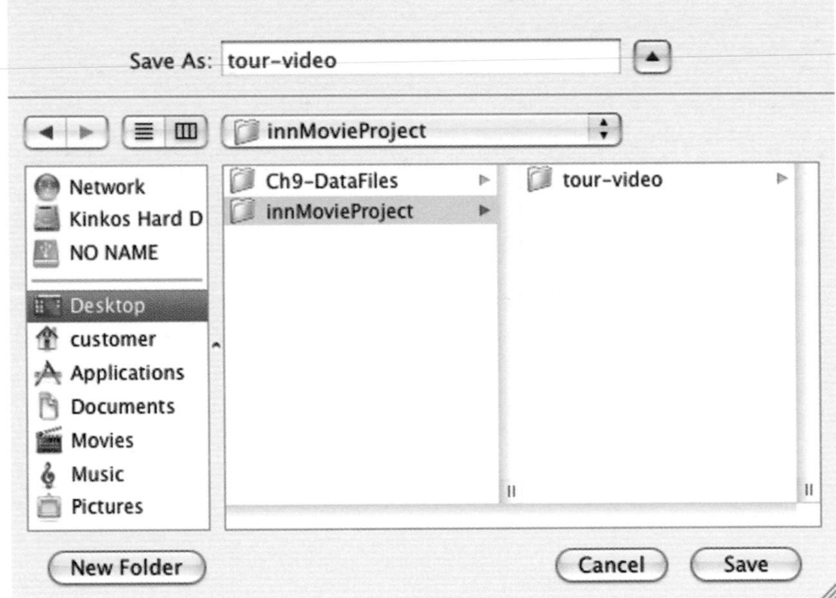

FIGURE 9-67

Dragging the icon to the Link box

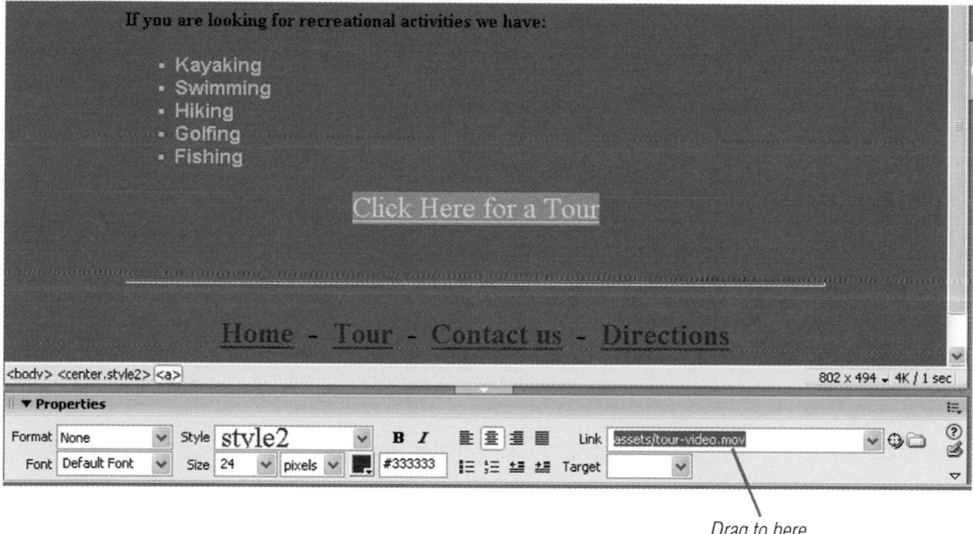

Link a movie to a Web page

1. Copy **tour-video.mov** from the **innMovieProject folder** to the assets folder of the InnWebsiteDW folder.
2. Start **Dreamweaver**, then display the **InnWebsiteDW site** in the Files panel.
3. Double-click **tour.htm** in the Files panel to open the Web page in the document window.
4. Scroll the document window to display the Video placeholder, click to select **Video placeholder**, then press **[delete]**.
5. Type **Click Here for a Tour**.
6. Select **Click Here for a Tour**, then use the Property inspector to change the font color to **#333333** and the size to **24**.
7. Verify **Click Here for a Tour** is selected, drag the **tour-video.mov** icon from the assets folder in the Files panel to the Link box as shown in Figure 9-67, then save the file.

   This creates a link between the Click Here for a Tour text and the tour-video.mov movie.
8. Press **[F12]** to view the Web page in a browser, then click the **Click Here for a Tour** text.
9. View the movie, close the media player, then close the browser window.
10. Return to the Dreamweaver document.

You added a .mov movie file to a Web page and linked it to text.

Embed a movie into a Web page

1. Click **File** on the menu bar, click **Save As**, type **tour-embed.htm**, then click **Save**.
2. Select the **Click Here for a Tour** text, then press **[delete]**.
3. Navigate to the folder containing the files for this chapter, then open **video-code.txt**.
4. Select the text, copy it, then display the Dreamweaver document.
5. Click the **Split button** Split on the Document toolbar.
6. Click to position the insertion point after the </center> tag as shown in Figure 9-68.

   Note: Your code may display differently. If so, click to position the insertion point before the <hr> tag.

(continued)

FIGURE 9-68
Positioning the pointer

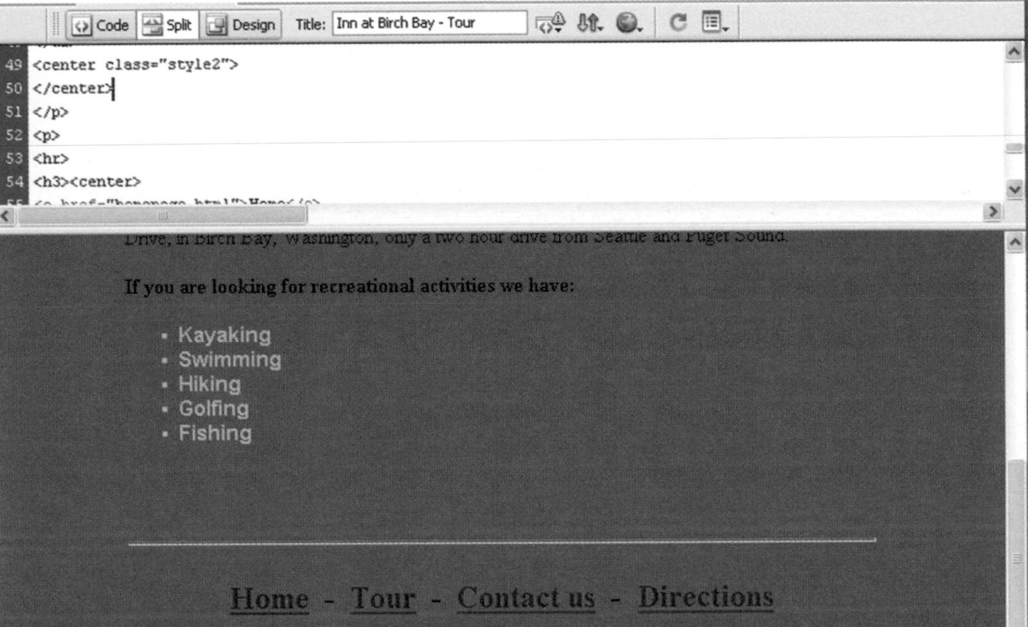

FIGURE 9-69

Movie displayed in a browser window

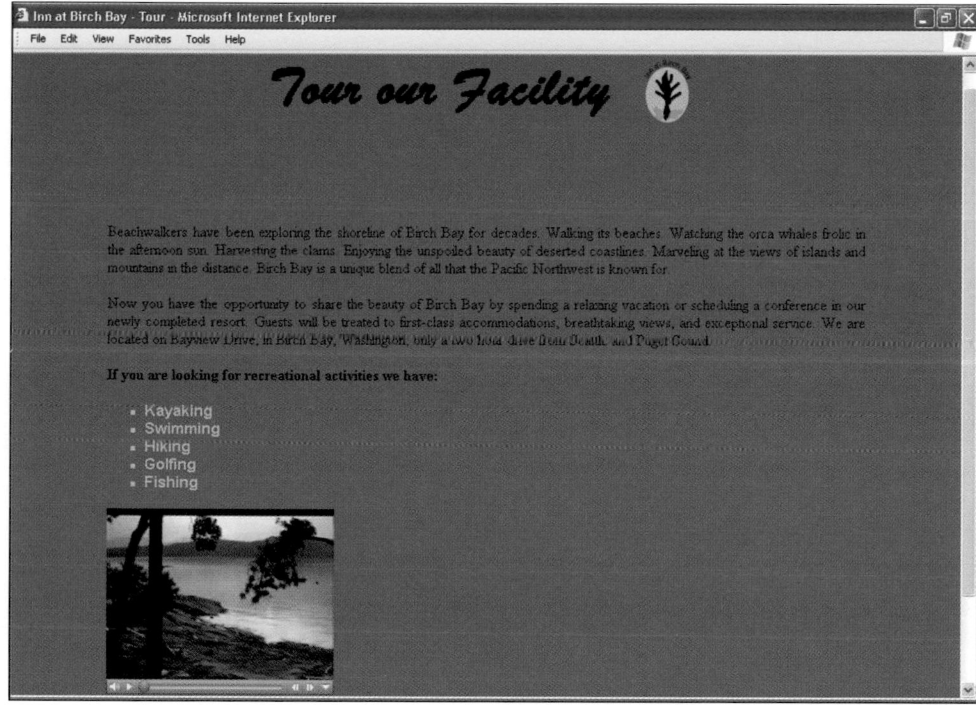

7. Press **[return]**.
8. Click **Edit** on the menu bar, then click **Paste**.
9. Click the **Design button** Design on the Document toolbar to close the split window, then save the file.
10. Press **[F12]** to view the Web page in a browser (see Figure 9-69), then play the movie.
11. Close the browser window, then return to the Dreamweaver document.

You embedded a .mov movie file into a Web page.

PROJECT BUILDER 1

You are an intern with a company that develops Web sites for clients. During your internship training, you learned how important video can be to Web pages. You have decided to study how other Web sites use video.

1. Connect to the Internet, go to *www.course.com*, navigate to the page for this book, click the Student Online Companion link, then click the link for this chapter.
2. Navigate through the site (see Figure 9-70) and note the use of video and video controls.
3. Open a document in a word processor, save the file as **Ch9pb1**, create a table with the column headings **Video** and **How would you describe the video?**, and the following row headings:
   - Introductory
   - Educational
   - Narration
   - Use of sound
   - Other
4. Complete the table by reviewing the videos found on the Web site.

One Step Beyond

5. What video controls are provided, if any?
6. Do you think the use of video was beneficial to the site? Why, or why not?
7. What improvements would you suggest for the use of video in the site?

Two Steps Beyond

8. Conduct a Web search for two companies that provide video clips.
9. Choose one subject and search those sites for available video clips on that subject.
10. Write a summary of each site and include the following in the summary:
    a. The name and URL for each company
    b. The approximate number of video clips available for the chosen subject
    c. Ease of finding the desired video clip
    d. Approximate cost of a video clip
    e. How video clips are distributed
    f. The terms of use (what is allowed and what is forbidden?)
    g. Which site would you evaluate as better and why?

FIGURE 9-70
The use of video on a Web site

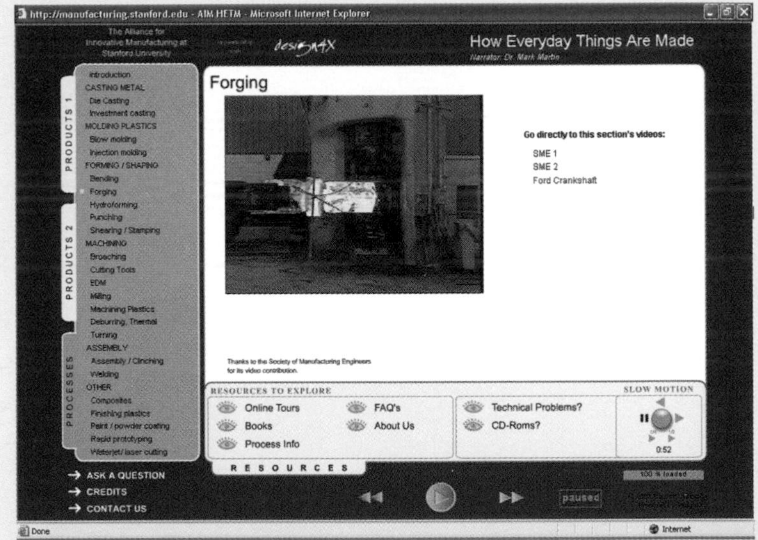

PROJECT BUILDER 2

You have been studying Web development. You decide it would be useful to add video to a Web page for a portfolio Web site. Complete the following steps to insert the movie into a Web page.

1. Using Windows Movie Maker 2 develop a movie of your choice. *Note*: you can use the sample files provided with the program. If you are a Mac user, complete this project using iMovie 3/4. Include the following in your movie, at least:
   a. One video clip
   b. Three pictures
   c. One sound
   d. Two different transition effects
   e. Two different special effects
2. Follow these guidelines:
   a. Create a new project and name it **mymovie**.
   b. Create a folder and name it **mymovie**.
   c. Add all of the assets, except the video clip(s) to the mymovie folder.
   d. Save the movie using the Best quality for playback on my computer setting.
   e. View the movie in a browser.

One Step Beyond

3. Using Dreamweaver, open mysitech9-video.htm (shown in Figure 9-71).
4. Add the following text: Click Here to Play a Video.
5. Center the text, change the size to 24, and change the color to red.
6. Link the text to the mymovie.wmv (mymovie.mov) file.
7. Save the Dreamweaver document with the filename **mymoviexx.htm** (where *xx* are your initials).
8. Preview the document in a browser.

Two Steps Beyond

9. Copy the html code from the video-code.txt document to the mymoviexx.htm file.
10. Change the code in the Dreamweaver document by replacing assets/tour-video.wmv (mov) with mymovie.wmv (mov) (Note: It is in two places in the code).
11. Save the file as **mymovieTwoxx.htm** (where *xx* are your initials).
12. Preview the document in a browser.

FIGURE 9-71
A Web page that will have a movie added

chapter 10

MARKUP, SCRIPTING, AND Programming for the Web

1. Review Markup Languages
2. Examine Scripting Languages and Scripting Environments
3. Explore Programming Languages

chapter 10 MARKUP, SCRIPTING, AND Programming for the Web

Introduction

Web developers and programmers have continually asked for greater extensibility than what has been possible with static HTML. Although many multimedia Web sites have been built using nothing but XHTML, today's Web has evolved into a sophisticated communication and data delivery medium well beyond what can be developed with XHTML alone. Scripting and programming languages provide extensibility and make it possible for Web developers and programmers to create interactive, feature-rich, multimedia Web sites. Today, Web developers and programmers must have skills using markup, scripting, and programming languages. They must also understand database structure and design as well as possess knowledge of the tools and technologies for creating databases and connecting them to the Web.

It is important to understand how Web content is delivered in order to understand how Web pages are developed when working with markup, scripting, and programming languages. A **Web server** is the computer on which the files for Web pages are stored and a **Web client** is the computer from which the user views the pages on a Web browser. Web pages are downloaded from Web servers to Web clients, where they are interpreted and displayed by a Web browser. When your Web page includes access to a script or program stored on a Web server, information must be sent from the Web client back to the Web server for processing, storage, and later retrieval.

Web developers or programmers write lines of code that create interactivity and animation, define structure, and respond to user actions. Most of the capabilities within the different scripting and programming languages overlap. In other words, you can achieve the same results using different languages.

Many Web sites on the Internet today are complex. Developing and maintaining complex Web sites is a challenge. Scripting and programming can make the task of developing and maintaining complex Web sites easier. This can be accomplished by setting up a standard template that can automate and simplify the process of adding content to a multimedia Web site.

For example, an online catalog may contain an image accompanied by a description, reference number, and price. Instead of designing each page of the catalog, the Web developer could design a template and then access the content dynamically through a database. Business transactions are also becoming more common on the Web, and applications created for the Web using scripting and programming languages help streamline many of these business functions. Customers can place orders, request information, check the status of an order, pay for a product or service, and even receive authorization to return a product via the Web. Scripts and programs provide a direct way of accessing information that exists within an organization, to collect information from users, or to generate sales through a Web site.

Markup, scripting, and programming languages (see Figure 10-1) are used to make a multimedia Web site a more interactive and interesting place to visit. Of course, the functionality of these languages is much broader in purpose than Web design and development. Therefore, the focus of this chapter will be on markup, scripting, and programming languages as they are used in preparing content and interactivity within a Web site. In this chapter, you will learn about the most commonly used markup languages, scripting languages and environments, and programming languages used to develop interactive, multimedia Web sites.

FIGURE 10-1

A combination of markup, scripting, and programming languages is used when creating interactive and interesting multimedia Web sites

xhtml (markup language)

JavaScript (scripting language)

form tag calls program on a Web server (program created using a programming language)

```
<xhtml>
<head>
<SCRIPT LANGUAGE="JavaScript">
<!--

function newImage(arg) {
        if (document.images) {
                rslt = new Image();
                rslt.src = arg;
                return rslt;
        }
}

function changeImages() {
        if (document.images && (preloadFlag == true)) {
                for (var i=0; i<changeImages.arguments.length; i+=2) {
                        document[changeImages.arguments[i]].src = changeImages.arguments[i+1];
                }
        }
}

var preloadFlag = false;
function preloadImages() {
        if (document.images) {
                home_over = newImage("images/home-over.gif");
                about_over = newImage("images/about-over.gif");
                tour_over = newImage("images/tour-over.gif");
                support_over = newImage("images/support-over.gif");
                contact_over = newImage("images/contact-over.gif");
                preloadFlag = true;
        }
}

// -->
</SCRIPT>
<script language="JavaScript">
<!--
function MM_reloadPage(init) {  //reloads the window if Nav4 resized
  if (init==true) with (navigator) {if ((appName=="Netscape")&&(parseInt(appVersion)==4)) {
    document.MM_pgW=innerWidth; document.MM_pgH=innerHeight; onresize=MM_reloadPage; }}
  else if (innerWidth!=document.MM_pgW || innerHeight!=document.MM_pgH) location.reload();
}
MM_reloadPage(true);
// -->
</script>
</HEAD>
<body bgcolor="ffffcc" text="000066" link="000066" vlink="ffcc00" alink="ffcc00" ONLOAD="preloadImages();">
<form action="/4dcgi/clients/user_edit.a4d?recNum=75965" method="POST" enctype="application/x-www-form-urlencoded" name="f_user_edit">
```

CONCEPT 1

REVIEW MARKUP Languages

What You'll Learn

In this lesson, you will learn about the different markup languages used to design multimedia Web sites.

A **markup language** is a full set of instructions that can be used to comprehensively describe the structural format of a piece of text or other media element. Markup languages are used to add tags to the electronic document, and these tags specify how the content will display in a browser. Markup tags are interpreted by applications, such as Web browsers. Markup tags have an immediate and specific effect. They may change the appearance of characters (for example, they may make them bold or italic) or they may change the position of a media element (for example, changing margins, indents, and alignment). They also detail the structure of a document, identifying components such as paragraphs, headings, sections, and titles. A discussion of the standard on which the most common markup languages are based, as well as a discussion of the most common markup languages, follows.

SGML

Standard Generalized Markup Language (SGML) is the standard for defining the most common markup languages. It is the most fully developed specification of markup languages for electronic documents. SGML provides a consistent and precise method of applying markup tags so that electronic documents can be exchanged and revised between different computer systems. SGML does not directly define or restrict the type of data contained in a document. It does not define markup tags nor does it provide a template for a particular type of document. Instead, it denotes a way of describing a markup language. This makes SGML flexible enough to meet the diverse needs of electronic data exchange. SGML itself is not a markup language; rather it is the standard on which the most common markup languages are based. All of the markup languages discussed next are derived from SGML. As a result, they all share similar characteristics including syntax, such as the use of bracketed tags (see Figure 10-2).

SGML's flexibility is both its strength and its weakness. Its flexibility to specify document structure for any application has led to its wide adoption as the standard for markup languages. Because it is so flexible many organizations have developed their own ways of implementing the SGML standard.

HTML and XHTML

As you learned in Chapter 4, **Hypertext Markup Language (HTML)** is the standard markup language used to create Web pages. HTML is a markup language not a programming language. HTML continues to develop and evolve based on the controls set by the World Wide Web Consortium (W3C). Each new version offers increased Web page functionality. The newest version, **Extensible Hypertext Markup Language (XHTML)**, provides support for XML and as a result it is stricter in structure and syntax than previous versions of HTML.

QUICKTIP

Most markup, scripting, and programming languages are case sensitive. Always pay attention to proper syntax when you are writing code.

FIGURE 10-2
All markup languages derived from SGML use bracketed tags

<html> </html>

<vrml> </vrml>

<xml> </xml>

<smil> </smil>

Which Language Is the Best?

No single language completely monopolizes Web programming. Because there are so many different ways to create the same interactive multimedia Web site, often the most difficult step is deciding which language or languages to use. The decision regarding which scripting and programming languages to use must take into consideration specific constraints, such as numerous protocols, formats (e.g., graphics), programming tasks, performance (both speed and size), security, and the basic ability to interface with other Web tools and languages.

Web developers and programmers generally use a combination of markup, scripting, and programming languages. Their choice of language is often specific to a particular task or it is simply used because it is the preferred language of the Web developer or programmer creating the Web site. Most of the time, the Web developer or programmer will use a combination of languages as it generally results in a stronger multimedia Web site.

Markup languages provide the basic structure of a Web page. Scripting and programming languages add flexibility. When you are writing code to create a multimedia Web site, you can be very specific in how you tailor the site to the target audience.

The look of a Web page is accomplished through the use of markup tags that specify how the browser will display text and other multimedia elements. All Web documents are formatted using markup tags (see Figure 10-3) and there are markup tags for almost any type of formatting desired.

> **QUICKTIP**
>
> Remember, different Web browsers and different versions of the same Web browser interpret HTML and other markup tags differently. Always test your Web pages before deploying them to the Internet community.

DHTML

Dynamic Hypertext Markup Language (DHTML) is a group of technologies used to create greater interactivity and page layout flexibility than is possible with XHTML alone. DHTML is more than a markup language. It includes XHTML, **JavaScript**, Cascading Style Sheets (CSS), and the **Document Object Model (DOM)**. DHTML allows for greater interactivity and extensibility on a Web site.

The Document Object Model (DOM) is a platform-neutral **application programming interface (API)** that describes the underlying framework of a document so that Web developers can access and manipulate objects in a standard way. Basically, the DOM gives Web designers and developers greater control over individual elements of a Web page. Because every element is an object, each object can be accessed separately and manipulated with DHTML. A standardized DOM solves many cross-compatibility problems associated with building dynamic, interactive Web pages, and it provides the necessary structure for Web pages created using DHTML to work reliably across browsers.

All of the major Web browsers support DHTML, however, they differ in terms of what each considers acceptable syntax and scripting code. This has made it difficult

FIGURE 10-3

Choose View>Source from the menu bar on a Web browser to view the markup tags for any Web page

```
File  Edit  Format  View  Help
<xhtml>
<head>
        <title>SVC - Skagit Valley College</title>
        <LINK rel="stylesheet" type="text/css" href="includes/style.css">
        <SCRIPT LANGUAGE="javascript">
                function opener(loc,name)
                {
                s=window.open(loc, name,
'toolbar=no,directories=no,menubar=yes,status=yes,scrollbars=yes,resizable=yes,width=35
0,height=400,left=300,top=50')
                s.focus()
                }
</SCRIPT>
        <SCRIPT LANGUAGE="javascript">
        function welcomePop() {
            if (document.all)
                var xMax = screen.width, yMax = screen.height;
            else{

                if (document.layers)
                    var xMax = window.outerWidth, yMax = window.outerHeight;
                else
                    var xMax = 640, yMax=480;
                }

            var xOffset = (xMax-50)/4, yOffset = yMax/4;

window.open('popup.asp','welcome','width=472,height=355,scrollbars=no,screenX='+xOffset
+',screenY='+yOffset+', top='+yOffset+',left='+xOffset+'');

            //return true;
        }
        </SCRIPT>
</head>
<body>
<div align="center">
<!--BANNER-->
<TABLE CELLSPACING="0" CELLPADDING="0" BORDER="0" width="780">
<TR>
    <TD>
        <IMG SRC="graphics/banner.jpg" WIDTH="780" HEIGHT="100" BORDER="0" ALT=""></TD>
</TR>
<TR>
    <TD bgcolor="#E9EFF7" height="20">
        <p align="right" style="margin-left: 4px; margin-right: 4px"><a class=link2
href="news.asp_Q_pagenumber_E_1318">Mount
        Vernon Campus</a>  | 
        <a class=link2 href="news.asp_Q_pagenumber_E_489">Whidbey Island
      Campus</a>  |  <a class=link2 href="news.asp_Q_pagenumber_E_520">San
Juan Center</a>  |  <a class=link2 href="news.asp_Q_pagenumber_E_619">South
```

for Web designers and developers to create Web pages using DHTML that look and respond the same way across all major Web browsers.

VRML

Virtual reality (VR) on the Web is created using the **Virtual Reality Modeling Language (VRML)** (pronounced "ver-mal"). It is a language that has been developed and maintained by the VRML Consortium, a combined effort of a group of companies and 3-D designers and programmers. VRML is a simple and accessible way to create interactive worlds using 3-D graphics and scenes on the Web (see Figure 10-4). It is the standard for 3-D Web content. It is gaining greater acceptance and, like all computer-based technologies, it continues to advance.

You can use any text editor or a number of VR programs to write VRML code. One of the most popular tools for creating virtual reality is **QuickTime VR**. This is Apple's photorealistic cross-platform virtual reality technology that makes it possible to explore places as if you were there.

FIGURE 10-4

Using VR on the Web, you can take a virtual tour of the oval office

QuickTime VR combines commercial photography and other media to convert photographs from flat, two-dimensional images into 3-D imagery complete with interactive components that enable viewers to explore and examine detailed virtual worlds with full panoramic views of objects and locations using a computer and mouse.

SMIL

Synchronized Multimedia Integration Language (SMIL) (pronounced "smile"), is a simple, platform-neutral markup language that lets Web designers and developers at all skill levels schedule audio, video (see Figure 10-5), text, and graphic files across a timeline without having to master development tools or complex programming languages. It is used to solve the problems encountered when coordinating multimedia elements on a timeline to display multimedia on a Web site.

SMIL offers control over synchronized multimedia by allowing individual components (such as audio, video, and graphics) to be played in relation to one another. What makes SMIL different from other Web-based multimedia presentation tools is that instead of forcing each component into a single file, the text-based SMIL code merely references each file. The start and end times of different media are specified relative to other events. For example, Web developers can specify actions such as "show image file A ten seconds after video file B starts and then play audio file C." Or, in a narrated presentation, a particular video clip can be played when the narrator in the audio starts talking about that clip. SMIL ensures that the two events are synchronized. Because the media files exist outside of the SMIL file, the SMIL file remains small and efficient, which

FIGURE 10-5
Examples of SMIL code used to control a movie clip

Purpose	Code
Start 20 seconds into the video	<video src="movie.mpg" clipBegin="20s"/>
Cut out the last 3 minute, 30-second scene	<video src="movie.mpg" clipEnd="26:30"/>
Show an interesting frame from the middle of the video	<video src="movie.mpg" clipBegin="14:55.7" clipEnd="14:55.7"/>

decreases download time and makes it easier to deliver low-bandwidth multimedia via the Web.

SMIL's text-based format also makes editing Web-based multimedia applications easy. If you want to change when the audio on a Web page begins to play, you can just edit the SMIL code. You don't have to rebuild the entire movie file from scratch. SMIL also lets you control the layout, appearance, and exit time of each file and it supports hyperlinks for interactivity.

XML

Extensible Markup Language (XML) is a markup language, but it is also a metalanguage. XML is a text-based language derived from SGML and designed by the W3C. It allows Web developers and programmers to define their own markup tags. In effect, XML is a system for defining other languages. Extensible by definition, it specifies the syntax for tags, but it does not specify the tags themselves. XML is a subset or simplified spin-off of SGML.

The extensibility of XML makes it possible for Web developers to create a set of tags specific to their tasks, and then share them throughout an industry (see Figure 10-6). Because companies and organizations can use XML to create original and unique

FIGURE 10-6

The extensibility of XML makes it possible for Web developers to create a set of tags specific to their tasks and needs

XML library for worker's compensation company

	Field on Transaction	Max Lngth
<?xml version="1.0"?>		
<CORRESPONDENCE>		
<KEY_FIELDS>		
<TRANS_TYPE>ADD</TRANS_TYPE>	TRANS_MODE	6
<DOC_KEY>20030531000MIGRATE168</DOC_KEY>	zcCaseNoteID	22
<DOC_VERSION>20030724142621</DOC_VERSION>	TRANS_DOCVERSION	14
<IW_NAME>Johns, Lance R.</IW_NAME>	zcWorkerLastFirstX	50
<CLAIM_NUMBER>W222195</CLAIM_NUMBER>	You get from RDBMS	25
<CASE_TYPE>VOC</CASE_TYPE>	You get from RDBMS	10
<BOS_IDENTIFIER>E30785</BOS_IDENTIFIER>	You get from RDBMS	10
<ATLAS_SYS_KEY>W222195-S-20030203-SCS</ATLAS_SYS_KEY>	You get from RDBMS	50
<BOS_SYS_KEY>8372872</BOS_SYS_KEY>	You get from Client Index?	64
</KEY_FIELDS>		
<DOC_ORDER>-2320031121.17221</DOC_ORDER>		
<CORR_DATE>05/31/2003</CORR_DATE>		
<FROM>Joe Counselor</FROM>		
<TO>Dr. Robert Whittaker</TO>		
<DESCRIPTION>Introductory letter to Dr. Whittaker</DESCRIPTION>		
<ATTACHMENT>		
<DOC_NAME>20030531000MIGRATE168_20040301092322.doc</DOC_NAME>		
</ATTACHMENT>		
<ATTACHMENT>		
<DOC_NAME>20030531000MIGRATE168_20040301092326.doc</DOC_NAME>		
</ATTACHMENT>		
<ATTACHMENT>		
<DOC_NAME>20030531000MIGRATE168_20040301092328.doc</DOC_NAME>		
</ATTACHMENT>		
</CORRESPONDENCE>		

tags, they will also be able to meet new changes and challenges within their industries as these arise.

While XHTML describes how to present a document's data, XML provides a common syntax for expressing structure within the data. In other words, it defines the data's actual content, meaning, or use. For example, an XHTML tag such as <h3>...</h3> specifies a certain typeface and size. Each time the <h3>...</h3> tag is applied to text, that text will be formatted according to the h3 specifications. XML, on the other hand, describes the content that appears within the tags. For example, a <price>...</price> tag might contain the cost of a product or service. The data would appear between the beginning and ending XML tags. The formatting for the price as it would appear on the Web page when displayed in the browser would come from the XHTML code, not the XML code.

With XHTML alone, content is closely tied to formatting, which is why we sometimes see disclaimers such as, "best viewed at 800 × 600" on Web pages. XML helps solve this problem because instead of specifying where to display something, you merely specify the document's structure. In other words, you may use XML to set the document's title and a list of related links, then any browser, microbrowser, or application is able to render a version of the document specifically tailored to that program. By using XHTML and XML together, formatting can be separated from the content, which means that the same XML source document can be written once, and then displayed in a variety of ways. This allows documents to be viewed by various browsers without having to be specifically rewritten for each one. So, the same XML source document can be formatted for a computer monitor, a cellular phone display, or translated into voice by a synthesized reader. And because an XML file will work on any communications device, it won't become obsolete as hardware and communications devices evolve.

XML also bypasses other limitations by offering a standard way to exchange data. For example, XML provides a way for databases from different vendors to exchange information across the Internet. Another XML strength is how it interacts with the Document Object Model (DOM) so that programmers are able to standardize the way in which dynamic content is scripted. In other words, they can use it to cause a specific media element on a Web page to behave in a certain way. As a result of the way in which XML structures data, it also improves search capabilities on the Web.

The use of XML is having a dramatic impact on the Web page development process. E-commerce is particularly influenced by XML because e-commerce relies extensively on search and data exchange capabilities via the Web.

WML

Wireless Markup Language (WML) is based on the **Handheld Device Markup Language (HDML)**, which in turn is a subset of HTML. It is also an XML application. Although similar in syntax to HTML (that is, in the use of tags for formatting), it is much more like XML (that is, in defining data). If you are transitioning from HTML to WML, with no prior knowledge of XML, you will probably find WML very unforgiving. WML is the current standard for Web delivery on wireless handheld devices.

WML uses a limited set of markup tags. These markup tags are based on the W3C's guidelines for wireless mobile access. Just as XHTML is read and interpreted by a browser installed on a computer, WML is read and interpreted by a **microbrowser** that is built in to a wireless handheld device (see Figure 10-7). WML is used to create content that conforms to the wireless world, which makes it possible for the microbrowser to interpret WML and render the information on a small display, such as that found on mobile phones and small terminals. Rendering an XHTML page takes quite a bit of processing power, which wireless handheld devices do not have, so WML code is compressed before it is delivered to wireless handheld devices. In essence, WML is to a microbrowser as XHTML is to a standard Web browser.

FIGURE 10-7

A microbrowser interprets WML and renders the information on a small display, such as those found on PDAs and mobile phones

What Is WAP?

Wireless Application Protocol (WAP) is a specification that allows users to access information via handheld wireless devices such as mobile phones and pagers. WAP supports most wireless networks and operating systems including PalmOS and Windows CE. WAP-enabled devices use small displays and microbrowsers to access the Internet. Using WAP, small files that accommodate the low memory constraints of handheld devices and the low-bandwidth constraints of a wireless-handheld network are delivered to the handheld device for viewing.

CONCEPT 2

EXAMINE SCRIPTING LANGUAGES and Scripting Environments

What You'll Learn

In this lesson, you will learn about the advantages and disadvantages of using client- and server-side scripting languages. You will also get a brief overview of the most commonly used scripting languages on the Web.

Scripts extend the capabilities of XHTML. They often reside within the XHTML code between a <script></script> container. Although scripts can be stored on the Web server, many **scripting languages** are used to write programs for the client-side. In fact, the term **client-side program** refers to uncompiled scripts that are processed and interpreted by the Web browser on the user's computer.

In general, scripting languages are not as powerful as programming languages because they are still restricted to interpretation by a Web browser or some other program. However, they are also not as difficult to learn. You can use scripts to perform tasks such as creating rollovers, automatically showing the date and time, sizing windows, opening new windows, and detecting which browser is being used to access the page.

Just like HTML, scripting languages have evolved over time. As a result, there are different scripting languages as well as different versions of the same scripting language that may or may not work properly on different browsers or different versions of the same browser. As with XHTML, it is important to test Web pages that contain scripts to ensure that they function as intended.

JavaScript

JavaScript was developed by Netscape to extend the capabilities of standard HTML. Although similar in name and to some extent syntax to the Java programming language by Sun Microsystems, JavaScript and Java are very different in their capabilities and execution. The most important point to note is that JavaScript is a scripting language that is executed on the Web client, whereas Java is a programming language used to create small programs that are called from the Web page but executed outside it.

JavaScript is an object-oriented scripting language. In an object-oriented scripting language, programmers describe data and procedures in terms of objects, methods, and properties. JavaScript allows developers to access objects such as images and links from within a Web page. These objects can then be manipulated or changed. JavaScript allows you to capture events such as mouse clicks, which you can use to perform actions based on user input. JavaScript is not used to create executable files that must be written for a specific computer platform. Instead JavaScript is interpreted by the user's browser.

JavaScript brings the Web to life by adding interactivity and dynamic content to your Web pages. JavaScript can be used to create rollovers (see Figure 10-8), do simple processing, deliver dynamic content, and set **cookies**, which store data on the Web client. Among other things, you can use JavaScript to do the following:

- Add scrolling messages
- Open a new pop-up window
- Verify data input from forms
- Create animation and dynamic images
- Insert mouse rollovers
- Create and read cookies
- Display the current date and time

FIGURE 10-8

JavaScript is used to create rollovers; at this Web site, when a user's mouse passes over a thumbnail tile, JavaScript instructs the Web browser to display a larger version to the right

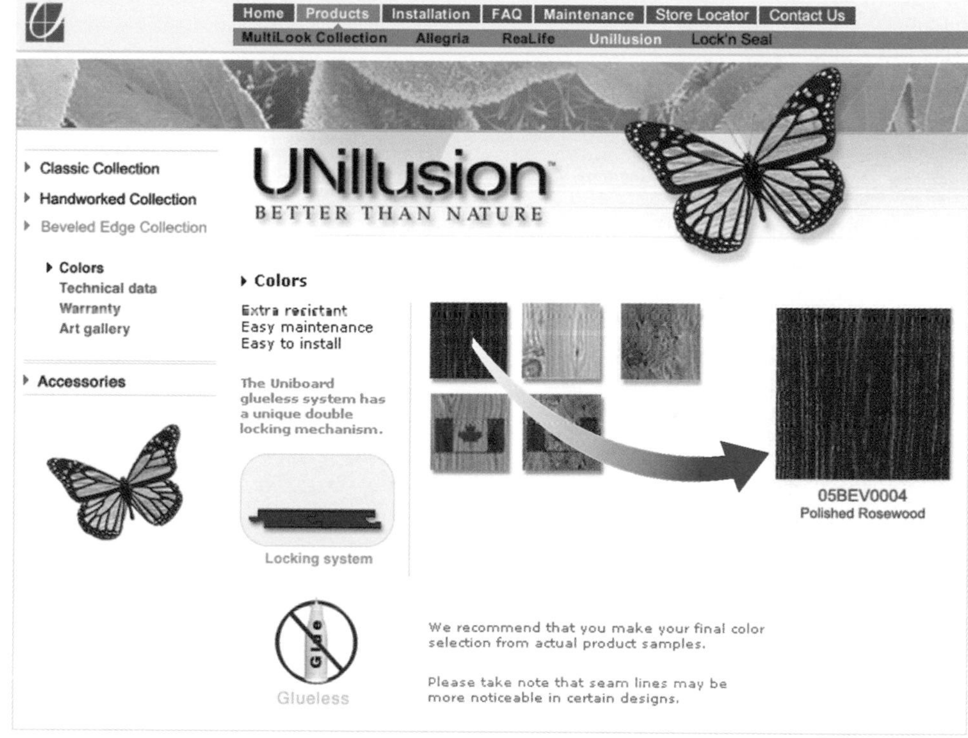

To use JavaScript you can either insert script code directly into your Web page by using the <script> </script> container (see Figure 10-9) or you can put it in an external file and use the <src> attribute with the file's URL to call it. You may use the <script></script> container as many times as needed within an XHTML file. Whether you insert the code directly inside your page or call an external file, the script tags will be used between the <head> and </head> or <body> and </body> tags.

Ideally, you can write JavaScript code once and it will work on any computer platform running any browser. Realistically, compatibility among different browsers and versions is always an issue. Just as new versions of browsers add and extend XHTML, JavaScript has been updated and extended to support newer browser capabilities. The <script> tag and <language> attribute can be used to specify which version of JavaScript to use.

QUICKTIP

By using comments in JavaScript you can request that the browser recognize the JavaScript version and ignore any script that it cannot support. If you do not do this, users who view your Web pages on a browser that does not support the version of JavaScript included will receive an error message.

FIGURE 10-9

JavaScript code is inserted directly into an XHTML document; the JavaScript code, shown here, sets a scrolling message and ensures that the values entered into the text boxes of a mortgage calculator are valid numbers

```
<head>
<title>Lab 10-2</title>
<script type="text/javascript">
<!--Hide from old browsers
var Msg = "  ---See us at Oak Wood Mortgage for all your financial and insurance needs!---  "
startAt = 0
function scrollingMsg() {
      document.Message.MsgBox.value = Msg.substring(startAt,Msg.length)+Msg.substring(0,startAt)
      startAt+=1
      if (startAt > Msg.length) {
           startAt = 0
      }
      window.setTimeout("scrollingMsg()",300)
}

var totalDebt = 0
var debt2income = 0

function validateInput(myForm) {
     var mPayment = parseInt(document.Ratio.MortPmt.value,10)
     if (isNaN(mPayment) || (mPayment < 1)) {
         alert("Monthly Payment not a valid entry")
         document.Ratio.MortPmt.value = ""
         document.Ratio.MortPmt.focus()
     }
     else {
           var mDebt = parseInt(document.Ratio.AmtDebt.value,10)
           if (isNaN(mDebt) || (mDebt < 1)) {
              alert("Amount of debt not a valid entry")
              document.Ratio.AmtDebt.value = ""
              document.Ratio.AmtDebt.focus()
           } else {
                  var mIncome = parseInt(document.Ratio.Income.value,10)
                  if (isNaN(mIncome) || (mIncome < 1)) {
                     alert("Income not a valid entry")
                     document.Ratio.Income.value = ""
                     document.Ratio.Income.focus()
                  } else {
                         TotalDebt(mPayment,mDebt, mIncome)
                    }
             }
      }
}

function TotalDebt(Pmt, Debt, Income) {
```

VBScript and ASP

Microsoft **VBScript** is a script version of Microsoft **Visual Basic (VB)** programming language. If you are already experienced in Visual Basic, you will find VBScript easy to learn. Even if you do not know Visual Basic, VBScript is fairly easy to learn.

Due in part to the popularity of the Visual Basic programming language, VBScript has become a widely used server-side scripting language for the Windows environment. Because VBScript is not cross-platform, its popularity on the client-side of the Web is limited. However, corporate intranets often support VBScript both on the client side and the server side. It is also the primary scripting language used for **Active Server Pages (ASP)**, a server-side scripting environment developed by Microsoft. In the ASP environment, you can combine XHTML and scripts to create dynamic and powerful Web pages. Active Server Pages are server-generated and can call other programs to perform a variety of different functions including accessing databases. Active Server Pages turn static XHTML pages into dynamic, database-driven Web sites.

The ASP environment has evolved into an open framework that does not require the use of proprietary Microsoft software to write the code. The ASP environment is not a scripting language; it is a scripting environment. You can use any text editor to create ASP code. Although VBScript is the most common choice for ASP coders, other scripting languages can be used to create Active Server Pages. Active Server Pages are easy to use and implement. The biggest drawback to the ASP environment is that, although it does not require proprietary software to write the code, it does require proprietary Web servers running Microsoft Web server software to deliver the code.

JSP

Similar to ASP, **Java Server Pages (JSP)** is the Java-based technology for generating dynamic Web pages with cross-platform and cross-Web-server support. JSP is a dynamic scripting environment for the Web. It is comparable to Microsoft's Active Server Pages but uses Java code instead of Visual Basic code.

The JSP environment is not a scripting language and therefore it is not the same as JavaScript. As you will recall, JavaScript is a client-side scripting language whereas JSP code resides on and is interpreted by the server. JSP is a perfect choice if you want the advantages of a dynamic Web-scripting, server-side environment to work on a Web server that does not offer native ASP support (i.e., a Web server other than those supported by Microsoft).

PHP

PHP (officially **PHP: Hypertext Preprocessor**) is a server-side scripting language for creating dynamic Web page components. PHP is widely used and is especially suited for Web development. PHP is open source and it runs on multiple platforms. PHP scripts are short bits of code embedded in the XHTML file and enclosed in special start and end tags that allow you to jump into and out of PHP mode.

PHP differs from client-side scripts in that the code is executed on the Web server. When a user opens a Web page, the PHP commands are processed on the Web server and the results are returned to the user's browser. Users receive only the results of running the script. Consequently, they have no way of viewing the underlying code. It is possible to configure your Web server to process all your XHTML files using PHP, which prevents users from viewing any of your source code.

You can use PHP to set cookies, manage authentication, and redirect users. It offers excellent connectivity to many databases as well as integration with various external libraries that let you generate PDF documents and parse XML.

There are several advantages to using PHP. Because PHP code is written directly into your Web pages, (see Figure 10-10) there is no need for a special development environment. Just use the <script language="php"></script> container, and the PHP engine will process everything between the tags and quickly return the results.

Common Gateway Interface (CGI)

Prior to the availability of scripting languages, collecting and processing user data required the use of a **Common Gateway Interface (CGI)**. CGI is a communication standard for data exchange between a Web server and server-side program. The CGI standard provides the rules for running external programs on a Web server. External programs are called gateways because they open up an outside world of information to the Web server.

In effect, CGI is the interface between applications and the Web server. It specifies how data is transferred from the Web server to the program and vice versa. It also serves as a server-side program used to collect and process data. Data from a form would have to travel from the Web browser to the CGI on the Web server. The CGI then processed the data and returned the results to the user in the form of a new Web page. This process occurred every time a user made changes to a Web form.

Sending data back and forth between the Web client and the Web server wastes time. By collecting and processing data on the user's system, scripting languages offer a way to add intelligence and interactivity to Web pages without burdening the Web server. Although you will still need to send the processed data to a CGI or comparable program, scripting languages have made this process more efficient by verifying the data on the Web client prior to submitting the data to the Web server.

FIGURE 10-10

Because PHP code is written directly into your XHTML files, there is no need for a special development environment

```
<?php
  require ('ActivEdit.inc');
  $ae = new ActivEdit;
  $ae->attributes["inc"]       = "/aephp/inc/";
  $ae->attributes["name"]      = "aecontone";
  $ae->attributes["image"]     = "1";
  $ae->attributes["baseurl"]   = "http://localhost/";
  $ae->attributes["imageurl"]  = "/aephp/inc/images/";
  $ae->attributes["imagepath"] = "c:/inetpub/wwwroot/aephp/inc/images/";
  $ae->attributes["upload"]    = "yes";
  $ae->attributes["tabview"]   = "true";

  $ae_control = $ae->printAE();

   //   Place the $ae_control within the form you want to use with ActivEdit
?>
<html>
<title> CFDEV.COM | ActivEdit Demo</title>

 <script>
 <!--
     function changeColor(newColor) {
     DHTMLSafe=aeObjects["aecontone"];
     DHTMLSafe.DOM.body.style.backgroundColor = newColor;
  document.all.colorPicker.selectedIndex = 0;
    }
 //-->
 </script>


<body>

<form name="test" action="save.php" method="POST">

 <select id="colorPicker" onChange="changeColor(this.options
[this.selectedIndex].value)">
  <option>Background Color
  <option value="0000FF">Blue
  <option value="FF0000">Red
  <option value="00FF00">Green
  <option value="000000">Black
 </select>

  <? print($ae_control); ?>
  <input type="submit" value="Click To View Submission">
</form>
</body>
</html>
```

This sample PHP code creates a drop-down list from which a user can select a background color

CONCEPT 3

EXPLORE PROGRAMMING Languages

What You'll Learn

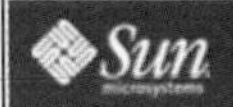

↓ Products & Services

Home > Products & Services > Software > Learn About >

Java Technology

The Java platform is **the** ideal platform for network computing. R
create a seamless, secure, networked platform for your busines

The Java platform benefits from a massive community of develo
through an open, community-based, standards organization kno

You can find Java technology in cell phones, on laptop compute
everywhere!

In this lesson, you will learn about the advantages and disadvantages of using programming languages for Web page development. You will also get a brief overview of several programming languages that can be used to develop multimedia Web sites.

As we have already discussed, Web pages are text files that are stored on a Web server. The Web server waits for a file request from a Web client, and then responds by sending the file to the Web browser on the client. Aside from scripts that might be embedded in XHTML files, there is nothing dynamic or interactive about the XHTML files sent to the client. They are simple text files. One way to make your Web pages more dynamic or interactive is to configure your Web page to request and run a script or program outside the Web page and possibly even on a different Web server (see Figure 10-11).

Programming languages used specifically for Web page development are used to write executable programs that are accessed or called from an XHTML file. In other words, Web pages are not programs, but programs can be called from within Web pages. These external programs can do just about anything you want or need them to do. They can play multimedia files, handle incoming forms, pull records from a database, and save data to a file. They extend the capabilities of a Web page beyond what is possible with markup and scripting languages.

As you decide whether to run a client-side script, a server-side script, or a program, you will find that each option has advantages and disadvantages. Dynamic updating and interactivity features, such as validating a data entry field, are probably best done with a client-side scripting language such as JavaScript, which is more responsive and delivers immediate feedback to the user. However, a client-side script runs on the user's machine. If you want information to pass from the Web client to the Web server, which you will need if you want to store information in a database, run server applications, or collect information about your Web site's visitors, your Web page will have to access server-side programs.

Security concerns should also play a role in your decision to use a client-side script, a server-side script, or a program. When you run client-side scripts, your Web server is safe because the client-side script does not access server resources. But a poorly written server-side script or program can open your site to ill-intended access. Therefore, your server-side scripts and programs must be vigilant in securing potential holes that might otherwise allow access to the Web server.

Another important consideration is the burden that server-side scripts and programs place on your Web server. With a server-side script or program, every new request for the script or program adds to the processing load of the Web server. This can result in lengthy response times if your site experiences heavy traffic. You obviously do not have to worry about this with client-side scripts.

If you need to store information in a server database or provide customized Web pages, server-side scripts or programs are usually the better solution. Often a combination of both client-side scripts and server-side scripts/programs are needed.

Perl

Practical Extraction and Report Language (Perl) is a powerful and flexible programming language. It is fairly easy to learn yet possesses almost limitless possibilities. As such, it has a tremendous following among Web developers. Many server-side programs are created in Perl. If you have ever filled out a form on the Web, you have probably interacted with Perl code as it is one of the most common programming languages for building CGI applications.

There are several reasons for Perl's popularity. There are Perl interpreters for the various operating systems that support Web servers. Perl is uniquely powerful when it comes to manipulating text. It is well designed for reading, parsing, manipulating, and outputting text. Perl programmers can borrow from a large library of publicly available modules. There are literally hundreds of different modules available that can interact with databases, perform commands like a Web browser, act as an e-mail client, manipulate graphics, and do just about anything else you might imagine. Perl can also handle encrypted Web data, including e-commerce transactions.

FIGURE 10-11
If you want your Web pages to do something dynamic or interactive, your Web page may have to request to run a script or program outside the Web page

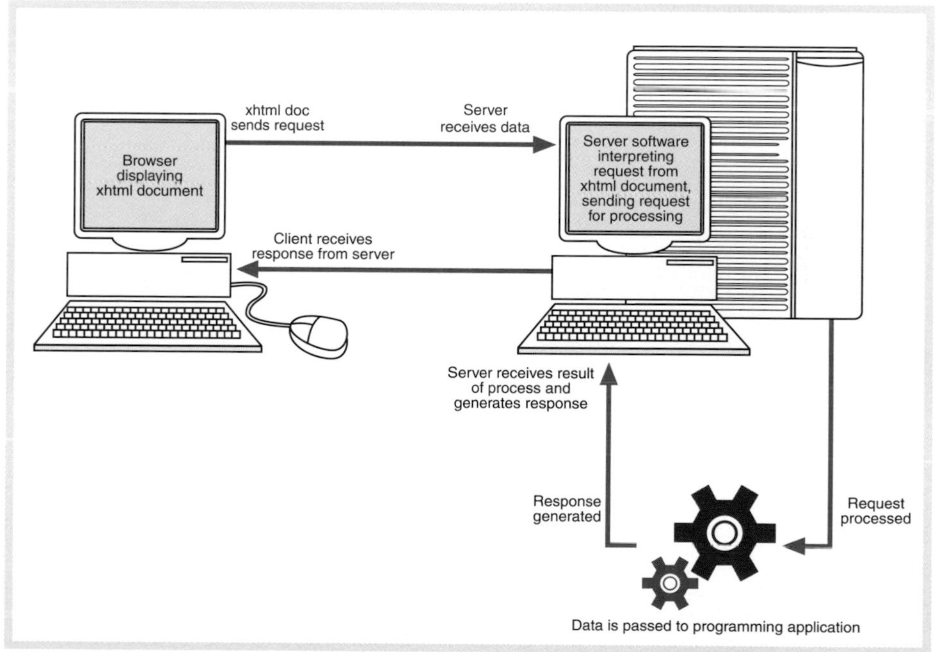

Java

Java is Sun Microsystems's full-fledged, object-oriented programming language (see Figure 10-12). Java is based on C++ but optimized for the distribution of program objects in a network environment such as the Internet. For development of content on the Web, Java is used primarily to create a special type of mini application, called an applet. **Applets** are small programs designed to be executed within another application or from a Web page (See Figure 10-13).

The first thing to remember is that Java is not the same as JavaScript. Although your browser can run both, they are handled quite differently. JavaScript is scripting code that you add to your XHTML code either in the Web page itself or in an external document that is called from the Web page. Your browser reads the code and executes it. Simply by viewing the XHTML source code, anyone can read the JavaScript code or the code that calls the JavaScript in an external document.

Java, on the other hand, is a **compiled language**. Before Java code can be run, it has to be processed by a special program to create an executable file or a Java applet. Although JavaScript is embedded within the XHTML document, Java applets are either executed on the Web server or sent alongside the XHTML document where they are executed on the Web client.

FIGURE 10-12

Java is a programming language developed by Sun Microsystems

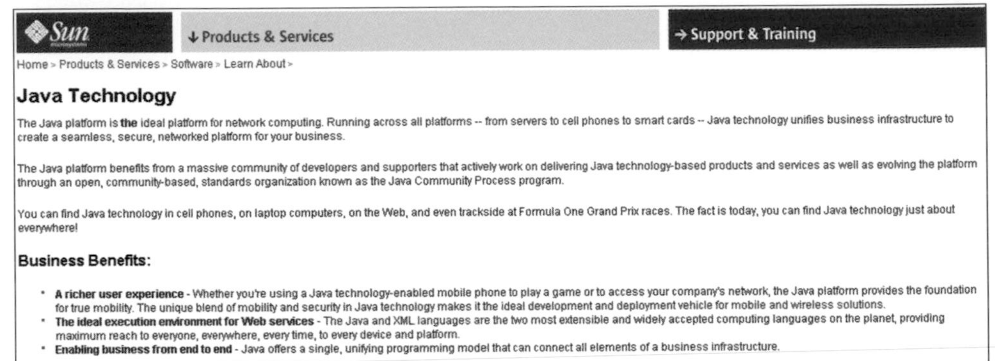

FIGURE 10-13

Java applets are called from the Web page; an applet is used to generate this graph from a function

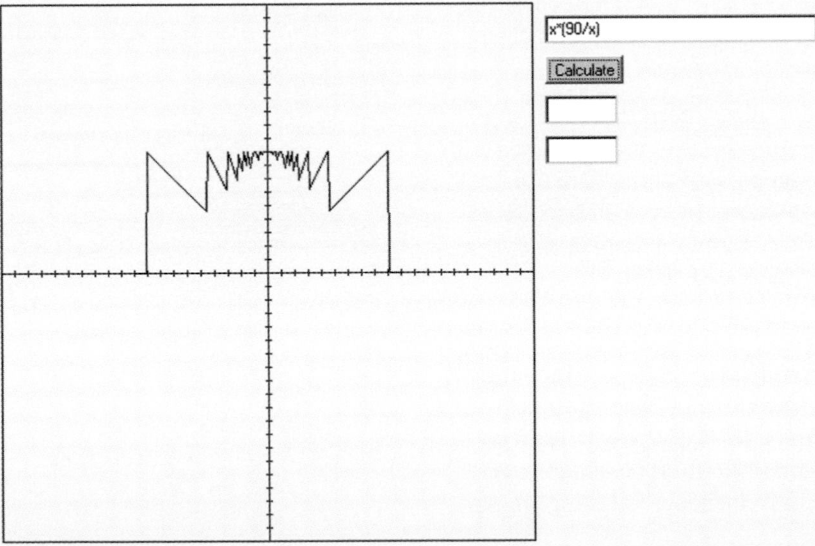

The uncompiled Java source code is contained in an editable file, which is separate from the Java applet file that contains the program to be run.

When you load a page that contains a Java applet, your Web browser actually loads the applet or the executable file. The Web browser has a special built-in engine that can execute this file and display the output on the page. The browser does not load the source file, which is not available to users.

Visual Basic

Visual Basic is a Microsoft programming language. Visual Basic is considered a high-level programming language, which means that almost all of the commands are English derivatives. You can use Visual Basic to create full-featured, powerful programs to do just about anything. Visual Basic includes many features specifically designed for database development and integration as well as the creation of server-side applications and components that are easily accessible from any Web browser on any platform.

C#

C# (pronounced "C sharp") is a modern, object-oriented language that enables programmers to quickly build a wide range of applications for the Microsoft .NET platform. It is similar in syntax to both C++ and Java and is considered by Microsoft as the natural evolution of the C and C++ languages. C# is touted as a language that incorporates the best of C, Visual Basic, C++, and Java. It extends the capabilities of these predecessors through object-oriented (OO) and component capabilities that are built directly in to the language structure. C# also supports XML and can be used to create components for Windows and the Web. Because Web programmers need languages that combine ease of use with high performance, C# offers the optimum productivity that Web developers need.

ActiveX

Another technology sometimes used on the Web is Microsoft's **ActiveX**. ActiveX is an extension of **object linking and embedding (OLE)**, a standard developed by Microsoft to create objects with one application and then link or embed them in another. Within a Web page that is ActiveX-enabled, you can link or embed objects from any application that supports ActiveX. In essence, the ActiveX component allows you to link to documents such as an Excel spreadsheet or Access database and then drop them into your Web page. Unlike Java, ActiveX is not platform independent. ActiveX works best in a Windows environment. Therefore, it is not as versatile as Java and some of the other programming languages mentioned previously. Though ActiveX is fine for intranets, where the platform is likely to be more consistent or at least more controllable, Java is a more adaptable language for the Internet.

Classifying Programming Languages

Programming languages are classified from low level to high level. In general, a **high-level programming language** is a programming language that is more user-friendly than a **low-level programming language**. The word "high" does not indicate that the language is superior, but rather it indicates that the syntax of the language is closer to an English derivative, whereas "low" indicates that the syntax is closer to machine language.

In general, high-level languages make complex programming easier, while low-level languages produce more efficient code. Note that the terms "high-level" and "low-level" are relative in that a language that is considered "high-level" today might be considered "low-level" tomorrow.

SUMMARY

A **Web server** is the computer on which the files for Web pages are stored and a **Web client** is the computer running a Web browser. A **markup language** is a full set of instructions that can be used to comprehensively describe the structural format of a piece of text or other media element. Markup instructions or tags are interpreted by Web browsers. **Standard Generalized Markup Language (SGML)** is a standard for defining document structures for markup schemes. SGML provides a consistent and precise method of applying markup so that electronic documents can be exchanged and revised between different computer systems, but it does not directly define or restrict the type of data contained in a document. Many markup languages are derivatives of SGML.

Hypertext Markup Language (HTML) and **Extensible Hypertext Markup Language (XHTML)** are markup languages used to create Web pages. **Dynamic Hypertext Markup Language (DHTML)** is a group of technologies combined to create greater interactivity and page layout flexibility. DHTML includes HTML, **JavaScript**, Cascading Style Sheets (CSS), and the **Document Object Model (DOM)**, a platform-neutral **application programming interface (API)**.

Virtual Reality Modeling Language (VRML) is a markup language used to create **virtual reality (VR)** on the Web. It offers a simple and accessible way to create interactive worlds for displaying 3-D graphics on the Web. Another popular tool for creating virtual reality on the Web is **QuickTime VR** by Apple.

Synchronized Multimedia Integration Language (SMIL) is a simple, platform-neutral markup language designed to let Web designers and developers schedule multimedia files across a timeline and deliver them via the Web. **Extensible Markup Language (XML)** is a meta-language that allows Web developers and programmers to define their own markup languages.

Wireless Markup Language (WML) is based on the **Handheld Device Markup Language (HDML)**. WML is read and interpreted by a **microbrowser** built in to a wireless handheld device. The microbrowser interprets WML and renders the information on a small display found on wireless handheld devices, such as mobile phones and small terminals. The standard for delivering WML files is **Wireless Application Protocol (WAP)**.

Scripting languages are used to write **scripts** that are interpreted by a Web browser. Scripts are processed on either the client side or the server side. **Client-side programs** are uncompiled scripts. You can use scripts to perform tasks such as creating rollovers, automatically showing the date and time, sizing windows, opening new windows, and detecting which browser is being used to access the page. Scripts can also be used to collect and process user data. **Common Gateway Interface (CGI)** is a communication standard for data exchange between a Web server and server-side program.

JavaScript was developed by Netscape to extend the capabilities of standard HTML and now XHTML. JavaScript allows you to add interactivity and dynamic content to your Web pages. JavaScript can be used to create rollovers, deliver dynamic content, and set **cookies**. **VBScript** is a scripting version of Microsoft Visual Basic (VB) that has become a widely used server-side scripting language for the Windows environment. It is also the primary scripting language used to create **Active Server Pages (ASP)**. **PHP** is a server-side scripting language, which means the code is executed on the Web server. **Java Server Pages (JSP)** is the Java-based technology for generating dynamic Web pages with cross-platform and cross-Web server support.

Programming languages for the Web are used to write executable programs that are accessed or called from a Web page.

Programming languages can be classified as **high-level** or **low-level programming languages**. **Practical Extraction and Report Language (Perl)** is a powerful and flexible programming language used extensively for building CGI applications. Another reason this program is popular is that there are Perl interpreters for nearly every operating system that supports Web servers. **Java** is Sun Microsystems's full-fledged, object-oriented programming language, which is used to build Java **applets**. Applets are small programs designed to be executed within another application or from a Web page. Java is a **compiled language** and should not be confused with JavaScript. **Visual Basic (VB)**, **C#**, and **ActiveX** are Microsoft technologies. VB and C# are high-level programming languages for creating server-side applications easily accessible from any Web browser, and ActiveX is an extension of **OLE (object linking and embedding)** that allows you to link or embed objects from a Web page to any application that supports ActiveX.

DESIGN PROJECT

Working with a Scripting Language

1. Add a Web Page with JavaScript to a Web Site

This is a continuation of the Design Project in Chapter 9.

The client The Inn at Birch Bay has reviewed the Web pages and has asked that a reservations page be added to the site. Specifically, the client would like visitors to be able to electronically select arrival and departure dates from a calendar, and then submit the dates along with their names and e-mail addresses. In addition, the client would like visitors to be able to specify flexibility related to the specified dates and be able to submit additional comments, such as a request for a bay view.

The WebsByCT multimedia development team has decided that this project would be ideal for you to learn how a scripting language can enhance the functionality of a Web page. The actual scripting has been completed by a programmer and you have been provided with a Web page containing the JavaScript code that meets the client's needs. Your role will be to study, in general, how the JavaScript code works. Then you will add the Web page containing the JavaScript to the Inn at Birch Bay Web site, test the page, and edit it.

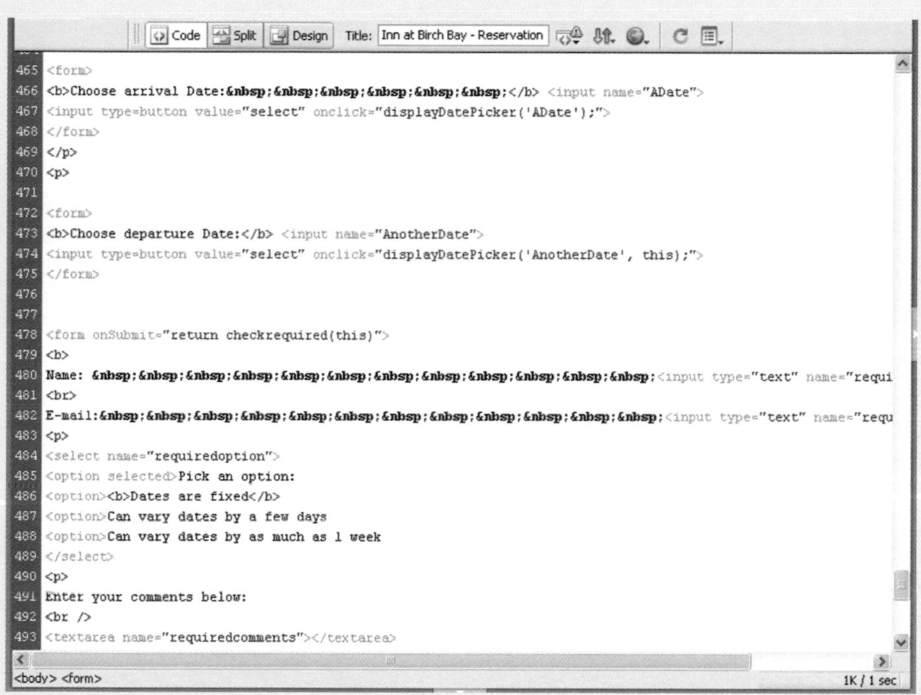
Code
Split
Design
Title: Inn at Birch Bay - Reservation
<form>
<b>Choose arrival Date: </b> <input name="ADate">
<input type=button value="select" onclick="displayDatePicker('ADate');">
</form>
</p>
<p>
<form>
<b>Choose departure Date:</b> <input name="AnotherDate">
<input type=button value="select" onclick="displayDatePicker('AnotherDate', this);">
</form>
<form onSubmit="return checkrequired(this)">
<b>
Name: <input type="text" name="requi

E-mail: <input type="text" name="requ
<p>
<select name="requiredoption">
<option selected>Pick an option:
<option><b>Dates are fixed</b>
<option>Can vary dates by a few days
<option>Can vary dates by as much as 1 week
</select>
<p>
Enter your comments below:

<textarea name="requiredcomments"></textarea>
<body> <form>
1K / 1 sec

Files
Files
Assets
InnWebsiteDW
Local view
Site - InnWebsiteDW (C:\InnWeb
assets
contactus.htm
directions.htm
homepage.htm
innmap.swf
reservations.htm
sitestyles.css
tour-embed.htm
tour.htm

Properties
Format Paragraph
Style None
Link reservations.htm
Font Default Font
Size None
Target
Page Properties...
List Item...

LESSON 1

ADD A WEB PAGE WITH JavaScript to a Web Site

What You'll Do

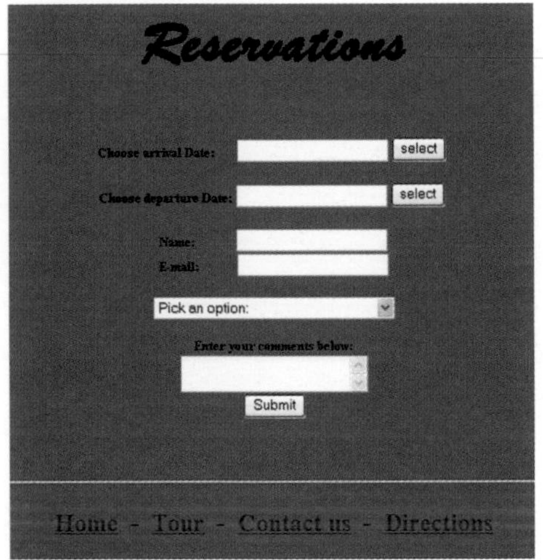

In this lesson, you will add a Web page containing JavaScript code to a Web site, test the code, and learn how to make changes in the forms that use the code.

The Completed Web Page

Figure 10-14 shows the Web page displayed in a browser with the forms that a visitor would complete. To the visitor the Web page appears to be one form, but to a programmer the Web page consists of three forms that are used to collect the data from the visitor. The first and second forms collect arrival date and departure date information. When a visitor clicks a select button, a calendar showing the current month opens. The visitor can select other months and other years for display. When the visitor clicks a date in the calendar, the date appears in the corresponding text box (arrival or departure). The third form is used to collect the visitor's name, e-mail address, information about date flexibility, and comments. To provide information about date flexibility, the visitor clicks the down arrow for the Pick an option box and chooses from a list of options. To submit comments, the visitor types comments into the Comments text box and clicks the Submit button. If the forms are incomplete, a warning message will open telling the visitor what information is still needed. When the visitor clicks the Submit button, the forms are sent to a server for processing.

The JavaScript Code

There are two major sections within the HTML document that relate to the JavaScript code, which is used to create the forms and make them interactive. The first section is the script tag that specifies the scripting language being used and contains the lines of code to set up variables and perform the necessary functions. The script tags are placed within the head element of the HTML document as follows:

```
<head>
        <script language="JavaScript">
        .
        .
        .
        </script>
```

An example of JavaScript code that creates the variables that format how a date is displayed follows. This code would be placed within script tags.

```
var defaultDateSeparator = "/";

var defaultDateFormat = "mdy"

var dateSeparator = defaultDateSeparator;

var dateFormat = defaultDateFormat;
```

Another example of JavaScript code that is used when the calendar is being created follows. The first part of that code specifies that if a Saturday has been displayed in the calendar, then a new row should be started. This code would also be placed within script tags.

```
if (thisDay.getDay() == 6)
```

The days are assigned numbers starting with Sunday (0), Monday (1), Tuesday (2), and so on.

FIGURE 10-14
The Web page displayed in a browser

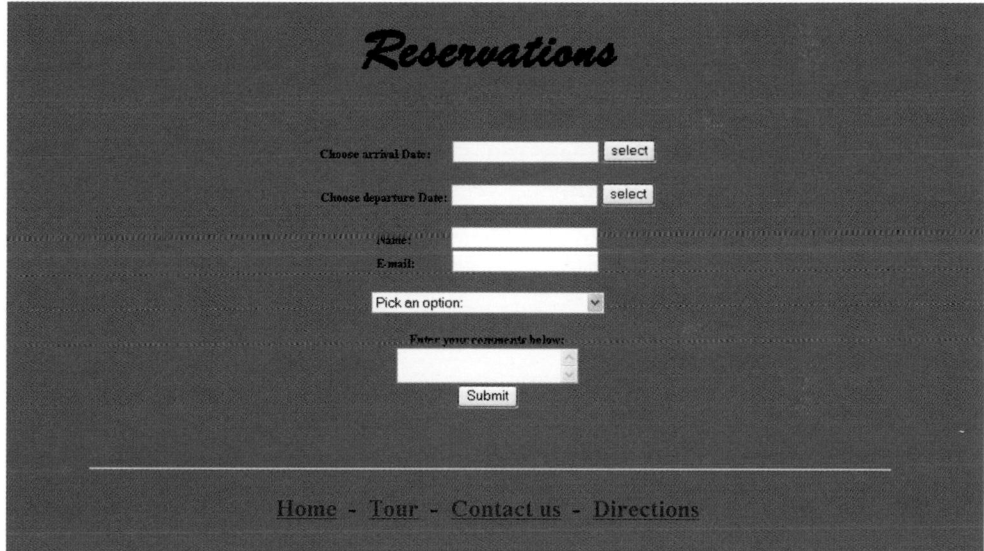

The second major section consists of the form tags. For the InnWebsite reservation page, there are three sets of form tags, one for each form in the document as shown in Figure 10-15. The form tags are placed in the body element of the html document. The first two sets of form tags contain the code to display the forms and accept the user input for the arrival and departure date. The third set of form tags contains the code to display the form and accept the user input for the name, e-mail, options, and comments.

The completed Web page containing the JavaScript code is named reservations.htm. You will copy this page from the location where you are storing the files for this chapter to the InnWebsite folder, and then link it to the Contact us page. Then you will test the page in a browser and edit the page by changing the options.

QUICKTIP

The exercises in this chapter were created with the screen resolution set at 1024 × 768. If your computer's screen resolution has a different setting, the figures in the book may appear different. You may want to verify the screen resolution on your computer and set it to 1024 × 768, if necessary.

FIGURE 10-15

The three sets of form tags

The first form collects information about the arrival date

```
<form>
<b>Choose arrival Date:      </b> <input name="ADate">
<input type=button value="select" onclick="displayDatePicker('ADate');">
</form>
<p>
```

The second form collects information about the departure date

```
<form>
<b>Choose departure Date:</b> <input name="AnotherDate">
<input type=button value="select" onclick="displayDatePicker('AnotherDate', this);">
</form>
```

The third form collects the user's name, e-mail address, flexibility regarding the dates listed in forms 1 and 2, and comments

```
<form onSubmit="return checkrequired(this)">
<b>
Name:             <input type="text"
name="requiredname">
<br />
E-mail:            <input type="text"
name="requiredemail">
<p>
<select name="requiredoption">
<option selected>Pick an option:
<option><b>Dates are fixed</b>
<option>Can vary dates by a few days
<option>Can vary dates as much as 1 week
</select>
<p>
Enter your comments below:
<br />
<textarea name="requiredcomments"></textarea>
<br />
<input type=submit value="Submit">
</form>
```

FIGURE 10-16
The selected text

FIGURE 10-17
Dragging the file to the Link box

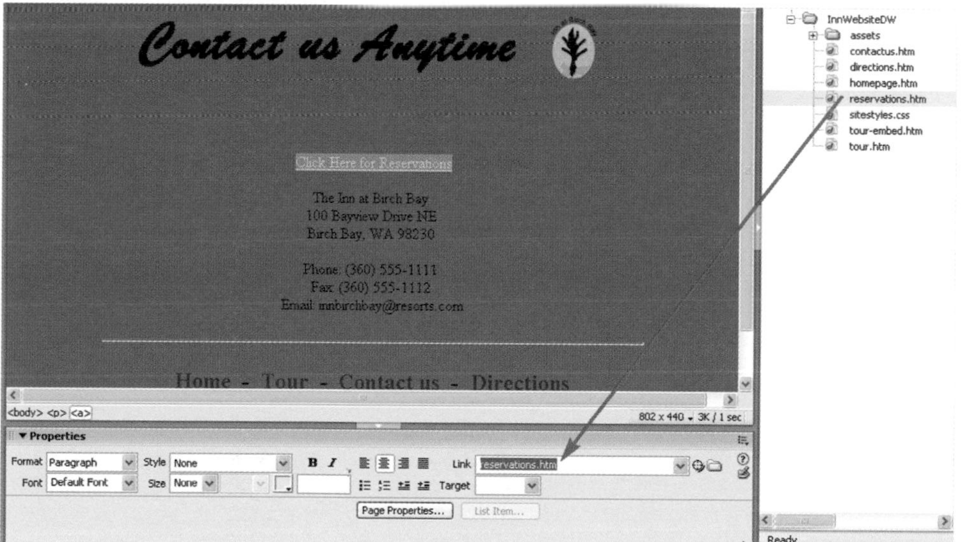

Add a Web page with JavaScript to a Web site

1. Navigate to the folder containing the files for this chapter, then copy **reservations.htm** to the InnWebsiteDW folder.
2. Start Dreamweaver, then display the InnWebsiteDW site in the Files panel.
3. Double-click **contactus.htm** in the Files panel to open the document.

   Note: If the body text is not centered, select the text and click the Align Center button in the Property inspector.
4. Select the text as shown in Figure 10-16, then press **[delete]**.
5. Type **Click Here for Reservations**.
6. Select **Click Here for Reservations**, then drag **reservations.htm** to the Link box as shown in Figure 10-17.
7. Click **File** on the menu bar, then click **Save**.

You added a Web page containing JavaScript code to a Web site.

Test JavaScript in a Web page

1. Press **[F12]** to display the document in a Web browser.
2. Click the **Click Here for Reservations link**. Note: If you have installed Windows XP Service Pack 2, you might need to allow blocked content to view the preview. To allow blocked content, click the Internet Security bar, and then select Allow Blocked Content.
3. Click the **select button** for the arrival Date, then select a date.

   Note: Mac users may have to scroll to see the calendar.
4. Click the **select button** for the departure Date, then select a date.
5. Click the **Submit button**, read the warning message, then click **OK**.
6. Type a name, click the **Submit button**, read the warning message as shown in Figure 10-18, then click **OK**.
7. Type an e-mail address, click the **Submit button**, read the warning message, then click **OK**.
8. Click the **list arrow** for Pick an option, click **Option 1**, click the **Submit button**, read the warning message, then click **OK**.

   Note: You will make changes to the list option choices in the next lesson so that the options have meaning to the visitor.
9. Type a comment in the comments box, then click the **Submit button**.
10. Close the browser, then return to Dreamweaver.

You tested the JavaScript in the Web page.

FIGURE 10-18
The message displayed by the JavaScript code

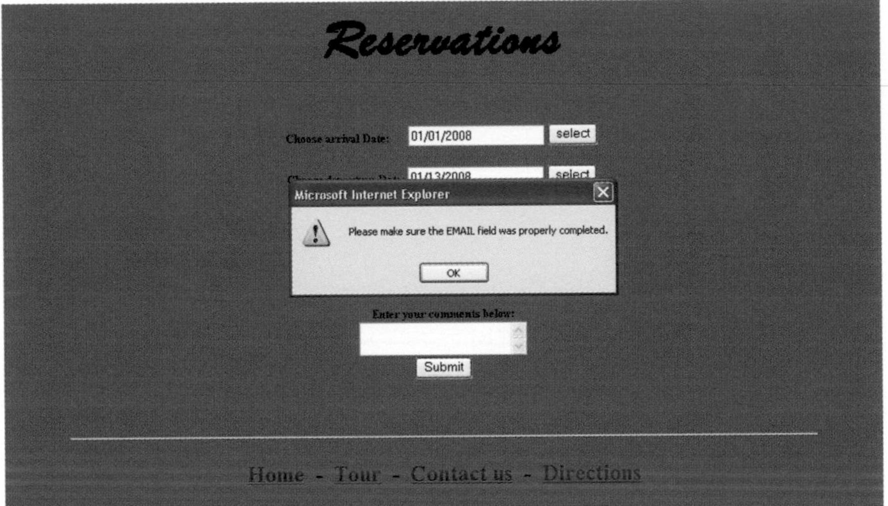

FIGURE 10-19

Selecting the text

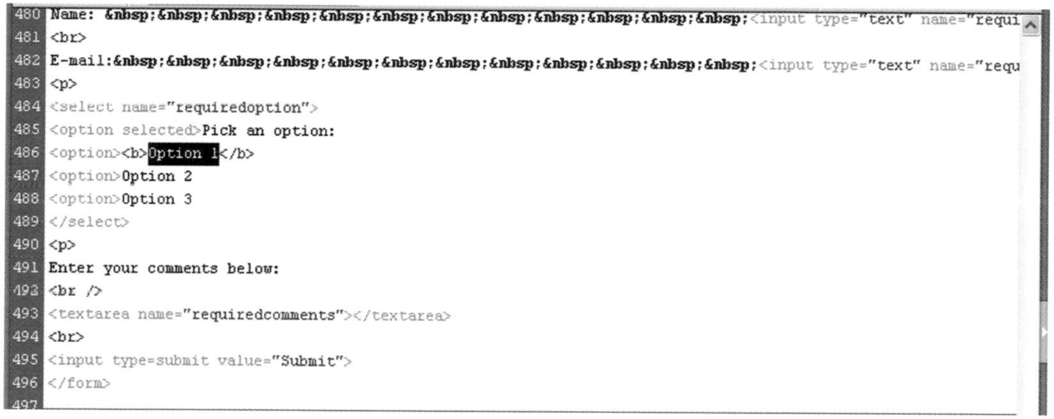

```
Name:             <input type="text" name="requi
<br>
E-mail:            <input type="text" name="requ
<p>
<select name="requiredoption">
<option selected>Pick an option:
<option><b>Option 1</b>
<option>Option 2
<option>Option 3
</select>
<p>
Enter your comments below:
<br />
<textarea name="requiredcomments"></textarea>
<br>
<input type=submit value="Submit">
</form>
```

Make a change to the form

1. Double-click **reservations.htm** in the Files panel to display it in Dreamweaver.
2. Click the **Pick an option box**, scrolling down if necessary.
3. Click the **Code button** to display the code.
4. Select **Option 1** as shown in Figure 10-19, then press **[delete]**.
5. Type **Dates are fixed**.
6. Select **Option 2**, press **[delete]**, then type **Can vary dates by a few days**.
7. Select **Option 3**, press **[delete]**, then type **Can vary dates as much as 1 week**.
8. Save the document.
9. Press **[F12]** to view the Web page in a browser.
10. Click the **list arrow** for Pick an option and notice the options have changed.
11. Close the browser and return to Dreamweaver.

You changed the form.

PROJECT BUILDER 1

1. Connect to the Internet, go to *www.course.com*, navigate to the page for this book, click the Student Online Companion link, then click the link for this chapter.
2. Navigate through the site (see Figure 10-20) and note the use of forms.
3. Open a document in a word processor, save the file as **Ch10pb1**, then answer the following questions for the home page.
   a. What components are used for the form(s): text input boxes, radio buttons, and so on?
   b. What is the purpose of the form(s)?
   c. What other criteria could be added to the form(s) to obtain the additional information?

One Step Beyond

4. View the source for the home page in a text editor, then answer the following questions or perform the following actions.
   a. Which language is being used to create the functionality of the forms?
   b. What is the exact HTML tag that is used to specify the language?
   c. In which section of the HTML document is the tag used to specify the language located?
   d. Copy and paste one complete section of script code from the text editor to your document.
   e. Copy and paste one complete section of form code from the text editor to your document.
   f. Find a line of code that refers to cgi and copy it to your document.
5. Save your document as **Ch10pb1-Onexx** (where *xx* are your initials).

Two Steps Beyond

6. Conduct a Web search for companies that provide JavaScript editors.
7. Choose one editor and write a summary that includes the following:
   a. The name and URL for the company
   b. The name of the editor
   c. A brief description of the major features of the editor
   d. The cost of the editor
8. Save the document as **Ch10pb1-Twoxx** (where *xx* are your initials).

FIGURE 10-20
The use of forms created with scripts in a Web page

PROJECT BUILDER 2

You have been studying Web development. You decide it would be useful to add a form to your Web page for a portfolio Web site. Complete the following steps to add a form to a Web page.

1. Conduct a Web search to find JavaScript code for a form that you would like to add to your Web page.
2. Write a summary of your Web search that includes:
   a. The source of the code (include the URL)
   b. The terms of use, including any copyright considerations
   c. What the code does
   d. Why you choose this code
3. Save the summary with the filename **Ch10pb2**.

One Step Beyond

4. Open Dreamweaver MX 2004 and insert the code in the body section of a new document.
5. Display the document in a browser and test the form.
6. Save the Dreamweaver document with the filename **Formpagexx.htm** (where *xx* are your initials).

Two Steps Beyond

7. Using Dreamweaver MX 2004, open mysiteCh10-script.htm (see Figure 10-21).
8. Insert the code in the document, replace the placeholder text "...form goes here..." with your form.
9. Save the document as **mysiteCh10-Twoxx.htm** (where *xx* are your initials).
10. Preview the document in a browser.

FIGURE 10-21
A Web page with placeholder text indicating where a form will be added

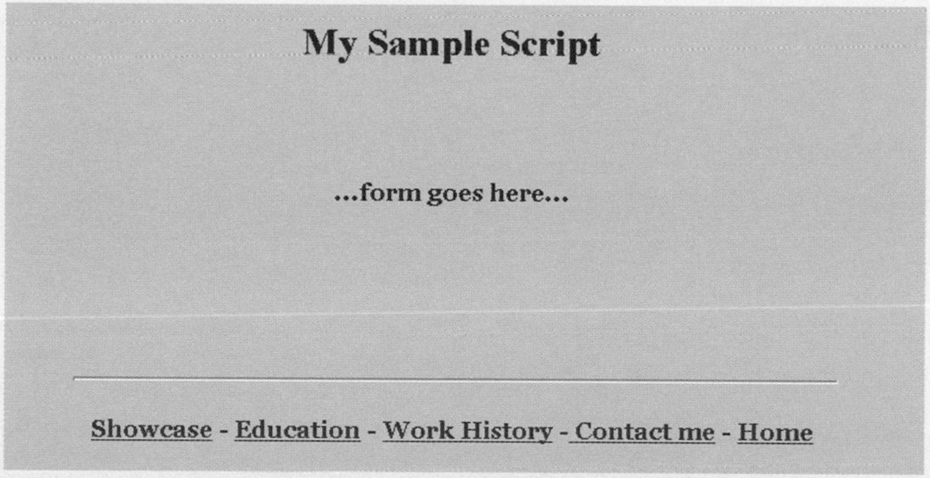

My Sample Script

...form goes here...

Showcase - Education - Work History - Contact me - Home

3-D modeling
Software program used to create or modify three-dimensional graphic images.

3-D sound
Sound that includes delays that attempt to simulate the time it would take for sound waves to reach the ear if the sound were happening live.

A

AAC (Advanced Audio Coding)
Audio file format at the core of the MPEG-4 specifications; format of choice for Internet, wireless, and digital broadcast arenas.

Absolute length unit
Length unit that is dependent on the viewing medium (monitor resolution, for example) and is useful only if the properties of the medium are known.

ACID
Music production software by Sony.

ActionScript
The Macromedia Flash built-in scripting language for creating customizable and engaging interactivity.

Active Server Pages (ASP)
An open application, server-side scripting environment developed by Microsoft; Active Server Pages are most commonly scripted using VBScript.

ActiveX
Microsoft technology used to extend object linking and embedding (OLE) on the Web.

Adobe Acrobat
The most common software program used to create Portable Document Format (PDF) files for the Web.

Adobe Acrobat Reader
Program that enables users to view Portable Document Format (PDF) files.

Adobe After Effects
A compositing software program that can help you create video and animation effects.

Adobe GoLive
Professional Web authoring and site management tool.

Adobe Illustrator
An industry-standard drawing program for creating vector graphics.

Adobe ImageReady
Software program specifically designed for producing and optimizing screen-based images and animation for the Web.

Adobe Photoshop
An industry-standard image editing and paint program.

Adobe Premiere
An industry-standard, nonlinear video-editing program used to capture and edit video.

AIFF
The Apple Audio Interchange Format for audio.

Alternate text
Text assigned to a media element on a Web site; alternate text is read by a screen reader.

Ambient sound
Sound used to reinforce messages and set the mood.

Amplitude
The distance between the valley and the peak of a waveform.

Analog sound
Continuous stream of sound waves.

Analog video
Video footage on videotape, videodisc, or laser disc that must be converted to a digital format before it can be recognized by the computer.

Analog-To-Digital Converter (ADC)
Equipment used to convert impulses to numbers that can be stored, understood, and manipulated by the computer.

Animated GIF
A special kind of GIF file known as GIF89a, used to create animated 2-D and 3-D images for Web pages.

Animation
A moving graphic image.

Animation codec
Compression algorithm developed to compress animation files.

Animation effect
Feature used with animation to create special effects.

Animation palette
Used to preview and set playback options for an animation.

Animation specialist
Multimedia team member responsible for creating 2-D or 3-D animation.

Apple Cinepak
A cross-platform compression scheme or codec that works well for cross-platform delivery of video on the Web.

Apple Final Cut Pro
A feature-rich, nonlinear video-editing application.

Apple iMovie
Nonlinear, video-editing package by Apple.

Applet
Tiny nonplatform-specific application called from a Web page.

Application Programming Interface (API)
Allows software developers to access the server software directly without having to go through a CGI first; increases form-processing speed and permits more extensive server customization.

Approach
Design consideration that determines how much direction the user will be provided.

ARPANET
Foundation of the Internet that was started by the military in the 1960s to create a decentralized communication network.

Art director
Multimedia team member responsible for creating the artwork for a project.

Aspect ratio
The ratio of width to height in the dimensions of a frame of video.

Asymmetrical balance
Achieved by arranging nonidentical elements on both sides of a centerline on the screen.

Attribute
Property that modifies an HTML tag.

AU
A 16-bit compressed audio format developed by Sun Microsystems.

Audio specialist
Multimedia team member responsible for ensuring that appropriate sound is delivered in real time.

Audio-Video Interleave (AVI)
Video file format by Microsoft supported within the Windows operating system environment.

Avid Media Composer
Worldwide standard software program used for high-end video editing.

Avid Xpress
Complete video-editing system.

B

Balance
Refers to the distribution of optical weight in layout.

Banding
Process that reduces colors without dithering; this results in areas of solid color.

Bandwidth
A measurement of the amount of data that can flow over a channel on a network.

BBEdit
High-performance text and Web page editor for the Macintosh.

Behavior
Ready-made scripts found in Web-based multimedia software programs.

Betacam SP
A high-quality video format used in professional video editing.

Bézier curve
Mathematically defined curves, named after Pierre Bézier, used to fine-tune a curve into almost any shape imaginable.

Bit
Binary digit.

Bit depth
The number of bits used to describe the color of a single pixel; the higher the bit depth, the more colors the image can contain.

Bit resolution
Measurement of the number of bits of stored information per pixel or how many tones or colors every pixel in a bitmap can

GLOSSARY

have. This is also referred to as bit depth, pixel depth, or color resolution.

Bitmap
A grid similar to graph paper from which each small square will be directly mapped back onto the computer screen as a pixel.

Bitmapped image
Graphic stored in memory as pixels.

Blending
The process of creating a series of intermediate colors and shapes between two selected objects.

Broadband
Internet connection with a high bandwidth.

Browser-safe color palette
See **Web-safe color palette**.

C

C#
An object-oriented programming language that enables programmers to quickly build a wide range of applications for the Microsoft .NET platform.

Capture
Digitize or convert to a number format that is recognizable by the computer.

Cascading Style Sheet (CSS)
A set of type specifications that can be applied to a block of text, a single Web page, or an entire Web site.

CD audio
Audio clips on CD.

Cel
A single frame in an animation.

Cel animation
Method of creating animation where key frames are created on cels or frames.

Client-side program
Uncompiled scripts (scripts that have not been compiled into standalone, executable programs) that are processed and interpreted by the Web browser on the user's computer.

Clip art
Commercially prepared drawings that come packaged with many application programs.

Clip audio
Audio files available for free or a fee; can be downloaded from the Web or purchased on CD.

Clip video
Video files available for free or a fee; can be downloaded from the Web or purchased on CD.

Codec
Compression/decompression algorithm used to compress data.

Co-location
A secure place to physically house hardware in a location other than in offices where the potential for fire, theft, or vandalism is much greater.

Color depth
See **color resolution**.

Color resolution
Measurement of the number of bits of stored information per pixel or how many tones or colors every pixel in a bitmap can have.

Commercial image provider
Business that finds and sells the rights to images.

Common Gateway Interface (CGI)
Communication standard for data exchange between a Web server and server-side gateway program; sets the rules for running external programs on a Web server.

Compile
Process of creating an executable file from program code.

Compiled language
Programming language in which the code must be compiled to be functional.

Compiling engine
Used to combine multiple still images into a single animation file.

Compression
A technique that mathematically reduces the size of a file.

Computational animation
Method of animating an object by varying its x- and y-coordinates.

Computer programmer
Person who creates underlying software programs called from a multimedia Web page.

Container
Two markup tags (beginning and ending tags) that enclose something between them.

Content sound
Sound in a multimedia application that furnishes information; narration and dialog are content sounds.

Content specialist
Multimedia team member who is responsible for providing some measure of authenticity or accuracy to the information in an interactive project.

Contextual cue
Design feature that enables users to know where they are within a Web site.

Continuous-tone image
Graphic such as a color photograph that has tonal variations

Conversion tool
Program that translates existing document formats into Web pages.

Cookie
Text file used to store data on a client computer.

Copyright
Ownership of rights to a creative work.

Copyright Act of 1976
Guidelines and regulations under which all original creative works are copyright protected.

Copyright law
Provides legal protection and grants certain rights to its owner.

Creative brief
A summary of the design strategy.

Crop
Process of removing areas of a photograph.

Cross-linking
Linking to related information.

Customer service
Assistance provided to Web site users.

Customer support personnel
People who respond to Web site users' questions and problems.

D

D1, D2, and D3
Common digital video standards.

Data transfer rate (dtr)
The time it takes for the data to be transferred from the processor and displayed on the monitor.

Database-driven organizational structure
Navigational structure based on an internal search engine that is used to locate information on a Web site.

Decibel (dB)
Smallest variation in amplitude that can be detected by the human ear.

Decorative
Classification of a type of font, such as script-type, that is more stylish and formal.

Default font
Font that will be used if the selected font is not available on the user's computer to display.

Design strategy
Planning document that includes the purpose and target audience of a multimedia Web site.

Digidesign Pro Tools
Powerful and popular high-end audio solution; complete, cross-platform package of hardware and software tools by Digidesign.

Digital audio
Sound that has been converted from an analog to a digital format.

Digital Audio Tape (DAT)
Media used to store digital audio data.

Digital Audio Tape (DAT) device
Device used to store digital audio data.

Digital camera
Camera that stores photographs in a digital format.

Digital Millennium Copyright Act (DMCA)
1998 act that updates U.S. copyright law for the digital age.

Digital Versatile Disc
See **DVD**.

Digital video
Video that is in a number format that can be interpreted by the computer.

Digital video camera
Video camera used to capture full-motion images as digital data.

Digital Video Disc
See **DVD**.

Digital-To-Analog (DAC) converter
Device that converts digital sound to analog sound.

Digitize
Process of capturing or converting data to a series of 0s and 1s that can be interpreted by a computer.

Digitizing tablet
A touch-sensitive board that converts points, lines, and curves drawn with a stylus to digital data.

Directed navigational structure
Tailored to the user by requesting information and then directing users based on their input.

Directory-based search engine
Search engine that catalogs only those Web sites that have been registered or submitted for review.

Distance learning
Training or instruction delivered over the Internet using a Web browser.

Dithering
The process of positioning different colored pixels side by side to create the illusion of a missing color.

DNS naming hierarchy
Structured arrangement of ascending authority for organizing domain names.

Document object model (DOM)
A platform-neutral application programming interface (API) that describes the underlying framework of a document so that Web developers can access and manipulate objects in a standard way.

Domain name
A pointer to a numeric IP address.

Domain name system
Registration system for domain names.

Downloaded
Files that are stored locally before they are played.

Drawing program
Software used to create and edit vector graphics.

DV
The Sony digital video-recording format that has been set as the standard by the major producers of video camera technologies.

DVD
Optical storage device that holds from 4.7 to 17 GB of data.

Dynamic Hypertext Markup Language (DHTML)
A group of technologies combined to create greater interactivity and page-layout flexibility using Javascript, Cascading Style Sheets (CSS), and the Document Object Model (DOM).

Dynamic Web site
Web site that provides information and offers some form of interactivity such as e-mail, searches, questionnaires, and order processing.

E

EA (Emblaze Audio)
A sound format developed specifically for the Internet by GEO for its Emblaze products.

E-commerce
Selling, advertising, and marketing products over the Web.

Editor
Multimedia team members responsible for providing a point of view and either originating or filtering information on a multimedia Web site.

Electronic portfolio (ePortfolio)
A compelling compilation of sample work and projects in a digital format to share with potential clients and employers.

Element
The combination of a tag with its attributes and values.

Embedded style
Style sheet in which all of the style information appears at the top of the Web page document, separated from the <body> of the code; also called an internal style.

Emphasis
The amount of focus placed on a multimedia element.

ePortfolio
See **electronic portfolio**.

Executive producer
Multimedia team member who is responsible for moving a project into and through production.

Extensible Hypertext Markup Language (XHTML)
The most recent version of HTML, which conforms to XML rules, thereby conforming to much stricter coding standards than HTML.

Extensible Markup Language (XML)
A markup language that describes the structure and content of a document and allows you to define your own markup tags.

External style
See **linked style**.

F

Fair use
Exclusionary right to use copyright images under certain circumstances such as research and instruction.

Frequently Asked Questions (FAQ)
A list of commonly asked questions and answers.

Feature creep
When new features that change the original specifications are added to a Web site and, therefore, increase the development time.

File Transfer Protocol (FTP)
The process by which files are transferred to a Web server.

Film loop
A series of animated frames looped to play over and over again.

Filters
Effects applied to an image or part of an image.

FireWire (also known as **IEEE 1394**)
A high-speed connector used to transfer video and sound from digital video cameras to computers.

Fireworks
See **Macromedia Fireworks**.

Flash
See **Macromedia Flash**.

Flash Player
See **Macromedia Flash Player**.

Flicker
When the illusion of motion fails and the animation appears as a rapid sequence of still images.

Flipbook approach
Method of creating animation in which a sequence of slightly different visual images is compressed and then played back to convey a sense of motion.

Flowchart
Multimedia planning document that illustrates the decision-making process that results as users make choices.

Font
A set of characters within a typeface that has specific characteristics associated with it, especially with respect to size (the height of the characters), weight (how dark the characters appear), and style (such as italic or condensed).

Font family
Fonts that are similar in appearance; for example, Times New Roman 12 point, bold, condensed is one font, and it is in the same font family as Times New Roman 16 point, light, expanded.

Frame
Navigation structure that divides a screen into multiple pages, thus enabling one region of a screen to remain constant while other regions of the screen change.

Frame rate
The speed at which individual frames are displayed.

Frame size
Size of a frame of video expressed in horizontal and vertical pixel dimensions, such as 800 x 600 pixels.

Frame-based animation
Method of creating animation where key frames are created on cels or frames.

Frames per second (fps)
Measurement used to determine the speed of both an animation and a video file.

Frequency
The number of peaks that occur in one second of sound; the frequency of a waveform determines its pitch.

Functionality
Ability to perform as intended.

G

Gamma correction
The ability to correct for differences in how computer monitors interpret color.

Gamma settings
Monitor specification that influences how bright items appear on the screen.

GIF89a
See **Animated GIF**.

Goal
Planning statement that supports the purpose of a multimedia Web site.

Gradient fill
A graduated blend between colors.

Graphic artist
See **Graphic designer**.

Graphic designer
Multimedia team member responsible for creating and designing all of the graphic images for a project.

Graphics Interchange File (GIF)
Graphic file format created by Compuserve for use on the Web. The GIF format supports only up to 256 colors.

Graphics program
Software program used to create or modify 2-D graphic images.

Graphics tablet
Converts points, lines, and curves from a sketch, drawing, or photograph to digital impulses and transmits them to a computer.

Grayscale image
Continuous-tone image consisting of only black, white, and gray data.

Group
To piece together objects so that they become one image.

H

Handheld Device Markup Language (HDML)
Standard on which WML is based.

HDTV (High Definition Television)
Video standard that supports a resolution of 1,200 horizontal lines with an aspect ratio (length:width) of 16:9.

Helper application
Tiny software program called from a Web page to play non-native content.

Hertz (Hz)
Measurement used to determine frequency.

Hexadecimal value
Refers to the base-16 number system used to reference color on Web pages.

Hi-8
The highest quality videotape format found in the consumer market.

Hierarchical organizational structure
Method of organization that follows a logical, branching structure.

High-level programming language
A programming language that is more user friendly than a low-level programming language.

Home page
The intended entry page of a Web site.

Hot spot
An area of a graphic or a section of text that links to another Web page when selected.

Hub and spokes navigational structure
Navigational structure that requires users to return to the home page in order to go to the other pages of the Web site.

Hue
Color in its purest form.

Hypergraphic
Graphic on a multimedia Web site that serves as a trigger to another screen, page, or topic.

Hyperlink
Text on a multimedia Web site that serves as a trigger to another screen, page, or topic.

Hypermedia
Multimedia element on a multimedia Web site that serves as a trigger to another screen, page, or topic.

Hypertext Markup Language (HTML)
The standard language used to create Web pages; designed to be a nonplatform-specific language that enables different computers running different operating systems and using different browsers to access the same page.

I

IEEE-1394
See **FireWire**.

Image editing program
Software used to manipulate images using a variety of features that combine painting, editing, and other image-composition tools.

Image map
Graphics that contain more than one trigger or hypermedia element.

Image resolution
The amount of information stored in each image; measured in pixels per inch (ppi).

ImageReady
See **Adobe ImageReady**.

Imported style
Style sheet that enables the use of one main style sheet as well as inline and embedded styles.

Indeo
The Intel compression scheme or codec.

Inline style
Style sheet inserted in the middle of an XHTML file that requires no style sheet code in the <head> section of the code.

Instructional specialist
Multimedia team member who is an expert in designing instructional projects for education or computer-based training.

Interactive multimedia
Multimedia applications that allow users to directly respond to and control any or all of the media elements.

Interactivity
The ability of the user to interact with the multimedia Web site.

Interface designer
Multimedia team member responsible for the look of the multimedia user interface.

Interlacing
Method of downloading a graphic so it appears blurry when first downloaded and then gradually increases in detail until it becomes completely clear.

Internal style
Style sheet in which style information appears at the top of the XHTML document, separated from the <body> section of the code.

Internet
A network of networks that connects millions of computers and people around the globe.

Internet Consortium for Assigned Names and Numbers (ICANN)
Organization charged by the U.S. Department of Commerce to control authorized domain registries.

Inter-page unity
The design that users encounter as they navigate from one page to another; provides consistency throughout a multimedia Web site.

Intranet
Private networks accessible only by the people within the organization or people with proper authorization to access the internal network.

Intra-page unity
How the various media elements on the same Web page are related to one another.

IP address (Internet Protocol)
A numeric address on the Internet that points to a specific location or Web page.

J

Jaggies
The stair-step-shaped edges that result when a bitmapped image is enlarged too much.

GLOSSARY

Java
Sun Microsystem independent programming languages used to create compact applications that users can access from a Web browser.

Java Server Pages (JSP)
The Java-based technology for generating dynamic Web pages with cross-platform and cross-Web-server support.

JavaScript
The Netscape scripting language used to create animation and interactivity on the Web.

Joint Photographic Experts Group (JPEG)
Graphic file format used to create compact bitmapped files.

K

Kerning
The amount of horizontal space between characters.

Keyframes
Frames that describe key events in the timeline of an animation.

Kilohertz (khz)
Measurement used to determine the frequency of a sound file.

L

Laser disc
Read-only optical storage technology that provides high-quality display of audio and video.

Layers
Different levels in a document; often used in image editing programs to create special effects in graphic files.

Leading
The amount of vertical space between lines of text.

Length unit
Used to define the length of an object on a Web page.

Letter-spacing property
CSS property used to control kerning.

Library
Storage location for multimedia elements.

LightWave 3D
A 3-D modeling program.

Line art
Images that contain only black and white pixels.

Linear
Sequential method of navigating through a multimedia Web site.

Linear organizational structure
Organizational structure that starts at the beginning and progresses through a set sequence of events until it reaches the end.

Line-height property
CSS property used to control leading.

Link
A reference to another Web page or Web site.

Link map
A schematic that illustrates the interconnectivity of Web pages within and external to a Web site.

Linked style
Style sheet in which the style code is stored in a file separate from the Web page so that multiple Web page files can be directed to one common style sheet document.

Livefeed
Analog or digital video signal delivered via cable or satellite.

Lossless compression
Mathematical algorithm that eliminates redundant data.

Lossy compression
Compression scheme in which expendable data is removed.

Low-level language
A programming language in which the syntax is closer to machine language.

M

Macromedia ColdFusion
Database management system by Macromedia.

Macromedia Dreamweaver
Web authoring program by Macromedia.

Macromedia Fireworks
Graphics program specifically designed for working with Web-based images and animation.

Macromedia Flash
Animation program designed specifically for creating full-motion animation with sound and interactivity for the Web.

Macromedia Flash Player
Plug-in needed to view Macromedia Flash content on the Web.

Macromedia FreeHand
Illustration or drawing program by Macromedia.

Macromedia HomeSite
Web editor by Macromedia.

Mapping software
Software used to create custom maps by geographic area, scale, and proposed perspective.

Markup language
Code used to specify how the content of a Web page will look.

Markup tag
Code that specifies how the browser will display text and other multimedia elements.

Metaphor
A figurative representation that links the content of a Web site to an established mental model.

Microbrowser
Interprets WML and renders the information on a small display such as those found on mobile phones and small terminals.

Microphone
Equipment used to translate analog signals into electrical impulses.

Microsoft Excel
Spreadsheet program by Microsoft.

Microsoft FrontPage
Web authoring program by Microsoft.

Microsoft Office
Office suite of applications by Microsoft.

Microsoft PowerPoint
Presentation software by Microsoft.

Microsoft Word
Word processing program by Microsoft.

MIDI
An internationally accepted file format used to store Musical Instrument Digital Interface (MIDI) data, which are instructions on how to replay music.

Mixman
Sound-editing program.

MNG (Multiple Image Network Graphics)
Animation file format that stores multiple images that are then streamed back for quick download and playback.

Modeling
Process used to create a 3-D object or scene.

Mono sound
Flat, unrealistic audio originating from a single channel.

Monochromatic
Color scheme that is created by designing with different shades of one color.

Monospaced font
Font in which each character takes up the exact same amount of horizontal space.

Morphing
Special technique that uses frames to create the illusion of one object changing into another.

Mosaic
The first cross-platform Web browser that fully exploited the Web's hypermedia capability.

Motion tweening
Tweening process used to create path-based animation.

Mouseover
Change that occurs on a Web page when the mouse pointer passes over a media element or text; it generally signifies that the item is a link to related or additional information.

MOV
QuickTime animation and video file format.

Movement
Relates to how the user's eye moves through the media elements on a Web page.

MP3
An open-standard technology that uses file compression to create near-CD quality audio files that are small enough to be distributed via the Web.

MPEG
Compression formats established by the Motion Picture Experts Group.

Multimedia
Using more than one media element; integrating text, graphics, animation, sound, and video.

Multitrack audio file
Digital audio file with multiple sound files stored on different tracks.

N

Navigation bar
A bar of buttons or text strategically placed and accessible from every page of a Web site for easy navigation.

Navigational structure
Means through which users know where they are, where they have been, and where they want to go on a Web site.

No balance
A design that has elements arranged on the screen without regard to the weight on either side of the centerline.

Nondestructive editing
Method of processing sound or video that maintains the original file.

Nonlinear
No prescribed or sequential path.

Nonlinear organizational structure
Organizational structure with no prescribed or sequential path; users can navigate from one topic to another in any order they choose.

NTSC (National Television Systems Committee)
Television and video standard in which video signals have a rate of 30 fps (29.97) and a single frame of video consists of 525 horizontal lines.

O

Object linking and embedding (OLE)
Term that describes a capability of software to import objects (embed) or maintain a path to an object or file (link).

Objective
Planning statement developed from the goals; must be clear, measurable, and obtainable.

Onion skinning
Animation technique that enables new images to be created by tracing over an existing image.

Open architecture
Software designed to be compatible with numerous software programs, extensions, and file formats.

Optical center
A point somewhere above the physical center of the screen.

Optical weight
The ability of a media element (such as a graphic, text, headline, or subhead) to attract the user's eye.

Optimized graphic
An image that has been saved in the smallest file size possible while still maintaining adequate quality for use on a Web page.

Optimizing
The process of making the image file sizes as small as possible for quick download via the Web while maintaining the quality of the image.

Organizational structure
The way in which information on a Web site is organized.

P

Paint program
Graphics program used to create bitmapped or raster graphics.

PAL (Phase Alternating Line)
Television and video standard in which video signals have a frame rate of 25 fps and a single frame of video consists of 625 horizontal lines.

Palette
Available color swatches for each pixel in an image.

Path-based animation
Type of animation that creates animated objects by following an object's transition over a line or vector; also called vector animation because it tracks the beginning, direction, and length that an object travels over a line or vector.

Pay-per-click
Search engine that gives priority placement to sites offering top bidding for keywords.

Peering
When a Web host has multiple Internet connections and can automatically route traffic to the fastest line out.

Performance
Quickness and efficiency of a Web site or Web server.

Perspective
View (top, front, or side) from which a 3-D image is rendered.

Photo CD
Multisession compact disc of digital images.

Photographer
Multimedia team member who shoots and captures appropriate, compelling, and high-quality photos to be used on the Web site.

PHP (Hypertext Preprocessor)
A server-side scripting language for creating dynamic Web pages; it is open source and cross-platform.

Pixel
Picture element represented by each small square or lighted dot on a monitor. A pixel is the smallest section of an image that can be independently displayed on a computer monitor.

Planning document
Includes flowcharts, site maps, link maps, wireframes, and storyboards; key to the creation and maintenance of a successful multimedia Web site.

Playback frame rate
The number of frames displayed per second when video is being viewed.

Playback rate
The number of images displayed per second when animation is being viewed.

Playback system
The specifications for displaying a multimedia Web site, which should include the operating systems, bandwidth speeds, and browsers for which the Web site is to be developed.

Player
Program that allows users to play non-native media content within a Web browser.

Plug-ins
See **Player**.

Pluginspage
Attribute that makes it possible for the Web page designer to better accommodate users by making it easy for them to download and install the appropriate plug-in or player if they do not already have it on their computer system.

Portable Document Format (PDF)
Electronic publishing tools used to create, edit, and read Portable Document Format (PDF) files.

Portable Document Software
Software used to create, edit, and read PDF files.

Portable Network Graphics (PNG)
Flexible graphic file format used on the Web. It supports a number of different color depths including 256 (8-bit) as well as millions of colors (24-bit or 32-bit).

Portfolio
A compelling compilation of sample work and projects to share with potential clients and employers.

Practical Extraction and Report Language (Perl)
A powerful and flexible programming language; has a tremendous following among Web developers.

Producer
See **Executive producer**.

Production manager
Multimedia team member who is responsible for forming a project, moving it into production, and overseeing its creation.

Production position
Multimedia position that requires skills in any or all of the following: markup, scripting, and programming languages; Web-based multimedia authoring programs, graphics, and typography; and artistic talent, a good sense of design, and good communication skills.

Program-based animation
Involves the use of programming and scripting languages to create animation.

Programming language
Used to create executable programs that are accessed or called from a Web page.

Progressive JPEG
Form of JPEG that gives a gradual image display, which offers a quicker preview to the user; similar to interlacing in the GIF format.

Project manager
Multimedia team member responsible for forming a project, moving it into production, and overseeing its creation.

Proportional font
Font in which each character takes up a varying amount of horizontal space.

Public domain
Artist work that can be used at the Web designer's discretion for no charge beyond the initial cost.

Purpose
Reason for creating a Web site.

Q

Quality-assurance
Multimedia positions responsible for testing a multimedia Web site.

QuickTime
Software-based video-delivery system by Apple that allows delivery of multimedia and video on the computer without using additional hardware.

QuickTime (MOV)
Platform-neutral, convenient, and powerful format for storing common digital media types such as audio and video.

QuickTime VR (QTVR)
Virtual reality software that allows developers to create entire 3-D interactive environments for the Web that include 3-D objects and full panoramic views of objects and locations.

R

RA, RAM, RM
see **RealMedia**.

Raster graphic
Another name for bitmapped graphic.

Rasterize
Process of converting a vector-based image to pixels or a bitmapped file format.

RealMedia (RM)
Popular format used for streaming media on the Internet.

Redbook
International storage standard for compact disc audio that allows audio segments on CDs to be addressed by minutes, seconds, and frames.

Refresh rate
Process of redrawing the screen each time items on the screen change.

Relative length unit
Defines the length of an object relative to another property, such as the size of the font.

Rendering
Process of capturing a view of a 3-D scene and saving it as a 2-D image.

Rendering program
Another name for 3-D modeling program.

Resolution
The number of binary bits processed for each sound wave or the number of pixels per inch used to store each graphic file.

Roundtrip
Term used to describe code that is not modified by a Web-authoring program, Web editor, or conversion program; the code remains clean—no unnecessary or unwanted tags are added.

S

Sales/marketing
Multimedia team member responsible for providing input and feedback about a multimedia Web site.

Sampling
The process of converting an analog sound to numbers.

Sampling rate (animation)
The actual number of different images that are recorded per second.

Sampling rate (audio)
Number of waveform samples per second; usually measured in kilohertz.

Sample size
The number of binary bits processed for each sound wave.

Sans serif
Typeface without serifs or perpendicular lines at the end of the character.

Scanner
Equipment used to digitize images so that they can be interpreted by the computer.

Script
Code interpreted by a Web browser that extends the capabilities of HTML and XHTML.

Script-based animation
Animation created through programming languages.

Scripting language
Used to write code for the client or server side that is interpreted by a Web browser.

Scripts
Planning document that contains all of the text and narration for a multimedia Web site.

Search engine
Tool used to find information on the Web.

Search feature
Text box or form in which users can enter specific words or combinations of words to locate information.

Search navigational structure
Navigational structure that incorporates a search feature.

Search term
Words or combinations of words entered by the user to search the Web site.

SECAM (Sequential Color with Memory)
Television and video standard in which video signals have a rate of 50 Hz with 625 horizontal lines per screen.

Security
Important consideration when choosing a Web host; data should be secure from hackers.

Serif
Typeface with serifs or perpendicular lines at the end of the character.

Shade
Color when light is added to it or subtracted from it.

Shading
The process of assigning surface properties such as color, texture, and finish to an object.

Shape tweening
Morphing that results when keyframes are created by the animator and the computer generates the between frames.

Shareware program
Program distributed based on the honor system—delivered free of charge; the developer usually requests that you pay a small fee if you like the program and use it regularly.

Site administration
Ability to update Web pages, manage files, collect orders, retrieve data from forms, get statistics, and perform other maintenance chores on a Web site.

Site map
Illustration of the relationship of the Web pages within a Web site.

Slide scanner
Input hardware that converts a slide or a negative to a digital image.

SMPTE (Society of Motion Picture and Television Engineers)
Industry-recognized timecode that measures video in hours, minutes, seconds, and frames; SMPTE is used to synchronize voice, music, and sound effects to the appropriate frames of video based on the frame rate.

Software
Computer instructions or programs.

GLOSSARY

Sorenson
High-end codec useful for compressing 24-bit video intended for CD or the Web.

Sound Forge
Sound-editing program by Sony.

Sound sampling
Process of converting analog sounds into numbers.

Sound wave
Vibrations that result from a sound.

Source code
Markup instructions in their original form.

Source frame rate
The speed at which video is recorded.

Specifications
Information on what will appear on each Web page, including the arrangement of each element and the functionality of each object; includes playback system, multimedia elements, functionality, and user interface.

Spider-based search engine
Search engine that automatically adds the contents of a Web site to its database.

Splash screen
Introductory Web page used to introduce and set a mood for the Web site before the user enters.

Staircasing
The stair-step-shaped edges that result when a bitmapped image is enlarged too much.

Standard Generalized Markup Language (SGML)
A standard for defining document structures for markup schemes.

Static Web sites
An electronic copy of a company brochure that includes no interactivity beyond simple hyperlinks.

Stereo sound
Dynamic and lifelike sound files with multiple channels.

Stock photography
Collections of digital photographs available on CD or the Web.

Stock photography house
Business that finds and sells the rights to images.

Stock video footage
Video footage offered by third parties.

Storage space
The capacity to hold data.

Storyboard
A diagram that describes the content and sequence of each page in a multimedia Web site.

Streamed
When sound or video is played while it is being downloaded.

Style
Formatting characteristic such as bold, italic, and underline.

Stylus
Special pen used with a digitizing tablet to make drawing easier than is possible with a mouse, trackball, or touchpad.

Surround sound
Sound that includes delays that attempt to simulate the time it would take for sound waves to reach the ears if the sound were happening live.

S-VHS
A video-editing format that offers higher quality video than VHS but slightly lower quality than Hi-8.

SWF
A compressed Macromedia Flash file format designed to efficiently deliver graphics and animation over the Web.

Symmetrical balance
Achieved by arranging elements as horizontal or vertical mirrored images on both sides of a centerline of a screen.

Synchronized Multimedia Integration Language (SMIL)
Simple, platform-neutral markup language designed to let Web designers and developers at all skill levels schedule audio, video, text, and graphic files across a timeline without having to master development tools or complex programming languages.

T

Tagged Image File Format (TIFF)
Widely used cross-platform bitmapped file format for print.

Target audience
The intended users of a multimedia Web site.

Technical support
Consideration in choosing a Web hosting company; refers to people with skills to assist you if there are technical problems with your Web site.

Template
A precise layout indicating where various media elements will appear on a Web page.

Tester
Multimedia team member responsible for testing the multimedia Web site.

Texture
Surfaces that are applied or mapped to models to give them shadows and provide special effects.

The 1976 Federal Copyright Act
See **Copyright Act of 1976**.

Theme
Contains a color scheme and generally consists of unified design elements for bullets, fonts, images, navigation bars, and other media elements.

Three-dimensional (3-D)
Having three properties—width, height, and depth.

Thumbnail image
A small image that is linked to a larger version of the same image.

Timeline
Used to develop and control multimedia elements.

Tone
The nature of a Web site, which might be humorous, serious, light, heavy, formal, or informal.

Tool palette
Box that contains electronic drawing tools such as pencils, paintbrushes, and erasers.

Trail effect
Result that occurs if the previous image is not completely erased when the image in the next frame appears on the screen.

Transparency
Characteristic of an image file that indicates an area with no pixel values.

Tweener
Artist who creates the frames between the keyframes.

Tweening
Process of filling in the frames between the keyframes to make an animation appear fluid.

Two-dimensional (2-D)
Having two properties—width and height.

Typeface
A set of characters, usually made up of alphabet letters, numerals, and symbols, that all follow the same rules within the set.

Typography
The communication of a message using typefaces and fonts.

U

Ungroup
When a graphic image is separated into all of the individual pieces used to create it.

Unity
Cohesiveness of a Web site whereby all of the multimedia elements are similar in design.

User interface
The means through which the user will navigate and interact with a multimedia Web site.

User profile
Creates a picture about the people who will be using the Web site—their online and offline habits.

V

Value
Assigned to an attribute in HTML or XHTML; determines the result of the modification made by the attribute.

VBScript
A scripting version of Microsoft Visual Basic or VB; the primary scripting language used for Active Server Pages (ASP).

Vector animation
See **Path-based animation**.

Vector graphic
Images that are created and recreated from mathematical models or formulas.

Vegas
Multitrack recording and audio arranging software program by Sony.

VHS
Lower-quality video format most often found in the consumer market; not really a usable format in video editing.

Video capture card
Converts an analog video signal from a camcorder, VCR, and livefeed to digital data that the computer can interpret.

Video disc
Analog technology for storing video; provides a random access feature.

Video specialist
Multimedia team member who may manage the entire process of shooting, capturing, and editing original video for use in interactive products.

Videographer
Multimedia team member who creates and records appropriate, compelling, and high-quality video to be used with interactive technology.

Virtual Reality (VR)
When multimedia is used to create artificial environments complete with 3-D images that can be explored and manipulated.

Virtual Reality Modeling Language (VRML)
The programming language used to create and view 3-D environments on the Web.

Vision
Dream or mental picture of a multimedia Web site.

Visual Basic
High-level programming language by Microsoft.

W

Warping
Special effect that results in distortion of an image.

WAV
Waveform sound file format developed by Microsoft and supported on the Windows platform without a player.

Waveform
The graphic representation of sound showing time on the horizontal axis and amplitude or strength on the vertical axis; includes the frequency, the amplitude, and the harmonic content of the sound.

Waveform audio
See **Waveform**.

Web
See **World Wide Web**.

Web architecture
The blueprint around which a consistent and functional Web site is developed.

Web authoring programs
Software programs that use a GUI (graphical user interface) to create Web pages.

Web-based multimedia
An online, interactive experience that incorporates two or more media elements including text, graphics, sound, animation, and video.

Web-based training
Training or instruction delivered over the Internet using a Web browser.

Web browser
Program that interprets the source code behind a Web page.

Web client
The user's computer.

Web designer
Multimedia team member responsible for refining the design process and efficiently creating a cohesive and well-planned multimedia Web site from the front-end.

Web developer
Multimedia team member who ensures that the communication between the front-end of the Web site and the back-end of the Web site is working.

Web master
Multimedia team member responsible for maintaining a Web server.

Web page editor
Software programs that allow Web designers to create Web pages using menus and buttons that represent markup and scripting tags.

Web portal
High-trafficked Web sites that serve as gateways to a multitude of other Web sites.

Web server
The computer on which the files for Web pages are stored.

Web site hosting
Storing the files for a Web site on a Web server with Internet access.

Web-safe color palette
The universal color palette shared by browsers; it contains 216 colors.

What You See Is What You Get (WYSIWYG)
Tools using a graphic user interface that generate code behind the scenes.

White space
Blank areas on a page where text and other media elements are not found.

Wireframe
A text-only skeletal structure of every click-through possibility of a Web site.

Wireless Application Protocol (WAP)
Standard used to provide Internet content and services to wireless clients.

Wireless Markup Language (XML)
A standard based on the Handheld Device Markup Language (HDML); similar to HTML but interpreted by a microbrowser that works on a handheld device.

WMA
Microsoft file format for encoding digital audio files.

World Wide Web
A worldwide network of linked documents.

World Wide Web Consortium (W3C)
Official standards committee that controls the changes and additions to standards that impact Web design and development.

Writer
Multimedia team member who writes the content for a Web page.

X

XML
See **Extensible Markup Language**.

INDEX

B

INDEX

E

F

G

H

J

K

L

M

P

Q

R

S

T

X

Z

Credit List for Multimedia for the Web

Chapter 1

Fig. 01-01	© Jim Cummins/CORBIS
Fig. 01-04a	Courtesy of Pixar
Fig. 01-04b	Courtesy of Pixar
Fig. 01-05	Courtesy Chris Conrad
Fig. 01-07	Courtesy of Greg Joly
Fig. 01-08	Courtesy of Amazon, Amazon, Amazon.com and the Amazon.com logo are registered trademarks of Amazon.com, Inc. or its affiliates.
Fig. 01-09	Courtesy Blackboard Inc., "Blackboard Inc. is the leading provider of course management software"
Fig. 01-10	Courtesy of NASA
Fig. 01-11	Courtesy of Direct Counseling Solutions
Fig. 01-12	Courtesy of MPOGD
Fig. 01-13	Crayola and the Serpentine and Chevron designs are registered trademarks, Gadget Headz and the smile design are trademarks of Binney & Smith, used with permission.
Fig. 01-14	Courtesy of the Art Institute of Colorado
Fig. 01-15	Credit Tiffany Beasi/www.tiffanybeasi.com
Fig. 01-16	Copyright Luc Beziat/Getty Images
Fig. 01-18	Courtesy Blackboard Inc., "Blackboard Inc. is the leading provider of course management software"
Fig. 01-19	Courtesy of the Griesser family at The Alpine Inn
Fig. 01-20	Courtesy of The Media
Fig. 01-21	Courtesy of Monster

Chapter 2

Fig. 02-03	Courtesy of Weider Publications
	Courtesy of Meredith Corporation
Fig. 02-04	Courtesy of The Quaker Oats Company
Fig. 02-05	Courtesy of Sun Microsystems
Fig. 02-06	Courtesy of Leader Dogs for the Blind
Fig. 02-08	Courtesy of Movement Arts
Fig. 02-09	www.google.com is a trademark of Google Inc.
	© Lands' End, Inc. and My Virtual Model™ 2005. Used with permission.
Fig. 02-18	Courtesy Blackboard Inc., "Blackboard Inc. is the leading provider of course management software"
Fig. 02-19	Courtesy of Lycos, Inc.
	Courtesy of Apple Computer, Inc.
Fig. 02-21	Courtesy of Adobe Systems Inc.

Fig. 02-22	Courtesy of the Hollywood Media Corp.
Fig. 02-25	Courtesy of fasterwhois.com
Fig. 02-26	Courtesy of Register.com
Fig. 02-28	Courtesy of Chimera Studio LLC
Fig. 02-29	Courtesy of Add Me, Inc,
Fig. 02-31	Courtesy of the Connor Hotel of Jerome, site built by Charles Platt
Fig. 02-32	Courtesy of MySite, Inc. a United Online Company

Chapter 3

Fig. 03-02	Courtesy of Amazon.com, Inc.
Fig. 03-03	Courtesy of Apple Computer, Inc.
Fig. 03-06	Copyright 2004 Dell, Inc. All Rights Reserved.
Fig. 03-08	Courtesy of Colgate-Palmolive Company
Fig. 03-10	Courtesy of Lynda.com
Fig. 03-11	Courtesy of blackat9.com
Fig. 03-14	Courtesy of Homer TLC
Fig. 03-15	Courtesy of Starbucks Corporation
Fig. 03-17a	Courtesy of Apple Computer, Inc.
Fig. 03-17b	Courtesy of Macromedia, Inc.
Fig. 03-18	Courtesy of verticalmoon.com and Courtesy of General Electric Company, www.geimaginationatwork.com <http://www.geimaginationatwork.com/>
Fig. 03-19	Courtesy of Beringer Blass Wine Estates
Fig. 03-20	Courtesy of Volkswagen of America, Inc.
Fig. 03-21	Courtesy of the Hollywood Media Corp.
Fig. 03-22	Courtesy of Nordstrom, Inc.

Chapter 4

Fig. 04-01	Courtesy of Starbucks Corporation
Fig. 04-04	Copyright 2005 Jupitermedia Corporation All Rights Reserved, http://www.webreference.com/xml/reference/xhtml.html
Fig. 04-06	Courtesy of Macromedia, Inc.
Fig. 04-11	Courtesy of Bare Bones Software, Inc.
Fig. 04-15	Courtesy of Macromedia, Inc.
Fig. 04-16	Courtesy of Macromedia, Inc.
Fig. 04-17	Courtesy of Adobe Systems Inc.
Fig. 04-18	Courtesy of Adobe Systems Inc.
Fig. 04-19	Courtesy of Adobe Systems Inc.

Fig. 04-21	Courtesy of Macromedia, Inc.
Fig. 04-22	Courtesy of Macromedia, Inc.
Fig. 04-23	Courtesy of Macromedia, Inc.
Fig. 04-24	Courtesy of Macromedia, Inc.
Fig. 04-25	Courtesy of Microsoft Corporation
Fig. 04-27	Courtesy of Virtual Training Company, Inc., www.vtc.com

Chapter 5

Fig. 05-01	Courtesy of EURO RSCG Worldwide
Fig. 05-04	Courtesy of Fonthead Design, Inc
Fig. 05-06a	Courtesy of The Boeing Company
Fig. 05-06b	Courtesy of Don Barnett, Nekton Design, www.donbarnett.com
Fig. 05-06c	Courtesy of GRAFCOMM, Inc.
Fig. 05-15	Courtesy of The Tech Museum of Innovation
Fig. 05-17	"Courtesy of John Webber"
Fig. 05-18a	Courtesy of Keynote NetMechanic
Fig. 05-18b	"Salon.com home page reproduced with permission."
Fig. 05-24a	Courtesy of CNET Networks
Fig. 05-24b	Courtesy of CNET Networks
Fig. 05-26	Courtesy of Visa International
	Copyright IBM Corporation. All rights reserved.
	Courtesy of Adobe Systems Inc.
	Courtesy of Macromedia, Inc.
	Courtesy of McDonald's Corporation and Affiliates. All rights reserved.
	Courtesy of the Coca-Cola Company. All rights reserved.
Fig. 05-27	Courtesy of Adobe Systems Inc.
Fig. 05-42	Courtesy of the National Geographic Society

Chapter 6

Fig. 06-01	Courtesy of Counterbalance Foundation
Fig. 06-03	Courtesy of Linspire, Inc. TM Linspire is a trademark of Linspire, Inc.
Fig. 06-04	Courtesy of Canon USA, Inc. All rights reserved.
Fig. 06-05	Courtesy Estman Kodak Company. All rights reserved.
Fig. 06-06	Courtesy of iStockphoto, Inc.
Fig. 06-07	Courtesy of Jupitermedia Corporation
Fig. 06-08	Courtesy of Wacom Technology Corporation
Fig. 06-10	Courtesy of Digimarc Corporation

Fig. 06-12 Courtesy of Rick darsey, www.darseydesign.com
Fig. 06-13 Courtesy of Cendant Timeshare
Fig. 06-20 Courtesy of Adobe Systems Inc.
Fig. 06-31- Fig. 06-32 Courtesy of 3D Render
Fig. 6-38 Photograph Courtesy of Rachel Biheller Bunin
Fig. 06-40 Courtesy of Fundy Communications
Fig. 06-79 Courtesy of American Automobile Association and Courtesy of Sierra Entertainment Inc.

Chapter 7

Fig. 07-01 Courtesy of Pearson Education, Adobe Press
Fig. 07-02 Courtesy of VA Software Corporation
Fig. 07-03 Courtesy of HowStuffWorks.com
Fig. 07-04 Courtesy of The Public Broadcasting Service
Fig. 07-05 Courtesy of Warner Brothers Entertainment
Fig. 07-06 Courtesy of Kevin Cappis
Fig. 07-13 Courtesy of Brunswick Corporation
Fig. 07-15- Fig. 07-16 Courtesy of Macromedia, Inc.
Fig. 07-17 Courtesy of ITCat Media, www.itcatmedia.com
Fig. 07-19- Fig. 07-20 Courtesy of Macromedia, Inc.
Fig. 07-23 Courtesy of Macromedia, Inc., Courtesy of Apple Computer, Inc.

Chapter 8

Fig. 08-01 Copyright Digital Vision/ Getty Images
Fig. 08-02 Courtesy of Apple Computer, Inc. and Courtesy of CNET
Fig. 08-03 Courtesy of Merriam-Webster Incorporated and Courtesy of Public Broadcasting Service
Fig. 08-04 Courtesy of Clevland Institute of Music
Fig. 08-08 Courtesy of Internet Magic
Fig. 08-11 Courtesy of SOS Publications Ltd.
Fig. 08-13 Courtesy of Comparisonics Corporation
Fig. 08-14 Courtesy of the Public Broadcasting Service
Fig. 08-15 Courtesy of Sirius Satellite Radio Inc.
Fig. 08-16 Courtesy of Akron Studios
Fig. 08-17 Courtesy of Bias, Inc.
Fig. 08-19- Fig. 08-22 Courtesy of Sony Pictures Digital Inc.
Fig. 08-24 Courtesy of RealNetworks, Inc. and Courtesy of Apple Computer, Inc. and Courtesy of Microsoft Corporation
Fig. 08-40 Courtesy of NASA

Chapter 9

Fig. 09-01	Copyright Jeff Greenberg/Alamy
Fig. 09-02	Copyright Joaquin Palting/ Photodisc/ Getty Images
Fig. 09-03	Courtesy of Valley Laser Eye Center
Fig. 09-04	Courtesy of Priority Electronics
Fig. 09-05	Courtesy of Canon USA, Inc. All rights reserved.
Fig. 09-10	Courtesy of Josh Sheppard, www.thestoryboardartist.com <http://www.thestoryboardartist.com/>
Fig. 09-20- Fig. 09-21	Courtesy of Adobe Systems Inc.
Fig. 09-22-Fig. 09-23	Courtesy of Apple Computer, Inc.
Fig. 09-24	Courtesy of Avid Technology, Inc.
Fig. 09-70	Courtesy of Design 4X and Stanford University

Chapter 10

Fig. 10-03	Courtesy of Skagit Valley College
Fig. 10-04	Courtesy of The United States Government, www.whitehouse.gov
Fig. 10-07	Courtesy of Palm, Inc.
Fig. 10-09	Courtesy of Uniboard Canada Inc.
Fig. 10-10	Courtesy of Robert Thrasher, www.cfdev.com
Fig. 10-12	Courtesy of Sun Microsystems
Fig. 10-13	Courtesy of Netarray
Fig. 10-20	Courtesy of Alki Tours